*N*EB

PROGRAMMING THE

WORLD WIDE WEB
2009

FIFTH EDITION

JUBILEE
CAMPUS
LRC

ROBERT W. SEBESTA
University of Colorado at Colorado Springs

Upper Saddle River Boston Columbus San Francisco New York
Indianapolis London Toronto Sydney Singapore Tokyo Montreal
Dubai Madrid Hong Kong Mexico City Munich Paris Amsterdam Cape Town

Editor in Chief: Michael Hirsch
Acquisitions Editor: Matt Goldstein
Editorial Assistant: Sarah Milmore
Managing Editor: Jeff Holcomb
Senior Production Supervisor: Meredith Gertz
Senior Media Producer: Bethany Tidd
Marketing Manager: Erin Davis
Marketing Coordinator: Kathryn Ferranti
Senior Manufacturing Buyer: Carol Melville
Text Design, Project Management,
    Production Coordination, Composition,
    and Illustrations: Gillian Hall, The Aardvark Group
Copyeditor: Kathleen Cantwell, C4 Technologies
Proofreader: Holly McLean-Aldis
Indexer: Jack Lewis
Cover Art Direction: Linda Knowles
Cover Design: Jodi Notowitz
Cover Image: ©Fotosearch

Many of the designations used by manufacturers and sellers to distinguish their products are claimed as trademarks. Where those designations appear in this book, and Addison-Wesley was aware of a trademark claim, the designations have been printed in initial caps or all caps.

The programs and applications presented in this book have been included for their instructional value. They have been tested with care, but are not guaranteed for any particular purpose. The publisher does not offer any warranties or representations, nor does it accept any liabilities with respect to the programs or applications.

If you purchased this book within the United States or Canada you should be aware that it has been wrongfully imported without the approval of the Publisher or the Author.

ISBN-13: 978-0-13-136476-9
ISBN-10: 0-13-136476-6
1 2 3 4 5 6 7 8 9 10—RRD—13 12 11 10 09

To Aidan

Contents

Preface

It is difficult to overestimate the effect the World Wide Web has had on the day-to-day lives of people, at least those in the developed countries. In just a few years, we have learned to use the Web for a myriad of disparate tasks, ranging from the mundane task of shopping for airline tickets to the crucial early-morning gathering of business news for a high-stakes day trader.

The speed at which millions of Web sites have appeared would seem to indicate that the technologies used to build them were sitting on the shelf, fully developed and ready to use, even before the Web was developed. Also, one might guess that the tens of thousands of people who built those sites were sitting around unemployed, waiting for an opportunity and already possessing the knowledge and abilities required to carry out this mammoth construction task when it appeared. Neither of these was true. The need for new technologies was quickly filled by a large number of entrepreneurs, some at existing companies and some who started new companies. A large part of the programmer need was filled, at least to the extent to which it has been filled, by new programmers, some straight from high school. Many, however, were previously employed by other sectors of the software development industry. All of them had to learn to use new languages and technologies.

Until recently, programmers learned Web software technologies through company in-house training, a scattering of courses focused on one specific Web technology at colleges and universities, or on their own. A visit to a local bookstore will turn up a large supply of books on those technologies aimed at the practicing professional. In the last few years college courses have appeared that attempt to cover a broad spectrum of Web programming technologies. One difficulty encountered by those teaching these courses is the lack of textbooks that are targeted to their needs. Most of the books that discuss Web programming were written for professionals, rather than college students. Such books are typically written to fulfill the needs of professionals, which are quite different from those of college students. One major difference between an academic book and a professional book lies in the assumptions made by the author about the prior knowledge and experience of the audience. The backgrounds of professionals vary widely, making it difficult to assume much of anything. On the other hand, a book written for junior computer science majors can make some definite assumptions about the background of the reader. This book is aimed at college students, not necessarily only computer science majors, but anyone who has taken at least two courses in programming. Although students are the primary target, the book is also useful for professional programmers who wish to learn Web programming.

The goal of this book is to provide the reader with a comprehensive introduction to the programming tools and skills required to build and maintain server sites on the Web. A wide variety of technologies are used in the construction of a Web site. There are now many books available for professionals that focus on these technologies. For example, there are dozens of books that specifically address only XHTML. The same is true for a half-dozen other technologies. This book provides an overview of how the Web works, as well as descriptions of many of the most widely used Web technologies.

The first four editions of this book were used to teach a junior-level Web programming course at the University of Colorado at Colorado Springs. The challenge for students in the course is to learn to use several different programming languages and technologies in one semester. A heavy load of programming exercises is essential to the success of the course. Students build a basic, static Web site using only XHTML as the first assignment. Throughout the remainder of the semester they add features to their site as the new technologies are discussed in the course. Our students' prior course work in Java, data structures, and assembly language are helpful, as is the fact that many of them know some XHTML before taking the course.

The most important prerequisite to the material of this book is a solid background in programming in some language that supports object-oriented programming. It is helpful to have some knowledge of a second programming language and a bit of UNIX, particularly if a UNIX-based Web server is used for the course. Familiarity with a second language makes learning the new languages easier.

Table of Contents

The book is organized into three parts, introduction (Chapter 1), client-side technologies (Chapters 2–8), and server-side technologies (Chapters 9–15).

Chapter 1 lays the groundwork for the rest of the book. A few fundamentals are introduced, including the history and nature of the Internet, the World Wide Web, browsers, servers, URLs, MIME types, and HTTP. Also included in Chapter 1 are brief overviews of the most important topics of the rest of the book.

Chapter 2 provides an introduction to XHTML, including images, links, lists, tables, frames, and forms. Small examples are used to illustrate the many XHTML elements that are discussed in this chapter.

The topic of Chapter 3 is Cascading Style Sheets, which provide the standard way of imposing style on the content specified in XHTML tags. Because of the size and complexity of the topic, the chapter does not cover all of the aspects of style sheets. The topics discussed are levels of style sheets, style specification formats, selector formats, property values, and color. Among the properties covered are those for fonts, lists, and margins. Small examples are used to illustrate the subjects being discussed.

Chapter 4 introduces the core of JavaScript, a powerful language that could be used for a variety of different applications. Our interest, of course, is its use in Web programming. Although JavaScript has become a large and complex language, we use the student's knowledge of programming in some other language to leverage our discussion, thereby providing a useful introduction to the language in a manageably small number of pages. Topics covered are the object model of JavaScript, its control statements, objects, arrays, functions, constructors, and pattern matching.

In Chapter 5 we discuss some of the features of JavaScript that are related to XHTML documents. Included is the use of the basic and DOM 2 event and event-handling model, which can be used in conjunction with some of the elements of XHTML documents.

One of the most exciting and interesting applications of JavaScript is for building dynamic XHTML documents using the Document Object Model (DOM). Chapter 6 provides descriptions of a collection of some of the document changes that can be made using JavaScript and the DOM. Included are element positioning, moving elements, changing the visibility of elements, changing the color, style, and size of text, changing the content of tags, changing the stacking order of overlapped elements, slow movement of elements, and dragging and dropping elements.

Chapter 7 presents an introduction to XML, which provides the means to design topic-specific markup languages that can be shared among users with common interests. Included are the syntax and document structure used by XML, data type definitions, namespaces, schemas, and the display of XML documents with both Cascading Style Sheets and XML Transformations. Also included is an introduction to Web services and XML processors.

Chapter 8 introduces the Flash development environment, which is used to create a wide variety of visual and audio presentations, particularly those that include animation. A series of examples are used to illustrate the development processes, including drawing figures, creating text, using color, creating motion and shape animations, and adding sound tracks to presentations.

Chapter 9 introduces PHP, a server-side scripting language that enjoys wide popularity, especially as a database access language. The basics of the language are discussed, as well as the use of cookies and session tracking. The use of PHP as a Web database access language is covered in Chapter 13.

Chapter 10 introduces Ajax, the relatively new technology that is used to build Web applications with extensive user interactions that are more efficient.

In addition to a thorough introduction to the concept and implementation of Ajax interactions, the chapter includes discussions of return document forms, Ajax toolkits, and Ajax security. Serveral examples are used to illustrate approaches to using Ajax.

Java Web software is discussed in Chapter 11. The chapter introduces the mechanisms for building Java servlets and presents several examples of how servlets can be used to present interactive Web documents. The NetBeans framework is introduced and used throughout the chapter. Two approaches to storing information on clients using servlets, cookies and session tracking, are introduced and illustrated with examples. Then JSP is introduced through a series of examples, including the use of code-behind files. This is followed by a discussion of JavaBeans and JavaServer Faces.

Chapter 12 is an introduction to ASP.NET, though it begins with a brief introduction to C#. ASP.NET Web controls and the many possible events and how they can be handled are among the topics discussed in this chapter. ASP.NET AJAX is also discussed. Finally, constructing Web services with ASP.NET is introduced.

Chapter 13 provides an introduction to database access through the Web. This chapter includes an introduction to the nature of relational databases, architectures for database access, the structured query language (SQL) and the free database system, MySQL. Then, two approaches to Web access to databases are discussed: using PHP and using Java JDBC. Both approaches are illustrated with complete examples. All of the program examples in the chapter use MySQL.

Chapter 14 introduces the Ruby programming language. Included are the scalar types and their operations, control statements, arrays, hashes, methods, classes, code blocks and iterators, and pattern matching. There is, of course, much more to Ruby, but the chapter includes sufficient material to allow the student to use Ruby for building simple programs and Rails applications.

Chapter 15 introduces the Rails framework, designed to make the construction of Web applications relatively quick and easy. Covered are simple document requests, both static and dynamic, applications that use databases, and Ajax use with Rails. Rails 2.0, which is not compatible with earlier versions of Rails, is used.

Appendix A introduces Java to those who have experience with C++ and object-oriented programming. Students who do not know Java can learn enough of the language from this appendix to allow them to understand the Java applets, servlets, JSP, and JDBC that appear in this book.

Appendix B is a list of over 140 named colors, along with their hex codings.

Appendix C discusses Java applets. First, the fundamentals of applet activities and the `paintComponent` method are introduced. Then, the `<object>` tag and applet parameters are discussed. Next, the appendix introduces the graphics that can be created by applets. Applets that can interact with the user through Swing widgets are then covered.

Support Materials

The supplements for the book are available at Addison-Wesley's Web site www.aw.com/cssupport. Support materials available to all readers of this book include

- A set of lecture notes in the form of PowerPoint files. The notes were developed to be the basis for class lectures on the book material.
- Code for example programs
- PowerPoint slides of all the figures

Additional support material including solutions to selected exercises are available only to instructors adopting this textbook for classroom use. Please contact your school's Pearson Education representative for information on obtaining access to this material.

Software Availability

Most of the software systems described in this book are available free to students. These include browsers, which provide interpreters for JavaScript and parsers for XML. Also, PHP, Ruby, and Java language processors, as well as the Rails framework, Java class libraries to support servlets, and Java JDBC, are available and free. ASP.NET is supported by the .NET software available from Microsoft. The Flash development environment is available for 30 days free from Adobe.

Differences Between the Fourth Edition and the Fifth Edition

The Fifth Edition differs significantly from the Fourth. A new chapter (8) on Flash was added. The chapter on Ajax was moved from Chapter 15 to Chapter 10, reflecting its increasing importance. This chapter was expanded by adding sections on return document forms, Ajax toolkits, and Ajax security. Also, the section on Rails/Ajax was moved from the Rails chapter (15) to the Ajax chapter (10). A section on ASP.NET AJAX was added to Chapter 12. The chapter on Rails (15) was heavily revised, in part to update it for Rails 2.0, which is not backward-compatible with the previous versions. Coverage on scaffolding and migrations was added to the chapter. Finally, the chapters on Perl and Perl/CGI were dropped from the book.

Throughout the book, numerous small changes were made to improve the correctness and clarity of the material.

Acknowledgments

The quality of this book was significantly improved as a result of the extensive suggestions, corrections, and comments provided by its reviewers. It was reviewed by:

R. Blank
CTO, Almer/Blank; Training Director,
The Rich Media Institute; Faculty,
USC Viterbi School of Engineering

Barry Burd
Drew University

William Cantor
Pennsylvania State University

Dunren Che
Southern Illinois University Carbondale

Brian Chess
Fortify Software

Randy Connolly
Mount Royal College

Mark DeLuca
Pennsylvania State University

Peter S. Kimble
University of Illinois

Chris Love
ProfessionalASPNET.com

Najib Nadi
Villanova University

Russ Olsen

Jamel Schiller
University of Wisconsin—Green Bay

Stephanie Smullen
University of Tennessee at Chattanooga

J. Reuben Wetherbee
University of Pennsylvania

Christopher C. Whitehead
Columbus State University

Matt Goldstein, Aquisitions Editor; Sarah Milmore, Editorial Assistant; Meredith Gertz, Senior Production Supervisor; and Erin Davis, Marketing Manager, all deserve my gratitude for their encouragement and help in completing the manuscript. Also, thanks to Gillian Hall of The Aardvark Group for quickly and accurately converting the collection of files I provided into a bound book.

Fundamentals

The lives of most inhabitants of industrialized countries, as well as some in unindustrialized countries, have been changed forever by the advent of the World Wide Web. Although this has had some downsides—for example, easier access to pornography and gambling and the ease with which those with destructive ideas can propagate those ideas to others—on balance, the changes have been enormously positive. Many use the Internet and the World Wide Web daily, communicating with friends, relatives, and business associates through e-mail, shopping for virtually anything that can be purchased anywhere, and digging up a limitless variety and amount of information, from movie theater schedules to hotel room prices in cities halfway around the world to the history and characteristics of the culture of some small and obscure society. Constructing the software and data that provide all of this information requires knowledge of several different technologies, such as markup languages and meta-markup languages, as well as programming skills in a myriad of different programming languages, some specific to the World Wide Web and some designed for general-purpose computing. This book is meant to provide the required background and a basis for acquiring the knowledge and skills necessary to build the World Wide Web sites that provide both the information users want and the advertising that pays for its presentation.

This chapter lays the groundwork for the remainder of the book. It begins with introductions to and some history of the Internet and the World Wide Web. Then, it discusses the purposes and some of the characteristics of Web browsers and servers. Next, it describes uniform resource locators (URLs), which specify addresses for resources available on the Web. Following this, it introduces Multipurpose Internet Mail Extensions, which provide ways in which file types can be specified—and which are required because of the many different formats in which information can be represented in files. Next, it discusses the Hypertext Transfer Protocol (HTTP), which provides the communication interface for connections between browsers and Web servers. Finally, the chapter provides brief overviews of some of the tools commonly used by Web programmers, including XHTML, XML, JavaScript, Flash, Servlets, JSP, JSF, ASP.NET, PHP, Ruby, Rails, and Ajax. All of these are discussed in far more detail in the remainder of the book (XHTML in Chapters 2 and 3; JavaScript in Chapters 4, 5, and 6; XML in Chapter 7; Flash in Chapter 8; PHP in Chapter 9; Ajax in Chapter 10; Servlets, JSP, and JSF in Chapter 11; Ruby in Chapters 14 and 15; and Rails in Chapter 15).

1.1   A Brief Introduction to the Internet

Virtually every topic discussed in this book is related to the Internet. Therefore, we begin with a quick introduction to the Internet itself.

1.1.1   Origins

In the 1960s the U.S. Department of Defense (DoD) became interested in developing a new large-scale computer network. The purposes of this network were communications, program sharing, and remote computer access for researchers working on defense-related contracts. One fundamental requirement was that the network be sufficiently robust so that even if some network nodes were lost due to sabotage, war, or some more benign reason, the network would continue to function. The DoD's Advanced Research Projects Agency (ARPA)[1] funded the construction of the first such network, which connected about a dozen ARPA-funded research laboratories and universities. The first node of this network was established at UCLA in 1969.

Because it was funded by ARPA, the network was named ARPAnet. Despite the initial intentions, the primary early use of ARPAnet was simple text-based communications through e-mail. Because ARPAnet was available only to labo-

---

1. ARPA was renamed Defense Advanced Research Projects Agency (DARPA) in 1972.

ratories and universities that conducted ARPA-funded research, the great majority of educational institutions were not connected. As a result, a number of other networks were developed during the late 1970s and early 1980s, with BITNET and CSNET among them. BITNET, which is an acronym for Because It's Time Network, began at the City University of New York. It was built initially to provide electronic mail and file transfers. CSNET, which is an acronym for Computer Science Network, connected the University of Delaware, Purdue University, the University of Wisconsin, RAND Corporation, and Bolt, Beranek, and Newman (a research company in Cambridge, Massachusetts). Its initial purpose was to provide electronic mail. For a variety of reasons, neither BITNET nor CSNET became a widely used national network.

A new national network, NSFnet, was created in 1986. It was sponsored, of course, by the National Science Foundation (NSF). NSFnet initially connected the NSF-funded supercomputer centers at five universities. Soon after being established, it became available to other academic institutions and research laboratories. By 1990, NSFnet had replaced ARPAnet for most nonmilitary uses, and a wide variety of organizations had established nodes on this network—by 1992 NSFnet connected more than 1 million computers around the world. In 1995 a small part of NSFnet returned to being a research network. The rest became known as the Internet, although this term was used much earlier for both ARPAnet and NSFnet.

1.1.2 What Is the Internet?

The Internet is a huge collection of computers connected in a communications network. These computers are of every imaginable size, configuration, and manufacturer. In fact, some of the devices connected to the Internet—such as plotters and printers—are not computers at all. The innovation that allows all of these diverse devices to communicate with each other is a single, low-level protocol, the Transmission Control Protocol/Internet Protocol (TCP/IP). TCP/IP became the standard for computer network connections in 1982, and it can be used directly to allow a program on one computer to communicate with a program on another computer via the Internet. In most cases, however, a higher-level protocol runs on top of TCP/IP. Nevertheless, it's important to know that TCP/IP provides the low-level interface that allows most computers (and other devices) connected to the Internet to appear exactly the same.[2]

Rather than connecting every computer on the Internet directly to every other computer on the Internet, normally the individual computers in an organization are connected to each other in a local network. One node on this local network is physically connected to the Internet. So, the Internet is actually a network of networks rather than a network of computers.

Obviously, all devices connected to the Internet must be uniquely identifiable.

---

2. TCP/IP is not the only communication protocol used by the Internet—UDP/IP is an alternative that is used in some situations.

1.1.3   Internet Protocol Addresses

For people, Internet nodes are identified by names; for computers, they are identified by numeric addresses. This exactly parallels the relationship between a variable name in a program, which is for people, and the variable's numeric memory address, which is for the machine.

The Internet Protocol (IP) address of a machine connected to the Internet is a unique 32-bit number. IP addresses usually are written (and thought of) as four 8-bit numbers, separated by periods. The four parts are separately used by Internet-routing computers to decide where a message must go next to get to its destination.

Organizations are assigned blocks of IPs, which they in turn assign to their machines that need Internet access—which now includes most computers. For example, a small organization may be assigned 256 IP addresses, such as `191.57.126.0` to `191.57.126.255`. Very large organizations, such as the Department of Defense, may be assigned 16 million IP addresses, which include IP addresses with one particular first 8-bit number, such as `12.0.0.0` to `12.255.255.255`.

Although people nearly always type domain names into their browsers, the IP works just as well. For example, the IP for United Airlines (`www.ual.com`) is `209.87.113.93`. So, if a browser is pointed at `http://209.87.113.93`, it will be connected to the United Airlines Web site.

In late 1998 a new IP standard, IPv6, was approved, although it has not yet been widely implemented. The most significant change was to expand the address size from 32 bits to 128 bits. This is a change that will soon be essential because the number of remaining unused IP addresses is diminishing rapidly. This new standard can be found at `ftp://ftp.isi.edu/in-notes/rfc2460.txt`.

1.1.4   Domain Names

Because people have difficulty dealing with and remembering numbers, machines on the Internet also have textual names. These names begin with the name of the host machine, followed by progressively larger enclosing collections of machines, called *domains*. There may be two, three, or more domain names. The first domain name, which appears immediately to the right of the hostname, is the domain of which the host is a part. The second domain name gives the domain of which the first domain is a part. The last domain name identifies the type of organization in which the host resides, which is the largest domain in the site's name. For organizations in the United States, `edu` is the extension for educational institutions, `com` specifies a company, `gov` is used for the U.S. government, and `org` is used for many other kinds of organizations. In other countries, the largest domain is often an abbreviation for the country—for example, `se` is used for Sweden, and `kz` is used for Kazakhstan.

Consider this sample address:

```
movies.comedy.marxbros.com
```

Here, `movies` is the hostname and `comedy` is `movies`'s local domain, which is a part of `marxbros`'s domain, which is a part of the `com` domain. The hostname and all of the domain names are together called a *fully qualified domain name*.

Because IP addresses are the addresses used internally by the Internet, the fully qualified domain name of the destination for a message, which is what is given by a browser user, must be converted to an IP address before the message can be transmitted on the Internet to the destination. These conversions are done by software systems called *name servers*, which implement the Domain Name System (DNS). Name servers serve a collection of machines on the Internet and are operated by organizations that are responsible for the part of the Internet to which those machines are connected. All document requests from browsers are routed to the nearest name server. If the name server can convert the fully qualified domain name to an IP address, it does so. If it cannot, the name server sends the fully qualified domain name to another name server for conversion. Like IP addresses, fully qualified domain names must be unique. Figure 1.1 shows how fully qualified domain names requested by a browser are translated into IPs before they are routed to the appropriate Web server.

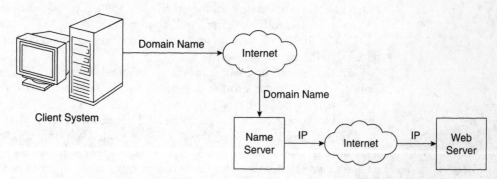

Figure 1.1   Domain name conversion

One way to determine the IP address of a Web site is by using `telnet` on the fully qualified domain name. This is illustrated in Section 1.7.1.

By the mid-1980s, a collection of different protocols that run on top of TCP/IP had been developed to support a variety of Internet uses. Among these, the most common were `telnet`, which was developed to allow a user on one computer on the Internet to log on to and use another computer on the Internet; File Transfer Protocol (`ftp`), which was developed to transfer files among computers on the Internet; Usenet, which was developed to serve as an electronic bulletin board; and `mailto`, which was developed to allow messages to be sent from the user of one computer on the Internet to other users on other computers on the Internet.

This variety of protocols, each with its own user interface and useful for only the purpose for which it was designed, restricted the growth of the Internet. Users were required to learn all the different interfaces to gain all the advantages of the Internet. Before long, however, a better approach developed: the World Wide Web.

1.2   The World Wide Web

This section provides a brief introduction to the evolution of the World Wide Web.

1.2.1   Origins

In 1989 a small group of people led by Tim Berners-Lee at CERN (Conseil European pour la Recherce Nucleaire, or the European Laboratory for Particle Physics) proposed a new protocol for the Internet as well as a system of document access to use it.[3] The intent of this new system, which the group named the World Wide Web, was to allow scientists around the world to use the Internet to exchange documents describing their work.

The proposed new system was designed to allow a user anywhere on the Internet to search for and retrieve documents from databases on any number of different document-serving computers. By late 1990, the basic ideas for the new system had been fully developed and implemented on a NeXT computer at CERN. In 1991 the system was ported to other computer platforms and released to the rest of the world.

For the form of its documents, the system used *hypertext*, which is text with embedded links to text in other documents to allow nonsequential browsing of textual material. The idea of hypertext had been developed earlier and had appeared in Xerox's NoteCards and Apple's HyperCard in the mid-1980s.

From here on, we will refer to the World Wide Web simply as "the Web." The units of information on the Web have been referred to by several different names; among them, the most common are *pages*, *documents*, and *resources*. Perhaps the best of these is *documents*, although that seems to imply only text. *Pages* is widely used, but it is misleading in that Web units of information often have more than one of the kind of pages that make up printed media. There is some merit to calling these units *resources* because that covers the possibility of nontextual information. This book will use *documents* and *pages* more or less interchangeably, but we prefer *documents* in most situations.

Documents are sometimes just text, usually with embedded links to other documents, but they often also include images, sound recordings, or other kinds of media. When a document contains nontextual information, it is called *hypermedia*.

In an abstract sense, the Web is a vast collection of documents, some of which are connected by links. These documents are accessed by Web browsers, introduced in Section 1.3, and are provided by Web servers, introduced in Section 1.4.

---

3. Although Berners-Lee's college degree (from Oxford) was in physics, his first stint at CERN was as a consulting software engineer. Berners-Lee was born and raised in London.

1.2.2   Web or Internet?

It is important to understand that the Internet and the Web are not the same thing. The *Internet* is a collection of computers and other devices connected by equipment that allows them to communicate with each other. The *Web* is a collection of software and protocols that has been installed on most, if not all, of the computers on the Internet. Each computer on the Internet is used either to request and display documents, or provide requested documents to requestors, or both. The Internet was quite useful before the Web was developed, and it is still useful without it. However, it is now the case that most users of the Internet use it through the Web.

1.3   Web Browsers

When two computers communicate over some network, in many cases one acts as a client and the other as a server. The client initiates the communication, which is often a request for information stored on the server, which sends that information back to the client. The Web, as well as many other systems, operates in this client/server configuration.

Documents provided by servers on the Web are requested by *browsers*, which are programs running on client machines. They are called browsers because they allow the user to browse the resources available on servers. The first browsers were text based—they were not capable of displaying any sort of graphic information, nor did they have a graphical user interface. This effectively constrained growth of Web use. In early 1993 this changed with the release of Mosaic, the first browser with a graphical user interface. Mosaic was developed at the National Center for Supercomputer Applications (NCSA) at the University of Illinois. This interface provided convenient access to the Web for users who were neither scientists nor software developers. The first release of Mosaic ran on UNIX systems using the X Window system. By late 1993 versions of Mosaic for Apple Macintosh and Microsoft Windows systems had been released. Finally, users of the computers connected to the Internet around the world had a powerful way to access anything on the Web anywhere in the world. The result of this power and convenience was explosive growth in Web usage.

A browser is a client on the Web because it initiates the communication with a server, which waits for a request from a client before doing anything. In the simplest case, a browser requests a static document from a server. The server locates the document and sends it to the browser, which displays it for the user. However, more complicated situations are common. For example, the server may provide a document that requests input from the user through the browser. After the user supplies the requested input, it is transmitted from the browser to the server, which may perform some computation using it and then return a new document to the browser to inform the user of the results of the computation. Sometimes a browser directly requests the execution of a program stored on the server. The output of the program is then returned to the browser.

Although the Web supports a variety of protocols, the most common one is the Hypertext Transfer Protocol (HTTP). HTTP provides a standard form of communication between browsers and Web servers. Section 1.7 provides an introduction to HTTP.

The most commonly used browsers are Microsoft Internet Explorer (IE), which runs only on PCs that use one of the Microsoft Windows operating systems,[4] and Firefox, which is available in versions for several different computing platforms, including Windows, Mac OS, and Linux. There are several other browsers available, such as the close relatives of Firefox, Mozilla Suite, and Netscape Navigator, as well as Opera and Apple's Safari. However, because the great majority of browsers now in use are either IE or Firefox, in this book we focus on those two.

1.4 Web Servers

Web servers are programs that provide documents to requesting browsers. Servers are slave programs: They act only when requests are made to them by browsers running on other computers on the Internet.

The most commonly used Web servers are Apache, which has been implemented for a variety of computer platforms, and Microsoft's Internet Information Server (IIS), which runs under Windows operating systems. As of April 2008, there were over 66 million active Web hosts in operation, about half of which were Apache, about 35 percent of which were IIS, and the remainder were spread thinly over a large number of others. (The third-place server was Google, with just over 6 percent.)[5]

1.4.1 Web Server Operation

Although having clients and servers is a natural consequence of information distribution, this configuration offers some additional benefits for the Web. Serving information does not take a great deal of time. On the other hand, displaying information on client screens is time consuming. Because Web servers need not be involved in this display process, they can handle many clients. So, it is both a natural and an efficient division of labor to have a small number of servers provide documents to a large number of clients.

Web browsers initiate network communications with servers by sending them URLs (discussed in Section 1.5). A URL can specify one of two different things: the address of a data file stored on the server that is to be sent to the client, or a program stored on the server that the client wants executed, with the output of the program returned to the client.

---

4. Actually, versions 4 and 5 of IE (IE4 and IE5) were also available for Macintosh computers, and IE4 was available for UNIX systems. However, IE6 and IE7 are currently available for Windows platforms only.

5. These statistics are from `http://www.netcraft.com`.

All the communications between a Web client and a Web server use the standard Web protocol, Hypertext Transfer Protocol (HTTP), which is discussed in Section 1.7.[6]

When a Web server begins execution, it informs the operating system under which it is running that it is now ready to accept incoming network connections through a specific port on the machine. While in this running state, the server runs as a background process in the operating system environment. A Web client, or browser, opens a network connection to a Web server, sends information requests and possibly data to the server, receives information from the server, and closes the connection. Of course, other machines exist between browsers and servers on the network—specifically, network routers and domain-name servers. This section, however, focuses on just one part of Web communication: the server.

Simply put, the primary task of a Web server is to monitor a communications port on its host machine, accept HTTP commands through that port, and perform the operations specified by the commands. All HTTP commands include a URL, which includes the specification of a host server machine. When the URL is received, it is translated into either a filename (in which case the file is returned to the requesting client) or a program name (in which case the program is run and its output is sent to the requesting client). This sounds pretty simple, but as is the case in many other simple-sounding processes, a large number of complicating details are involved.

All current Web servers have a common ancestry: the first two servers, developed at CERN in Europe and NCSA at the University of Illinois. Currently, the most common server configuration is Apache running on some version of UNIX.

1.4.2 General Server Characteristics

Most available servers share common characteristics, regardless of their origin or the platform on which they run. This section provides brief descriptions of some of these characteristics.

The file structure of a Web server has two separate directories. The root of one of these is called the *document root*. The file hierarchy that grows from the document root stores the Web documents to which the server has direct access and normally serves to clients. The root of the other directory is called the *server root*. This directory, along with its descendant directories, stores the server and its support software.

The files stored directly in the document root are those available to clients through top-level URLs. Typically, clients do not access the document root directly in URLs; rather, the server maps requested URLs to the document root, whose location is not known to clients. For example, suppose that the site name is www.tunias.com (not a real site, at least not yet), which happens to be a UNIX-based system. Further suppose that the document root is named

---

6. Some of these communications use the secure version of HTTP, HTTPS.

topdocs and is stored in the /admin/web directory, making its address /admin/web/topdocs. A request for a file from a client with the URL http://www.tunias.com/petunias.html will cause the server to search for the file with the file path /admin/web/topdocs/petunias.html. Likewise, the URL http://www.tunias.com/bulbs/tulips.html will cause the server to search for the file with the address /admin/web/topdocs/bulbs/tulips.html.

Many servers allow part of the servable document collection to be stored outside the directory at the document root. The secondary areas from which documents can be served are called *virtual document trees*. For example, the original configuration of a server might store all its servable documents from the primary system disk on the server machine. Later, the collection of servable documents might outgrow that disk, in which case part of the collection could be stored on a secondary disk. This secondary disk might reside on the server machine or on some other machine on a local area network. To support this arrangement, the server is configured to direct request URLs with a particular file path to a storage area separate from the document-root directory. Sometimes files of different types of content, such as images, are stored outside the document root.

Early servers provided few services other than the basic process of returning requested files or the output of programs whose execution had been requested. The list of additional services has grown steadily over the years. Contemporary servers are large and complex systems that provide a wide variety of client services. Many servers can support more than one site on a computer, potentially reducing the cost of each site and making their maintenance more convenient. Such secondary hosts are called *virtual hosts*.

Some servers can serve documents that are in the document root of other machines on the Web; in this case, they are called *proxy servers*.

Although Web servers were originally designed to support only the HTTP protocol, many now support ftp, gopher, news, and mailto. In addition, nearly all Web servers can interact with database systems through Common Gateway Interface (CGI) programs and server-side scripts.

1.4.3 Apache

Apache began as the NCSA server, httpd, with some added features. The name Apache has nothing to do with the Native American tribe of the same name. Rather, it came from the nature of its first version, which was *a patch*y version of the httpd server. As seen in the usage statistics given at the beginning of this section, Apache is the most widely used Web server. The primary reasons for this are as follows: It is an excellent server because it's both fast and reliable. Furthermore, it is open-source software, which means it is free and is managed by a large team of volunteers, a process that efficiently and effectively maintains the system. Finally, it is one of the best available servers for Unix-based systems, which are the most popular for Web servers.

Apache is capable of providing a long list of services beyond the basic process of serving documents to clients. When Apache begins execution, it reads its configuration information from a file and sets its parameters to operate accordingly. A new copy of Apache includes default configuration information for a "typical" operation. The site manager modifies this configuration information to fit his or her particular needs and tastes.

For historical reasons, there are three configuration files in an Apache server: `httpd.conf`, `srm.conf`, and `access.conf`. Only one of these, `httpd.conf`, actually stores the directives that control an Apache server's behavior. The other two point to `httpd.conf`. This file contains the list of directives that specify the server's operation. These directives are described at `http://httpd.apache.org/docs/2.2/mod/quickreference.html`.

1.4.4   IIS

Although Apache has been ported to the Windows platforms, it is not the most popular server on those systems. Because the Microsoft IIS server is supplied as part of Windows—and because it is a reasonably good server—most Windows-based Web servers use IIS. Apache and IIS provide similar varieties of services.

From the point of view of the site manager, the most important difference between Apache and IIS is that Apache is controlled by a configuration file that is edited by the manager to change Apache's behavior. With IIS, server behavior is modified by changes made through a window-based management program, named the IIS snap-in, which controls both IIS and `ftp`. This program allows the site manager to set parameters for the server.

Under Windows XP and Vista, the IIS snap-in is accessed by going to Control Panel, Administrative Tools, and IIS Admin. Clicking on this last selection takes you to a window that allows starting, stopping, or pausing IIS. This same window allows IIS parameters to be changed when the server has been stopped.

1.5   Uniform Resource Locators

Uniform (or universal)[7] resource locators (URLs) are used to identify documents (resources) on the Internet. There are many different kinds of resources, identified by different forms of URLs.

1.5.1   URL Formats

All URLs have the same general format:

scheme:object-address

The scheme is often a communications protocol. Common schemes include `http`, `ftp`, `gopher`, `telnet`, `file`, `mailto`, and `news`. Different schemes use

---

7. Fortunately, resource addresses are usually referred to as URLs, so whether it is *uniform* or *universal* is usually irrelevant.

object addresses that have differing forms. Our main interest is in the HTTP protocol, which supports the Web. It is used to request and send eXtensible Hypertext Markup Language (XHTML) documents. In the case of HTTP, the form of the object address of a URL is as follows:

//fully-qualified-domain-name/path-to-document

Another scheme of interest to us is `file`. The `file` protocol means that the document resides on the machine running the browser. This is useful for testing documents to be made available on the Web, without actually making them visible to any other browser. When `file` is the protocol, the fully qualified domain name is omitted, making the form of such URLs as follows:

`file://`*path-to-document*

Because the focus of this book is on XHTML documents, the remainder of the discussion of URLs is limited to the HTTP protocol.

The hostname is the name of the server computer that stores the document (or provides access to it on some other computer). Messages to a host machine must be directed to the appropriate process running on the host for handling. Such processes are identified by their associated port numbers. The default port number of Web server processes is 80. If a server has been configured to use some other port number, it is necessary to attach that port number to the hostname in the URL. For example, if the Web server is configured to use port 800, the hostname must have `:800` attached.

URLs can never have embedded spaces.[8] Also, there is a collection of special characters that cannot appear in a URL, including semicolons, colons, and ampersands (`&`). To include a space or one of the disallowed special characters in a URL, the character must be coded as a percent sign (`%`) followed by the two-digit hexadecimal ASCII code for the character. For example, if `San Jose` is a domain name, it must be typed as `San%20Jose` (20 is the hexadecimal ASCII code for a space). All of the details of URLs can be found at `http://www.w3.org/Addressing/URL/URI_Overview.html`.

1.5.2   URL Paths

The path to the document for the HTTP protocol is similar to a path to a file or directory in the file system of an operating system: a sequence of directory names and a filename, all separated by whatever separator character the operating system uses. For UNIX servers, the path is specified with forward slashes; for Windows servers, it is specified with backward slashes. Most browsers allow the user to specify the separators incorrectly—for example, using forward slashes in a path to a document file on a Windows server.

The path in a URL can differ from a path to a file because a URL need not include all directories on the path. A path that includes all directories along the

---

8. Actually, some browsers incorrectly accept spaces in URLs, although this is nonstandard behavior.

way is called a *complete path*. In most cases, the path to the document is relative to some base path that is specified in the configuration files of the server. Such paths are called *partial paths*. For example, if the server's configuration specifies that the root directory for files it can serve is `files/f99`, the previous URL is specified as follows:

```
http://www.gumboco.com/storefront.html
```

If the specified document is a directory rather than a single document, the directory's name is followed immediately by a slash, as in the following:

```
http://www.gumboco.com/departments/
```

Sometimes a directory is specified (with the trailing slash) but its name is not given, as in the following example:

```
http://www.gumboco.com/
```

The server then searches at the top level of the directory in which servable documents are normally stored for something it recognizes as a home page. By convention, this is often a file named `index.html`. The home page usually includes links that allow the user to find the other related servable files on the server.

If the directory does not have a file that the server recognizes as being a home page, a directory listing is constructed and returned to the browser.

1.6 Multipurpose Internet Mail Extensions

A browser needs some way of determining the format of a document it receives from a Web server. Without knowing the form of a document, the browser would be unable to render it, because different document formats require different rendering tools. The forms of these documents are specified with the Multipurpose Internet Mail Extensions (MIME).

1.6.1 Type Specifications

MIME was developed to specify the format of different kinds of documents to be sent using Internet mail. These could be various kinds of text, video data, or sound data. Because the Web has similar needs, MIME was adopted as the way to specify document types transmitted over the Web. A Web server attaches a MIME format specification to the beginning of the document that it is about to provide to a browser. When the browser receives the document from a Web server, it uses the included MIME format specification to determine what to do with the document. If the content is text, for example, the MIME code tells the browser that it is text and also indicates the particular kind of text it is. If the content is sound, the MIME code tells the browser that it is sound and then gives the particular representation of sound so that the browser can choose a program to which it has access to produce the transmitted sound.

MIME specifications have the following form:

type/subtype

The most common MIME types are `text`, `image`, and `video`. The most common text subtypes are `plain` and `html`. Some common image subtypes are `gif` and `jpeg`. Some common video subtypes are `mpeg` and `quicktime`. A list of MIME specifications is stored in the configuration files of every Web server. In the remainder of this book, when we say *document type*, we mean both the document's type and its subtype.

Servers determine the type of a document by using the filename's extension as the key into a table of types. For example, the extension `.html` tells the server that it should attach `text/html` to the document before sending it to the requesting browser.[9]

Browsers also maintain a conversion table for looking up the type of a document by its filename extension. However, this is used only when the server does not specify a MIME type, which may be the case for some older servers. In all other cases, the browser gets the document type from the MIME header provided by the server.

1.6.2   Experimental Document Types

Experimental subtypes are sometimes used. The name of an experimental subtype begins with `x-`, as in `video/x-msvideo`. Any Web provider can add an experimental subtype by having its name added to the list of MIME specifications stored in the Web provider's server. For example, a Web provider might have a handcrafted database whose contents he or she wants to make available to others through the Web. Of course, this raises the issue of how the browser can display the database. As might be expected, the Web provider must supply a program that the browser can call when it needs to display the contents of the database. These programs either are external to the browser, in which case they are called *helper applications*, or are code modules that are inserted into the browser, in which case they are called *plug-ins*.

Every browser has a set of MIME specifications it can handle. All can deal with `text/plain` (unformatted text) and `text/html` (HTML files), among others. It sometimes occurs that a particular browser cannot handle some specific document type, even though the type is widely used. These cases are handled in the same way as the experimental types described previously. The browser determines the helper application or plug-in it needs by examining the browser configuration file, which provides an association between file types and their required helpers or plug-ins. If the browser does not have an application or a plug-in that it needs to render a document, an error message is displayed.

A browser can indicate to the server the document types it prefers to receive, as discussed in Section 1.7.

---

9. This is not necessarily correct. XHTML documents also use the `.html` file extension, but strictly speaking should use a different MIME type.

1.7 The Hypertext Transfer Protocol

All Web communications transactions use the same protocol—the Hypertext Transfer Protocol (HTTP). The current version of HTTP is 1.1. It is formally defined as RFC 2616, which was approved in June 1999. RFC 2616 is available at the Web site for the World Wide Web Consortium (W3C), `http://www.w3.org`. This section provides a brief introduction to HTTP.

HTTP consists of two phases, the request and the response. Each HTTP communication (request or response) between a browser and a Web server consists of two parts, a header and a body. The header contains information about the communication; the body contains the data of the communication, if there is any.

1.7.1 The Request Phase

The general form of an HTTP request is as follows:

1. HTTP method   Domain part of the URL   HTTP version
2. Header fields
3. Blank line
4. Message body

The following is an example of the first line of an HTTP request:

```
GET  /storefront.html  HTTP/1.1
```

Only a few request methods are defined by HTTP, and even a smaller number of these are typically used. Table 1.1 lists the most commonly used methods.

Table 1.1 HTTP request methods

Method	Description
GET	Returns the contents of the specified document
HEAD	Returns the header information for the specified document
POST	Executes the specified document, using the enclosed data
PUT	Replaces the specified document with the enclosed data
DELETE	Deletes the specified document

Among the methods given in Table 1.1, GET and POST are the most frequently used. POST was originally designed for tasks such as posting a news article to a newsgroup. Its most common use now is to send form data from a browser to a server, along with a request to execute a program on the server that will process the form data.

Following the first line of an HTTP communication is any number of header fields, most of which are optional. The format of a header field is the field name followed by a colon and the value of the field. There are four categories of header fields:

1. *General*: For general information, such as the date
2. *Request*: Included in request headers
3. *Response*: For response headers
4. *Entity*: Used in both request and response headers

One common request field is the `Accept` field, which specifies a preference of the browser for the MIME type of the requested document. More than one `Accept` field can be specified if the browser is willing to accept documents in more than one format. For example:

```
Accept: text/plain
Accept: text/html
Accept: image/gif
```

A wildcard character, the asterisk (*), can be used to specify that part of a MIME type can be anything. For example, if any kind of text is acceptable, the `Accept` field could be as follows:

```
Accept: text/*
```

The `Host: hostname` request field gives the name of the host. The `Host` field is required for HTTP 1.1. The `If-Modified-Since: date` request field specifies that the requested file should be sent only if it has been modified since the given date.

If the request has a body, the length of that body must be given with a `Content-length` field, which gives the length of the response body in bytes. `POST` method requests require this field because they send data to the server.

The header of a request must be followed by a blank line, which is used to separate the header from the body of the request. Requests that use the `GET`, `HEAD`, and `DELETE` methods do not have bodies. In these cases, the blank line signals the end of the request.

A browser is not necessary to communicate with a Web server; `telnet` also can be used. Consider the following command, given at the command line of any widely used operating system:

```
> telnet blanca.uccs.edu http
```

This command creates a connection to the `http` port on the `blanca.uccs.edu` server. The server responds with the following:[10]

```
Trying 128.198.162.60 ...
Connected to blanca
Escape character is '^]'.
```

The connection to the server is now complete, and HTTP commands can be given. For example:

---

10. Notice that this `telnet` request returns the IP of the server.

```
GET /respond.html HTTP/1.1
Host: blanca.uccs.edu
```

The header of the response to this request is given in Section 1.7.2.

1.7.2   The Response Phase

The general form of an HTTP response is as follows:

1. Status line
2. Response header fields
3. Blank line
4. Response body

The status line includes the HTTP version used, a three-digit status code for the response, and a short textual explanation of the status code. For example, most responses begin with the following:

```
HTTP/1.1  200  OK
```

The status codes begin with 1, 2, 3, 4, or 5. The general meanings of the five categories specified by these first digits are shown in Table 1.2.

Table 1.2   First digits of HTTP status codes

First Digit	Category
1	Informational
2	Success
3	Redirection
4	Client error
5	Server error

One of the more common status codes is one users never want to see: 404 Not Found, which means the requested file could not be found. Of course, 200 OK is what users want to see, because it means the request was handled without error. The 500 code means the server has encountered a problem and was not able to fulfill the request.

After the status line, the server sends a response header, which can contain several lines of information about the response, each in the form of a field. The only essential field of the header is Content-type.

The following is the response header for the request given near the end of Section 1.7.1:

```
HTTP/1.1  200  OK
Date: Tues, 18 May 2004 16:45:13 GMT
Server: Apache (Red-Hat/Linux)
Last-modified: Tues, 18 May 2004 16:38:38 GMT
ETag: "1f1223-16c-92dc9f80"
Accept-ranges: bytes
Content-length: 364
Connection: close
Content-type: text/html, charset=ISO-8859-1
```

The response header must be followed by a blank line, as is the case for request headers. The response data follows the blank line. In the preceding example, the response body would be the HTML file, `respond.html`.

In HTTP versions prior to 1.1, when a server finished sending a response to the client, the communications connection was closed. However, the default operation of HTTP 1.1 is that the connection is kept open for a time so that a client can make several requests over a short period of time without needing to reestablish the communications connection with the server. This change led to significant increases in the efficiency of the Web.

1.8 Security

It does not take a great deal of contemplation to realize that the Internet and the Web are fertile grounds for security problems. On the Web server side, anyone on the planet with a computer, a browser, and an Internet connection can request the execution of software on the server computer. He or she can also access data and databases stored on the server computer. On the browser end, the problem is similar: Any server to which the browser points can download software that is to be executed on the browser host machine. Such software potentially can access parts of the memory and memory devices attached to that machine that are not related to the needs of the original browser request. In effect, on both ends, it is like allowing any number of total strangers into your house and preventing them from leaving anything in the house, taking anything from the house, or altering anything in the house. The larger and more complex the design of the house, the more difficult it will be to prevent any of those activities. The same is true for Web servers and browsers: The larger and more complex they are, the more difficult it is to prevent security breaches. Today's browsers and Web servers are indeed large and complex software systems, so security is a significant problem in Web applications.

The subject of Internet and Web security is extensive and complicated, so much so that more than a few books that discuss it have been written. Therefore, in this one section of one chapter of one book, there can be no more than a brief sketch of some of the subtopics of security.

One of the aspects of Web security is the matter of getting one's data from the browser to the server and having the server deliver data back to the browser without anyone or any device intercepting or corrupting that data along the way. Consider just the simplest case, that of transmitting a credit card number to a company from which a purchase is being made. The security issues for this transaction are as follows:

1. *Privacy*—it must not be possible for the credit card number to be stolen on its way to the company's server.

2. *Integrity*—it must not be possible for the credit card number to be modified on its way to the company's server.

3. *Authentication*—it must be possible for both the purchaser and the seller to be certain of each other's identity.

4. *Nonrepudiation*—it must be possible to prove legally that the message was actually sent and received.

The basic tool to support privacy and integrity is encryption. Data to be transmitted is converted, or encrypted into a different form, which is virtually impossible to decrypt for someone (or some computer) who is not supposed to access the data. So, if data is intercepted while en route between Internet nodes, the interceptor cannot use the data because he or she cannot decrypt it. Both encryption and decryption are done with a key and a process (applying the key to the data). Encryption is not a process first developed for the Internet. Julius Caesar used a crude encryption process on the messages he sent to his field generals while at war. Until the middle 1970s, the process used the same key for both encryption and decryption. Because both the sender and receiver used the same key, the initial problem was how to transmit the key from the sender to the receiver.

This problem was solved in 1976 by Whitfield Diffie and Martin Hellman of Stanford University, who developed public-key encryption. In *public-key encryption*, a public key and a private key are used, the public key to encrypt messages and the private key to decrypt messages. A communicator, say Joe, has an inversely related pair of keys, one public and one private. The public key can be distributed to all organizations that might send Joe messages. All of them can use the public key to encrypt messages to Joe, who can decrypt the messages with his matching private key. This works because the private key need never be transmitted, and also because it is virtually impossible to compute the private key from its public key. The technical wording for this is that it is "computationally infeasible" to determine the private key from its public key.

The most widely used public-key algorithm is named RSA, developed in 1977 by three MIT professors, Ron Rivest, Adi Shamir, and Leonard Adleman, the first letters of whose last names were used to name the algorithm. Most large companies now use RSA for e-commerce.

Another completely different security problem for the Web is the intentional and malicious destruction of data on computers attached to the Internet. The number of different ways this can be done has increased steadily over the life span of the Web. Their sheer numbers have also grown rapidly. There is now a continuous stream of new and increasingly devious denial-of-service (DoS), viruses, and worms being discovered, which have caused billions of dollars of damage, primarily to businesses that use the Web heavily. Of course, huge damage also has been done to home computer systems through Web intrusions.

DoS attacks can be created simply by flooding a Web server with requests, overwhelming its ability to operate correctly. Most DoS attacks are conducted using networks of virally infected "zombie" computers, whose owners are unaware of their sinister use. So, DoS and viruses are often related.

Viruses are programs that often arrive in a system in attachments to e-mail messages or attached to free downloaded programs. Then they attach to other programs. When executed, they replicate and can themselves overwrite memory and attached memory devices, destroying programs and data alike. Two viruses that were extensively destructive appeared in 2000 and 2001, the ILOVEYOU virus and the CodeRed virus, respectively.

Worms damage memory, like viruses, but spread on their own, rather than being attached to other files. Perhaps the most famous worm so far has been the Blaster worm, launched in 2003.

DoS, virus, and worm attacks are created by malicious people referred to as *hackers*. The incentive for these people apparently is simply the feeling of pride and accomplishment they derive from being able to cause huge amounts of damage by outwitting the designers of Web software systems.

Protection against viruses and worms is provided by antivirus software, which must be updated frequently so that it can detect and protect against the continuous stream of new viruses and worms.

1.9   The Web Programmer's Toolbox

This section provides an overview of the most common tools used in Web programming—some are programming languages, some are not. The tools discussed are XHTML, a markup language, along with a few high-level markup document editing systems; XML, a meta-markup language; JavaScript, PHP, and Ruby, which are programming languages; JSF, ASP.NET, and Rails, which are development frameworks for Web-based systems; Flash, a technology for creating and displaying graphics and animation in XHTML documents; AJAX, a Web technology that uses JavaScript and XML.

Web programs and scripts are divided into two categories, client side and server side, according to where they are interpreted or executed. XHTML and XML are client-side languages; PHP and Ruby are server-side languages; JavaScript is most often a client-side language, although it can be used for both.

We begin with the most basic tool, XHTML.

1.9.1   Overview of XHTML

At the onset, it is important to realize that XHTML is not a programming language—it cannot be used to describe computations. Its purpose is to describe the general form and layout of documents to be displayed by a browser.

The word *markup* comes from the publishing world, where it is used to describe what production people do with a manuscript to specify to a printer how the text, graphics, and other elements in the book should appear in printed form. XHTML is not the first markup language used with computers. TeX and LaTeX are older markup languages for use with text; they are now used primarily to specify how mathematical expressions and formulas should appear in print.

An XHTML document is a mixture of content and controls. The controls are specified by the tags of XHTML. The name of a tag specifies the category of its content. Most XHTML tags consist of a pair of syntactic markers that are used to delimit particular kinds of content. The pair of tags and their content together is called an *element*. For example, a paragraph element specifies that its content, which appears between its opening tag, `<p>`, and its closing tag, `</p>`, is a paragraph. A browser has a default style (font, font style, font size, and so forth) for paragraphs, which is used to display the content of a paragraph element.

Some tags include attribute specifications that provide some additional information for the browser. In the following example, the attribute specifies the location of its image content:

```
<img src = "redhead.jpg"/>
```

In this case, the image document stored in `redhead.jpg` is to be displayed at the position in the document in which this tag appears.

XHTML 1.0 was introduced in early 2000 by the W3C as an alternative to HTML 4.01, which was at that time (and still is) the latest version of HTML. XHTML 1.0 is nothing more than HTML 4.01 with stronger syntactic rules. These stronger rules are those of XML (see Section 1.9.4). The current version, XHTML 1.1, was released in May 2001 as a replacement for XHTML 1.0, although for various reasons, XHTML 1.0 is still widely used. Chapter 2, "Introduction to XHTML," provides a description of a large subset of XHTML.

1.9.2   Tools for Creating XHTML Documents

XHTML documents can be created with a general-purpose text editor. There are two kinds of tools that can simplify this task: XHTML editors and what-you-see-is-what-you-get (WYSIWYG, pronounced *wizzy-wig*) XHTML editors.

XHTML editors provide shortcuts to producing repetitious tags such as those used to create the rows of a table. They also may provide a spell-checker and a syntax-checker, and they may color code the XHTML in the display to make it easier to read and edit.

A more powerful tool for creating XHTML documents is a WYSIWYG XHTML editor. Using a WYSIWYG XHTML editor, the writer can see the document that the XHTML describes while writing the XHTML. WYSIWYG XHTML editors are very useful for beginners who want to create simple documents without learning XHTML and for users who want to prototype the appearance of a document. On the other hand, these editors sometimes produce poor-quality XHTML. In some cases, they create proprietary tags that some browsers will not recognize.

Two examples of WYSIWYG XHTML editors are Microsoft FrontPage and Adobe Dreamweaver. Both allow the user to create XHTML-described documents without requiring the user to know XHTML. They cannot handle all of the tags of XHTML, but they are very useful for creating many of the common features of documents. Between the two, FrontPage is by far the most widely used. Information on Dreamweaver is available at `http://www.adobe.com/;` information on FrontPage is available at `http://www.microsoft.com/frontpage/`.

1.9.3   Plug-ins and Filters

Two different kinds of converters can be used to create XHTML documents. *Plug-ins*[11] are programs that can be integrated with a word processor. Plug-ins add new capabilities to the word processor, such as toolbar buttons and menu elements that provide convenient ways to insert XHTML into the document being created or edited. After such insertions, the document is displayed using the XHTML. So, the plug-in makes the word processor appear to be an XHTML editor that provides WYSIWYG XHTML document development. The end result of this process is an XHTML document. The plug-in also makes available all the tools that are inherent to the word processor during XHTML document creation, such as a spell-checker and a thesaurus.

A second kind of converter is a *filter*, which converts an existing document in some form, such as LaTeX or Microsoft Word, to XHTML. Filters are never part of the editor or word processor that created the document. This is an advantage because they can be platform-independent. For example, a Word-Perfect user working on a Macintosh computer can provide documents that can be later converted to XHTML using a filter running on a UNIX platform. The disadvantage of filters is that creating XHTML documents with a filter is a two-step process: First you create the document and then you use a filter to convert it to XHTML.

Neither plugs-ins nor filters produce XHTML documents that, when displayed by browsers, have the identical appearance of that produced by the word processor.

The two advantages of both plug-ins and filters, however, are that existing documents produced with word processors can be easily converted to XHTML

---

11. The word *plug-in* applies to many different software systems that can be added to or embedded in other software systems. For example, many different plug-ins can be added to Web browsers.

and that users can produce XHTML documents using a word processor with which they are familiar. This obviates the need to learn to format text using XHTML directly. For example, once you learn to create tables with your word processor, it is easier to use that process than to learn to define tables directly in XHTML.

The XHTML output produced by both filters and plug-ins often must be modified, usually using a simple text editor, to perfect the appearance of the displayed document in the browser. Because this new XHTML file cannot be converted to its original form (regardless of how it was created), you will have two different source files for a document. This inevitably leads to version problems during maintenance of the document. This is clearly a disadvantage of using converters.

1.9.4   Overview of XML

HTML is defined using the Standard Generalized Markup Language (SGML), which is a language for defining markup languages (such languages are called meta-markup languages). XML (eXtensible Markup Language) is a simplified version of SGML, designed to allow users to easily create markup languages that fit their own needs. XHTML is defined using XML. Whereas XHTML users must use the predefined set of tags and attributes, when a user creates his or her own markup language using XML, the set of tags and attributes is designed for the application at hand. For example, if a group of users wants a markup language to describe data about weather phenomena, that language could have tags for cloud forms, thunderstorms, and low-pressure centers. The content of these tags would be restricted to relevant data. If such data is described using XHTML, cloud forms could be put in generic tags, but then they could not be distinguished from thunderstorm elements, which would also be in the same generic tags.

Whereas XHTML describes the overall layout and some presentation hints for general information, XML-based markup languages describe data and its meaning through their individualized tags and attributes. XML does not specify any presentation details.

The great advantage of XML is that application programs can be written to use the meanings of the tags in the given markup language to find specific kinds of data and process it accordingly. The syntax rules of XML, along with the syntax rules for a specific XML-based markup language, allow documents to be validated before any application attempts to process their data. This means that all documents that use a specific markup language can be checked to determine whether they are in the standard form for such documents. This greatly simplifies the development of application programs that process the data in XML documents.

1.9.5   Overview of JavaScript

JavaScript is a client-side scripting language whose primary uses in Web programming are to validate form data and to create dynamic XHTML documents.

The name JavaScript is misleading because the relationship between Java and JavaScript is tenuous, except for some of the syntax. One of the most important differences between JavaScript and most common programming languages is that JavaScript is dynamically typed. This is virtually the opposite of strongly typed languages such as C++ and Java.

JavaScript "programs" are usually embedded in XHTML documents.[12] These XHTML documents are downloaded when they are requested by browsers. The JavaScript code in an XHTML document is interpreted by an interpreter embedded in the browser on the client.

One of the most important applications of JavaScript is to dynamically create and modify documents. JavaScript defines an object hierarchy that matches a hierarchical model of an XHTML document. Elements of an XHTML document are accessed through these objects, providing the basis for dynamic documents.

Chapter 4, "The Basics of JavaScript," provides a more detailed look at JavaScript. Chapter 5, "JavaScript and XHTML Documents," and Chapter 6, "Dynamic Documents with JavaScript," discuss the use of JavaScript to provide access to and dynamic modification of XHTML documents.

1.9.6   Overview of Flash

There are two components of Flash, the authoring environment, which is a development framework, and the player. Developers use the authoring environment to create static graphics, animated graphics, text, sound, and interactivity to be part of standalone HTML documents or to be part of other XHTML documents. These documents are served by Web servers to browsers, which use the Flash player plug-in to display the documents. Much of this development is done by clicking buttons, choosing menu items, and dragging and dropping graphics.

Flash makes animation very easy. For example, for motion animation, the developer needs only to supply the beginning and ending positions of the figure to be animated—Flash builds the intervening figures. The interactivity of a Flash application is implemented with ActionScript, a dialect of JavaScript.

Flash is now the leading technology for delivering graphics and animation on the Web. It has been estimated that nearly 99 percent of the world's computers used to access the Internet have a version of the Flash player installed as a plug-in in their browsers.

---

12. We quote the word *programs* to indicate that these are not programs in the general sense of the self-contained collections of C++ or C code we normally call programs.

1.9.7 Overview of Servlets, JavaServer Pages, and JavaServer Faces

There are many computational tasks in a Web interaction that must occur on the server, such as processing order forms and accessing server-resident databases. A Java class called a *servlet* can be used for these applications. A servlet is a compiled Java class, an object of which is executed on the server system when requested by the XHTML document being displayed by the browser. A servlet produces an XHTML document response, some parts of which are static and are generated by simple output statements, while other parts are created dynamically when the servlet is called.

When an HTTP request is received by a Web server, the Web server examines the request. If a servlet must be called, the Web server passes the request to the servlet processor, called a *servlet container*. The servlet container determines which servlet must be executed, makes sure it is loaded, and calls it. As the servlet handles the request, it generates an XHTML document as its response, which is returned to the server through the response object parameter.

Java can also be used as a server-side scripting language. An XHTML document with embedded Java scriptlets is one form of JavaServer Pages (JSP). JSP, which is built on top of servlets, provides alternative ways of constructing dynamic Web documents.

JSP takes an opposite approach to that of servlets: Instead of embedding XHTML in Java code that provides dynamic documents, code of some form is embedded in XHTML documents to provide the dynamic parts of a document. These different forms of code make up the different approaches used by JSP. The basic capabilities of servlets and JSP are the same.

When requested by a browser, a JSP document is processed by a software system called a *JSP container*. Some JSP containers compile the document when the document is loaded on the server; others compile them only when they are requested. The compilation process translates a JSP document into a servlet and then compiles the servlet. So, JSP is actually a simplified approach to writing servlets.

JavaServer Faces (JSF), designed by Sun Microsystems, adds another layer to the JSP technology. The most important contribution of JSF is an event-driven user interface model for Web applications. Client-generated events can be handled by server-side code with JSF.

Servlets, JSP, and JSF are discussed in Chapter 11, "Java Web Software."

1.9.8 Overview of Active Server Pages .NET

Active Server Pages .NET (ASP.NET) is a Microsoft framework for building server-side dynamic documents. ASP.NET documents are supported by programming code executed on the Web server. As we saw in Section 1.9.7, JSF uses Java to describe the dynamic generation of XHTML documents, as well as computation associated with user interactions with documents. ASP.NET provides an alternative to JSF, with two major differences: First, ASP.NET allows the server-side programming code to be written in any of the .NET languages. Second, in ASP.NET all programming code is compiled, which allows it to execute much faster than interpreted code.

Every ASP.NET document is compiled into a class. From a programmer's point of view, developing dynamic Web documents (and the supporting code) in ASP.NET is similar to developing non-Web applications. Both involve defining classes based on library classes, implementing interfaces from a library, and calling methods defined in library classes. An application class uses and interacts with existing classes. In ASP.NET, this is exactly the same for Web applications. Web documents are designed by designing classes.

ASP.NET is discussed in Chapter 12, "Introduction to ASP.NET."

1.9.9 Overview of PHP

PHP is a server-side scripting language specifically designed for Web applications. PHP code is embedded in XHTML documents, as is the case with JavaScript. With PHP, however, the code is interpreted on the server before the XHTML document is delivered to the requesting client. A requested document that includes PHP code is preprocessed to interpret the PHP code and insert its output into the XHTML document. The browser never sees the embedded PHP code and is not aware that a requested document originally included PHP code.

PHP is similar to JavaScript, both in terms of its syntactic appearance and in terms of the dynamic nature of its strings and arrays. Both JavaScript and PHP use dynamic data typing, meaning that the type of a variable is controlled by the most recent assignment to it. PHP's arrays are a combination of dynamic arrays and hashes (associative arrays). The language includes a large number of predefined functions for manipulating arrays.

PHP allows simple access to XHTML form data, so form processing is easy with PHP. PHP also provides support for many different database management systems. This makes it an excellent language for building programs that need Web access to databases.

1.9.10 Overview of Ruby

Ruby (Thomas, et al., 2005) is an object-oriented interpreted scripting language designed by Yukihiro Matsumoto (a.k.a. Matz) in the early 1990s and released in 1996. Since then it has continually evolved and its level of usage has grown rapidly. The original motivation for Ruby was dissatisfaction of its designer with the earlier languages, Perl and Python.

The primary characterizing feature of Ruby is that it is a pure object-oriented language, just as is Smalltalk. Every data value is an object and all operations are via method calls. The operators in Ruby are only syntactic mechanisms to specify method calls for the corresponding operations. Because they are methods, many of the operators can be redefined by user programs. All classes, whether predefined or user-defined, can be subclassed.

Both classes and objects in Ruby are dynamic in the sense that methods can be dynamically added to either. This means that both classes and objects can have different sets of methods at different times during execution. So, different instantiations of the same class can behave differently.

The syntax of Ruby is related to that of Eiffel and Ada. There is no need to declare variables, because dynamic typing is used. In fact, all variables are references and do not have types, though the objects they reference do.

Our interest in Ruby is based on Ruby's use with the Web development framework, Rails (see Section 1.9.11). Rails was designed for use with Ruby, and it is Ruby's primary use in Web programming. Programming in Ruby is introduced in Chapter 14, "Introduction to Ruby."

Ruby is culturally interesting because it is the first programming language designed in Japan that has achieved relatively widespread use.

1.9.11 Overview of Rails

Rails is a development framework for Web-based applications that access databases. A framework is a system in which much of the more-or-less standard software parts are furnished by the framework, so they need not be written by the applications developer. ASP.NET and JSF are also development frameworks for Web-based applications. Rails, whose more official name is Ruby on Rails, was developed by David Heinemeier Hansson in the early 2000s and was released to the public in July 2004. Since then, it has rapidly gained widespread interest and usage. Rails is based on the Model-View-Controller (MVC) architecture for applications, which clearly separates the presentation and the data model from program logic.

Rails applications are tightly bound to relational databases. Many Web applications are closely integrated with database access, so this is a widely applicable architecture.

Rails can be and often is used in conjunction with Ajax. Rails uses the JavaScript framework Prototype to support Ajax and interactions with the JavaScript model of the document being displayed by the browser. Rails also provides other support for developing Ajax, including producing visual effects.

Rails was designed to be used with Ruby and makes use of the strengths of that language. Furthermore, Rails is written in Ruby. Using Rails is introduced in Chapter 15, "Introduction to Rails."

1.9.12 Overview of Ajax

Ajax, shorthand for *A*synchronous *Ja*vaScript + *XML*, has been around for a few years, but did not acquire its catchy name until 2005.[13] The idea of Ajax is rela-

---

13. Ajax was named by Jesse James Garrett, who has on numerous occasions stated that Ajax is shorthand, not an acronym. Thus, we spell it Ajax, not AJAX.

tively simple, but it results in a different way of viewing and building Web interactions. This new approach results in an enriched Web experience for those using a certain category of Web interactions.

In a traditional (as opposed to Ajax) Web interaction, the client sends messages to the server, either by clicking a link in the document being displayed by the browser or by submitting forms to the server. After the link has been clicked or the form has been submitted, the client waits until the server responds with a new document. The entire browser display is then replaced by the new document. Complicated documents take a significant amount of time to be transmitted from the server to the client and more time to be rendered by the browser. In Web applications that require frequent interactions with the client and remain active for a significant amount of time, the delay for receiving and rendering a complete response document can be disruptive to the user.

In an Ajax Web application, there are two variations from the traditional Web interaction. First, the communication from the browser to the server is asynchronous; that is, the browser need not wait for the server to respond, the browser user can continue whatever he or she was doing while the server finds and transmits the requested document and the browser renders the new document. Second, the document provided by the server usually is only a relatively small part of the displayed document, and therefore it takes less time to be transmitted and rendered. These two changes can result in much faster interactions between the browser and the server.

The x in Ajax, XML, is there because in many cases the data supplied by the server is in the form of an XML document, which provides the new data to be placed in the displayed document. However, in some cases it is plain text, which may be either data or even JavaScript code. It can also be XHTML.

The goal of Ajax is to have Web-based applications become closer to desktop (client resident) applications, in terms of the speed of interactions and the quality of the user experience. Wouldn't we all like our Web-based applications to be as responsive as our word processors?

Ajax has some advantages over the competing technologies of ASP.NET and JSP. First and foremost, the technologies that support Ajax are already resident in nearly all Web browsers and servers. This is in contrast to both ASP.NET and JSP, which still have far-from-complete coverage. Second, using Ajax does not require learning a new tool or language. Rather, it requires only a new way of thinking about Web interactions.

Ajax is discussed in more depth in Chapter 10, "Introduction to Ajax."

Summary

The Internet began in the late 1960s as the ARPAnet, which was eventually replaced by NSFnet for nonmilitary users. NSFnet later became known as the Internet. There are now millions of computers around the world connected to the Internet. Although much of the network control equipment is different and many kinds of computers are connected, all of these connections are made through the TCP/IP protocol, making them all appear, at least at the lowest level, the same to the network.

Two kinds of addresses are used on the Internet: IP addresses for computers, which are four-part numbers; and fully qualified domain names for people, which are words separated by periods. Fully qualified domain names are translated to IP addresses by name servers running DNS. A number of different information interchange protocols have been created, including telnet, ftp, and mailto.

The Web began in the late 1980s at CERN as a means for physicists to efficiently share the results of their work with colleagues at other locations. The fundamental idea of the Web is to transfer hypertext documents among computers using the HTTP protocol on the Internet.

Browsers request XHTML documents from Web servers and display them for users. Web servers find and send requested documents to browsers. All documents are addressed on the Internet using URLs; the specific protocol to be used is the first field of the URL. URLs also include the fully qualified domain name and a file path to the specific document on the server. The type of a document that is delivered by a Web server appears in the first line of the document as a MIME specification. Web sites can create their own experimental MIME types, provided that they also furnish a program that allows the browser to present the document's contents to the user.

HTTP is the standard protocol for Web communications. HTTP requests are sent on the Internet from browsers to Web servers; HTTP responses are sent from Web servers to browsers to fulfill those requests. The most commonly used HTTP requests are GET and POST, both of which require URLs.

Web programmers use several languages to create the documents that servers can provide to browsers. The most basic of these is XHTML, the standard markup language for describing how Web documents should be presented by browsers. Tools that can be used without specific knowledge of XHTML are available to create XHTML documents. A plug-in is a program that can be integrated with a word processor to make it possible to use the word processor to create XHTML. A filter converts a document written in some other format to XHTML. XML is a meta-markup language that provides a standard way to define new markup languages.

JavaScript is a client-side scripting language that can be embedded in XHTML to describe simple computations. JavaScript code is interpreted by the browser on the client machine; it provides access to the elements of an XHTML document, as well as the ability to change those elements dynamically.

Flash is a framework for building animation into XHTML documents. A browser must have a Flash player plug-in to be able to display the movies created with the Flash framework.

Servlets are server-side Java programs that can be used for form processing and database access. JSP is an approach to building dynamic documents. JSP documents are translated into servlets. JSF is a development framework for JSP.

ASP.NET is a Web development framework. The code used in ASP.NET documents, which is executed on the server, can be written in any .NET programming language.

PHP is the server-side equivalent to JavaScript. It is an interpreted language whose code is embedded in XHTML documents. It is used primarily for form processing and database access from browsers.

Ruby is a relatively recent object-oriented scripting language that is introduced here primarily because of its use in Rails, a Web applications framework. Rails provides a significant part of the code required to build Web applications that access databases, allowing the developer to spend his or her time on the specifics of the application without the drudgery of dealing with all of the housekeeping details.

Ajax is an approach to building Web applications in which partial document requests are handled asynchronously. Ajax can significantly increase the speed of user interactions, so it is most useful for building systems that have frequent interactions.

Review Questions

1.1 What is the task of a DNS name server?

1.2 What was one of the fundamental requirements for the new national computer network proposed by the DoD in the 1960s?

1.3 What is a virtual host?

1.4 What protocol is used by all computer connections to the Internet?

1.5 Describe a fully qualified domain name.

1.6 What is the purpose of `telnet`?

1.7 In the first proposal for the Web, what form of information was to be interchanged?

1.8 What is hypertext?

1.9 What is the form of an IP address?

1.10 What category of browser, introduced in 1993, led to a huge expansion of Web usage?

1.11 What is the document root of a Web server?

1.12 What is the server root of a Web server?

1.13 What is a virtual document tree?

1.14 What is a proxy server?

1.15 In what common situation is the document returned by a Web server created after the request is received?

1.16 How do partial paths to documents work in Web servers?

1.17 When a browser requests a directory without giving its name, what is the name of the file that is normally returned by the Web server?

1.18 What response header field is most often required?

1.19 What is the purpose of a MIME type specification in a request/response transaction between a browser and a server?

1.20 What does the file protocol specify?

1.21 What must a Web server furnish the browser when it returns a document with an experimental MIME type?

1.22 Prior to HTTP 1.1, how long were connections between browsers and servers normally maintained?

1.23 Describe the purposes of the five most commonly used HTTP methods.

1.24 What is the purpose of the `Accept` field in an HTTP request?

1.25 What important capability is lacking in a markup language?

1.26 Is it practically possible to compute the private key associated with a given public key?

1.27 What is the difference between a virus and a worm?

1.28 How many different tags are predefined in an XML-based markup language?

1.29 What is the primary use of Flash?

1.30 What appears to motivate a hacker to create and disseminate a virus?

1.31 What is a filter XHTML converter?

1.32 What problem is addressed by using a public key approach to encryption?

1.33 Why must code generated by a filter often be modified by hand before use?

1.34 What is the great advantage of XML over XHTML for describing data?

1.35 What is the relationship between Java and JavaScript?

1.36 Where are servlets executed, on the server or on the browser?

1.37 What are the most common applications of JavaScript?

1.38 Where is JavaScript most often interpreted, on the server or on the browser?

1.39 What is a plug-in?

1.40 Where are Flash movies interpreted, on the server or on the browser?

1.41 In what language are servlets written?

1.42 What is the purpose of JSF?

1.43 What is the purpose of ASP.NET?

1.44 Which programming languages are used in Ajax applications?

1.45 In what language is the code in an ASP.NET document usually written?

1.46 In what way are JSP documents the opposite of servlets?

1.47 In what country was Ruby developed?

1.48 Where is PHP code interpreted, on the server or on the browser?

1.49 What is the purpose of Rails?

1.50 For what particular kind of Web application was Rails designed?

1.51 In what fundamental way does an Ajax Web application differ from a traditional Web application?

1.52 In what ways is Ruby more object-oriented than Java?

1.53 In what ways is PHP similar to JavaScript?

Exercises

1.1 Search the Web for information on the history of the following technologies and write a brief overview of those histories.

a. TCP/IP

b. SGML

c. XHTML

d. ARPAnet

e. BITNET

f. XML

g. JavaScript

h. Flash

i. Servlets

j. JSP

k. JSF

l. Rails

m. Ajax

1.2 For the following products, what brand do you have access to, what is its version number, and what is the latest available version?

a. Browser
b. Web server
c. JavaScript
d. PHP
e. Servlets
f. ASP.NET
g. Ruby
h. Rails

CHAPTER

2

Introduction to XHTML

This chapter introduces the most commonly used subset of the eXtensible Hypertext Markup Language (XHTML). Due to the simplicity of XHTML, the discussion moves quickly. The chapter begins with a brief history of the evolution of HTML and XHTML, followed by a description of the form of tags and the structure of an XHTML document. Then tags used to specify the presentation of text are discussed, including those for line breaks, paragraph breaks, headings, and block quotations, as well as tags for specifying the style and relative size of fonts. This is followed by a description of the formats and uses of images in Web documents. Next, hypertext links are introduced. Three kinds of lists—ordered, unordered, and definition—are then covered. After that, the

XHTML tags and attributes used to specify tables are discussed. The next section of the chapter introduces forms, which provide the means to collect information from Web clients. Finally, the last section describes the syntactic differences between HTML and XHTML.

2.1 Origins and Evolution of HTML and XHTML

HTML is defined using the Standard Generalized Markup Language (SGML), which is an International Standards Organization (ISO) standard notation for describing text-formatting languages.[1] The original intent of HTML was different from those of other text-formatting languages, which dictate all of the presentation details of text, such as font style, size, and color. Rather, HTML was designed to specify document structure at a higher and more abstract level, necessary because HTML-specified documents had to be displayable on a variety of computer systems, often using different browsers.

The addition of style sheets to HTML in the late 1990s advanced its capabilities closer to those of other text-formatting languages by providing a way to include the specification of presentation details. These are introduced in Chapter 3, "Cascading Style Sheets."

2.1.1 Versions of HTML and XHTML

The original version of HTML was designed, in conjunction with the structure of the Web and the first browser, at Conseil European pour la Recerce Nucleaire or European Laboratory for Particle Physics (CERN). Use of the Web began its meteoric rise in 1993 with the release of MOSAIC, the first graphical Web browser. Not long after MOSAIC was commercialized and marketed by Netscape, Microsoft began developing its browser, Internet Explorer (IE). The release of IE marked the beginning of a four-year marketing competition between Netscape and Microsoft. During this time, both companies worked feverously to develop their own extensions to HTML in an attempt to gain market advantage. This naturally led to incompatible versions of HTML, both between the two developers and also between older and newer releases within the same company. All of these differences made it a serious challenge to Web content providers to design HTML documents that could be viewed by the different browsers.

In late 1994 Tim Berners-Lee, who developed the initial version of HTML, started the World Wide Web Consortium (W3C), which had as one of its primary purposes to develop and distribute standards for Web technologies, starting with HTML. The first HTML standard, HTML 2.0, was released in 1995. It was followed by HTML 3.2 in early 1997. Up to this point, W3C was playing catch up, and HTML 3.2 was really just a reflection of the then-current features

---

1. Not all text-formatting languages are based on SGML; for example, PostScript and LaTeX are not.

that had been developed by Netscape and Microsoft. Fortunately, after 1997 the evolution of HTML was dominated by W3C, in part because Netscape had surrendered from their browser competition with Microsoft. The browsers produced by the two companies have since drifted ever closer to W3C standards.

The latest version of HTML, 4.01 was approved by W3C in late 1999. The XHTML 1.0 standard was approved in early 2000. XHTML 1.0 is a redefinition of HTML 4.01 using XML.[2] XHTML 1.0 is actually three standards, Strict, Transitional, and Frameset. The Strict standard requires all of XHTML 1.0 be followed. The Transitional standard allows deprecated features of XHTML 1.0 to be included. The Frameset standard allows the collection of frame elements and attributes to be included, although they have been deprecated. The XHTML 1.1 standard was recommended by W3C in May 2001. This standard, primarily a modularization of XHTML 1.0, drops some of the features of its predecessor, most notably frames. XHTML 2.0 was getting close to release at the time of this writing.[3]

There is a problem with the MIME types used to serve XHTML documents. In fact, most XHTML documents are currently served with the `html/text` MIME type, which is incorrect. This creates problems with validation for XHTML 1.1 documents, but not XHTML 1.0 Strict documents.[4] To avoid this issue, all documents in this book are written against the XHTML 1.0 Strict standard.

The latest versions of the most popular browsers, Microsoft Internet Explorer 7 (IE7) and Firefox 2 (FX2), come close to supporting all of XHTML 1.1.

The addition of presentation details through style sheets in HTML 4.0 made some features of earlier versions obsolete. These features, as well as some others, have been *deprecated*, meaning that they will be dropped from HTML at some time in the future. Deprecating a feature is a warning to users to stop using the feature because it will not be supported forever. Although even the latest releases of browsers still support the deprecated parts of HTML, we do not include descriptions of them in this book.

2.1.2 HTML versus XHTML

There are some commonly heard arguments for using HTML rather than XHTML, especially XHTML 1.0 Strict. First, because of its lax syntax rules, HTML is much easier to write, whereas XHTML requires a level of discipline many of us naturally resist. Second, because of the huge number of HTML documents available on the Web, browsers will continue to support it as far as one can see into the future. However, some older browsers have problems with some parts of XHTML.

---

2. XML (eXtensible Markup Language) is the topic of Chapter 7, "Introduction to XML."

3. The W3C Web site is `http://www.w3.org`.

4. Validation is discussed in Section 2.5.3.

On the other hand, there are strong reasons why one should use XHTML. One of the most compelling is that quality and consistency in any endeavor, be it electrical wiring, software development, or Web document development, rely on standards. HTML has few syntactic rules, and HTML processors (for example, browsers) do not enforce the rules it does have. Therefore, HTML authors have a high degree of freedom to create documents using their own syntactic preferences. Because of this, HTML documents lack consistency, both in low-level syntax and overall structure. Conversely, XHTML has strict syntactic rules that impose a consistent structure on all XHTML documents. Furthermore, the fact that there are a large number of poorly structured HTML documents on the Web is a poor excuse for generating more.

Another significant reason for using XHTML is that when you create an XHTML document, its syntactic correctness can be checked, either by an XML browser or by a validation tool (see Section 2.4). This checking process may find errors that could otherwise go undetected until after the document is posted on a site and requested by a client, possibly then only by a specific browser.

The argument that XHTML is difficult to write correctly is obviated by the availability of XHTML editors, which provide a simple and effective approach to creating syntactically correct XHTML documents.[5]

It is also possible to convert legacy HTML documents to XHTML documents using software tools. Tidy, which is available at `http://tidy.sourceforge.net`, is one such tool.

The remainder of this chapter provides an introduction to the most commonly used tags and attributes of XHTML 1.0.

2.2 Basic Syntax

The fundamental syntactic units of HTML are called *tags*. In general, tags are used to specify categories of content. For each category, a browser has default presentation specifications for the specified content. The syntax of a tag is the tag's name surrounded by angle brackets (<>). Tag names must be written in all lowercase letters. Most tags appear in pairs: an opening tag and a closing tag. The name of a closing tag is the name of its corresponding opening tag with a slash attached to the beginning. For example, if the tag's name is p, the corresponding closing tag is named /p. Whatever appears between a tag and its closing tag is the *content* of the tag. A browser display of an XHTML document shows the content of all of the document's tags; it is the information the document is meant to portray. Not all tags can have content.

The opening tag and its closing tag together specify a container for the content they enclose. The container and its content together are called an *element*. For example, consider the following element:

```
<p> This is extremely simple. </p>
```

---

5. One such editor system is available at `http://www.xstandard.com`.

The paragraph tag, `<p>`, marks the beginning of the content, and the `</p>` tag marks the end of the content of the paragraph element.

Attributes, which are used to specify alternative meanings of a tag, can appear between an opening tag's name and its right-pointed bracket. They are specified in keyword form, which means that the attribute's name appears, followed by an equals sign and the attribute's value. Attribute names, like tag names, are written in lowercase letters. Attribute values must be delimited by double quotes.

Comments in programs increase the readability of those programs. Comments in XHTML have the same purpose. They can appear in XHTML in the following form:

```
<!-- anything except two adjacent dashes -->
```

Browsers ignore XHTML comments—they are for people only. Comments can be spread over as many lines as are needed. For example, you could have the following comment:

```
<!-- PetesHome.html
This document describes the home page of Pete's Pickles
-->
```

Besides comments, several other kinds of text may appear in an XHTML document but be ignored by browsers. Browsers ignore all unrecognized tags. They also ignore line breaks. Line breaks that show up in the displayed content can be specified but only with tags designed for that purpose. The same is true for multiple spaces and tabs.

Programmers find XHTML a bit frustrating. In a program, the statements specify exactly what the computer must do. XHTML tags are treated more like suggestions to the browser. If a reserved word is misspelled in a program, the error is usually detected by the language implementation system, and the program is not executed. However, a misspelled tag name results in the tag being ignored by the browser, with no indication to the browser user that anything has been left out. Browsers are even allowed to ignore tags that they recognize. Furthermore, the browser user can configure his or her browser to react to specific tags in different ways.

2.3 Standard XHTML Document Structure

Every XHTML document must begin with an `xml` declaration element that simply identifies the document as being one based on XML. This element includes an attribute that specifies the version number, which is still 1.0. The `xml` declaration usually includes a second attribute, `encoding`, which specifies the encoding used for the document. In this book, we use the Unicode encoding, `utf-8`. Following is the `xml` declaration element, which should be the first line of every XHTML document:

```
<?xml version = "1.0" encoding = "utf-8"?>
```

Note that this declaration must begin in the first character position of the document file.

Immediately following the `xml` declaration element is an SGML `DOCTYPE` command, which specifies the particular SGML document-type definition (DTD) with which the document complies, among other things.[6] The following command states that the document in which it is included complies with the XHTML 1.0 Strict standard:

```
<!DOCTYPE html PUBLIC "-//W3C//DTD XHTML 1.0 Strict//EN"
   "http://www.w3.org/TR/xhtml11/DTD/xhtml1-strict.dtd">
```

A complete explanation of the `DOCTYPE` command requires more effort, both to write and to read, than is justified at this stage of our introduction to XHTML.

XHTML documents must include the four tags `<html>`, `<head>`, `<title>`, and `<body>`. The `<html>` tag identifies the root element of the document. So, XHTML documents always have an `<html>` tag immediately following the `DOCTYPE` command, and they always end with the closing `html` tag, `</html>`. The `html` element includes an attribute, `xmlns`, that specifies the XHTML namespace, as shown in the following:

```
<html xmlns = "http://www.w3.org/1999/xhtml">
```

Although the `xmlns` attribute's value looks like a URL, it does not specify a document. It is just a name that happens to have the form of a URL. Namespaces are discussed in Chapter 7, "Introduction to XML."

An XHTML document consists of two parts, named the *head* and the *body*. The `<head>` element contains the head part of the document, which provides information about the document rather than its content. The body of a document provides the content of the document, which itself includes tags and attributes.

The content of the title element is displayed by the browser at the top of its display window, usually in the browser window's title bar.

2.4   Basic Text Markup

This section describes how the text content of an XHTML document can be formatted with XHTML tags. By *formatting*, we mean layout and some presentation details. For now, we will ignore the other kinds of content that can appear in an XHTML document.

2.4.1   Paragraphs

Text is normally organized into paragraphs in the body of a document. In fact, the XHTML standard does not allow text to be placed directly in a document body. Textual paragraphs appear as the content of a paragraph element, speci-

---

6. A document-type definition specifies the syntax rules for a particular category of XHTML documents.

fied with the tag `<p>`. In displaying the content of a paragraph, the browser puts as many words as will fit on the lines in the browser window. The browser supplies a line break at the end of each line. As stated in Section 2.2, line breaks embedded in text are ignored by the browser. For example, the following paragraph might[7] be displayed by a browser, as shown in Figure 2.1.

```
<p>
   Mary had
a
     little lamb, its fleece was white as snow. And
 everywhere that
  Mary went, the lamb
 was sure to go.
</p>
```

Mary had a little lamb, its fleece was white as snow. And everywhere that Mary went, the lamb was sure to go.

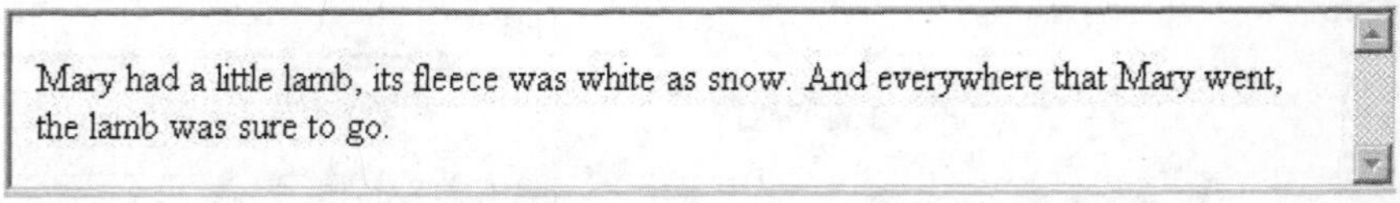

Figure 2.1 Filling lines

Notice that multiple spaces in the source paragraph element are replaced by single spaces in the display of Figure 2.1.

The following is our first example of a complete XHTML document:

```
<?xml version = "1.0" encoding = "utf-8"?>
<!DOCTYPE html PUBLIC "-//W3C//DTD XHTML 1.0 Strict//EN"
  "http://www.w3.org/TR/xhtml11/DTD/xhtml11-strict.dtd">

<!-- greet.html
     A trivial document
     -->
<html xmlns = "http://www.w3.org/1999/xhtml">
  <head> <title> Our first document </title>
  </head>
  <body>
    <p>
      Greetings from your Webmaster!
    </p>
  </body>
</html>
```

---

7. We say "might" because the width of the display that the browser uses determines how many words will fit on a line.

Figure 2.2 shows a browser display of `greet.html`.

Greetings from your Webmaster!

Figure 2.2 Display of `greet.html`

If the content of a paragraph tag is displayed at a position other than the beginning of the line, the browser breaks the current line and inserts a blank line. For example, the following line would be displayed, as shown in Figure 2.3.

```
<p> Mary had a little lamb, </p> <p> its fleece was
white as snow. </p>
```

Mary had a little lamb,

its fleece was white as snow.

Figure 2.3 The paragraph element

2.4.2   Line Breaks

When the content of a paragraph element is displayed at a position other than at the beginning of a line, the browser breaks the current line and inserts a blank line. Sometimes text requires a line break without the preceding blank line. This is exactly what the break tag does. The break tag differs from the paragraph tag in that it can have no content and therefore has no closing tag (because it would serve no purpose). The break tag is specified as `<br />`. The slash indicates that the tag is both an opening and closing tag. The space before the slash represents the absent content.[8]

Consider the following:

```
<p>
Mary had a little lamb, <br />
   its fleece was white as snow.
</p>
```

This would be displayed as shown in Figure 2.4.

---

8. Some older browsers have trouble with the tag `<br/>` but not with `<br />`.

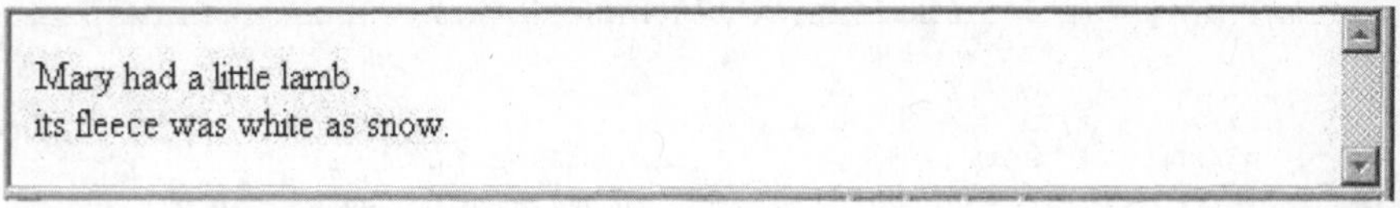

Figure 2.4 Line breaks

2.4.3   Preserving Whitespace

Sometimes it is desirable to preserve the whitespace in text, that is, to prevent the browser from eliminating multiple spaces and ignoring embedded line breaks. This can be specified with the `pre` tag. For example,

```
<p><pre>
Mary
    had a
        little
            lamb
</pre>
```

This would be displayed as shown in Figure 2.5. Notice that the content of the `pre` element is shown in monospace, rather than in the default font.

Figure 2.5 The `pre` element

A `pre` element can contain virtually any other tags, except those that cause a paragraph break, such as paragraph elements.

2.4.4   Headings

Text is often separated into sections in documents by beginning each section with a heading. Larger sections sometimes have headings that appear more prominent than headings for sections nested inside them. In XHTML, there are six levels of headings, specified by the tags `<h1>`, `<h2>`, `<h3>`, `<h4>`, `<h5>`, and `<h6>`, where `<h1>` specifies the highest-level heading. Headings are displayed in a boldface font whose default size depends on the number in the heading tag. On most browsers, `<h1>`, `<h2>`, and `<h3>` use font sizes that are larger than that of the default size of text, `<h4>` uses the default size, and `<h5>` and `<h6>` use smaller sizes. The heading tags always break the current line, so their content always appears on a new line. Browsers usually insert some vertical space before and after all headings.

The following example illustrates the use of headings:

```
<?xml version = "1.0" encoding = "utf-8"?>
<!DOCTYPE html PUBLIC "-//W3C//DTD XHTML 1.0 Strict//EN"
  "http://www.w3.org/TR/xhtml11/DTD/xhtml11-strict.dtd">

<!-- headings.html
     An example to illustrate headings
     -->
<html xmlns = "http://www.w3.org/1999/xhtml">
  <head> <title> Headings </title>
  </head>
  <body>
    <h1> Aidan's Airplanes (h1) </h1>
    <h2> The best in used airplanes (h2) </h2>
    <h3> "We've got them by the hangarful" (h3) </h3>
    <h4> We're the guys to see for a good used airplane (h4) </h4>
    <h5> We offer great prices on great planes (h5) </h5>
    <h6> No returns, no guarantees, no refunds,
         all sales are final! (h6) </h6>
  </body>
</html>
```

Figure 2.6 shows a browser display of headings.html.

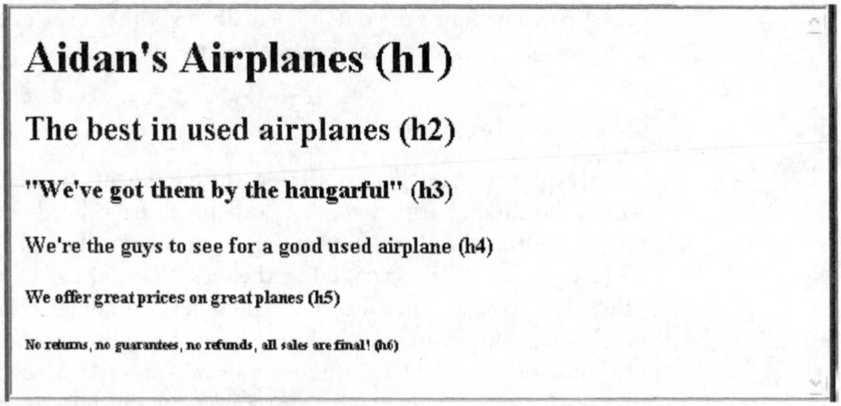

Figure 2.6 Display of headings.html

2.4.5   Block Quotations

Sometimes we want a block of text to be set off from the normal flow of text in a document. In many cases, such a block is a long quotation. The `<blockquote>` tag is designed for this situation. Browser designers determine how the content of `<blockquote>` can be made to look different from the surrounding text. In many cases, the block of text is indented, either on the left or right side or both. Another possibility is that the block is set in italic. Consider the following sample document:

```
<?xml version = "1.0" encoding = "utf-8"?>
<!DOCTYPE html PUBLIC "-//W3C//DTD XHTML 1.0 Strict//EN"
   "http://www.w3.org/TR/xhtml1/DTD/xhtml1-strict.dtd">


<!-- blockquote.html
      An example to illustrate a blockquote
      -->
<html xmlns = "http://www.w3.org/1999/xhtml">
  <head> <title> Blockquotes </title>
  </head>
  <body>
    <p>
      Abraham Lincoln is generally regarded as one of the greatest
      presidents of the U.S. His most famous speech was delivered
      in Gettysburg, Pennsylvania, during the Civil War. This
      speech began with
    </p>
    <blockquote>
      <p>
        "Fourscore and seven years ago our fathers brought forth on
        this continent, a new nation, conceived in Liberty, and
        dedicated to the proposition that all men are created equal.
      </p>
      <p>
        Now we are engaged in a great civil war, testing whether
        that nation or any nation so conceived and so dedicated,
        can long endure."
      </p>
    </blockquote>
    <p>
      Whatever one's opinion of Lincoln, no one can deny the
      enormous and lasting effect he had on the U.S.
    </p>
  </body>
</html>
```

Figure 2.7 shows a browser display of `blockquote.html`.

Abraham Lincoln is generally regarded as one of the greatest presidents of the U.S. His most famous speech was delivered in Gettysburg, Pennsylvania, during the Civil War. This speech began with

> "Fourscore and seven years ago our fathers brought forth on this continent, a new nation, conceived in Liberty, and dedicated to the proposition that all men are created equal.
>
> Now we are engaged in a great civil war, testing whether that nation or any nation so conceived and so dedicated, can long endure."

Whatever one's opinion of Lincoln, no one can deny the enormous and lasting effect he had on the U.S.

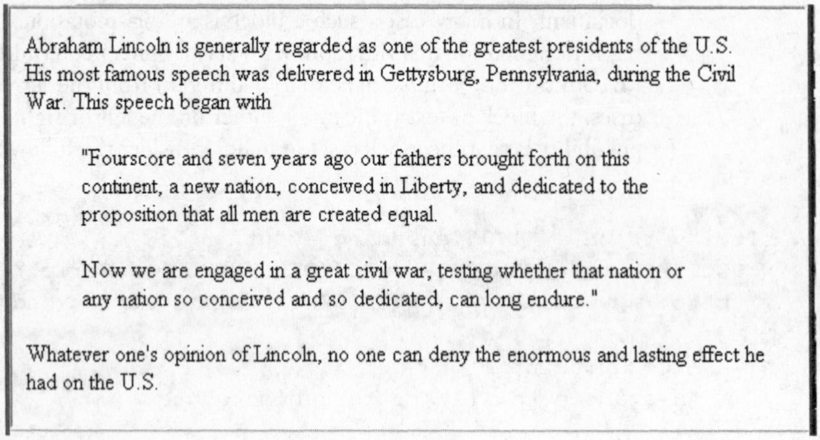

Figure 2.7 Display of `blockquote.html`

2.4.6   Font Styles and Sizes

Early Web designers used a collection of tags to set font styles and sizes. For example, `<i>` specified italics and `<b>` specified bold. Since the advent of cascading style sheets (see Chapter 3, "Cascading Style Sheets"), use of these tags has become passé. There are a few tags for fonts that are still in widespread use, called *content-based style tags*. They are called content-based because the tag indicates the particular kind of text that appears in their content. In the following, three of the most commonly used content-based tags are described.

The emphasis tag, `<em>`, specifies that its textual content is special and should be displayed in some way that indicates this. Most browsers use italic for such content.

The strong tag, `<strong>` is like the emphasis tag, but more so. Browsers often set the content of strong elements in bold.

The `<code>` tag is used to specify a monospace font, usually used for program code. For example,

```
cost = quantity * price
```

would be displayed as shown in Figure 2.8.

```
cost = quantity * price
```

Figure 2.8 The `<code>` element

Subscript and superscript characters can be specified by the `<sub>` and `<sup>` tags, respectively. These are not content-based tags. For example,

```
X<sub>2</sub><sup>3</sup> + y<sub>1</sub><sup>2</sup>
```

would be displayed as shown in Figure 2.9.

$$x_2{}^3 + y_1{}^2$$

Figure 2.9 The `<sub>` and `<sup>` elements

Character-modifying tags are not affected by `<blockquote>` except when there is a conflict. For example, if the text content of `<blockquote>` is set in italic and a part of that text is made the content of an `<em>` tag, the `<em>` tag would have no effect.

XHTML tags are categorized as being either block or inline. The content of an *inline* tag appears on the current line. So, an inline tag does not implicitly include a line break. One exception is `br`, which is an inline tag, but its entire purpose is to insert a line break in the content. A *block* tag breaks the current line so that its content appears on a new line. The heading and block quote tags are block tags, whereas `<em>` and `<strong>` are inline tags. In XHTML, block tags cannot appear in the content of inline tags. Therefore, a block tag can never be nested directly in an inline tag. Also, inline tags and text cannot be directly nested in body or form elements. Only block tags can be nested directly in body or form elements. That is why the example `greet.html` has the text content of its body nested in a paragraph element.

2.4.7   Character Entities

XHTML provides a collection of special characters that are sometimes needed in a document but cannot be typed as themselves. In some cases, these characters are used in XHTML in some special way, for example >, <, and &. In other cases, the characters do not appear on keyboards, such as the small raised circle that represents "degrees" in a reference to temperature. Finally, there is the nonbreaking space, which browsers regard as a hard space—they do not squeeze them out like they do other multiple spaces. These special characters are defined as *entities*, which are codes for the characters. An entity in a document is replaced by its associated character by the browser. Table 2.1 lists some of the most commonly used entities.

Table 2.1 Some commonly used entities

Character	Entity	Meaning
&	&	Ampersand
<	<	Less than
>	>	Greater than
"	"	Double quote
'	'	Single quote (apostrophe)
$\frac{1}{4}$	¼	One quarter
$\frac{1}{2}$	½	One half
$\frac{3}{4}$	¾	Three quarters
°	°	Degree
(space)		Nonbreaking space

2.4.8   Horizontal Rules

The parts of a document can be separated from each other, making the document easier to read, by placing horizontal lines between them. Such lines are called *horizontal rules*, and the block tag that creates them is `<hr />`. The `<hr />` tag causes a line break (ending the current line) and draws a line across the screen. The browser chooses the thickness, length, and horizontal placement of the line. Typically, browsers display lines that are three pixels thick.

Note again the slash in the `<hr />` tag, indicating that this tag has no content and no closing tag.

2.4.9   The meta Element

The meta element is used to provide additional information about a document. The meta tag has no content; rather, all of the provided information is specified through attributes. The two attributes that are used to provide information are name and content. The user makes up a name as the value of the name attribute and specifies information through the content attribute. One commonly chosen name is keywords; the value of the content attribute associated with the key words are those that a document author believes characterizes his or her document. For example,

```
<meta name = "keywords"  content = "binary trees,
linked lists, stacks" />
```

Web search engines use the information provided with the meta element to categorize Web documents in their indices. So, if the author of a document seeks widespread exposure for the document, one or more `meta` elements are included to ensure that it will be found by at least some Web search engines. For example, if an entire book were published as a Web document, it might have the following `meta` elements:

```
<meta name = "Title" content = "Don Quixote" />
<meta name = "Author"  content = "Miguel Cervantes" />
<meta  name = "keywords"  content = "novel,
 Spanish literature, groundbreaking work" />
```

2.5 Images

The inclusion of images in a document can dramatically enhance its appearance (although images slow the document-download process considerably for clients who do not have high-speed Internet access). The image is stored in a file, which is specified by an XHTML request. The image is inserted into the display of the document by the browser.

2.5.1   Image Formats

The two most common methods of representing images are Graphic Interchange Format (GIF, pronounced like the first syllable of *jif-fy*) and Joint Photographic Experts Group (JPEG, pronounced *jay-peg*) format. Most contemporary browsers can render images in either of these two formats. Files in both of these formats are compressed to reduce storage needs and provide faster transfer over the Internet.

The GIF format was developed by the CompuServe network service provider for the specific purpose of moving images. It uses 8-bit color representations for pixels, allowing a pixel to have 256 different colors. If you are not familiar with color representations, this may seem to be entirely adequate. However, with the color displays on most contemporary computers, this leaves a huge number of colors that can be displayed but that cannot be represented in a GIF image. Files containing GIF images use the `.gif` (or `.GIF`) extension on their names. GIF images can be made to appear transparent.

The JPEG format uses 24-bit color representations for pixels, which allows JPEG images to include more than 16 million different colors. Files that store JPEG images use the `.jpg` (or `.JPG` or `.jpeg`) extension on their names. The compression algorithm used by JPEG is better at shrinking an image than the one used by GIF. This compression process actually loses some of the color accuracy of the image, but because there is so much to begin with, the loss is rarely discernable by the user. Because of this powerful compression process, even though a JPEG image has much more color information than a GIF image of the same subject, the JPEG image can be smaller than the GIF image. Because of this, JPEG images are often preferred to GIF images. The disadvantage of JPEG is that it does not support transparency.

A third image format is now gaining popularity—Portable Network Graphics (PNG, pronounced *ping*). PNG was designed in 1996 as a free replacement for GIF after the patent owner for GIF, Unisys, suggested it may begin charging royalties for documents that included GIF images.[9] Actually, PNG provides a good replacement for both GIF and JPEG because it has the best characteristics of each (the possibility of transparency, as provided by GIF, and the same large number of colors as JPEG). One drawback of PNG is that because its compression algorithm does not sacrifice picture clarity, its images require more space than comparable JPEG images.[10] Support for PNG in the earlier IE browsers was unacceptably poor, which kept many developers from using PNG. However, IE7 is much better than IE6 at displaying PNG images (although its support is still not perfect). Information on PNG can be found at `www.w3.org/ Graphics/PNG`.

2.5.2   The `<img />` Tag

The image tag, `<img />`, which is an inline tag, specifies an image that is to appear in a document. In its simplest form, the image tag includes two attributes: `src`, which specifies the file containing the image; and `alt`, which specifies text to be displayed when it is not possible to display the image. If the file is in the same directory as the XHTML file of the document, the value of `src` is just the image's filename. In many cases, image files are stored in a subdirectory of the directory where the XHTML files are stored. For example, the image files might be stored in a subdirectory named `images`. If the image file's name is `stars.jpg` and it is stored in the `images` subdirectory, the value of `src` would be as follows:

```
"images/stars.jpg"
```

Some seriously aged browsers are not capable of displaying images. When such a browser finds an `<img />` tag, it simply ignores its content, possibly leaving the user confused by the text in the neighborhood of where the image was supposed to be. Also, graphical browsers, which *are* capable of displaying images, may have image downloading disabled by the browser user. This is done when the Internet connection is slow and the user chooses not to wait for images to download. It is also done by visually impaired users. In any case, it is helpful to have some text displayed in place of the ignored image. For these reasons, the `alt` attribute is required by XHTML.

Two optional attributes of `img`, `width` and `height`, can be included to specify (in pixels) the size of the rectangle for the image. These can be used to scale the size of the image (that is, to make it larger or smaller). Care must be taken to ensure that the image is not distorted in the resizing. For example, if the image is square, the `width` and `height` attribute values must be equal.

---

9. The patent expired in the United States in 2003.

10. Space is not the direct issue; download time, which depends on file size, is the real issue.

The following is an example of an image element:

```
<img src = "c210.jpg"  alt = "Picture of a Cessna 210" />
```

The following example extends the airplane ad document to include information about a specific airplane and its image.

```
<?xml version = "1.0" encoding = "utf-8"?>
<!DOCTYPE html PUBLIC "-//W3C//DTD XHTML 1.0 Strict//EN"
  "http://www.w3.org/TR/xhtml1/DTD/xhtml1-strict.dtd">

<!-- image.html
     An example to illustrate an image
     -->
<html xmlns = "http://www.w3.org/1999/xhtml">
  <head> <title> Images </title>
  </head>
  <body>
    <h1> Aidan's Airplanes </h1>
    <h2> The best in used airplanes </h2>
    <h3> "We've got them by the hangarful" </h3>
    <h2> Special of the month </h2>
    <p>
      1960 Cessna 210 <br />
      577 hours since major engine overhaul<br />
      1022 hours since prop overhaul <br /><br />
      <img src = "c210new.jpg"  alt = "Picture of a Cessna 210" />
      <br />
      Buy this fine airplane today at a remarkably low price
      <br />
      Call 999-555-1111 today!
    </p>
  </body>
</html>
```

Figure 2.10 shows a browser display of `image.html`.

There is much more to the `<img />` tag than we have led you to believe. In fact, the `<img />` tag can include up to 30 different attributes. For descriptions of the rest, visit `http://www.w3.org/TR/html401/index/attributes.html`.

2.5.3 XHTML Document Validation

The W3C provides a convenient Web-based way to validate XHTML documents against its standards. The URL of the service is `http://validator.w3.org/file-upload.html`. Figure 2.11 shows a browser display of `file-upload.html`.

Figure 2.10 Display of `image.html`

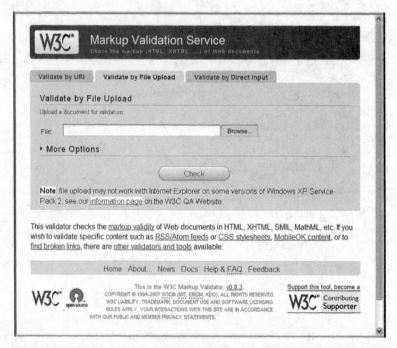

Figure 2.11 Display of `file-upload.html`, the W3C HTML validation document

The filename of the document to be validated is entered (including the pathname) or found by browsing. We recommend that the *More Options* button be clicked and the *Show Source* checkbox be checked, because that causes the validation system to furnish a listing of the document in which the lines are numbered. These numbers are referenced in the report provided by the validation system. When the *Check* button is clicked, the specified file is uploaded to the `validator` server, where the validation system is run on it.

Figure 2.12 shows a browser display of the document returned by the validation system for our sample document `image.html`. Notice that we cut the source listing off in the figure, simply to prevent the figure from spanning more than one page.

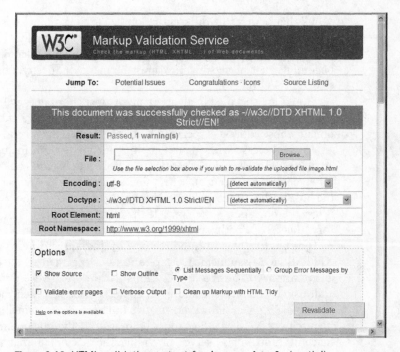

Figure 2.12 HTML validation output for `image.html` (partial)

One of the most common errors made in crafting XHTML documents is putting text or elements where they do not belong. For example, putting text directly in a body element is illegal. The XHTML validation system is a valuable tool for producing documents that adhere to W3C standards. The specific standard against which the document is checked is given in the `DOCTYPE` command. Because the `DOCTYPE` command in `image.html` specifies the `xhtml1-strict.dtd` DTD, this document is checked against the XHTML 1.0 Strict standard.

2.6 Hypertext Links

A hypertext link in an XHTML document, which we simply call a *link* here, acts as a pointer to some particular place in some Web resource. That resource can be an XHTML document anywhere on the Web, or it may be the document currently being displayed. Without links, Web documents would be boring and tedious to read. There would be no convenient way for the browser user to get from one document to a logically related document. Most Web sites consist of many different documents, all logically linked. Therefore, links are essential to building an interesting Web site.

2.6.1 Links

A link that points to a different resource specifies the address of that resource. Such an address might be a filename, a directory path and a filename, or a complete URL. If a link points to a specific place in any document other than the beginning, that place somehow must be marked. Specifying such places is discussed in Section 2.6.2.

Links are specified in an attribute of an anchor tag (`<a>`), which is an inline tag. The anchor tag that specifies a link is called the *source* of that link. The document whose address is specified in a link is called the *target* of that link.

As is the case with many tags, the anchor tag can include many different attributes. However, for creating links only one is required, `href` (an acronym for hypertext `reference`). The value assigned to `href` specifies the target of the link. If the target is in another document in the same directory, the target is just the document's filename. If the target document is in some other directory, the UNIX pathname conventions are used. So, an XHTML file named `c210data.html` in a subdirectory of the directory in which the source XHTML file—say, named `airplanes`—is specified in the `href` attribute as `airplanes/c210data.html`. This is the relative method of document addressing. Absolute file addresses could be used in which the entire pathname for the file is given. However, relative links are easier to maintain, especially if a hierarchy of XHTML files must be moved. If the document is on some other machine (not on the server providing the document that includes the link), obviously the complete URL must be used.

The content of an anchor tag, which becomes the clickable link the user sees, is restricted to text, line breaks, images, and headings. Although some browsers allow other nested tags, that is not standard XHTML and should not be used if you want your documents to be correctly displayed by all browsers. Links are usually implicitly rendered in a different color than the surrounding text. Sometimes they are also underlined. When the mouse cursor is placed over the anchor-tag content and the left mouse button is pressed, the link is taken by the browser. If the target is in a different document, that document is loaded and displayed, replacing the currently displayed document. If the target is in the current document, the document is scrolled by the browser to display the target of the link. As an example, consider the following document, which adds a link to the document displayed in Figure 2.10:

```
<?xml version = "1.0" encoding = "utf-8"?>
<!DOCTYPE html PUBLIC "-//W3C//DTD XHTML 1.0 Strict//EN"
  "http://www.w3.org/TR/xhtml1/DTD/xhtml1-strict.dtd">

<!-- link.html
     An example to illustrate a link
     -->
<html xmlns = "http://www.w3.org/1999/xhtml">
  <head> <title> A link </title>
  </head>
  <body>
    <h1> Aidan's Airplanes </h1>
    <h2> The best in used airplanes </h2>
    <h3> "We've got them by the hangarful" </h3>
    <h2> Special of the month </h2>
    <p>
      1960 Cessna 210 <br />
      <a href = "C210data.html"> Information on the Cessna 210 </a>
    </p>
  </body>
</html>
```

In this case, the target is a complete document that is stored in the same directory as the XHTML document. Figure 2.13 shows a browser display of `link.html`. When the link shown in Figure 2.13 is clicked, the browser displays the screen shown in Figure 2.14.

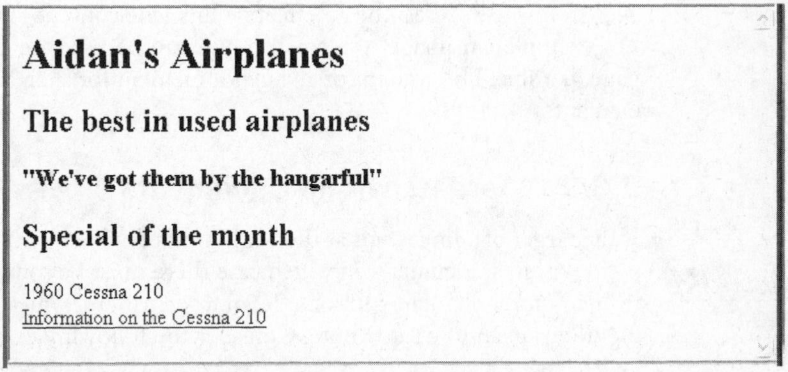

Aidan's Airplanes

The best in used airplanes

"We've got them by the hangarful"

Special of the month

1960 Cessna 210
Information on the Cessna 210

Figure 2.13 Display of `link.html`

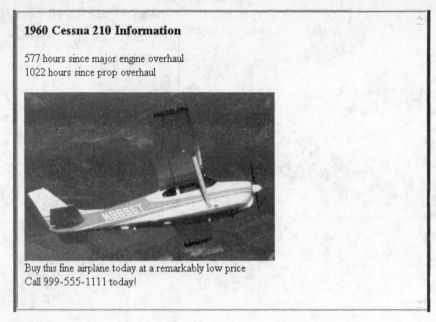

1960 Cessna 210 Information

577 hours since major engine overhaul
1022 hours since prop overhaul

Buy this fine airplane today at a remarkably low price
Call 999-555-1111 today!

Figure 2.14 Following the link from `link.html`

Links can include images in their content, in which case the browser displays the image with the link:

```
<a href = "c210data.html" >
  <img src = "small-airplane.jpg"
      alt = "An image of a small airplane" />
    Information on the Cessna 210
</a>
```

An image itself can be an effective link (the content of the anchor element). For example, an image of a small house can be used for the link to the home page of a site. The content of an anchor element for such a link is just the image element.

2.6.2 Targets within Documents

If the target of a link is not at the beginning of a document, it must be some element within a document, in which case there must be some means of specifying it. The target element can include an `id` attribute, which can then be used to identify it in an `href` attribute. Consider the following example:

```
<h2 id = "avionics"> Avionics </h2>
```

Nearly all elements can include an `id` attribute. The value of an `id` attribute must be unique within the document.

If the target is in the same document as the link, the target is specified in the `href` attribute value by preceding the `id` value with a pound sign (#), as in the following example:

```
<a href = "#avionics"> What about avionics? </a>
```

When the `What about avionics?` link is taken, the browser moves the display so that the h2 element whose `id` is `avionics` is at the top.

When the target is a part or fragment of another document, the name of the part is specified at the end of the URL, separated by a pound sign (#), as in this example:

```
<a href = "AIDAN1.html#avionics"> Avionics </a>
```

2.6.3   Using Links

One common use of links to parts of the same document is to provide a table of contents in which each entry has a link. This provides a convenient way for the user to get to the various parts of the document simply and quickly. Such a table of contents is implemented as a stylized list of links, using the list specification capabilities of XHTML, which are discussed in Section 2.7.

Links exemplify the true spirit of hypertext. The reader can click on links to learn more about a particular subtopic of interest and then return to the location of the link. Designing links requires some care because they can be annoying if the designer tries too hard to convince the user to take them. For example, making them stand out too much from the surrounding text can be distracting. A link should blend into the surrounding text as much as possible so that reading the document without clicking any of the links is easy and natural.

2.7   Lists

We frequently make and use lists in daily life—for example, to-do lists and grocery lists. Likewise, both printed and displayed information is littered with lists. XHTML provides simple and effective ways to specify lists in documents. The primary supported list types are those with which most people are already familiar: unordered lists such as grocery lists and ordered lists such as the assembly instructions for a new bookshelf. Definition lists can also be defined. The tags to specify unordered, ordered, and definition lists are described in this section.

2.7.1   Unordered Lists

The `<ul>` tag, which is a block tag, creates an unordered list. Each item in a list is specified with an `<li>` tag (li is an acronym for *list item*). Any tags can appear in a list item, including nested lists. When displayed, each list item is implicitly preceded with a bullet. For example, consider the following:

```
<?xml version = "1.0" encoding = "utf-8"?>
<!DOCTYPE html PUBLIC "-//W3C//DTD XHTML 1.0 Strict//EN"
  "http://www.w3.org/TR/xhtml1/DTD/xhtml1-strict.dtd">


<!-- unordered.html
     An example to illustrate an unordered list
     -->
<html xmlns = "http://www.w3.org/1999/xhtml">
  <head> <title> Unordered list </title>
  </head>
  <body>
    <h3> Some Common Single-Engine Aircraft </h3>
    <ul>
      <li> Cessna Skyhawk </li>
      <li> Beechcraft Bonanza </li>
      <li> Piper Cherokee </li>
    </ul>
  </body>
</html>
```

Figure 2.15 shows a browser display of unordered.html.

Some Common Single-Engine Aircraft

- Cessna Skyhawk
- Beechcraft Bonanza
- Piper Cherokee

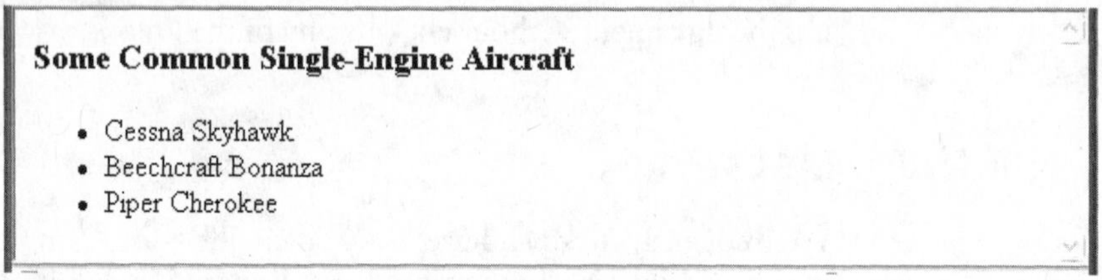

Figure 2.15 Display of unordered.html

2.7.2   Ordered Lists

Ordered lists are those in which the order of items is important. This ordered-ness of a list is shown in the display of the list by the implicit attachment of a sequential value to the beginning of each item. The default sequential values are Arabic numerals, beginning with 1.

An ordered list is created within the block tag <ol>. The items are specified and displayed just like those for unordered lists, except that the items in an ordered list are preceded by sequential values instead of bullets. Consider the following example of an ordered list:

```
<?xml version = "1.0" encoding = "utf-8"?>
<!DOCTYPE html PUBLIC "-//W3C//DTD XHTML 1.0 Strict//EN"
  "http://www.w3.org/TR/xhtml1/DTD/xhtml1-strict.dtd">

<!-- ordered.html
     An example to illustrate an ordered list
     -->
<html xmlns = "http://www.w3.org/1999/xhtml">
  <head> <title> Ordered list </title>
  </head>
  <body>
    <h3> Cessna 210 Engine Starting Instructions </h3>
    <ol>
      <li> Set mixture to rich </li>
      <li> Set propeller to high RPM </li>
      <li> Set ignition switch to "BOTH" </li>
      <li> Set auxiliary fuel pump switch to "LOW PRIME" </li>
      <li> When fuel pressure reaches 2 to 2.5 PSI, push
           starter button
      </li>
    </ol>
  </body>
</html>
```

Figure 2.16 shows a browser display of `ordered.html`.

Cessna 210 Engine Starting Instructions

1. Set mixture to rich
2. Set propeller to high RPM
3. Set ignition switch to "BOTH"
4. Set auxiliary fuel pump switch to "LOW PRIME"
5. When fuel pressure reaches 2 to 2.5 PSI, push starter button

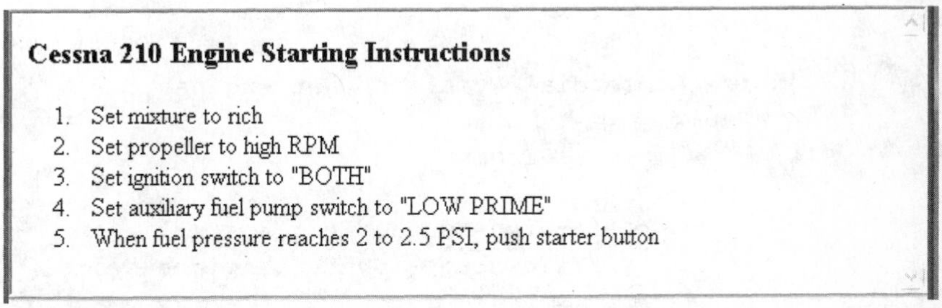

Figure 2.16 Display of `ordered.html`

As noted earlier, lists can be nested. However, a list cannot be directly nested; that is, an `<ol>` tag cannot immediately follow an `<ol>` tag. Rather, the nested list must be the content of an `<li>` element. The following example illustrates nested ordered lists:

```
<?xml version = "1.0" encoding = "utf-8"?>
<!DOCTYPE html PUBLIC "-//W3C//DTD XHTML 1.0 Strict//EN"
  "http://www.w3.org/TR/xhtml1/DTD/xhtml1-strict.dtd">

<!-- nested_lists.html
     An example to illustrate nested lists
     -->
<html xmlns = "http://www.w3.org/1999/xhtml">
  <head> <title> Nested lists </title>
  </head>
  <body>
    <h3> Aircraft Types </h3>
    <ol>
      <li> General Aviation (piston-driven engines)
        <ol>
          <li> Single-Engine Aircraft
            <ol>
              <li> Tail wheel </li>
              <li> Tricycle </li>
            </ol> <br />
          </li>
          <li> Dual-Engine Aircraft
            <ol>
              <li> Wing-mounted engines </li>
              <li> Push-pull fuselage-mounted engines </li>
            </ol>
          </li>
        </ol> <br />
      </li>
      <li> Commercial Aviation (jet engines)
        <ol>
          <li> Dual-Engine
            <ol>
              <li> Wing-mounted engines </li>
              <li> Fuselage-mounted engines </li>
            </ol> <br />
          </li>
          <li> Tri-Engine
            <ol>
              <li> Third engine in vertical stabilizer </li>
              <li> Third engine in fuselage </li>
            </ol>
```

```
        </li>
      </ol>
    </li>
  </ol>
 </body>
</html>
```

Figure 2.17 shows a browser display of `nested_lists.html`.

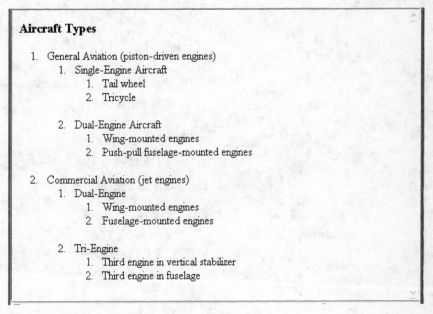

Aircraft Types

1. General Aviation (piston-driven engines)
   1. Single-Engine Aircraft
      1. Tail wheel
      2. Tricycle

   2. Dual-Engine Aircraft
      1. Wing-mounted engines
      2. Push-pull fuselage-mounted engines

2. Commercial Aviation (jet engines)
   1. Dual-Engine
      1. Wing-mounted engines
      2. Fuselage-mounted engines

   2. Tri-Engine
      1. Third engine in vertical stabilizer
      2. Third engine in fuselage

Figure 2.17 Display of `nested_lists.html`

One problem with the nested lists shown in Figure 2.17 is that all three levels use the same sequence values. Chapter 3 describes how style sheets can be used to specify different kinds of sequence values for different lists.

The `nested_lists.html` example uses nested ordered lists. There are no restrictions on list nesting, provided the nesting is not direct. For example, ordered lists can be nested in unordered lists and vice versa.

2.7.3   Definition Lists

As the name implies, definition lists are used to specify lists of terms and their definitions, such as in glossaries. A definition list is given as the content of a `<dl>` tag, which is a block tag. Each term to be defined in the definition list is given as the content of a `<dt>` tag. The definitions themselves are specified as the content of `<dd>` tags. The defined terms of a definition list are usually displayed on the left margin; the definitions are usually shown on the line or lines following the term, which are indented. Consider the following example:

```
<?xml version = "1.0" encoding = "utf-8"?>
<!DOCTYPE html PUBLIC "-//W3C//DTD XHTML 1.0 Strict//EN"
  "http://www.w3.org/TR/xhtml1/DTD/xhtml1-strict.dtd">


<!-- definition.html
     An example to illustrate definition lists
     -->
<html xmlns = "http://www.w3.org/1999/xhtml">
  <head> <title> Definition lists </title>
  </head>
  <body>
    <h3> Single-Engine Cessna Airplanes </h3>
    <dl>
      <dt> 152 </dt>
      <dd> Two-place trainer </dd>
      <dt> 172 </dt>
      <dd> Smaller four-place airplane </dd>
      <dt> 182 </dt>
      <dd> Larger four-place airplane </dd>
      <dt> 210 </dt>
      <dd> Six-place airplane - high performance </dd>
    </dl>
  </body>
</html>
```

Figure 2.18 shows a browser display of `definition.html`.

Single-Engine Cessna Airplanes

152

    Two-place trainer

172

    Smaller four-place airplane

182

    Larger four-place airplane

210

    Six-place airplane - high performance

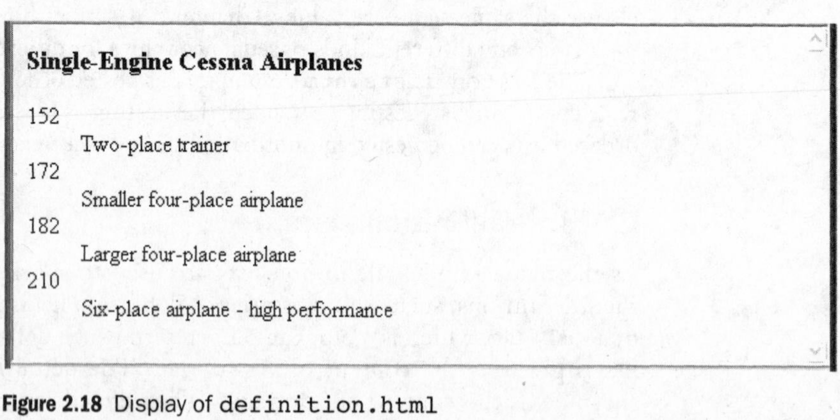

Figure 2.18 Display of `definition.html`

2.8 Tables

Tables are common fixtures in printed documents, books, and of course, Web documents. Tables provide a highly effective way of presenting many kinds of information.

A table is a matrix of cells. The cells in the top row often contain column labels; those in the leftmost column often contain row labels; most of the rest of the cells contain the data of the table. The content of a cell can be almost any document element, including text, headings, horizontal rules, images, and nested tables.

2.8.1 Basic Table Tags

A table is specified as the content of the block tag `<table>`. The most common attribute for the `<table>` tag is `border`. There are two kinds of lines in tables: the line around the outside of the whole table is called the *border*; the lines that separate the cells from each other are called *rules*. A table that does not include the `border` attribute will be a matrix of cells with neither a border nor rules. The browser has default widths for table borders and rules, which are used if the `border` attribute is assigned the value `"border."` Otherwise, a number can be given as `border`'s value, which specifies the border width in pixels. For example, `border = "3"` specifies a border 3 pixels wide. A `border` value of `"0"` specifies no border and no rules. The rule lines are set at 1 pixel when any non-zero `border` value is specified. All table borders are beveled to give a three-dimensional appearance, although this is ineffective when narrow border widths are used.

In most cases, a displayed table is preceded by a title, which is given as the content of a `<caption>` tag, which can immediately follow the opening `<table>` tag. The cells of a table are specified one row at a time. Each row of a table is specified with a row tag, `<tr>`. Within each row, the row label is specified by the table heading tag, `<th>`. Although the `<th>` tag has *heading* in its name, we call them *labels* to avoid confusion with headings created with the `<hx>` tags. Each data cell of a row is specified with a table data tag, `<td>`. The first row of a table usually has the table's column labels. For example, if a table has three data columns and their column labels are `Apple`, `Orange`, and `Screwdriver`, the first row can be specified by the following:

```
<tr>
   <th> Apple </th>
   <th> Orange </th>
   <th> Screwdriver </th>
</tr>
```

Each data row of a table is specified with a heading tag and one data tag for each data column. For example, the first data row for our work-in-progress table might be as follows:

```
<tr>
  <th> Breakfast </th>
  <td> 0 </td>
  <td> 1 </td>
  <td> 0 </td>
</tr>
```

In tables that have both row and column labels, the upper-left corner cell is often empty. This empty cell is specified with a table header tag that includes no content (either `<th></th>` or just `<th />`).

The following document describes the whole table:

```
<?xml version = "1.0" encoding = "utf-8"?>
<!DOCTYPE html PUBLIC "-//W3C//DTD XHTML 1.0 Strict//EN"
  "http://www.w3.org/TR/xhtml1/DTD/xhtml1-strict.dtd">

<!-- table.html
     An example of a simple table
     -->
<html xmlns = "http://www.w3.org/1999/xhtml">
  <head> <title> A simple table </title>
  </head>
  <body>
    <table border = "border">
      <caption> Fruit Juice Drinks </caption>
      <tr>
        <th> </th>
        <th> Apple </th>
        <th> Orange </th>
        <th> Screwdriver </th>
      </tr>
      <tr>
        <th> Breakfast </th>
        <td> 0 </td>
        <td> 1 </td>
        <td> 0 </td>
      </tr>
      <tr>
        <th> Lunch </th>
        <td> 1 </td>
        <td> 0 </td>
        <td> 0 </td>
      </tr>
      <tr>
        <th> Dinner </th>
```

```
            <td> 0 </td>
            <td> 0 </td>
            <td> 1 </td>
        </tr>
    </table>
  </body>
</html>
```

Figure 2.19 shows a browser display of this table.

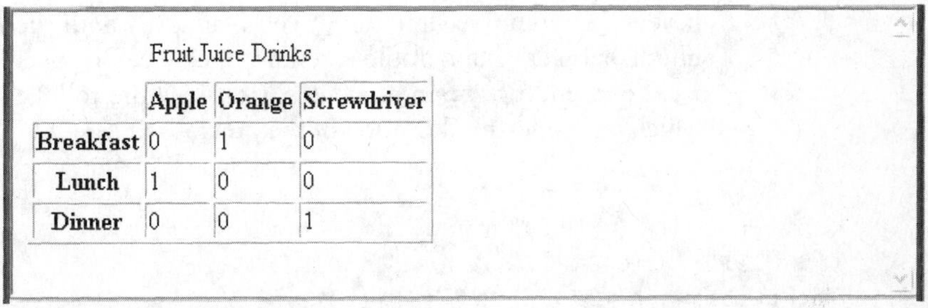

Figure 2.19 Display of `table.html`

2.8.2   The `rowspan` and `colspan` Attributes

In many cases, tables have multiple levels of row or column labels in which one label covers two or more secondary labels. For example, consider the display of a partial table shown in Figure 2.20. In this table, the upper-level label **Fruit Juice Drinks** spans the three lower-level label cells. Multiple-level labels can be specified with the `rowspan` and `colspan` attributes.

Figure 2.20 Two levels of column labels

The `colspan` attribute specification in a table header or table data tag tells the browser to make the cell as wide as the specified number of rows below it in the table. For the previous example, the following code could be used:

```
<tr>
  <th colspan = "3"> Fruit Juice Drinks </th>
</tr>
```

```
<tr>
  <th> Apple </th>
  <th> Orange </th>
  <th> Screwdriver </th>
</tr>
```

If there are fewer cells in the rows above or below the spanning cell than the colspan attribute specifies, the browser stretches the spanning cell over the number of cells that populate the column in the table.[11] The rowspan attribute of the table heading and table data tags does for rows what colspan does for columns.

A table that has two levels of column labels and also has row labels must have an empty upper-left corner cell that spans both the multiple rows of column labels and the multiple columns. Such a cell is specified by including both rowspan and colspan attributes. Consider the following table specification, which is a minor modification of the previous table:

```
<?xml version = "1.0" encoding = "utf-8"?>
<!DOCTYPE html PUBLIC "-//W3C//DTD XHTML 1.0 Strict//EN"
  "http://www.w3.org/TR/xhtml1/DTD/xhtml1-strict.dtd">

<!-- cell_span.html
     An example to illustrate rowspan and colspan
     -->
<html xmlns = "http://www.w3.org/1999/xhtml">
  <head> <title> Rowspan and colspan </title>
  </head>
  <body>
    <table border = "border">
      <caption> Fruit Juice Drinks and Meals </caption>
      <tr>
        <td rowspan = "2"> </td>
        <th colspan = "3"> Fruit Juice Drinks </th>
      </tr>
      <tr>
        <th> Apple </th>
        <th> Orange </th>
        <th> Screwdriver </th>
      </tr>
      <tr>
        <th> Breakfast </th>
        <td> 0 </td>
        <td> 1 </td>
```

---

11. Some browsers add empty row cells to allow the specified span to occur.

```
          <td> 0 </td>
      </tr>
      <tr>
        <th> Lunch </th>
        <td> 1 </td>
        <td> 0 </td>
        <td> 0 </td>
      </tr>
      <tr>
        <th> Dinner </th>
        <td> 0 </td>
        <td> 0 </td>
        <td> 1 </td>
      </tr>
    </table>
  </body>
</html>
```

Figure 2.21 shows a browser display of `cell_span.html`.

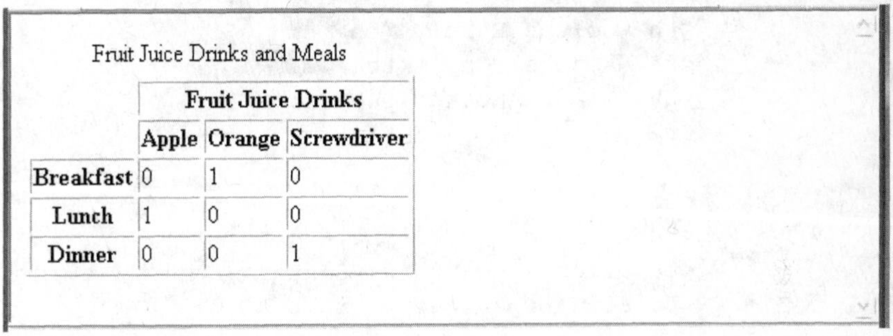

Fruit Juice Drinks and Meals			
	Fruit Juice Drinks		
	Apple	**Orange**	**Screwdriver**
Breakfast	0	1	0
Lunch	1	0	0
Dinner	0	0	1

Figure 2.21 Display of `cell_span.html`: multiple-labeled columns and labeled rows

2.8.3   The `align` and `valign` Attributes

The placement of the content within a table cell can be specified with the `align` and `valign` attributes in the `<tr>`, `<th>`, and `<td>` tags. The `align` attribute has the possible values `left`, `right`, and `center`, with the obvious meanings for horizontal placement of the content within a cell. The default alignment for `th` cells is `center`; for `td` cells, it is `left`. If `align` is specified in a `<tr>` tag, it applies to all of the cells in the row. If it is included in a `<th>` or `<td>` tag, it applies only to that cell.

The `valign` attribute of the `<th>` and `<td>` tags has the possible values `top` and `bottom`. The default vertical alignment for both headings and data is `center`. Because `valign` applies only to a single cell, there is never any point in specifying `center`.

The following example illustrates the `align` and `valign` attributes:

```
<?xml version = "1.0" encoding = "utf-8"?>
<!DOCTYPE html PUBLIC "-//W3C//DTD XHTML 1.0 Strict//EN"
  "http://www.w3.org/TR/xhtml1/DTD/xhtml1-strict.dtd">

<!-- cell_align.html
     An example to illustrate align and valign
     -->
<html xmlns = "http://www.w3.org/1999/xhtml">
  <head> <title> Alignment in cells </title>
  </head>
  <body>
    <table border = "border">
      <caption> The align and valign attributes </caption>
      <tr align = "center">
        <th> </th>
        <th> Column Label </th>
        <th> Another One </th>
        <th> Still Another One </th>
      </tr>
      <tr>
        <th> align </th>
        <td align = "left"> Left </td>
        <td align = "center"> Center </td>
        <td align = "right"> Right </td>
      </tr>
      <tr>
        <th> <br /> valign <br /> <br /> </th>
        <td> Default </td>
        <td valign = "top"> Top </td>
        <td valign = "bottom"> Bottom </td>
      </tr>
    </table>
  </body>
</html>
```

Figure 2.22 shows a browser display of `cell_align.html`.

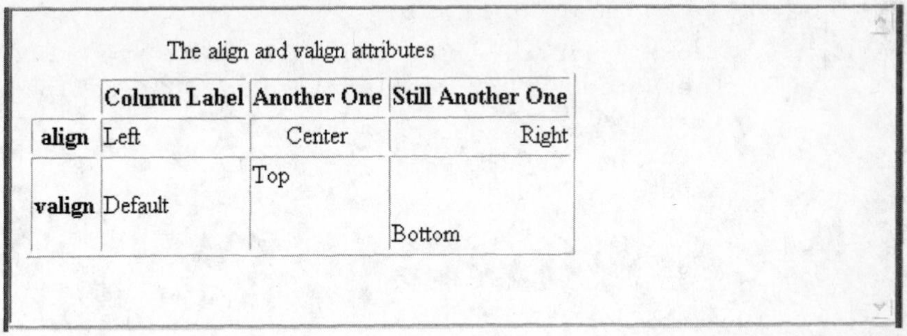

The align and valign attributes

	Column Label	Another One	Still Another One
align	Left	Center	Right
valign	Default	Top	Bottom

Figure 2.22 Display of `cell_align.html`: the `align` and `valign` attributes

2.8.4 The cellpadding and cellspacing Attributes

The table tag has two attributes that can be used to specify the spacing between the content of a table cell and the cell's edge and the spacing between adjacent cells. The `cellpadding` attribute is used to specify the spacing between the content of a cell and the inner walls of the cell. This is often used to prevent text in a cell from being too close to the edge of the cell. The `cellspacing` attribute is used to specify the distance between cells in a table.

The following document, `space_pad.html`, illustrates the `cellpadding` and `cellspacing` attributes:

```
<?xml version = "1.0" encoding = "utf-8"?>
<!DOCTYPE html PUBLIC "-//W3C//DTD XHTML 1.0 Strict//EN"
  "http://www.w3.org/TR/xhtml1/DTD/xhtml1-strict.dtd">

<!-- space_pad.html
     An example that illustrates the cellspacing and
     cellpadding table attributes
     -->
<html xmlns = "http://www.w3.org/1999/xhtml">
  <head> <title> Cell spacing and cell padding </title>
  </head>
  <body>
    <b>Table 1 (space = 10, pad = 30) </b><br /><br />
    <table border = "5"  cellspacing = "10"  cellpadding = "30">
      <tr>
        <td> Small spacing, </td>
        <td> large padding </td>
      </tr>
    </table>
```

```
            <br /><br /><br /><br />
            <b>Table 2 (space = 30, pad = 10) </b><br /><br />
            <table border = "5"  cellspacing = "30"  cellpadding = "10">
              <tr>
                <td> Large spacing, </td>
                <td> small padding </td>
              </tr>
            </table>
        </body>
</html>
```

Figure 2.23 shows a browser display of `space_pad.html`.

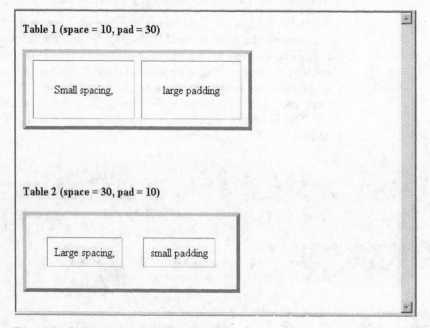

Figure 2.23 Display of `space_pad.html`

2.8.5   Table Sections

Tables naturally occur in two and sometimes three parts: header, body, and footer (not all tables have a natural footer). These three parts can be denoted in XHTML with the `thead`, `tbody`, and `tfoot` elements. The header includes the column labels, regardless of the number of levels in those labels. The body includes the data of the table, including the row labels. The footer, when it appears, sometimes has the column labels repeated after the body. In some tables, the footer contains totals for the columns of data above. A table can have multiple body sections, in which case the browser may delimit them with horizontal lines that are thicker than the rule lines within a body section.

2.9 Forms

The most common way for a user to communicate information from a Web browser to the server is through a form. Forms, which are modeled on the paper forms that people frequently are required to fill out, can be described in XHTML and displayed by the browser. XHTML provides tags to generate the commonly used objects on a screen form. These objects are called *controls* or *widgets*. There are controls for single-line and multiple-line text collection, checkboxes, radio buttons, and menus, among others. All control tags are inline tags. Most controls are used to gather information from the user in the form of either text or button selections. Each control can have a value, usually given through user input. Together, the values of all of the controls (that have values) in a form are called the *form data*. Every form requires a *Submit* button (see Section 2.9.5). When the user clicks the *Submit* button, the form data is encoded and sent to the Web server for processing. Form processing is discussed in several subsequent chapters (Chapters 9, 11, and 12).

2.9.1   The <form> Tag

All of the components of a form appear in the content of a `<form>` tag. `<form>`, which is a block tag, can have several different attributes, only one of which, `action`, is required. The `action` attribute specifies the URL of the application on the Web server that is to be called when the user clicks the *Submit* button. In this chapter, our examples of form elements will not have corresponding application programs, so the value of their `action` attributes will be the empty string (`""`).

The `method` attribute of `<form>` specifies one of the two techniques, `get` or `post`, used to pass the form data to the server. `get` is the default, so if no `method` attribute is given in the `<form>` tag, `get` will be used. The alternative technique is `post`. In both techniques, the form data is coded into a text string when the user clicks the *Submit* button.

When the `get` method is used, the browser attaches the query string to the URL of the HTTP request, so the form data is transmitted to the server with the URL. The browser inserts a question mark at the end of the actual URL just before the first character of the query string so that the server can easily find the beginning of the query string. The `get` method can also be used to pass parameters to the server when forms are not involved (this cannot be done with `post`). One disadvantage of the `get` method is that some servers place a limit on the length of the URL string and truncate any characters past the limit. So, if the form has more than a few controls, `get` is not a good choice.

When the `post` method is used, the query string is passed by some other method to the form processing program. There is no length limitation for the query string with the `post` method, so obviously it is the better choice when there are more than a few controls in the form. There are also some security concerns with `get` that are not a potential problem with `post`.

2.9.2   The `<input>` Tag

Many of the commonly used controls are specified with the inline tag `<input>`, which is used for text, passwords, checkboxes, radio buttons, and the action buttons *Reset*, *Submit*, and *plain*. The text, password, checkboxes, and radio controls are discussed in this section. The action butons are discussed in Section 2.9.5.

The one attribute of `<input>` that is required for all of the controls discussed in this section is `type`, which specifies the particular kind of control. The control's kind is its type name, such as `checkbox`. All of the previously listed controls except *Reset* and *Submit* also require a `name` attribute, which becomes the name of the value of the control within the form data. The controls for checkboxes and radio buttons require a `value` attribute, which initializes the value of the control.

A text control, which we usually refer to as a text box, creates a horizontal box into which the user can type a line of text. Text boxes are often used to gather information from the user, such as the user's name and address. The default size of a text box is often 20 characters. Because the default size can vary among browsers, it is a good idea to include a size on each text box. This is done with the `size` attribute of `<input>`. If the user types more characters than will fit in the box, the box is scrolled. If you do not want the box to be scrolled, you can include the `maxlength` attribute to specify the maximum number of characters that the browser will accept in the box. Any additional characters are ignored. For example, consider the following text box:

```
<form action = "">
  <p>
    <input type = "text"  name = "Name"  size = "25" />
  </p>
</form>
```

Suppose the user typed the following line:

```
Alfred Paul von Frickenburger
```

The text box would collect the whole string, but the string would be scrolled to the right, leaving the following shown in the box:

```
ed Paul von Frickenburger
```

The left end of the line would be part of the value of `Name`, even though it does not appear in the box. The ends of the line can be viewed in the box by moving the cursor off the ends of the box.

Notice that controls cannot appear directly in the form content—they must be placed in some block container, such as a paragraph.

Now consider a similar text box that includes a `maxlength` attribute.

```
<form action = "">
  <p>
    <input type = "text"  name = "Name"  size = "25"
           maxlength = "25" />
  </p>
</form>
```

If the user typed the same name as in the previous example, the resulting value of the `Name` text box would be as follows:

```
Alfred Paul von Frickenbu
```

No matter what was typed after the u in that person's last name, the value of `Name` would be as shown.

If the contents of a text box should not be displayed when it is entered by the user, a password control can be used. For example:

```
<input type = "password"  name = "myPassword"
       size = "10" maxlength = "10" />
```

In this case, regardless of what characters are typed into a password control, only bullets or asterisks are displayed by the browser.

There are no restrictions on the characters that can be typed into a text box. So, the string `"?!34,:"` could be entered into the text box meant for names. Therefore, the entered contents of text boxes nearly always must be validated, either on the browser or on the server to which the form data is passed for processing, or both.

Text boxes, as well as most other control elements, should be labeled. Labeling could be done by simply inserting text into the approximate places in the form. For example:

```
Phone: <input type = "text"  name = "phone" />
```

This effectively labels the text box, but there are several ways the labeling could be better. For one thing, there is no connection between the label and the control. Therefore, they could become separated in maintenance changes to the document. A control and its label can be connected by putting the control and its label in the content of a label element. For example:

```
<label> Phone: <input type = "text"  name = "phone" />
</label>
```

Now, the text box and its label are encapsulated together. There are several other benefits of this approach to labeling controls. First, browsers often render the text content of a label element differently to make it stand out. Second, if the text content of a label element is selected, the cursor is implicitly moved to the control in the content of the label. This is an aid to new Web users. Third, the text content of a label element can be rendered by a speech synthesizer on the client machine when selected. This can be a great aid to a user with a visual disability.

Checkbox and radio controls are used to collect multiple-choice input from the user. A checkbox control is a single button that is either on or off (checked or not). If a checkbox button is on, the value associated with the name of the button is the string assigned to its `value` attribute. A checkbox button does not contribute to the form data if it is off. Every checkbox button requires a `name` attribute and a `value` attribute in its `<input>` tag. For form processing on the server, the name identifies the button and the value is its value (if it is checked). The attribute `checked`, which is assigned the value `checked`, specifies that the checkbox button is initially on. In many cases, checkboxes appear in lists, with every one in the list having the same name. Checkbox elements should appear in label elements, for the same reasons that text boxes should. Consider the following example:

```
<?xml version = "1.0" encoding = "utf-8"?>
<!DOCTYPE html PUBLIC "-//W3C//DTD XHTML 1.0 Strict//EN"
  "http://www.w3.org/TR/xhtml1/DTD/xhtml1-strict.dtd">

<!-- checkbox.html
     An example to illustrate a checkbox
     -->
<html xmlns = "http://www.w3.org/1999/xhtml">
  <head> <title> Checkboxes </title>
  </head>
  <body>
    <p>
      Grocery Checklist
    </p>
    <form action = "">
      <p>
        <label> <input type = "checkbox"  name = "groceries"
               value = "milk"  checked = "checked" /> Milk </label>
        <label> <input type = "checkbox"  name = "groceries"
               value = "bread" /> Bread </label>
        <label> <input type = "checkbox"  name = "groceries"
               value= "eggs" /> Eggs </label>
      </p>
    </form>
  </body>
</html>
```

Figure 2.24 shows a browser display of `checkbox.html`.

Grocery Checklist

☑ Milk ☐ Bread ☐ Eggs

Figure 2.24 Display of `checkbox.html`

If the user does not turn on any of the checkbox buttons in our example, `milk` will be the value for `groceries` in the form data. If the `milk` checkbox is left on and the `eggs` checkbox is also turned on by the user, the values of `groceries` in the form data would be `milk` and `eggs`.

Radio buttons are closely related to checkbox buttons. The difference between a group of radio buttons and a group of checkboxes is that only one radio button can be on or pressed at any time. Every time a radio button is pressed, the button in the group that was previously on is turned off. Radio buttons are named after the mechanical push buttons on the radios of cars of the 1950s—when you pushed one button on such a radio, the previously pushed button was mechanically forced out. The `type` value for radio buttons is `radio`. All radio buttons in a group must have the `name` attribute set in the `<input>` tag, and all radio buttons in a group must have the same name value. A radio button definition may specify which button is to be initially in the pressed, or on, state. This is indicated by including the `checked` attribute, set to the value `checked`, in the `<input>` tag of the button's definition. If no radio button in a group is specified as being checked, the browser usually checks the first button in the group. Consider the following radio button example:

```
<?xml version = "1.0" encoding = "utf-8"?>
<!DOCTYPE html PUBLIC "-//W3C//DTD XHTML 1.0 Strict//EN"
  "http://www.w3.org/TR/xhtml1/DTD/xhtml1-strict.dtd">

<!-- radio.html
     An example to illustrate radio buttons
     -->
<html xmlns = "http://www.w3.org/1999/xhtml">
  <head> <title> Radio </title>
  </head>
  <body>
    <p>
      Age Category
    </p>
```

```
<form action = "">
  <p>
    <label><input type = "radio"  name = "age"
          value = "under20" checked = "checked" />
          0-19 </label>
    <label><input type = "radio"  name = "age"
          value = "20-35" /> 20-35 </label>
    <label><input type = "radio"  name = "age"
          value = "36-50" /> 36-50 </label>
    <label><input type = "radio"  name = "age"
          value = "over50" /> Over 50 </label>
  </p>
</form>
</body>
</html>
```

Figure 2.25 shows a browser display of `radio.html`.

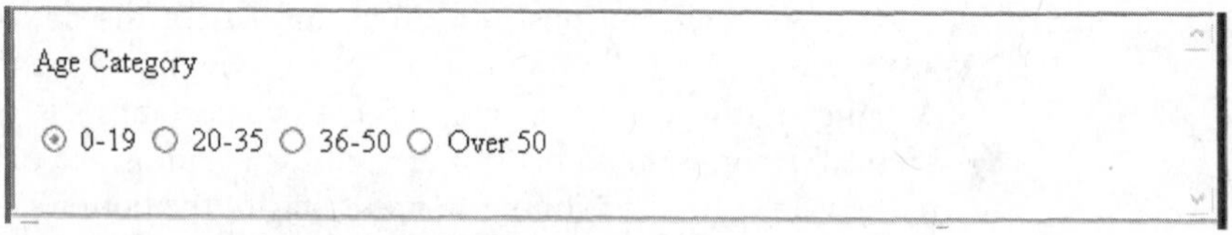

Age Category

⊙ 0-19   ○ 20-35   ○ 36-50   ○ Over 50

Figure 2.25 Display of `radio.html`

2.9.3   The `<select>` Tag

Checkboxes and radio buttons are effective methods for collecting multiple-choice data from a user. However, if the number of possible choices is large, the displayed form becomes too long to display. In these cases, a menu should be used. A menu is specified with a `<select>` tag (rather than with the `<input>` tag). There are two kinds of menus: those in which only one menu item can be selected at a time (which are related to radio buttons) and those in which multiple menu items can be selected at a time (which are related to checkboxes). The default option is the one related to radio buttons. The other option can be specified by adding the `multiple` attribute. The `multiple` attribute must be set to the value `"multiple"`. When only one menu item is selected, the value sent in the form data is the value of the `name` attribute of the `<select>` tag and the chosen menu item. When multiple menu items are selected, the value for the menu in the form data includes all selected menu items. If no menu item is selected, no value for the menu is included in the form data. The `name` attribute, of course, is required in the `<select>` tag.

The `size` attribute can be included in the `<select>` tag. `size` specifies the number of menu items that are to be displayed for the user. If no `size` attribute is specified, the value 1 is used. If the value for the `size` attribute is 1 and `multiple` is not specified, just one menu item is displayed with a downward scroll arrow. If the scroll arrow is clicked, the menu is displayed as a pop-up menu. If either `multiple` is specified or the `size` attribute is set to a number larger than 1, the menu is usually displayed as a scrolled list.

Each of the items in a menu is specified with an `<option>` tag, nested in the select element. The content of an `<option>` tag is the value of the menu item, which is just text (no tags may be included). The `<option>` tag can include the `selected` attribute, which specifies that the item is preselected. The value assigned to `selected` is "selected." This preselection can be overridden by the user. The following document describes a menu with the default value (1) for `size`:

```
<?xml version = "1.0" encoding = "utf-8"?>
<!DOCTYPE html PUBLIC "-//W3C//DTD XHTML 1.0 Strict//EN"
  "http://www.w3.org/TR/xhtml1/DTD/xhtml1-strict.dtd">


<!-- menu.html
     An example to illustrate menus
     -->
<html xmlns = "http://www.w3.org/1999/xhtml">
  <head> <title> Menu </title>
  </head>
  <body>
    <p>
      Grocery Menu - milk, bread, eggs, cheese
    </p>
    <form action = "">
      <p>
        With size = 1 (the default)
        <select name = "groceries">
          <option> milk </option>
          <option> bread </option>
          <option> eggs </option>
          <option> cheese </option>
        </select>
      </p>
    </form>
  </body>
</html>
```

Figure 2.26 shows a browser display of menu.html. Figure 2.27 shows a browser display of menu.html after clicking the scroll arrow. Figure 2.28 shows a browser display of menu.html after modification to set `size` to "2."

Figure 2.26 Display of menu.html (default size of 1)

Figure 2.27 Display of menu.html after the scroll arrow is clicked

Figure 2.28 Display of menu.html with size set to 2

When the multiple attribute of the `<select>` tag is set, adjacent options can be chosen by dragging the mouse cursor over them while the left mouse button is held down. Nonadjacent options can be selected by clicking them while holding down the keyboard *Control* key.

2.9.4 The `<textarea>` Tag

In some situations, a multiline text area is needed. The `<textarea>` tag is used to create such a control. The text typed into the area created by `<textarea>` is not limited in length, and there is implicit scrolling when needed, both vertically and horizontally. The default size of the visible part of the text in a text area is often quite small, so the rows and cols attributes should usually be included and set to reasonable sizes. If some default text is to be included in the text area, it can be included as the content of the text area element. The following document describes a text area whose window is 40 columns wide and 3 lines tall:

```
<?xml version = "1.0" encoding = "utf-8"?>
<!DOCTYPE html PUBLIC "-//W3C//DTD XHTML 1.0 Strict//EN"
  "http://www.w3.org/TR/xhtml1/DTD/xhtml1-strict.dtd">

<!-- textarea.html
     An example to illustrate a textarea
     -->
<html xmlns = "http://www.w3.org/1999/xhtml">
  <head> <title> Textarea </title>
  </head>
  <body>
    <p>
      Please provide your employment aspirations
    </p>
    <form action = "handler">
      <p>
        <textarea name = "aspirations"  rows = "3"  cols = "40">
          (Be brief and concise)
        </textarea>
      </p>
    </form>
  </body>
</html>
```

Figure 2.29 shows a browser display of `textarea.html` after some text has been typed into the area.

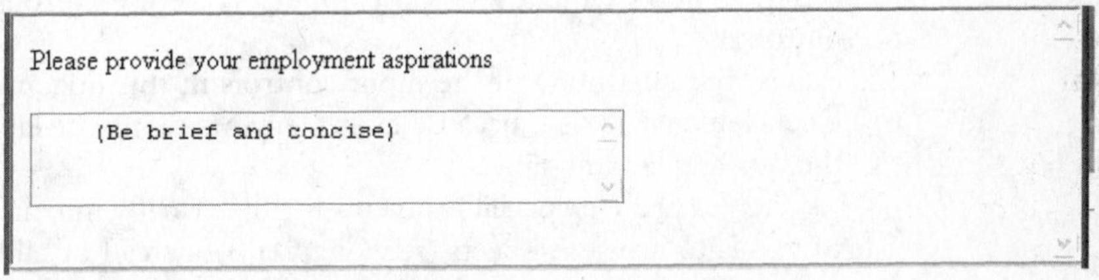

Figure 2.29 Display of `textarea.html` after some text entry

2.9.5   The Action Buttons

The *Reset* button clears all of the controls in the form to their initial states. The *Submit* button has two actions: First, the form data is encoded and sent to the server. Second, the server is requested to execute the server-resident program specified in the `action` attribute of the `<form>` tag. The purpose of such a server-resident program is to process the form data and return some response to the user. Every form requires a *Submit* button. The *Submit* and *Reset* buttons are created with the `<input>` tag, as shown in the following example:

```
<form action = "">
  <p>
    <input type = "submit"  value = "Submit Form" />
    <input type = "reset"  value = "Reset Form" />
  </p>
</form>
```

Figure 2.30 shows a browser display of *Submit* and *Reset* buttons.

Figure 2.30 *Submit* and *Reset* buttons

A *plain* button has the type `button`. *Plain* buttons are used to choose an action.

2.9.6   A Complete Form Example

The following document describes a form for taking sales orders for popcorn. Three text boxes are used at the top of the form to collect the buyer's name and address. These are placed in a borderless table to force the text boxes to align vertically. A second table is used to collect the actual order. Each row of this table names a product with the content of a `<td>` tag, displays the price with another `<td>` tag, and uses a text box with `size` set to 2 to collect the quantity ordered. The payment method is input by the user through one of four radio buttons.

Notice that none of the input controls in this document are embedded in label elements. This is because table elements cannot be labeled, except by using the row and column labels.

Tables present special problems for the visually impaired. The best solution to this is to use style sheets (see Chapter 3) instead of tables to lay out tabular information.

```
<?xml version = "1.0"  encoding = "utf-8" ?>
<!DOCTYPE html PUBLIC "-//W3C//DTD XHTML 1.0 Strict//EN"
   "http://www.w3.org/TR/xhtml1/DTD/xhtml1-strict.dtd">

<!-- popcorn.html
```

```
        This describes a popcorn sales form document>
        -->
<html xmlns = "http://www.w3.org/1999/xhtml">
  <head> <title> Popcorn Sales Form </title>
  </head>
  <body>
    <h2> Welcome to Millennium Gymnastics Booster Club Popcorn
        Sales
    </h2>

<!-- The next line gives the address of the CGI program -->
    <form action = "">
<!-- A borderless table of text boxes for name and address -->
      <table>
        <tr>
          <td> Buyer's Name: </td>
          <td> <input type = "text"  name = "name"
                      size = "30" />
          </td>
        </tr>
        <tr>
          <td> Street Address: </td>
          <td> <input type = "text"  name = "street"
                      size = "30" />
          </td>
        </tr>
        <tr>
          <td> City, State, Zip: </td>
          <td> <input type = "text"  name = "city"
                      size = "30" />
          </td>
        </tr>
      </table>
    <p />

<!-- A bordered table for item orders -->
      <table border = "border">

<!-- First, the column headings -->
        <tr>
          <th> Product Name </th>
          <th> Price </th>
          <th> Quantity </th>
        </tr>

<!-- Now, the table data entries -->
```

```
            <tr>
               <td> Unpopped Popcorn (1 lb.) </td>
               <td> $3.00 </td>
               <td> <input type = "text"  name = "unpop"
                        size ="2" />
               </td>
            </tr>
            <tr>
               <td> Caramel Popcorn (2 lb. canister) </td>
               <td> $3.50 </td>
               <td> <input type = "text"  name = "caramel"
                        size = "2" />
               </td>
            </tr>
            <tr>
               <td> Caramel Nut Popcorn (2 lb. canister) </td>
               <td> $4.50 </td>
               <td> <input type = "text"  name = "caramelnut"
                        size = "2" />
               </td>
            </tr>
            <tr>
               <td> Toffey Nut Popcorn (2 lb. canister) </td>
               <td> $5.00 </td>
               <td> <input type = "text"  name = "toffeynut"
                        size = "2" />
               </td>
            </tr>

         </table>
         <p />

<!-- The radio buttons for the payment method -->
         <h3> Payment Method: </h3>
         <p>
            <label> <input type = "radio"  name = "payment"
                        value = "visa"  checked = "checked" />
                        Visa
            </label>
            <br />
            <label> <input type = "radio"  name = "payment"
                        value = "mc" /> Master Card
            </label>
            <br />
```

```
            <label> <input type = "radio"  name = "payment"
                          value = "discover" /> Discover
            </label>
            <br />
            <label> <input type = "radio"  name = "payment"
                          value = "check" /> Check
            </label>
            <br />
        </p>

<!-- The submit and reset buttons -->
        <p>
          <input type = "submit"  value = "Submit Order" />
          <input type = "reset"  value = "Clear Order Form" />
        </p>
    </form>
  </body>
</html>
```

Figure 2.31 shows a browser display of popcorn.html.

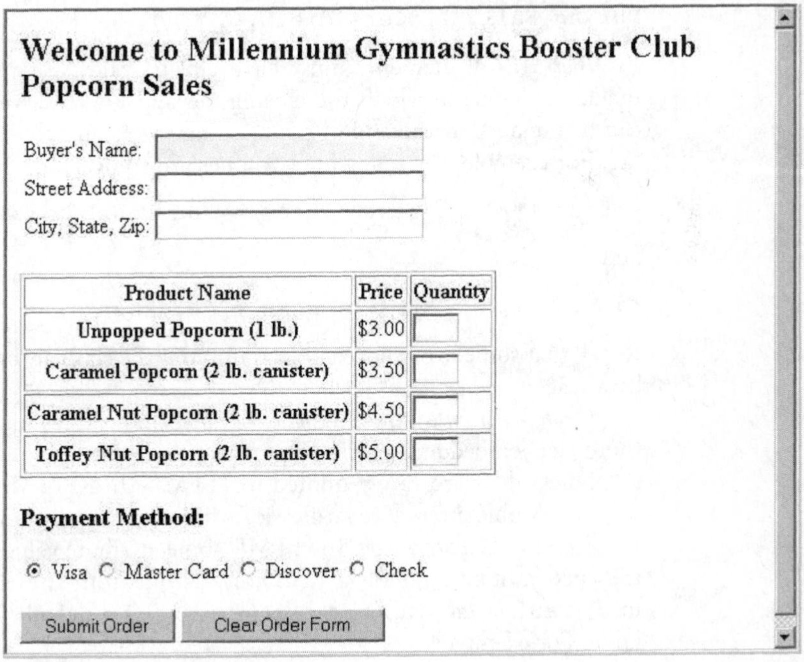

Figure 2.31 Display of popcorn.html

Chapter 9, "Introduction to PHP," has a PHP script for processing the data from the same form.

2.10   Syntactic Differences between HTML and XHTML

There are some significant differences between the syntactic rules of HTML (or lack thereof) and those of XHTML. This section describes these differences.

Case sensitivity. In HTML tag and attribute names are case insensitive, meaning that <FORM>, <form>, and <Form> are equivalent. In XHTML all tag and attribute names must be in lowercase.

Closing tags. In HTML closing tags may be omitted if the processing agent (usually a browser) can infer their presence. For example, in HTML paragraph elements often do not have closing tags. The appearance of another opening paragraph tag is used to infer the closing tag on the previous paragraph. For example:

```
<p>
During Spring, flowers are born. ...
<p>
During Fall, flowers die. ...
```

In XHTML all elements must have closing tags. For elements that do not include content, in which the closing tag appears to serve no purpose, a slash can be included at the end of the opening tag as an abbreviation of the closing tag. For example, the following two lines are equivalent:

```
<input type = "text"  name = "address" > </input>
```

and

```
<input type = "text"  name = "address" />
```

Recall that some browsers can be confused if the slash at the end is not preceded by a space.

Quoted attribute values. In HTML attribute values must be quoted only if there are embedded special characters or whitespace characters. Numeric attribute values are rarely quoted in HTML. In XHTML all attribute values must be double quoted, regardless of what characters are included in the value.

Explicit attribute values. In HTML some attribute values are implicit; that is, they need not be explicitly stated. For example, if the border attribute appears in a <table> tag without a value, it specifies a default width border on the table. For example:

```
<table border>
```

This is illegal in XHTML, in which such an attribute is assigned a string of the name of the attribute. For example:

```
<table border = "border">
```

Other such attributes are `checked`, `multiple`, and `selected`.

`id` *and* `name` *attributes*. HTML markup often uses the `name` attribute for elements. This attribute was deprecated for some elements in HTML 4.0. The `id` attribute was added to nearly all elements with this same version of HTML. In XHTML the use of `id` is encouraged, and the use of `name` is discouraged. In fact, the `name` attribute was removed for the anchor and map elements in XHTML 1.1. However, form elements must still use the `name` attribute because it is used in processing form data.

Element nesting. Although HTML has rules against improper nesting of elements, they are not enforced. Examples of nesting rules are: 1) an anchor element cannot contain another anchor element, and a form element cannot contain another form element; 2) if an element appears inside another element, the closing tag of the inner element must appear before the closing tag of the outer element; 3) block elements cannot be nested in inline elements; 4) text cannot be directly nested in body or form elements; and 5) list elements cannot be directly nested in list elements. In XHTML these nesting rules are strictly enforced.

All of the XHTML syntactic rules are checked by the W3C validation software.

Summary

XHTML was derived from SGML. Without the style sheets described in Chapter 3, XHTML is capable of specifying only the general layout of documents, with few presentation details. The current version of XHTML is XHTML 1.1; it was released in 2001.

The tags of XHTML specify how content is to be arranged in a display by a browser (or other XHTML processor). Most tags consist of opening and closing tags to encapsulate the content that is to be affected by the tag. XHTML documents have two parts, the head and the body. The head describes some things about the document but does not include any content. The body includes the content and the tags and attributes to describe the layout of that content.

Line breaks in text are ignored by browsers. The browser fills lines in its display window and provides line breaks when needed. Line breaks can be specified with the `<br />` tag. Paragraph breaks can be specified with `<p>`. Headings can be created with the `<hx>` tags, where *x* can be any number from 1 to 6. The `<blockquote>` tag is used to set off a section of text. The `<sub>` and `<sup>` tags are used to create subscripts and superscripts, respectively. Horizontal lines can be specified with the `<hr />` tag.

Images in GIF, JPEG, or PNG format can be inserted into documents from files where they are stored with the `<img />` tag. The `alt` attribute of `<img />` is used to present a message to the user when his or her browser is unable (or unwilling) to present the associated image.

Links support hypertext by allowing a document to "point to" other documents, enabling the user to move easily from one document to another. The target of a link can be a different part of the current document or the top or some other part of a different document.

XHTML supports both unordered lists, using the `<ul>` tag, and ordered lists, using the `<ol>` tag. Both of these kinds of lists use the `<li>` tag to define list elements. The `<dl>` tag is used to describe definition lists. The `<dt>` and `<dd>` tags are used to specify the terms and their definitions, respectively.

Tables are easy to create with XHTML, using a collection of tags designed for that purpose. `<table>` is used to create a table, `<tr>` is used to create table rows, `<th>` is used to create label cells, and `<td>` is used to create data cells in the table. The `colspan` and `rowspan` attributes, which can appear in both `<th>` and `<td>` tags, provide the means of creating multiple levels of column and row labels, respectively. The `align` and `valign` attributes of the `<tr>`, `<th>`, and `<td>` tags are used to tell the browser exactly where to put data or label values within their respective table cells. The `cellpadding` and `cellspacing` attributes are used to specify the distance between the content of a cell and its boundary and the distance between cells in a table, respectively.

XHTML forms are sections of documents that contain controls used to collect input from the user. The data specified in a form can be sent to a server-resident program in either of two methods, `get` or `post`. The most commonly used controls (text boxes, checkboxes, passwords, radio buttons, and the action buttons *Submit*, *Reset*, and *plain*) are specified with the `<input>` tag. The *Submit* button is used to indicate that the form data is to be sent to the server for processing. The *Reset* button is used to clear all of the controls in a form. The text box control is used to collect one line of input from the user. Checkboxes are one or more buttons used by the user to select one or more elements of a list. Radio buttons are like checkboxes, except that within a collection, only one button can be on at a time. A password is a text box whose content is never displayed by the browser.

Menus are used to allow the user to select items from a list when the list is too long to use checkboxes or radio buttons. Menu controls are created with the `<select>` tag. A text area control, which is created with the `<textarea>` tag, creates a multiple line text-gathering box, with implicit scrolling in both directions.

Review Questions

2.1 What does the `<code>` tag specify for its content?

2.2 What does it mean for a tag or attribute of XHTML to be deprecated?

2.3 What is the form of an XHTML comment?

2.4 How does a browser treat line breaks in text to be displayed?

2.5 What tag is used to define a link?

2.6 What is the difference in the effect of a paragraph tag and a break tag?

2.7 How do browsers usually set block quotations differently from normal text?

2.8 What are the differences between the JPEG and GIF image formats?

2.9 What is the form of the value of the `href` attribute in an anchor tag when the target is a fragment of a document other than the one in which the link appears?

2.10 What are the two required attributes of an `<img   />` tag?

2.11 What is the purpose of the `alt` attribute of `<img   />`?

2.12 What attribute is required in all anchor tags?

2.13 Which heading tags use fonts that are smaller than the normal text font size?

2.14 Does XHTML allow nested links?

2.15 What is the drawback of specifying the `multiple` attribute with a menu?

2.16 How is the target of a link usually identified in a case where the target is in the currently displayed document, but not at its beginning?

2.17 What is the default bullet form for the items in an unordered list?

2.18 What tags are used to define the terms and their definitions in a definition list?

2.19 What is specified when the `border` attribute of a `<table>` tag is set to `border`?

2.20 What is the default size of a text control's text box?

2.21 What is the purpose of the `colspan` attribute of the `<th>` tag?

2.22 What are the `align` and `valign` attributes of the `<tr>`, `<th>`, and `<td>` tags used for?

2.23 What is the purpose of the `rowspan` attribute of the `<td>` tag?

2.24 What is the difference between the `cellspacing` and `cellpadding` attributes?

2.25 How are scroll bars specified for text area controls?

2.26 What are controls?

2.27 Which controls discussed in this chapter are created with the `<input>` tag?

2.28 What is the difference between the `size` and `maxlength` attributes of `<input>` for text controls?

2.29 What is the difference in behavior between a group of checkbox buttons and a group of radio buttons?

2.30 What are the default sequence values for the items in an ordered list?

2.31 Under what circumstances is a menu used instead of a radio button group?

Exercises

2.1 Create, test, and validate an XHTML document for yourself, including your name, home town, and birthday. If you are a student, you must include your major and your grade level. If you work, you must include your employer, your employer's address, and your job title. This document must use several headings and `<em>`, `<strong>`, `<hr  />`, `<p>`, and `<br  />` tags.

2.2 Add pictures of yourself and at least one other image (your parents, spouse, or pet) to the document created for Exercise 2.1.

2.3 Add a second document to the document created for Exercise 2.1 that describes part of your background, using `background` as the link content. This document should have a few paragraphs of your personal or work history.

2.4 Create, test, and validate an XHTML document to describe an unordered list of your typical grocery shopping list. (If you've never written such a list, use your imagination.)

2.5 Create, test, and validate an XHTML document to describe an unordered list of at least four countries. Each element of the list must have a nested list of at least three cities in the country.

2.6 Create, test, and validate an XHTML document to describe an ordered list of your five favorite TV shows.

2.7 Modify the list of Exercise 2.6 to add nested, unordered lists of at least two actors and/or actresses in your favorite TV shows.

2.8 Create, test, and validate an XHTML document to describe an ordered list with the following contents: The highest level should be the names of your parents, with your mother first. Under each parent, you must have a nested, ordered list with the brothers and sisters of your parents, in order by age, eldest first. Each of the nested lists must have nested lists that list the children of your uncles and aunts (your cousins)—under the proper parents, of course. Regardless of how many aunts, uncles, and cousins you actually have, there must be at least three list items in each sublist below each of your parents and below each of your aunts and uncles.

2.9 Create, test, and validate an XHTML document to describe a table with the following contents: The columns of the table must have the headings Dog, Cat, Horse, and Rabbit. The rows must have the labels Height, Weight, Typical Life Span, and Color. You can make up the data cell values.

2.10 Modify, test, and validate an XHTML document from Exercise 2.9 to add a second-level column label, Animal, and a second-level row label, Characteristics.

2.11 Create, test, and validate an XHTML document that defines a table with columns for State, State Bird, State Flower, and State Tree. There must be at least five states as rows in the table. You must include attribute specifications for `cellpadding` and `cellspacing`.

2.12 Create, test, and validate an XHTML document that defines a table that has two levels of column labels: an overall label, Meals; and three secondary labels, Breakfast, Lunch, and Dinner. There must be two levels of row labels: an overall label, Foods; and four secondary labels, Bread, Main Course, Vegetable, and Dessert. The cells of the table must contain a number of grams for each of the food categories.

2.13 Create, test, and validate an XHTML document that is the home page of a business, Cookies Unlimited, that sells cookies. This document must include images and descriptions of at least three different kinds of cookies. There must be at least one unordered list, one ordered list, and one table. Detailed descriptions of the different cookies must be stored in separate documents that are accessible through links from the home document. You must discuss several occasions when cookies could be served, and include sales pitches for them.

2.14 Create, test, and validate an XHTML document that has a form with the following controls:

a. A text box to collect the user's name

b. Four checkboxes, one each for the following items:

   i. A pair of tennis shoes for $59.99

   ii. A pair of dress shoes for $129.99

   iii. A pair of slippers for $14.99

   iv. A pair of cowboy boots for $299.99

c. A collection of three radio buttons that are labeled as follows:

   i. Visa

   ii. Mastercard

   iii. Discover

CHAPTER

3

Cascading Style Sheets

This chapter introduces the concept of a style sheet and explains how style sheets fit into the philosophy of XHTML and the structure of XHTML documents. An introduction to the three levels of style sheets and the format of style specifications follows. Then, the many varieties of property value forms are described. Next, specific properties for fonts and lists are introduced and illustrated. A discussion of the properties for specifying colors, background images, and text alignment follows. The box model of document elements is then discussed, along with borders and the associated padding and margin properties.

The chapter's next section describes two tags, `<span>` and `<div>`, that are used to delimit the scope of style sheet specifications. These tags are used in full examples in Chapter 6, "Dynamic Documents with JavaScript." Finally, the last section of the chapter provides an overview of the resolution process for conflicting style specifications.

3.1 Introduction

We have said that XHTML is concerned primarily with content rather than the details of how that content is presented by browsers. That is not entirely true, even with the tags discussed in Chapter 2, "Introduction to XHTML." Some of those tags—for example, `<code>`—specify presentation details, or style. However, these presentation specifications can be more precisely and more consistently described with style sheets. Furthermore, many of the tags and attributes that can be used for describing presentation details have been deprecated in favor of style sheets.

Most XHTML tags have associated properties, which store presentation information for browsers. Browsers use default values for these properties if the document does not specify values. For example, the `<h2>` tag has the `font-size` property, for which a browser could have the default value of 18 points. A style sheet could specify that the `font-size` property for `<h2>` be set to 20 points, which would override the default value. The new value could apply to one occurrence of an `<h2>` element or all such occurrences in the document, depending on how the property value is set.

The idea of a style sheet is not new—word processors and desktop publishing systems have long used style sheets to impose a particular style on documents. The first style-sheet specification for use in XHTML documents, dubbed Cascading Style Sheets (CSS1), was developed in 1996 by the W3C. In mid-1998, the second standard, CSS2, was released. CSS2 added many properties and property values to CSS1. It also extended presentation control to media other than Web browsers, such as printers. Most, but not all of CSS1 has been implemented by Internet Explorer 7 (IE7) and FireFox 2 (FX2), but support for CSS2 is far from complete, especially in IE7. As a result of the incomplete implementation (and perhaps a lack of interest) of parts of CSS2, W3C decided to develop a new standard, CSS2.1, which would reflect the level of acceptance of CSS2 by the browser implementors. CSS2.1 is now at the "working draft" stage. CSS3 has been in development since the late 1990s.

This chapter is restricted to a subset of the CSS1 properties and property values, along with a few from CSS2 that are supported by one or both of the two most popular browsers. Unless otherwise stated, all of the examples in the chapter work correctly for both IE7 and FX2 browsers.

Perhaps the most important benefit of style sheets is their capability of imposing consistency on the style of Web documents. For example, they allow the author to specify that all occurrences of a particular tag use the same presentation style.

XHTML style sheets are called *cascading* style sheets because they can be defined at three different levels to specify the style of a document. Lower-level style sheets can override higher-level style sheets, so the style of the content of a tag is determined in effect through a cascade of style-sheet applications.

3.2 Levels of Style Sheets

The three levels of style sheets, in order from lowest level to highest level, are *inline, document level*, and *external*. Inline style sheets apply to the content of a single XHTML element, document-level style sheets apply to the whole body of a document, and external style sheets can apply to the bodies of any number of documents. Inline style sheets have precedence over document style sheets, which have precedence over external style sheets. For example, if an external style sheet specifies a value for a particular property of a particular tag, that value is used until a different value is specified in either a document style sheet or an inline style sheet. Likewise, document style sheet property values can be overridden by different property values in an inline style sheet. In effect, the properties of a specific tag are those that result from a merge of all applicable style sheets, with lower-level style sheets having precedence in cases of conflicting specifications. There are other ways style specification conflicts can occur. These and their resolution are discussed in Section 3.13.

If no style sheet information is specified, the browser default property values are used.

As is the case with tags and tag attributes, a particular browser may not be capable of using the property values specified in a style sheet. For example, if the value of the `font-size` property of a paragraph is set to 18 points, but the browser can only display the particular font being used in sizes up to 16 points, the browser obviously cannot fulfill the property specification. In this case, the browser either would substitute an alternative value or would simply ignore the given font size value.

Inline style specifications appear within the opening tag and apply only to the content of that tag. This fine-grain application of style defeats one of the primary advantages of style sheets—that of imposing a uniform style on the tags of at least one whole document. Another disadvantage of inline style sheets is that they result in style information, which is expressed in a language distinct from XHTML markup, being embedded in various places in documents. It is much better to keep style specifications separate from XHTML markup. For this reason, among others, W3C deprecated inline style sheets in XHTML 1.1.[1] Therefore, inline style specifications should be used sparingly. This chapter discusses inline style sheets, but we follow our own advice and make little use of them in our examples.

---

1. Being placed on the list of deprecated features is a warning to users to restrict their use, because sometime in the future they will be discontinued.

Document-level style specifications appear in the document head section and apply to the entire body of the document. This is obviously an effective way to impose a uniform style on the presentation of all of the content of a document.

In many cases, it is desirable to have a style sheet apply to more than one document. This is the purpose of external style sheets. External style sheets are not part of any of the documents to which they apply. They are stored separately and are referenced in all documents that use them. External style sheets are written as text files with the MIME type `text/css`. They can be stored on any computer on the Web. The browser fetches external style sheets just as it fetches documents. The `<link>` tag is used to specify external style sheets. Within `<link>`, the `rel` attribute is used to specify the relationship of the linked-to document to the document in which the link appears. The `href` attribute of `<link>` is used to specify the URL of the style sheet document, as in the following example:

```
<link rel = "stylesheet"  type = "text/css"
      href = "http://www.cs.usc.edu/styles/wbook.css" />
```

The link to an external style sheet must appear in the head of the document. If the external style sheet resides on the Web server computer, only its path address must be given as the value of `href`. An example of an external style sheet appears in Section 3.6.

The `@import` directive is an alternative way to use style specifications from other files. The form is the following:

```
@import url(filename);
```

Notice that the filename is not quoted. There are two differences between `link` and `@import`: (1) `@import` can appear only at the beginning of the content of a `style` element,[2] and (2) the imported file can contain markup, as well as style rules. In fact, sometimes the imported file contains other `@import` directives, along with some style rules.

External style sheets can be validated with the service provided at `http://jigsaw.w3.org/css-validator/validator-upload.html`.

3.3 Style Specification Formats

The format of a style specification depends on the level of style sheet. Inline style specifications appear as values of the `style` attribute of a tag,[3] the general form of which is as follows:

```
style = "property_1:value_1;  property_2:value_2;  ...;
         property_n:value_n;"
```

---

2. The `style` element is discussed in Section 3.3.

3. The `style` attribute is deprecated in the XHTML 1.1 recommendation.

Although it is not required, it is recommended that the last property/value pair be followed by a semicolon.

Document style specifications appear as the content of a style element within the header of a document, although the format of the specification is quite different from that of inline style sheets. The general form of the content of a style element is as follows:[4]

```
<style type = "text/css">
  rule_list
</style>
```

The `type` attribute of the `<style>` tag tells the browser the type of style specification, which is always `text/css`. The type of style specification is necessary because there are other kinds of style sheets. For example, JavaScript, which can be embedded in an XHTML document, also provides style sheets that can appear in style elements.

Each style rule in a rule list has two parts: a selector, which indicates the tag or tags affected by the rule, and a list of property/value pairs. The list has the same form as the quoted list for inline style sheets, except the list is delimited by braces rather than double quotes. So, the form of a style rule is as follows:

```
selector {property_1:value_1; property_2:value_2; ...;
          property_n:value_n;}
```

If a property is given more than one value, those values usually are separated with spaces. For some properties, however, multiple values are separated with commas.

Like all other kinds of coding, complicated CSS rule lists should be documented with comments. Of course, XHTML comments cannot be used here, because CSS is not XHTML. Therefore, a different form of comment is needed. CSS comments are introduced with /* and terminated with */.[5] For example:

```
<style type = "text/css">
  /* Styles for the initial paragraph */
  ...
  /* Styles for other paragraphs */
  ...
</style>
```

External style sheets have a form similar to that of document style sheets. The external file consists of a list of style rules. An example of an external style sheet appears in Section 3.6.

---

4. Browsers so old that they do not recognize the `<style>` tag may display the content of the style element at the top of the document. There are now so few such browsers in use that we ignore the issue here. Those who are concerned put the rule list in an XHTML comment.

5. This form of comment is adopted from the C programming language and some of its descendants.

3.4   Selector Forms

The selector can have a variety of forms, which are described in this section.

3.4.1   Simple Selector Forms

The simplest selector form is a single element name, such as `h1`. In this case, the property values in the rule apply to all occurrences of the named element. The selector could be a list of element names, separated by commas, in which case the property values apply to all occurrences of all of the named elements. Consider the following examples, in which the property is `font-size` and the property value is a number of points:

```
h1 {font-size: 24pt;}
h2, h3 {font-size: 20pt;}
```

The first of these specifies that the text content of all `h1` elements must be set in 24-point font size. The second specifies that the text content of all `h2` and `h3` elements must be set in 20-point font size.

Selectors can also specify that the style should only apply to elements in certain positions in the document. This is done by listing the element hierarchy in the selector, with only whitespace separating the element names. For example, the rule

```
form em {font-size: 14pt;}
```

only applies its style to the content of emphasis elements that are nested in a form element in the document. This is a *contextual* selector (sometimes called a *descendant* selector).

3.4.2   Class Selectors

Class selectors are used to allow different occurrences of the same tag to use different style specifications. A style class is defined in a style element by giving it a name, which is attached to the tag's name with a period. For example, if you want two paragraph styles in a document—say, `normal` and `warning`—you could define these two classes in the content of a `<style>` tag as follows:

```
p.normal  {property-value list}
p.warning {property-value list}
```

Within the document body, the particular style class that you want is specified with the `class` attribute of the affected tag—in the preceding example, the paragraph tag. For example, you might have the following:

```
<p class = "normal">
A paragraph of text that we want to be presented in
'normal' presentation style
</p>
```

```
<p class = "warning">
A paragraph of text that is a warning to the reader, which
should be presented in an especially noticeable
presentation style
</p>
```

3.4.3   Generic Selectors

Sometimes it is convenient to have a class of style specifications that applies to the content of more than one kind of tag. This is done by using a generic class, which is defined without a tag name in its name. In place of the tag name, you use the name of the generic class, which must begin with a period. For example:

.sale   *{property-value list}*

Now, in the body of a document, you could have the following:

```
<h3 class = "sale"> Weekend Sale </h3>
...
<p class = "sale">
...
</p>
```

3.4.4   id Selectors

An id selector allows the application of a style to one specific element. The general form of an id selector is as follows:[6]

#specific-id   {property-value list}

As you would probably guess, the style specified in the id selector applies to the element with the specific id. For example:

```
#section14 {font-size: 20}
```

specifies a font size of 20 points to the element

```
<h2 id = "section14">1.4 Calico Cats </h2>
```

CSS2 added still more selector forms. However, because of the lack of browser support for them, they are not discussed here.

3.4.5   Universal Selectors

The universal selector, denoted by an asterisk (*), applies its style to all elements in the document. For example:

```
* {color: red;}
```

makes all elements in the document red.

The universal selection is not often useful.

---

6. For the oddly curious reader, the Bell Labs name for the # symbol is *octothorpe*. It was named that when it was first put on the telephone dial, for some reason unknown to the author.

3.4.6 Pseudo Classes

Pseudo classes are styles that apply when something happens rather than because the target element simply exists. CSS1 included some pseudo classes, and CSS2 added more. Unfortunately, support for the pseudo classes is sorely lacking, at least among the most popular browsers. However, two pseudo classes, hover and focus, are supported by FX2, so we introduce them here. IE7 supports hover, but not focus.

While the names of style classes and generic classes begin with a period, the names of pseudo classes begin with colons. The style of the hover pseudo class applies when its associated element has the mouse cursor over it. The style of the focus pseudo class applies when its associated element has focus.[7] For example, consider the following document:

```
<?xml version = "1.0" encoding = "utf-8"?>
<!DOCTYPE html PUBLIC "-//W3C//DTD XHTML 1.0 Strict//EN"
  "http://www.w3.org/TR/xhtml1/DTD/xhtml1-strict.dtd">

<!-- pseudo.html
     Illustrates the :hover and :focus pseudo classes.
     :hover works for IE7, but :focus does not.
     Both work for FX2
     -->
<html xmlns = "http://www.w3.org/1999/xhtml">
  <head> <title> Pseudo Classes </title>
    <style type = "text/css">
      input:hover {color: red;}
      input:focus {color: green;}
    </style>
  </head>
  <body>
    <form action = "">
      <p>
        <label>
          Your name:
          <input type = "text"  />
        </label>
      </p>
    </form>
  </body>
</html>
```

---

7. An element acquires focus when the user places the mouse cursor over it and clicks the left mouse button.

In `pseudo.html`, the content of an input element (a text box) is colored red when the mouse cursor is placed over its content. This happens only when the text box does not have focus. If no text has been typed into the text box, the hover pseudo class has no effect. When the text box acquires focus, the text turns green and stays that color until the left mouse button is clicked outside the box.

3.5 Property Value Forms

CSS1 includes 60 different properties in seven categories: fonts, lists, alignment of text, margins, colors, backgrounds, and borders. As you probably would guess, not all of these properties are discussed here. The complete details of all properties and property values can be found at the W3C Web site.

Property values can appear in a variety of forms. Key word property values are used when there are only a few possible values and they are predefined—for example, `large`, `medium`, and `small`. Key word values are not case sensitive, so `Small`, `SmAlL`, and `SMALL` are all the same as `small`.

Number values are used when no meaningful units can be attached to a numeric property value. A number value either can be an integer or a sequence of digits with a decimal point and can be preceded by a sign (+ or −).

Length values are specified as number values that are followed immediately by a two-character abbreviation of a unit name. There can be no space between the number and the unit name. The possible unit names are `px` for pixels, `in` for inches, `cm` for centimeters, `mm` for millimeters, `pt` for points (a point is 1/72 inch), and `pc` for picas, which are 12 points. Note that on a display, the `in`, `cm`, `mm`, `pt`, and `pc` are approximate measures. Their actual values depend on screen resolution. There are also two relative length values: `em`, which is the value of the current font size in pixels, and `ex`, which is the height of the letter x.

Percentage values are used to provide a measure that is relative to the previously used measure for a property value. Percentage values are numbers that are followed immediately by a percent sign (`%`). For example, if the font size were set to `75%`, it would make the new current size for the font 75 percent of its previous value. Font size would stay at the new value until changed again. Percentage values can be signed. If preceded by a plus sign, the percentage is added to the previous value; if negative, the percentage is subtracted.

URL property values use a form that is slightly different from references to URLs in links. The actual URL, which can be either absolute or relative, is placed in parentheses and preceded by `url`, as in the following:

```
url(tetons.jpg)
```

There can be no space between `url` and the left parenthesis.

Color property values can be specified as color names, as six-digit hexadecimal numbers, or in RGB form. RGB form is just the word `rgb` followed by a parenthesized list of three numbers that specify the levels of red, green, and blue. The RGB values can be given as either decimal numbers between 0 and 255 or as percentages. Hexadecimal numbers must be preceded with pound signs (#), as in `#43AF00`. For example, powder blue could be specified with

```
fuchsia
```

or

```
rgb(255, 0, 255)
```

or

```
#FF00FF
```

CSS2 specifies that some property values are inherited by elements nested in the element for which the values are specified. For example, the property `background-color` is not inherited but `font-size` is. Using a style sheet to set a value for an inheriting property for the `<body>` tag effectively sets it as a default property value for the whole document. For example:

```
body {font-size: 16pt}
```

Unless overridden by a style sheet that applies to paragraph elements, every paragraph element in the body of this document would inherit the font size of 16 points.

3.6   Font Properties

The font properties are among the most commonly used of the style-sheet properties. Virtually all XHTML documents include text, which is often used in a variety of different situations. This creates a need for text in many different fonts, font styles, and sizes. The font properties allow us to specify these different forms.

3.6.1   Font Families

The `font-family` property is used to specify a list of font names. The browser uses the first font in the list that it supports. For example, the following could be specified:

```
font-family: Arial, Helvetica, Futura
```

In this case, the browser will use Arial if it supports that font. If not, it will use Helvetica if it supports it. If the browser supports neither Arial nor Helvetica, it will use Futura if it can. If the browser does not support any of the specified fonts, it will use an alternative of its choosing.

A generic font can be specified as a `font-family` value. The possible generic fonts and examples of each are shown in Table 3.1. Each browser has a font defined for each of these generic names. A good approach to specifying fonts is to use a generic font as the last font in the value of a `font-family` property. For example, because Arial, Helvetica, and Futura are sans-serif fonts,[8] the example above would be better as follows:

```
font-family: Arial, Helvetica, Futura, sans-serif
```

---

8. Serifs are non-structural decorations that may appear at the ends of strokes in a character. Sans-serif fonts do not have serifs.

Table 3.1   Generic fonts

Generic Name	Examples
`serif`	`Times New Roman, Garamond`
`sans-serif`	`MS Arial, Helvetica`
`cursive`	`Caflisch Script, Zapf-Chancery`
`fantasy`	`Critter, Cottonwood`
`monospace`	`Courier, Prestige`

If a font name has more than one word, the whole name should be delimited by single quotes,[9] as in the following example:

```
font-family: 'Times New Roman'
```

In practice, the quotes may not be mandatory, but their use is recommended because they may be required in the future.

3.6.2   Font Sizes

The `font-size` property does what its name implies. For example, the following property specification sets the font size for text to 10 points:

```
font-size: 10pt
```

Many relative `font-size` values are defined; namely, `xx-small`, `x-small`, `small`, `medium`, `large`, `x-large`, and `xx-large`. In addition, `smaller` or `larger` can be specified. Furthermore, the value can be a percentage, which would be relative to the current font size.

The disadvantage of the relative font sizes is the lack of strict font size control. Different browsers can use different values for them. For example, `small` might mean 10 points on one browser and 8 points on another. On the other hand, using a specific font size has the risk that some browsers may not support the particular size, causing the document to appear different on different browsers.

3.6.3   Font Variants

The default value of the `font-variant` property is `normal`, which specifies the usual character font. This property can be set to `small-caps` to specify small cap characters. Small cap characters are all uppercase, but the letters that are normally uppercase are somewhat larger than those that are normally lowercase.

---

9. Single quotes are used here because, in the case of inline style sheets, the whole property list is delimited by double quotes.

3.6.4   Font Styles

The `font-style` property is most commonly used to specify italic, as in the following:

```
font-style: italic
```

An alternative to `italic` is `oblique`, but when displayed, the two are nearly identical, so `oblique` is not a terribly useful font style. In fact, some browsers do not support oblique, so they display all oblique fonts in italic.

3.6.5   Font Weights

The `font-weight` property is used to specify the degree of boldness. For example:

```
font-weight: bold
```

Besides `bold`, the values `normal` (the default), `bolder`, and `lighter` can be specified. The `bolder` and `lighter` values are taken as relative to the current level of boldness. Specific numbers also can be given in multiples of 100 from 100 to 900, where 400 is the same as `normal` and 700 is the same as `bold`.

3.6.6   Font Shorthands

If more than one font property must be specified, the values can be stated in a list as the value of the `font` property—the browser has the responsibility for determining from the forms of the values which properties to assign. For example, consider the following specification:

```
font: bold 14pt 'Times New Roman' Palatino
```

This specifies that the font weight should be `bold`, the font size should be 14 points, and either Times New Roman or Palatino font should be used, with precedence given to Times New Roman.

The order in which the property values are given in a `font` value list is important. The order must be as follows: the font names must be last, the font size must be second last, and the font style, font variant, and font weight, when they are included, can be in any order but must precede the font size and font names. Only the font size and the font family are required in the `font` value list.

The XHTML document `fonts.html` illustrates some aspects of style-sheet specification of the font properties in headings and paragraphs using a document style sheet.

Figure 3.1 shows a browser display of `fonts.html`.

```
<?xml version = "1.0" encoding = "utf-8"?>
<!DOCTYPE html PUBLIC "-//W3C//DTD XHTML 1.0 Strict//EN"
  "http://www.w3.org/TR/xhtml1/DTD/xhtml1-strict.dtd">

<!-- fonts.html
     An example to illustrate font properties
     -->
<html xmlns = "http://www.w3.org/1999/xhtml">
  <head> <title> Font properties </title>
    <style type = "text/css">
      p.major {font-size: 14pt;
               font-style: italic;
               font-family: 'Times New Roman';
              }
      p.minor {font: 10pt bold 'Courier New';}
      h2 {font-family: 'Times New Roman';
          font-size: 24pt; font-weight: bold}
      h3 {font-family: 'Courier New'; font-size: 18pt}
    </style>
  </head>
  <body>
    <p class = "major">
      If a job is worth doing, it's worth doing right.
    </p>
    <p class = "minor">
      Two wrongs don't make a right, but they certainly
      can get you in a lot of trouble.
    </p>
    <h2> Chapter 1 Introduction </h2>
    <h3> 1.1 The Basics of Computer Networks </h3>
  </body>
</html>
```

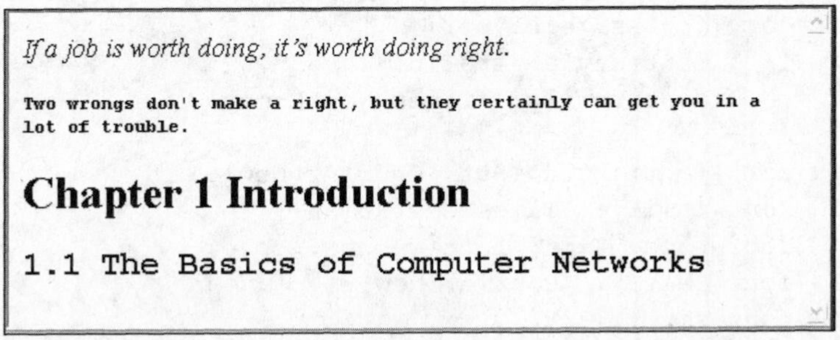

If a job is worth doing, it's worth doing right.

Two wrongs don't make a right, but they certainly can get you in a
lot of trouble.

Chapter 1 Introduction

1.1 The Basics of Computer Networks

Figure 3.1 Display of fonts.html

The following document is a revision of fonts.html, fonts2.html, which uses an external style sheet in place of the document style sheet used in fonts.html. The external style sheet, styles.css, follows the revised document.

```
<?xml version = "1.0" encoding = "utf-8"?>
<!DOCTYPE html PUBLIC "-//W3C//DTD XHTML 1.0 Strict//EN"
  "http://www.w3.org/TR/xhtml1/DTD/xhtml1-strict.dtd">

<!-- fonts2.html
     An example to test external style sheets
     -->
<html xmlns = "http://www.w3.org/1999/xhtml">
  <head> <title> External style sheets </title>
    <link rel = "stylesheet"  type = "text/css"
          href = "styles.css" />
  </head>
  <body>
    <p class = "major">
      If a job is worth doing, it's worth doing right.
    </p>
    <p class = "minor">
      Two wrongs don't make a right, but they certainly
      can get you in a lot of trouble.
    </p>
    <h2> Chapter 1 Introduction </h2>
    <h3> 1.1 The Basics of Computer Networks </h3>
  </body>
</html>
```

```
/* styles.css - an external style sheet
     for use with fonts2.html
  */
p.major {font-size: 14pt;
         font-style: italic;
         font-family: 'Times New Roman';
        }
p.minor {font: bold 10pt 'Courier New';}
h2 {font-family: 'Times New Roman';
    font-size: 24pt; font-weight: bold}
h3 {font-family: 'Courier New';
    font-size: 18pt}
```

3.6.7   Text Decoration

The `text-decoration` property is used to specify some special features of text. The available values are `line-through`, `overline`, `underline`, and `none`, which is the default. Many browsers implicitly underline links. The `none` value can be used to avoid this. Note that `text-decoration` is not inherited. The following document, `decoration.html`, illustrates the `line-through`, `overline`, and `underline` values.

```
<?xml version = "1.0" encoding = "utf-8"?>
<!DOCTYPE html PUBLIC "-//W3C//DTD XHTML 1.0 Strict//EN"
  "http://www.w3.org/TR/xhtml1/DTD/xhtml1-strict.dtd">

<!-- decoration.html
     An example that illustrates several of the
     possible text decoration values
     -->
<html xmlns = "http://www.w3.org/1999/xhtml">
  <head> <title> Text decoration </title>
    <style type = "text/css">
      p.delete {text-decoration: line-through}
      p.cap {text-decoration: overline}
      p.attention {text-decoration: underline}
    </style>
  </head>
  <body>
    <p class = "delete">
      This illustrates line-through
    </p>
    <p class= "cap">
      This illustrates overline
    </p>
    <p class = "attention">
      This illustrates underline
    </p>
  </body>
</html>
```

Figure 3.2 shows a browser display of `decoration.html`.

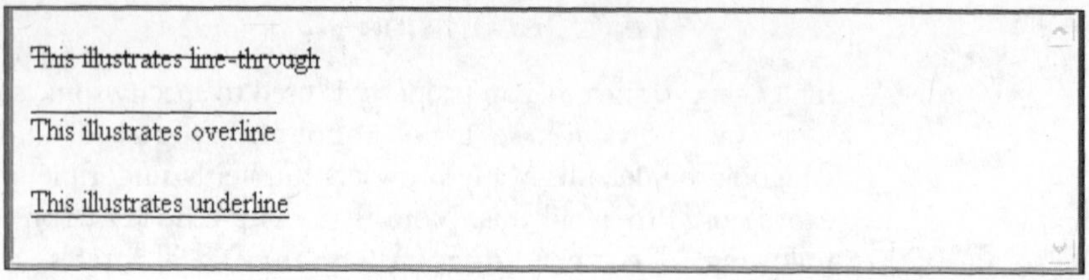

This illustrates line-through

This illustrates overline

This illustrates underline

Figure 3.2 Display of `decoration.html`

The `letter-spacing` property controls the amount of space between characters in text. The possible values of `letter-spacing` are any length property values, for example 3px.

3.7 List Properties

Two presentation details of lists can be specified in XHTML documents: the shape of the bullets that precede the items in an unordered list and the sequencing values that precede the items in an ordered list. The `list-style-type` property is used to specify both of these.

The `list-style-type` property of an unordered list can be set to `disc`, `circle`, `square`, or `none`. A `disc` is a small filled circle, a `circle` is an unfilled circle, and a `square` is a filled square. The default property value for bullets is `disc`. For example, the following illustrates a document style sheet to set the bullet type in all items in unordered lists to `square`:

```
<!-- bullets1 -->
<style type = "text/css">
  ul {list-style-type: square}
</style>
...
<h3> Some Common Single-Engine Aircraft </h3>
  <ul>
    <li> Cessna Skyhawk </li>
    <li> Beechcraft Bonanza </li>
    <li> Piper Cherokee </li>
  </ul>
```

Style classes can be defined to allow different list items to have different bullet types:

```
<!-- bullets2 -->
<style type = "text/css">
  li.disc {list-style-type: disc}
  li.square {list-style-type: square}
```

```
      li.circle {list-style-type: circle}
</style>
...
<h3> Some Common Single-Engine Aircraft </h3>
  <ul>
    <li class = "disc"> Cessna Skyhawk </li>
    <li class = "square"> Beechcraft Bonanza </li>
    <li class = "circle"> Piper Cherokee </li>
  </ul>
```

Figure 3.3 shows a browser display of these two lists.

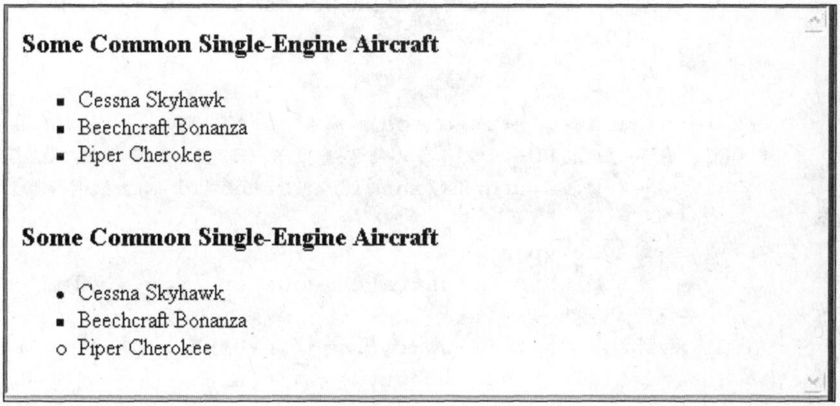

Figure 3.3 Examples of unordered lists

Bullets in unordered lists are not limited to discs, squares, and circles. Any image can be used in a list item bullet. Such a bullet is specified with the list-style-image property, whose value is specified with the url form. For example, if small_plane.gif is a small image of an airplane that is stored in the same directory as the XHTML document, it could be used as follows:

```
<style type = "text/css">
  li.image {list-style-image: url(small_airplane.gif)}
</style>
  ...
  <li class = "image"> Beechcraft Bonanza </li>
```

When ordered lists are nested, it is best to use different kinds of sequence values for the different levels of nesting. The list-style-type property can be used to specify the types of sequencing values. Table 3.2 lists the different possibilities defined by CSS1.

Table 3.2 Possible sequencing values for ordered lists

Property Values	Sequence Type	First Four Values
`decimal`	Arabic numerals	1, 2, 3, 4
`upper-alpha`	Uppercase letters	A, B, C, D
`lower-alpha`	Lowercase letters	a, b, c, d
`upper-roman`	Uppercase Roman numerals	I, II, III, IV
`lower-roman`	Lowercase Roman numerals	i, ii, iii, iv

The following example illustrates the use of different sequence value types in nested lists.

```
<?xml version = "1.0" encoding = "utf-8"?>
<!DOCTYPE html PUBLIC "-//W3C//DTD XHTML 1.0 Strict//EN"
  "http://www.w3.org/TR/xhtml1/DTD/xhtml1-strict.dtd">

<!-- sequence_types.html
     An example to illustrate sequence type styles
     -->
<html xmlns = "http://www.w3.org/1999/xhtml">
  <head> <title> Sequence types </title>
    <style type = "text/css">
      ol {list-style-type: upper-roman;}
      ol ol {list-style-type: upper-alpha;}
      ol ol ol {list-style-type: decimal;}
    </style>
  </head>
<body>
  <h3> Aircraft Types </h3>
  <ol>
    <li> General Aviation (piston-driven engines)
      <ol>
        <li> Single-Engine Aircraft
          <ol>
            <li> Tail wheel </li>
            <li> Tricycle </li>
          </ol>
        </li>
        <li> Dual-Engine Aircraft
          <ol>
            <li> Wing-mounted engines </li>
            <li> Push-pull fuselage-mounted engines </li>
```

```
          </ol>
        </li>
      </ol>
    </li>
    <li> Commercial Aviation (jet engines)
      <ol>
        <li> Dual-Engine
          <ol>
            <li> Wing-mounted engines </li>
            <li> Fuselage-mounted engines </li>
          </ol>
        </li>
        <li> Tri-Engine
          <ol>
            <li> Third engine in vertical stabilizer </li>
            <li> Third engine in fuselage </li>
          </ol>
        </li>
      </ol>
    </li>
  </ol>
</body>
</html>
```

Figure 3.4 shows a browser display of `sequence_types.html`.

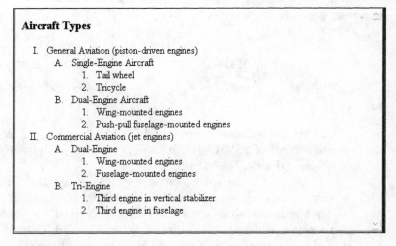

Figure 3.4 Display of `sequence_types.html`

CSS2.1 added more sequence types such as `armenian` and `lower-greek`, but they are not yet supported by the popular browsers.

3.8   Color

If older browsers and older client machines and CSS validation are taken into account, color is not a simple issue. For one thing, the document may be displayed on monitors of widely varying capabilities. Also, the document may be rendered by browsers that have different abilities to deal with colors. Finally, most color names recognized by browsers prevent CSS validation. This section provides an introduction to how Web sites can deal with these difficulties.

3.8.1   Color Groups

Three levels of collections of colors might be used by an XHTML document. The smallest useful set of colors includes only those that have standard names and are guaranteed to be correctly displayable by all browsers on all color monitors. This collection of sixteen colors is called the *named colors*. These are the only color names that allow CSS validation. The names and hexadecimal codes for these named colors are shown in Table 3.3.

Table 3.3   Named colors

Name	Hexadecimal Code	Name	Hexadecimal Code
aqua	00FFFF	navy	000080
black	000000	olive	808000
blue	0000FF	purple	800080
fuchsia	FF00FF	red	FF0000
gray	808080	silver	C0C0C0
green	008000	teal	008080
lime	00FF00	white	FFFFFF
maroon	800000	yellow	FFFF00

Most Web browsers now recognize 140 named colors, although these names are not part of a W3C standard and prevent CSS validation. This collection of colors is given in Appendix B.

A larger set of colors, called the *Web palette*, includes 216 colors. These colors, which are often called Web-safe colors, are displayable by Windows- and Macintosh-based browsers but may not be correctly displayed with some older terminals used on UNIX systems. Elements of this set of colors have hexadecimal values for red, green, and blue that are restricted to 00, 33, 66, 99, CC, and FF. These numbers allow all combinations of all increments of 20 percent of each of the three basic colors, red, green, and blue. The colors of the Web palette can be viewed at http://www.web-source.net/216_color_chart.htm. Note that use of these names prevent CSS validation.

When the limitations of older browsers and monitors are not a consideration, 24-bit (or six-hexadecimal-digit) numbers can be used to specify any one of 16 million colors. When a color is specified that the browser or monitor cannot display, a (hopefully) similar color will be used.

3.8.2   Color Properties

The color property is used to specify the foreground color of XHTML elements. For example, consider the following small table:

```
<style type = "text/css">
  th.red {color: red}
  th.orange {color: orange}
</style>
  ...
<table border = "5px">
  <tr>
    <th class = "red"> Apple </th>
    <th class = "orange"> Orange </th>
    <th class = "orange"> Screwdriver </th>
  </tr>
</table>
```

The background-color property is used to set the background color of an element, where the element could be the whole body of the document. For example, consider the following paragraph element:

```
<style type = "text/css">
  p.standout {font-size: 24pt; color: blue;
              background-color: red">
</style>
...
<p class = "standout">
  To really make it stand out, use a red background!
</p>
```

When displayed by a browser, this might appear as shown in Figure 3.5.

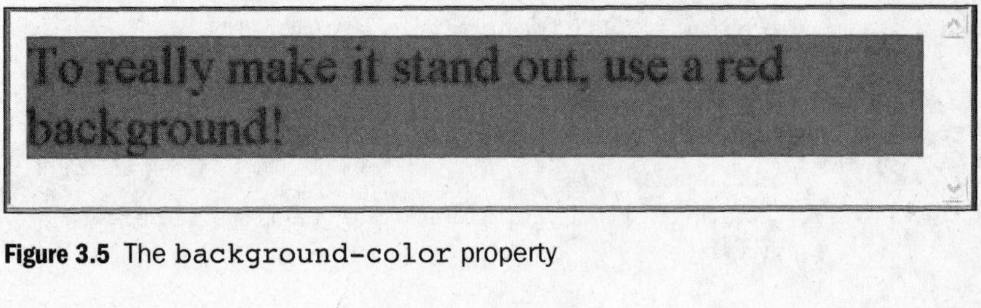

To really make it stand out, use a red background!

Figure 3.5 The background-color property

3.9 Alignment of Text

The first line of a paragraph can be indented using the `text-indent` property. This property takes either a length or a percentage value. For example:

```
<style type = "text/css">
  p.indent {text-indent: 0.5in}
</style>
...
<p class = "indent">
  Now is the time for all good Web programmers to begin
  using cascading style sheets for all presentation
  details in their documents. No more deprecated tags
  and attributes, just nice, precise style sheets.
</p>
```

This paragraph would be displayed as follows:

```
      Now is the time for all good Web programmers to begin
using cascading style sheets for all presentation details
in their documents. No more deprecated tags and attributes,
just nice, precise style sheets.
```

The `text-align` property, for which the possible keyword values are `left`, `center`, `right`, and `justify`, is used to arrange text horizontally. For example, the following document-level style sheet entry causes the content of paragraphs to be aligned on the right margin:

```
p {text-align: right}
```

The default value for `text-align` is `left`.

The `float` property is used to specify that text should flow around some element, often an image or table. The possible values for `float` are `left`, `right`, and `none`, which is the default. For example, suppose we want an image to be on the right side of the display and have text flow around its left side. To specify this, the `float` property of the image is set to `right`. Because the default value for `text-align` is `left`, `text-align` need not be set for the text. In the following example, the text of a paragraph is specified to flow to the left of an image until the bottom of the image is reached, at which point the paragraph text flows across the whole window.

```
<?xml version = "1.0" encoding = "utf-8"?>
<!DOCTYPE html PUBLIC "-//W3C//DTD XHTML 1.0 Strict//EN"
  "http://www.w3.org/TR/xhtml1/DTD/xhtml1-strict.dtd">

<!-- float.html
    An example to illustrate the float property
    -->
```

```html
<html xmlns = "http://www.w3.org/1999/xhtml">
  <head> <title> The float property </title>
    <style type = "text/css">
      img {float: right}
    </style>
  </head>
  <body>
    <p>
      <img src = "c210new.jpg"  alt = "Picture of a Cessna 210" />
    </p>
    <p>
      This is a picture of a Cessna 210. The 210 is the flagship
      single-engine Cessna aircraft. Although the 210 began as a
      four-place aircraft, it soon acquired a third row of seats,
      stretching it to a six-place plane. The 210 is classified
      as a high-performance airplane, which means its landing
      gear is retractable and its engine has more than 200
      horsepower. In its first model year, which was 1960,
      the 210 was powered by a 260-horsepower fuel-injected
      six-cylinder engine that displaced 471 cubic inches.
      The 210 is the fastest single-engine airplane ever
      built by Cessna.
    </p>
  </body>
</html>
```

When rendered by a browser, float.html might appear as shown in Figure 3.6, depending on the width of the browser display window.

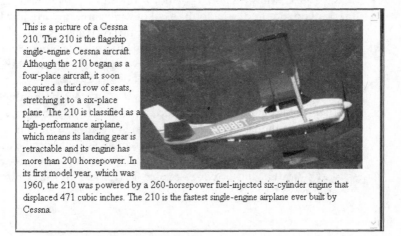

Figure 3.6 Display of float.html

3.10 The Box Model

Virtually all document elements can have borders. These borders have various styles such as color and width. Furthermore, the amount of space between the content of an element and its border, known as *padding*, can be specified, as well as the space between the border and an adjacent element, known as the *margin*. This model is shown in Figure 3.7.

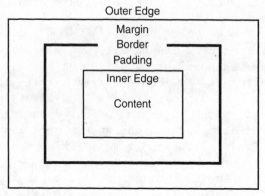

Figure 3.7 The box model

3.10.1 Borders

Every element has a property, `border-style`, that controls whether the element's content has a border, as well as the style of the border.[10] CSS1 requires that borders be available for any element, but the only required style is `solid` (the default style when the border attribute of a table element is set to `border` or a pixel width). CSS2 provides several different border styles, among them `dotted`, `dashed`, and `double`, all of which are supported by IE7 and FX2. The default value for `border-style` is `none`, which is why the contents of elements do not normally have borders. The styles of one particular side of an element can be set with `border-top-style`, `border-bottom-style`, `border-left-style`, and `border-right-style`.

The `border-width` property is used to specify the thickness of a border. Its possible values are `thin`, `medium` (the default), `thick`, or a length value in pixels. Setting `border-width` sets the thickness of all four sides of an element. The width of each of the four borders of an element can be different. These are specified with `border-top-width`, `border-bottom-width`, `border-left-width`, and `border-right-width`. All of the border width properties are part of CSS1.

---

10. Recall that the border on a table can be set with the `border` attribute of the table element.

The color of a border is controlled by the `border-color` property, which is part of CSS1. Once again, the individual borders of an element can be colored differently through the CSS2 properties, `border-top-color`, `border-bottom-color`, `border-left-color`, and `border-right-color`. All of the border color properties are supported by IE7 and FX2.

The following document, `borders.html`, illustrates borders, using a table and a short paragraph as examples. Notice that if a table has a border that was

```
<?xml version = "1.0" encoding = "utf-8"?>
<!DOCTYPE html PUBLIC "-//W3C//DTD XHTML 1.0 Strict//EN"
  "http://www.w3.org/TR/xhtml1/DTD/xhtml1-strict.dtd">

<!-- borders.html
     An example of a simple table with various borders
     -->
<html xmlns = "http://www.w3.org/1999/xhtml">
  <head> <title> Table borders </title>
    <style type = "text/css">
      table {border-top-width: medium;
             border-bottom-width: thick;
             border-top-color: red;
             border-bottom-color: blue;
             border-top-style: dotted;
             border-bottom-style: dashed;
            }
      p {border-style: dashed; border-width: thin;
         border-color: green
        }
    </style>
  </head>
  <body>
    <table border = "5">
      <caption> Fruit Juice Drinks </caption>
      <tr>
        <th> </th>
        <th> Apple </th>
        <th> Orange </th>
        <th> Screwdriver </th>
      </tr>
      <tr>
        <th> Breakfast </th>
        <td> 0 </td>
        <td> 1 </td>
        <td> 0 </td>
      </tr>
```

```
      <tr>
        <th> Lunch </th>
        <td> 1 </td>
        <td> 0 </td>
        <td> 0 </td>
      </tr>
      <tr>
        <th> Dinner </th>
        <td> 0 </td>
        <td> 0 </td>
        <td> 1 </td>
      </tr>
    </table>
    <p>
      Now is the time for all good Web programmers to
      learn to use style sheets.
    </p>
  </body>
</html>
```

specified with its `border` attribute, the border properties override the original border. In this example, the table has a regular 5-pixel border, but the top and bottom borders are replaced by those specified with the border properties.

The display of `borders.html` is shown in Figure 3.8.

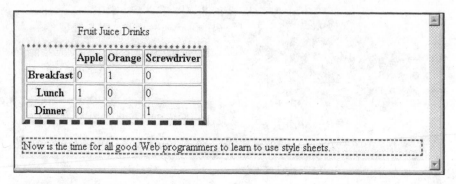

Figure 3.8 Borders

If the `border` attribute had been left out of the `table` element in `borders.html`, the table would have a top border and a bottom border only. It would not have left and right borders, nor would it have borders around the cells.

3.10.2 Margins and Padding

Recall from the box model that *padding* is the space between the content of an element and its border. The *margin* is the space between the border of an element and the element's neighbor. When there is no border, the margin plus the padding is the space between the content of an element and its neighbor. In this scenario, it may appear that there is no difference between padding and margins. However, there is a difference when the element has a background. In this case, the background extends into the padding but not into the margin.

The margin properties are named `margin`, which applies to all four sides of an element, `margin-left`, `margin-right`, `margin-top`, and `margin-bottom`. The padding properties are named `padding`, which applies to all four sides, `padding-left`, `padding-right`, `padding-top`, and `padding-bottom`.

The following example, `marpads.html`, illustrates several combinations of margins and padding, both with and without borders.

```
<?xml version = "1.0" encoding = "utf-8"?>
<!DOCTYPE html PUBLIC "-//W3C//DTD XHTML 1.0 Strict//EN"
  "http://www.w3.org/TR/xhtml1/DTD/xhtml1-strict.dtd">

<!-- marpads.html
     An example to illustrate margins and padding
     -->
<html xmlns = "http://www.w3.org/1999/xhtml">
  <head> <title> Margins and Padding </title>
    <style type = "text/css">
      p.one   {margin: 0.2in;
               padding: 0.2in;
               background-color: #C0C0C0;
               border-style: solid;
              }
      p.two   {margin: 0.1in;
               padding: 0.3in;
               background-color: #C0C0C0;
               border-style: solid;
              }
      p.three {margin: 0.3in;
               padding: 0.1in;
               background-color: #C0C0C0;
               border-style: solid;
              }
```

```
        p.four   {margin:0.4in;
                  background-color: #C0C0C0;}
        p.five   {padding: 0.4in;
                  background-color: #C0C0C0;
                  }
    </style>
  </head>
  <body>
    <p>
      Here is the first line.
    </p>
    <p class = "one">
      Now is the time for all good Web programmers to
      learn to use style sheets. <br /> [margin = 0.2in,
      padding = 0.2in]
    </p>
    <p class = "two">
      Now is the time for all good Web programmers to
      learn to use style sheets. <br /> [margin = 0.1in,
      padding = 0.3in]
    </p>
    <p class = "three">
      Now is the time for all good Web programmers to
      learn to use style sheets. <br /> [margin = 0.3in,
      padding = 0.1in]
    </p>
    <p class = "four">
      Now is the time for all good Web programmers to
      learn to use style sheets. <br /> [margin = 0.4in,
      no padding, no border]
    </p>
    <p class = "five">
      Now is the time for all good Web programmers to
      learn to use style sheets. <br /> [padding = 0.4in,
      no margin, no border]
    </p>
    <p>
      Here is the last line.
    </p>
  </body>
</html>
```

Figure 3.9 shows a browser display of marpads.html.

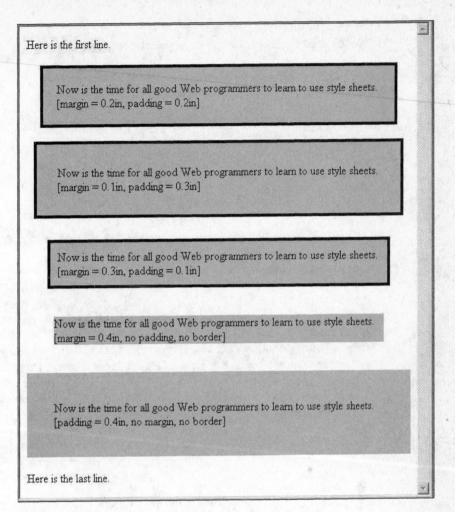

Figure 3.9 Display of `marpads.html`

3.11 Background Images

The `background-image` property is used to place an image in the background of an element. For example, an image of an airplane might be an effective background for text about the airplane. Consider the following example:

```
<?xml version = "1.0" encoding = "utf-8"?>
<!DOCTYPE html PUBLIC "-//W3C//DTD XHTML 1.0 Strict//EN"
  "http://www.w3.org/TR/xhtml1/DTD/xhtml1-strict.dtd">
```

```
<!-- back_image.html
    An example to illustrate background images
    -->
<html xmlns = "http://www.w3.org/1999/xhtml">
  <head> <title> Background images </title>
    <style type = "text/css">
       body {background-image: url(c172.gif);}
       p {margin-left: 30px; margin-right: 30px;
          margin-top: 50px; font-size: 14pt;}
    </style>
  </head>
  <body>
    <p>
       The Cessna 172 is the most common general aviation airplane
       in the world. It is an all-metal, single-engine piston,
       high-wing four-place monoplane. It has fixed-gear and is
       categorized as a non-high-performance aircraft. The current
       model is the 172R.
       The wingspan of the 172R is 36'1". Its fuel capacity is 56
       gallons in two tanks, one in each wing. The takeoff weight
       is 2,450 pounds. Its maximum useful load is 837 pounds.
       The maximum speed of the 172R at sea level is 142 mph.
       The plane is powered by a 360 cubic inch gasoline engine
       that develops 160 horsepower. The climb rate of the 172R
       at sea level is 720 feet per minute.
    </p>
  </body>
</html>
```

Figure 3.10 shows a browser display of back_image.html.

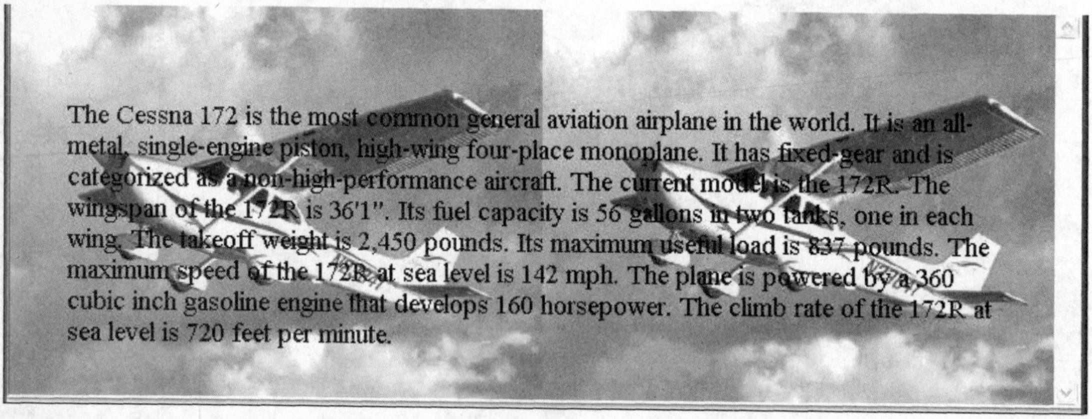

Figure 3.10 Display of back_image.html

Text over a background image can be difficult to read if the image has areas that are nearly the same color as the text. Therefore, care must be taken in selecting background images. In many cases, images with various kinds of textures in light gray colors are best.

In the example, notice that the background image is replicated as necessary to fill the area of the element. This replication is called *tiling*. Tiling can be controlled with the `background-repeat` property, which can take the value `repeat` (the default), `no-repeat`, `repeat-x`, or `repeat-y`. The `no-repeat` value specifies that just one copy of the image is to be displayed. The `repeat-x` value means that the image is to be repeated horizontally; `repeat-y` means to repeat vertically. Additionally, the position of a nonrepeated background image can be specified with the `background-position` property, which can take a large number of different values. The key word values are `top`, `center`, `bottom`, `left`, and `right`. These can be used in many different combinations. The simplest uses of these are to use one key word to specify the horizontal placement and one to specify the vertical placement, such as `top left`, `bottom right`, and `top center`. If only one key word is given, the other is assumed to be `center`. So, `top` is equivalent to `top center` (or `center top`), and `left` is the same as `center left` (or `left center`).

3.12 The `<span>` and `<div>` Tags

In many situations, we want to apply special font properties to less than a whole paragraph of text. For example, it is often useful to have a word or phrase in a line appear in a different font size or color. The `<span>` tag is designed for just this purpose. Unlike most other tags, there is no default layout for the content of `<span>`. So, in the following example, the word `total` is not displayed differently from the rest of the paragraph:

```
<p>
  It sure is fun to be in <span> total </span>
  control of text
</p>
```

The purpose of `<span>` is to change property values of part of a line of content. For example:

```
<style type = "text/css" >
  .spanred {font-size: 24pt;
          font-family: Ariel; color: red}
</style>
...
<p>
  It sure is fun to be in
  <span class = "spanred"> total </span>
  control of text
</p>
```

The display of this paragraph is shown in Figure 3.11.

It sure is fun to be in total control of text

Figure 3.11 The `<span>` tag

It is common for documents to have sections, each consisting of some number of paragraphs, that have their own presentation styles. Using style classes on paragraphs, you can do this with what has already been discussed. It is more convenient, however, to be able to apply a style to a section of a document rather than each paragraph. This can be done with the `<div>` tag. As with `<span>`, there is no implied layout for the content of the `<div>` tag, so its primary use is to specify presentation details for a section or division of a document.

Consider the following example, in which a section, or division, of a document is to use a specific paragraph style:

```
<div class = "primary">
  <p>
  ...
  </p>
  <p>
  ...
  </p>
  <p>
  ...
  </p>
</div>
```

The span and div elements are used in examples in Chapter 6.

3.13 Conflict Resolution

When there are two different values for the same property on the same element, there is an obvious conflict that the browser (or other XHTML processor) must resolve. So far, we have only considered one way in which this conflict can occur: when style sheets at two or more levels specify different values for the same property on the same element. This particular kind of conflict is resolved by the precedence of the three different levels of style sheets. In-line style sheets have precedence over document and external style sheets, and document style sheets have precedence over external style sheets. However, property value conflicts can occur in several other ways. For example, a conflict may occur within a single style sheet. Consider the following style specifications, which are next to each other in the same document-level style sheet:

```
h3 {color: blue;}
body h3 {color: red;}
```

Both of these apply to all `h3` elements in the body of the document.

Inheritance is another source of potential property value conflicts. These can occur if a property on a particular element has a value assigned by some style sheet and also inherits a value for that same property. Therefore, some method of resolving conflicts caused by inheritance must be available.

There can be several different origins of the specification of property values. For example, they may come from a style sheet written by the author of the document itself, but they may also come from the browser user and from the browser. For example, an FX2 user can set a minimum font size in the *Tools-Options-Advanced* window. Furthermore, browsers allow their users to write and use their own style sheets. Property values with different origins can have different precedences.

In addition, every property value specification has a particular *specificity*, depending on the particular kind of selector that is used to set it, and those specificities have different levels of precedence. These different levels are used to resolve conflicts among different specifications.

Finally, property value specifications can be marked as being important, by including `!important` in the specification. For example,

```
p.special {font-style: italic !important; font-size: 14}
```

In this specification, `font-style: italic` is important, but `font-size: 14` is normal. Whether a specification has been marked as being important is called the *weight* of the specification. The weight can be either normal or important. Obviously, this is another way to specify the relative precedence that a specification should have in resolving conflicts.

The details of property value conflict resolution, which are complex, will not be discussed here. Rather, the following is a relatively brief overview of process of property value conflict resolution.

Conflict resolution is a multistage sorting process. The first step in the process is to gather the syle specifications from the three possible levels of style sheets. These specifications are sorted into order by the relative precedence of the style sheet levels. Next, all of the available specifications (those from style sheets, those from the user, and those from the browser) are sorted by origin and weight. This is done according to the following rules, in which the first has the highest precedence:

1. Important declarations with user origin
2. Important declarations with author origin
3. Normal declarations with author origin
4. Normal declarations with user origin
5. Any declarations with browser (or other user agent) origin

Note that user-origin specifications are considered to have the highest precedence. The rationale for this is that such specifications often are declared because of some diminished capability of the user, most often a visual impairment.

If there are conflicts after the sorting described above, the next step in their resolution is a sort by specificity. This sort is based on the following rules, in which the first has the highest precedence:

1. id selectors
2. Class and pseudo-class selectors
3. Contextual selectors (more element type names means they are more specific)
4. Universal selectors

If there are still conflicts, they are resolved by giving precedence to the most recently seen specification. For this process, the specifications in an external style sheet are considered to occur at the point in the document where the link element or @import rule that references the external style sheet appears. For example, if a style sheet specifies the following, and there are no further conflicting specifications before the element is displayed, the value used will be the last (in this case, 10pt):

```
p {font-size: 12pt}
p {font-size: 10pt}
```

The whole sorting process that is used to resolve style specification conflicts is called *the cascade*.

Summary

Cascading style sheets were introduced to provide a uniform and consistent way to specify presentation details in XHTML documents. Many of the style tags and attributes designed for specifying styles that had crept into HTML were deprecated in HTML 4.0 in favor of style sheets. Style sheets can appear at three levels: inline, which apply only to the content of one specific tag; document, which apply to all appearances of specific tags in the body of a document; and external, which are stored in files by themselves and can apply to any number of documents. The property values in inline style sheets are specified in the string value of the style attribute. Document style sheets are specified in a comment that is the content of a `<style>` tag in the head of the document. External style sheets appear in separate files. Both document-level and external style specifications have the form of a list of style rules. Each style rule has a list of the names of tags and a list of property/value pairs. The property/value pairs apply to all occurrences of the named tags.

A style class, which is defined in the content of a `<style>` tag, allows different occurrences of the same tag to have different property values. A generic style-class specification allows tags with different names to use the same presentation style. A pseudo class takes effect when a particular event occurs. There are many different property value forms, including lengths, percentage values, URLs, and colors. Several different properties are related to fonts. The `font-family` property specifies one or more font names. Because different browsers support different sets of fonts, there are five generic font names. Each browser supports at least one font in each generic category. The `font-size` property can specify a length value or one of a number of different named size categories. The `font-style` property can be set to `italic` or `normal`. The `font-weight` property is used to specify the degree of boldness of text. The `font` property provides an abbreviated form for font-related properties. The `text-decoration` property is used to specify underlining, overlining, and line-through text.

The `list-style-type` property is used to specify the bullet form for items in unordered lists. It is also used to specify the sequence type for the items in ordered lists.

A Web content designer must be concerned with the color capabilities of clients' browsers and monitors. The safest set of colors includes just 16 basic colors, all of which have standard names. A much larger set of relatively safe Web colors is the Web palette, which includes 216 colors. The foreground and background colors of the content of a document are specified by the `color` and `background-color` properties, respectively.

The first line of a paragraph can be indented with `text-indent`. Text can be aligned with the `text-align` property, whose values are `left`, `right`, and `justify`, which means both left and right alignment. When the `float` property is set to `left` or `right`, text can be made to flow around it on the right or left, respectively, in the display window.

Borders can be specified to appear around any element. These borders can appear in any color and any of the forms—dotted, solid, dashed, or double. The margin, which is the space between the border (or the content of the element if it has no border) and the element's neighbor, can be set with the margin properties. The padding, which is the space between the content of an element and its border (or neighbor if it has no border) can be set with the padding properties.

The `background-image` property is used to place an image in the background of an element.

The `<span>` tag provides a way to include an inline style sheet that applies to a range of text that is smaller than a line or a paragraph. The `<div>` tag provides a way to define a section of a document that has its own style properties.

Conflict resolution for property values is a complicated process, using the origin of specifications, their specificity, inheritance, and the relative position of specifications.

Review Questions

3.1   What attributes are required in a link to an external style sheet?

3.2   What is the advantage of document-level style sheets over inline style sheets?

3.3   What is the purpose of external style sheets?

3.4   What is the purpose of a generic class?

3.5   What is the format of an inline style sheet?

3.6   What is the format of an external style sheet?

3.7   What is the form of comments within the rule list of a document-level style sheet?

3.8   What is the format of a document-level style sheet, and where does it appear?

3.9   What is the purpose of a style class selector?

3.10 Why is a list of font names given as the value of a `font-family` property?

3.11 In what order must property values appear in the list of a `font` property?

3.12 How is the `list-style-type` property used with unordered lists?

3.13 Are key word property values case sensitive or case insensitive?

3.14 What are the possible values of the `list-style-type` property when it is used with ordered lists?

3.15 What are the five generic fonts?

3.16 If you want text to flow around the right side of an image, which value, `right` or `left`, must be assigned to the `float` property of the image?

3.17 Why must background images be chosen with care?

3.18 In what ways can text be modified with `text-decoration`?

3.19 Which has higher precedence, a user-origin specification or a browser specification?

3.20 What are the possible values for the `text-align` property?

3.21 What are the three ways color property values can be specified?

3.22 What purpose does the `text-indent` property serve?

3.23 What properties are used to set margins around elements?

3.24 If you want a background image to be repeated vertically but not horizontally, what value must be set to what property?

3.25 If there are two conflicting specifications in a document-level style sheet, which of the two has precedence?

3.26 What properties and what values must be used to put a dotted border around a text box, where the border is red and thin on the left and blue and thick on the right?

3.27 What is the purpose of the `<div>` tag?

3.28 What layout information does a `<span>` tag by itself indicate to the browser?

3.29 Which has higher precedence, an id selector or a universal selector?

Exercises

3.1 Create an external style sheet for the chapters of this book.

3.2 Create and test an XHTML document that displays a table of basketball scores from a collegiate basketball conference in which the team names have one of the primary colors of their respective schools. The winning scores must appear larger and in a different font than the losing scores. The team names must be in a script font.

3.3 Create and test an XHTML document that includes at least two images and enough text to precede the images, flow around them (one on the left and one on the right), and continue after the last image.

3.4 Create and test an XHTML document that has at least a half page of text and that has a small box of text embedded on the right margin, with the main text flowing around the small box. The embedded text must appear in a smaller font and also must be set in bold.

3.5 Create and test an XHTML document that has six short paragraphs of text that describe various aspects of the town in which you live. You must define three different paragraph styles, p1, p2, and p3. The p1 style must use left and right margins of 20 pixels, a background color of gray, and a foreground color of blue. The p2 style must use left and right margins of 30 pixels, a background color of black, and a foreground color of white. The p3 style must use a text indent of 1 centimeter, a background color of green, and a foreground color of blue. The first and third paragraph must use p1, the second and fourth must use p2, and the third and fifth must use p3.

3.6 Create and test an XHTML document that describes nested ordered lists of pets. The outer list must have three entries: cat, dog, and horse. Inside each of these three lists there must be two sublists of breed. The cat sublists are Siamese and Persian; the dog sublists are Poodle and German Shepherd; the horse sublists are Arabian horse and Colorado

Ranger. Each breed sublist must have at least three entries, each of which is the name of a particular animal that fits the category. The outer list must use uppercase Roman numerals, the middle lists must use uppercase letters, and the inner lists must use Arabic numerals. The background color for the cat list must be pink; for the dog list it must be blue; for the horse list, it must be red. All of the styles must be in a document style sheet.

3.7   Rewrite the document of Exercise 3.6 to put all style sheet information in an external style sheet. Validate your external style sheet with the W3C CSS validation service.

3.8   Rewrite the document of Exercise 3.6 to use inline style sheets only.

3.9   Create and test an XHTML document that contains at least five lines of text from a magazine story. Every verb in the text must be red, every noun must be blue, and every preposition must be yellow.

3.10 Create and test an XHTML document that describes an unordered list of at least five popular music CDs. The bullet for each CD must be a small image of the album's cover. Find the images on the Web.

3.11 Modify the XHTML document, `nested_lists.html` in Section 2.7.2, to make the different levels of lists different colors using a document style sheet.

3.12 Using a document style sheet, modify the XHTML document, `definition.html` in Section 2.7.3, to set the font in the `dt` elements to Verdana 12-point font and the `dd` elements to Arial 12-point bold font.

The Basics of JavaScript

This chapter takes you on a quick tour of the basics of JavaScript, introducing its most important concepts and constructs, but leaving out many of the details of the language. Topics discussed include the following: primitive data types and their operators and expressions, screen output and keyboard input, control statements, objects and constructors, arrays, functions, and pattern matching. In spite of this chapter's brevity, if you are an experienced programmer, you should be able to learn how to be an effective JavaScript programmer by studying this chapter, along with Chapter 5, "JavaScript and XHTML Documents," and Chapter 6, "Dynamic Documents with JavaScript." More comprehensive descriptions of JavaScript can be found in the numerous books devoted solely to JavaScript.

4.1 Overview of JavaScript

This section discusses the origins of JavaScript, a few of its characteristics, and some of its uses. Included are a comparison of JavaScript and Java and a brief introduction to event-driven programming.

4.1.1   Origins

JavaScript, which was originally named LiveScript, was developed by Netscape. In late 1995 LiveScript became a joint venture of Netscape and Sun Microsystems and its name was changed to JavaScript. Netscape's JavaScript has gone through extensive evolution, moving from version 1.0 to version 1.5, primarily by adding many new features. A language standard for JavaScript was developed in the late 1990s by the European Computer Manufacturers Association (ECMA) as ECMA-262. This standard has also been approved by the International Standards Organization (ISO) as ISO-16262. The ECMA-262 standard is now in version 3, which corresponds to Netscape's version 1.5 of JavaScript. Microsoft's JavaScript is named JScript. The FireFox 2 (FX2) and Internet Explorer 7 (IE7) browsers both implement languages that conform to ECMA-262 version 3. The current standard specification can be found at

```
http://www.ecma-international.org/publications/
standards/Ecma-262.htm
```

The official name of the standard language is ECMAScript. Because it is nearly always called JavaScript elsewhere, we will use that term exclusively in this book.

JavaScript can be divided into three parts: the core, client side, and server side. The *core* is the heart of the language, including its operators, expressions, statements, and subprograms. *Client-side* JavaScript is a collection of objects that support control of a browser and interactions with users. For example, with JavaScript, an XHTML document can be made to be responsive to user inputs such as mouse clicks and keyboard use. *Server-side* JavaScript is a collection of objects that make the language useful on a Web server; for example, to support communication with a database management system.

Server-side JavaScript is used far less frequently than client-side JavaScript. Therefore, this book does not cover server-side JavaScript.

Client-side JavaScript is an XHTML-embedded scripting language. We refer to every collection of JavaScript code as a *script*. An XHTML document can include any number of embedded scripts.

4.1.2   JavaScript and Java

Although JavaScript's name appears to connote a close relationship with Java, JavaScript and Java are actually very different. One important difference is support for object-oriented programming. Although JavaScript is sometimes said to be an object-oriented language, its object model is quite different from that of Java and C++, as you will see in Section 4.2. In fact, JavaScript does not support the object-oriented software development paradigm.

Java is a strongly typed language. Types are all known at compile time, and operand types are checked for compatibility. Variables in JavaScript need not be declared and are dynamically typed, making compile-time type checking impossible. One more important difference between Java and JavaScript is that objects in Java are static in the sense that their collection of data members and methods is fixed at compile time. JavaScript objects are dynamic—the number of data members and methods of an object can change during execution.

The main similarity between Java and JavaScript is the syntax of their expressions, assignment statements, and control statements.

4.1.3   Uses of JavaScript

The original goal of JavaScript was to provide programming capability at both the server and the client ends of a Web connection. Since then, JavaScript has grown into a full-fledged programming language that can be used for a variety of application areas. This book focuses on client-side JavaScript.

Client-side JavaScript can serve as an alternative for some of what is done with server-side programming, in which computational capability resides on the server and is requested by the client. Client-side JavaScript, on the other hand, is embedded in XHTML documents (either physically or logically) and is interpreted by the browser. This transfer of load from the often-overloaded server to the normally underloaded client can obviously benefit all other clients. Client-side JavaScript cannot replace all server-side computing. In particular, while server-side software supports file operations, database access, and networking, client-side JavaScript supports none of these.

JavaScript can be used as an alternative to Java applets.[1] JavaScript has the advantage of being easier to learn and use than Java. Also, Java applets are downloaded separately from the XHTML documents that call them; many JavaScript scripts, however, are an integral part of the XHTML document, so no secondary downloading is necessary. On the other hand, Java applets are far more capable of producing graphics in browser displays than are JavaScript scripts.

Interactions with users through form elements, such as buttons and menus, can be conveniently described in JavaScript. Because button clicks and mouse movements are easily detected with JavaScript, they can be used to trigger computations and provide feedback to the user. For example, when a user moves the

---

1. Java applets are discussed in Appendix C.

mouse curser from a text box, JavaScript can detect that movement and check the appropriateness of the text box's value (which presumedly was just filled by the user). Even without forms, user interactions are both possible and simple to program in JavaScript. These interactions, which take place in dialog windows, include getting input from the user and allowing the user to make choices through buttons. It is also easy to generate new content in the browser display dynamically.

Another interesting capability of JavaScript was made possible by the development of the Document Object Model (DOM), which allows JavaScript scripts to access and modify the CSS properties and content of any element of a displayed XHTML document, making formally static documents highly dynamic. Various techniques for designing dynamic XHTML documents with JavaScript are discussed in Chapter 6, "Dynamic Documents with JavaScript."

Much of what JavaScript scripts typically do is event driven, meaning that the actions often are executed in response to actions of the browser user, among them mouse clicks and form submissions. This sort of computation supports user interactions through the XHTML form elements on the client display. The mechanics of event-driven computation in JavaScript are discussed in detail in Chapter 5.

4.1.4   Browsers and XHTML/JavaScript Documents

If an XHTML document does not include embedded scripts, the browser reads the lines of the document and renders its window according to the tags, attributes, and content it finds. When a JavaScript script is encountered in the document, the browser uses its JavaScript interpreter to "execute" the script. When the end of the script is reached, the browser goes back to reading the XHTML document and displaying its content.

There are two different ways to embed JavaScript in an XHTML document, implicitly or explicitly. *Explicit embedding* means that the JavaScript code physically resides in the XHTML document. This approach has several disadvantages. Mixing two completely different kinds of code in the same document makes the document difficult to read. Also, in some cases, the person who creates and maintains the XHTML is distinct from the person who creates and maintains the JavaScript. Having two different people, doing two different jobs, working on the same document can lead to many problems. To avoid these, the JavaScript can be placed in its own file, separate from the XHTML document. This is called *implicit embedding*. Implicit embedding has the advantage of hiding the script from the browser user. It also avoids the problem of hiding scripts from older browsers, which is discussed later in this section. Except for the first simple example, which illustrates explicit embedding of JavaScript in an XHTML document, all of the JavaScript example scripts in this chapter are implicitly embedded.

When JavaScript scripts are explicitly embedded, they can appear in either part of an XHTML document, the head or the body, depending on the purpose of the script. Scripts that produce content only when requested or that react to user interactions are placed in the head of the document. Generally, this means function definitions and code associated with form elements such as buttons. On the other hand, scripts that are to be interpreted just once, when the interpreter finds them, are placed in the document body. Accordingly, the interpreter notes the existence of scripts that appear in the head of a document, but it does not interpret them while processing the head. Scripts that are found in the body of a document are interpreted as they are found. When implicit embedding is used, these same guidelines apply to the XHTML code that references the external JavaScript files.

4.2   Object Orientation and JavaScript

As stated previously, JavaScript is not an object-oriented programming language. Rather, it is an object-based language. JavaScript does not have classes. Its objects serve both as objects and as models of objects. Without classes, JavaScript cannot have class-based inheritance, as is supported in object-oriented languages such as C++ and Java. It does, however, support a technique that can be used to simulate some of the aspects of inheritance. This is done with the prototype object; thus, this form of inheritance is called *prototype-based inheritance*. Prototype-based inheritance is not discussed in this book.

Without class-based inheritance, JavaScript cannot support polymorphism. A polymorphic variable can reference related objects of different classes within the same class hierarchy. A method call through such a polymorphic variable can be dynamically bound to the method in the object's class.[2]

Despite the fact that JavaScript is not an object-oriented language, much of its design is rooted in the concepts and approaches used in object-oriented programming. Specifically, client-side JavaScript deals in large part with documents and document elements, which are modeled with objects.

4.2.1   JavaScript Objects

In JavaScript, objects are collections of properties, which correspond to the members of classes in Java and C++. Each property is either a data property or a function or method property. Data properties appear in two categories: primitive values and references to other objects. (In JavaScript, variables that refer to objects are often called *objects* rather than *references*.) Sometimes we will refer to the data properties simply as *properties;* we often refer to the method properties simply as *methods* or *functions*. We prefer to call subprograms that are called through objects methods and subprograms that are not called through objects functions.

The more general category of object properties is other objects. JavaScript uses nonobject types for some of its simplest data types; these types are called

---

2. This is often called *dynamic binding*. It is an essential part of full support for object-oriented programming in a language.

primitives. Primitives are used because they often can be implemented directly in hardware, resulting in faster operations on their values (faster than if they were treated as objects). Primitives are like the simple scalar variables of non-object-oriented languages such as C. C++, Java, and JavaScript all have both primitives and objects; JavaScript's primitives are described in Section 4.4.

All objects in a JavaScript program are indirectly accessed through variables. Such a variable is like a reference in Java. All primitive values in JavaScript are accessed directly—these are like the scalar types in Java and C++. These are often called *value types.* The properties of an object are referenced by attaching the name of the property to the variable that references the object. For example, if myCar is a variable that is referencing an object that has the property engine, the engine property can be referenced with myCar.engine.

The root object in JavaScript is Object. It is the ancestor, through prototype inheritance, of all objects. Object is the most generic of all objects, having some methods but no data properties. All other objects are specializations of Object, and all inherit its methods (although they are often overridden).[3]

A JavaScript object appears, both internally and externally, as a list of property/value pairs. The properties are names; the values are data values or functions. All functions are objects and are referenced through variables. The collection of properties of a JavaScript object is dynamic—properties can be added or deleted at any time.

Every object is characterized by its collection of properties, although objects do not have types in any formal sense. Recall that Object is characterized by having no properties. Futher discussions of objects appear in Sections 4.7 and 4.11.

4.3 General Syntactic Characteristics

In this book all JavaScript scripts are embedded, either directly or indirectly, in XHTML documents. Scripts can appear directly as the content of a <script> tag. The type attribute of <script> must be set to "text/javascript". The JavaScript script can be indirectly embedded in an XHTML document using the src attribute of a <script> tag, whose value is the name of a file that contains the script. For example:

```
<script type = "text/javascript" src = "tst_number.js" >
</script>
```

Notice that the script element requires the closing tag, even though it has no content when the src attribute is included.

There are some situations when a small amount of JavaScript code is embedded in an XHTML document. Furthermore, some documents have a

---

3. It sounds like a contradiction when we say that all objects inherit methods from Object, although we said earlier that Object has no properties. The answer to this paradox lies in the design of prototype inheritance in JavaScript. Every object has a prototype object associated with it. It is Object's prototype object that defines the methods that are inherited by all other objects.

large number of places where JavaScript code is embedded. Therefore, it is sometimes inconvenient and cumbersome to place all JavaScript code in a separate file.

In JavaScript, identifiers, or names, are similar to those of other common programming languages. They must begin with a letter, an underscore (_), or a dollar sign ($).[4] Subsequent characters may be letters, underscores, dollar signs, or digits. There is no length limitation for identifiers. As is the case with most C-based languages, the letters in a variable name in JavaScript are case sensitive, meaning that FRIZZY, Frizzy, FrIzZy, frizzy, and frizZy are all distinct names. However, by convention, programmer-defined variable names do not include uppercase letters.

JavaScript has 25 reserved words, which are listed in Table 4.1.

Table 4.1 JavaScript reserved words

break	delete	function	return	typeof
case	do	if	switch	var
catch	else	in	this	void
continue	finally	instanceof	throw	while
default	for	new	try	with

Besides its reserved words, another collection of words is reserved for future use in JavaScript—these can be found at the ECMA Web site. In addition, JavaScript has a large collection of predefined words, including alert, open, java, and self.

JavaScript has two forms of comments, both of which are used in other languages. First, whenever two adjacent slashes (//) appear on a line, the rest of the line is considered a comment. Second, both single- and multiple-line comments can be written using /* to introduce the comment and */ to terminate it.

There are two issues regarding embedding JavaScript in XHTML documents. First, there are some browsers still in use that recognize the <script> tag but do not have JavaScript interpreters. These browsers simply ignore the contents of the script element and cause no problems. Second, there are still a few browsers in use that are so old they do not recognize the <script> tag. Such a browser would display the contents of the script element as if it were just text. It has been customary to enclose the contents of all script elements in XHTML comments to avoid this problem. Because there are so few browsers that do not recognize the <script> tag, we believe this is no longer a problem. However, the XHTML validator also has a problem with embedded JavaScript. When the embedded JavaScript happens to include recognizable tags—for

---

4. Dollar signs are not intended to be used by user-written scripts, although it is legal.

example <br /> tags in the output of the JavaScript—they often cause validation errors. Therefore, we still enclose embedded JavaScript in XHTML comments when we explicitly embedded JavaScript.

The XHTML comment introduction (<!--) works as a hiding prelude to JavaScript code. However, the syntax for closing a comment that encloses JavaScript code is special. It is the usual XHTML comment closer, but it must be on its own line and must be preceded by two slashes (which makes it a JavaScript comment). The following XHTML comment form hides the enclosed script from browsers that do not have JavaScript interpreters, but makes it visible to browsers that do support JavaScript:

```
<!--
-- JavaScript script --
// -->
```

There are other problems with putting embedded JavaScript in comments in XHTML documents. These are discussed in Chapter 6. The best solution to all of these problems is to put all JavaScript scripts of significant size in separate files and embed them implicitly.

The use of semicolons in JavaScript is unusual. The JavaScript interpreter tries to make semicolons unnecessary, but it does not always work. When the end of a line coincides with what could be the end of a statement, the interpreter effectively inserts a semicolon there. But this can lead to problems. For example, consider the following:

```
return
x;
```

The interpreter will insert a semicolon after `return`, making `x` an illegal orphan. The safest way to organize JavaScript statements is to put each on its own line whenever possible and terminate each statement with a semicolon. If a statement does not fit on a line, be careful to break the statement at a place that will ensure that the first line does not have the form of a complete statement.

The following is a complete, but trivial XHTML document that simply greets the client who requests it. There is but one line of JavaScript in the document, the call to `write` through the `document` object to display the message.

```
<?xml version = "1.0" encoding = "utf-8"?>
<!DOCTYPE html PUBLIC "-//W3C//DTD XHTML 1.0 Strict//EN"
   "http://www.w3.org/TR/xhtml1/DTD/xhtml1-strict.dtd">

<!-- hello.html
     A trivial hello world example of XHTML/JavaScript
     -->
```

```
<html xmlns = "http://www.w3.org/1999/xhtml">
  <head>
    <title> Hello world </title>
  </head>
  <body>
    <script type = "text/javascript">
      <!--
      document.write("Hello, fellow Web programmers!");
      // -->
    </script>
  </body>
</html>
```

4.4 Primitives, Operations, and Expressions

The primitive data types, operations, and expressions of JavaScript are similar to those of other common programming languages. Therefore, our discussion of them is brief.

4.4.1 Primitive Types

JavaScript has five primitive types: Number, String, Boolean, Undefined, and Null.[5] All primitive values have one of these types. JavaScript includes predefined objects that are closely related to the Number, String, and Boolean types, named `Number`, `String`, and `Boolean`. (Is this confusing yet?) These objects are called *wrapper objects*. Each contains a property that stores a value of the corresponding primitive type. The purpose of the wrapper objects is to provide properties and methods that are convenient for use with values of the primitive types. In the case of `Number`, the properties are more useful; in the case of `String`, the methods are more useful. Because JavaScript coerces values between the Number type and `Number` objects and between the String type and `String` objects, the methods of `Number` and `String` can be used on variables of the corresponding primitive types. In fact, in most cases you can simply treat Number and String type values as if they were objects.

The difference between primitives and objects is shown in the following example. Suppose that `prim` is a primitive variable with the value 17 and `obj` is a `Number` object whose property value is 17. Figure 4.1 shows how `prim` and `obj` are stored.

---

5. Undefined and Null are often called *trivial* types, for reasons that will be obvious when these types are discussed in Section 4.4.3.

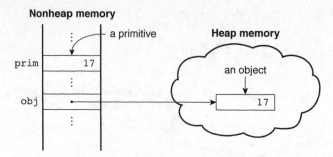

Figure 4.1 Primitives and objects

4.4.2   Numeric and String Literals

All numeric literals are values of type Number. The numeric values of Java-Script are represented internally in double-precision floating-point form. Because of this single numeric data type, numeric values in JavaScript are often called *numbers*. Literal numbers in a script can have the forms of either integer or floating-point values. Integer literals are strings of digits. Floating-point literals can have decimal points or exponents or both. Exponents are specified with an uppercase or lowercase e and a possibly signed integer literal. The following are legal numeric literals:

```
72    7.2    .72    72.    7E2    7e2    .7e2    7.e2    7.2E-2
```

Integer literals can be written in hexadecimal form by preceding their first digit with either 0x or 0X (the first character is zero, not "oh").

A string literal is a sequence of zero or more characters delimited by either single quotes (') or double quotes ("). String literals can include characters specified with escape sequences, such as \n and \t. If you want an actual single-quote character in a string literal that is delimited by single quotes, the embedded single quote must be preceded by a backslash:

```
'You\'re the most freckly person I\'ve ever met'
```

A double quote can be embedded in a double-quoted string literal by preceding it with a backslash. An actual backslash character in any string literal must be itself backslashed, as in the following example:

```
"D:\\bookfiles"
```

There is no difference between single-quoted and double-quoted literal strings. The null string (one with no characters) can be denoted with either ' ' or " ". All string literals are primitive values.

4.4.3   Other Primitive Types

The only value of type Null is the reserved word null, which indicates no value. A variable is null if it has not been explicitly declared or assigned a value.

If an attempt is made to use the value of a variable whose value is null, it will cause a runtime error.

The only value of type Undefined is `undefined`. Unlike `null`, there is no reserved word `undefined`. If a variable has been explicitly declared, but not assigned a value, it has the value `undefined`. If the value of an undefined variable is displayed, the word `"undefined"` is displayed.

The only values of type Boolean are `true` and `false`. These values are usually computed as the result of evaluating a relational or Boolean expression (see Section 4.6.1). The existence of both the Boolean primitive type and the `Boolean` object can lead to some confusion (also discussed in Section 4.6.1).

4.4.4   Declaring Variables

One of the characteristics of JavaScript that sets it apart from most common non-scripting programming languages is that it is dynamically typed. This means that a variable can be used for anything. Variables are not typed, values are. A variable can have the value of any primitive type, or it can be a reference to any object. The type of the value of a particular appearance of a variable in a program is determined by the interpreter. In many cases, the interpreter converts the type of a value to whatever is needed for the context in which it appears.

A variable can be declared either by assigning it a value, in which case the interpreter implicitly declares it to be a variable, or by listing it in a declaration statement that begins with the reserved word `var`. Initial values can be included in a `var` declaration, as with some of the variables in the following declaration:

```
var counter,
    index,
    pi = 3.14159265,
    quarterback = "Elway",
    stop_flag = true;
```

We recommend that all variables be explicitly declared.

As stated previously, a variable that has been declared, but not assigned a value, has the value `undefined`.

4.4.5   Numeric Operators

JavaScript has the typical collection of numeric operators. These are the binary operators + for addition, – for subtraction, * for multiplication, / for division, and % for modulus. The unary operators are plus (+), negate (–), decrement (--), and increment (++). The increment and decrement operators can be either prefix or postfix.[6] As with other languages that have the increment and decrement unary operators, the prefix and postfix uses are not always equivalent.

---

6. *Prefix* means that the operator precedes its operand; *postfix* means that the operator follows its operand.

Consider an expression consisting of a single variable and one of these operators. If the operator precedes the variable, the value of the variable is changed and the expression evaluates to the new value. If the operator follows the variable, the expression evaluates to the current value of the variable, and then the value of the variable is changed. For example, if the variable a has the value 7, the value of the following expression is 24:

```
(++a) * 3
```

But the value of the following expression is 21:

```
(a++) * 3
```

In both cases, a is set to 8.

All numeric operations are done in double-precision floating point.

The *precedence rules* of a language specify which operator is evaluated first when two operators with different precedence are adjacent in an expression. Adjacent operators are separated by a single operand. For example, in the following * and + are adjacent:

```
a * b + 1
```

The *associativity rules* of a language specify which operator is evaluated first when two operators with the same precedence are adjacent in an expression. The precedence and associativity of the numeric operators of JavaScript are given in Table 4.2.

Table 4.2 Precedence and associativity of the numeric operators

Operator	Associativity
++, --, unary -, unary +	Right (though it is irrelevant)
*, /, %	Left
Binary +, binary -	Left

The first operators listed have the highest precedence.

As examples of operator precedence and associativity, consider the following code:

```
var a = 2,
    b = 4,
    c,
    d;
c = 3 + a * b;
// * is first, so c is now 11 (not 24)
d = b / a / 2;
// / associates left, so d is now 1 (not 4)
```

Parentheses can be used to force any desired precedence. For example, the addition will be done before the multiplication in the following expression:

```
(a + b) * c
```

4.4.6   The Math Object

The Math object provides a collection of properties of Number objects and methods that operate on Number objects. The Math object has methods for the trigonometric functions, such as sin (for sine) and cos (for cosine), as well as for other commonly used mathematical operations. Among these are floor, to truncate a number; round, to round a number; and max, to return the largest of two given numbers. The floor and round methods are used in the example script in Section 4.10. All of the Math methods are referenced through the Math object, as in Math.sin(x).

4.4.7   The Number Object

The Number object includes a collection of useful properties that have constant values. Table 4.3 lists the properties of Number. These properties are referenced through Number. For example:

```
Number.MIN_VALUE
```

Table 4.3   Properties of Number

Property	Meaning
MAX_VALUE	Largest representable number
MIN_VALUE	Smallest representable number
NaN	Not a number
POSITIVE_INFINITY	Special value to represent infinity
NEGATIVE_INFINITY	Special value to represent negative infinity
PI	The value of π

Any arithmetic operation that results in an error (for example, division by zero) or that produces a value that cannot be represented as a double-precision floating-point number, such as one that is too large (overflow), returns the value "not a number," which is displayed as NaN. If NaN is compared for equality against any number, the comparison fails. Surprisingly, in a comparison, NaN is not equal to itself. To determine whether a variable has the NaN value, the predefined predicate function isNaN() must be used. For example, if the variable a has the NaN value, isNaN(a) returns true.

The `Number` object has a method, `toString`, which it inherits from `Object` but overrides. The `toString` method converts the number through which it is called to a string. Because numeric primitives and `Number` objects are always coerced to the other when necessary, `toString` can be called through a numeric primitive. For example:

```
var price = 427,
    str_price;
...
str_price = price.toString();
```

4.4.8 The String Catenation Operator

JavaScript strings are not stored or treated as arrays of characters; rather, they are unit scalar values. String catenation is specified with the operator denoted by a plus sign (+). For example, if the value of `first` is `"Freddie"`, the value of the following expression is `"Freddie Freeloader"`:

```
first + " Freeloader"
```

4.4.9 Implicit Type Conversions

The JavaScript interpreter performs several different implicit type conversions. Such conversions are called *coercions*. In general, when a value of one type is used in a position that requires a value of a different type, JavaScript attempts to convert the value to the type that is required. The most common examples of these conversions involve primitive string and number values.

If either operand of a + operator is a string, the operator is interpreted as a string catenation operator. If the other operand is not a string, it is coerced to a string. For example, consider the following expression:

```
"August " + 1977
```

In this expression, because the left operand is a string, the operator is considered to be a catenation operator. This forces string context on the right operand, so the right operand is implicitly converted to a string. Therefore, this expression evaluates to the following:

```
"August 1997"
```

The number `1977` in the following expression is also coerced to a string:

```
1977 + "August"
```

Now consider the following expression:

```
7 * "3"
```

In this expression the operator is one that is only used with numbers. This forces numeric context on the right operand. Therefore, JavaScript attempts to convert it to a number. In this example the conversion succeeds, and the value of this expression is 21. If the second operand were a string that could not be converted to a number, such as "August", the conversion would produce NaN, which would be the value of the expression.

When used as a number, null is 0. Unlike in C and C++, however, null is not the same as 0. When used as a number, undefined is interpreted as NaN (see Section 4.4.7).

4.4.10 Explicit Type Conversions

There are several different ways to force type conversions, primarily between strings and numbers. Strings that contain numbers can be converted to numbers with the String constructor, as in the following:

```
var str_value = String(value);
```

This conversion could also be done with the toString method, which has the advantage that it can be given a parameter to specify the base of the resulting number (although the base of the number to be converted is taken to be decimal). For example:

```
var num = 6;
var str_value = num.toString();
var str_value_binary = num.toString(2);
```

In the first conversion, the result is "6"; in the second, it is "110".

A number also can be converted to a string by catenating it with the empty string.

Strings can be explicitly converted to numbers in a variety of ways. The Number constructor can be used, as in the following:

```
var number = Number(aString);
```

The same conversion could be specified by subtracting zero from the string, as in the following:

```
var number = aString - 0;
```

Both of these conversions have the following restriction: The number in the string cannot be followed by any character except a space. For example, if the number happens to be followed by a comma, the conversion will not work. JavaScript has two predefined string functions that do not have this problem. These two, parseInt and parseFloat, are not String methods, so they are not called through String objects; however, they operate on the strings given as parameters. The parseInt function searches its string parameter for an integer literal. If one is found at the beginning of the string, it is converted to a number and returned. If the string does not begin with a valid integer literal, NaN is returned. The parseFloat function is similar to parseInt, but it searches for a floating-point literal, which could have a decimal point or an exponent or both. In both parseInt and parseFloat, the numeric literal could be followed by any nondigit character without causing any problems.

Because of the coercions JavaScript normally does, as discussed in Section 4.4.9, `parseInt` and `parseFloat` are not often needed.

4.4.11   String Properties and Methods

Because JavaScript coerces primitive string values to and from `String` objects when necessary, the differences between the `String` object and the String type have little effect on scripts. `String` methods can always be used through String primitive values, as if the values were objects. The `String` object includes one property, `length`, and a large collection of methods.

The number of characters in a string is stored in the `length` property as follows:

```
var str = "George";
var len = str.length;
```

In this code, `len` is set to the number of characters in `str`, 6. In the expression `str.length`, `str` is a primitive variable, but we treated it as if it were an object (referencing one of its properties). In fact, when `str` is used with the `length` property, JavaScript implicitly builds a temporary `String` object with a property whose value is that of the primitive variable. After the second statement is executed, the temporary `String` object is discarded.

A few of the most commonly used `String` methods are shown in Table 4.4.

Table 4.4   `String` methods

Method	Parameters	Result
charAt	A number	Returns the character in the `String` object that is at the specified position
indexOf	One-character string	Returns the position in the `String` object of the parameter
substring	Two numbers	Returns the substring of the `String` object from the first parameter position to the second
toLowerCase	None	Converts any uppercase letters in the string to lowercase
toUpperCase	None	Converts any lowercase letters in the string to uppercase

Note that for the `String` methods, character positions start at zero.

For example, suppose `str` has been defined as follows:

```
var str = "George";
```

The following expressions have the shown values:

```
str.charAt(2)  is 'o'
str.indexOf('r')  is 3
```

```
str.substring(2, 4)  is 'org'
str.toLowerCase()  is 'george'
```

Several `String` methods associated with pattern matching are described in Section 4.12.

4.4.12 The `typeof` Operator

The `typeof` operator returns the type of its single operand. This is quite useful in some circumstances in a script. `typeof` produces to `"number"`, `"string"`, or `"boolean"` if the operand is of primitive type Number, String, or Boolean, respectively. If the operand is an object or `null`, `typeof` produces `"object"`. This illustrates a fundamental characteristic of JavaScript—objects do not have types. If the operand is a variable that has not been assigned a value, `typeof` produces `"undefined"`, reflecting the fact that variables themselves are not typed. Notice that the `typeof` operator always returns a string. The operand for `typeof` can be placed in parentheses, making it appear to be a function. Therefore, `typeof x` and `typeof(x)` are equivalent.

4.4.13 Assignment Statements

The assignment statement in JavaScript is exactly like the assignment statement in other common C-based programming languages. There is a simple assignment operator, denoted by =, and a host of compound assignment operators, such as += and /=. For example, the statement

```
a += 7;
```

means the same as the following:

```
a = a + 7;
```

When considering assignment statements, it is important to remember that JavaScript has two kinds of values—primitives and objects. A variable can refer to a primitive value, such as the number 17, or an object, as shown in Figure 4.1. Objects are allocated on the heap, and variables that refer to them are essentially reference variables. When used to refer to an object, a variable stores an address only. Therefore, assigning the address of an object to a variable is fundamentally different from assigning a primitive value to a variable.

4.4.14 The `Date` Object

There are occasions when information about the current date and time is useful in a program. Likewise, sometimes it is convenient to be able to create objects that represent a specific date and time and manipulate them. These capabilities are available in JavaScript through the `Date` object and its rich collection of methods. In the following, we describe this object and some of its methods.

A `Date` object is created, naturally, with the `new` operator and the `Date` constructor, which has several forms. Because we focus on uses of the current date and time, we use only the simplest `Date` constructor, which takes no parameters and builds an object with the current date and time for its properties. For example:

```
var today = new Date();
```

The date and time properties of a `Date` object are in two forms, local and Coordinated Universal Time (UTC, which was formerly named Greenwich Mean Time). We only deal with local time in this section.

Table 4.5 shows the methods, along with the descriptions, that retrieve information from a `Date` object.

Table 4.5   Methods for the `Date` object

Method	Returns
`toLocaleString`	A string of the `Date` information
`getDate`	The day of the month
`getMonth`	The month of the year, as a number in the range of 0 to 11
`getDay`	The day of the week, as a number in the range of 0 to 6
`getFullYear`	The year
`getTime`	The number of milliseconds since January 1, 1970
`getHours`	The number of the hour, as a number in the range of 0 to 23
`getMinutes`	The number of the minute, as a number in the range of 0 to 59
`getSeconds`	The number of the second, as a number in the range of 0 to 59
`getMilliseconds`	The number of the millisecond, as a number in the range of 0 to 999

The use of the `Date` object is shown in Section 4.6.

4.5   Screen Output and Keyboard Input

A JavaScript script is interpreted when the browser finds the script or a reference to a separate script file in the body of the XHTML document. Thus, the normal output screen for JavaScript is the same as the screen in which the content of the host XHTML document is displayed. JavaScript models the XHTML document with the `Document` object. The window in which the browser displays an XHTML document is modeled with the `Window` object. The `Window` object includes two properties, `document` and `window`. The document property refers to the Document object. The window property is self referential; it refers to the Window object.

The Document object has several properties and methods. The most interesting and useful of its methods, at least for now, is write, which is used to create script output, which is dynamically created XHTML document content.[7] This content is specified in the parameter to write. For example, the following produces the screen shown in Figure 4.2:

```
document.write("The result is: ", result, "<br />");
```

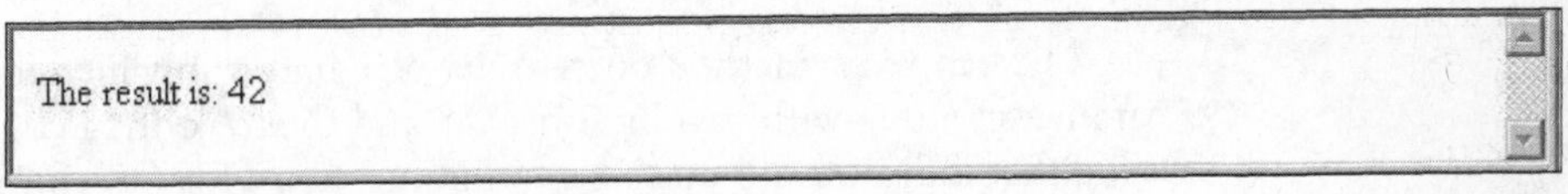

The result is: 42

Figure 4.2 An example of the output of document.write

Because write is used to create XHTML code, the only useful punctuation in its parameter is in the form of XHTML tags. Therefore, the parameter to write often includes <br />. The writeln method implicitly adds "\n" to its parameter, but since browsers ignore line breaks when displaying XHTML, is has no effect on the output.[8]

The parameter to write can include any XHTML tags and content. The parameter is simply given to the browser, which treats it exactly like any other part of the XHTML document. The write method actually can take any number of parameters. Multiple parameters are concatenated and placed in the output.

As stated previously, the Window object is the JavaScript model for the browser window. Window includes three methods that create dialog boxes for three specific kinds of user interactions. The default object for JavaScript is the Window object currently being displayed, so calls to these methods need not include an object reference.

The alert method opens a dialog window and displays its parameter in that window. It also displays an *OK* button. The parameter string to alert is not XHTML code; it is plain text. Therefore, the string parameter to alert may include \n but never should include <br />. As an example of an alert, consider the following code, which produces the dialog window shown in Figure 4.3:

```
alert("The sum is:" + sum + "\n");
```

---

7. The XML Document Object Model does not require XML agents (processors) to implement write, although that was likely the intention. Therefore, if an XHTML document is served as XML, some browsers may reject any embedded calls to write. However, most XHTML documents are now served as HTML and we believe most browsers will implement write for their XML parsers, so we will use write in many of our examples.

8. The writeln method is useful only if the browser is used to view a non-XHTML document, which is rarely done.

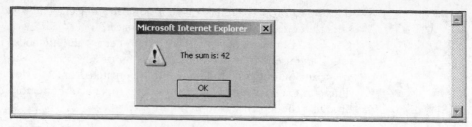

Figure 4.3 An example of the output of `alert`

The `confirm` method opens a dialog window in which it displays its string parameter, along with two buttons, *OK* and *Cancel*. `confirm` returns a Boolean value that indicates the user's button input: `true` for *OK* and `false` for *Cancel*. This method is often used to offer the user the choice of continuing some process. For example, the following statement produces the screen shown in Figure 4.4:

```
var question =
    confirm("Do you want to continue this download?");
```

After the user presses one of the buttons in the `confirm` dialog window, the script can test the variable, `question`, and react accordingly.

Figure 4.4 An example of the output of `confirm`

The `prompt` method creates a dialog window that contains a text box. The text box is used to collect a string of input from the user, which `prompt` returns as its value. The window also includes two buttons, *OK* and *Cancel*. `prompt` takes two parameters: the string that prompts the user for input and a default string in case the user does not type a string before pressing one of the two buttons. In many cases, an empty string is used for the default input. Consider the following example:

```
name = prompt("What is your name?", "");
```

Figure 4.5 shows the screen created by this call to `prompt`.

Figure 4.5 An example of the output of `prompt`

`alert`, `prompt`, and `confirm` cause the browser to wait for a user response. In the case of `alert`, the *OK* button must be pressed for the Java-Script interpreter to continue. The `prompt` and `confirm` methods wait for either *OK* or *Cancel* to be pressed.

The following example XHTML and JavaScript files, `roots.html`, and `roots.js`, illustrate some of the JavaScript features described so far. The Java-Script script gets the coefficients of a quadratic equation from the user with `prompt` and computes and displays the real roots of the given equation. If the roots of the equation are not real, the value `NaN` is displayed. This value comes from the `sqrt` function, which returns `NaN` when given a negative parameter. This corresponds mathematically to the equation not having real roots.

```
<?xml version = "1.0"  encoding = "utf-8" ?>
<!DOCTYPE html PUBLIC "-//W3C//DTD XHTML 1.0 Strict//EN"
   "http://www.w3.org/TR/xhtml1/DTD/xhtml1-strict.dtd">

<!-- roots.html
     A document for roots.js
     -->
<html xmlns = "http://www.w3.org/1999/xhtml">
  <head>
    <title> roots.html </title>
  </head>
  <body>
    <script type = "text/javascript"  src = "roots.js" >
    </script>
  </body>
</html>
```

```
// roots.js
//    Compute the real roots of a given quadratic
//    equation. If the roots are imaginary, this script
//    displays NaN, because that is what results from
//    taking the square root of a negative number

// Get the coefficients of the equation from the user
var a = prompt("What is the value of 'a'? \n", "");
var b = prompt("What is the value of 'b'? \n", "");
var c = prompt("What is the value of 'c'? \n", "");

// Compute the square root and denominator of the result
var root_part = Math.sqrt(b * b - 4.0 * a * c);
var denom = 2.0 * a;

// Compute and display the two roots
var root1 = (-b + root_part) / denom;
var root2 = (-b - root_part) / denom;
document.write("The first root is: ", root1, "<br />");
document.write("The second root is: ", root2, "<br />");
```

In the examples in the remainder of this chapter, the XHTML document that uses the associated JavaScript file is not shown.

4.6 Control Statements

This section introduces the flow-control statements of JavaScript. Before discussing the control statements, we must describe the control expressions, which provide the basis for controlling the order of execution of statements. Once again, the similarity of these JavaScript constructs to their counterparts in Java and C++ makes them easy to learn for those who are familiar with one of those languages.

Control statements often require some syntactic container for sequences of statements whose execution they are meant to control. In JavaScript, that container is the compound statement. A *compound statement* in JavaScript is a sequence of statements delimited by braces. A *control construct* is a control statement and the statement or compound statement whose execution it controls.

Unlike several related languages, JavaScript does not allow compound statements to create local variables. If a variable is declared in a compound statement, access to it is not confined to that compound statement. Such a variable is visible in the whole XHTML document.[9] Local variables are discussed in Section 4.9.2.

---

9. The exception to this rule is if the variable is declared in a function.

4.6.1   Control Expressions

The expressions upon which statement flow control can be based include primitive values, relational expressions, and compound expressions. The result of evaluating a control expression is one of the Boolean values `true` or `false`. If the value of a control expression is a string, it is interpreted as `true` unless it is either the empty string (`""`) or a zero string (`"0"`). If the value is a number, it is `true` unless it is zero (`0`). If the special value, `NaN`, is interpreted as a Boolean, it is false. If `undefined` is used as a Boolean, it is false. When interpreted as a Boolean, `null` is false. When interpreted as a number, `true` has the value `1` and `false` has the value `0`.

A relational expression has two operands and one relational operator. Table 4.6 lists the relational operators.

Table 4.6   Relational operators

Operation	Operator
Is equal to	==
Is not equal to	!=
Is less than	<
Is greater than	>
Is less than or equal to	<=
Is greater than or equal to	>=
Is strictly equal to	===
Is strictly not equal to	!==

If the two operands are not of the same type and the operator is neither `===` nor `!==`, JavaScript will attempt to convert the operands to a single type. In the case in which one operand is a string and the other is a number, JavaScript attempts to convert the string to a number. If one operand is Boolean and the other is not, the Boolean value is converted to a number (`1` for `true`, `0` for `false`).

The last two operators in Table 4.6 disallow type conversion of either operand. Thus, the expression `"3" === 3` evaluates to `false`, while `"3" == 3` evaluates to `true`.

Comparisons of variables that reference objects are rarely useful. If `a` and `b` reference different objects, `a == b` is never true, even if the objects have identical properties. `a == b` is true only if `a` and `b` reference the same object.

JavaScript has operators for the AND, OR, and NOT Boolean operations. These are `&&` (AND), `||` (OR), and `!` (NOT). Both `&&` and `||` are short-circuit operators, as they are in Java and C++. This means that if the value of the first operand of either `||` or `&&` determines the value of the expression, the second operand is not evaluated, and the Boolean operator does nothing. JavaScript also has bitwise operators, but they are not discussed in this book.

The properties of the object `Boolean` must not be confused with the primitive values `true` and `false`. If a `Boolean` object is used as a conditional expression, it evaluates to `true` if it has any value other than `null` or `undefined`. The `Boolean` object has a method, `toString`, which it inherits from `Object`, that converts the value of the object through which it is called to one of the strings `"true"` or `"false"`.

The precedence and associativity of all operators discussed so far in this chapter are shown in Table 4.7.

Table 4.7   Operator precedence and associativity

Operators	Associativity
`++`, `--`, unary `-`	Right
`*`, `/`, `%`	Left
`+`, `-`	Left
`>`, `<`, `>=` ,`<=`	Left
`==`, `!=`	Left
`===`,`!==`	Left
`&&`	Left
`||`	Left
`=`, `+=`, `-=`, `*=`, `/=`, `&&=`, `||=`, `%=`	Right

Highest-precedence operators are listed first.

4.6.2   Selection Statements

The selection statements (`if-then` and `if-then-else`) of JavaScript are similar to those of the common programming languages. Either single statements or compound statements can be selected. For example:

```
if (a > b)
    document.write("a is greater than b <br />");
else {
    a = b;
    document.write("a was not greater than b <br />",
                "Now they are equal <br />");
}
```

4.6.3   The switch Statement

JavaScript has a switch statement that is similar to that of Java. The form of this construct follows:

```
switch (expression) {
    case value_1:
        // statement(s)
    case value_2:
        // statement(s)
    ...
    [default:
        // statement(s)]
}
```

In any case segment, the statement(s) can be either a statement sequence or a compound statement.

The semantics of a switch construct are as follows: The expression is evaluated when the switch statement is reached in execution. The value is compared to the values in the cases in the construct (those values that immediately follow the case reserved words). If one matches, control is transferred to the statements immediately following that case value. Execution then continues through the remainder of the construct. In the great majority of situations, it is intended that only the statements in one case be executed in each execution of the construct. To implement this, a break statement appears as the last statement in each sequence of statements following a case. The break statement is exactly like the break statement in Java and C++. It transfers control out of the compound statement in which it appears.

The control expression of a switch statement could evaluate to a number, a string, or a Boolean value. Case labels also can be numbers, strings, or Booleans, and different case values can be of different types. Consider the following script, which includes a switch construct. The XHTML file that includes this script is very simple and thus is not shown.

```
// borders2.js
//    An example of a switch statement for table border
//    size selection

var bordersize;
bordersize = prompt("Select a table border size \n" +
                "0 (no border) \n" +
                "1 (1 pixel border) \n" +
                "4 (4 pixel border) \n" +
                "8 (8 pixel border) \n");
```

```javascript
switch (bordersize) {
  case "0": document.write("<table>");
            break;
  case "1": document.write("<table border = '1'>");
            break;
  case "4": document.write("<table border = '4'>");
            break;
  case "8": document.write("<table border = '8'>");
            break;
  default:  document.write("Error - invalid choice: ",
                            bordersize, "<br />");
}

document.write("<caption> 2007 NFL Divisional",
                " Winners </caption>");
document.write("<tr>",
                "<th />",
                "<th> American Conference </th>",
                "<th> National Conference </th>",
                "</tr>",
                "<tr>",
                "<th> East </th>",
                "<td> New England Patriots </td>",
                "<td> Dallas Cowboys </td>",
                "</tr>",
                "<tr>",
                "<th> North </th>",
                "<td> Pittsburgh Steelers </td>",
                "<td> Green Bay Packers </td>",
                "</tr>",
                "<tr>",
                "<th> West </th>",
                "<td> San Diego Chargers </td>",
                "<td> Seattle Seahawks </td>",
                "</tr>",
                "<tr>",
                "<th> South </th>",
                "<td> Indianapolis Colts </td>",
                "<td> Tampa Bay Buccaneers </td>",
                "</tr>",
                "</table>");
```

The entire table element is produced with `write`. Alternatively, we could have given all of the elements for the table, except the `<table>` and `</table>` tags, directly as XHTML in the XHTML document. Because `<table>` is in the content of the script element, the validator would not see it. Therefore, the `</table>` tag would also need to be hidden.

Browser displays of the prompt dialog box and the output of `borders2.js` are shown in Figures 4.6 and 4.7, respectively.

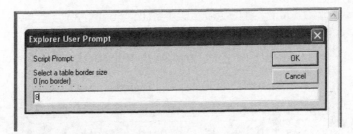

Figure 4.6 Dialog box from `borders2.js`

	American Conference	National Conference
East	New England Patriots	Dallas Cowboys
North	Pittsburgh Steelers	Green Bay Packers
West	San Diego Chargers	Seattle Seahawks
South	Indianapolis Colts	Tampa Bay Buccaneers

2007 NFL Divisional Winners

Figure 4.7 Display of `borders2.js`

4.6.4   Loop Statements

The JavaScript `while` and `for` statements are similar to those of Java and C++. The general form of the `while` statement is as follows:

```
while (control expression)
    statement or compound statement
```

The general form of the `for` statement is as follows:

```
for (initial expression; control expression; increment expression)
    statement or compound statement
```

Both the initial expression and the increment expression of the `for` statement can be multiple expressions, separated by commas. The initial expression of a `for` statement can include variable declarations. Such variables are visible in the entire script unless the `for` statement is in a function definition, in which case the variable is visible in the whole function. The following illustrates a simple `for` construct:

```
var sum = 0,
    count;
for (count = 0; count <= 10; count++)
    sum += count;
```

The following is an example that illustrates the `Date` object and a simple `for` loop:

```javascript
// date.js
//   Illustrates the use of the Date object by
//   displaying the parts of a current date and
//   using two Date objects to time a calculation

// Get the current date
var today = new Date();

// Fetch the various parts of the date
var dateString = today.toLocaleString();
var day = today.getDay();
var month = today.getMonth();
var year = today.getFullYear();
var timeMilliseconds = today.getTime();
var hour = today.getHours();
var minute = today.getMinutes();
var second = today.getSeconds();
var millisecond = today.getMilliseconds();

// Display the parts
document.write(
  "Date: " + dateString + "<br />",
  "Day: " + day + "<br />",
  "Month: " + month + "<br />",
  "Year: " + year + "<br />",
  "Time in milliseconds: " + timeMilliseconds + "<br />",
  "Hour: " + hour + "<br />",
  "Minute: " + minute + "<br />",
  "Second: " + second + "<br />",
  "Millisecond: " + millisecond + "<br />");
```

```
// Time a loop
var dum1 = 1.00149265, product = 1;
var start = new Date();

for (var count = 0; count < 10000; count++)
  product = product + 1.000002 * dum1 / 1.00001;

var end = new Date();
var diff = end.getTime() - start.getTime();
document.write("<br />The loop took " + diff +
               " milliseconds <br />");
```

A display of `date.js` is shown in Figure 4.8.

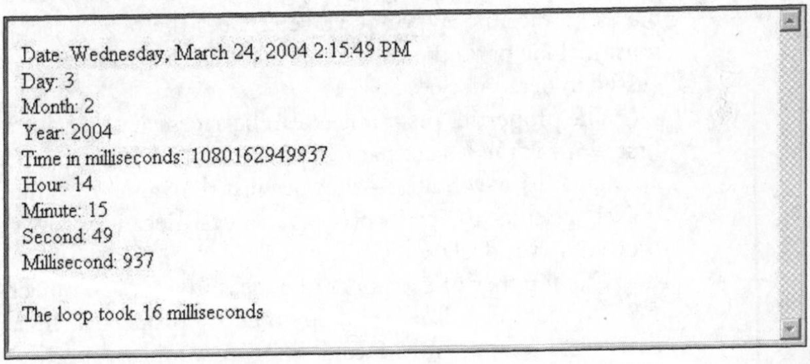

```
Date: Wednesday, March 24, 2004 2:15:49 PM
Day: 3
Month: 2
Year: 2004
Time in milliseconds: 1080162949937
Hour: 14
Minute: 15
Second: 49
Millisecond: 937

The loop took 16 milliseconds
```

Figure 4.8 Display of `date.js`

In addition to the `while` and `for` loop statements, JavaScript also has a `do-while` statement, whose form is as follows:

do *statement or compound statement*
while (*control expression*)

The `do-while` statement is related to the `while` statement, but the test for completion is logically (and physically) at the end rather than at the beginning of the loop construct. The body of a `do-while` construct is always executed at least once. The following is an example of a `do-while` construct:

```
do {
    count++;
    sum = sum + (sum * count);
} while (count <= 50);
```

JavaScript includes one more loop statement, the `for-in` statement, which is most often used with objects. The `for-in` statement is discussed in Section 4.7.

4.7 Object Creation and Modification

Objects are often created with a `new` expression, which must include a call to a constructor method. The constructor that is called in the `new` expression creates the properties that characterize the new object. In an object-oriented language such as Java, the `new` operator creates a particular object, meaning an object with a type and a specific collection of members. Thus, in Java, the constructor initializes members but does not create them. In JavaScript, however, the `new` operator creates a blank object, or one with no properties. Furthermore, JavaScript objects do not have types. The constructor both creates and initializes the properties.

The following statement creates an object that has no properties:

```
var my_object = new Object();
```

In this case, the called constructor is that of `Object`, which endows the new object with no properties, although it does have access to some inherited methods. The variable `my_object` references the new object. Calls to constructors must include parentheses, even if there are no parameters. Constructors are discussed in detail in Section 4.11.

The properties of an object can be accessed using dot notation, in which the first word is the object name and the second is the property name. Properties are not actually variables—they are just the names of values. They are used with object variables to access property values. Because properties are not variables, they are never declared.

The number of members of a class in a typical object-oriented language is fixed at compile time. The number of properties in a JavaScript object is dynamic. At any time during interpretation, properties can be added to or deleted from an object. A property for an object is created by assigning a value to that property. Consider the following example:

```
// Create an Object object
var my_car = new Object();
// Create and initialize the make property
my_car.make = "Ford";
// Create and initialize model
my_car.model = "Contour SVT";
```

This code creates a new object, `my_car`, with two properties, `make` and `model`.

There is an abbreviated way to create an object and its properties. For example, the object referenced with `my_car` above could be created with the following statement:

```
var my_car = {make: "Ford", model: "Contour SVT"};
```

Notice that this statement includes neither the `new` operator nor the call to the `Object` constructor.

Because objects can be nested, you can create a new object that is a property of `my_car` with properties of its own as follows:

```
my_car.engine = new Object();
my_car.engine.config = "V6";
my_car.engine.hp = 200;
```

Properties can be accessed in two ways. First, any property can be accessed in the same way it is assigned a value, using the object-dot-property notation. Second, the property names of an object can be accessed as if they were elements of an array, using the property name (as a string literal) as a subscript. For example, consider the following statements:

```
var prop1 = my_car.make;
var prop2 = my_car["make"];
```

After executing these two statements, the variables `prop1` and `prop2` both have the value `"Ford"`.

If an attempt is made to access a property of an object that does not exist, the value `undefined` is used. A property can be deleted with `delete`, as in the following example:

```
delete my_car.model;
```

JavaScript has a loop statement, `for-in`, that is perfect for listing the properties of an object. The form of `for-in` is as follows:

for (*identifier* in *object*)
  statement or compound statement

Consider the following example:

```
for (var prop in my_car)
  document.write("Name: ", prop, "; Value: ",
                 my_car[prop], "<br />");
```

The variable, `prop`, takes on the values of the properties of the `my_car` object, one for each iteration. So, this code lists all of the values of the properties of `my_car`.

4.8 Arrays

In JavaScript, arrays are objects that have some special functionality. Array elements can be primitive values or references to other objects, including other arrays. JavaScript arrays have dynamic lengths.

4.8.1 Array Object Creation

`Array` objects, unlike most other JavaScript objects, can be created in two distinct ways. The usual way to create any object is with the `new` operator and a call to a constructor. In the case of arrays, the constructor is named `Array`:

```
var my_list = new Array(1, 2, "three", "four");
var your_list = new Array(100);
```

In the first declaration, an `Array` object of length 4 is created and initialized. Notice that the elements of an array need not have the same type. In the second declaration, a new `Array` object of length 100 is created, without actually creating any elements. Whenever a call to the `Array` constructor has a single parameter, that parameter is taken to be the number of elements, not the initial value of a one-element array.

The second way to create an `Array` object is with a literal array value, which is a list of values enclosed in brackets:

```
var my_list_2 = [1, 2, "three", "four"];
```

The array `my_list_2` has the same values as the `Array` object `my_list` created previously with new.

4.8.2   Characteristics of `Array` Objects

The lowest index of every JavaScript array is zero. Array element access is specified with numeric subscript expressions placed in brackets. The length of an array is the highest subscript to which a value has been assigned, plus 1. For example, if `my_list` is an array with four elements and the following statement is executed, the new length of `my_list` will be 48.

```
my_list[47] = 2222;
```

The length of an array is both read- and write-accessible through the `length` property, which is added to every array object by the `Array` constructor. Consequently, the length of an array can be set to whatever you like by assigning the `length` property as follows:

```
my_list.length = 1002;
```

Now, the length of `my_list` is 1002, regardless of what it was previously. Assigning a value to the `length` property can lengthen, shorten, or not affect the array's length (if the value assigned happens to be the same as the previous length of the array).

So, an array can be made to grow by setting its `length` property to a larger value; one can be made to shrink by setting its `length` property to a smaller value.

Only the assigned elements of an array actually occupy space. For example, if it is convenient to use the subscript range of 100 to 150 (but not 0 to 99), an array of length 151 can be created. But if only the elements indexed 100 to 150 are assigned values, the array will require the space of 51 elements, not 151. The `length` property of an array is not necessarily the number of allocated elements. For example, the following statement sets the `length` property of `new_list` to 1002, but `new_list` may have no elements that have values or occupy space:

```
new_list.length = 1002;
```

To support JavaScript's dynamic arrays, all array elements are allocated dynamically from the heap. Assigning a value to an array element that did not previously exist creates that element.

The following example, `insert_names.js`, illustrates JavaScript arrays. This script has an array of names, which are in alphabetical order. It uses `prompt` to get new names, one at a time, and inserts them into the existing array. Our approach is to move elements down one at a time, starting at the end of the array, until the correct position for the new name is found. Then the new name is inserted, and the new array is displayed. Notice that each new name

```javascript
// insert_names.js
//    This script has an array of names, name_list,
//    whose values are in alphabetical order. New
//    names are input through a prompt. Each new
//    name is inserted into the name_list array,
//    after which the new list is displayed.

// The original list of names
var name_list = new Array("Al", "Betty", "Kasper",
                            "Michael", "Roberto", "Zimbo");
var new_name, index, last;

// Loop to get a new name and insert it
while (new_name =
        prompt("Please type a new name", "")) {
  last = name_list.length - 1;

// Loop to find the place for the new name
  while (last >= 0 && name_list[last] > new_name) {
    name_list[last + 1] = name_list[last];
    last--;
  }

// Insert the new name into its spot in the array
  name_list[last + 1] = new_name;

// Display the new array
  document.write("<p><b>The new name list is:</b> ",
                "<br />");
  for (index = 0; index < name_list.length; index++)
    document.write(name_list[index], "<br />");
  document.write("</p>");
} //** end of the outer while loop
```

causes the array to grow by one element. This is caused by assigning a value to the element following what was the last allocated element.

4.8.3 Array Methods

`Array` objects have a collection of useful methods, most of which are described here. The `join` method converts all of the elements of an array to strings and catenates them into a single string. If no parameter is provided to `join`, the values in the new string are separated by commas. If a string parameter is provided, it is used as the element separator. Consider the following example:

```
var names = new Array["Mary", "Murray", "Murphy", "Max"];
...
var name_string = names.join(" : ");
```

The value of `name_string` is now `"Mary : Murray : Murphy : Max"`.

The `reverse` method does what you would expect: It reverses the order of the elements of the `Array` object through which it is called.

The `sort` method coerces the elements of the array to strings, if they are not already strings, and sorts them alphabetically. For example consider the following statement:

```
names.sort();
```

The value of `names` is now `["Mary", "Max", "Murphy", "Murray"]`. Section 4.9.4 discusses the use of `sort` for different orders and for nonstring elements.

The `concat` method catenates its actual parameters to the end of the `Array` object on which it is called. Consider the following code:

```
var names = new Array["Mary", "Murray", "Murphy", "Max"];
...
var new_names = names.concat("Moo", "Meow");
```

The `new_names` array now has length 6, with the elements of `names`, along with `"Moo"` and `"Meow"` as its fifth and sixth elements.

The `slice` method does for arrays what the `substring` method does for strings. It returns the part of the `Array` object specified by its parameters, which are used as subscripts. The returned array has the elements of the `Array` object through which it is called from the first parameter up to, but not including the second parameter. For example, consider the following:

```
var list = [2, 4, 6, 8, 10];
...
var list2 = list.slice(1, 3);
```

The value of `list2` is now `[4, 6]`. If `slice` is given just one parameter, the returned array has all of the elements of the object, starting with the specified index. Consider the following example:

```
var list = ["Bill", "Will", "Jill", "dill"];
...
var listette = list.slice(2);
```

The value of listette is ["Jill", "dill"].

When the toString method is called through an Array object, each of the elements of the object is converted (if necessary) to a string. These strings are catenated, separated by commas. So, for Array objects, the toString method behaves much like join.

The push, pop, unshift, and shift methods of Array allow the easy implementation of stacks and queues in arrays. The pop and push methods remove and add an element to the high end of an array, respectively. For example, consider the following code:

```
var list = ["Dasher", "Dancer", "Donner", "Blitzen"];
var deer = list.pop();     // deer is "Blitzen"
list.push("Blitzen");
  // This puts "Blitzen" back on list
```

The shift and unshift methods remove and add an element to the beginning of an array, respectively. For example, assume that list is created as previously and consider the following code:

```
var deer = list.shift(); // deer is now "Dasher"
list.unshift("Dasher");  // This puts "Dasher" back on list
```

A two-dimensional array is implemented in JavaScript as an array of arrays. This can be done with the new operator or with nested array literals, as shown in the script nested_arrays.js:

```
// nested_arrays.js
//   An example illustrating an array of arrays

// Create an array object with three arrays as its elements
var nested_array = [[2, 4, 6], [1, 3, 5], [10, 20, 30]
                   ];

// Display the elements of nested_list
for (var row = 0; row <= 2; row++) {
  document.write("Row ", row, ":  ");

  for (var col = 0; col <=2; col++)
    document.write(nested_array[row][col], " ");

  document.write("<br />");
}
```

Figure 4.9 shows a browser display of `nested_arrays.js`.

```
Row 0: 2 4 6
Row 1: 1 3 5
Row 2: 10 20 30
```

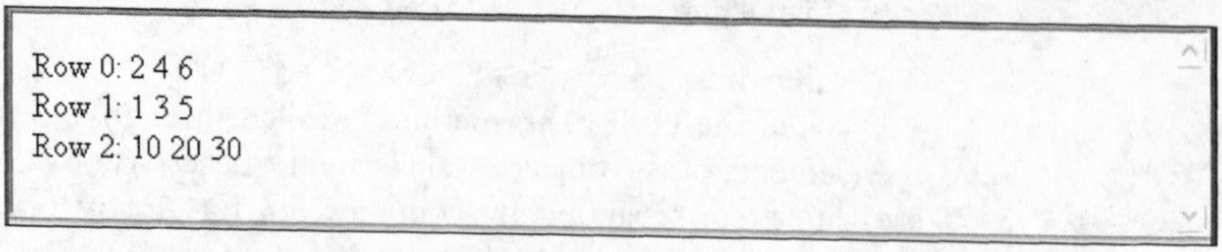

Figure 4.9 Display of `nested_arrays.js`

4.9 Functions

JavaScript functions are similar to those of other C-based languages such as C and C++. This section describes these functions.

4.9.1 Fundamentals

A *function definition* consists of the function's header and a compound statement that describes its actions. This compound statement is called the *body* of the function. A function *header* consists of the reserved word `function`, the function's name, and a parenthesized list of parameters, if there are any. The parentheses are required, even if there are no parameters.

A `return` statement returns control from the function in which it appears to the function's caller. Optionally, it includes an expression, whose value is returned to the caller. A function body may include one or more `return` statements. If there are no `return` statements in a function, or if the specific `return` that is executed does not include an expression, the returned value is `undefined`. This is also the case if execution reaches the end of the function body without executing a `return` statement (which is legal).

Syntactically, a call to a function with no parameters is the function's name followed by an empty pair of parentheses. A call to a function that returns `undefined` is a standalone statement. A call to a function that returns a useful value appears as the operand in an expression (often the whole right side of an assignment statement). For example, if `fun1` is a parameterless function that returns `undefined`, and if `fun2`, which also has no parameters, returns a useful value, they can be called with the following code:

```
fun1();
result = fun2();
```

JavaScript functions are objects, so variables that reference them can be treated as other object references. They can be passed as parameters, assigned to other variables, and be the elements of an array. Consider the following example:

```
function fun() { document.write(
              "This surely is fun! <br/>");}
```

```
ref_fun = fun;      // Now, ref_fun refers to the fun object
fun();              // A call to fun
ref_fun();          // Also a call to fun
```

Because JavaScript functions are objects, their references can be properties in other objects, in which case they act as methods.

To ensure that the interpreter sees the definition of a function before it sees a call to the function, which is required in JavaScript, function definitions are placed in the head of an XHTML document (either explicitly or implicitly). Normally, but not always, calls to functions appear in the document body.

4.9.2 Local Variables

The *scope* of a variable is the range of statements over which it is visible. When JavaScript is embedded in an XHTML document, the scope of a variable is the range of lines of the document over which the variable is visible.

A variable that is not declared with a `var` statement is implicitly declared by the JavaScript interpreter at the time it is first encountered in the script. Variables that are implicitly declared, even if the implicit declaration occurs within a function definition, have *global scope*—that is, they are visible in the entire XHTML document (or entire file if the script is in its own file). Variables that are explicitly declared outside function definitions also have global scope. As stated earlier, we recommend that all variables be explicitly declared.

It is usually best for variables that are used only within a function to have *local scope*, meaning that they are visible and can be used only within the body of the function. Any variable explicitly declared with `var` in the body of a function has local scope.

If a variable that is defined both as a local variable and as a global variable appears in a function, the local variable has precedence, effectively hiding the global variable with the same name. This is the advantage of local variables: When you make up their names, you need not be concerned that a global variable with the same name may exist somewhere in the collection of scripts in the XHTML document.

Although JavaScript function definitions can be nested, the need for nested functions in client-side JavaScript is minimal. Furthermore, they can greatly complicate scripts. Therefore, we do not recommend the use of nested functions and do not discuss them.

4.9.3 Parameters

The parameter values that appear in a call to a function are called *actual parameters*. The parameter names that appear in the header of a function definition, which correspond to the actual parameters in calls to the function, are called *formal parameters*. JavaScript uses the pass-by-value parameter-passing method. When a function is called, the values of the actual parameters specified in the call are, in effect, copied into their corresponding formal parameters, which behave exactly like local variables. Because references are passed as the actual parameters for objects, the function has access to the objects and can change them, thereby providing the semantics of pass-by-reference parameters. However, if a reference to an object is passed to a function and the function changes its corresponding formal parameter (rather than the object to which it points), it has no affect on the actual parameter. For example, suppose an array is passed as a parameter to a function, as in the following:

```
function fun1(my_list) {
  var list2 = new Array(1, 3, 5);
  my_list[3] = 14;
  ...
  my_list = list2;
  ...
}
...
var list = new Array(2, 4, 6, 8)
fun1(list);
```

The first assignment to `my_list` in `fun1` changes the object to which `my_list` refers, which was created in the calling code. However, the second assignment to `my_list` changes it to refer to a different array object. This does not change the actual parameter in the caller.

Because of JavaScript's dynamic typing, there is no type checking of parameters. The called function can itself check the types of parameters with the `typeof` operator. However, recall that `typeof` cannot distinguish between different objects. The number of parameters in a function call is not checked against the number of formal parameters in the called function. In the function, excess actual parameters that are passed are ignored; excess formal parameters are set to `undefined`.

All parameters are communicated through a property array, `arguments`, which, like other array objects, has a property named `length`. By accessing `arguments.length`, a function can determine the number of actual parameters that were passed. Because the `arguments` array is accessible directly, all actual parameters specified in the call are available, including actual parameters that do not correspond to any formal parameters (because there were more actual parameters than formal parameters). Consider the following example:

```
// params.js
//   The params function and a test driver for it.
//   This example illustrates a variable number of
//   function parameters

// Function params
// Parameters: A variable number of parameters
```

```
// Returns: nothing
// Displays its parameters
function params(a, b) {
  document.write("Function params was passed ",
      arguments.length, " parameter(s) <br />");
  document.write("Parameter values are: <br />");

  for (var arg = 0; arg < arguments.length; arg++)
    document.write(arguments[arg], "<br />");

  document.write("<br />");
}

// A test driver for function params
params("Mozart");
params("Mozart", "Beethoven");
params("Mozart", "Beethoven", "Tchaikowsky");
```

Figure 4.10 shows a browser display of params.js.

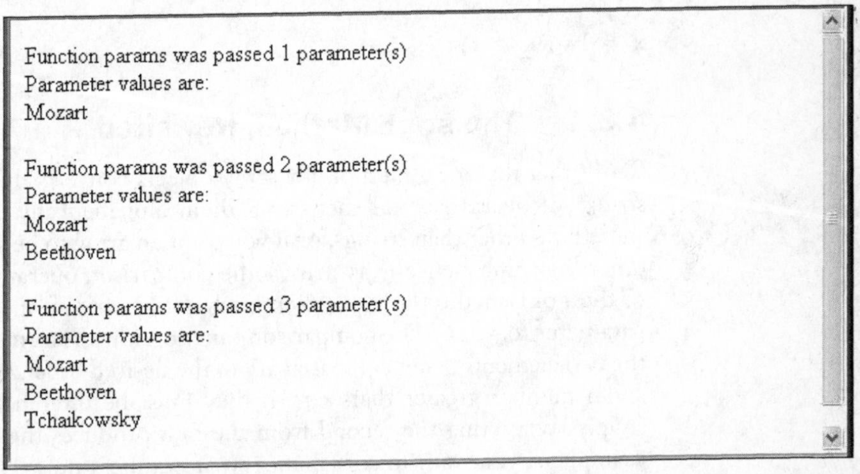

Function params was passed 1 parameter(s)
Parameter values are:
Mozart

Function params was passed 2 parameter(s)
Parameter values are:
Mozart
Beethoven

Function params was passed 3 parameter(s)
Parameter values are:
Mozart
Beethoven
Tchaikowsky

Figure 4.10 Display of params.js

There is no elegant way in JavaScript to pass a primitive value by reference. One inelegant way is to put the value in an array and pass the array. This works because arrays are objects. For example, consider the following script:

```
// Function by10
//      Parameter: a number, passed as the first element
//                 of an array
```

```
// Returns: nothing
// Effect: multiplies the parameter by 10

function by10(a) {
    a[0] *= 10;
}
...
var x;
var listx = new Array(1);
...
listx[0] = x;
by10(listx);
x = listx[0];
```

Another way to have a function change the value of a primitive type actual parameter is to have the function return the new value as follows:

```
function by10_2(a) {
    return 10 * a;
}
...
var x;
...
x = by10_2(x);
```

4.9.4   The sort Method, Revisited

Recall that the sort method for array objects converts the array's elements to strings, if necessary, and then sorts them alphabetically. If you need to sort something other than strings, or if you want an array to be sorted in some order other than alphabetically as strings, the comparison operation must be supplied to the sort method by the caller. Such a comparison operation is passed as a parameter to sort. The comparison function must return a negative number if the two elements being compared are in the desired order, zero if they are equal, and a number greater than zero if they must be interchanged. For numbers, simply subtracting the second from the first produces the required result. For example, if you want to sort the array of numbers num_list into descending order using the sort method, you could use the following:

```
// Function num_order
// Parameter: Two numbers
// Returns: If the first parameter belongs before the
//          second in descending order, a negative number
//          If the two parameters are equal, 0
//          If the two parameters must be
//          interchanged, a positive number
function num_order(a, b) {return b - a;}
```

```
// Sort the array of numbers, list, into
// ascending order
  num_list.sort(num_order);
```

Rather than defining a comparison function elsewhere and passing its name, the function definition can appear as the actual parameter in the call to sort. This is shown in the script in Section 4.10.

4.10 An Example

The following is an example of an XHTML document containing a JavaScript function to compute the median of an array of numbers. The function first sorts the array using the sort method. If the given array has an odd length, the median is the middle element. The middle element is determined by dividing the length by 2 and truncating the result using floor. If the length is even, the median is the average of the two middle elements. The result of the average computation is rounded to an integer using round.

```
// medians.js
//    A function and a function tester
//    Illustrates array operations

// Function median
//    Parameter: An array of numbers
//    Result: The median of the array
//    Return value: none
function median(list) {
  list.sort(function (a, b) {return a - b;});
  var list_len = list.length;

// Use the modulus operator to determine whether
//    the array's length is odd or even
// Use Math.floor to truncate numbers
// Use Math.round to round numbers
  if ((list_len % 2) == 1)
    return list[Math.floor(list_len / 2)];
  else
    return Math.round((list[list_len / 2 - 1] +
                       list[list_len / 2]) / 2);
} // end of function median

// Test driver
var my_list_1 = [8, 3, 9, 1, 4, 7];
var my_list_2 = [10, -2, 0, 5, 3, 1, 7];
```

```
var med = median(my_list_1);
document.write("Median of [", my_list_1, "] is: ",
               med, "<br />");
med = median(my_list_2);
document.write("Median of [", my_list_2, "] is: ",
               med, "<br />");
```

Figure 4.11 shows a browser display of medians.js.

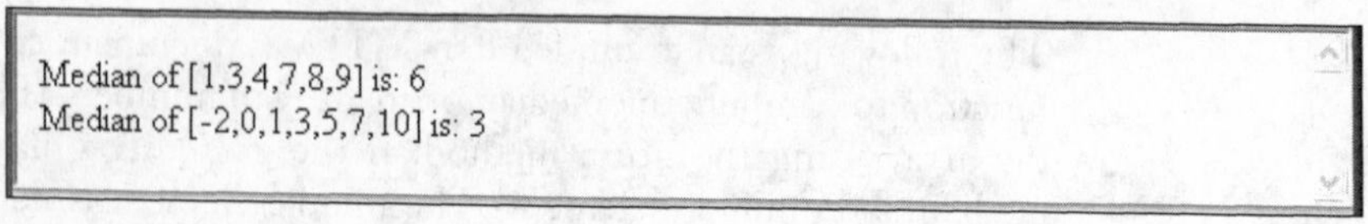

Median of [1,3,4,7,8,9] is: 6
Median of [-2,0,1,3,5,7,10] is: 3

Figure 4.11 Display of medians.js

One significant side effect of the median function is that it leaves the given array in ascending order. This may not always be acceptable. If not, the array could be moved to a local array in median before the sorting operation.

Notice that this script uses Math.floor to determine the median of an odd-length list. If the list subscripts began at 1, this would be wrong; because they begin at 0, it is correct.

4.11 Constructors

JavaScript constructors are special methods that create and initialize the properties for newly created objects. Every new expression must include a call to a constructor, whose name is the same as that of the object being created. As you saw in Section 4.8, for example, the constructor for arrays is named Array. Constructors are actually called by the new operator, which immediately precedes them in the new expression.

Obviously, a constructor must be able to reference the object on which it is to operate. JavaScript has a predefined reference variable for this purpose, named this. When the constructor is called, this is a reference to the newly created object. The this variable is used to construct and initialize the properties of the object. For example, consider the following constructor:

```
function car(new_make, new_model, new_year) {
    this.make = new_make;
    this.model = new_model;
    this.year = new_year;
}
```

This constructor could be used as in the following:

```
my_car = new car("Ford", "Contour SVT", "2000");
```

So far, we have considered only data properties. If a method is to be included in the object, it is initialized the same way as if it were a data property. For example, suppose you wanted a method for `car` objects that listed the property values. A function that could serve as such a method could be written as follows:

```
function display_car() {
    document.write("Car make: ", this.make, "<br/>");
    document.write("Car model: ", this.model, "<br/>");
    document.write("Car year: ", this.year, "<br/>");
}
```

The following line must be added to the `car` constructor:

```
this.display = display_car;
```

Now, the code `my_car.display();` would produce the following:

```
Car make: Ford
Car model: Contour SVT
Car year: 2000
```

The collection of objects created using the same constructor is related to the concept of class in an object-oriented programming language. All such objects have the same set of properties and methods, at least initially. These objects can diverge from each other through user code changes. Furthermore, there is no convenient way to determine in the script whether two objects have the same set of properties and methods.

4.12 Pattern Matching Using Regular Expressions

JavaScript has powerful pattern-matching capabilities based on regular expressions. There are two approaches to pattern matching in JavaScript: one that is based on the `RegExp` object and one that is based on methods of the `String` object. The regular expressions used by these two approaches are the same. They are based on the regular expressions of the Perl programing language. This book covers only the `String` methods for pattern matching.

As stated previously, patterns are specified in a form that is based on regular expressions, which were developed to define members of a simple class of formal languages. Elaborate and complex patterns can be used to describe specific strings or categories of strings. Patterns, which are sent as parameters to the pattern-matching methods, are delimited with slashes.

The simplest pattern-matching method is `search`, which takes a pattern as a parameter. The `search` method returns the position in the `String` object (through which it is called) where the pattern matched. If there is no match, `search` returns –1. Most characters are normal, which means that in a pattern they match themselves. The position of the first character in the string is 0. For example, consider the following:

```
var str = "Rabbits are furry";
var position = str.search(/bits/);
if (position >= 0)
    document.write("'bits' appears in position", position,
                    "<br />");
else
    document.write("'bits' does not appear in str <br />");
```

The output of this code is as follows:

```
'bits' appears in position 3
```

4.12.1 Character and Character-Class Patterns

The "normal" characters are those that are not metacharacters. Metacharacters are characters that have special meanings in some contexts in patterns. The following are the pattern metacharacters:

```
\ | ( ) [ ] { } ^ $ * + ? .
```

Metacharacters can themselves be matched by being immediately preceded by a backslash.

A period matches any character except newline. So, the following pattern matches "snowy", "snowe", and "snowd", among others:

```
/snow./
```

To match a period in a string, the period must be backslashed in the pattern. For example, the pattern `/3\.4/` matches `3.4`. The pattern `/3.4/` would match `3.4` and `374`, among others.

It is often convenient to be able to specify classes of characters rather than individual characters. Such classes are defined by placing the desired characters in brackets. Dashes can appear in class definitions, making it easy to specify sequences of characters. For example, the following character class matches 'a', 'b', or 'c':

```
[abc]
```

The following character class matches any lowercase letter from 'a' to 'h':

```
[a-h]
```

If a circumflex character (^) is the first character in a class, it inverts the specified set. For example, the following character class matches any character except the letters 'a', 'e', 'i', 'o', and 'u':

```
[^aeiou]
```

Because they are frequently used, some character classes are predefined and can be specified by their names. These are shown in Table 4.8, which gives the names of the classes, their literal definitions as character classes, and descriptions of what they match.

Table 4.8 Predefined character classes

Name	Equivalent Pattern	Matches
\d	[0-9]	A digit
\D	[^0-9]	Not a digit
\w	[A-Za-z_0-9]	A word character (alphanumeric)
\W	[^A-Za-z_0-9]	Not a word character
\s	[\r\t\n\f]	A whitespace character
\S	[^ \r\t\n\f]	Not a whitespace character

Consider the following examples of patterns that use predefined character classes:

```
/\d\.\d\d/      // Matches a digit, followed by a period,
                // followed by two digits
/\D\d\D/        // Matches a single digit
/\w\w\w/        // Matches three adjacent word characters
```

In many cases, it is convenient to be able to repeat a part of a pattern, often a character or character class. To repeat a pattern, a numeric quantifier, delimited by braces, is attached. For example, the following pattern matches xyyyyz:

```
/xy{4}z/
```

There are also three symbolic quantifiers: asterisk (*), plus (+), and question mark (?). An asterisk means zero or more repetitions, a plus sign means one or more repetitions, and a question mark means one or none. For example, the following pattern matches strings that begin with any number of x's (including zero), followed by one or more y's, possibly followed by z:

```
/x*y+z?/
```

The quantifiers are often used with the predefined character class names, as in the following pattern, which matches a string of one or more digits followed by a decimal point and possibly more digits:

```
/\d+\.\d*/
```

As another example, consider the following pattern:

```
/[A-Za-z]\w*/
```

This pattern matches the identifiers in some programming languages (a letter, followed by zero or more letters, digits, or underscores).

There is one additional named pattern that is often useful. This is \b (boundary), which matches the boundary position between a word character (\w) and a nonword character (\W), in either order. For example, the following pattern matches "A tulip is a flower" but not "A frog isn't":

```
/\bis\b/
```

It does not match the second string because the 'is' is followed by another word character (n).

The boundary pattern is different from the named character classes in that it does not match a character; it matches a position between two characters.

4.12.2 Anchors

Frequently, it is useful to be able to specify that a pattern must match at a particular position in a string. The most common example of this is requiring a pattern to match at one specific end of the string. A pattern is tied to a string position with an anchor. A pattern can be specified to match only at the beginning of the string by preceding it with a circumflex (^) anchor. For example, the following pattern matches "pearls are pretty" but does not match "My pearls are pretty":

```
/^pearl/
```

A pattern can be specified to match at the end of a string only by following the pattern with a dollar sign anchor. For example, the following pattern matches "I like gold" but does not match "golden":

```
/gold$/
```

Anchor characters are like boundary-named patterns. They do not match specific characters in the string; rather, they match positions before, between, or after characters. When a circumflex appears in a pattern at a position other than the beginning of the pattern or at the beginning of a character class, it has no special meaning (it matches itself). Likewise, if a dollar sign appears in a pattern at a position other than the end of the pattern, it has no special meaning.

4.12.3 Pattern Modifiers

Modifiers can be attached to patterns to change how they are used, thereby increasing their flexibility. The modifiers are specified as letters just after the right delimiter of the pattern. The i modifier makes the letters in the pattern match either uppercase or lowercase letters in the string. For example, the pattern /Apple/i matches 'APPLE', 'apple', 'APPle', and any other combination of uppercase and lowercase spellings of the word "apple."

The x modifier allows whitespace to appear in the pattern. Because comments are considered whitespace, this provides a way to include explanatory comments in the pattern. For example:

```
/\d+           # The street number
\s             # The space before the street name
[A-Z][a-z]+    # The street name
/x
```

This pattern is equivalent to the following:

```
/\d+\s[A-Z][a-z]+/
```

4.12.4 Other Pattern-Matching Methods of String

The replace method is used to replace substrings of the String object that match the given pattern. The replace method takes two parameters: the pattern and the replacement string. The g modifier can be attached to the pattern if the replacement is to be global in the string, in which case the replacement is done for every match in the string. The matched substrings of the string are made available through the predefined variables $1, $2, and so on. For example, consider the following statements:

```
var str = "Fred, Freddie, and Frederica were siblings";
str.replace(/Fre/g, "Boy");
```

In this example, str is set to "Boyd, Boyddie, and Boyderica were siblings", and $1, $2, and $3 are all set to "Fre".

The match method is the most general of the String pattern-matching methods. The match method takes a single parameter, a pattern. It returns an array of the results of the pattern-matching operation. If the pattern has the g modifier, the returned array has all of the substrings of the string that matched. If the pattern does not include the g modifier, the following returned array has the match as its first element, and the remainder of the array has the matches of parenthesized parts of the pattern, if there are any:

```
var str =
  "Having 4 apples is better than having 3 oranges";
var matches = str.match(/\d/g);
```

In this example, matches is set to [4, 3].

Now consider a pattern that has parenthesized subexpressions.

```
var str = "I have 428 dollars, but I need 500";
var matches = str.match(/(\d+)([^\d]+)(\d+)/);
document.write(matches, "<br />");
```

The following is the value of the matches array after this code is interpreted:

```
["428 dollars, but I need 500", "428",
"dollars, but I need ", "500"]
```

In this result array, the first element, `"428 dollars, but I need 500"`, is the match; the second, third, and fourth elements are the parts of the string that matched the parenthesized parts of the pattern, `(\d+)`, `([^\d]+)`, and `(\d+)`.

The `split` method of `String` splits its object string into substrings, based on a given string or pattern. The substrings are returned in an array. For example, consider the following code:

```
var str = "grapes:apples:oranges";
var fruit = str.split(":");
```

In this example, `fruit` is set to `[grapes, apples, oranges]`.

As mentioned at the beginning of this section, there is a second way to do pattern matching in JavaScript. A pattern can be a `RegExp` object, in which case the methods of that object are used and the string on which the pattern is to be matched is sent as the parameter to the method. The use of `RegExp` objects for pattern matching is not discussed in this book.

4.13 Another Example

One of the common uses for JavaScript is to check the format of input from XHTML forms, which is discussed in detail in Chapter 5. The following example illustrates the use of a simple function to check a given string that is supposed to contain a phone number to determine whether its format is correct. The function uses a simple pattern match to check the phone number.

```javascript
// forms_check.js
//    A function tst_phone_num is defined and tested.
//    This function checks the validity of phone
//    number input from a form

// Function tst_phone_num
//    Parameter: A string
//    Result: Returns true if the parameter has the form of a legal
//            seven-digit phone number (3 digits, a dash, 4 digits)

function tst_phone_num(num) {

// Use a simple pattern to check the number of digits and the dash
  var ok = num.search(/^\d{3}-\d{4}$/);

  if (ok == 0)
    return true;
  else
    return false;
```

```
}   // end of function tst_phone_num

// A script to test tst_phone_num
var tst = tst_phone_num("444-5432");
if (tst)
  document.write("444-5432 is a legal phone number <br />");
else
  document.write("Error in tst_phone_num <br />");

tst = tst_phone_num("444-r432");
if (tst)
  document.write("Program error <br />");
else
  document.write(
            "444-r432 is not a legal phone number <br />");

tst = tst_phone_num("44-1234");
if (tst)
  document.write("Program error <br />");
else
  document.write("44-1234 is not a legal phone number <br /");
```

Figure 4.12 shows a browser display of `forms_check.js`.

444-5432 is a legal phone number
444-r432 is not a legal phone number
44-1234 is not a legal phone number

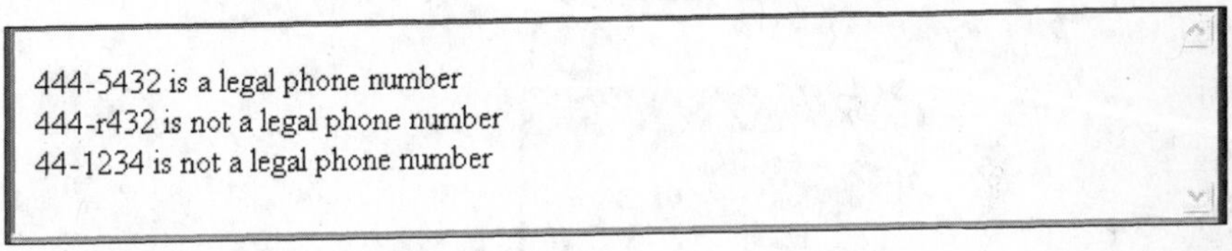

Figure 4.12 Display of `forms_check.js`

4.14 Errors in Scripts

The JavaScript interpreter is capable of detecting various errors in scripts. These are primarily syntax errors, although uses of undefined variables are also detected. Debugging a script is a bit different from debugging a program in a more typical programming language, mostly because errors that are detected by the JavaScript interpreter are found while the browser is attempting to display a document. In most cases, a script error causes the browser to not display the document and does not produce an error message. Without a diagnostic message, you must simply examine the code to find the problem. This is, of course, unacceptable for all but the smallest and simplest scripts. Fortunately, there are ways to get some debugging assistance.

The default settings for IE7 provide no debugging help for JavaScript. However, this can be changed as follows: Select *Internet Options* from the *Tools* menu and choose the *Advanced* tab there. This opens a window with a long list of checkboxes. Uncheck the *Disable script debugging* box and check the *Display a notification about every script error* box. Then press the *Apply* button in this window. Starting then and continuing until the browser is closed, JavaScript errors will cause the browser to open and display a small window with an explanation of the problem. For example, consider the following sample XHTML document:

```
// debugdemo.js
//    An example to illustrate debugging help

var row;
row = 0;

while(row != 4 {
  document.write("row is ", row, "<br />");
  row++;
}
```

Notice the syntax error in the `while` statement (missing right parenthesis). Figure 4.13 shows the browser display of what happens when an attempt is made to display `debugdemo.js`.

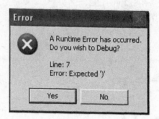

Figure 4.13 Display of `debugdemo.js` with Internet Explorer 7

The FX2 browser has a special console window that displays script errors. Select *Tools and Error Console* to open this window. When using this browser to display documents that include JavaScript, this window should be kept open. After an error message has appeared and has been used to fix a script, press the *Clear* button on the console. Otherwise, the old error message will remain there and possibly cause confusion about subsequent problems. An example of the FX2 JavaScript Console window is shown in Figure 4.14.

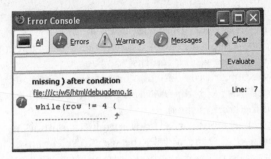

Figure 4.14 Display of the FireFox 2 error console

The more interesting and challenging programming problems are only detectable during execution or interpretation. For these problems, a debugger is used. Both IE7 and FX2 have debuggers for JavaScript.

The JavaScript debugger for FX2, which was produced by Mozilla and is named Venkman, is available at `http://www.mozilla.org/projects/venkman/`. Another JavaScript debugger, named Firebug, is available for FX2 at `https://addons.mozilla.org/en-US/firefox/addon/1843`. Firebug also includes a CSS debugger.

Summary

Client-side JavaScript scripts are embedded in XHTML files as the content of `<script>` tags. The `type` attribute of `<script>` must be set to `"text/javascript"`. A file containing a script can be included by specifying its name as the value of the `<script>` attribute `src`. The script itself must appear in a special XHTML comment.

Values in JavaScript are either primitives or objects. The primitive types are Number, String, Boolean, Undefined, and Null. Numbers are represented in double-precision floating-point format. The Number, String, and Boolean types have corresponding objects named `Number`, `String`, and `Boolean`, which act as wrapper objects. String literals can use either single or double quotes as delimiters.

JavaScript is dynamically typed, which is not the same as being a typeless language. Variables are typeless, but the values they reference are typed. The type of the value referenced by a variable can change every time a new value is assigned to the variable. It is best to declare all variables explicitly.

The `Number` object includes a collection of useful properties such as `MIN_VALUE` and `PI`. The `Math` object has many methods for commonly used operations on numbers, such as `round` and `cos`. The catenation operator, `+`, creates a new string by putting the two operand strings together. The `String` property `length` stores the number of characters in a string. There are `String` methods to return the character at a specified position in the string, the position of a specified character in the string, and a specified substring of the string. There are a large number of other `String` methods.

The `typeof` operator returns the type name of its operand if the operand is a primitive type; otherwise, it returns `"object"`.

The `Date` object provides the current time and date. It includes a large number of methods to produce various parts of time and date, such as the day of the week and the hour of the day.

The `alert` method of `Window` produces output in a dialog box. The `confirm` method of `Window` asks the user to select either an *OK* button or a *Cancel* button. The `prompt` method of `Window` asks the user for textual input. The `document.write` method dynamically produces XHTML content. The control statements of JavaScript are closely related to those of other common programming languages. Included is a `switch` statement.

Arrays in JavaScript are objects, as they are in Java. They have dynamic length. An `Array` object can be created in a `new` expression, which includes a call to the `Array` constructor, or by simply assigning an `Array` literal to a variable. `Array` literals are lists of values enclosed in brackets. Every `Array` object has a `length` property, which is both readable and writable. The property stores the number of elements in the array. `Array` objects have a collection of useful methods, among which are `join`, which joins the elements of an array in a string; `reverse`, which reverses the order of elements in an array; `sort`, which converts the elements of the array to strings and sorts them alphabetically; and `slice`, which returns a specified part of the array. The array methods `pop`, `push`, `shift`, and `unshift` were designed to implement stacks and queues in arrays.

Function definitions name their formal parameters, but do not include type names. All functions return values, but the type of the value is not specified in the function's definition. Variables declared in a function with `var` are local to that function. Parameters are passed by value, resulting in pass-by-value semantics for primitives and pass-by-reference semantics for objects. The `arguments` property stores the values of the passed parameters. Neither the types of the parameters nor the number of parameters are checked by the JavaScript interpreter.

The regular expressions used in the pattern-matching facilities of JavaScript are modeled on the regular expressions of Perl. Pattern matches are specified by one of the three methods—`search`, `replace`, or `match`—of the `String` object. The regular expressions, or patterns, are made up of special characters, normal characters, character classes, and operators. Patterns are delimited with slashes. Character classes are delimited with brackets. If a circumflex appears at the left end of a character class, it inverts the meaning of the characters in the class. Several of the most common character classes are predefined. Subpatterns can be followed by numeric or symbolic quantifiers. Patterns can be anchored at the left or right end of the string against which the pattern is being matched. The `search` method searches its object string for the pattern given as its parameter. The `replace` method replaces matches in its object string with its second parameter. The `match` method searches its object string for the given pattern and returns an array of all matches.

Review Questions

4.1 Describe the two ways to embed a JavaScript script in an XHTML document.

4.2 Describe briefly three major differences between Java and JavaScript.

4.3 What are the two categories of properties in JavaScript?

4.4 Describe briefly the basic process of event-driven computation.

4.5 Why does JavaScript have two categories of data variables, primitives and objects?

4.6 Describe briefly three major uses of JavaScript on the client side.

4.7 What are the two forms of JavaScript comments?

4.8 Why are JavaScript scripts sometimes hidden in XHTML documents by putting them in XHTML comments?

4.9 If the value `undefined` is used as a Boolean expression, is it interpreted as `true` or `false`?

4.10 What are the five primitive data types in JavaScript?

4.11 Do single-quoted string literals have any different characteristics than double-quoted string literals?

4.12 What purpose do rules of operator associativity serve in a programming language?

4.13 In what circumstances would a variable have the value `undefined`?

4.14 What purpose do rules of operator precedence serve in a programming language?

4.15 Describe the purpose and characteristics of `NaN`.

4.16 Why is `parseInt` not used more often?

4.17 What are the three possible forms of control expressions in JavaScript?

4.18 What value does `typeof` return for an object operand?

4.19 Describe the operation of the prompt method.

4.20 What is the usual end-of-line punctuation for the string operand to alert?

4.21 What is the usual end-of-line punctuation for the string operand to `document.write`?

4.22 What is a control construct?

4.23 What is the difference between == and ===?

4.24   What is the difference between a constructor in Java and one in JavaScript?

4.25   Explain what short-circuit evaluation of an expression means.

4.26   What is the difference between a `while` statement and a `do-while` statement?

4.27   When is a JavaScript constructor called?

4.28   What is the semantics of a `break` statement?

4.29   What properties does an object created with a `new` operator and the `Object` constructor have?

4.30   Describe the two ways an `Array` object can be created.

4.31   Describe the two ways the properties of an object can be referenced.

4.32   Describe the semantics of the `for-in` statement.

4.33   What relationship is there between the value of the `length` property of an `Array` object and the actual number of existing elements in the object?

4.34   Describe the semantics of the join method of `Array`.

4.35   What is the advantage of using local variables in functions?

4.36   Describe the semantics of the `slice` method when it is given just one parameter.

4.37   How is a new property of an object created?

4.38   What value is returned by a function that contains no `return` statement?

4.39   Define the scope of a variable in a JavaScript script embedded in an XHTML document when the variable is not declared in a function.

4.40   What is the form of a nested array literal?

4.41   Is it possible to reference global variables in a JavaScript function?

4.42   What parameter-passing method does JavaScript use?

4.43   Does JavaScript check the types of actual parameters against the types of their corresponding formal parameters?

4.44   Describe the two end-of-line anchors.

4.45   How can a function access actual parameter values for those actual parameters that do not correspond to any formal parameter?

4.46   What is one way in which primitive variables can be passed by reference to a function?

4.47 What exactly does the `String` method `match` do?

4.48 In JavaScript, what exactly does a constructor do?

4.49 What are the predefined character classes, and what do they mean?

4.50 What does the `i` pattern modifier do?

4.51 What is a character class in a pattern?

4.52 What exactly does the `String` method `replace` do?

4.53 What are the symbolic quantifiers, and what do they mean?

Exercises

Write, `test`, and debug (if necessary) JavaScript scripts for the following problems. When required to write functions, you must include a script to test the function with at least two different data sets. In all cases, for testing, you must write an XHTML file that references the JavaScript file.

4.1 *Output*: A table of the numbers from 15 to 25 and their squares and cubes, using alert.

4.2 *Output*: The first 10 Fibonacci numbers, which are defined as in the following sequence:

$$1,1,2,3,\ldots$$

where each number in the sequence after the second is the sum of the two previous numbers. You must use document `.write` to produce the output.

4.3 *Input*: Four numbers, using `prompt` to get each.

Output: The largest of the four input numbers.

Hint: Use the predefined function `Math. max`.

4.4 Modify the script of Exercise 4.2 to input a number, n, using `prompt`, which calculates the sum of the Fibonacci number required as output.

4.5 *Input*: A text string, using `prompt`.

Output: Either `"Legal name"` or `"Illegal name"`, depending on whether the input names fit the required format, which is

        `Last name, first name, initial`

where neither of the names can have more than 25 characters.

4.6 *Input*: A line of text, using `prompt`.

Output: The words of the input text, in alphabetical reverse order.

4.7 Modify the script for Exercise 4.6 to get a second input from the user, which is either `"ascending"` or `"descending"`. Use this input to determine how to sort the input words starting with vowels (a,e,i,o,u) first and then the words starting with non-vowels.

4.8 *Function*: `zeros`

Parameter: An array of numbers.

Result: The given array must be modified to retain only zero values.

Returns: `true` if the given array included zero values; `false` otherwise.

4.9 *Function*: `e_names`

Parameter: An array of names, represented as strings.

Returns: The number of names in the given array that end in either `"ss"` or `"l"`.

4.10 *Function*: `second_vowel`

Parameter: A string.

Returns: The position in the string of the second left vowel.

4.11 *Function*: `counter`

Parameter: An array of numbers.

Returns: The numbers of values less than one, one, and values greater than zero in the given array.

Note: You must use a `switch` statement in the function.

4.12 *Function*: `tst_name`

Parameter: A string.

Returns: `true` if the given string has the form

```
string1, string2, string3 letter
```

where both strings must be all lowercase letters except the first letter, and `letter` must be uppercase; `false` otherwise.

4.13 *Function*: `sum`

Parameter: An array of arrays of numbers.

Returns: the sum of the array of numbers.

4.14 *Function*: `ascender`

Parameter: A number.

Returns: The number with its digits in the ascending order.

JavaScript and XHTML Documents

Client-side JavaScript does not include language constructs that are not in core JavaScript. Rather, it defines the collection of objects, methods, and properties that allow scripts to interact with XHTML documents on the browser. This chapter describes some of these features and illustrates their use with examples.

The chapter begins with a description of the execution environment of client-side JavaScript, which means the object hierarchy that corresponds to the structure of documents. Then it gives a brief overview of the Document Object Model (DOM), noting that you need not know the details of this model to be able to use client-side JavaScript. Next, the techniques for accessing XHTML document elements in JavaScript are discussed. The fundamental concepts of events and event handling are then introduced, using the DOM 0 event model. Although the event-driven model of computation is not a new idea in programming, it has become more important to programmers with the advent of Web programming. Next, the chapter describes the relationships between event objects, XHTML tag attributes, and tags, primarily by means of two tables.

Applications of basic event handling are introduced through a sequence of complete XHTML/JavaScript examples. The first of these illustrates handling the `load` event from a body element. The next two examples demonstrate the use of the `click` event created when radio buttons are pressed. This is followed by an example that uses the `blur` event to compare passwords that are input twice. The next example demonstrates the use of the `change` event to validate the format of input to a text box. The last example shows the use of the `blur` event to prevent user changes to the values of text box elements.

Next, the event model of DOM 2 is discussed, using a revision of an earlier example to illustrate the new features of this model. The chapter then introduces the use of the `navigator` object to determine which browser is being used. Finally, a few of the methods and properties used to traverse and modify DOM structures are briefly intoduced.

Nearly all of the JavaScript in the examples in this chapter is in separate files. Therefore, each of the examples consists of an XHTML document and one or two JavaScript files.

5.1 The JavaScript Execution Environment

A browser displays an XHTML document in a window on the screen of the client. The JavaScript `Window` object represents the window that displays the document.

All JavaScript variables are properties of some object. The properties of the `Window` object are visible to all JavaScript scripts that appear either implicitly or explicitly in the window's XHTML document, so they include all of the global variables. When a global variable is created in a client-side script, it is created as a new property of the `Window` object. The `Window` object provides the largest enclosing referencing environment for JavaScript scripts.

There can be more than one `Window` object. In this book, however, we deal only with scripts with a single `Window` object.

The JavaScript `Document` object represents the displayed XHTML document. Every `Window` object has a property named `document`, which is a reference to the `Document` object that the window displays. The `Document` object is used more often than any other object in client-side JavaScript. Its `write` method was used extensively in Chapter 4, "The Basics of JavaScript."

Every `Document` object has a `forms` array, each element of which represents a form in the document. Each `forms` array element has an `elements` array as a property, which contains the objects that represent the XHTML form elements, such as buttons and menus. The JavaScript objects associated with the elements in a document can be addressed in a script in several ways. These are discussed in Section 5.3.

`Document` objects also have property arrays for anchors, links, images, and applets. There are many other objects in the object hierarchy below a `Window` object, but in this chapter we are primarily interested in documents, forms, and form elements.

5.2 The Document Object Model

The Document Object Model (DOM) has been under development by the W3C since the mid-1990s. DOM Level 3 (usually referred to as DOM 3) is the current approved version. The original motivation for the standard DOM was to provide a specification that would make Java programs and JavaScript scripts that deal with XHTML documents portable among various browsers.

Although the W3C never produced such a specification, DOM 0 is the name often used to describe the document model used by the early browsers that supported JavaScript. Specifically, DOM 0 is the version of the document model implemented in the Netscape 3.0 and Internet Explorer 3.0 browsers. The DOM 0 model was partially documented in the HTML 4 specification.

DOM 1, the first W3C DOM specification, issued in October 1998, focused on the XHTML and XML (see Chapter 7, "Introduction to XML") document model. DOM 2, issued in November 2000, specifies a style sheet object model and defines how style information attached to a document can be manipulated. It also includes document traversals and provides a complete and comprehensive event model. DOM 3, issued in 2004, deals with content models for XML (DTDs and schemas), document validation, and document views and formatting, as well as key events and event groups. As stated previously, DOM 0 is supported by all JavaScript-enabled browsers. DOM 2 is nearly completely supported by Firefox 2 (FX2), but Internet Explorer 7 (IE7) leaves significant parts either unimplemented or implemented in a nonstandard way. No part of DOM 3 is covered in this book.

The DOM is an application programming interface (API) that defines an interface between XHTML documents and application programs. It is an abstract model because it must apply to a variety of application programming languages. Each language that interfaces with the DOM must define a binding to that interface. The actual DOM specification consists of a collection of interfaces, including one for each document tree node type. These interfaces are similar to Java interfaces and C++ abstract classes. They define the objects, methods, and properties that are associated with their respective node types. With the DOM, users can write code in programming languages to create documents, move around in their structures, and change, add, or delete elements and their content.

Documents in the DOM have a treelike structure, but there can be more than one tree in a document (though that is unusual). Because the DOM is an abstract interface, it does not dictate that documents must be implemented as trees or collections of trees. Therefore, in an implementation, the relationships among the elements of a document could be represented in any number of different ways.

A language that is designed to support the DOM must have a binding to the DOM constructs. This binding amounts to a correspondence between constructs in the language and elements in the DOM. In the JavaScript binding to the DOM, the elements of a document are objects, with both data and operations. The data are called *properties*, and the operations are, naturally, called *methods*. For example, the following element would be represented as an object with two properties, type and name, with the values "text" and "address", respectively:

```
<input type = "text"  name = "address">
```

In most cases, the property names in JavaScript are the same as their corresponding attribute names in XHTML.

Both of the two most popular browsers, IE7 and FX2, provide a way of viewing the DOM structure of a displayed document. For IE7, a special addition must be downloaded and installed in the browser. This addition, named IE Developer Toolbar, can be downloaded from http://go.microsoft.com/fwlink/?LinkId=92716. After downloading this tool, installing it, and restarting the browser, the following steps will show the DOM structure of any displayed document. First, after displaying a document, click the >> icon just right of the *Tools* icon on the lower toolbar of the display, which shows the *Tools* icons that are not displayed. Click the *IE Developer Toolbar* in the menu that appears when >> was clicked. The lower left area of the resulting display will show an elided version of the DOM structure.[1] By clicking on all of the eliding icons (square boxes that have plus signs in them), the whole structure will be displayed. Consider the following simple document:

```
<?xml version = "1.0" encoding = "utf-8" ?>
<!DOCTYPE html PUBLIC "-//W3C//DTD XHTML 1.0 Strict//EN"
  "http://www.w3.org/TR/xhtml1/DTD/xhtml1-strict.dtd">
<!-- table2.html
     A simple table to demonstrate DOM trees
     -->
<html xmlns = "http://www.w3.org/1999/xhtml">
  <head> <title> A simple table </title>
  </head>
  <body>
    <table border = "border">
      <tr>
```

---

1. Eliding abstracts away parts of the structure. An elided part can be restored to the display.

```
        <th> </th>
        <th> Apple </th>
        <th> Orange </th>
      </tr>
      <tr>
        <th> Breakfast </th>
        <td> 0 </td>
        <td> 1 </td>
      </tr>
    </table>
  </body>
</html>
```

The display of this document and its complete DOM structure is shown in Figure 5.1.

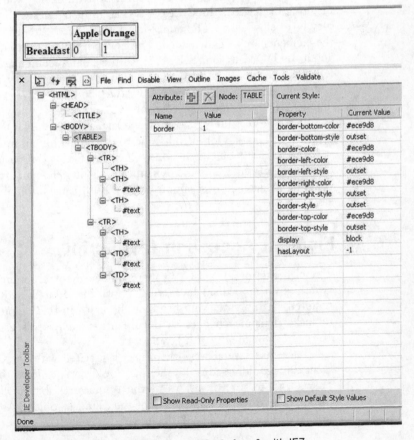

Figure 5.1 The DOM structure for `table2.html` with IE7

Below the display of the document there are three areas, the left of which shows the DOM structure. The middle area displays the attribute values of any selected element in the structure. The table element has been selected in the DOM structure, so the attribute in the attribute display area is border, with a value of 1. The attributes of other elements can be displayed by selecting those elements. The right area displays the CSS style properties of any selected element in the structure. In Figure 5.1, the table element has been selected, so the style properties are those of the table element. With the whole display, one can view virtually everything about the DOM structure for the displayed document. The FX2 browser must be installed with a custom option to allow it to be used to inspect the DOM structure of a document. This option is chosen by selecting the *Dom Inspector* box of the *Optional Components* window during installation. When installed with this option, the DOM structure can be viewed by clicking the *Tools* button at the top of the display and selecting the *DOM Inspector* menu item. This opens a new window that is similar to the IE7 window for DOM viewing. To view the display of the chosen document in the same window, the *Inspect* button in the upper-right corner of the display must be clicked. The resulting display has three areas—two large rectangles with the document display box below them. The upper-left area is the DOM structure. As with IE7, the elements are initially elided. The upper-right area is to display information about the DOM structure. By clicking the small rectangular icon in the upper-left corner of this area, a menu drops down showing the available information, which includes the *DOM Node*, *Box Model*, and *CSS Style Rules*, among others. The FX2 DOM Inspector display of table2.html is shown in Figure 5.2.

Anything resembling a complete explanation of the DOM is far beyond the scope of this book. Our introduction to the DOM here is intended only to provide the basis for our discussion of how JavaScript can be used to respond to document-related events and dynamically modify element attributes, styles, and content.[2] A detailed description of the DOM can be found at the W3C Web site.

5.3 Element Access in JavaScript

The elements of an XHTML document have corresponding objects that are visible to an embedded JavaScript script. The addresses of these objects are required, both by the event handling discussed in this chapter and by the code to make dynamic changes to documents, which is discussed in Chapter 6, "Dynamic Documents with JavaScript."

There are several ways the object associated with an XHTML form element can be addressed in JavaScript. The original (DOM 0) way is to use the forms and elements arrays of the Document object, which is referenced through the document property of the Window object. As an example, consider the following XHTML document:

---

2. We will discuss modifications of style properties in Chapter 6.

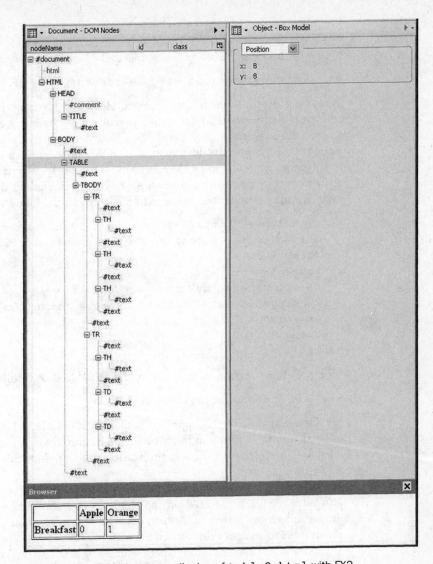

Figure 5.2 The DOM Inspector display of `table2.html` with FX2

```
<html xmlns = "http://www.w3.org/1999/xhtml">
  <head> <title> Access to form elements </title>
  </head>
  <body>
    <form action = "">
      <input type = "button"  name = "turnItOn" />
    </form>
  </body>
</html>
```

We refer to the address of the JavaScript object that is associated with an XHTML element as the *DOM address* of the element. The DOM address of the button in this example, using the forms and elements arrays, is as follows:

```
var dom = document.forms[0].elements[0];
```

The problem with this approach to element addressing is that the DOM address is defined by address elements that could change; namely, the forms and elements arrays. For example, if a new button were added before the turnItOn button in the document, the DOM address shown would be wrong.

Another approach to DOM addressing is to use element names. For this, the element and its enclosing elements, up to but not including the body element, must include name attributes. For example, consider the following document:

```
<html xmlns = "http://www.w3.org/1999/xhtml">
  <head> <title> Access to form elements </title>
  </head>
  <body>
    <form name = "myForm"  action = "">
      <input type = "button"  name = "turnItOn" />
    </form>
  </body>
</html>
```

Using the name attributes, the button's DOM address is as follows:

```
var dom = document.myForm.turnItOn;
```

One drawback of this approach is that the XHTML 1.1 standard does not allow the name attribute in the form element, even though the attribute is now legal for form elements. This is a validation problem, but it causes no difficulty for browsers.

Although name attributes are not allowed on form elements, name attributes are often required on the elements in a form. The server-side programs and scripts that process form data use a widget's name attribute value to identify the form data value associated with the widget.

Yet another approach to element addressing is to use the JavaScript method getElementById, which is defined in DOM 1. Because an element's identifier (id) is unique in the document, this approach works, regardless of how deeply the element is nested in other elements in the document. For example, if the id attribute of our button is set to "turnItOn", the following could be used to get the DOM address of that button element:

```
var dom = document.getElementById("turnItOn");
```

The parameter of getElementById can be any expression that evaluates to a string. In many cases, it is a variable.

Because ids are most useful for DOM addressing and names are required for form-processing code, form elements often have both ids and names, both set to the same value.

Buttons in a group of checkboxes often share the same name. The buttons in a radio button group *always* have the same name. In these cases, the names of the individual buttons obviously cannot be used in their DOM addresses. Of course, each radio button and checkbox can have an id, which would make it easy to address using getElementById. However, using this approach does not provide a convenient way to search a group of radio buttons or checkboxes to determine which is checked.

An alternative to both names and ids is provided by the implicit arrays associated with each checkbox and radio button group. Every such group has an array, which has the same name as the group name, that stores the DOM addresses of the individual buttons in the group. These arrays are properties of the form in which the buttons appear. To access the arrays, the DOM address of the form object first must be obtained. For example:

```
<form id = "vehicleGroup">
  <input type = "checkbox"  name = "vehicles"
         value = "car" />  Car
  <input type = "checkbox"  name = "vehicles"
         value = "truck" />  Truck
  <input type = "checkbox"  name = "vehicles"
         value = "bike" />  Bike
</form>
```

The implicit array, vehicles, has three elements, which reference the three objects associated with the three checkbox elements in the group. This array provides a convenient way to search the list of checkboxes in a group. The checked property of a checkbox object is set to true if the button is checked. For the preceding sample checkbox group, the following code would count the number of checkboxes that were checked:

```
var numChecked = 0;
var dom = document.getElementById("vehicleGroup");
for (index = 0; index < dom.vehicles.length; index++)
  if (dom.vehicles[index].checked)
    numChecked++;
```

Radio buttons can be addressed and handled exactly as the checkboxes in the above code have been addressed and handled.

5.4 Events and Event Handling

The HTML 4.0 standard provided the first specification of an event model for documents. This is sometimes referred to as the DOM 0 event model. Although the DOM 0 event model is limited in scope, it is the only one that is supported by all browsers that support JavaScript. A complete and comprehensive event model was specified by DOM 2. The DOM 2 model is supported by the FX2 browser. However, inexplicably, IE7 does not support it. Our discussion of events and event handling is divided into two parts, one for the DOM 0 model and one for the DOM 2 model. We describe the DOM 2 standard, even though IE7 does not support it. We hope that Microsoft will soon recognize the error of its ways and implement the DOM 2 event model in its IE8 browser.

5.4.1 Basic Concepts of Event Handling

One important use of JavaScript for Web programming is to detect certain activities of the browser and the browser user and provide computation when these activities occur. These computations are specified using a special form of programming called *event-driven programming*. In conventional (non-event-driven) programming, the code itself specifies the order in which that code is executed, although the order is usually affected by the program's input data. In event-driven programming, parts of the program are executed at completely unpredictable times, often triggered by user interactions with the executing program.

An *event* is a notification that something specific has occurred, either with the browser, such as the completion of the loading of a document, or because of a browser user action, such as a mouse click on a form button. Strictly speaking, an event is an object that is implicitly created by the browser and the JavaScript system in response to something happening.

An *event handler* is a script that is implicitly executed in response to the appearance of an event. Event handlers enable a Web document to be responsive to browser and user activities. One of the most common uses of event handlers is to check for simple errors and omissions in user input to the elements of a form, either when they are changed or when the form is submitted. This saves the time of sending the form data to the server, where its correctness then must be checked by a server-resident program or script before it can be processed.

If you are familiar with the exceptions and exception-handling capabilities of a programming language such as C++ or Java, you should see the close relationship between events and exceptions. Both events and exceptions occur at unpredictable times, and both often require some specific program actions.

Because events are JavaScript objects, their names are case sensitive. The names of all event objects have only lowercase letters. For example, `click` is an event, but `Click` is not.

Events are created by activities associated with specific XHTML elements. For example, the `click` event can be caused by the browser user clicking a radio button or the link of an anchor tag, among other things. Thus, an event's name is only part of the information pertinent to handling the event. In most cases, the specific XHTML element that caused the event is also needed.

The process of connecting an event handler to an event is called *registration*. There are two distinct approaches to event handler registration, one that assigns tag attributes and one that assigns handler addresses to object properties. These are further discussed and shown in Sections 5.5 and 5.6.

The write method of document should never be used in an event handler. Remember that a document is displayed as its XHTML code is parsed by the browser. Events usually occur after the whole document is displayed. If write appears in an event handler, the content produced by it might be placed over the top of the existing document.

The remainder of this section and Sections 5.5 to 5.7 describe the DOM 0 event model and some of its uses.

5.4.2   Events, Attributes, and Tags

HTML 4 defined a collection of events, which browsers implement and with which JavaScript can deal. These events are associated with XHTML tag attributes, which can be used to connect the events to handlers. The attributes have names that are closely related to their associated events. Table 5.1 lists the most commonly used events and their associated tag attributes.

Table 5.1   Events and their tag attributes

Event	Tag Attribute
blur	onblur
change	onchange
click	onclick
dblclick	ondblclick
focus	onfocus
keydown	onkeydown
keypress	onkeypress
keyup	onkeyup
load	onload
mousedown	onmousedown
mousemove	onmousemove
mouseout	onmouseout
mouseover	onmouseover
mouseup	onmouseup
reset	onreset
select	onselect
submit	onsubmit
unload	onunload

In many cases, the same attribute can appear in several different tags. The circumstances under which an event is created are related to a tag and an attribute, and they can be different for the same attribute when it appears in different tags.

An XHTML element is said to *get focus* when the user puts the mouse cursor over it and clicks the left mouse button. An element can also get focus when the user tabs to the element. Focus on an element can be forced with the `focus` method, which is described in Section 5.7.2. When a text element has focus, any keyboard input goes into that element. Obviously, only one text element can have focus at one time. An element becomes blurred when the user moves the cursor away from the element and clicks the left mouse button, or tabs away from the element. An element obviously becomes blurred when another element gets focus. Several nontext elements can also have focus, but the condition is less useful in those cases.

Table 5.2 shows the most commonly used attributes related to events, tags that can include the attributes, and the circumstances under which the associated events are created. Only a few of the situations shown in Table 5.2 are discussed in this chapter.

Table 5.2   Event attributes and their tags

Attribute	Tag	Description
onblur	`<a>`	The link loses the input focus
	`<button>`	The button loses the input focus
	`<input>`	The input element loses the input focus
	`<textarea>`	The text area loses the input focus
	`<select>`	The selection element loses the input focus
onchange	`<input>`	The input element is changed and loses the input focus
	`<textarea>`	The text area is changed and loses the input focus
	`<select>`	The selection element is changed and loses the input focus
onclick	`<a>`	The user clicks on the link
	`<input>`	The input element is clicked
ondblclick	Most elements	The user double clicks the left mouse button
onfocus	`<a>`	The link acquires the input focus
	`<input>`	The input element receives the input focus
	`<textarea>`	A text area receives the input focus
	`<select>`	A selection element receives the input focus

Table 5.2   Event attributes and their tags   *(continued)*

Attribute	Tag	Description
onkeydown	`<body>`, form elements	A key is pressed down
onkeypress	`<body>`, form elements	A key is pressed down and released
onkeyup	`<body>`, form elements	A key is released
onload	`<body>`	The document is finished loading
onmousedown	Most elements	The user clicks the left mouse button
onmousemove	Most elements	The user moves the mouse cursor within the element
onmouseout	Most elements	The mouse cursor is moved away from being over the element
onmouseover	Most elements	The mouse cursor is moved over the element
onmouseup	Most elements	The left mouse button is unclicked
onreset	`<form>`	The reset button is clicked
onselect	`<input>`	The mouse cursor is moved over the element
	`<textarea>`	The text area is selected within the text area
onsubmit	`<form>`	The *Submit* button is pressed
onunload	`<body>`	The user exits the document

As mentioned previously, there are two ways to register an event handler in the DOM 0 event model. One of these is by assigning the event handler script to an event tag attribute, as in the following example:

```
<input type = "button" id = "myButton"
       onclick = "alert('You clicked my button!');" />
```

In many cases, the handler consists of more than a single statement. For these, often a function is used, and the literal string value of the attribute is the call to the function as follows:

```
<input type = "button" id = "myButton"
       onclick = "myButtonHandler();" />
```

The event handler could also be registered by the assignment to the associated event property on the button object as follows:

```
document.getElementById("myButton").onclick =
                                   myButtonHandler;
```

This statement must follow both the handler function and the form element so that JavaScript has seen both before assigning the property. Notice that only the name of the handler function is assigned to the property—it is neither a string nor a call to the function.

5.5 Handling Events from Body Elements

The events most often created by body elements are load and unload. As our first example of event handling, we consider the simple case of producing an alert message when the body of the document has been loaded. In this case, we use the onload attribute of <body> to specify the event handler.

```
<?xml version = "1.0"  encoding = "utf-8" ?>
<!DOCTYPE html PUBLIC "-//W3C//DTD XHTML 1.0 Strict//EN"
   "http://www.w3.org/TR/xhtml1/DTD/xhtml1-strict.dtd">

<!-- load.html
     A document for load.js
     -->
<html xmlns = "http://www.w3.org/1999/xhtml">
  <head>
    <title> load.html </title>
    <script type = "text/javascript"  src = "load.js" >
    </script>
  </head>
  <body onload="load_greeting();">
    <p />
  </body>
</html>
```

```
// load.js
//   An example to illustrate the load event

// The onload event handler
function load_greeting () {
  alert("You are visiting the home page of \n" +
        "Pete's Pickled Peppers \n" + "WELCOME!!!");
}
```

Figure 5.3 shows a browser display of load.html.

The unload event is probably more useful than the load event. It is used to do some cleanup before a document is unloaded, such as when the browser user goes on to some new document. For example, if the document opened a second browser window, that window should be closed by an unload event handler.

Figure 5.3 Display of load.html

5.6 Handling Events from Button Elements

Buttons in a Web document provide an effective way to collect simple input from the browser user. The most commonly used event created by button actions is click. Section 5.4.2 includes an example of a plain button.

Consider the following example of a set of radio buttons that enables the user to choose information about a specific airplane. The click event is used in this example to trigger a call to alert, which presents a brief description of the selected airplane. In this example, the calls to the event handlers send the value of the pressed radio button to the handler. This is another way the handler can determine which of a group of radio buttons is pressed.

```
<?xml version = "1.0" encoding = "utf-8" ?>
<!DOCTYPE html PUBLIC "-//W3C//DTD XHTML 1.0 Strict//EN"
  "http://www.w3.org/TR/xhtml1/DTD/xhtml1-strict.dtd">

<!-- radio_click.hmtl
     A document for radio_click.js
     Creates four radio buttons that call the planeChoice
     event handler to display descriptions
     -->
<html xmlns = "http://www.w3.org/1999/xhtml">
  <head>
    <title> radio_click.html </title>
  <script type = "text/javascript"  src = "radio_click.js" >
  </script>
  </head>
  <body>
    <h4> Cessna single-engine airplane descriptions </h4>
    <form id = "myForm"  action = "">
      <p>
```

```
               <label> <input type = "radio"  name = "planeButton"
                           value = "152"
                           onclick = "planeChoice(152)" />
          Model 152 </label>
          <br />
          <label> <input type = "radio"  name = "planeButton"
                           value = "172"
                           onclick = "planeChoice(172)" />
          Model 172 (Skyhawk) </label>
          <br />
          <label> <input type = "radio"  name = "planeButton"
                           value = "182"
                           onclick = "planeChoice(182)" />
          Model 182 (Skylane) </label>
          <br />
          <label> <input type = "radio"  name = "planeButton"
                           value = "210"
                           onclick = "planeChoice(210)" />
          Model 210 (Centurian) </label>
        </p>
      </form>
    </body>
</html>
```

```
// radio_click.js
//    An example of the use of the click event with radio buttons,
//    registering the event handler by assignment to the button
//    attributes

// The event handler for a radio button collection
function planeChoice (plane) {

// Produce an alert message about the chosen airplane
  switch (plane) {
    case 152:
      alert("A small two-place airplane for flight training");
      break;
    case 172:
      alert("The smaller of two four-place airplanes");
      break;
    case 182:
      alert("The larger of two four-place airplanes");
      break;
    case 210:
```

```
        alert("A six-place high-performance airplane");
        break;
      default:
        alert("Error in JavaScript function planeChoice");
        break;
    }
  }
}
```

Figure 5.4 shows a browser display of `radio_click.html`. Figure 5.5 shows the `alert` window that results from choosing the Model 182 radio button in `radio_click.html`.

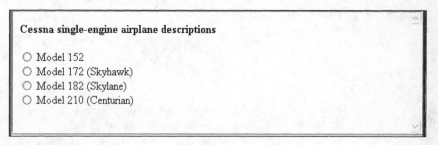

Figure 5.4 Display of `radio_click.html`

Figure 5.5 The result of pressing the Model 182 button in `radio_click.html`

In `radio_click.html` the event handler is registered by assigning its call to the `onclick` attribute of the radio buttons. The specific button that was clicked is identified by the parameter sent in the handler call in the button element. An alternative to using the parameter would be to include code in the handler to determine which radio button was pressed.

The next example, `radio_click2.html`, whose purpose is the same as that of `radio_click.html`, registers the event handler by assigning the name of the handler to the event properties of the radio button objects. For example, the following registers the handler on the first radio button:

```
document.getElementById("myForm").elements[0].onclick = planeChoice;
```

Recall that this statement must follow both the handler function and the XHTML form specification so that JavaScript has seen both before assigning to the property. The following example uses three files, one for the XHTML, one for the script for the event handlers, and one for the script to register the handlers.

```
<!-- radio_click2.hmtl
     A document for radio_click2.js
     -->
<html xmlns = "http://www.w3.org/1999/xhtml">
  <head>
    <title> radio_click2.html </title>

<!-- Script for the event handler -->
    <script type = "text/javascript"  src = "radio_click2.js" >
    </script>

  </head>
  <body>
    <h4> Cessna single-engine airplane descriptions </h4>
    <form id = "myForm"  action = "">
      <p>
        <label> <input type = "radio"  name = "planeButton"
                       value = "152" />
        Model 152 </label>
        <br />
        <label> <input type = "radio"  name = "planeButton"
                       value = "172" />
        Model 172 (Skyhawk) </label>
        <br />
        <label> <input type = "radio"  name = "planeButton"
                       value = "182" />
        Model 182 (Skylane) </label>
        <br />
        <label> <input type = "radio"  name = "planeButton"
                       value = "210" />
        Model 210 (Centurian) </label>
      </p>
    </form>

<!-- Script for registering the event handlers -->
    <script type = "text/javascript"  src = "radio_click2r.js" >
    </script>

  </body>
</html>
```

```javascript
// radio_click2.js
//    An example of the use of the click event with radio buttons,
//    registering the event handler by assigning an event property

// The event handler for a radio button collection
function planeChoice (plane) {

// Put the DOM address of the elements array in a local variable
  var dom = document.getElementById("myForm");

// Determine which button was pressed
  for (var index = 0; index < dom.planeButton.length;
       index++) {
    if (dom.planeButton[index].checked) {
      plane = dom.planeButton[index].value;
      break;
    }
  }

// Produce an alert message about the chosen airplane
  switch (plane) {
    case "152":
      alert("A small two-place airplane for flight training");
      break;
    case "172":
      alert("The smaller of two four-place airplanes");
      break;
    case "182":
      alert("The larger of two four-place airplanes");
      break;
    case "210":
      alert("A six-place high-performance airplane");
      break;
    default:
      alert("Error in JavaScript function planeChoice");
      break;
  }
}
```

```
// radio_click2r.js
//   The event registering code for radio_click2
var dom = document.getElementById("myForm");
dom.elements[0].onclick = planeChoice;
dom.elements[1].onclick = planeChoice;
dom.elements[2].onclick = planeChoice;
dom.elements[3].onclick = planeChoice;
```

In `radio_click2r.js` (the JavaScript file that registers the event handlers), the form elements (radio buttons in this case) are addressed as elements of the `elements` array. An alternative would be to give each radio button an id attribute and register the handler using the id. For example, the first radio button could be defined as follows:

```
<input type = "radio"  name = "planeButton" value = "152"
    id = "152" />
```

Then the event handler registration would be as follows:

```
var dom = document.getElementById("myForm");
dom.getElementById("152").onclick = planeChoice;
dom.getElementById("172").onclick = planeChoice;
dom.getElementById("182").onclick = planeChoice;
dom.getElementById("210").onclick = planeChoice;
```

There is no way to specify parameters on the handler function when it is registered by assigning its name to the event property. Therefore, event handlers that are registered this way cannot use parameters—clearly a disadvantage of this approach. In `radio_click2.js`, the handler includes a loop to determine which radio button created the `click` event.

There are two advantages to registering handlers as properties over registering them in XHTML attributes. First, it is good to keep XHTML and JavaScript separated in the document. This allows a kind of modularization of XHTML documents, resulting in a cleaner design that will be easier to maintain. Second, having the handler function registered as the value of a property allows for the possibility of changing it during use. This could be done by registering a different handler for the event when some other event occurred. This would be impossible if the handler were registered using XHTML.

5.7 Handling Events from Text Box and Password Elements

Text boxes and passwords can create four different events: blur, focus, change, and select.

5.7.1 The Focus Event

Suppose JavaScript is used to precompute the total cost of an order and display it to the customer before the order is submitted to the server for processing. An unscrupulous user may be tempted to change the total cost before submission, thinking that somehow an altered (and lower) price would not be noticed at the server end. Such a change to a text box can be prevented by an event handler that blurs the text box every time the user attempts to put it in focus. Blur can be forced on an element with the blur method. The following example illustrates this process:

```
<?xml version = "1.0"  encoding = "utf-8" ?>
<!DOCTYPE html PUBLIC "-//W3C//DTD XHTML 1.0 Strict//EN"
  "http://www.w3.org/TR/xhtml1/DTD/xhtml1-strict.dtd">

<!-- nochange.html
     A document for nochange.js
     -->
<html xmlns = "http://www.w3.org/1999/xhtml">
  <head> <title> nochange.html </title>

<!-- Script for the event handlers -->
    <script type = "text/javascript"  src = "nochange.js" >
    </script>

  </head>
  <body>
    <form action = "">
      <h3> Coffee Order Form </h3>

<!-- A bordered table for item orders -->
      <table border = "border">

<!-- First, the column headings -->
        <tr>
          <th> Product Name </th>
          <th> Price </th>
          <th> Quantity </th>
        </tr>
```

```
<!-- Now, the table data entries -->
      <tr>
        <th> French Vanilla (1 lb.) </th>
        <td> $3.49 </td>
        <td> <input type = "text"  id = "french"
                     size ="2" /> </td>
      </tr>
      <tr>
        <th> Hazlenut Cream (1 lb.) </th>
        <td> $3.95 </td>
        <td> <input type = "text"  id = "hazlenut"
             size = "2" /> </td>
      </tr>
      <tr>
        <th> Colombian (1 lb.) </th>
        <td> $4.59 </td>
        <td> <input type = "text"  id = "colombian"
             size = "2" /></td>
      </tr>
    </table>

<!-- Button for precomputation of the total cost -->
    <p>
      <input type = "button"  value = "Total Cost"
            onclick = "computeCost();" />
      <input type = "text"  size = "5"  id = "cost"
            onfocus = "this.blur();" />
    </p>

<!-- The submit and reset buttons -->
    <p>
      <input type = "submit"  value = "Submit Order" />
      <input type = "reset"  value = "Clear Order Form" />
    </p>
  </form>
 </body>
</html>
```

```
// nochange.js
//   This script illustrates using the focus event
//   to prevent the user from changing a text field

// The event handler function to compute the cost
```

```
function computeCost() {
  var french = document.getElementById("french").value;
  var hazlenut = document.getElementById("hazlenut").value;
  var colombian = document.getElementById("colombian").value;

// Compute the cost
  document.getElementById("cost").value =
  totalCost = french * 3.49 + hazlenut * 3.95 +
            colombian * 4.59;
}  //* end of computeCost
```

In this example, the button labeled `Total Cost` allows the user to precompute the total cost of the order. The event handler for this button gets the values (input quantities) of the three kinds of coffee and computes the total cost. The cost value is placed in the text box's value property, and it is then displayed for the user. Whenever this text box acquires focus, it is forced to blur with the `blur` method, which prevents the user from changing the value.

5.7.2 Validating Form Input

One of the common uses of JavaScript is to check the values provided in forms by users to determine whether the values are sensible. Without client-side checks of such values, form values must be transmitted to the server for processing without any prior reality checks. The program or script on the server that processes the form data checks for invalid input data. When invalid data is found, the server must transmit that information back to the browser, which then must ask the user to resubmit corrected input. It is obviously more efficient to perform input data checks and carry on this user dialog entirely on the client. This approach shifts this task from the usually busy server to the client, which in most cases is only lightly used. It also results in less network traffic because it avoids sending bad data to the server, only to have it returned without being processed. Furthermore, detecting incorrect form data on the client results in quicker responses to users. Validity checking of form data is often also performed on the server, in part because client-side validity checking can be subverted by an unscrupulous user. Also, for some data, validity is crucial. One example is if the data is to be put in a database where invalid data could corrupt the database. Even though form data is checked on the server, any errors that can be detected and corrected on the client save server and network time.

When a user fills in a form input element incorrectly and a JavaScript event-handler function detects the error, the function should do several things. First, it should produce an `alert` message indicating the error to the user and reminding the user of the correct format for the input. Next, it should cause the input element to be put in focus, which positions the cursor in the element. This is done with the `focus` method, which must be called through the DOM address of the element. For example, if the element's `id` is `phone`, the element can be put in focus with the following statement:

```
document.getElementById("phone").focus();
```

This puts the cursor in the `phone` text box. Finally, the function should select the element, which highlights the text in the element. This is done with the `select` method, as in the following example:

```
document.getElementById("phone").select();
```

If an event handler returns `false`, that tells the browser not to perform any default actions of the event. For example, if the event is a click on the *Submit* button, the default action is to submit the form data to the server for processing. If user input is being validated in an event handler that is called when the `submit` event occurs and some of the input is incorrect, the handler should return `false` to avoid sending the bad data to the server. We use the convention that event handlers that check form data always return `false` if they detect an error, and `true` otherwise.

When a form requests a password from the user and that password will be used in future sessions, the user is often asked to enter the password a second time for verification. A JavaScript function can be used to check that the two entered passwords are the same.

The form in the following example includes the two password input elements, along with *Reset* and *Submit* buttons. The JavaScript function that checks the passwords is called either when the *Submit* button is pressed, using the `onsubmit` event to trigger the call, or when the second text box loses focus, using the `blur` event. The function performs two different tests. First, it determines whether the user typed the initial password (in the first input box) by testing the value of the element against the empty string. If no password has been typed into the first field, the function calls `alert` to produce an error message, calls `focus` on the field, and returns `false`. The second test is to determine whether the two typed passwords are the same. If they are different, the function calls `alert` to generate an error message, calls both `focus` and `select` on the first password field, and returns `false`. If they are the same, it returns `true`. Following is the XHTML document that creates the text boxes for the passwords, as well as the *Reset* and *Submit* buttons, and the two scripts for the event handlers for `pswd_chk.html` and the event handler registrations.

```
<?xml version = "1.0" encoding = "utf-8" ?>
<!DOCTYPE html PUBLIC "-//W3C//DTD XHTML 1.0 Strict//EN"
  "http://www.w3.org/TR/xhtml1/DTD/xhtml1-strict.dtd">

<!-- pswd_chk.html
     A document for pswd_chk.ps
     Creates two text boxes for passwords
     -->
```

```html
<html xmlns = "http://www.w3.org/1999/xhtml">
  <head>
    <title> Illustrate password checking> </title>
    <script type = "text/javascript"  src = "pswd_chk.js" >
    </script>
  </head>
  <body>
    <h3> Password Input </h3>
    <form id = "myForm"  action = "" >
      <p>

      <label> Your password
        <input type = "password" id = "initial"
               size = "10" />
      </label>
      <br /><br />

      <label> Verify password
        <input type = "password"  id = "second"
               size = "10" />
      </label>
      <br /><br />

      <input type = "reset"  name = "reset" />
      <input type = "submit"  name = "submit" />
      </p>
    </form>

<!-- Script for registering the event handlers  -->
    <script type = "text/javascript"  src = "pswd_chkr.js">
    </script>

  </body>
</html>
```

```javascript
// pswd_chk.js
//   An example of input password checking, using the submit
//   event

// The event handler function for password checking
function chkPasswords() {
  var init = document.getElementById("initial");
  var sec = document.getElementById("second");
  if (init.value == "") {
```

```
          alert("You did not enter a password \n" +
                "Please enter one now");
          init.focus();
          return false;
      }
      if (init.value != sec.value) {
          alert("The two passwords you entered are not the same \n" +
                "Please re-enter both now");
          init.focus();
          init.select();
          return false;
      } else
          return true;
  }
```

```
// pswd_chkr.js
//   Register the event handlers for pswd_chk.html

document.getElementById("second").onblur = chkPasswords;
document.getElementById("myForm").onsubmit = chkPasswords;
```

Figure 5.6 shows a browser display of `pswd_chk.html` after the two password elements have been input but before *Submit Query* has been clicked.

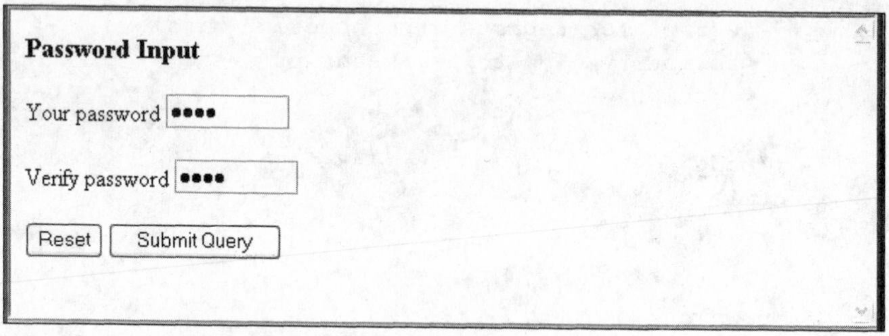

Figure 5.6 Display of `pswd_chk.html` after it has been filled out

Figure 5.7 shows a browser display that results from pressing the *Submit Query* button on `pswd_chk.html` after different passwords have been entered.

Figure 5.7 Display of `pswd_chk.html` after *Submit Query* has been clicked

We now consider an example that checks the validity of the form values for a name and phone number obtained from text widgets. Functions are used to check the form of each input when the values of the text boxes are changed, which is detected by the appearance of a `change` event.

In both cases, if an error is detected, an `alert` message is generated and both `focus` and `select` are called to prompt the user to fix the input. The `alert` message includes the correct format. The correct format for the name is last-name, first-name, middle-initial, where the first and last names must begin with uppercase letters and have at least one lowercase letter. Both must be followed immediately by a comma and possibly one space. The middle initial must be uppercase. It may or may not be followed by a period. There can be no characters before or after the whole name. The pattern for matching such names is as follows:

```
/^[A-Z][a-z]+, ?[A-Z][a-z]+, ?[A-Z]\.?$/
```

Note the use of the anchors, ^ and $, on the ends of the pattern. This prevents any leading or trailing characters. Also, notice the question marks after the spaces (following the first and last names) and after the period. Recall that the question mark qualifier means zero or one of the qualified subpattern. The period is backslashed so it matches only a period.

The correct format of the phone number is three digits and a dash, followed by three digits and a dash, followed by four digits. As with names, no characters can precede or follow the phone number. The pattern for phone numbers is as follows:

```
/^\d{3}-\d{3}-\d{4}$/
```

The following is the XHTML document, `validator.html`, that displays the text boxes for a customer's name and phone number.

```
<?xml version = "1.0" encoding = "utf-8" ?>
<!DOCTYPE html PUBLIC "-//W3C//DTD XHTML 1.0 Strict//EN"
  "http://www.w3.org/TR/xhtml1/DTD/xhtml1-strict.dtd">

<!-- validator.html
     A document for validator.js
     Creates text boxes for a name and a phone number
     -->
<html xmlns = "http://www.w3.org/1999/xhtml">
  <head>
    <title> Illustrate form input validation> </title>
    <script type = "text/javascript"  src = "validator.js" >
    </script>
  </head>
  <body>
    <h3> Customer Information </h3>
    <form action = "">
      <p>
        <label>
          <input type = "text"  id = "custName" />
          Name (last name, first name, middle initial)
        </label>
        <br /><br />

        <label>
          <input type = "text"  id = "phone" />
          Phone number (ddd-ddd-dddd)
        </label>
        <br /><br />

        <input type = "reset"  id = "reset" />
        <input type = "submit"  id = "submit" />
      </p>
    </form>
    <script type = "text/javascript"  src = "validatorr.js">
    </script>
  </body>
</html>
```

The following are the scripts for the event handlers and event registration for `validator.html`.

```
// validator.js
//    An example of input validation using the change and submit
//    events

// The event handler function for the name text box
function chkName() {
  var myName = document.getElementById("custName");

// Test the format of the input name
//    Allow the spaces after the commas to be optional
//    Allow the period after the initial to be optional
  var pos = myName.value.search(
          /^[A-Z][a-z]+, ?[A-Z][a-z]+, ?[A-Z]\.?$/);
  if (pos != 0) {
    alert("The name you entered (" + myName.value +
          ") is not in the correct form. \n" +
          "The correct form is: " +
          "last-name, first-name, middle-initial \n" +
          "Please go back and fix your name");
    myName.focus();
    myName.select();
    return false;
  } else
    return true;
}

// The event handler function for the phone number text box
function chkPhone() {
  var myPhone = document.getElementById("phone");

// Test the format of the input phone number
  var pos = myPhone.value.search(/^\d{3}-\d{3}-\d{4}$/);
  if (pos != 0) {
    alert("The phone number you entered (" + myPhone.value +
          ") is not in the correct form. \n" +
          "The correct form is: ddd-ddd-dddd \n" +
          "Please go back and fix your phone number");
    myPhone.focus();
    myPhone.select();
    return false;
  } else
    return true;
}
```

```
// validatorr.js
//   Register the event handlers for validator.html

document.getElementById("custName").onchange = chkName;
document.getElementById("phone").onchange = chkPhone;
```

Figure 5.8 shows the browser screen of `validator.html` after entering a name in the correct format, followed by an invalid telephone number. The screen is shown before the user causes the phone text field to lose focus, either by pressing *e* or by clicking the left mouse button outside the phone text field.

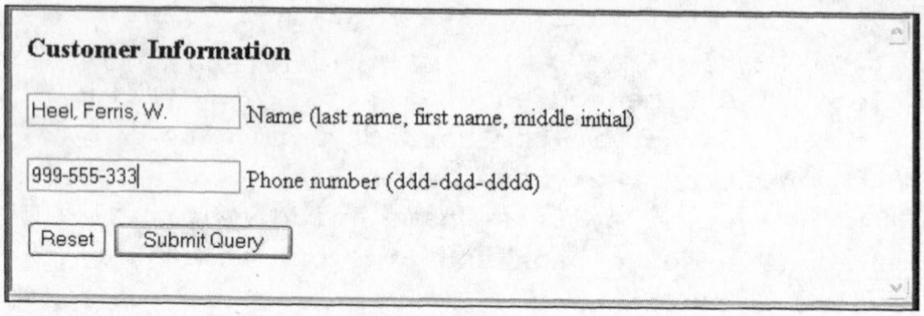

Figure 5.8 Display of `validator.html`, with an invalid phone number, while the phone text field has focus

Figure 5.9 shows the `alert` dialog box generated by pressing the *e* button in the phone text field of the screen of Figure 5.8.

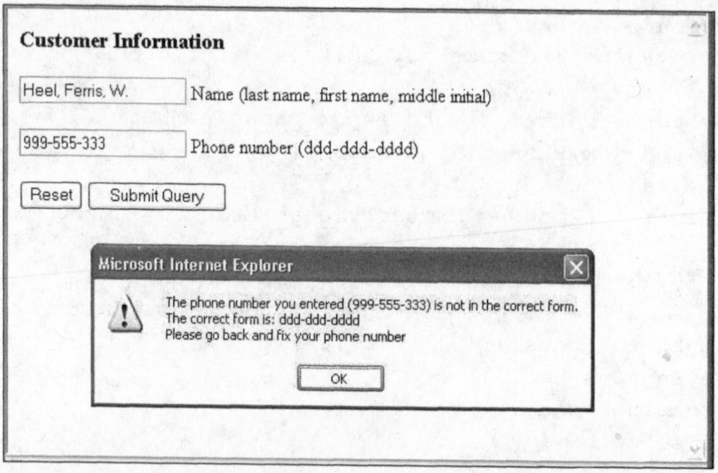

Figure 5.9 The message created by entering an invalid telephone number in `validator.html`

5.8 The DOM 2 Event Model

The DOM 2 event model does not include the features of the DOM 0 event model. However, there is no chance that support for those features will be dropped from browsers anytime soon. Therefore, Web authors should not hesitate to continue to use them. On the other hand, the DOM 2 event model is more sophisticated and powerful than DOM 0. The drawback of using the DOM 2 model is that Microsoft has yet to provide support for it in its browsers.

The DOM 2 model is a modularized interface. One of the DOM 2 modules is `Events`, which includes several submodules. The most commonly used are `HTMLEvents` and `MouseEvents`. The interfaces and events defined by these modules are as follows:

Module	Event Interface	Event Types
`HTMLEvents`	`Event`	`abort, blur, change, error, focus, load, reset, resize, scroll, select, submit, unload`
`MouseEvents`	`MouseEvent`	`click, mousedown, mousemove, mouseout, mouseover, mouseup`

When an event occurs and an event handler is called, an object that implements the event interface associated with the event type is implicitly passed to the handler. (Section 5.8.1 explains how a handler is chosen to be called.) The properties of this object have information associated with the event.

The DOM 2 event model is relatively complex. This section covers only the basics of the model. A description of the rest of the model can be found at the W3C's Web site.

5.8.1 Event Propagation

The connection between an event and the handler that deals with it is very simple in the DOM 0 event model. When the browser senses an event has occurred, the object associated with the element that caused the event is checked for event handlers. If that object has a registered handler for the particular event that occurred, that handler is executed. The event-handler connection for the DOM 2 event model is much more complicated.

Briefly, what happens is as follows. An event object is created at some node in the document tree. For that event, that node is called the *target node*. Event creation causes a three-phase process to begin.

The first of these phases is called the *capturing phase*. The event created at the target node starts at the document root node and propagates down the tree to the target node. If there are any handlers for the event registered on any node encountered in this propagation, including the document node but not the target node, these handlers are checked to determine whether they are enabled. (Section

5.8.2 explains how a handler can be defined to be enabled.) Any enabled handler for the event that is found during capturing is executed (whether it is enabled or not). When the event reaches the target node, the second phase, called the *target node phase*, takes place. In this phase, the handlers registered for the event at the target node are executed. This is similar to what happens with the DOM 0 event model. After execution of any appropriate handlers at the target node, the third phase begins. This is the *bubbling phase*, in which the event bubbles back up the document tree to the document node. On this trip back up the tree, any handler registered for the event at any node on the way is executed (whether it is enabled or not).

Not all events bubble. For example, the `load` and `unload` events do not bubble. On the other hand, all of the mouse events do. In general, if it makes sense to handle an event farther up the document tree than the target node, the event bubbles; otherwise, it does not.

Any handler can stop the event from further propagation, using the `stopPropagation` method of the event object.

Bubbling is an idea that was borrowed from exception handling. In a large and complicated document, having event handlers for every element would require a great deal of code. Much of this code would be redundant, both in the handlers and in the registering of handlers for events. Therefore, it makes sense to define a way for a single handler to deal with events created from a number of similar or related elements. The concept is that events can be propagated to some central place for handling rather than always being handled locally. In the DOM, the natural central place for event handling is at the document or window level, so that is the direction of bubbling.

Many events cause the browser to perform some action; for example, a mouse click on a link causes the document referenced in the link to replace the current document. In some cases, we want to prevent this action from taking place. For example, if a value in a form is found to be invalid by a *Submit* button event handler, we do not want the form to be submitted to the server. In the DOM 0 event model, the action is prevented by having the handler return `false`. The DOM 2 events interface provides a method, `preventDefault`, that accomplishes the same thing.

5.8.2   Event Handler Registration

The DOM 0 event model uses two different ways of registering event handlers. First, the handler code can be assigned as a string literal to the event's associated attribute in the element. Second, the name of the handler function can be assigned to the property associated with the event. Handler registration in the DOM 2 event model is performed by the method `addEventListener`, which is defined in the `EventTarget` interface, which is implemented by all objects that descend from `Document`.[3]

---

3. The name of this method includes "listener" rather than "handler" because in the DOM 2 specification handlers are called *listeners*. This is also the term used in Java for widget event handlers.

The `addEventListener` method takes three parameters, the first of which is the name of the event as a string literal. For example, `"mouseup"` and `"submit"` would be legitimate first parameters. The second parameter is the handler function. This could be specified as the function code itself or as the name of a function that is defined elsewhere. Note that this parameter is not a string type, so it is not quoted. The third parameter is a Boolean value that specifies whether the handler is enabled for calling during the capturing phase. If the value `true` is specified, the handler is enabled for the capturing phase. In fact, an enabled handler can *only* be called during capturing. If the value is `false`, the handler can be called either at the target node or on any node reached during bubbling.

When a handler is called, it is passed a single parameter, the `event` object. For example, suppose we want to register the event handler `chkName` on the text element whose `id` is `custName` for the `change` event. The following call accomplishes this:

```
document.custName.addEventListener(
                "change", chkName, false);
```

In this case, we want the handler to be called at the target node, which is `custName` in this example, so we passed `false` as the third parameter.

Sometimes it is convenient to have a temporary event handler. This can be done by registering the handler for the time when it is to be used, and then deleting that registration. The `removeEventListener` method deletes the registration of an event handler. This method takes the same parameters as `addEventListener`.

With the DOM 0 event model, when an event handler is registered to a document node, the handler becomes a method of the object that represents that node. This makes every use of `this` in the handler a reference to the target node. FX2 browsers implement event handlers for the DOM 2 model in this same way. However, this is not required by the DOM 2 model, so some other browsers may not use this approach, making the use of `this` in a handler potentially nonportable. The safe alternative is to use the `currentTarget` property of `Event`, which will always reference the object on which the handler is being executed. If the handler is called through the object of the target node, `currentTarget` is the target node. However, if the handler is called during capturing or bubbling, `currentTarget` is the object through which the handler is called, which is not the target node object. Another property of `Event`, `target`, is a reference to the target node.

The `MouseEvent` interface inherits from the `Event` interface. It adds a collection of properties related to mouse events. The most useful of these are `clientX` and `clientY`, which have the *x* and *y* coordinates of the mouse cursor, relative to the upper-left corner of the client area of the browser window. The whole browser window is taken into account, so if the user has scrolled down the document, the `clientY` value is measured from the top of the document, not the top of the current display.

5.8.3   An Example of the DOM 2 Event Model

The following example is a revision of the validator.html document validator.js script from Section 5.7, which used the DOM 0 event model. Because this version uses the DOM 2 event model, it does not work with IE7. Notice that no call to preventDefault appears in this document. The only event handled here is change, which has no default actions, so there is nothing to prevent.

```
<?xml version = "1.0" encoding = "utf-8" ?>
<!DOCTYPE html PUBLIC "-//W3C//DTD XHTML 1.0 Strict//EN"
  "http://www.w3.org/TR/xhtml1/DTD/xhtml1-strict.dtd">

<!-- validator2.html
     A document for validator2.js
     Creates text boxes for a name and a phone number
     Note: This document does not work with IE7
     -->
<html xmlns = "http://www.w3.org/1999/xhtml">
  <head>
    <title> Illustrate form input validation with DOM 2> </title>
<!-- Script to define the event handlers -->
    <script type = "text/javascript"  src = "validator2.js" />
  </head>
  <body>
    <h3> Customer Information </h3>
    <form action = "">
      <p>
        <label>
          <input type = "text"  id = "custName" />
          Name (last name, first name, middle initial)
        </label>
        <br /><br />

        <label>
          <input type = "text"  id = "phone" />
          Phone number (ddd-ddd-dddd)
        </label>
        <br /><br />

        <input type = "reset" />
        <input type = "submit"  id = "submitButton" />
      </p>
    </form>
```

```
<!-- Script for registering event handlers -->
   <script type = "text/javascript"  src = "validator2r.js" />
 </body>
</html>
```

```
// validator2.js
//    An example of input validation using the change and submit
//    events, using the DOM 2 event model
//    Note: This document does not work with IE7

// ************************************************************ //
// The event handler function for the name text box
function chkName(event) {

// Get the target node of the event
  var myName = event.currentTarget;

// Test the format of the input name
// Allow the spaces after the commas to be optional
// Allow the period after the initial to be optional
  var pos = myName.value.search(
          /^[A-Z][a-z]+, ?[A-Z][a-z]+ ?[A-Z]\.?$/);
  if (pos != 0) {
    alert("The name you entered (" + myName.value +
          ") is not in the correct form. \n" +
          "The correct form is: " +
          "last-name, first-name, middle-initial \n" +
          "Please go back and fix your name");
    myName.focus();
    myName.select();
  }
}

// ************************************************************ //
// The event handler function for the phone number text box
function chkPhone(event) {

// Get the target node of the event
  var myPhone = event.currentTarget;

// Test the format of the input phone number
  var pos = myPhone.value.search(/^\d{3}-\d{3}-\d{4}$/);
```

```
    if (pos != 0) {
        alert("The phone number you entered (" + myPhone.value +
            ") is not in the correct form. \n" +
            "The correct form is: ddd-ddd-dddd \n" +
            "Please go back and fix your phone number");
        myPhone.focus();
        myPhone.select();
    }
}
```

```
// validator2r.js
//    The last part of validator2. Registers the
//    event handlers
//    Note: This script does not work with IE6

// Get the DOM addresses of the elements and register
//    the event handlers
    var customerNode = document.getElementById("custName");
    var phoneNode = document.getElementById("phone");
    customerNode.addEventListener("change", chkName, false);
    phoneNode.addEventListener("change", chkPhone, false);
```

Note that the two event models can be mixed in a document. If a DOM 0 feature happens to be more convenient than the corresponding DOM 2 feature, there is no reason it cannot be used. Chapter 6 includes an example of the use of the DOM 2 event model for something that is more difficult to do with the DOM 0 event model.

5.9 The navigator Object

The navigator object indicates which browser is being used to view the XHTML document. The browser's name is stored in the appName property of the navigator object. The version of the browser is stored in the appVersion property of the navigator object. These properties allow the script to determine which browser is being used and to use processes appropriate to that browser. The following example illustrates the use of navigator, in this case just to display the browser name and version number:

```
<?xml version = "1.0"  encoding = "utf-8" ?>
<!DOCTYPE html PUBLIC "-//W3C//DTD XHTML 1.0 Strict//EN"
  "http://www.w3.org/TR/xhtml1/DTD/xhtml1-strict.dtd">

<!-- navigate.html
     A document for navigate.js
     Calls the event handler on load
     -->
<html xmlns = "http://www.w3.org/1999/xhtml">
  <head>
    <title> navigate.html </title>
    <script type = "text/javascript"  src = "navigate.js" >
    </script>
  </head>
  <body onload = "navProperties()">
  </body>
</html>
```

```
// navigate.js
//  An example of using the navigator object

// The event handler function to display the browser name
//  and its version number
function navProperties() {
  alert("The browser is: " + navigator.appName + "\n" +
    "The version number is: " + navigator.appVersion + "\n");
}
```

Figure 5.10 shows the result of displaying navigate.html with FX2. Figure 5.11 shows the result of displaying navigate.html with IE7. Notice that the version number of IE7 is 4. Microsoft intentionally set the version number to 4 because of some compatibility issues with earlier browsers. One would hope that future versions of IE will use the correct version number. Firefox is not any better in this regard. Using FX2, it displays version 5.0.

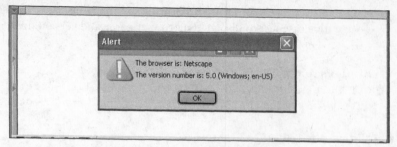

Figure 5.10 The `navigator` properties `appName` and `appVersion` for Firefox 2

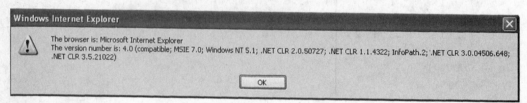

Figure 5.11 The `navigator` properties `appName` and `appVersion` for Internet Explorer 7

5.10 DOM Tree Traversal and Modification

There are many objects, properties, and methods associated with DOM 2 document representations that we have not discussed. One collection of these is defined in the `Node` interface, which is implemented by all node objects in the DOM structure. Some of these can be used to traverse and modify the DOM tree structure of the document being displayed. In this section a few of the most useful of these are briefly described. All of the properties and methods mentioned here are supported by both IE7 and FX2.

5.10.1 DOM Tree Traversal

The `parentNode` property has the DOM address of the parent node of the node through which it is referenced. The `childNodes` property is an array of the child nodes of the node through which it is referenced. For example, if the document has an unordered list with the id `mylist`, the number of list items in the list can be displayed with the following code:

```
var nod = document.getElementById("mylist");
var listitems = nod.childNodes.length;
document.write("Number of list itmes is: " +
               listitems + "<br />");
```

The `previousSibling` property has the DOM address of the previous sibling node of the node through which it is referenced. The `nextSibling` has the DOM address of the previous sibling node of the node through which it is referenced. The `firstChild` and `lastChild` properties have the DOM addresses of the first and last child nodes of the node through which they are referenced. The `nodeType` property has the type of the node through which it is referenced.

5.10.2 DOM Tree Modification

The following methods allow JavaScript code to modify an existing DOM tree structure. The `insertBefore(newChild, refChild)` places the `newChild` node before the `refChild` node. The `replaceChild(newChild, oldChild)` method replaces the `oldChild` with the `newChild` node. The `removeChild(oldChild)` method removes the specified node from the DOM structure. The `appendChild(newChild)` method adds the given node to the end of the list of siblings of the node through which it is called.

Summary

The highest levels of the execution environment of client-side JavaScript are represented with the `Window` and `Document` objects. The `Document` object includes a `forms` array property, which includes references to all forms in the document. Each element of the `forms` array has an `elements` array, which includes references to all elements in the form.

The DOM is an abstract interface whose purpose is to provide a language-independent way to access the elements of an XHTML document. Also included are the means to navigate around the structure in which the XHTML elements appear. XHTML tags are represented in JavaScript as objects; tag attributes are represented as properties.

There are three different ways to access XHTML elements in JavaScript: through the `forms` and `elements` arrays, through the names of the element and its enclosing elements, and through the `getElementById` method.

Events are simply notifications that something specific has happened that may require some special processing. Event-handling code provides that special processing. There are two distinct event models currently in use. The first is the model implemented by all browsers that support JavaScript, which we refer to as the DOM 0 model. The second is the more elaborate and powerful model defined in DOM 2.

With the DOM 0 model, there are two ways to register an event handler. First, an attribute of the tag that defines the XHTML element can be assigned the handler code. Second, the property associated with the event of the object that represents the XHTML element can be assigned the name of a function that implements the handler. The `write` method of `document` should not be used in event handlers.

With the DOM 0 model, each event has an associated tag attribute. A particular attribute may appear in several different tags. Each of these appearances is identified as a different event occurrence. The load and unload events are often used with the <body> tag to perform some operation when a document has been loaded or unloaded, respectively. The click event is used for all of the different XHTML buttons, as well as the link of an anchor tag. Form input can be conveniently checked using the change event. The submit event can also be used to check form data just before the form is submitted.

The DOM 2 event model defines three phases of event processing: capturing, target node, and bubbling. During the capturing phase, the event object travels from the document root to the target node, where the event was created. During the bubbling phase, the event travels back up the document tree to the root, triggering any handlers registered on nodes that are encountered. Event handlers can be set to allow them to be triggered during the capturing phase. Event-handler registration is done with the addEventListener method, which sets whether capturing-phase triggering will take place. Events can be unregistered with the removeEventListener method. The currentTarget property of Event has the object through which the handler was called. The target property has the target node object. The mouseEvent object has two properties, clientX and clientY, which have the coordinates of the position of the mouse cursor in the browser display window when a mouse event occurs.

The navigator object has information about which browser is being used, as well as its version number and other related information.

There are many objects, methods, and properties defined in DOM 2 that are used to traverse and modify the DOM tree structure of a document.

Review Questions

5.1 What is an event handler?

5.2 Global variables in JavaScript are properties of what object?

5.3 What is an event?

5.4 Why should document.write not be used in an event handler?

5.5 What is the origin of the DOM 0 event model?

5.6 What are the two ways in which an event handler can be associated with an event generated by a specific XHTML element in the DOM 0 event model?

5.7 How are XHTML elements and attributes represented in the JavaScript binding to DOM?

5.8 In what ways can an XHTML element acquire focus?

5.9 Describe the approach to addressing XHTML elements using forms and elements.

5.10 Describe the approach to addressing XHTML elements using `getElementById`.

5.11 What exactly does the `select` function do?

5.12 What is the disadvantage of assigning event handlers to event properties?

5.13 What are the advantages of assigning event handlers to event properties?

5.14 Why is it good to use JavaScript to check the validity of form inputs before the form data is sent to the server?

5.15 Describe the approach to addressing XHTML elements using `name` attributes.

5.16 What three things should be done when a form input element is found to have incorrectly formatted data?

5.17 What exactly does the `focus` function do?

5.18 What happens when an event handler for the `onsubmit` event returns `false`?

5.19 What event is used to trigger an event handler that checks the validity of input for a text button in a form?

5.20 What purpose does the `navigator` object have?

5.21 How is an event handler registered so that it will be called during the capturing phase?

5.22 What event propagation takes place in the DOM 0 event model?

5.23 Give two examples of default actions of events.

5.24 Explain the first two parameters of the `addEventListener` method.

5.25 How can an event handler be unregistered?

5.26 Explain the three phases of event processing in the DOM 2 event model.

5.27 What exactly do the `clientX` and `clientY` properties store?

Exercises

5.1 Modify the `radio_click.html` example to have seven buttons, labeled *Sunday, Monday, Tuesday, Wednesday, Thursday, Friday,* and *Saturday.* The event handlers for these buttons must produce messages stating the chosen favorite day. The event handler must be implemented as a function, whose name must be assigned to the `onclick` attribute of the radio button elements. The chosen day must be sent to the event handler as a parameter.

5.2   Rewrite the document for Exercise 5.1 to assign the event handler to the event property of the button element. This requires the chosen day to be obtained from the value property of the button element rather than through the parameter.

5.3   Develop, test, and validate an XHTML document that has checkboxes for motherboard ($59 each), hard disk ($49 each), and keyboard ($39 each), along with a *Submit* button. Each of the checkboxes should have its own `onclick` event handler. These handlers must add the cost of their product to a total cost. An event handler for the *Submit* button must produce an `alert` window with the message *Your total cost is $xxx*, where *xxx* is the total cost of the chosen product, including 5 percent sales tax. This handler must return `false` (to avoid actual submission of the form data).

5.4   Develop, test, and validate an XHTML document that is similar to that of Exercise 5.3. In this case, use radio buttons rather than checkboxes. These text boxes take a number, which is the purchased number of the particular product. The rest of the document should behave exactly like that of Exercise 5.3.

5.5   Add reality checks to the text boxes of the document in Exercise 5.4. The checks on the text box inputs should ensure that the input values are numbers in the range of 0 to 499.

5.6   Range checks for element inputs can be represented as new properties of the object that represents the element. Modify the document in Exercise 5.5 to add a max property value of 499 and a min property value of 0. Your event handler must use the properties for the range checks on values input through the text boxes.

5.7   Develop, test, and validate an XHTML document that collects the following information from the user: last name, first name, middle initial, age (restricted to be greater than 20), and weight (restricted to the range of 60–150). You must have event handlers for the form elements that collect this information that check the input data for correctness. Messages in `alert` windows must be produced when errors are detected.

5.8   Revise the document of Exercise 5.1 to use the DOM 2 event model.

5.9   Revise the document of Exercise 5.3 to use the DOM 2 event model.

CHAPTER

6

Dynamic Documents with JavaScript

Informally, a dynamic XHTML document is one that in some way can be changed while it is being displayed by a browser. The most common client-side approach to providing dynamic documents is to use JavaScript to manipulate the objects of the Document Object Model (DOM). Changes to documents can occur when explicitly requested by user interactions, or at regular timed intervals, or when browser events occur.

XHTML elements can be initially positioned at any given location on the browser display. If they're positioned in a specific way, elements can be dynamically moved to new positions on the display. Elements can be made to disappear and reappear. The colors of the background and the foreground (the elements) of a document can be changed. The font, font size, and font style of displayed text can be changed. Even the content of an element can be changed. Overlapping elements in a document can be positioned in a specific top-to-bottom stacking order, and their stacking order can be dynamically changed. The position of the mouse cursor on the browser display can be determined when the mouse is clicked. Elements can be made to move slowly around the display screen. Finally, elements can be defined to allow the user to drag and drop them anywhere in the display window. This chapter discusses the JavaScript code that can create all of these effects.

6.1 Introduction

Dynamic XHTML is not a new markup language. It is a collection of technologies that allows dynamic changes to documents defined with XHTML. Specifically, a *dynamic XHTML document* is one whose tag attributes, tag contents, or element style properties can be changed by user interaction or the occurrence of a browser event after the document has been and is still being displayed. Such changes can be made with an embedded script that accesses the elements of the document as objects in the associated DOM structure.

Support for dynamic XHTML is not uniform across the various browsers. As in Chapter 5, "JavaScript and XHTML Documents," the discussion is restricted to W3C-standard approaches rather than including features defined by a particular browser vendor. All of the examples in this chapter, except the document in Section 6.11, use the DOM 0 event model and work on both Internet Explorer 7 (IE7) and Firefox 2 (FX2) browsers. The example in Section 6.11 uses the DOM 2 event model because it cannot be designed in a standard way using the DOM 0 event model. Because IE7 does not support the DOM 2 event model, this example does not work with IE7.

This chapter discusses user interactions through XHTML documents using client-side JavaScript. Chapters 8–10 discuss user interactions through XHTML documents using server-side technologies.

6.2 Positioning Elements

Before the browsers that implemented HTML 4.0 appeared, Web site authors had little control over how HTML elements were arranged in documents. In many cases, the elements found in the HTML file were simply placed in the document the way text is placed in a document with a word processor—fill a row, start a new row, fill it, and so forth. HTML tables provide a framework of columns for arranging elements, but they lack flexibility and also take a considerable time to display.[1] This lack of powerful and efficient element placement

---

1. Frames provide another way to arrange elements, but they were deprecated in XHTML 1.0 and eliminated in XHTML 1.1.

control ended when Cascading Style Sheets–Positioning (CSS-P) was released by the W3C in 1997.

CSS-P is completely supported by IE7 and FX2. It provides the means not only to position any element anywhere in the display of a document, but also to move an element to a new position in the display dynamically, using JavaScript to change the positioning style properties of the element. These style properties, which are appropriately named `left` and `top`, dictate the distance from the left and top of some reference point to where the element is to appear. Another style property, `position`, interacts with `left` and `top` to provide a higher level of control of placement and movement of elements. The `position` property has three possible values: `absolute`, `relative`, and `static`.

6.2.1 Absolute Positioning

The `absolute` value is specified for `position` when the element is to be placed at a specific place in the document display without regard to the positions of other elements. For example, if a paragraph of text is to appear 100 pixels from the left edge of the display window and 200 pixels from the top, the following could be used:

```
<p style = "position: absolute; left: 100px; top: 200px">
    -- text --
</p>
```

One use of absolute positioning is to superimpose special text over a paragraph of ordinary text to create an effect similar to a watermark on paper. A larger italicized font, with space between the letters in a light gray color, could be used for the special text, allowing both the ordinary text and the special text to be legible. The following XHTML document provides an example that implements this approach. In this example, a paragraph of normal text that describes apples is displayed. Superimposed on this paragraph is the somewhat subliminal message "APPLES ARE GOOD FOR YOU."

```
<?xml version = "1.0" encoding = "utf-8"?>
<!DOCTYPE html PUBLIC "-//W3C//DTD XHTML 1.0 Strict//EN"
  "http://www.w3.org/TR/xhtml1/DTD/xhtml1-strict.dtd">

<!-- absPos.html
     Illustrates absolute positioning of elements
     -->
<html xmlns = "http://www.w3.org/1999/xhtml">
  <head>
    <title> Absolute positioning </title>
    <style type = "text/css">
```

```
/* A style for a paragraph of text */
    .regtext {font-family: Times; font-size: 14pt; width: 600px}

/* A style for the text to be absolutely positioned */
    .abstext {position: absolute; top: 25px; left: 50px;
             font-family: Times; font-size: 24pt;
             font-style: italic; letter-spacing: 1em;
             color: rgb(102,102,102); width: 500px}
    </style>
  </head>
  <body>
    <p class = "regtext">
      Apple is the common name for any tree of the genus Malus,
      of the family Rosaceae. Apple trees grow in any of the
      temperate areas of the world. Some apple blossoms are white,
      but most have stripes or tints of rose. Some apple blossoms
      are bright red. Apples have a firm and fleshy structure that
      grows from the blossom. The colors of apples range from
      green to very dark red. The wood of apple trees is fine-
      grained and hard. It is, therefore, good for furniture
      construction. Apple trees have been grown for many
      centuries. They are propogated by grafting because they
      do not reproduce themselves.
    </p>
    <p class = "abstext">
      APPLES ARE GOOD FOR YOU
    </p>
  </body>
</html>
```

Figure 6.1 shows a display of absPos.html.

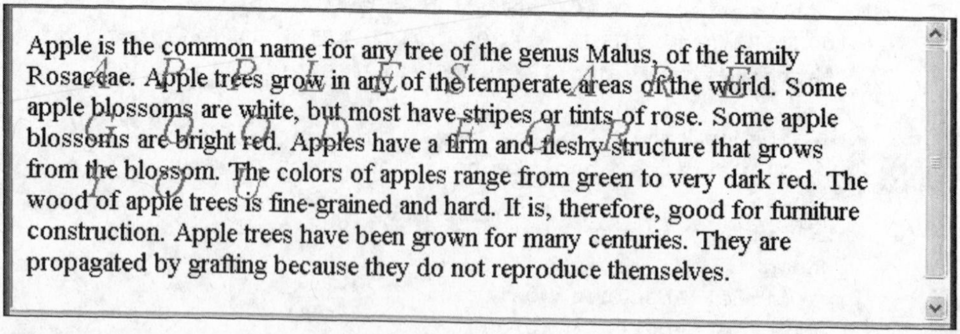

Figure 6.1 Display of absPos.html

Notice that a `width` property value is included in the style for both the regular and the special text. This property is used here to ensure that the special text is uniformly embedded in the regular text. Without it, the text would extend to the right end of the browser display window. And, of course, the width of the window could vary widely from client to client and even from minute to minute on the same client because the user can resize the browser window at any time.

When an element is absolutely positioned inside another positioned element (one that has the `position` property specified), the `top` and `left` property values are measured from the upper-left corner of the enclosing element (rather than the upper-left corner of the browser window).

To illustrate nested element placement, the document `absPos.html` is modified to place the regular text 100 pixels from the top and 100 pixels from the left. The special text is nested inside the regular text by using `<div>` and `<span>` tags. The modified document, which is named `absPos2.html`, follows:

```
<?xml version = "1.0" encoding = "utf-8"?>
<!DOCTYPE html PUBLIC "-//W3C//DTD XHTML 1.0 Strict//EN"
  "http://www.w3.org/TR/xhtml1/DTD/xhtml1-strict.dtd">


<!-- absPos2.html
     Illustrates nested absolute positioning of elements
     -->
<html xmlns = "http://www.w3.org/1999/xhtml">
  <head>
    <title> Nested absolute positioning </title>
    <style type = "text/css">

/* A style for a paragraph of text */
    .regtext {font-family: Times; font-size: 14pt; width: 500px;
            position: absolute; top: 100px; left: 100px;}

/* A style for the text to be absolutely positioned */
    .abstext {position: absolute; top: 25px; left: 50px;
            font-family: Times; font-size: 24pt;
            font-style: italic; letter-spacing: 1em;
            color: rgb(102,102,102); width: 400px;}
    </style>
  </head>
  <body>
    <div class = "regtext">
      Apple is the common name for any tree of the genus Malus,
      of the family Rosaceae. Apple trees grow in any of the
      temperate areas of the world. Some apple blossoms are white,
```

```
          but most have stripes or tints of rose. Some apple blossoms
          are bright red. Apples have a firm and fleshy structure that
          grows from the blossom. The colors of apples range from
          green to very dark red. The wood of apple trees is fine-
          grained and hard. It is, therefore, good for furniture
          construction. Apple trees have been grown for many
          centuries. They are propagated by grafting because they
          do not reproduce themselves.
          <span class = "abstext">
            APPLES ARE GOOD FOR YOU
          </span>
        </div>
      </body>
    </html>
```

Figure 6.2 shows a display of `absPos2.html`.

Apple is the common name for any tree of the genus Malus, of the
family Rosaceae. Apple trees grow in any of the temperate areas of
the world. Some apple blossoms are white, but most have stripes
or tints of rose. Some apple blossoms are bright red. Apples have
a firm and fleshy structure that grows from the blossom. The
colors of apples range from green to very dark red. The wood of
apple trees is fine-grained and hard. It is, therefore, good for
furniture construction. Apple trees have been grown for many
centuries. They are propagated by grafting because they do not
reproduce themselves.

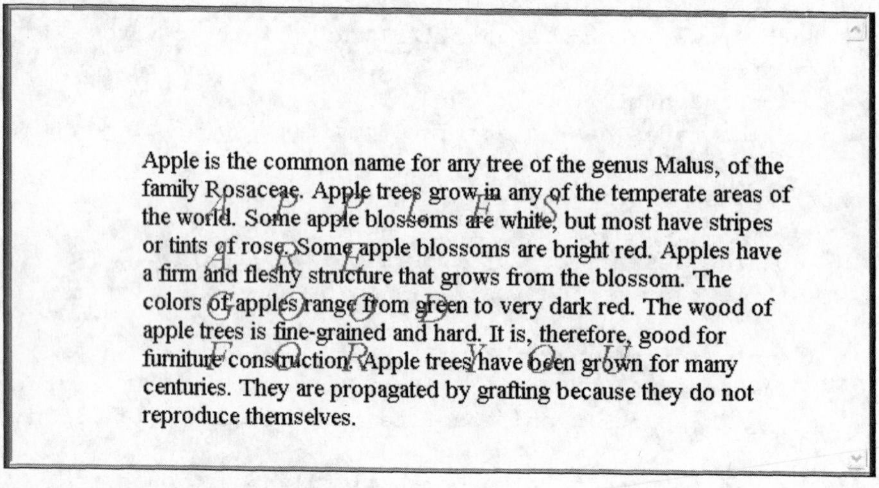

Figure 6.2 Display of `absPos2.html`

6.2.2   Relative Positioning

An element that has the `position` property set to `relative` but does not
specify `top` and `left` property values is placed in the document as if the
`position` attribute were not set at all. However, such an element can be moved
later. If the `top` and `left` properties are given values, they displace the element
by the specified amount from the position where it would have been placed (if
`top` and `left` had not been set). For example, suppose that two buttons are
placed in a document, and the `position` attribute has its default value, which is

static. They would appear next to each other in a row, assuming the current row has sufficient horizontal space for them. If position has been set to relative and the second button has its left property set to 50px, the effect would be to move it 50 pixels farther to the right than it otherwise would have appeared.

In both the case of an absolutely positioned element inside another element and the case of a relatively positioned element, negative values of top and left displace the element upward and to the left, respectively.[2]

Relative positioning can be used for a variety of special effects in element placement. For example, it can be used to create superscripts and subscripts by placing the values to be raised or lowered in <span> tags and displacing them from their regular positions. In the following example, a line of text is set in a normal font style in 24-point size. Embedded in the line is one word that is set in italic, 48-point, red font. Normally, the bottom of the special word would align with the bottom of the rest of the line. In this case, the special word is to be vertically centered in the line, so its position property is set to relative and its top property is set to 10 pixels, which lowers it by that amount relative to the surrounding text. The XHTML document to specify this, which is named relPos.html, follows:

```
<?xml version = "1.0" encoding = "utf-8"?>
<!DOCTYPE html PUBLIC "-//W3C//DTD XHTML 1.0 Strict//EN"
  "http://www.w3.org/TR/xhtml1/DTD/xhtml1-strict.dtd">


<!-- relPos.html
     Illustrates relative positioning of elements
     -->
<html xmlns = "http://www.w3.org/1999/xhtml">
  <head>
    <title> Relative positioning </title>
  </head>
  <body style = "font-family: Times; font-size: 24pt;">
    <p>
      Apples are <span style =
              "position: relative; top: 10px;
               font-family: Times; font-size: 48pt;
               font-style: italic; color: red;">
      GOOD </span> for you.
    </p>
  </body>
</html>
```

---

2. Of course, if the left or top properties are set to negative values for an absolutely positioned element, only part of the element will be visibly displayed.

Figure 6.3 shows a display of `relPos.html`.

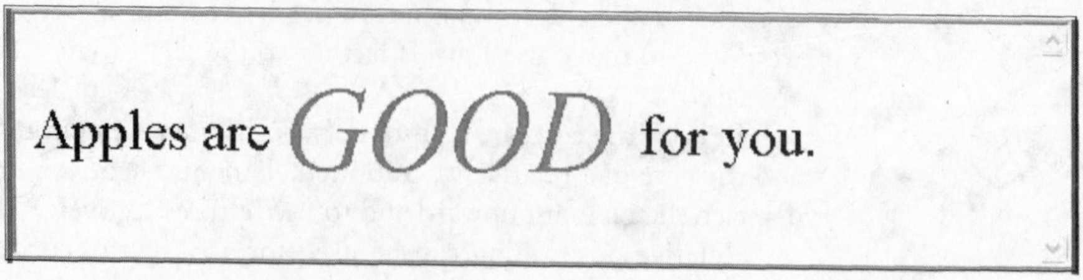

Figure 6.3 Display of `relPos.html`

6.2.3 Static Positioning

The default value for the `position` property is `static`. A statically positioned element is placed in the document as if it had the `position` value of `relative`. The difference is that a statically positioned element cannot have its `top` or `left` properties initially set or changed later. Therefore, a statically placed element cannot be displaced from its normal position and cannot be moved from that position later.

6.3 Moving Elements

As stated previously, an XHTML element whose `position` property is set to either `absolute` or `relative` can be moved. Moving an element is simple: Changing the `top` or `left` property values causes the element to move on the display. If its `position` is set to `absolute`, the element moves to the new values of `top` and `left`; if its `position` is set to `relative`, it moves from its original position by distances given by the new values of `top` and `left`.

In the following example, an image is absolutely positioned in the display. The document includes two text boxes labeled `x coordinate` and `y coordinate`. The user can enter new values for the `left` and `top` properties of the image in these boxes. When the *Move It* button is pressed, the values of the `left` and `top` properties of the image are changed to the given values, and the element is moved to its new position.

A JavaScript function, stored in a separate file, is used to change the values of `left` and `top` in our example. Although it is not necessary in our example, the id of the element to be moved is sent to the moving function, just to illustrate that the function could be used on any number of different elements. The values of the two text boxes are also sent to the function as parameters. The actual parameter values are the DOM addresses of the text boxes, with the `value` attribute attached, which provides the complete DOM addresses of the text box values. Notice that `style` is attached to the DOM address of the image to be moved because `top` and `left` are style properties. Because the input `top` and `left` values from the text boxes are just string representations of numbers, but the `top` and `left` properties must end with some unit abbreviation, the event handler catenates `"px"` to each value before assigning it to the `top` and `left` properties.

```
<?xml version = "1.0" encoding = "utf-8" ?>
<!DOCTYPE html PUBLIC "-//W3C//DTD XHTML 1.0 Strict//EN"
   "http://www.w3.org/TR/xhtml1/DTD/xhtml1-strict.dtd">

<!-- mover.html
     Uses mover.js to move an image within a document
     -->
<html xmlns = "http://www.w3.org/1999/xhtml">
  <head>
    <title> Moving elements </title>
    <script type = "text/javascript"  src = "mover.js" >
    </script>
  </head>
  <body>
    <form action = "">
      <p>
        <label>
          x coordinate:
          <input type = "text"  id = "leftCoord" size = "3" />
        </label>
        <br />
        <label>
          y coordinate:
          <input type = "text"  id = "topCoord" size = "3" />
        </label>
        <br />
        <input type = "button"  value = "Move it"
               onclick =
                 "moveIt('nebula',
                 document.getElementById('topCoord').value,
                 document.getElementById('leftCoord').value)" />
      </p>
    </form>
    <div id = "nebula"  style = "position: absolute;
         top: 115px; left: 0;">
      <img src = "../images/ngc604.jpg"
           alt = "(Picture of a nebula)" />
    </div>
  </body>
</html>
```

```
// mover.js
//    Illustrates moving an element within a document

// The event handler function to move an element
function moveIt(movee, newTop, newLeft) {
  dom = document.getElementById(movee).style;

// Change the top and left properties to perform the move
//   Note the addition of units to the input values
  dom.top = newTop + "px";
  dom.left = newLeft + "px";
}
```

Figures 6.4 and 6.5 show the initial and new positions of an image in mover.html.

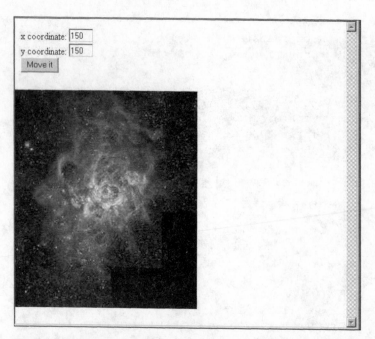

Figure 6.4 Display of mover.html (before pressing the *Move It* button)

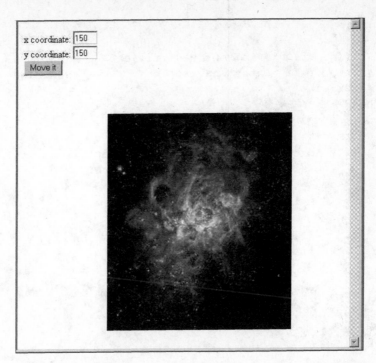

Figure 6.5 Display of `mover.html` (after pressing the *Move It* button)

6.4 Element Visibility

Document elements can be specified to be visible or hidden with the value of their `visibility` property. The two possible values for `visibility` are, quite naturally, `visible` and `hidden`. The appearance or disappearance of an element can be controlled by the user through a widget.

The following example displays an image and allows the user to toggle (with a button) causing the image to appear and not appear in the document display. Once again, the event handler is in a separate file.

```
<?xml version = "1.0"  encoding = "utf-8" ?>
<!DOCTYPE html PUBLIC "-//W3C//DTD XHTML 1.0 Strict//EN"
   "http://www.w3.org/TR/xhtml1/DTD/xhtml1-strict.dtd">

<!-- showHide.html
     Uses showHide.js
     Illustrates visibility control of elements
     -->
```

```
<html xmlns = "http://www.w3.org/1999/xhtml">
  <head>
    <title> Visibility control </title>
    <script type = "text/javascript"  src = "showHide.js" >
    </script>
  </head>
  <body>
    <form action = "">
      <div id = "saturn"  style = "position: relative;
          visibility: visible;">
        <img src = "../images/saturn.jpg"
            alt = "(Picture of Saturn)" />
      </div>
      <p>
        <br />
        <input type = "button"  value = "Toggle Saturn"
            onclick = "flipImag()" />
      </p>
    </form>
  </body>
</html>
```

```
// showHide.js
//    Illustrates visibility control of elements

// The event handler function to toggle the visibility
//    of the images of Saturn
function flipImag() {
  dom = document.getElementById("saturn").style;

// Flip the visibility adjective to whatever it is not now
 if (dom.visibility == "visible")
   dom.visibility = "hidden";
 else
   dom.visibility = "visible";
}
```

6.5 Changing Colors and Fonts

The background and foreground colors of the document display can be dynamically changed, as can the font properties of the text.

6.5.1   Changing Colors

Dynamic changes to colors are relatively simple. In the following example, the user is presented with two text boxes into which color specifications can be typed—one for the document background color and one for the foreground color. The colors can be specified by any of the three ways that color properties can be given anywhere else. A JavaScript function, which is called (using the onchange event) whenever one of the text boxes is changed, makes the change in the document's appropriate color property, backgroundColor or color. The first of the two parameters to the function specifies whether the new color is for the background or foreground; the second specifies the new color. The new color is the value property of the text box that was changed by the user.

In this example, the calls to the handler functions are in the XHTML text box elements. This approach allows a simple way to reference the element's DOM address. The JavaScript this variable in this situation is a reference to the object that represents the element in which it is referenced. A reference to such an object is its DOM address. Therefore, in a text element, the value of this is the DOM address of the text element. So, in the example, this.value is used as an actual parameter to the handler function. Because the call is in an input element, this.value is the DOM address of the value of the input element.

```
<?xml version = "1.0"  encoding = "utf-8" ?>
<!DOCTYPE html PUBLIC "-//W3C//DTD XHTML 1.0 Strict//EN"
  "http://www.w3.org/TR/xhtml1/DTD/xhtml1-strict.dtd">

<!-- dynColors.html
     Uses dynColors.js
     Illustrates dynamic foreground and background colors
     -->
<html xmlns = "http://www.w3.org/1999/xhtml">
  <head>
    <title> Dynamic colors </title>
    <script type = "text/javascript"  src = "dynColors.js" >
    </script>
  </head>
  <body>
    <p style = "font-family: Times; font-style: italic;
                font-size: 24pt" >
      This small page illustrates dynamic setting of the
      foreground and background colors for a document
    </p>
    <form action = "">
      <p>
```

```
            <label>
              Background color:
              <input type = "text"  name = "background" size = "10"
                     onchange = "setColor('background', this.value)" />
            </label>
            <br />
            <label>
              Foreground color:
              <input type = "text"  name = "foreground" size = "10"
                     onchange = "setColor('foreground', this.value)" />
            </label>
            <br />
        </p>
      </form>
    </body>
</html>
```

```
// dynColors.js
//    Illustrates dynamic foreground and background colors

// The event handler function to dynamically set the
// color of background or foreground
function setColor(where, newColor) {
  if (where == "background")
    document.body.style.backgroundColor = newColor;
  else
    document.body.style.color = newColor;
}
```

6.5.2 Changing Fonts

Web users are accustomed to having links in documents change color when the cursor is placed over them. Any property of a link can be changed by using the mouse event mouseover to trigger JavaScript event handlers. Thus, the font style and font size, as well as the color and background color of a link, can be changed when the cursor is placed over the link. The link can be changed back to its original form when an event handler is triggered with the mouseout event. In the following example, the only element is a sentence with an embedded link. The foreground color for the document is the default black. The link is presented in blue. When the mouse cursor is placed over the link, its color changes to red and its font style changes to italic. Notice that the event handlers in this example are embedded in the markup. This is one of those cases where the small amount of JavaScript needed does not justify putting it in a separate file.

```
<?xml version = "1.0"  encoding = "utf-8" ?>
<!DOCTYPE html PUBLIC "-//W3C//DTD XHTML 1.0 Strict//EN"
  "http://www.w3.org/TR/xhtml1/DTD/xhtml1-strict.dtd">

<!-- dynLink.html
     Illustrates dynamic font styles and colors for links
     -->
<html xmlns = "http://www.w3.org/1999/xhtml">
  <head>
    <title> Dynamic fonts for links </title>
    <style type = "text/css">
      .regText {font: Times; font-size: 16pt;}
    </style>
  </head>
  <body>
    <p class = "regText">
      The state of
      <a style = "color: blue;"
        onmouseover = "this.style.color = 'red';
                       this.style.font = 'italic 16pt Times';"
        onmouseout = "this.style.color = 'blue';
                      this.style.font = 'normal 16pt Times';">
        Washington
      </a>
      produces many of our nation's apples.
    </p>
  </body>
</html>
```

Figures 6.6 and 6.7 show browser displays of the `dynLink.html` document with the mouse cursor not over and then over the link.

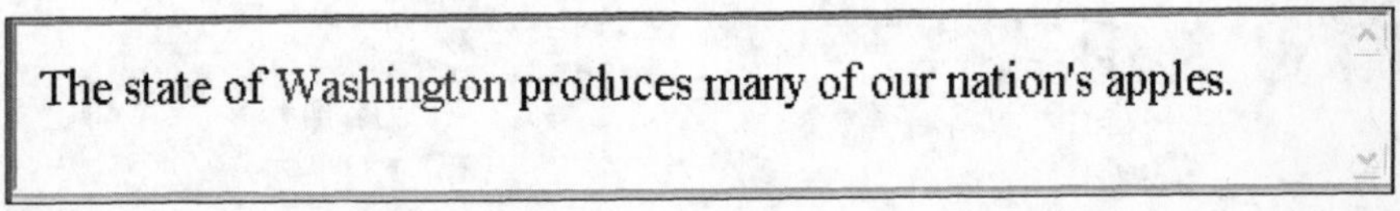

The state of Washington produces many of our nation's apples.

Figure 6.6 Display of `dynLink.html` with the cursor not over the link

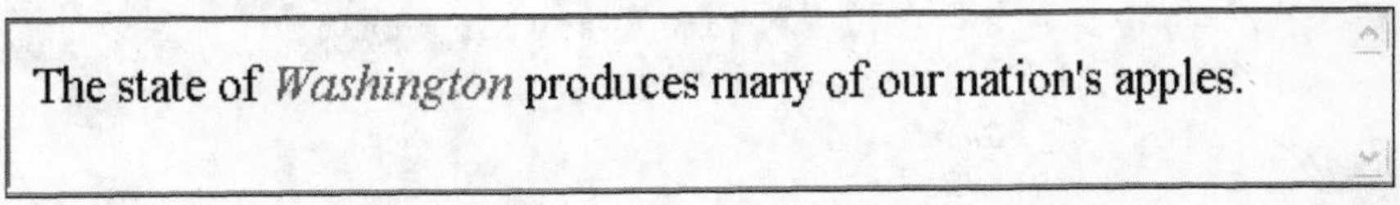

The state of *Washington* produces many of our nation's apples.

Figure 6.7 Display of `dynLink.html` with the mouse cursor over the link

6.6 Dynamic Content

We have explored the options of dynamically changing the positions of elements, their visibility, and the colors, background colors, and styles of text fonts. This section investigates changing the content of XHTML elements. The content of an element is accessed through the `value` property of its associated JavaScript object. So, changing the content of an element is not essentially different from changing other properties of the element. We now develop an example that illustrates one use of dynamic content.

Assistance to a browser user filling out a form can be provided by an associated text area, often called a *help box*. The content of the help box can change, depending on the placement of the mouse cursor. When the cursor is placed over a particular input field, the help box can display advice on how the field is to be filled in. When the cursor is moved away from an input field, the help box content can be changed to simply indicate that assistance is available.

In our example, an array of messages that can be displayed in the help box is defined in JavaScript. When the mouse cursor is placed over an input field, the `mouseover` event is used to call a function that changes the help box content to the appropriate value (the one associated with the input field). The appropriate value is specified with a parameter sent to the handler function. The `mouseout` event is used to trigger the change of the content of the help box back to the "standard" value.

```
<?xml version = "1.0" encoding = "utf-8" ?>
<!DOCTYPE html PUBLIC "-//W3C//DTD XHTML 1.0 Strict//EN"
  "http://www.w3.org/TR/xhtml1/DTD/xhtml1-strict.dtd">

<!-- dynValue.html
     Uses dynValue.js
     Illustrates dynamic values
     -->
<html xmlns = "http://www.w3.org/1999/xhtml">
  <head>
    <title> Dynamic values </title>
    <script type = "text/javascript"  src = "dynValue.js" >
    </script>
  </head>
  <body>
    <form action = "">
      <p style = "font-weight: bold">
        <span style = "font-style: italic">
          Customer information
        </span>
        <br /><br />
```

```
            <label>
              Name:
              <input type = "text"  onmouseover = "messages(0)"
                     onmouseout = "messages(4)" />
            </label>
            <br />
            <label>
              Email:
              <input type = "text"  onmouseover = "messages(1)"
                     onmouseout = "messages(4)" />
            </label>
            <br /> <br />
            <span style = "font-style: italic">
              To create an account, provide the following:
            </span>
            <br /> <br />
            <label>
              User ID:
              <input type = "text"  onmouseover = "messages(2)"
                     onmouseout = "messages(4)" />
            </label>
            <br />
            <label>
              Password:
              <input type = "password"
                     onmouseover = "messages(3)"
                     onmouseout = "messages(4)" />
            </label>
            <br />
            <textarea id = "adviceBox"  rows = "3"  cols = "50"
                      style = "position: absolute; left: 250px;
                      top: 0px">
This box provides advice on filling out the form
on this page. Put the mouse cursor over any input
field to get advice.
            </textarea>
            <br /><br />
            <input type = "submit"  value = "Submit" />
            <input type = "reset"  value = "Reset" />
          </p>
        </form>
      </body>
</html>
```

```
// dynValue.js
//    Illustrates dynamic values

var helpers = ["Your name must be in the form: \n \
 first name, middle initial., last name",
  "Your email address must have the form: \
user@domain",
  "Your user ID must have at least six characters",
  "Your password must have at least six \
characters and it must include one digit",
  "This box provides advice on filling out\
the form on this page. Put the mouse cursor over any \
 input field to get advice"]

// ************************************************************
// The event handler function to change the value of the
// textarea

function messages(adviceNumber) {
  document.getElementById("adviceBox").value =
                                    helpers[adviceNumber];
}
```

Note that the backslash characters that terminate some of the lines of the literal array of messages specify that the string literal is continued on the next line.

Figure 6.8 shows a browser display of the document defined in dynValue.html when the mouse cursor is over the *User ID* input field.

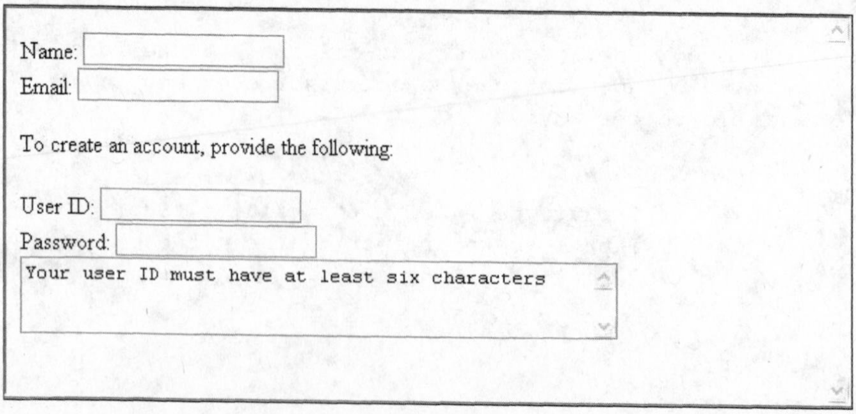

Figure 6.8 Display of dynValue.html with the cursor over *User ID*

6.7 Stacking Elements

The top and left properties allow the placement of an element anywhere in the two dimensions of the display of a document. Although the display is restricted to two physical dimensions, the effect of a third dimension is possible through the simple concept of stacked elements, such as that used to stack windows in windowing systems. Although multiple elements can occupy the same space in the document, one is considered to be on top and is displayed. The top element hides the parts of the lower elements on which it is superimposed. The placement of elements in this third dimension is controlled by the z-index attribute of the element. An element whose z-index is greater than that of an element in the same space will be displayed over the other element, effectively hiding the element with the smaller z-index value. The JavaScript style property associated with the z-index attribute is zIndex.

In the following example, three images are placed on the display so that they overlap. In the XHTML description of this, each image tag includes an onclick attribute, which is used to trigger the execution of a JavaScript handler function. First the function defines DOM addresses for the last top element and the new top element. Then the function sets the zIndex value of the two elements so that the old top element has a value of 0 and the new top element has the value 10, effectively putting it at the top. The script keeps track of which image is currently on top with the global variable top, which is changed every time a new element is moved to the top with the toTop function. Note that the zIndex value, as in the case with other properties, is a string.

```
<?xml version = "1.0"  encoding = "utf-8" ?>
<!DOCTYPE html PUBLIC "-//W3C//DTD XHTML 1.0 Strict//EN"
  "http://www.w3.org/TR/xhtml1/DTD/xhtml1-strict.dtd">

<!-- stacking.html
     Uses stacking.js
     Illustrates dynamic stacking of images
     -->
<html xmlns = "http://www.w3.org/1999/xhtml">
  <head>
    <title> Dynamic stacking of images </title>
    <script type = "text/javascript"  src = "stacking.js" >
    </script>
    <style type = "text/css">
      .plane1 {position: absolute; top: 0; left: 0;
               z-index: 0;}
      .plane2 {position: absolute; top: 50px; left: 110px;
               z-index: 0;}
      .plane3 {position: absolute; top: 100px; left: 220px;
               z-index: 0;}
```

```
        </style>
      </head>
      <body>
        <p>
          <img class = "plane1"  id = "C172"
               src = "../images/c172.gif"
               alt = "(Picture of a C172)"
               onclick = "toTop('C172')" />
          <img class = "plane2"  id = "cix"
               src = "../images/cix.gif"
               alt = "(Picture of a Citation airplane)"
               onclick = "toTop('cix')" />
          <img class = "plane3"  id = "C182"
               src = "../images/c182.gif"
               alt = "(Picture of a C182)"
               onclick = "toTop('C182')" />
        </p>
      </body>
    </html>
```

```
// stacking.js
//   Illustrates dynamic stacking of images
var top = "C172";

// The event handler function to move the given element
// to the top of the display stack
function toTop(newTop) {

// Set the two dom addresses, one for the old top
// element and one for the new top element
  domTop = document.getElementById(top).style;
  domNew = document.getElementById(newTop).style;

// Set the zIndex properties of the two elements, and
// reset top to the new top
  domTop.zIndex = "0";
  domNew.zIndex = "10";
  top = newTop;
}
```

Figures 6.9, 6.10, and 6.11 show the document described by `stacking.html` in three of its possible configurations.

Figure 6.9 The initial display of `stacking.html` (photographs courtesy of Cessna Aircraft Company)

Figure 6.10 The display of `stacking.html` after clicking the second image (photographs courtesy of Cessna Aircraft Company)

Figure 6.11 The display of `stacking.html` after clicking the bottom image (photographs courtesy of Cessna Aircraft Company)

6.8 Locating the Mouse Cursor

Recall from Chapter 5 that every event that occurs in an XHTML document creates an event object. This object includes some information about the event. A mouse-click event is an implementation of the `MouseEvent` interface, which defines two pairs of properties that provide geometric coordinates of the position of the element in the display that created the event. One of these pairs, `clientX` and `clientY`, gives the coordinates of the element relative to the upper-left corner of the browser display window, in pixels. The other pair, `screenX` and `screenY`, also gives coordinates of the element but relative to the client computer's screen. Obviously, the former pair is usually more useful than the latter.

In the following example, `where.html`, two pairs of text boxes are used to display these four properties every time the mouse button is clicked. The handler is triggered by the `onclick` attribute of the body element. An image is displayed just below the display of the coordinates, but only to make the screen more interesting.

The call to the handler in this example sends `event`, which is a reference to the event just created in the element, as a parameter. This is a bit of magic, because the event object is implicitly created. In the handler, the formal parameter is used to access the coordinate properties. Note that the handling of the event object is not implemented the same way in the popular browsers. The

Firefox browsers send it as a parameter to event handlers, whereas Microsoft browsers make it available as a global property. The code in where.html works for both of these approaches by sending it in the call to the handler. It is available in the call with Microsoft browsers because it is visible there as a global variable. Of course, for a Microsoft browser, it need not be sent at all.

```
<?xml version = "1.0"  encoding = "utf-8" ?>
<!DOCTYPE html PUBLIC "-//W3C//DTD XHTML 1.0 Strict//EN"
  "http://www.w3.org/TR/xhtml1/DTD/xhtml1-strict.dtd">

<!-- where.html
     Uses where.js
     Illustrates x and y coordinates of the mouse cursor
     -->
<html xmlns = "http://www.w3.org/1999/xhtml">
  <head>
    <title> Where is the cursor? </title>
    <script type = "text/javascript"  src = "where.js" >
    </script>
  </head>
  <body onclick = "findIt(event)">
    <form action = "">
      <p>
        Within the client area: <br />
        x:
        <input type = "text"  id = "xcoor1"  size = "4" />
        y:
        <input type = "text"  id = "ycoor1"  size = "4" />
        <br /><br />
        Relative to the origin of the screen coordinate system:
        <br />
        x:
        <input type = "text"  id = "xcoor2"  size = "4" />
        y:
        <input type = "text"  id = "ycoor2"  size = "4" />
      </p>
    </form>
    <p>
      <img src = "../images/c172.gif"  alt = "(Picture of C172)" />
    </p>
  </body>
</html>
```

```
// where.js
//    Show the coordinates of the mouse cursor position
//    in an image and anywhere on the screen when the mouse
//    is clicked

// The event handler function to get and display the
//    coordinates of the cursor, both in an element and
//    on the screen
function findIt(evt) {
    document.getElementById("xcoor1").value = evt.clientX;
    document.getElementById("ycoor1").value = evt.clientY;
    document.getElementById("xcoor2").value = evt.screenX;
    document.getElementById("ycoor2").value = evt.screenY;
}
```

Figure 6.12 shows a browser display of where.html.

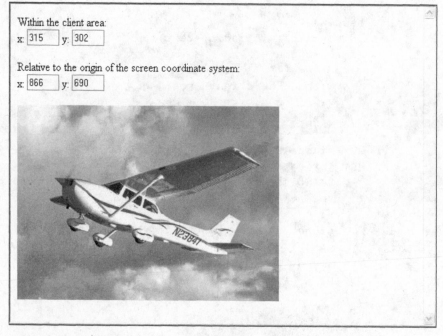

Figure 6.12 Display of where.html (the cursor was in the tail section of the plane)

One interesting note about the cursor-finding example is that with IE7, the mouse clicks are ignored if the mouse cursor is below the last element on the display. The FX2 browser always responds the same way regardless of where the cursor is on the display.

6.9 Reacting to a Mouse Click

The following is another example related to reacting to mouse clicks. In this case, the mousedown and mouseup events are used to show and hide the message "Please don't click here!" on the display under the mouse cursor whenever the mouse button is clicked, regardless of where the cursor is at the time. The offsets (-130 for left and -25 for top) modify the actual cursor position so that the message is approximately centered over the cursor position.

```
<?xml version = "1.0"  encoding = "utf-8" ?>
<!DOCTYPE html PUBLIC "-//W3C//DTD XHTML 1.0 Strict//EN"
   "http://www.w3.org/TR/xhtml1/DTD/xhtml1-strict.dtd">


<!-- anywhere.html
     Uses anywhere.js
     Display a message when the mouse button is pressed,
     no matter where it is on the screen
     -->
<html xmlns = "http://www.w3.org/1999/xhtml">
  <head>
    <title> Sense events anywhere </title>
    <script type = "text/javascript"  src = "anywhere.js" >
    </script>
  </head>
  <body onmousedown = "displayIt(event);"
        onmouseup = "hideIt();">
    <p>
      <span id= "message"
            style = "color: red; visibility: hidden;
                     position: relative;
                     font-size: 20pt; font-style: italic;
                     font-weight: bold;">
          Please don't click here!
      </span>
      <br /><br /><br /><br /><br /><br /><br /><br />
      <br /><br /><br /><br /><br /><br /><br /><br />
    </p>
  </body>
</html>
```

```
// anywhere.js
//    Display a message when the mouse button is pressed,
//    no matter where it is on the screen

// The event handler function to display the message
function displayIt(evt) {
  var dom = document.getElementById("message");
  dom.style.left = (evt.clientX - 130) + "px";
  dom.style.top = (evt.clientY - 25) + "px";
  dom.style.visibility = "visible";
}

// *****************************************************
// The event handler function to hide the message
function hideIt() {
  document.getElementById("message").style.visibility =
      "hidden";
}
```

6.10 Slow Movement of Elements

So far, only element movements that happen instantly have been considered. These movements are controlled by changing the top and left properties of the element to be moved. The only way to move an element slowly is to move it by small amounts many times, with the moves separated by small amounts of time. JavaScript has two Window methods that are capable of this: setTimeout and setInterval.

The setTimeout method takes two parameters: a string of JavaScript code to be executed and a number of milliseconds of delay before executing the given code. For example, consider the following call:

```
setTimeout("mover()", 20);
```

This causes a 20-millisecond delay, after which the function mover is called.

The setInterval method has two forms. One form takes two parameters, exactly as does setTimeout. It executes the given code repeatedly, using the second parameter as the interval in milliseconds between executions. The second form of setInterval takes a variable number of parameters. The first parameter is the name of a function to be called, the second is the interval in milliseconds between the calls to the function, and the remaining parameters are used as actual parameters to the function being called.

The example presented here, moveText.html, moves a string of text from one position (100, 100) to a new position (300, 300). The move is accomplished by using setTimeout to call a mover function every millisecond until the final position (300, 300) is reached. The initial position of the text is set in the span element that specifies the text. The `onload` attribute of the body element is used to call a function, `initText`, to initialize the x and y coordinates for the initial position to the `left` and `top` properties of the element and call the mover function.

The mover function, named `moveText`, takes the current coordinates of the text as parameters, moves them one pixel toward the final position, and then calls itself with the new coordinates using `setTimeout`. The recomputation of the coordinates is complicated by the fact that we want the code to work regardless of the direction of the move.

One consideration with this script is that the coordinate properties are stored as strings with units attached. For example, if the initial position of an element is (100, 100), its `left` and `top` property values both have the string value `"100px"`. To change the properties arithmetically, the properties must be numbers. Therefore, the property values are converted to numbers in the `initText` function by stripping the nondigit unit parts. Then, before the `left` and `top` properties are set to the new coordinates, the units abbreviation (in this case, `"px"`) is catenated back on to the coordinates.

It is interesting that in this example, placing the event handler in a separate file avoids a problem that would occur if the JavaScript were embedded in the markup. The problem is the use of XHTML comments to hide JavaScript and having possible parts of XHTML comments embedded in the JavaScript. For example, if the JavaScript statement `x--;` is embedded in an XHTML comment, the validator complains that the `--` in the statement is an invalid comment declaration. In the JavaScript code of the following example, the statement `x--;` is used to move the x-coordinate of the text being moved.

In the code file, `moveTextfuns.js`, note the complexity of the call to the `moveText` function in the call to `setTimeout`. This is required because the call to `moveText` must be built from static strings with the values of the variables `x` and `y` catenated in.

The JavaScript script for `moveText.html` is as follows:

```xml
<?xml version = "1.0" encoding = "utf-8"?>
<!DOCTYPE html PUBLIC "-//W3C//DTD XHTML 1.0 Strict//EN"
  "http://www.w3.org/TR/xhtml1/DTD/xhtml1-strict.dtd">

<!-- moveText.html
     Uses moveTextfuns.js
     Illustrates a moving text element
     -->
<html xmlns = "http://www.w3.org/1999/xhtml">
  <head>
    <title> Moving text </title>
    <script type = "text/javascript"
            src = "moveTextfuns.js">
    </script>
  </head>
```

```html
<!-- Call the initializing function on load, giving the
     destination coordinates for the text to be moved
     -->
  <body onload = "initText()">

<!-- The text to be moved, including its initial position -->
    <p>
      <span id = 'theText' style =
               "position: absolute; left: 100px; top: 100px;
                font: bold 20pt 'Times Roman';
                color: blue;"> Jump in the lake!
      </span>
    </p>
  </body>
</html>
```

```javascript
//************************************************************
// This is moveTextfuns.js - used with moveText.html
   var dom, x, y, finalx = 300, finaly = 300;

// *********************************************** //
// A function to initialize the x and y coordinates
//  of the current position of the text to be moved,
//  and then call the mover function
   function initText() {
       dom = document.getElementById('theText').style;

   /* Get the current position of the text */
       var x = dom.left;
       var y = dom.top;

   /* Convert the string values of left and top to
      numbers by stripping off the units */
       x = x.match(/\d+/);
       y = y.match(/\d+/);

   /* Call the function that moves it */
       moveText(x, y);
   } /*** end of function initText */

// *********************************************** //
// A function to move the text from its original
//  position to (finalx, finaly)
   function moveText(x, y) {
```

```
    /* If the x coordinates are not equal, move
       x toward finalx */
    if (x != finalx)
        if (x > finalx) x--;
        else if (x < finalx) x++;

    /* If the y coordinates are not equal, move
       y toward finaly */
    if (y != finaly)
        if (y > finaly) y--;
        else if (y < finaly) y++;

    /* As long as the text is not at the destination,
       call the mover with the current position */
    if ((x != finalx) || (y != finaly)) {

    /* Put the units back on the coordinates before
       assigning them to the properties to cause the
       move */
        dom.left = x + "px";
        dom.top = y + "px";

    /* Recursive call, after a 1-millisecond delay */
        setTimeout("moveText(" + x + "," + y + ")", 1);
    }

} /*** end of function moveText */
```

6.11 Dragging and Dropping Elements

One of the more powerful effects of event handling is allowing the user to drag and drop elements around the display screen. The mouseup, mousedown, and mousemove events can be used to implement this. Changing the top and left properties of an element, as seen earlier in this chapter, causes the element to move. To illustrate drag and drop, an example that creates a magnetic poetry system is developed, showing two static lines of a poem and allowing the user to create the last two lines from a collection of movable words.

This example uses a mixture of the DOM 0 and DOM 2 event models. The DOM 0 model is used for the call to the handler for the mousedown event. The rest of the process is designed with the DOM 2 model. The mousedown event handler, grabber, takes the Event object as its parameter. It gets the element to be moved from the currentTarget property of the Event object and puts it in a global variable so it is available to the other handlers. Then it determines the coordinates of the current position of the element to be moved and computes the difference between them and the coordinates of the position of the mouse cursor. These two differences, which are used by the handler for mousemove to actually move the element, are also placed in global variables. The `grabber` handler also registers the event handlers for mousemove and mouseup. These two handlers are named `mover` and `dropper`, respectively. The `dropper` handler disconnects mouse movements from the element-moving process by unregistering the handlers `mover` and `dropper`. The following is the document we have just described:

```
<?xml version = "1.0"  encoding = "utf-8" ?>
<!DOCTYPE html PUBLIC "-//W3C//DTD XHTML 1.0 Strict//EN"
  "http://www.w3.org/TR/xhtml1/DTD/xhtml1-strict.dtd">

<!-- dragNDrop.html
     An example to illustrate the DOM 2 Event model
     Allows the user to drag and drop words to complete
     a short poem
     Does not work with IE7
     -->
<html xmlns = "http://www.w3.org/1999/xhtml">
  <head>
    <title> Drag and drop </title>
    <script type = "text/javascript"  src = "dragNdrop.js" >
    </script>
  </head>
  <body style = "font-size: 20;">
    <p>
      Roses are red <br />
      Violets are blue <br />

        <span style = "position: absolute; top: 200px; left: 0px;
                       background-color: lightgrey;"
            onmousedown = "grabber(event);"> candy </span>
        <span style = "position: absolute; top: 200px; left: 75px;
                       background-color: lightgrey;"
            onmousedown = "grabber(event);"> cats </span>
        <span style = "position: absolute; top: 200px; left: 150px;
                       background-color: lightgrey;"
            onmousedown = "grabber(event);"> cows </span>
        <span style = "position: absolute; top: 200px; left: 225px;
                       background-color: lightgrey;"
            onmousedown = "grabber(event);"> glue </span>
        <span style = "position: absolute; top: 200px; left: 300px;
                       background-color: lightgrey;"
            onmousedown = "grabber(event);"> is </span>
```

```
            <span style = "position: absolute; top: 200px; left: 375px;
                      background-color: lightgrey;"
               onmousedown = "grabber(event);"> is </span>
            <span style = "position: absolute; top: 200px; left: 450px;
                      background-color: lightgrey;"
               onmousedown = "grabber(event);"> meow </span>
            <span style = "position: absolute; top: 250px; left: 0px;
                      background-color: lightgrey;"
               onmousedown = "grabber(event);"> mine </span>
            <span style = "position: absolute; top: 250px; left: 75px;
                      background-color: lightgrey;"
               onmousedown = "grabber(event);"> moo </span>
            <span style = "position: absolute; top: 250px; left: 150px;
                      background-color: lightgrey;"
               onmousedown = "grabber(event);"> new </span>
            <span style = "position: absolute; top: 250px; left: 225px;
                      background-color: lightgrey;"
               onmousedown = "grabber(event);"> old </span>
            <span style = "position: absolute; top: 250px; left: 300px;
                      background-color: lightgrey;"
               onmousedown = "grabber(event);"> say </span>
            <span style = "position: absolute; top: 250px; left: 375px;
                      background-color: lightgrey;"
               onmousedown = "grabber(event);"> say </span>
            <span style = "position: absolute; top: 250px; left: 450px;
                      background-color: lightgrey;"
               onmousedown = "grabber(event);"> so </span>
            <span style = "position: absolute; top: 300px; left: 0px;
                      background-color: lightgrey;"
               onmousedown = "grabber(event);"> sticky </span>
            <span style = "position: absolute; top: 300px; left: 75px;
                      background-color: lightgrey;"
               onmousedown = "grabber(event);"> sweet </span>
            <span style = "position: absolute; top: 300px; left: 150px;
                      background-color: lightgrey;"
               onmousedown = "grabber(event);"> syrup </span>
            <span style = "position: absolute; top: 300px; left: 225px;
                      background-color: lightgrey;"
               onmousedown = "grabber(event);"> too </span>
            <span style = "position: absolute; top: 300px; left: 300px;
                      background-color: lightgrey;"
               onmousedown = "grabber(event);"> yours </span>
         </p>
      </body>
   </html>
```

```
// dragNDrop.js
//    An example to illustrate the DOM 2 Event model
//    Allows the user to drag and drop words to complete
//    a short poem
//    Does not work with IE7

// Define variables for the values computed by
// the grabber event handler but needed by mover
// event handler
      var diffX, diffY, theElement;

// ********************************************************
// The event handler function for grabbing the word
function grabber(event) {

// Set the global variable for the element to be moved
  theElement = event.currentTarget;

// Determine the position of the word to be grabbed,
// first removing the units from left and top
  var posX = parseInt(theElement.style.left);
  var posY = parseInt(theElement.style.top);

// Compute the difference between where it is and
// where the mouse click occurred
  diffX = event.clientX - posX;
  diffY = event.clientY - posY;

// Now register the event handlers for moving and
// dropping the word
  document.addEventListener("mousemove", mover, true);
  document.addEventListener("mouseup", dropper, true);

// Stop propagation of the event and stop any default
// browser action
  event.stopPropagation();
  event.preventDefault();

}  //** end of grabber

// ********************************************************
// The event handler function for moving the word
function mover(event) {

// Compute the new position, add the units, and move the word
```

```
      theElement.style.left = (event.clientX - diffX) + "px";
      theElement.style.top = (event.clientY - diffY) + "px";

// Prevent propagation of the event
   event.stopPropagation();
}   //** end of mover

// ****************************************************
// The event handler function for dropping the word
function dropper(event) {

// Unregister the event handlers for mouseup and mousemove
   document.removeEventListener("mouseup", dropper, true);
   document.removeEventListener("mousemove", mover, true);

// Prevent propagation of the event
   event.stopPropagation();
}   //** end of dropper
```

Figure 6.13 shows a browser display of `dragNDrop.html`.

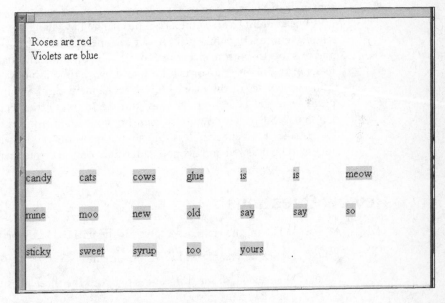

Figure 6.13 Display of `dragNDrop.html`

Note that the drag-and-drop process can be written with the DOM 0 event model. However, it can only be made portable by having the script detect which browser is being used and using different code for the different browsers. We have chosen to write it with the DOM 2 event model rather than deal with that untidy situation. Before long, it is hoped that all browsers will implement the DOM 2 model.

Summary

The CSS-P standard enables us initially to place XHTML elements wherever we want in a document and then move them later. Elements can be positioned at any given location in the display of a document if their `position` property is set to `absolute` or `relative`. Absolute positioning is used to place an element at a position in the display of the document relative to the upper-left corner of the display, using the `left` and `top` properties of the element. Relative positioning is used to place an element at a specified offset from the `top` and `left` coordinates of where it would have gone with the default static positioning. Relative positioning also allows an element to be moved later. Static positioning, which is the default, disallows both specific initial placement and dynamic moving of the element. An XHTML element can be made to disappear and reappear by changing its `visibility` property.

The color of the background of a document is stored in its `backgroundColor` property; the color of an element is stored in its `color` property. Both of these can be dynamically changed. The font, font size, and font style of text also can be changed.

The content of an element can be changed by changing its `value` property. An element in a document can be set to appear to be in front of other elements, and this top-to-bottom stacking order can be dynamically changed. The coordinates of the mouse cursor can be found every time a mouse button is pressed, using properties of the event object. An element can be animated, at least in a crude way, by changing its `top` and `left` properties repeatedly by small amounts. Such an operation can be controlled by the `Window` method `setTimeout`. Event handlers for the mouse events can be written to allow elements to be dragged and dropped anywhere on the display screen by the user.

Review Questions

6.1 What are the standard values for the `visibility` property?

6.2 Define a dynamic XHTML document.

6.3 Describe all of the differences between the three possible values of the `position` property.

6.4 If you know the id of an XHTML element, how can you get the DOM address of that element in JavaScript?

6.5 In what additional way can you obtain the DOM addresses of radio buttons and checkboxes?

6.6 What is CSS-P?

6.7 What properties control the foreground and background colors of a document?

6.8 What events can be used to change a font when the mouse cursor is moved over and away from an element?

6.9 To move an element to the top of the display, do you set its `z-index` property to a large number or a small number?

6.10 What property has the content of an element?

6.11 If you have a variable that has the id of an XHTML element, how can you get the DOM address of that element in JavaScript?

6.12 What JavaScript variable is associated with the `z-index` property?

6.13 What exactly is stored in the `clientX` and `clientY` properties after a mouse click?

6.14 Describe the parameters and actions of the `setTimeout` function.

6.15 What exactly is stored in the `screenX` and `screenY` properties after a mouse click?

Exercises

Write, test, validate, and debug (if necessary) the following documents:

6.1 The document must have a paragraph of at least 20 lines of text that describe you. This paragraph must be centered on the page and have space for 30 characters per line only. A light gray image of yourself must be superimposed over the center of the text as a nested element.

6.2 Modify the document described in Exercise 6.1 to add four buttons. These buttons must be labeled *East*, *West*, *North*, and *South*. When they're pressed, the buttons must move your image to the specified corner of the text. Initially, your image must appear in the north (upper) corner of the text.

6.3 Modify the document described in Exercise 6.2 to make the buttons toggle their respective copies of your image on and off so that, at any time, the document may include none, one, ten, twenty, or thirty copies of your image. The initial document should have no images shown.

6.4 The document must have a paragraph of text that describes your home. Choose at least four different phrases (three to six words) of this paragraph and make them change font, font style, color, and font size when the mouse cursor is placed over them. Each of the different phrases must change to different fonts, font styles, colors, and font sizes.

6.5 The document must display an image and four buttons. The buttons should be labeled simply *1, 2, 3,* and *4*. When pressed, each button should change the content of the image to that of a different image.

6.6 The document must contain three short paragraphs of text, stacked on top of each other, with only enough of each showing so that the mouse cursor can always be placed over some part of them. When the cursor is placed over the exposed part of any paragraph, it should rise to the top to become completely visible.

6.7 Modify the document of Exercise 6.6 so that when a paragraph is moved from the bottom stacking position, it returns to its original position rather than to the top.

6.8 The document must have a small image of Mona Lisa, which must appear when the mouse button is clicked at the position of the mouse cursor, regardless of the position of the cursor at the time.

6.9 The document must contain the statement "Save time with TIME-SAVER 1.8" which continuously moves back and forth across the top of the display.

6.10 Modify the document of Exercise 6.9 to make the statement change color between green and blue every third step of its movement (assuming each move is 1 pixel long).

6.11 Modify the `mover` example in Section 6.10 to input the starting, middle, and ending position of the element to be moved.

Introduction to XML

Some people consider the eXtensible Markup Language (XML) to be one of the most important among the parade of technologies developed to support the World Wide Web. Clearly, it has already had far-reaching effects on the storage and processing of data. XML consists of a collection of related technologies specified by recommendations developed by the W3C. This chapter provides introductions to the most important of these.

The chapter begins with a brief discussion of the origins of XML followed by a description of some of its characteristics. Then the general syntactic structure of XML documents is described. Next, the chapter details the purpose and form of document type definitions (DTDs), including the declarations of elements, attributes, and entities. A DTD provides the elements and attributes for a markup language, as well as the rules for how the elements can appear in documents. This is followed by a description of XML namespaces. Next, XML Schema is introduced. XML Schema provides a more elaborate way to describe the structure of XML documents than DTDs. Two different approaches to formatting XML documents, CSS and XSLT style sheets, are then discussed and illustrated with examples. Actually, XSLT style sheets are used to transform XML documents. The target of the transformations we describe is an XHTML document, which can include CSS style specifications for display. Finally, we discuss the issues associated with reading and processing XML documents. Keep in mind that this chapter describes only a small part of XML and its associated technologies.

7.1 Introduction

A meta-markup language is a language for defining markup languages. The Standard Generalized Markup Language (SGML) is a meta-markup language for defining markup languages that can describe a wide variety of document types. In 1986 SGML was approved as an International Standards Organization (ISO) standard. In 1990 SGML was used as the basis for the development of HTML as the standard markup language for Web documents. In 1996 the World Wide Web Consortium (W3C) began work on XML, another meta-markup language. The first XML standard, 1.0, was published in February 1998. The second, 1.1, was published in 2004. Because this newer version is not yet widely supported, only the 1.0 version is described in this chapter.

Part of the motivation for the development of XML was the deficiencies of HTML. The purpose of HTML is to describe the layout of information in Web documents. For this purpose, HTML defines a collection of tags and attributes. An HTML user is restricted to use that set of tags and attributes only. One problem with HTML is that it was defined to describe the layout of information without considering its meaning. So, regardless of the kind of information being described with HTML, only its general form and layout can be described in a document. For example, suppose that a document stores a list of used cars for sale, and the color and price are included for each car. With HTML, those two pieces of information about a car could be stored as the content of paragraph elements, but there would be no way to find them in the document because paragraph tags could have been used for many different kinds of information. To describe a particular kind of information, it would be necessary to have tags indicating the meaning of the element's content. That would allow processing of specific categories of information in a document. For example, if the price of a used car is stored as the content of an element named `price`, an application could find all cars in the document that cost less than $20,000. Of course, no markup language could possibly include meaningful tags for all of the different kinds of information that might be stored in documents.

Another potential problem with HTML is that it enforces few restrictions on the arrangement or order of tags in a document. For example, an opening tag can appear in the content of an element, but its corresponding closing tag can appear after the end of the element in which it is nested. An example of this is as follows:

```
<strong> Now <em> is </strong> the time </em>
```

Note that although this problem was evident in HTML 4, which was in use when XML was developed, it is not a problem with XHTML, for obvious reasons.

One solution that addresses the deficiencies of HTML is for each group of users with common document needs to develop its own set of tags and attributes and then use the SGML standard to define a new markup language to meet those needs. Each application area would have its own markup language. The problem with this is that SGML is too large and complex to make this approach feasible. SGML includes a large number of capabilities that are only rarely used. A program capable of parsing SGML documents would be very large and costly to develop. In addition, SGML requires that a formal definition be provided with each new markup language. So, although having area-specific markup languages is a good idea, basing them on SGML is not.

An alternative solution to the problems of HTML is to define a simplified version of SGML and allow users to define their own markup languages based on it. XML was designed to be that simplified version of SGML. In this context, "users" means organizations of people with common data description and processing needs (rather than individual users). For example, chemists need to store chemical data in a standard way, providing a way to share data with other chemists and allowing all to use data processing tools that work on chemical data stored in the same standard format, regardless of its origin. Likewise, this is the case for many other groups with their own kinds of data to represent and process.

It is important to understand that XML was not meant to be a replacement for HTML. In fact, they have different goals. Whereas HTML is a markup language that is meant to describe the layout of general information, as well as provide some guidance for how it should be displayed, XML is a meta-markup language that provides a framework for defining specialized markup languages. HTML itself can be defined as an XML markup language. In fact, XHTML is an XML-based version of HTML.

XML is far more than a solution to the deficiencies of HTML. It provides a simple and universal way of storing any textual data. Data stored in XML documents can be electronically distributed and processed by any number of different applications. These applications are relatively easy to write because of the standard ways in which the data is stored. Therefore, XML is a universal data interchange language.

XML is not a markup language; it is a meta-markup language that specifies rules for creating markup languages. As a result, XML includes no tags. When designing a markup language using XML, the designer must define a collection of tags that are useful in the intended area. As with XHTML, an XML tag and its content, together with the closing tag, are called an *element*.

Strictly speaking, a markup language designed with XML is called an *XML application*. However, a program that processes information stored in a document formatted with an XML application is also called an application. To avoid confusion, we will refer to an XML-based markup language as a *tag set*. We call documents that use an XML-based markup language *XML documents*.

XML documents can be written by hand using a simple text editor. This approach is, of course, impractical for large data collections, documents for which are likely to be written by programs. A browser has a default presentation style for every XHTML element, which makes it possible for the browser to display any XHTML document, whether or not CSS information is included. However, a browser cannot be expected to have default presentation styles for elements it has never seen. Therefore, the data in an XML document can be displayed by browsers only if the presentation styles are provided by style sheets of some kind.

Application programs that process the data in XML documents must analyze the document before they gain access to the data. This analysis is performed by an XML processor, which has several tasks, one of which is to parse XML documents, a process that isolates the constituent parts (such as tags, attributes, and data strings) and provides them to an application. XML processors are described in Section 7.10.

Unlike most documents produced by word processing systems, XML documents have no hidden specifications. Therefore, XML documents are plain text, which is easily readable by both people and application programs (although there are no compelling reasons for people to read them).

At the time of this writing (late 2008), the vast majority of Web clients use either Internet Explorer 6 (IE6), Internet Explorer 7 (IE7), Firefox (FX), or Firefox 2 (FX2) browsers, all of which support basic XML.

7.2 The Syntax of XML

The syntax of XML can be thought of at two distinct levels. First, there is the general low-level syntax of XML that imposes its rules on all XML documents. The other syntactic level is specified by either document type definitions (DTDs) or XML schemas. DTDs and XML schemas specify the set of tags and attributes that can appear in a particular document or collection of documents, and also the orders and arrangements in which they can appear. So, either a DTD or an XML schema can be used to define an XML-based markup language. DTDs are described in Section 7.4. XML schemas are discussed in Section 7.6. This section describes the first level of XML syntax, that which applies to all XML documents.

An XML document can include several different kinds of statements. The most common of these are the data elements of the document. XML documents may also include markup declarations, which are instructions to the XML parser, and processing instructions, which are instructions for an application program that will process the data described in the document.

All XML documents begin with an XML declaration, which looks like a processing instruction but technically is not one. The XML declaration identifies the document as being XML and provides the version number of the XML standard being used. It may also specify an encoding standard. The XML declaration appears as the first line of all XHTML documents in this book.

Comments in XML are the same as in HTML. They cannot contain two adjacent dashes, for obvious reasons.

XML names are used to name elements and attributes. An XML name must begin with a letter or an underscore and can include digits, hyphens, and periods. XML names are case sensitive, so Body, body, and BODY are all distinct names. There is no length limitation for XML names.

A small set of syntax rules applies to all XML documents. XHTML uses the same rules, and the XHTML markup in this book complies with them.

Every XML document defines a single root element, whose opening tag must appear on the first line of XML code. All other elements of an XML document must be nested inside the root element. The root element of every XHTML document is html, but in XML it has whatever name the author chooses. XML tags, like those of XHTML, are surrounded by angle brackets.

Every XML element that can have content must have a closing tag. Elements that do not include content must use a tag with the following form:

<element_name />

As is the case with XHTML, XML tags can have attributes, which are specified with name/value assignments. As with XHTML, all attribute values must be enclosed by either single or double quotation marks.

An XML document that strictly adheres to these syntax rules is considered *well formed*. Consider the following simple but complete example:

```
<?xml version = "1.0" encoding = "utf-8"?>
<ad>
  <year> 1960 </year>
  <make> Cessna </make>
  <model> Centurian </model>
  <color> Yellow with white trim </color>
  <location>
    <city> Gulfport </city>
    <state> Mississippi </state>
  </location>
</ad>
```

Notice that none of the tags in this document is defined in XHTML—all are designed for the specific content of the document. This document defines an XML tag set. This illustrates that an XML-based markup language can be defined without a DTD or an XML schema, although it is an informal definition of a tag set (in this case, no attributes were defined) with no structure rules.

When designing an XML document, the designer is often faced with the choice between adding a new attribute to an element or defining a nested element. In some cases, there is no choice. For example, if the data in question is an image, a reference to it can only be an attribute because such a reference cannot be the content of an element (because images are binary data and XML documents can contain only text). In other cases, it may not matter whether an attribute or a nested element is used. However, there are some situations in which there is a choice and one is clearly better than the other.

In some cases, nested tags are better than attributes. A document or category of documents for which tags are being defined might need to grow in structural complexity in the future. Nested tags can be added to any existing tag to describe its growing size and complexity. Nothing can be added to an attribute, however. Attributes cannot describe structure at all, so a nested element should be used if the data in question has some substructure of its own. A nested element should be used if the data is subdata of the parent element's content rather than information about the data of the parent element.

There is one situation in which an attribute should always be used: for identifying numbers or names of elements, exactly as the `id` and `name` attributes are used in XHTML. An attribute also should be used if the data in question is one value from a given set of possibilities. Finally, attributes should be used if there is no substructure or if it is really just information about the element.

The following versions of an element named `patient` illustrate three possible choices between tags and attributes:

```
<!-- A tag with one attribute -->
<patient name = "Maggie Dee Magpie">
  ...
</patient>


<!-- A tag with one nested tag -->
<patient>
  <name> Maggie Dee Magpie </name>
  ...
</patient>


<!-- A tag with one nested tag, which contains
     three nested tags -->
<patient>
  <name>
    <first> Maggie </first>
    <middle> Dee </middle>
    <last> Magpie </last>
  </name>
  ...
</patient>
```

In this example, the third choice is probably the best because it provides easy access to all of the parts of the data, which may be needed. Also, there is no compelling reason to use attributes in this structure.

7.3   XML Document Structure

An XML document often uses two auxiliary files: one that defines its tag set and structural syntactic rules and one that contains a style sheet to describe how the content of the document is to be printed or displayed. The structural syntactic rules are given as either a DTD or an XML schema. Two approaches to style specification are discussed in Sections 7.8 and 7.9.

An XML document consists of one or more entities, which are logically related collections of information, ranging in size from a single character to a book chapter. One of these entities, called the *document entity*, is always physically in the file that represents the document. The document entity can be the entire document, but in many cases it includes references to the names of entities that are stored elsewhere. For example, the document entity for a technical article might contain the beginning material and ending material but have references to the article body sections, which are entities stored in separate files. Every entity except the document entity must have a name.

There are several reasons to break a document into multiple entities. It is good to define a large document as a number of smaller parts to make it more manageable. Also, if the same data appears in more than one place in the document, defining it as an entity allows any number of references to a single copy of the data. This avoids the problem of inconsistency among the occurrences. Finally, many documents include information that cannot be represented as text, such as images. Such information units are usually stored as binary data. If a binary data unit is logically part of a document, it must be a separate entity because XML documents cannot include binary data. Such entities are called *binary entities*.

When an XML processor encounters the name of a nonbinary entity in a document, it replaces the name with the value it references. Binary entities can be handled only by applications that deal with the document, such as browsers. XML processors deal only with text.

Entity names can be any length. They must begin with a letter, a dash, or a colon. After the first character, a name can have letters, digits, periods, dashes, underscores, or colons. A reference to an entity is its name with a prepended ampersand and an appended semicolon. For example, if `apple_image` is the name of an entity, `&apple_image;` is a reference to it.

One of the common uses of entities is to allow characters that are normally used as markup delimiters to appear as themselves in a document. Because this is a common need, XML includes the entities that are predefined for XHTML, the most common of which are shown in Table 2.1 (in Chapter 2). User-defined entities can be defined only in DTDs, which are discussed in Section 7.4.

When several predefined entities must appear near each other in an XML document, their references clutter the content and make it difficult to read. In such cases, a character data section can be used. The content of a character data section is not parsed by the XML parser, so any tags it may include are not recognized as tags. This makes it possible to include special markup delimiter characters directly in the section without using their entity references. The form of a character data section is as follows:

```
<![CDATA[ content ]]>
```

For example, instead of

```
The last word of the line is &gt;&gt;&gt; here
&lt;&lt;&lt;.
```

the following could be used:

```
<![CDATA[The last word of the line is >>> here <<<]]>
```

The opening key word of a character data section is not just CDATA; it is in effect [CDATA[. An important consequence of this is that there cannot be any spaces between the [and the C, or between the A (the last character of CDATA) and the second [. The only thing that cannot appear in the content of a CDATA section is the closing delimiter,]]>.

Because the content of a character data section is not parsed by the XML parser, any entity references that are included are not expanded. For example, the content of the line

```
<![CDATA[The form of a tag is &lt;tag name&gt;]]>
```

is as follows:

```
The form of a tag is &lt;tag name&gt;
```

7.4 Document Type Definitions

A document type definition (DTD) is a set of structural rules called *declarations*, which specify a set of elements and attributes that can appear in the document as well as how and where these elements and attributes may appear. DTDs also provide entity definitions. Not all XML documents need a DTD. Use of a DTD is related to the use of an external style sheet for XHTML documents. External style sheets are used to impose a uniform style over a collection of documents. DTDs are used when the same tag set definition is used by a collection of documents, perhaps by a collection of users, and the documents must have a consistent and uniform structure.

A document can be tested against the DTD to determine if it conforms to the rules the DTD describes. Application programs that process the data in the collection of XML documents can be written to assume the particular document form. Without such structural restrictions, developing such applications would be difficult, if not impossible.

A DTD can be embedded in the XML document whose syntax rules it describes, in which case it is called an *internal DTD*. The alternative is to have the DTD stored in a separate file, in which case it is called an *external DTD*. Because external DTDs allow use with more than one XML document, they are preferable. A group of users defines a DTD for their particular kind of data and they all use that DTD, which imposes structural uniformity across all of their documents. Another reason to put a DTD in a different file is to separate the DTD, which is not XML, from the XML code of the document—that is, to avoid two different notations from appearing in the same document.

It is common knowledge that the earlier errors in software systems are found, the less expensive it is to fix them. The situation is similar in the case of DTDs. A DTD with an incorrect or inappropriate declaration can have widespread consequences. Fixing the DTD and all copies of it is the first and simplest step. After the correction of the DTD is completed, all documents that use the DTD must be tested against the DTD and often modified to conform to the changed DTD. Changes to associated style sheets also might be necessary.

Syntactically, a DTD is a sequence of declarations. Each declaration has the form of a markup declaration:

```
<!keyword ... >
```

Four possible key words can be used in a declaration: ELEMENT, used to define tags; ATTLIST, used to define tag attributes; ENTITY, used to define entities; and NOTATION, used to define data type notations. The first three of these kinds of declarations are described in the following sections. Because of their infrequent use, NOTATION declarations are not discussed.

7.4.1 Declaring Elements

The element declarations of a DTD have a form that is related to that of the rules of context-free grammars, also known as Backus-Naur form (BNF).[1] BNF is used to define the syntactic structure of programming languages. A DTD describes the syntactic structure of a particular set of documents, so it is natural for its rules to be similar to those of BNF.

Each element declaration in a DTD specifies the structure of one category of elements. The declaration provides the name of the element whose structure is being defined, along with the specification of the structure of that element. Although an XML document actually is a string of characters, it is often convenient to think of it in terms of a general tree. An element is a node in such a tree, either a leaf node or an internal node. If the element is a leaf node, its syntactic description is its character pattern. If the element is an internal node, its syntactic description is a list of its child elements, each of which can be a leaf node or an internal node.

The form of an element declaration for elements that contain elements is as follows:

```
<!ELEMENT element_name (list of names of child elements)>
```

For example, consider the following declaration:

```
<!ELEMENT memo (from, to, date, re, body)>
```

---

1. BNF is named after its primary designer, John Backus, and Peter Naur, who helped by providing some small modifications.

This element declaration would describe the document tree structure shown in Figure 7.1.

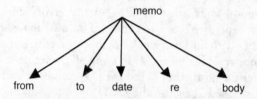

Figure 7.1 An example of the document tree structure for an element definition

In many cases, it is necessary to specify the number of times that a child element may appear. This can be done in a DTD declaration by adding a modifier to the child element specification. These modifiers, described in Table 7.1, are borrowed from regular expressions. Any child element specification can be followed by one of the modifiers.

Table 7.1 Child element specification modifiers

Modifier	Meaning
+	One or more occurrences
*	Zero or more occurrences
?	Zero or one occurrence

Consider the following DTD declaration:

```
<!ELEMENT person (parent+, age, spouse?, sibling*)>
```

In this example, a `person` element is specified to have the following child elements: one or more `parent` elements, one `age` element, possibly a `spouse` element, and zero or more `sibling` elements.

The leaf nodes of a DTD specify the data types of the content of their parent nodes, which are elements. In most cases, the content of an element is type PCDATA, for *parsable* character *data*. Parsable character data is a string of any printable characters except less than (<), greater than (>), and ampersand (&). Two other content types can be specified: EMPTY and ANY. The EMPTY type is used to specify that the element has no content. This is used for elements similar to the XHTML `img` element. The ANY type is used when the element may contain literally any content. The form of a leaf element declaration is as follows:

```
<!ELEMENT element_name (#PCDATA)>
```

7.4.2   Declaring Attributes

The attributes of an element are declared separately from the element declaration in a DTD. An attribute declaration must include the name of the element to which the attribute belongs, the attribute's name, and its type. Also, it may include a default value. The general form of an attribute declaration is as follows:

```
<!ATTLIST  element_name  attribute_name  attribute type  [default_value]>
```

If more than one attribute is declared for a given element, the declarations can be combined, as in the following example:

```
<!ATTLIST  element_name
           attribute name_1  attribute type  default_value_1
           attribute_name_2  attribute_type  default_value_2
           ...
           attribute_name_n  attribute_type  default_value_n
>
```

There are ten different attribute types. For this chapter, only one, CDATA, will be used. This type is just any string of characters that does not include less than, greater than, or ampersand characters.

The default value in an attribute declaration can specify either an actual value or a requirement for the value of the attribute in the XML document. Table 7.2 lists the possible default values.

Table 7.2 Possible default values for attributes

Value	Meaning
A value	The quoted value, which is used if none is specified in an element
#FIXED value	The quoted value, which every element will have and which cannot be changed
#REQUIRED	No default value is given; every instance of the element must specify a value
#IMPLIED	No default value is given (the browser chooses the default value); the value may or may not be specified in an element

For example, suppose the DTD included the following attribute specifications:

```
<!ATTLIST airplane places CDATA "4">
<!ATTLIST airplane engine_type CDATA #REQUIRED>
<!ATTLIST airplane price CDATA #IMPLIED>
<!ATTLIST airplane manufacturer CDATA #FIXED "Cessna">
```

The following XML element is valid for this DTD:

```
<airplane places = "10" engine_type = "jet"> </airplane>
```

Attributes that include #FIXED in the DTD may or may not be specified in particular element instances.

7.4.3 Declaring Entities

Entities can be defined so that they can be referenced anywhere in the content of an XML document, in which case they are called *general entities*. The pre-defined entities are all general entities. Entities can also be defined so that they can be referenced only in DTDs, in which case they are called *parameter entities*.

The form of an entity declaration that appears in a DTD follows:

```
<!ENTITY [%] entity_name "entity_value">
```

When the optional percent sign (%) is present in an entity declaration, it specifies that the entity is a parameter entity rather than a general entity.

Consider the following example of an entity. Suppose that a document includes a large number of references to the full name of President Kennedy. You could define an entity to represent his complete name as follows:

```
<!ENTITY jfk "John Fitzgerald Kennedy">
```

Any XML document that uses a DTD that includes this declaration can specify the complete name with just the reference &jfk;.

When an entity is longer than a few words, such as a section of a technical article, its text is defined outside the DTD. In such cases, the entity it is called an *external text entity*. The form of the declaration of an external text entity follows:

```
<!ENTITY entity_name SYSTEM "file_location">
```

The keyword SYSTEM specifies that the definition of the entity is in a different file, which is specified as the string following SYSTEM.

7.4.4 A Sample DTD

As an example of a DTD, consider a booklet of ads for used airplanes. In this case, the DTD describes the form of the booklet and each of its ads:

```
<?xml version = "1.0" encoding = "utf-8"?>

<!-- planes.dtd - a document type definition for
                  the planes.xml document, which specifies
                  a list of used airplanes for sale  -->

<!ELEMENT planes_for_sale (ad+)>
```

```
<!ELEMENT ad (year, make, model, color, description,
              price?, seller, location)>
<!ELEMENT year (#PCDATA)>
<!ELEMENT make (#PCDATA)>
<!ELEMENT model (#PCDATA)>
<!ELEMENT color (#PCDATA)>
<!ELEMENT description (#PCDATA)>
<!ELEMENT price (#PCDATA)>
<!ELEMENT seller (#PCDATA)>
<!ELEMENT location (city, state)>
<!ELEMENT city (#PCDATA)>
<!ELEMENT state (#PCDATA)>

<!ATTLIST seller phone CDATA #REQUIRED>
<!ATTLIST seller email CDATA #IMPLIED>

<!ENTITY c "Cessna">
<!ENTITY p "Piper">
<!ENTITY b "Beechcraft">
```

Some XML parsers check documents that have DTDs to ensure that the documents conform to the structure specified in the DTDs. These parsers are called *validating parsers*. Not all XML parsers are validating parsers. If an XML document specifies a DTD and is parsed by a validating XML parser, and the parser determines that the document conforms to the DTD, the document is called *valid*.

Handwritten XML documents often are not well formed, which means that they do not follow XML's syntactic rules. These errors are detected by all XML parsers, which must report them. Because errors are common, it is important to check that XML documents are well formed before making them available to site visitors. XML parsers are not allowed to either repair or ignore errors. Validating XML parsers detect and report all inconsistencies in documents relative to their DTDs. XML parsers are discussed in Section 7.10.

7.4.5   Internal and External DTDs

Recall that a DTD can appear inside an XML document or in an external file, as is the case with planes.dtd. If the DTD is included in the XML code, it must be introduced with <!DOCTYPE *root_name* [and terminated with]>. For example, the structure of the planes XML document with its DTD included is as follows:

```
<?xml version = "1.0" encoding = "utf-8"?>
    <!DOCTYPE planes [
        <!-- The DTD for planes -->
    ]>
```

```
<!-- The planes XML document -->
```

When the DTD is in a separate file, the XML document refers to it with a DOCTYPE declaration as its second line. This declaration has the following form:

```
<!DOCTYPE XML_document_root_name SYSTEM "DTD_file_name">
```

For the planes example, assuming that the DTD is stored in the file named planes.dtd, this declaration would be as follows:

```
<!DOCTYPE planes_for_sale SYSTEM "planes.dtd">
```

The following is an example of an XML document that is valid for the planes DTD:

```
<?xml version = "1.0" encoding = "utf-8"?>

<!-- planes.xml - A document that lists ads for
                  used airplanes -->

<!DOCTYPE planes_for_sale SYSTEM "planes.dtd">
<planes_for_sale>
  <ad>
    <year> 1977 </year>
    <make> &c; </make>
    <model> Skyhawk </model>
    <color> Light blue and white </color>
    <description> New paint, nearly new interior,
        685 hours SMOH, full IFR King avionics </description>
    <price> 23,495 </price>
    <seller phone = "555-222-3333"> Skyway Aircraft </seller>
    <location>
      <city> Rapid City, </city>
      <state> South Dakota </state>
    </location>
  </ad>
  <ad>
    <year> 1965 </year>
    <make> &p; </make>
    <model> Cherokee </model>
    <color> Gold </color>
    <description> 240 hours SMOH, dual NAVCOMs, DME,
        new Cleveland brakes, great shape </description>
    <seller phone = "555-333-2222"
        email = "jseller@www.axl.com">
        John Seller </seller>
```

```
    <location>
      <city> St. Joseph, </city>
      <state> Missouri </state>
    </location>
  </ad>
</planes_for_sale>
```

7.5 Namespaces

It is often convenient to construct XML documents that use tag sets that are defined for and used by other documents. When a tag set is available and appropriate for a particular XML document or class of documents, it is better to use it than to invent a new collection of element types. For example, suppose you must define an XML markup language for a furniture catalog with <chair>, <sofa>, and <table> tags. The catalog document must also include several different tables of specific furniture pieces, wood types, finishes, and prices. It obviously would be convenient to use XHTML table tags to define these tables rather than inventing a new vocabulary for them.

One problem with using different markup vocabularies in the same document is that collisions between names that are defined in two or more of those tag sets could result. An example of this is having a <table> tag for a category of furniture and a <table> tag from XHTML for information tables. Clearly, software systems that process XML documents must be capable of unambiguously recognizing the element names in those documents. To deal with this problem, the W3C has developed a standard for XML namespaces at (http://www.w3.org/TR/REC-xml-names).

An *XML namespace* is a collection of element and attribute names used in XML documents. The name of a namespace usually has the form of a uniform resource identifier (URI).[2] A namespace for the elements and attributes of the hierarchy rooted at a particular element is declared as the value of the attribute xmlns. The form of a namespace declaration for an element follows:

<element_name xmlns[:*prefix*] = URI>

The square brackets indicate that what is within them is optional. The prefix, if included, is the name that must be attached to the names in the declared namespace. If the prefix is not included, the namespace is the default for the document.

A prefix is used for two reasons. First, most URIs are too long to be typed on every occurrence of every name from the namespace. Second, a URI includes characters that are illegal in XML. Note that the element for which a namespace is declared is usually the root of a document. For example, all

---

2. A URL is a URI that happens to be the Internet address of some resource.

XHTML documents in this book declare the `xmlns` namespace on the root element, `html`:

```
<html xmlns = "http://www.w3.org/1999/xhtml">
```

This defines the default namespace for XHTML documents, which is `http://www.w3.org/1999/xhtml`.

As an example of a prefixed namespace declaration, consider the following:

```
<birds  xmlns:bd = "http://www.audubon.org/names/species">
```

Within the `birds` element, including all of its children elements, the names from the given namespace must be prefixed with `bd`, as in the following:

```
<bd:lark>
```

If an element has more than one namespace declaration, they are declared as in the following example:

```
<birds  xmlns:bd = "http://www.audubon.org/names/species"
        xmlns:html = "http://www.w3.org/1999/xhtml" >
```

In this tag, the standard XHTML namespace has been added to the `birds` element. One of the namespaces can be specified as the default by omitting the prefix in any namespace declaration.

Consider the following example in which two namespaces are declared. The first is declared to be the default namespace; the second defines the prefix, `cap`.

```
<states>
   xmlns = "http://www.states-info.org/states"
   xmlns:cap = "http://www.states-info.org/state-capitals"
   <state>
     <name> South Dakota </name>
     <population> 754844 </population>
     <capital>
       <cap:name> Pierre </cap:name>
       <cap:population> 12429 </cap:population>
     </capital>
   </state>
   <!-- More states -->
</states>
```

Each state element has name and population child elements from both namespaces.

Attribute names are not included in namespaces because attribute names are local to elements, so a tag set may use the same attribute name in more than one element without causing ambiguity.

If an XML document uses a DTD and a prefixed name, the DTD must define an element with exactly the same prefix and name.

Because of their form, it is tempting to think that a namespace is a Web resource that lists element names. But that is never the case. The standard namespaces (e.g., `http://www.w3.org/1999/xhtml`) often are valid URLs, but they are documents that describe far more than a set of element names. User-defined namespace names do not need to use the URI form, although that is a good way to prevent conflicts with namespace names.

7.6   XML Schemas

DTDs have several disadvantages. One is that DTDs are written in a syntax unrelated to XML, so they cannot be analyzed with an XML processor. Also, it can be confusing for people to deal with two different syntactic forms, one that defines a document and one that defines its structure. Another disadvantage is that DTDs do not allow restrictions on the form of data that can be the content of a particular tag. For example, if the content of an element represents time, regardless of the form of the time data, a DTD can only specify that it is text, which could be anything. In fact, the content of an element could be an integer number, a floating-point number, or a range of numbers. All of these would be specified as text. With DTDs, there are only ten data types, none of which is numeric.

Several alternatives to DTDs have been developed to attempt to overcome their weaknesses. The XML Schema standard, which was designed by the W3C, is one of these alternatives. We have chosen to discuss it because of its W3C support and the likelihood that it will become the primary successor to the DTD-based system. An XML schema is an XML document, so it can be parsed with an XML parser. It also provides far more control over data types than do DTDs. The content of a specific element can be required to be any one of 44 different data types. Furthermore, the user can define new types with constraints on existing data types. For example, a numeric data value can be required to have exactly seven digits.

To promote the transition from DTDs to XML schemas, XML Schema was designed to allow any DTD to be automatically converted to an equivalent XML schema.

7.6.1   Schema Fundamentals

Schemas can conveniently be related to the idea of a class and an object in an object-oriented programming language. A schema is similar to a class definition; an XML document that conforms to the structure defined in the schema is similar to an object of the schema's class. In fact, XML documents that conform to a specific schema are considered instances of that schema.

Schemas have two primary purposes. First, a schema specifies the structure of its instance XML documents, including which elements and attributes may appear in the instance document, as well as where and how often they may appear. Second, a schema specifies the data type of every element and attribute in its instance XML documents. This is the area in which schemas far outshine DTDs.

It has been said that XML schemas are "namespace centric." There is some truth to that depiction. In XML schemas, as in XML, namespaces are represented by names that have the form of URIs. Because they must be unique, it is customary to use URIs that start with the author's Web site address for namespaces. For example, for namespaces used in this section we use the prefix `"http://cs.uccs.edu/"`. To this we add whatever name connotes the specific application.

7.6.2   Defining a Schema

Schemas themselves are written using a collection of tags, or a vocabulary, from a namespace that is, in effect, a schema of schemas. The name of this namespace is `http://www.w3.org/2001/XMLSchema`. Some of the elements in this namespace are `element`, `schema`, `sequence`, and `string`.

Every schema has `schema` as its root element. As stated, the `schema` element specifies the namespace for the schema of schemas from which the schema's elements and attributes will be drawn. It often also specifies a prefix that will be used for the names in the schema. This namespace specification appears as follows:

```
xmlns:xsd = "http://www.w3.org/2001/XMLSchema"
```

This provides the prefix `xsd` for the names from the namespace for the schema of schemas.

A schema defines a namespace in the same sense as a DTD defines a tag set. The name of the namespace defined by a schema must be specified with the `targetNamespace` attribute of the `schema` element. Every top-level (not nested) element that appears in a schema places its name in the target namespace. The target namespace is specified by assigning a namespace to the target namespace attribute, as in the following:

```
targetNamespace = "http://cs.uccs.edu/planeSchema"
```

If the elements and attributes that are not defined directly in the schema element (they are nested inside top-level elements) are to be included in the target namespace, schema's `elementFormDefault` must be set to `qualified`, as in the following:

```
elementFormDefault = "qualified"
```

The default namespace, which is the source of the unprefixed names in the schema, is given with another `xmlns` specification, but this time without the prefix. For example:

```
xmlns = "http://cs.uccs.edu/planeSchema"
```

An example of a complete opening tag for a schema is as follows:

```
<xsd:schema
<!-- The namespace for the schema itself (prefix is xsd) -->
  xmlns:xsd = http://www.w3.org/2001/XMLSchema
<!-- The namespace where elements defined here will be placed -->
  targetNamespace = http://cs.uccs.edu/planeSchema
<!-- The default namespace for this document (no prefix) -->
  xmlns = http://cs.uccs.edu/planeSchema
<!-- We want to put non-top-level elements in the target namespace -->
  elementFormDefault = "qualified">
```

In this example, the target namespace and the default namespace are the same.

One alternative to the preceding opening tag would be to make the XMLSchema names the default so that they do not need to be prefixed in the schema. Then the names in the target namespace would need to be prefixed. The following schema tag illustrates this:

```
<schema
  xmlns = "http://www.w3.org/2001/XMLSchema"
  targetNamespace = "http://cs.uccs.edu/planeSchema"
  xmlns:plane = "http://cs.uccs.edu/planeSchema"
  elementFormDefault = "qualified">
```

Notice that the name schema in this tag name does not need to be prefixed because its namespace is now the default. However, all of the names being created by this schema must be prefixed, both in the schema and in its instances.

7.6.3 Defining a Schema Instance

An instance of a schema must include specifications of the namespaces it uses. These are given as attribute assignments in the tag for its root element. First, an instance document normally defines its default namespace to be the one defined in its schema. For example, if the root element is planes, we could have the following:

```
<planes
  xmlns = http://cs.uccs.edu/planeSchema
  ... >
```

The second attribute specification in the root element of an instance document is for the schemaLocation attribute. This attribute is used to name the standard namespace for instances, which includes the name XMLSchema-instance. This namespace corresponds to the XMLSchema namespace used for schemas. The following attribute assignment specifies the XMLSchema-instance namespace and defines the prefix, xsi, for it:

```
xmlns:xsi = "http://www.w3.org/2001/XMLSchema-instance"
```

Third, the instance document must specify the filename of the schema where the default namespace is defined. This is accomplished with the `schemaLocation` attribute, which takes two values: the namespace of the schema and the filename of the schema. This attribute is defined in the `XMLSchema-instance` namespace, so it must be named with the proper prefix. For example:

```
xsi:schemaLocation = "http://cs.uccs.edu/planeSchema
                      planes.xsd"
```

This is a peculiar attribute assignment in that it assigns two values, which are separated only by whitespace.

Altogether, the opening root tag of an XML instance of the `planes.xsd` schema, where the root element name in the instance is `planes`, could appear as follows:

```
<planes
   xmlns = "http://cs.uccs.edu/planeSchema"
   xmlns:xsi = "http://www.w3.org/2001/XMLSchema-instance"
   xsi:schemaLocation = "http://cs.uccs.edu/planeSchema
                         planes.xsd">
```

The purpose of both DTDs and XML schemas is to provide a technique for standardization of the tag set and structure of families of XML documents. Conformance checking of an XML document against an XML schema can be done with any one of several available validation programs. One of these, named `xsv`, is discussed in Section 7.6.7. An XML schema validation program performs two kinds of conformance checks: First, it checks to determine whether the schema is valid relative to the schema of schemas, `XMLSchema`. Second, it checks to determine whether the XML document conforms to the syntactic rules specified in the schema of which the document is an instance.

7.6.4 An Overview of Data Types

There are two categories of user-defined XML schema data types: simple and complex. A *simple data type* is one whose content is restricted to strings. A simple type cannot have attributes or include nested elements. The string restriction seems like it would make simple types a very narrow type category, but in fact it does not because a large collection of predefined data types is included in the category. Some of these are mentioned in this section. A *complex type* can have attributes and include other data types as child elements.

The XML Schema defines 44 data types, 19 of which are primitive and 25 of which are derived. The primitive data types include `string`, `Boolean`, `float`, `time`, and `anyURI`. The predefined derived types include `byte`, `long`, `decimal`, `unsignedInt`, `positiveInteger`, and `NMTOKEN`. User-defined data types are defined by specifying restrictions on an existing type, which is then called a *base type*. Such user-defined types are *derived types*. Constraints in derived types are given in terms of the *facets* of the base type. For example, the `integer` primitive data type has eight possible facets: `totalDigits`, `maxInclusive`, `maxExclusive`, `minInclusive`, `minExclusive`, `pattern`, `enumeration`, and `whitespace`. Examples of user-defined data types are given in Section 7.6.5. A list of all predefined data types can be found at `http://www.w3.org/TR/xmlschema-2/#built-in-datatypes`.

Both simple and complex types can be *named* or *anonymous*. If anonymous, a type cannot be used outside the element in which it is declared.

Elements in a DTD are all global. Each has a unique name and is defined exactly once. The context of a reference to a DTD element is irrelevant. By contrast, context is essential to defining the meaning of a reference to an element in an XML schema.

Data declarations in an XML schema can be either local or global. A *local declaration* is one that appears inside an element that is a child of the `schema` element; that is, a declaration in a grandchild element of `schema` (or a more distant descendant) is a local declaration. A locally declared element is visible only in that element. This means that local elements with the same name can appear in any number of different elements with no interference among them. A *global declaration* is one that appears as a child of the `schema` element. Global elements are visible in the whole schema in which they are declared.

7.6.5   Simple Types

Elements are defined in an XML schema with the `element` tag, which is from the `XMLSchema` namespace. Recall that the prefix `xsd` is normally used for names from this namespace. An element that is named includes the `name` attribute for that purpose. The other attribute that is necessary in a simple element declaration is `type`, which is used to specify the type of content allowed in the element. For example:

```
<xsd:element name = "engine"  type = "xsd:string" />
```

An instance of the schema in which the engine element is defined could have the following element:

```
<engine> inline six cylinder fuel injected </engine>
```

An element can be given a default value using the `default` attribute. For example:

```
<xsd:element name = "engine"   type = "xsd:string"
             default = "fuel injected V-6"  />
```

Elements can have constant values, meaning that the content of the defined element in every instance document has the same value. Constant values are given with the `fixed` attribute, as in the following example:

```
<xsd:element name = "plane"   type = "xsd:string"
             fixed = "single wing"  />
```

We now turn our attention to user-defined data types, which are constrained predefined types. A simple user-defined data type is described in a `simpleType` element, using facets. Facets must be specified in the content of a `restriction` element, which gives the base type name. The facets themselves are given in elements named for the facets, using the `value` attribute to specify the value of the facet. For example, the following declares a user-defined type, `firstName`, for strings of fewer than 11 characters:

```
<xsd:simpleType name = "firstName">
  <xsd:restriction base = "xsd:string">
    <xsd:maxLength value = "10" />
  </xsd:restriction>
</xsd:simpleType>
```

The `length` facet is used to restrict the string to an exact number of characters. The `minLength` facet is used to specify a minimum length. The number of digits of a decimal number can be restricted with the `precision` facet. For example:

```
<xsd:simpleType name = "phoneNumber">
  <xsd:restriction base = "xsd:decimal">
    <xsd:precision value = "7" />
  </xsd:restriction>
</xsd:simpleType>
```

7.6.6 Complex Types

Most XML documents include nested elements, so few XML schemas do not have complex types. Although there are several categories of complex element types, the discussion here is restricted to those called *element-only elements*, which can have elements in their content but no text. All complex types can have attributes.

Complex types are defined with the `complexType` tag. The elements that are the content of an element-only element must be contained in an ordered group, an unordered group, a choice, or a named group. Ordered and unordered groups are discussed here.

The `sequence` element is used to contain an ordered group of elements. For example, consider the following type definition:

```
<xsd:complexType name = "sports_car">
  <xsd:sequence>
    <xsd:element name = "make"  type = "xsd:string" />
    <xsd:element name = "model"  type = "xsd:string" />
    <xsd:element name = "engine"  type = "xsd:string" />
    <xsd:element name = "year"  type = "xsd:decimal" />
  </xsd:sequence>
</xsd:complexType>
```

A complex type whose elements are an unordered group is defined in an `all` element.

Elements and `all` and `sequence` groups can include attributes to specify the numbers of occurrences. These attributes are `minOccurs` and `maxOccurs`. The possible values of `minOccurs` are the non-negative integers, including zero. The possible values for `maxOccurs` are the non-negative integers plus the value `unbounded`, which has the obvious meaning.

Consider the following complete example of a schema:

```
<?xml version = "1.0" encoding = "utf-8"?>

<!-- planes.xsd
     A simple schema for planes.xml
     -->
<xsd:schema
  xmlns:xsd = "http://www.w3.org/2001/XMLSchema"
  targetNamespace = "http://cs.uccs.edu/planeSchema"
  xmlns = "http://cs.uccs.edu/planeSchema"
  elementFormDefault = "qualified">

  <xsd:element name = "planes">
    <xsd:complexType>
      <xsd:all>
        <xsd:element name = "make"
                     type = "xsd:string"
                     minOccurs = "1"
                     maxOccurs = "unbounded" />
      </xsd:all>
    </xsd:complexType>
  </xsd:element>
</xsd:schema>
```

Notice that we use the `all` element to contain the single element of the complex type, `planes`. `sequence` could have been used instead. Because there is only one contained element, it makes no difference.

An XML instance that conforms to the `planes.xsd` schema follows:

```
<?xml version = "1.0" encoding = "utf-8"?>

<!-- planes1.xml
     A simple XML document for illustrating a schema
     The schema is in planes.xsd
     -->
```

```
<planes
  xmlns = "http://cs.uccs.edu/planeSchema"
  xmlns:xsi = "http://www.w3.org/2001/XMLSchema-instance"
  xsi:schemaLocation = "http://cs.uccs.edu/planeSchema
                        planes.xsd">
    <make> Cessna </make>
    <make> Piper </make>
    <make> Beechcraft </make>
</planes>
```

If we want the year element in the sports_car element that was defined earlier to be a derived type, the derived type could be defined as another global element and we could refer to it in the sports_car element. For example, the year element could be defined as follows:

```
<xsd:element name = "year">
  <xsd:simpleType>
    <xsd:restriction base = "xsd:decimal">
      <xsd:minInclusive value = "1900" />
      <xsd:maxInclusive value = "2007" />
    </xsd:restriction>
  </xsd:simpleType>
</xsd:element>
```

With the year element defined globally, the sports_car element can be defined with a reference to the year with the ref attribute, as shown in the following:

```
<xsd:complexType name = "sports_car">
  <xsd:sequence>
    <xsd:element name = "make"   type = "xsd:string" />
    <xsd:element name = "model"  type = "xsd:string" />
    <xsd:element name = "engine" type = "xsd:string" />
    <xsd:element ref = "year" />
  </xsd:sequence>
</xsd:complexType>
```

7.6.7   Validating Instances of Schemas

An XML schema provides a definition of a category of XML documents. However, developing a schema is of limited value unless there is some mechanical way to determine whether a given XML instance document conforms to the schema. Several XML schema validation tools are available. One of them is named xsv, an acronym for XML Schema Validator. It was developed by Henry S. Thompson and Richard Tobin at the University of Edinburgh in Scotland. If the schema and instance document are available on the Web, xsv can be used online, like the XHTML validation tool at the W3C Web site. This tool can also be downloaded and run on any computer. The Web site for `xsv` is `http://www.w3.org/XML/Schema#XSV`.

The output of `xsv` is an XML document. When run from the command line, the output document appears on the screen with no formatting, so it is a bit difficult to read. The following is the output of `xsv` when run on `planes.xml`:

```
<?XML version='1.0' encoding = 'utf-8'?>
<xsv docElt='{http://cs.uccs.edu/planeSchema}planes'
     instanceAssessed='true'
     instanceErrors = '0'
     rootType='[Anonymous]'
     schemaErrors='0'
     schemaLocs='http://cs.uccs.edu/planeSchema -> planes.xsd'
     target='file:/c:/wbook2/xml/planes.xml'
     validation='strict'
     version='XSV 1.197/1.101 of 2001/07/07 12:10:19'
     xmlns='http://www.w3.org/2000/05/xsv' >

  <importAttempt URI='file:/c:wbook2/xml/planes.xsd'
             namespace='http://cs.uccs.edu/planeSchema'
             outcome='success' />

</xsv>
```

The actual output from `xsv` is displayed with no formatting: Each line is filled to the right end of the screen, and attribute values are broken across line boundaries in several places.

There is one useful thing to know about validation with `xsv`: If the schema is not in the correct format, the validator will report that it could not find the specified schema.

7.7 Displaying Raw XML Documents

An XML-enabled browser, or any other system that can deal with XML documents, cannot possibly know how to format the tags defined in the document (after all, someone just made them up). Therefore, if an XML document is displayed without a style sheet that defines presentation styles for the document's tags, the displayed document will not have formatted content. Contemporary browsers include default style sheets that are used when no style sheet is specified in the XML document. The display of such an XML document is only a somewhat stylized listing of the XML. The FX2 browser display of the `planes.xml` document is shown in Figure 7.2.

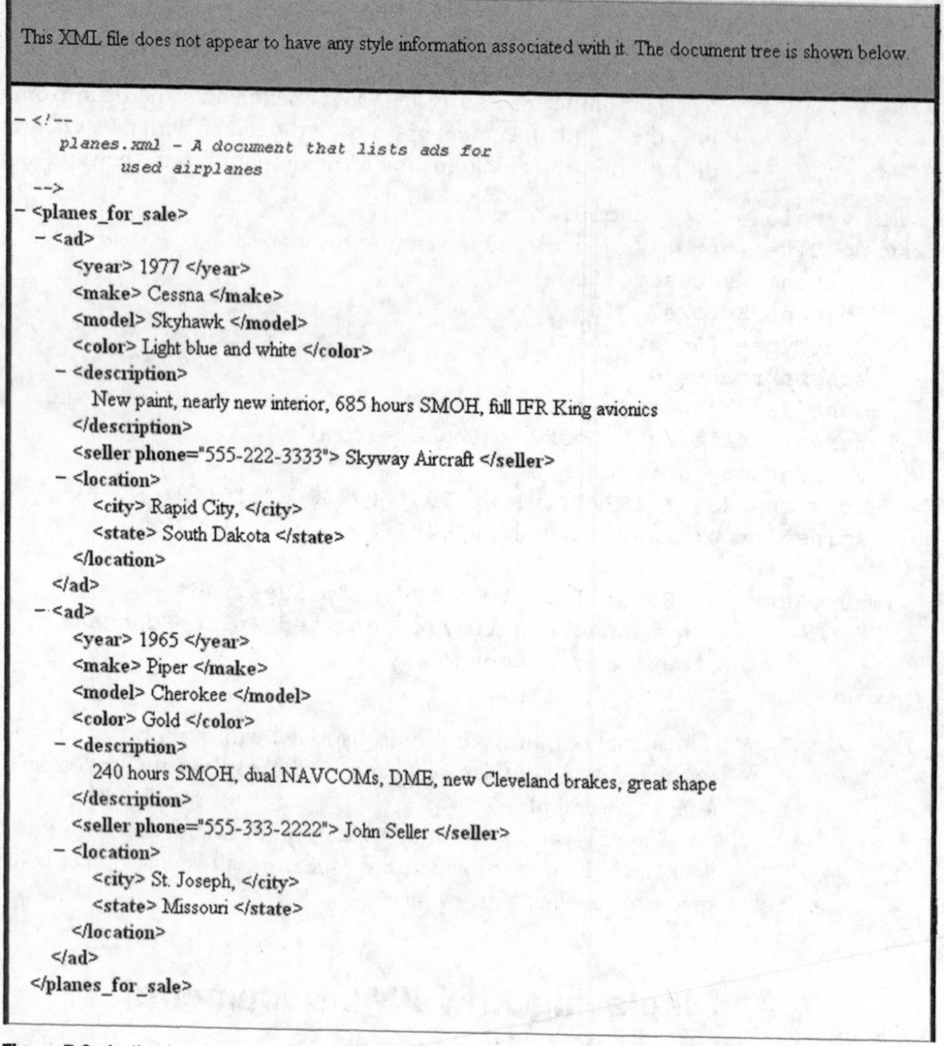

This XML file does not appear to have any style information associated with it. The document tree is shown below.

```
- <!--
    planes.xml - A document that lists ads for
         used airplanes
  -->
- <planes_for_sale>
  - <ad>
      <year> 1977 </year>
      <make> Cessna </make>
      <model> Skyhawk </model>
      <color> Light blue and white </color>
    - <description>
        New paint, nearly new interior, 685 hours SMOH, full IFR King avionics
      </description>
      <seller phone="555-222-3333"> Skyway Aircraft </seller>
    - <location>
        <city> Rapid City, </city>
        <state> South Dakota </state>
      </location>
    </ad>
  - <ad>
      <year> 1965 </year>
      <make> Piper </make>
      <model> Cherokee </model>
      <color> Gold </color>
    - <description>
        240 hours SMOH, dual NAVCOMs, DME, new Cleveland brakes, great shape
      </description>
      <seller phone="555-333-2222"> John Seller </seller>
    - <location>
        <city> St. Joseph, </city>
        <state> Missouri </state>
      </location>
    </ad>
  </planes_for_sale>
```

Figure 7.2 A display of an XML document with the FX2 default style sheet

Some of the elements in the display shown in Figure 7.2 are preceded by dashes. These elements can be elided (temporarily removed) by placing the mouse cursor over the dash and clicking the left mouse button. For example, if the mouse cursor is placed over the dash to the left of the first <ad> tag and the left mouse button is clicked, the result is as shown in Figure 7.3.

It is unusual to display a raw XML document. This is usually done to review and check the structure and content of the document during its development.

> This XML file does not appear to have any style information associated with it. The document tree is shown below.

```
- <!--
      planes.xml - A document that lists ads for
            used airplanes
  -->
- <planes_for_sale>
  + <ad></ad>
  - <ad>
      <year> 1965 </year>
      <make> Piper </make>
      <model> Cherokee </model>
      <color> Gold </color>
    - <description>
        240 hours SMOH, dual NAVCOMs, DME, new Cleveland brakes, great shape
      </description>
      <seller phone="555-333-2222"> John Seller </seller>
    - <location>
        <city> St. Joseph, </city>
        <state> Missouri </state>
      </location>
    </ad>
  </planes_for_sale>
```

Figure 7.3 The document of Figure 7.2 with the first ad element elided

IE7 under XP SP2 and Vista by default restrict the eliding process. By clicking the information bar (which appears at the top of the display when eliding is attempted) and then clicking *Allow Blocked Content*, the eliding is allowed.

7.8 Displaying XML Documents with CSS

Style sheet information can be provided to the browser for an XML document in two ways. First, a Cascading Style Sheet (CSS) file that has style information for the elements in the XML document can be developed. Second, the XSLT style sheet technology, which was developed by the W3C, can be used. Although using CSS is effective, XSLT provides far more power over the appearance of the document's display. On the other hand, XSLT is not yet available on all of the most commonly used browsers. XSLT is discussed in Section 7.9.

The form of a CSS style sheet for an XML document is simple: It is just a list of element names, each followed by a brace-delimited set of the element's

CSS attributes. This is the form of the rules in a CSS document style sheet. The following shows a CSS style sheet for the `planes` XML document:

```
<!-- planes.css - a style sheet for the planes.xml document -->
ad { display: block; margin-top: 15px; color: blue;}
year, make, model { color: red; font-size: 16pt;}
color {display: block; margin-left: 20px; font-size: 12pt;}
description {display: block; margin-left: 20px; font-size: 12pt;}
seller { display: block; margin-left: 15px; font-size: 14pt;}
location {display: block; margin-left: 40px; }
city {font-size: 12pt;}
state {font-size: 12pt;}
```

The only style property in this style sheet that has not been discussed earlier in this book is `display`, which is used to specify whether an element is to be displayed inline or in a separate block. These two options are specified with the values `inline` and `block`. The `inline` value is the default. When `display` is set to `block`, the content of the element is usually separated from its sibling elements by line breaks.

The connection of an XML document to a CSS style sheet is established with the processing instruction `xml-stylesheet`, which specifies the particular type of the style sheet via its `type` attribute and the name of the file that stores the style sheet via its `href` attribute. For the `planes` example, this processing instruction is as follows:

```
<?xml-stylesheet type = "text/css" href = "planes.css" ?>
```

Figure 7.4 shows the display of `planes.xml` using the `planes.css` style sheet.

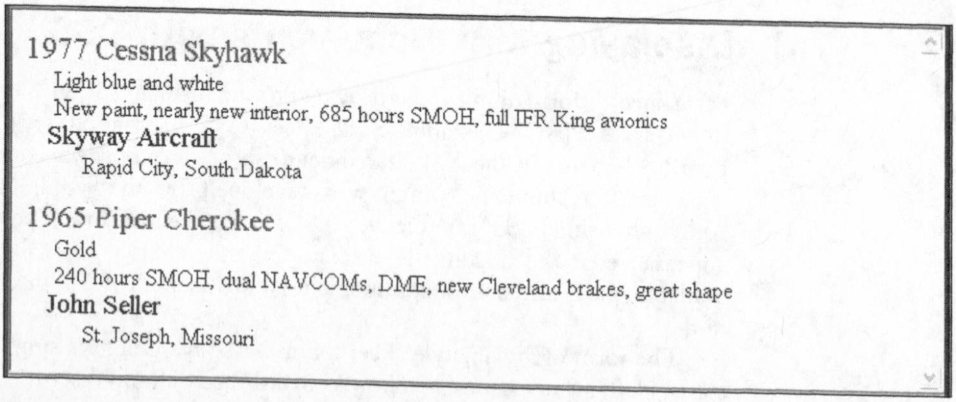

1977 Cessna Skyhawk
    Light blue and white
    New paint, nearly new interior, 685 hours SMOH, full IFR King avionics
Skyway Aircraft
    Rapid City, South Dakota

1965 Piper Cherokee
    Gold
    240 hours SMOH, dual NAVCOMs, DME, new Cleveland brakes, great shape
John Seller
    St. Joseph, Missouri

Figure 7.4 The result of using a CSS style sheet to format `planes.xml`

7.9 XSLT Style Sheets

The eXtensible Stylesheet Language (XSL) is a family of recommendations for defining XML document transformations and presentation. It consists of three related standards: XSL Transformations (XSLT), XML Path Language (XPath), and XSL Formatting Objects (XSL-FO). Each of these has an importance and use of its own. Together, they provide a powerful means of formatting XML documents. Because XSL-FO is not yet widely used, it is not discussed in this book.

XSLT style sheets are used to transform XML documents into different forms or formats, perhaps using different DTDs. One common use for XSLT is to transform XML documents into XHTML documents, primarily for display. In the transformation of an XML document, element content can be moved and/or modified, sorted, or converted to attribute values, among other things. XSLT style sheets are XML documents, so they can be validated against DTDs. They can even be transformed using other XSLT style sheets. The XSLT standard is given at `http://www.w3.org/TR/xslt`. XSLT style sheets and their uses are the primary topics of this section.

XPath is a language for expressions, which are often used to identify parts of XML documents, such as specific elements that are in specific positions in the document or elements that have particular attribute values. XSLT requires such expressions to specify transformations. XPath is also used for XML document querying languages, such as XQL, and for building new XML document structures using XPointer. The XPath standard is given at `http://www.w3.org/TR/xpath`. This chapter uses simple XPath expressions in the discussion of XSLT but does not explore them further.

7.9.1 Overview of XSLT

XSLT is actually a functional-style programming language. Included in XSLT are functions, parameters, names to which values can be bound, selection constructs, and conditional expressions for multiple selection. The syntactic structure of XSLT is XML, so each statement is specified with an element. This makes XSLT documents appear very different from programs in a typical imperative programming language, but not completely different from programs written in the LISP-based functional languages COMMON LISP and Scheme.

XSLT processors take as input an XML document and an XSLT document. The XSLT document is the program to be executed; the XML document is the input data to the program. Parts of the XML document are selected, possibly modified, and merged with parts of the XSLT document to form a new document, which is sometimes called an *XSL document*. Note that the XSL document is also an XML document, which could be again the input to an XSLT processor. The output document can be stored for future use by applications, or it may be immediately displayed by an application, often a browser. Neither the XSLT document nor the input XML document is changed by the XSLT processor.

The transformation process by an XSLT processor is shown in Figure 7.5.

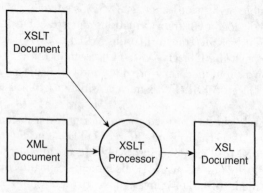

Figure 7.5 XSLT processing

An XSLT document consists primarily of one or more templates, which use XPath to describe element/attribute patterns in the input XML document. Each template has associated with it a section of XSLT "code," which is "executed" when a match to the template is found in the XML document. So, each template describes a function that is executed whenever the XSLT processor finds a match to the template's pattern.

An XSLT processor sequentially examines the input XML document, searching for parts that match one of the templates in the XSLT document. XML documents consist of nodes, where nodes are elements, attributes, comments, text, and processing instructions. If a template matches an element, the element is not processed until the closing tag is found. When a template matches an element, the child elements of that element may or may not be processed.

One XSLT model of processing XML data is called the *template-driven model*, which works well when the data consists of multiple instances of highly regular data collections, as with files of records. XSLT can also deal with irregular and recursive data, using template fragments in what is called the *data-driven model*. A single XSLT style sheet can include the mechanisms for both the template- and data-driven models. The discussion of XSLT in this chapter is restricted to the template-driven model.

To keep the complexity of the discussion manageable, the focus is on transformations that are related to presentation. The examples in this section were processed with the XSLT processor that is part of IE7.

7.9.2 XSL Transformations for Presentation

Although XSLT style sheets can be used to control page layout, including orientation, writing direction, margins, and page numbering, this chapter discusses only the simplest of formatting specifications for the smallest units of information. XSLT includes more than 50 formatting object (element) types and more than 230 properties, so it is a large and complex tag set.

In this section we assume that the XSLT processor processes an XML document with its associated XSLT style sheet document and produces as its output document an XHTML document to display.

An XML document that is to be used as data to an XSLT style sheet must include a processing instruction to inform the XSLT processor that the style sheet is to be used. The form of this instruction is as follows:

```
<?xml-stylesheet type = "text/xsl" href =
                              "XSL_stylesheet_name" ?>
```

As a simple example of an XML document that can be used to illustrate XSLT formatting, consider the following:

```
<?xml version = "1.0" encoding = "utf-8"?>
<!-- xslplane.xml -->
<?xml-stylesheet type = "text/xsl"  href = "xslplane.xsl" ?>
<plane>
  <year> 1977 </year>
  <make> Cessna </make>
  <model> Skyhawk </model>
  <color> Light blue and white </color>
</plane>
```

Notice that this document specifies `xslplane.xsl` as its XSLT style sheet.

An XSLT style sheet is an XML document whose root element is the special-purpose element `stylesheet`. The `stylesheet` tag defines namespaces as its attributes and encloses the collection of elements that defines its transformations. It also identifies the document as an XSLT document. The namespace for all XSLT elements is specified with a W3C URI. If the style sheet includes XHTML elements, the style sheet tag also specifies the XHTML namespace. Consider the following style sheet tag:

```
<xsl:stylesheet xmlns:xsl =
              "http://www.w3.org/1999/XSL/Transform"
              xmlns = "http://www.w3.org/1999/xhtml">
```

Notice that the prefix for XSLT elements is `xsl` and the default namespace is that for XHTML.

A style sheet document must include at least one `template` element. The template opening tag includes a `match` attribute to specify an XPath expression to select a node in the XML document. The content of a template element specifies what is to be placed in the output document. If a template element is thought of as a subprogram, the opening tag states where the subprogram is to be applied, and the content of the element specifies the body of the subprogram.

In most XSLT documents, a template is included to match the root node of the XML document. This can be done in two ways, one being to use the XPath expression "/", as in the following:

```
<xsl:template match = "/">
```

Notation similar to that used to specify UNIX directory addresses is used. The alternative to using "/" is to use the actual root of the document. In the example, `xslplane.xml`, the document root is `plane`. Every XSLT style sheet should include a template for the root node. If the output of the XSLT processor is an XHTML document, the template that matches the root node is used to create the XHTML header of the output document. The header code appears as the content of the template element. An example of a complete template element follows:

```
<xsl:template match = "plane">
<html><head><title> Example </title></head><body>
...
</body></html>
</xsl:template>
```

To produce complete XHTML documents as output from XSLT documents, the `output` element can be included prior to the first template. This element can include `doctype-public` and `doctype-system` attributes to specify the two parts of the `DOCTYPE` declaration, respectively. For the sake of brevity, `output` elements are not included in the XSLT examples in this chapter.

Style sheets nearly always have templates for specific nodes of the XML document, which are descendants of the root node, as in the following example:

```
<xsl:template match = "year">
```

XPath expressions that begin with the slash are absolute addresses within the document. Those that do not begin with a slash are relative addresses. The value `"year"` in the preceding example is obviously a relative address. Relative addresses are relative to the "current" node of the XML document, which is the last node found by the XSLT processor in the XML document.

The template for the root node is implicitly applied. However, all other templates in an XSLT document must be explicitly applied to the XML document. This can be done in several ways. The `apply-templates` element applies appropriate templates to the descendant nodes of the current node. This element can include a `select` attribute to specify the descendant nodes whose templates should be applied. If no `select` attribute is included, the XSLT processor will apply a template to every descendant node. For those nodes for which the XSLT document has not defined a template, a default template is used. For example, both text and attributes have default templates that output them as text.

Template elements include two distinct kinds of elements: those that literally contain content and those that specify content to be copied from the associated XML document. XSLT elements that represent XHTML elements often are used to specify content. These have the appearance of their associated XHTML elements. For example, consider the following XHTML element:

```
<span style = "font-size: 14pt"> Merry Christmas! </span>
```

All XSLT elements that represent XHTML elements are copied by the XSLT processor to the output document being generated. Note that all XHTML elements that appear in an XSLT document must conform to the syntactic restrictions that apply to XML (and XHTML) elements.

In many cases, the content of an element of the XML document is to be copied to the output document. This is done with the value-of element, which uses a select attribute to specify the element of the XML document whose contents are to be copied. For example:

```
<xsl:value-of select = "AUTHOR" />
```

This element specifies that the content of the AUTHOR element of the XML document is to be copied to the output document. Because the value-of element cannot have content, it is terminated with a slash and a right angle bracket.

The select attribute can specify any node of the XML document. This is an advantage of XSLT formatting over CSS, in which the order of data as stored is the only possible order of display.

The attribute value "." for the select attribute of value-of means to select all elements within the current element, just the current node if it contains no nested elements.[3]

The following is a complete XSLT style sheet for the XML document xslplane.xml, shown previously:

```
<?xml version = "1.0" encoding = "utf-8"?>
<!-- xslplane1.xsl
     An XSLT stylesheet for xslplane.xml using child templates
     -->
<xsl:stylesheet version = "1.0"
            xmlns:xsl = "http://www.w3.org/1999/XSL/Transform"
            xmlns = "http://www.w3.org/1999/xhtml">

<!-- The template for the whole document (the plane element) -->
  <xsl:template match = "plane">
    <html><head><title> Style sheet for xslplane.xml </title>
    </head><body>
    <h2> Airplane Description </h2>

<!-- Apply the matching templates to the elements in plane -->
```

---

3. If select = "." is included in an <xsl:apply-templates> tag, it does nothing because apply-templates implicitly specifies all immediate child nodes.

```
            <xsl:apply-templates />
            </body></html>
       </xsl:template>

<!-- The templates to be applied (by apply-templates) to the
       elements in the plane element -->
    <xsl:template match = "year">
        <span style = "font-style: italic; color: blue;"> Year:
        </span>
        <xsl:value-of select = "." /> <br />
    </xsl:template>
    <xsl:template match = "make">
        <span style = "font-style: italic; color: blue;"> Make:
        </span>
        <xsl:value-of select = "." /> <br />
    </xsl:template>
    <xsl:template match = "model">
        <span style = "font-style: italic; color: blue;"> Model:
        </span>
        <xsl:value-of select = "." /> <br />
    </xsl:template>
    <xsl:template match = "color">
        <span style = "font-style: italic; color: blue;"> Color:
        </span>
        <xsl:value-of select = "." /> <br />
    </xsl:template>
</xsl:stylesheet>
```

Figure 7.6 shows an IE7 display of the output document created by the XSLT processor from `xslplane.xml` with `xslplane1.xsl`.

Airplane Description

Year: 1977
Make: Cessna
Model: Skyhawk
Color: Light blue and white

Figure 7.6 An output document from the XSLT processor

The XSLT document, `xslplane1.xsl`, is more general and complex than necessary for the simple use for which it was written. There is actually no need to include templates for all of the child nodes of `plane`, because the `select` clause of the `value-of` element finds them. The following XSLT document, `xslplane2.xsl`, produces the same output as `xslplane1.xsl`.

```
<?xml version = "1.0" encoding = "utf-8"?>
<!-- xslplane2.xsl
     An XSLT Stylesheet for xslplane.xml using implicit templates
     -->
<xsl:stylesheet version = "1.0"
                xmlns:xsl = "http://www.w3.org/1999/XSL/Transform"
                xmlns = "http://www.w3.org/1999/xhtml">

<!-- The template for the whole document (the plane element) -->
  <xsl:template match = "plane" >
    <html><head><title> Style sheet for xslplane.xml </title>
    </head><body>
    <h2> Airplane Description </h2>
    <span style = "font-style: italic; color: blue;"> Year:
    </span>
    <xsl:value-of select = "year" /> <br />
    <span style = "font-style: italic; color: blue;"> Make:
    </span>
    <xsl:value-of select = "make" /> <br />
    <span style = "font-style: italic; color: blue;"> Model:
    </span>
    <xsl:value-of select = "model" /> <br />
    <span style = "font-style: italic; color: blue;"> Color:
    </span>
    <xsl:value-of select = "color" /> <br />
    </body></html>
  </xsl:template>
</xsl:stylesheet>
```

Now an XML document that includes a collection of data elements with the same structure is considered. For example, a document named `airplanes.xml` could have a list of airplane descriptions. The XSLT template used for one plane can be used repeatedly with the `for-each` element, which uses a `select` attribute to specify an element in the XML data. The value of the `select` attribute is a pattern, which is a path expression that specifies an element. Any child elements of the specified element are included.

Consider the following XML document:

```xml
<?xml version = "1.0" encoding = "utf-8"?>
<!-- xslplanes.xml -->
<?xml-stylesheet type = "text/xsl" href = "xslplanes.xsl" ?>
<planes>
  <plane>
    <year> 1977 </year>
    <make> Cessna </make>
    <model> Skyhawk </model>
    <color> Light blue and white </color>
  </plane>
  <plane>
    <year> 1975 </year>
    <make> Piper </make>
    <model> Apache </model>
    <color> White </color>
  </plane>
  <plane>
    <year> 1960 </year>
    <make> Cessna </make>
    <model> Centurian </model>
    <color> Yellow and white </color>
  </plane>
  <plane>
    <year> 1956 </year>
    <make> Piper </make>
    <model> Tripacer </model>
    <color> Blue </color>
  </plane>
</planes>
```

The following XSLT style sheet processes the previous XML data document:

```xml
<?xml version = "1.0" encoding = "utf-8"?>
<!-- xslplanes.xsl -->
<xsl:stylesheet version = "1.0"
             xmlns:xsl = "http://www.w3.org/1999/XSL/Transform"
             xmlns = "http://www.w3.org/1999/xhtml" >

<!-- The template for the whole document (the planes element) -->
  <xsl:template match = "planes">
    <h2> Airplane Descriptions </h2>
```

```
<!-- Apply the following to all occurrences of the plane element -->
    <xsl:for-each select = "plane">
      <span style = "font-style: italic"> Year: </span>
      <xsl:value-of select = "year" /> <br />
      <span style = "font-style: italic"> Make: </span>
      <xsl:value-of select = "make" /> <br />
      <span style = "font-style: italic"> Model: </span>
      <xsl:value-of select = "model" /> <br />
      <span style = "font-style: italic"> Color: </span>
      <xsl:value-of select = "color" /> <br /> <br />
    </xsl:for-each>

  </xsl:template>
</xsl:stylesheet>
```

Figure 7.7 shows an IE7 display of the document produced by an XSLT processor on `xslplanes.xml`, using the `xslplanes.xsl` style sheet.

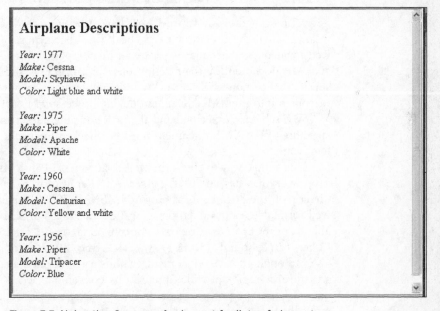

Figure 7.7 Using the `for-each` element for lists of elements

XSLT provides a simple way to sort the elements of the XML document before sending them or their content to the output document. This is done with the `sort` element, which can take several attributes. The `select` attribute specifies the node that is used for the key of the sort. The `data-type` attribute is used to specify whether the key is to be sorted as text ("text") or numerically ("number"). By default, it sorts in ascending order. The order attribute can be set to "descending" to produce the reverse order. By inserting the following single line into the xslplanes.xsl document, the output will appear in ascending numeric order of the year of the airplane:

```
<xsl:sort  select = "year"  data-type = "number" />
```

7.10   XML Processors

So far this chapter has discussed the structure of XML documents, the rules for writing them, the DTD and XML Schema approaches to specifying the particular tag sets and structure of collections of XML documents, and the CSS and XSLT methods of displaying the contents of XML documents. That is tantamount to telling a long story about how data can be stored and displayed, without providing any hint on how it may be processed. Although this section does not discuss processing data stored in XML documents, it does introduce approaches to making that data conveniently available to application programs that process that data.

7.10.1   The Purposes of XML Processors

Several purposes of XML processors have already been discussed. They are as follows: First, the processor must check the basic syntax of the document for well-formedness. Second, the processor must replace all references to entities in an XML document by their definitions. Third, DTDs and XML schemas can specify that certain values in an XML document have default values, which must be copied into the XML document during processing. Fourth, when a DTD or an XML schema is specified and the processor includes a validating parser, the structure of the XML document must be checked to ensure that its structure is legitimate.

One simple way to check the well-formedness of an XML document is with a browser that has an XML parser. Another way is to run an XML parser directly on the document. Microsoft's MSXML XML parser, which checks for well-formedness and validation against either DTDs or XML schemas, is available at http://msdn2.microsoft.com/en-US/xml/bb291077.aspx. Others can be found at http://www.w3.org/XML/Schema.

Although an XML document exhibits a regular and elegant structure, that structure does not provide applications convenient access to the document's data. Because the process of the initial syntactic analysis required to expose the embedded data must be repeated for every application that processes XML documents, it was recognized early on that standard syntax analyzers for XML documents were needed. Actually, the syntax analyzers themselves need not be standard; rather, they should expose the data of XML documents in a standard application programmer interface (API). This need led to the development of two different standard APIs for XML processors. Because there are different needs and uses of XML applications, having two standards is not a negative. The two APIs parallel the two kinds of output that are produced by the syntax analyzers of compilers for programming languages. Some of these syntax analyzers produce a stream of the syntactic structures of an input program. Others produce a parse tree of the input program that shows the hierarchical structure of the program in terms of its syntactic structures.

7.10.2 The SAX Approach

The Simple API for XML (SAX) standard, which was released in May 1998, was developed by an XML users group, XML-DEV. Although not developed or supported by any standards organization, SAX has been widely accepted as a de facto standard and is now widely supported by XML processors.

The SAX approach to processing is called *event processing*. The processor scans the XML document from beginning to end. Every time a syntactic structure of the document is recognized, the processor signals an event to the application by calling an event handler for the particular structure that was found. The syntactic structures of interest naturally include opening tags, attributes, text, and closing tags. The interfaces that describe the event handlers form the SAX API.

7.10.3 The DOM Approach

The natural alternative to the SAX approach to XML document parsing is to build a hierarchical syntactic structure of the document. Given the use of DOM representations of XHTML documents to create dynamic documents in Chapter 6, "Dynamic Documents with JavaScript," this is a familiar idea. In the case of XHTML, the browser parses the document and builds the DOM tree. In the case of XML, the parser part of the XML processor builds the DOM tree. In both cases, the nodes of the tree are represented as objects that can be accessed and processed or modified by the application. When parsing is complete, the complete DOM representation of the document is in memory and can be accessed in a number of different ways, including tree traversals of various kinds as well as random accesses.

The DOM representation of an XML document has several advantages over the sequential listing provided by SAX parsers. First, it has an obvious advantage if any part of the document must be accessed more than once by the application. Second, if the application must perform any rearrangement of the document, that can most easily be done if the whole document is accessible at the same time. Third, accesses to random parts of the document are possible. Finally, because the parser sees the whole document before any processing takes place, this approach avoids any processing of a document that is later found to be invalid (according to a DTD or XML schema).

In some situations, the SAX approach has advantages over the DOM method. The DOM structure is stored entirely in memory. For large documents, this requires a great deal of memory. In fact, because there is no limit on the size of an XML document, there may be some documents that cannot be parsed this way. This is not a problem with the SAX approach. Another advantage of the SAX method is speed—it is faster than the DOM approach.

The process of building the DOM structure of an XML document requires some syntactic analysis of the document, similar to that done by SAX parsers. In fact, most DOM parsers include a SAX parser as a front end.

7.11 Web Services

The movement toward Web services began in earnest when Microsoft Chairman Bill Gates introduced a concept he called BizTalk in 1999. BizTalk later was renamed .NET. The idea was to provide the technologies to allow different software in different places, written in different languages and resident on different platforms, to connect and interoperate.

The Web began as a Web service focused on information, and is still primarily just that. Through two fundamental HTTP methods, GET and POST, and a vast collection of public markup documents, information is provided to anyone with an Internet connection and a computer running a browser. The more general concept of a Web service is a similar technology for services. Rather than deploying documents through a Web server, services are deployed (through the same Web server). Rather than documents, access to software components is provided. Components are not downloaded, but they are run on the Web server as a remote service. In most cases, the components are remotely callable methods.

Web services are of course not a completely new idea. Remote Procedure Call (RPC) is an earlier and closely related concept. RPC was invented to allow distributed components to communicate. There are two successful (widely used) RPC technologies, DCOM and CORBA. Both, however, are too complex to provide a simple and convenient way to support interoperability among the components of different systems. DCOM is proprietary, supported only by Microsoft software systems. CORBA is designed to be cross-platform, but it requires a great deal of manual integration work. DCOM uses the Object Remote Procedure Call (ORPC) protocol to interface components. CORBA uses Object Management Group's Internet Inter-ORB Protocol (IIOP). Needless to say, these two protocols are not compatible. Therefore, neither DCOM nor CORBA supports the goal of Web services—universal component interoperability.

The dream of Web services is that there will be protocols that allow all components to interoperate entirely under the control of the computers, without human intervention. This means that when a software system needs a service, it can implicitly find one on the Web and use it. Standard non-proprietary protocols and languages to support this dream have been developed, although they are not yet widely used. Web services are now being offered by a number of large software companies, including Microsoft, Amazon, and Google.

There are three roles that are required to provide and use Web services: service providers, service requestors, often called consumers, and a service registry. A service provider must develop and deploy software that provides a service.

This service must have a standard description. The W3C language designed for writing such descriptions is Web Services Definition Language (WSDL, pronounced "wiz´-dul"), which is an XML-based format. The WSDL description is published on a Web server, similar to a Web-accessible document. It is used to describe the specific operations provided by the Web service, as well as the protocols for the messages the Web service can send and receive. The descriptions of data, both input and output, in a WSDL description are often written using XML Schema.

A Web services registry is created with another standard protocol, Universal Description, Discovery, and Integration Service (UDDI). UDDI also provides methods of querying a Web services registry to determine what specific services are available. So, a requestor queries a registry with a WSDL query, to which the registry responds with the protocol of how the requestor may interact with the requested Web service. UDDI has two kinds of clients, service providers and clients who want to find and use Web services.

SOAP is an XML tag set that defines the forms of messages and RPCs. SOAP was originally an acronym for Standard Object Access Protocol, designed to describe data objects. However, it is now a name for the XML tag set with wider use in Web services communications. The root element of a SOAP document is `Envelope`, so SOAP documents are often called envelopes. The body of a SOAP message is either a request, which is an RPC, or a response, which contains values returned from the called method, or service. SOAP messages are sent with the HTTP POST method.

Most Web services are developed using powerful tools, such as Microsoft's Visual Studio and Sun's NetBeans.

Web services consumers are clients of the service. Such a client could be a Web application, a non-Web application, or another Web service. The architecture of a Web service client includes a proxy running on the client machine. The proxy is a local substitute for the remote Web service. Once the proxy has been constructed, compiled, and referenced in the client, the client can call the methods of the remote Web service, although the calls will actually be received locally by the proxy. So, the client actually interacts with the proxy and the proxy interacts through the Internet with the remote Web service. The client acts like it is calling the remote Web service, but in fact is calling the proxy.

Chapter 12, "Introduction to ASP.NET," discusses ASP.NET approaches to defining and using Web services.

Summary

XML is a simplified version of SGML, which is a meta-markup language. XML provides a standard way for a group of users to define the structure of their data documents, using a subject-specific markup language.

XML documents can include elements, markup declarations, and processing instructions. Every XML document has the form of a single document tree, so there can be just one root element.

An XML document is a document entity that can include any number of references to other entities defined elsewhere. An entity can be several different things, including plain text and references to images.

A DTD is a document that describes the syntactic structure of an XML document or collection of documents that uses a particular tag set. A validating XML parser compares a document it is analyzing to its DTD, if one is specified. If no DTD is specified for an XML document, only well-formedness can be checked during parsing. A DTD has declarations for elements, attributes, entities, and notations. An element declaration specifies the name of the element and its structure. If an element represents an internal node in the document tree, its structure is a list of the children nodes. Any internal node can include a modifier that specifies the number of times that its children nodes can or must appear. A leaf node's structure is usually either empty or plain text.

A DTD attribute declaration specifies the attribute's name, the name of its associated element, the type of its values, and optionally, a default value. In many cases, the type of an attribute value is simply text. The default value can be an actual value, but it may also specify something about the value. There are several predefined entities that represent the special characters that are used as markup delimiters. A character data section can be used to allow these special characters to appear as themselves, without using entities. A DTD specification could appear embedded in an XML document, but this makes it inconvenient to use for other documents.

An XML document can include the predefined element names for some other application, such as the names of the elements of XHTML. To avoid name clashes between these different sources of names, XML uses the concepts of namespaces and name prefixes, which indicate the namespace of a name in a document. Namespaces are specified in declarations as URIs. A default namespace can be declared for a document. Names from the default namespace can be used without being prefixed.

XML schemas provide an alternative to DTDs. XML schemas allow much stricter control over the structure and especially the data types of an XML document. A schema defines the structure of a class of XML documents. The documents that conform to a specific schema are considered instances of that schema. A schema, which is an XML document, is an instance of a schema, `XMLSchema`. A schema specifies a target namespace with the `targetNamespace` attribute. The target namespace is also often named as the default namespace. Schemas can define simple and complex data types. Simple data types cannot contain other elements or attributes. One common category of complex types are those that can contain other elements but no text. There are many predefined types. Users are allowed to define new simple types as constrained versions of existing simple types, using facets. Users can also define new complex types. Instances of schemas can be validated with several different validation programs that are now available, among them `xsv`.

An XML parser includes a default style sheet, which is used when no other style sheet is specified by the document being parsed. The default style sheet simply produces a somewhat stylized listing of the XML. CSS style sheets can be used with XML documents to provide formatting information. Such a CSS style sheet has the form of an external CSS style sheet for XHTML.

XML documents can also be formatted with XSLT style sheets. XSLT style sheets specify document transformations and can include XHTML and CSS presentation information. XSLT style sheets define templates into which XML document elements are mapped. An XSLT processor creates an output document from the XML document and the XSLT style sheet. If the style sheet includes XHTML style specifications, the document will have style information embedded in its elements. XSLT style sheets actually are XML applications. An XSLT style sheet can have a template that is reused for any number of occurrences of a document branch in the associated XML document.

XML applications require that the nodes (tags, attributes, text, and so forth) of the XML document are provided in some standard way by the XML parser. The two ways in which this is done are the SAX approach, which calls an event handler for each node it finds, and the DOM approach, which provides a complete tree structure of the whole document.

A Web service is a method that resides and is executed on a Web server, but which can be called from any computer on the Web. The standard technologies to support Web services are WSDL, UDDI, SOAP, and XML.

Review Questions

7.1 What is a facet?

7.2 Is XML more closely related to SGML or HTML?

7.3 What is the main deficiency of HTML?

7.4 Under what circumstances are attributes better than nested tags?

7.5 What is the goal of HTML?

7.6 What is the goal of XML?

7.7 Explain the three types that can be used to describe data in an element declaration.

7.8 What are the two primary tasks of a validating XML parser?

7.9 What is SOAP?

7.10 Under what circumstances are nested tags better than attributes?

7.11 Why should a document be broken into multiple entities?

7.12 What is a binary entity?

7.13 How does an XML parser handle binary entities?

7.14 What is the purpose of a DTD?

7.15 Why is it better to find an error in a DTD before it is used?

7.16 What is a document entity?

7.17 What are the four possible keywords in a DTD declaration?

7.18 What are the meanings of the modifiers (+, *, and ?) that can be used in element declarations?

7.19 What are the four possible parts of an attribute declaration in a DTD?

7.20 Describe the meanings of the default attribute values #REQUIRED and #IMPLIED.

7.21 What is the difference between general and parameter entities?

7.22 What three namespaces are normally named in an XML schema?

7.23 Why do some special characters have predefined entity references?

7.24 What is the syntactic form of an internal DTD?

7.25 What is the markup vocabulary of a markup language?

7.26 What is an XML namespace?

7.27 What is the purpose of a character data section?

7.28 What are the two primary advantages of XML schemas over DTDs?

7.29 From where do the names used in defining an XML schema come?

7.30 How does the XML parser distinguish between a general entity and a parameter entity?

7.31 What is the form of the assignment to the schemaLocation attribute?

7.32 What are the differences between simple and complex XML schema types?

7.33 What is UDDI?

7.34 Define local and global declarations in an XML schema.

7.35 What are the four categories of complex types in an XML schema?

7.36 What is the difference between the sequence and all schema elements?

7.37 Why would you use a CSS style sheet for an XML document?

7.38 How does an XSLT processor use an XSLT style sheet with an XML document?

7.39 What does the keyword SYSTEM specify in an entity declaration?

7.40 What does the select attribute of the value-of element do?

7.41 What is a template element of an XSLT style sheet?

7.42 What two kinds of elements are included in XSLT style sheets?

7.43 What does the `value-of` XSLT element do?

7.44 What does the `for-each` element of an XSLT style sheet do?

7.45 What is produced by a SAX parser?

7.46 What advantages does a DOM parser have over a SAX parser?

7.47 Explain the ultimate goal of Web services.

7.48 What advantages does a SAX parser have over a DOM parser?

7.49 Describe the three roles required to provide and use Web services.

7.50 What is produced by a DOM parser?

Exercises

Write, test, and debug (if necessary) the following documents.

7.1 Create a DTD for a catalog of trucks, where each `truck` has the child elements `make`, `model`, `year`, `color`, `engine`, `number_of_wheels`, `transmission_type`, and `accessories`. The `engine` element has the attribute `number_of_cylinders` and `fuel` (gasoline or diesel). The accessories element has the attributes `radio`, `air_conditioning`, `power_windows`, `power_steering`, and `power_brakes`, each of which is required and has the possible values `yes` and `no`. Entities must be declared for the names of popular truck models.

7.2 Create an XML document with at least three instances of the `truck` element defined in the DTD of Exercise 7.1. Process this document using the DTD of Exercise 7.1 and produce a display of the raw XML document.

7.3 Create an XML schema for the XML document described in Exercises 7.1 and 7.2.

7.4 Create a CSS style sheet for the XML document of Exercise 7.2 and use it to create a display of that document.

7.5 Create an XSLT style sheet for one truck element of the XML document of Exercise 7.2 and use it to create a display of that element.

7.6 Modify the XSLT style sheet of Exercise 7.5 to format all the `truck` elements in the XML document of Exercise 7.2 and use it to create a display of the whole document.

7.7 Design an XML document to store information about students in a college. Information about students must include name (in three parts), Social Security number, age, major, home address—including street, city, state, and zip code—college address (in the same sub-parts as for the home address), grade-point average, and expected graduation date. Both attributes and nested tags must be included. Make up sample data for at least four students.

7.8 Write a DTD for the document described in Exercise 7.7 with the following restrictions: name, Social Security number, age, major, and home address are required. All the other elements are optional, as are middle names.

7.9 Create a CSS style sheet for the XML document of Exercise 7.7 and use it to create a display of that document.

7.10 Create an XSLT style sheet for one `student` element of the XML document of Exercise 7.7 and use it to create a display of that element.

7.11 Modify the XSLT style sheet of Exercise 7.6 to format all the `student` elements in the XML document of Exercise 7.7 and use it to create a display of the whole document.

CHAPTER

8

Introduction to Flash

This chapter introduces the Flash authoring environment. This is a complex and powerful tool for creating rich interactive and animated content for a wide variety of applications, including Web sites. There are two fundamental parts to Flash, the Flash authoring environment, used to create Flash applications, which are called movies, and the Flash player, a program that can be embedded in various software systems, including as a plug-in in Web browsers. The Flash player displays movies, much as a Web browser displays XHTML documents. When the target of a Flash movie is the Web, it is embedded as an `object` element in an HTML file. Although there are other uses of Flash movies, this chapter only deals with embedding them in HTML documents. Because of the complexity of Flash, we only provide an introduction to some of its most commonly used features. Many books are dedicated to describing Flash. The structure of this chapter is that of a tutorial—after an overview of Flash, the reader is led through several sequences of actions that produce example Flash movies.

The chapter begins with a brief discussion of how Flash came into existence. Next, the primary parts of the Flash authoring environment are introduced. Then, the most commonly used Flash drawing tools, including those for producing geometric figures, lines, hand-drawn figures, and text are described. The remainder of the chapter uses examples to illustrate some of the uses of the authoring environment.

The first example illustrates text and static figures. The next uses motion animation to build a movie, to which later is added a sound clip. Then, shape animation is illustrated with a simple example. Finally, two buttons are added to a movie with animation to allow the user to control its animation.

A copy of the latest version of the Flash authoring environment can be obtained as a 30-day trial from `http://www.adobe.com/products/flash`. There are Flash tutorials available, both in the Flash environment and at other sites on the Web.

8.1 Origins and Uses of Flash

In the mid-1990s a product named FutureSplash Animator was created by adding animation capabilities to an earlier drawing program named SmartSketch. The first copy of the FutureSplash Animator was shipped in the summer of 1996. At the same time, Macromedia was developing and selling a multimedia player named ShockWave. In late 1996 Macromedia bought FutureSplash Animator, which then became Flash 1.0. In 2005 Adobe bought Macromedia. Flash has evolved and grown steadily over the last 13 years.

Flash is now used to create movies, television, games, instructional media, presentations, and content for the Web, including for mobile devices.

The interactivity of a Flash application is implemented with a programming language, ActionScript, which is now in version 3.0. ActionScript is compliant with ECMA-262, which is the ISO name for JavaScript. Therefore, readers of this book are already familiar with the basics of ActionScript.

Flash is now the leading technology for delivering graphics, animation, and video on the Web. It has been estimated that nearly 99% of the world's computers used to access the Internet have a version of the Flash player installed as a plug-in in their browsers.

The current version of the Flash authoring environment is Flash CS3. The current version of the Flash player is version 9, although version 10 may be in use by the time this book is printed. The Flash player is free—it can be downloaded from `http://www.adobe.com`.

8.2 A First Look at the Flash Authoring Environment

Assuming the Flash authoring environment has been installed, starting it is a simple matter of double-clicking the desktop icon for Flash. This produces the welcome screen shown in Figure 8.1.

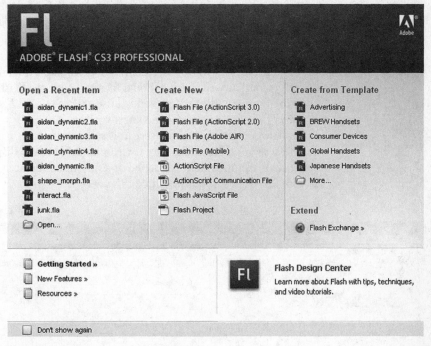

Figure 8.1 The Flash welcome screen

The top part of the welcome screen has four areas, each with a title, *Open a Recent Item*, *Create New*, *Create from Template*, and *Extend*. On the initial use of Flash, there are no recent items, so there is no list beneath the *Open a Recent Item* title. After one or more Flash files have been created, the most recently used of those will appear in this list, followed by an *Open* button. Clicking *Open* opens a dialog box (provided by the operating system) for the directory where Flash files are stored. This shows the files previously created but not listed in the *Recent Item* list. Most of the files in the *Recent Item* list and in the dialog box fall into three categories, Flash movies, with the file name extension `.swf`, Flash documents with the file name extension `.fla`, or files that contain ActionScript code, with the file name extension, `.as`. Clicking either one of the recent Flash document files or one chosen from the dialog box displayed when *Open* is clicked will open that file for modification. If a movie file name in this list is clicked, the Flash player is launched and the movie is played.

The middle top area of the welcome screen, titled *Create New*, has a list of createable files. To create a new Flash file, the first of these is usually chosen. It creates a Flash file that uses the current version of the scripting language, ActionScript 3.0. Note that ActionScript 3.0 is incompatible with earlier versions of ActionScript and cannot be interpreted by Flash players prior to version 9. *Create New* is the only entry of this area discussed here.

The right top area of the welcome screen, titled *Create from Template*, allows a Flash movie to be made according to a premade pattern. This chapter does not discuss templates.

At the center right part of the screen is the title *Extend* over the *Flash Exchange* button. This button is actually a hyperlink to a document that lists third-party extensions, as well as contributed files and code for Flash development.

At the bottom left of the screen is a list of three links. These are tutorials for new users, the new features of the latest version, and other resources for users.

The lower right area of the screen is self explanatory.

The screen of the authoring environment, which is displayed when either an existing Flash document is opened or a new one is created, is shown in Figure 8.2. This screen is sometimes called the *workspace*.

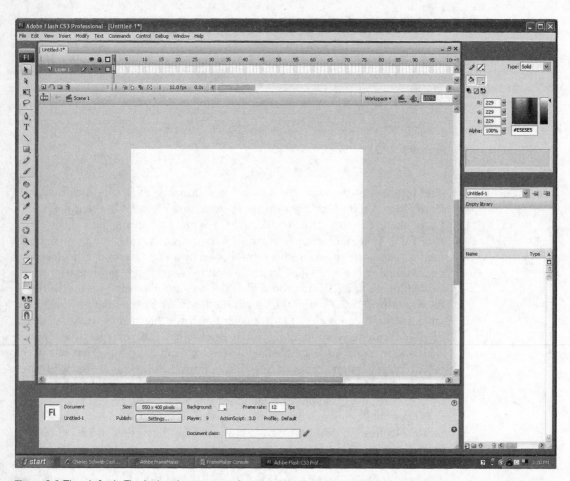

Figure 8.2 The default Flash development environment

At this point, only the general areas of the workspace will be discussed. Details will be explained when they are needed and used in examples of movie development later in the chapter. Across the top of the workspace is a menu bar of the kind found at the top of many applications, with menu titles such as *File*, *Edit*, and *Help*.

The large white rectangle at the center of the workspace is the *stage*, which is where the parts of a movie are displayed. Attached (or docked) to the left and right sides and bottom of the stage are panels that are often used in development of a Flash movie. These panels can be closed, opened, resized, and moved to customize the workspace.

Immediately below the menu bar is the timeline, which initially consists of a row of white rectangles with numbers above every fifth rectangle. Each one of the rectangles represents a frame of the to-be-constructed movie. To the left of both the numbers and the frame rectangles are some icons, which will be described as needed later. Notice that also to the left of the row of frames is the label *Layer 1*. There can be any number of layers of frames. When a new layer is added, it appears above the currently selected layer. Each of these layers can be given descriptive names, rather than the default names Layer 1, Layer 2, and so forth. Changing a layer's name is dicussed later. When the movie is played, the content of the layers is displayed, layer on top of layer. Multiple layers allow the various parts of the movie to be treated separately. For example, a graphic figure in one layer could be animated while the figures in other layers are left stationary.

The rectangle covering the number of the first frame (frame 1) is red and has a red line protruding downward. This indicates the position of the *playhead*—the frame that is currently being displayed on the stage in the authoring environment. The playhead can be dragged with the mouse cursor to display any frame in the movie. Initially, a movie has just frame 1. Everything that appears on the stage is called an *asset*.

Attached to the left of the stage is the tools panel. This group of tool icons can be displayed in two columns, rather than one, by clicking the double arrow button above the Flash icon (*Fl*) to the left of the menu bar. This button is labeled with two small triangles that initially point to the right (they change direction when clicked). The tools panel, when displayed in two columns, is shown in Figure 8.3, which includes a brief description of each tool.

Perhaps the most frequently used tool is the *Selection Tool* at the top (or top left, if the tools are displayed in two columns) of the panel of tool icons. It is used to select elements on the stage.

The tabbed panel at the bottom of the workspace is called the Properties Inspector. Its three tabs are *Properties*, *Filters*, and *Parameters*. It initially appears with the *Properties* tab clicked, as shown in Figure 8.2. When nothing on the stage is selected, this panel can be used to change the default values of the size of the stage, the background color of the stage, and the frame rate, which is the speed at which the document's movie will be played, in frames per second (fps).

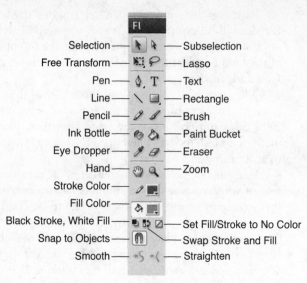

Figure 8.3 The tools panel

When the Properties Inspector has the *Properties* tab selected, we will call the panel the *properties panel*. When any text or graphic figure on the stage is selected, its properties are shown in the properties panel. Different figures have different properties panels. The *Filters* tab provides ways to apply special effects to text, among other things. The *Parameters* tab displays parameters of components, such as buttons. Some assets do not have parameters.

The panel on the lower-right side of the workspace displays the contents of the movie's library. The library panel can show the library of any movie. The library is further discussed in Section 8.3.4.

The panel on the upper-right side of the workspace is the *Color* panel, which can be used to set the colors for both stroke and fill. The *stroke color* is the color that will be used for the lines drawn on the stage, including the outlines of graphical figures. In XHTML this is called the foreground color. The *fill color* is the color that will be used to fill graphical figures on the stage. The choice between stroke and fill is made by clicking the appropriate button in the upper-left corner of the *Color* panel (a pencil for stroke and a paint bucket below the pencil for fill). There are several ways of choosing the colors. The button immediately to the right of the stroke and fill choice buttons opens a window showing a palette of all of the Web-safe colors, from which one can be selected. Another option for specifying a color is to choose the numeric values for red, green, and blue with the sliders that appear when the check mark to the right of a number is clicked. A color can also be specified by entering the hex number of the color in the text box in the lower-right area of the color panel.

The transparency of a color can also be selected in the *Color* panel. A text box labeled *Alpha* accepts a percentage number, which will become the amount of transparency, with 0% being completely transparent and 100% being completely solid.

Other panels can be added to the Flash development environment display by selecting them from the *Window* menu.

8.3 Drawing Tools

Flash has convenient tools for drawing graphic figures on the stage. The most commonly used of these are briefly described in this section.

8.3.1 Predefined Figures

Predefined figures are placed on the stage using the rectangle tool in the tools panel. If the mouse cursor is placed over the icon for the *Rectangle Tool* and the left mouse button is held down, a menu of shapes is displayed, as shown in Figure 8.4.

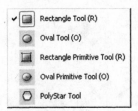

Figure 8.4 The rectangle tool menu

In the following paragraphs, we briefly describe the five tools in the rectangle tool menu.

Rectangles can be easily created, modified, and moved about on the stage. To begin, the mouse cursor is placed over the *Rectangle Tool* menu button in the tools panel and held down for a short time. This displays the rectangle tool menu, from which the *Rectangle Tool* menu button can be selected. Next, the stroke style, stroke color, and fill color are selected. The colors can be chosen with the stroke and fill color buttons in the tools menu or in the properties panel. Note that the square with the red diagonal line in the color swatch window indicates no color. If this is chosen for the stroke color, the figure will have no border; if it is chosen for the fill color, the figure will not be filled. Of course, if a rectangle has neither stroke color nor fill color, it will be invisible on the stage. The buttons in the properties panel are exactly like the corresponding buttons in the tools menu. The stroke style can only be selected in the properties panel, with which one can select any of seven different styles, including plain lines, dashed lines, and dotted lines.

After choosing the stroke style, stroke color, and fill color, the cursor is placed in the stage area. Holding down the left mouse button starts the drawing; letting it up stops it. If we want a perfect square (all sides of equal length), the *Shift* key can be held down while drawing a rectangle.

Drawing ovals is similar to drawing rectangles. Circles are drawn while holding down the *Shift* key. Drawing a polygon or star is a bit different, because these figures have more options, which are chosen in the properties panel. To begin, the *Polystar Tool* must be chosen from the rectangle tool menu. Then the parameters of the figure are chosen in the window that appears when the *Options* button, which appears in the lower center of the properties panel, is clicked. Either a polygon or star is chosen from the *Style* menu. Then the number of points can be set—it defaults to 5. Finally, if the figure is a star, the star point size can be chosen—it defaults to 0.5. The star point size is a measure of the width of the points on stars. The first row of Figure 8.5 shows a polygon and three stars, all with five sides or points. The second row shows the same figures as the first, except the polygon has seven sides and the stars have seven points.

Figure 8.5 Polygons and stars

The leftmost stars in Figure 8.5 have a point width of 0.25, the middle stars have a point width of 0.5, and the rightmost stars have a point width of 0.75.

A drawn figure can be modified by selecting it and changing its properties in the properties panel. Its stroke color, fill color, stroke style, size, and position can be changed. When the parameters of the figure are changed in the properties panel, the figure changes immediately. The stroke, or border of a figure, is selected by choosing the *Select Tool* in the tools menu and then clicking the left mouse button with the cursor on the stroke of the figure. One of the strokes of a figure can be selected with a single click with the select cursor on that stroke. The whole stroke of a figure is selected by double clicking any of the figure's strokes. Any part of the stroke of a figure can be modified by selecting it, holding down the mouse key, and moving the cursor. Figure 8.6 shows two modified figures. In the first, the two vertical sides have been pulled to the right. In the second, three of the points of a six-point star have been extended.

Figure 8.6 Modified figures

A single click with the select cursor inside a figure selects its fill. A complete figure, stroke and fill, is selected by double clicking with the select cursor inside the figure.

The *Rectangle Primitive Tool* is used to construct rectangles, like the *Rectangle Tool*, but the drawn figures are of a different kind. Both primitive and non-primitive rectangles are created from a master template, which has a set of parameters that determine its characteristics. The difference between primitive and non-primitive rectangles is that the non-primitive ones are disconnected from the master template as soon as they are created. This has two effects: First, a rectangle that has been disconnected can be changed with the *Selection Tool*— the sides can be moved, removed, or bent in any direction, as shown in Figure 8.6. However, because it is no longer connected to the master template, the master template parameters cannot be changed. The parameters of the master template for rectangles control the radius of the corners. So, the corners of a primitive rectangle can be changed by changing these parameters in the properties panel, but its sides cannot be bent with the *Selection Tool*. The properties panel for a primitive rectangle is shown in Figure 8.7.

Figure 8.7 The properties panel for a primitive rectangle

The radius of any corner of a rectangle can be changed in either direction, positive or negative. The corner radius is initially set to zero, which specifies a right angle corner. Changing it to positive values rounds the corner in the usual way. Changing it to negative values rounds the corner to the inside. Figure 8.8 shows a primitive rectangle with the upper-left corner set to a radius of 30 and the upper-right corner set to a radius of –30.

Figure 8.8 A primitive rectangle with positive and negative corner radii

The *Oval Primitive Tool* is similar to the *Rectangle Primitive Tool*—it creates ovals that remain connected to the master template for ovals. The properties panel for primitive ovals is shown in Figure 8.9.

Figure 8.9 The properties panel for a primitive oval

The difference in the properties panel between a primitive oval and a non-primitive oval is shown in the controls in the lower center of the panel. The *Start angle* and *End angle* control where the drawing of the outline of the oval begin and end. Setting the *Start angle* at 30 leaves a pie-shaped piece out of the oval starting at 0 degrees, which is straight to the right on the screen. and ending at 30 degrees clockwise from there. Setting the *End angle* to 330 leaves a pie-shaped piece out of the oval beginning at 30 degrees above straight right and ending at 30 degrees below straight right. Such an oval is shown in Figure 8.10.

Figure 8.10 A primitive oval with *Start angle* at 30 and *End angle* at 330

The inner radius of an oval is its inside border, which is initially set at zero, which means there is no inner border. Setting the The *Inner radius* parameter to a positive number increases the size of the inner border. Figure 8.11 shows the same oval as is shown in Figure 8.10, except the *Inner radius* has been set to 40.

Figure 8.11 A primitive oval with *Inner radius* set to 40, *Start angle* to 30, and *End angle* to 330

It should be obvious that many different figures can be created with the primitive and non-primitive tools from the *Rectangle Tool* set.

When a figure is placed on the stage, a black dot appears in the first frame of the timeline. The first frame is initially a keyframe. The dot indicates that this frame is now a *populated keyframe*, which means it has user-defined content.

Flash supports both bitmap and vector figures. Vector figures can be created and edited in Flash, but bitmap figures must be imported and cannot be edited (although their sizes can be changed). Therefore, if a bitmap figure must be modified, that modification must be done outside Flash, after which it is re-imported. The Web image formats, GIF, JPEG, and PNG, are all bitmap formats. Many of the Microsoft clip art figures are WMFs (for Windows Meta-Files), which have both bitmap and vector components.

8.3.2   Lines and Hand Drawings

Lines are drawn on the stage with the *Line Tool* from the tools menu, whose icon is a diagonal line from upper-left to lower-right. This tool simply draws straight lines. The parameters of the line are specified in the properties panel. The syle of the line is chosen from the menu of solid lines, dashed lines, dotted lines, and so forth. The thickness of the line can be specified with the slide just left of the line style menu.

Freehand drawing can be done with either the *Pencil Tool*, the *Pen Tool*, or the *Brush Tool*. Only the *Pencil Tool* will be discussed here. There are three optional modes for the *Pencil Tool*. When the *Pencil Tool* is selected, two small icons appear at the bottom of the tools panel (when they are displayed in two columns). The left of these new icons is for drawing objects. The right icon is the *Pencil Mode*, which when selected, displays a menu with three items.The three items are *Straighten*, *Smooth*, and *Ink*. Each has an icon, which is also displayed. The *Straighten* option fits straight and curved line segments to whatever is drawn when the mouse button is released after drawing. This allows the designer to draw rough circles, ellipses, rectangles, and squares, and have the system convert them to perfect figures. The *Smooth* option smooths whatever is drawn after the mouse button is released. This is useful for removing jitters from a hand-drawn figure. The *Ink* option leaves exactly what is drawn on the stage. Naturally, *Ink* is the default.

8.3.3 Text

Placing text on the stage is straightforward. After clicking the *Text Tool*, a narrow text box is created under the cursor when the left mouse button is clicked with the cursor on the stage. As text is entered into the box, the box extends in width to accommodate the entered text, but the text will not wrap to an additional line. Each corner of the box can be dragged to lengthen the box. When the box is lengthened, the upper-right corner mark is changed from a small circle to a small square and the box is changed to wrap mode. In wrap mode, if the entered text will not fit into the box, the excess characters are wrapped onto an additional line, extending the box on its bottom side. If the square at the upper-right corner of a text box that has been enlarged is double-clicked, the box reverts to its previous size. The default parameters of the entered text can be changed in the properties panel, a special version of which for text appears when the *Text Tool* is clicked. This panel is shown in Figure 8.12.

Figure 8.12 The properties panel for the *Text Tool*

The most frequently used parts of the properties panel for the *Text Tool* are the following: At the upper-left of the panel is a menu whose default displayed value is *Static Text*. The other options in this menu are *Dynamic* and *Input*. *Dynamic* is for text fields that will be changed during display. *Input* is for text fields that will accept user input. *Static* is for text that cannot be changed while it is displayed. Only *Static* text is discussed and used here.

Immediately to the right of this menu is another menu for font. Any one of the fonts that have been installed on the computer can be chosen from this menu. Immediately to the right of the font menu is the font size menu, which is a list of numbers that represent point size. Just to the right of the font size menu is a button for choosing the color of the font. To the right of the color button are buttons for boldface and italic font syles. To the right of the style buttons are the usual paragraph alignment buttons. These are followed by two more buttons, the *Edit format* option and *Text direction*. The icon of the first is a paragraph mark and the second is made up of the letters A, b, c, and d, arranged in a square. When clicked, the *Edit format* button opens a small window with menus to change the format option of the text. When clicked, the *Text orientation* button opens a menu that allows the text to be displayed vertically, rather than horizontally.

In the lower-left corner of the properties panel are the text field width and height, as well as the x and y coordinates of the text field on the stage. There is a button and a menu just below the left end of the font menu. When clicked, the button turns into a slider that specifies the letter spacing for the text, where 0 means normal spacing, positive numbers mean greater than normal spacing, and negative numbers mean less than normal spacing. Under the right end of the font menu is another menu, which is used to select *Normal*, *Superscript*, or *Subscript*, where *Normal* is the default.

8.3.4 Libraries and Symbols

Every Flash document has a library. The library stores a variety of things that could be part of a movie. Graphic figures created in Flash can be stored in the library as symbols. Other possible things in the library include imported sounds, video clips, and bitmaps. For now, only graphics symbols will be discussed. Any symbol in the library can be dragged to the stage to become part of the movie. Such items are called *instances*, because only one copy need be stored in the library, although multiple instances can appear in the movie. This can save considerable memory if a graphic figure appears several times in the movie.

The contents of the library of a document is displayed in the *Library* panel. Initially, only a narrow view of the *Library* panel is displayed. This can be changed to a wide, complete view by clicking the *Wide Library View* button on the *Library* panel, which appears as a small square above the slide bar on the lower-right side of the panel. The view can be returned to the narrow view by clicking the *Narrow Library View* button, which appears as a small vertical bar just below the *Wide Library View* button.

The specific library that is being displayed is shown in the menu at the top of the *Library* panel. Initially, the displayed library is that of the currently open active document. The library of any open but inactive document can be displayed and any symbol from any of these libraries can be placed in the current movie. The contents of a library can be organized into folders and subfolders, but that is not covered in this book.

If a figure is created on the stage, it is a vector graphic figure. It can be converted to a symbol and placed in the library. To do this, first the figure on the stage is selected. Then *Modify/Convert to Symbol* is selected from the menu at the top of the workspace. This opens a dialog box, as shown in Figure 8.13.

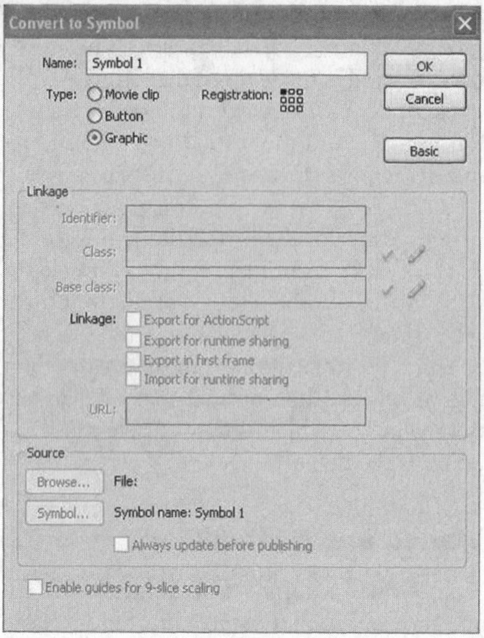

Figure 8.13 The *Convert to Symbol* dialog box

In this dialog box, the symbol is renamed by replacing the default name, which is *Symbol1*. This dialog box has two modes, basic and advanced. In basic mode, only the top part of the dialog box is displayed. This part has the symbol's name and type, as well as *OK* and *Cancel* buttons. In advanced mode, the bottom part of the dialog box is also displayed, none of which is discussed in this chapter. The modes can be interchanged by clicking the *Basic* button if in advanced mode, and by clicking the *Advanced* button if in basic mode. Then *OK* is clicked.

8.4   An Example—Static Graphics

This section demonstrates the use of Flash to build a static movie with graphic figures and text. Without animation, a movie occupies a single frame. A movie usually has multiple layers, each with a different part of the scene being depicted. However, when there is no animation, a movie often has just a single layer. This example will have a single frame with a single layer.

The example of this section is a banner for an ad document for used airplanes. To begin, we open a new Flash document and resize the stage to 700 by 350 pixels. This creates a stage that is 700 pixels wide and 350 pixels tall. To resize the stage, click on the *Size* button in the properties panel when the stage has been selected. This opens a *Document Properties* window that includes width and height dimensions. These can be changed to resize the stage.

Next, we add a text box to the upper center of the stage, with the company's name and slogan. These are shown in Figure 8.14.

Figure 8.14 The text of the movie

The next things we add to the movie are two small airplane figures, one to be placed on each side of the text. These are obtained from a free clip art Web site, in this case `http://office.microsoft.com/en-us/clipart/default.aspx`. External clip art can be placed in a movie by selecting *File/Import*, which provides four options. The easiest way to place external bitmap graphic figures into a movie is to import them directly to the stage. This places the figure both on the stage and in the library. If the figure is not to be animated, that is all there is to it. If the external figure is a vector graphic figure, for example, a WMF figure, it is better to import it to the library and then drag one or more instances of it to the stage.[1] For our example, we import one bitmap airplane figure to the stage (and library) and one vector graphic airplane figure to the library. Then we rename the figures (in the library) `airplane1` and `airplane2`. The *Library* panel now appears as in Figure 8.15.

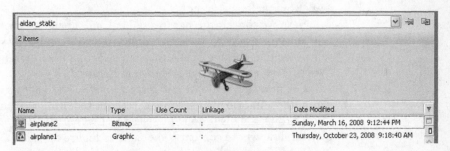

Figure 8.15 The library after importing two figures

---

1. Importing a vector graphic figure to the stage causes some problems.

Notice that one of the figures (`airplane1`) appears as a graphic—it is actually a WMF file—and the other (`airplane2`) appears as a bitmap—it is actually a PNG file.

Imported graphic figures are often converted to symbols, which saves space if they appear more than once in a movie. It also makes it possible to animate them. However, our example movie here is static, so the airplane graphics are not converted to symbols.

Next, we drag an instance of `airplane1` to the stage. The new stage is as shown in Figure 8.16.

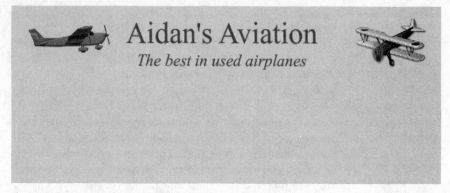

Figure 8.16 The stage after adding the clip art airplanes

One of the motivations for the example movie is to announce a sale at Aidan's Aviation. To make this known, we add another figure to the movie, in this case a star with the word `Sale` inside. We begin by drawing an eight-pointed star on the stage and then stretching four of its points to flatten its appearance. A point is stretched by selecting the *Selection Tool*, pressing the left mouse button with the mouse cursor over the point of the star, and dragging it away from the star's center.

Next, we convert the star to a symbol and, finally use the *Text Tool* to put the relevant text inside it. The star is converted to a symbol by selecting the whole star by double-clicking inside the star, selecting *Modify* and clicking *Convert to Symbol*. The resulting stage is shown in Figure 8.17.

The next step is to save and test the movie. Flash allows movies to be tested within the authoring environment, without requiring that the movie be loaded into a browser. This is done by selecting *Control/Test Movie*. The resulting display window, whose content is the same as Figure 8.17, is shown in Figure 8.18. Notice in Figure 8.18 that the name of the movie is `aidan_static`.

Figure 8.17 The complete sale announcement

Figure 8.18 The test of the movie, `aidan_static`

There are a variety of ways to publish a movie. These are accessed by selecting *File/Publish/Settings*. The dialog window that results is shown in Figure 8.19.

If the movie is to be placed on a Web site, it needs to be published as a Flash file and as HTML. Because this is the usual choice, these two buttons are checked by default. The *GIF, JPEG,* and *PNG* buttons are used to produce images of the movie. The *Windows Projector* button creates a file that can be executed under Windows. This file, when executed, plays the movie without a Flash player being installed on the computer on which it is executed. The *Macintosh Projector* button creates a similar file for Macintosh computers.

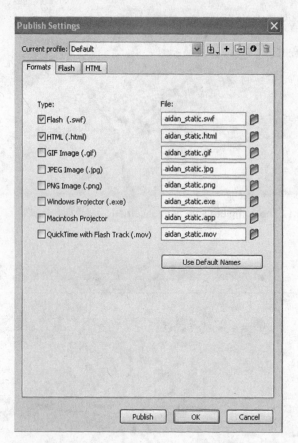

Figure 8.19 The *Publish Settings* dialog window

If only the *Flash* and *HTML* buttons are checked, several files are created in the directory where the Flash document resides. The Flash movie is in the file `aidan_static.swf`, where the `swf` extension is an acronym for Shockwave Flash (Shockwave was the previous name for Flash). Incidentally, `swf` is pronounced "swiff." The HTML file is implicitly named `aidan_static.html`, although that could be changed to whatever the author likes. The other created file contains a JavaScript script that allows Flash movies to be played in Microsoft browsers without requiring interaction by the user. The name of this file is `AC_RunActiveContent.js`.

If the browser of the system on which the Flash movie was built is pointed to the HTML document, the movie will be played on that browser.

A movie can be published just as a `swf` file and inserted into an HTML document using the HTML object element.

Following is the HTML file, `aidan_static.html`, produced by Flash for our movie:

```html
<html xmlns="http://www.w3.org/1999/xhtml" xml:lang="en"
      lang="en">
<head>
<meta http-equiv="Content-Type" content="text/html;
      charset=iso-8859-1" />
<title>aidan_static</title>
<script language="javascript">AC_FL_RunContent = 0;</script>
<script src="AC_RunActiveContent.js" language="javascript">
</script>
</head>
<body bgcolor="#00ffff">
<script language="javascript">
if (AC_FL_RunContent == 0) {
alert("This page requires AC_RunActiveContent.js.");
} else {
  AC_FL_RunContent(
    ...
  ); //end AC code
}
</script>
<noscript>
  <object classid="clsid:d27cdb6e-ae6d-11cf-96b8-444553540000"
          codebase="http://download.macromedia.com/pub/shockwave/
                    cabs/flash/swflash.cab#version=9,0,0,0"
          width="750" height="300" id="aidan_static" align="middle">
    <param name="allowScriptAccess" value="sameDomain" />
    <param name="allowFullScreen" value="false" />
    <param name="movie" value="aidan_static.swf" />
    <param name="quality" value="high" />
    <param name="bgcolor" value="#00ffff" />
    <embed src="aidan_static.swf" quality="high" bgcolor="#00ffff"
           width="750" height="300"
           name="aidan_static" align="middle"
           allowScriptAccess="sameDomain"
           allowFullScreen="false"
           type="application/x-shockwave-flash"
           pluginspage="http://www.macromedia.com/go/getflashplayer" />
  </object>
</noscript>
</body>
</html>
```

The HTML file produced by Flash does not use Windows end-of-line characters, so in Windows the format of the file is difficult to read. The listing above was created by converting the end-of-line characters and then doing some reformatting. Also, some unnecessary comments were removed and the long list of parameters to the JavaScript function AC_FL_RunContent also were removed.

In many cases, an XHTML document consists of the HTML produced by Flash, as well as XHTML written by a Web designer. The hand-written XHTML can be added to the HTML document from Flash. As an example, we next modify the HTML document from the aidan_static movie by adding a small amount of text. The style element for this addition is as follows:

```
<style type = "text/css">
  p.special {text-indent: "2.5in"; font-family: 'Times New Roman';
            font-size: 24pt; font-style: italic; color: "red";
            text-decoration: "underline";}
  p.list {text-indent: "1in"; font-family: 'Times New Roman';
         font-size: 16pt; color: "blue";}
</html>
```

The content for the addition is as follows:

```
<!-- Content added to the Flash-produced file for the
     aidan_static movie -->
<p></p><p></p>
<p class = "special">
  Specials of the Week
</p>
<p></p>
<p class = "list">
1. 1960 Cessna 210 <span style = "position: absolute; left: 3in">
   $49,000 </span>
</p>
<p class = "list">
2. 1977 Piper Commanche <span style = "position: absolute; left:
   3in">  $72,000 </span>
</p>
<p class = "list">
3. 1980 Cessna 182RG <span style = "position: absolute; left: 3in">
   $81,000 </span>
</html>
```

The display of the new version of `aidan_static`, named `aidan_static2.html`, is shown in Figure 8.20.

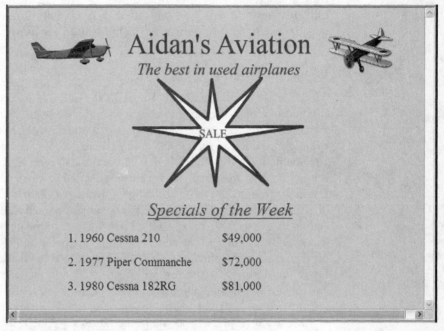

Figure 8.20 The display of `aidan_static2.html`

8.5   An Example—Animation and Sound

The example movie of this section is similar to the static movie of Section 8.4, but with modifications to animate part of it and to add sound to it.

8.5.1   Introduction to Animation

When a movie has multiple frames, those frames are displayed by the Flash player in sequence, repeatedly, from first to last, where the first is frame 1. Flash animation is created by the player showing sequences of frames, where each has a slightly changed appearance. Early animated movies (film movies for theaters) were made by hand painting long sequences of slightly differing scenes and photographing each in its own frame on film. With Flash, the author needs only to create the changing parts of the beginning and ending frames. Flash creates the intervening frames that morph the first frame into the last. These intervening frames are created through a process called *tweening*.

In the example movie of Section 8.4, all of the assets in the movie are in the same layer. This is unusual, because most movies have multiple layers. In fact, it is normal to place each asset in its own layer, because this allows each to be treated separately and differently, especially with regard to animation. Specifically, placing different assets in different layers allows some assets to be animated while others are static over the life span of the movie.

8.5.2 Moving a Figure

The example of this section is similar to the example in Section 8.4—a banner that provides the name of a company and announces a sale. Instead of two stationary airplane figures, this movie will have just one airplane, but it will move across the stage from left to right. This motion is created by placing one instance of the airplane figure in frame 1 at the left end of the stage and copying it to frame 50 at the right end of the stage. Then tweening is used to create the airplane figure in frames 2 through 49, each succeeding figure moved slightly to the right.

We begin by creating a new Flash document named `aidan_dynamic1` and setting its size to 700 by 400 pixels. Then we change the name of the initial layer to *name*. After frame 1 is selected, the company name and slogan text are placed on the stage, with sufficient space left above the text for the animated airplane figure. To ensure that the text will not accidentally be deleted and to disallow any other assets from being placed in the *name* layer, we lock the layer by clicking the dot to the right of the layer's name that is below the small lock icon, which is on the same row as the frame numbers. When this dot is clicked, the dot turns into a figure of a small lock.

The next step is to create a new layer for the animated airplane figure. Upper layers have precedence over lower layers. In effect, the bottom layer is displayed first, then progressively the upper layers are revealed. So, graphic figures in a layer above can hide a figure in a lower layer. If no two layers have overlapping objects, which will be the case in the example here, then the order of layers is irrelevant. A new layer is created by selecting *Insert/Timeline/Layer* or by clicking the *Insert Layer* button at the bottom left of the layers panel. (The name *Insert Layer* appears when the cursor is over the button.) This creates a new layer directly above the selected layer. If you want the new layer to be below the current bottom layer, drag it there with the mouse cursor after it has been created. In the example, the new layer is created and dragged to the bottom. Then we rename the layer *animation1*. This is done by double-clicking the layer name, editing it, and pressing *Enter*.

Next, we need a figure of a small airplane. We import a WMF vector graphic figure of an airplane to the library with *File/Import/Import to Library*. After importing the figure and selecting frame 1 of the *animation1* layer, we drag an instance of it on to the stage. Then, we convert it to a symbol with *Modify/Convert to Symbol*. In the resulting dialog box we set the type of the symbol to *Movie clip*. The other choices are *Button* and *Graphic*. It is not a button, so that should not be its type. The difference between movie clips and graphics is complex and mostly beyond the scope of this book. Briefly, a movie clip runs in its own timeline and allows a sound track. Because of its support for sound tracks, which we will add later, we make our symbol a movie clip. We name this figure *airplane1*.

It is a common practice to import graphic figures to the stage and then convert them to symbols, rather than importing them to the library, dragging an instance of them to the stage, and then converting them to symbols. Importing to the stage works for bitmap figures. However, importing a WMF figure, or any other vector graphic figure to the stage leads to difficulties, so we import our WMF figure to the library.

The Flash player always begins by displaying the assets of the first frame of the movie. If the movie has but one frame, as is the case with the `aidan_static` example of Section 8.4, that is all that is ever displayed. To make the movie change, assets must be placed in other frames. When the Flash player plays a movie with multiple frames, it displays them in sequence, repeatedly.

To create the airplane animation for our movie, we must create a new keyframe. A *keyframe* is a frame in which there is something new or changed. (Frame 1 is implicitly a keyframe.) A new keyframe is created at frame 50 by right-clicking frame 50 of the *animation1* layer and selecting *Insert Keyframe* from the menu that appears. This creates a new keyframe in frame 50 and copies the contents of the previous keyframe (from frame 1 in this case) into the new keyframe. Then with frame 50 of the *animation1* layer selected, we drag the airplane figure instance from the upper-left corner of the stage to the upper right corner of the stage. If frame 1 is selected, the airplane is where we initially put it, in the upper-left corner of the stage. If we drag the playhead from frame 1 to frame 49, the airplane remains displayed in the upper-left corner. So, at this point we have the airplane figure displayed in the upper-left corner for frames 1 to 49. Then it jumps to the upper-right corner for frame 50.

To create reasonable animation, the frames between 1 and 50 must be filled with copies of the airplane figure at positions between the first and fiftieth frames. We could do this manually, but it would be very tedious. Flash provides two kinds of support for creating the in between frames for animation, motion, and shape. These are called *motion tweening* and *shape tweening*. Motion tweening can be used for symbol instances; shape tweening is used for figures drawn on the stage.

To animate the airplane, which was converted to a symbol, *motion tweening* is used to create the frames between 1 and 50. This is done by selecting a frame between the two ends, say frame 25, in the *animation1* layer. This opens the frame version of the properties panel, which has a menu labeled *Tween*. If this menu is clicked, it shows three items, *None*, *Motion*, and *Shape*. We will consider the *Shape* option in Section 8.5.4. But for now we want to move the airplane figure, which is a symbol, so we choose *Motion*. Flash then displays an arrow starting at frame 1 of the timeline and extending to frame 50 in the *animation1* layer. This causes Flash to create frames between 1 and 50, each with the airplane figure moved slightly to the right of its position in the preceding frame. The animation can be checked by selecting the playhead on the top of the timeline and moving it between frame 1 and 50.

One remaining issue for the airplane image animation is that the rest of the assets of the movie, in this case only the text, are shown only when the playhead is over frame 1. To make it remain throughout the movie, it must be placed in all of the frames between 2 and 50. This is done by clicking the *name* layer in frame 1 and selecting *Insert/Timeline/Frame*. Now if the playhead is dragged from frame 1 to frame 50, the airplane image moves and the text remains while showing all of the frames.

Now we can save and test the movie. Unfortunately, we cannot show the animated movie in this static book.

8.5.3   More Animation

We now add another animated figure to the movie of Section 8.5.2. We will add the star from the example, `aidan_static` (Section 8.4) to the movie `aidan_dynamic1`. The star will be made to grow and shrink as the movie is played. We begin by adding a new layer for the star. This is done by selecting *Insert/Timeline/Layer* or by clicking the *Insert Layer* button at the bottom left of the layers panel. The name of this layer is then changed to *animate2*. While frame 1 in the new layer is selected, we draw a 12-pointed star with a dark blue stroke color and a white fill onto the stage. After creating the star, the six points on the left and right sides are stretched to make the star slightly flat, rather than circular, as was done with the star figure in Section 8.4. The star is then selected and converted to a symbol, by selecting *Modify/Convert to Symbol*. The symbol is named *star* and its type is set to *Movie Clip*. Then the text, SALE, in red, bold, 24 point font is added to the center of the star. The text is added in the *name* layer, where the company name and slogan text appears. The stage now appears as shown in Figure 8.21.

The next step in creating the animated star is to create two new keyframes in the *animate2* layer, one at frame 25 and one at frame 50. These are created by selecting the frame number and the desired layer (*animate2*), and then *Insert/Timeline/Keyframe*. Both of these implicitly get copies of the star in frame 1. (If a keyframe is accidentally created in the wrong frame, it can be removed by selecting the keyframe and then selecting *Modify/Timeline/Clear Keyframe*.) Next, we must modify the star in frame 25. We want the star to start (in frame 1) large, then shrink to a smaller size by frame 25, and then grow back to its original size by frame 50. To build the smaller star, we select frame 25 and select the star image on the stage. This displays the properties of the star figure in the properties panel. In the lower-left corner of this panel, the size of the figure is given in pixels. Next, we select the *Free Transform Tool*, which is just below the *Selection Tool* (if the tools are displayed in two columns). Its icon (in Windows) is a red dashed square with a triangular tool on the left side. Selecting this tool displays a rectangle with black squares on the corners and embedded in the sides. These can be dragged to change the size of the figure. Dragging a corner toward the center with the *Shift* key held down changes the figure proportionally, so it retains its original shape. This is how we make a smaller version of the star. We now have a large star in frames 1 and 50 and a smaller star in frame 25.

Figure 8.21 The ad with the star (`aidan_dynamic1`)

Finally, we create the tween frames. First, we select frame 12 in the *animation2* layer. In the *Properties* panel, we select *Motion* from the *Tween* menu. This creates all of the tween figures between frames 1 and 25. Then, we do the same in frame 37, which creates the tween figures between frames 25 and 50. Motion tweening (rather than shape tweening) is chosen because the shape of the star need not be changed (and because symbols cannot be shape tweened).

The next step is to save the document and test its movie by dragging the playhead from frame 1 to frame 50. The small airplane should still fly across the top of the stage from left to right. Also, the star at the bottom should shrink and grow as the airplane moves across the stage. Then, we use *Control/Test Movie* to again test the movie. Finally, we publish the movie as HTML and as a Flash document. As one more test, we point the browser at the HTML file, which produces the same movie as *Test Movie*.

8.5.4   Shape Animation

In Sections 8.5.2 and 8.5.3, motion-tweened animation was illustrated. We demonstrate shape-tweened animation in this section. The example will be simple: a red circle will be morphed into a blue square, which is then morphed into a green triangle.

We begin by creating a new movie named `shape_morph`. The initial layer is renamed *morph*. In frame 1 we draw a circle with a dark red stroke color and a light red fill on the stage. Then, we create a blank keyframe in frame 25 by right-clicking frame 25 of the morph layer and selecting *Insert Blank Keyframe* from the menu that appears. The blank keyframe, when selected, hides everything already on the stage. We use a blank keyframe here because we do not want it to inherit the content of any other keyframe. After selecting frame 25, we draw a square about the same size as the circle, this time with a dark blue stroke color and a light blue fill. Initially, we need not worry about it being in the same position as the circle. Next, we create the frames to transition the circle to the square. We select frame 12 and then select the *Shape* item of the *Tween* menu of the *Properties* panel.

After the frames have been filled, the figures may need to be aligned with each other. This can be done by first clicking the *Edit Multiple Frames* button, whose icon appears below the timeline—it is two small filled squares, one overlaying the other. This places two square brackets on the timeline. Next, we drag the right bracket to frame 50. Then, we click Control-A to select all elements on stage. Finally, we select *Modify/Align*. From the resulting menu we select *Horizontal Center*. Then, we select *Modify/Align* again and select *Vertical Center*. Now, all three figures are centered on the stage.

Next, we create a new blank keyframe in frame 50 and draw a triangle (a three-sided polygon) in that frame. The triangle uses a dark green stroke color and a light green fill. We then select frame 37 to create the tweening figures between the square and the triangle.

Both shape and motion animation can be made smoother by placing the animated assets farther apart on the timeline. For example, in the shape morphing example, the square could have been placed in frame 50 and the triangle in frame 100. This would have resulted in many more frames in the movie, thereby smoothing the transitions.

Animation created from discrete pictures, like that of movie films and Flash movies, are effective because, if the pictures change fast enough, the human brain fills in between the displayed pictures. If the actual pictures change too slowly, the animation appears jerky, because the brain no longer fills in between them. If the pictures change too quickly, the picture becomes blurred. The speed of the Flash player is controlled by the movie being played. The frame rate, which is the number of frames displayed per second, has a default value of 12 frames per second (fps). The frame rate can be changed in the properties panel when the stage has been selected.

The standard frame rate for film is 24 fps, but older versions of the Flash player were not able to play movies that fast. Version 9 of the Flash player can display movies far faster than 24 fps. For example, the movie `aidan_dynamic2` can be played at 100 fps, but at that speed the animated airplane is a blur. It would take many more frames in the movie to make it appear realistic at that frame rate. However, Flash movies with a large number of frames require larger files for storage and longer times to download. Furthermore, if a movie has complex animation and the frame rate is high, the CPU of the host of the player can become overwhelmed.

8.5.5   Sound

Sound clips can be added to a Flash movie. The first step to adding sound is to import the sound file to the library of the movie. Sound clips are widely available on the Web. To import a sound file, select *File/Import/Import to Library* and then select the sound file. The sound file will then appear in the *Library* panel as a new entry. If the new entry is clicked, the waveform of the sound file will appear in the window above the library's list of assets. When adding sounds to the timeline, it is best to place the sounds in their own layer in a movie, because that makes them easier to manage.

As an example, we will add a sound clip to the example movie of Section 8.5.3. We begin by opening that movie, *aidan_dynamic1*, and saving it in *aidan_dynamic2*. We then add a new layer (*Insert/Timeline/Layer*) and name it *sound*. We place the new layer at the bottom of the list of layers, to make it easy to find.

In the case of this example, the chosen sound clip was too long. Sound clips can be shortened by removing parts of either or both ends. This is done in the properties panel displayed when the keyframe of the beginning of the clip placed is clicked. This panel is shown in Figure 8.22.

Figure 8.22 The properties panel for editing sound clips

This panel shows the properties of the sound clip. Included is a *Edit* button, which when clicked displays the window shown in Figure 8.23.

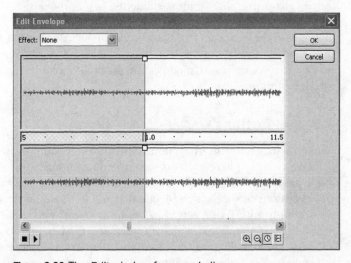

Figure 8.23 The *Edit* window for sound clips

Notice that the left half of the display is shaded. This shows the part of the clip that we trimmed by sliding the small rectangle on the center scale to the right. For this example, the right end was also significantly trimmed. This clip was actually 26.5 seconds long, as shown in the bottom of Figure 8.22. Since our animation is quite short, we made the sound layer similarly short. The length of the sound is shown by the length of the soundwave in the sound layer of the timeline, as shown in Figure 8.24.

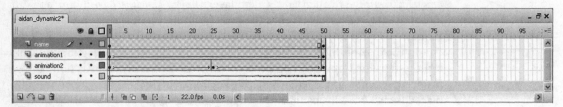

Figure 8.24 The timeline showing the sound layer

When the movie `aidan_dynamic2` is played, the sound clip, which is the sound of a small airplane taking off, is heard.

8.6   User Interactions

In Chapters 5 and 6 JavaScript is used to allow the user to interact with XHTML documents through graphical elements to control the presentation details of how they are displayed, among other things. The Flash dialect of Java Script, ActionScript, can be used to implement control of the content of a Flash movie, also through graphical elements, or components. Most commonly, in Flash these components are buttons. However, a variety of components can be placed in a Flash movie. They can be used for virtually any user interaction. In this section, simple buttons and their associated ActionScript code are illustrated with an example that allows the user to control the animation of a movie through buttons.

8.6.1   Actions

Actions associated with user interactions through components are programmed in ActionScript. There are two ways to add ActionScript to a Flash movie: as frame actions, which is code associated with particular keyframes of the movie, and as custom classes, which is code that resides in an external file. In this book we deal only with frame actions. Actions are similar to those written to implement user interactions with components in Chapter 5, "JavaScript and XHTML Documents." Flash component interactions create events and the associated actions are programmed as event handler functions. The event handlers are registered on the components using the DOM 2 event model function, `addEventListener`.

Because the user interactions implemented in Flash usually control the player, there are methods predefined in ActionScript for player control. Among these are `nextFrame()`, which instructs the player to play the next frame, `gotoAndStop`(frame number), `gotoAndPlay`(frame number), `play()`, and `stop()`, which do what their names imply. The parameter to `gotoAndStop` and `gotoAndPlay` can be a frame label, which can be created in another layer. These methods are usually called through the graphic figure symbols defined for the movie.

Actions are usually added to a new layer of the movie, often named *actions*. When such a layer has ActionScript associated with it in a keyframe, that keyframe is displayed in the timeline with a lowercase 'a'. Action layers are usually locked to prevent the accidental placement of graphic figures or other assets in them. Being locked does not prevent the placement of ActionScript in the layer.

ActionScript is written in a workspace window named *Actions*, which is accessed by selecting *Window/Actions*. The upper-left panel of this window, which is titled *ActionScript 3.0* (assuming the movie was created for ActionScript 3.0), is a menu of buttons that create skeletal ActionScript constructs. This is part of a tool named *Script Assist*, which helps create ActionScript code. Because we assume the reader is already versed in JavaScript, we do not describe how to use Script Assist in this book. The main panel of the *Actions* window is where ActionScript code is typed. Above this panel is a row of buttons, only one of which is of interest at this stage, *Check syntax*, whose symbol is a check mark (✔). This tool is used to check the correctness of the syntax of the code in the main panel before the author uses the player to test it.

8.6.2   Flash Components

In Flash, components can be designed by the programmer. For example, a button can be designed by choosing a graphic figure to represent the button, such as a circle, an ellipse, or a square. There are also a collection of predefined components available in the workspace. Among these are simple buttons, checkboxes, sliders, and radio buttons. We only deal with predesigned components here.

8.6.3   An Example

Our example to illustrate user interactions will be simple—we begin with just the animated airplane figure and the business title from the previous examples. To this we will add two buttons, one to stop the airplane and one to restart its motion.

We begin by opening `aidan_dynamic1` and saving it as `interact`. The first step is to add a layer for the buttons and one for actions. These are added by selecting *Insert/Timeline/Layer*. The names we chose for these layers are *buttons* and *actions*.

Next, we create the two buttons in the button layer by dragging *Button* component to the lower-left corner of the stage. The components are found in the window opened by selecting *Window/Components/User Interface*. This window is shown in Figure 8.25.

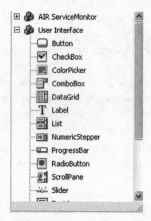

Figure 8.25 The *Window/Component* window

After creating the two buttons, we change their labels to *start airplane* and *stop airplane*. The label of a button is changed by selecting the button and then selecting *Window/Component Inspector*. The window that results is shown in Figure 8.26.

The labels are changed by typing in the new labels in the *label* entry's *Value* box.

Figure 8.26 The *Window/Component Inspector* window

The next step is to give the airplane figure an instance name. This is done by selecting the airplane figure on the stage and typing a name in the *Instance Name* box in the properties panel. We chose the name *airplaneMC*, for *airplane movie clip*.

The instances of the buttons must have their *Instance Name* boxes changed in their property panels. The *Instance Name* box appears just above the size and position boxes in the properties panel. For the example, they are named *stopbutton* and *startbutton*.

The workspace, minus the library and color panels, with the stop button selected is shown in Figure 8.27.

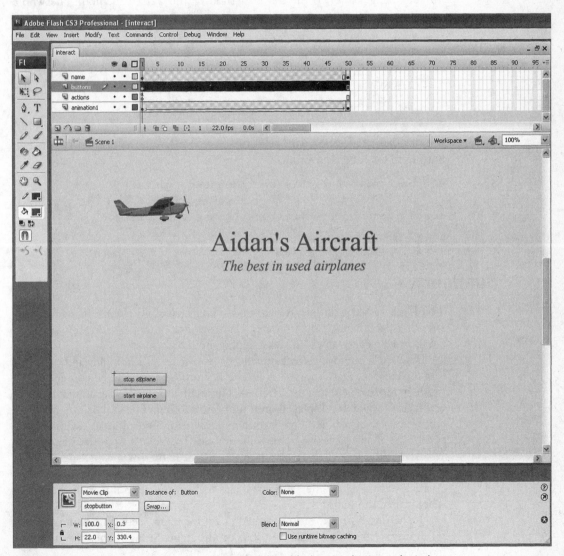

Figure 8.27 The workspace for the `interact` movie, with the stop button selected

Now, we must write the code to control the airplane figure on the stage. First, we select frame 1 of the *actions* layer. Then, we select *Window/Actions* to open the *Actions* window. We are now ready to type the code in the code panel. The first thing to do is add a call to the `stop` function, which will pause the player at frame 1 of the movie. Next, we type the event handler for the click event of the buttons. We name the handler function `handleClick`. This function takes the formal parameter for the event object, which is of type `MouseEvent`. The body of the event handler contains two selection constructs. Each of these checks to determine whether the target of the raised event is one specific button. The then clause of each selection is a call through the button instance name either to the `stop` method or the `start` method. The whole handler function follows:

```
function handleClick(bEvent: MouseEvent) {
  if (bEvent.target == stopbutton)
     airplaneMC.stop();
  if (bEvent.target == startbutton)
     airplaneMC.play();
}
```

The last of the necessary code is the registrations of the handler for the two buttons. This code is as follows:

```
stopbutton.addEventListener(MouseEvent.CLICK,
                            handleClick);
startbutton.addEventListener(MouseEvent.CLICK,
                            handleClick);
```

Summary

The Flash system consists of two fundamental parts, an environment for constructing documents, called movies, that can include both static and animated parts, and a player, which resides as a plug-in in browsers.

The Flash authoring environment, or workspace, is a complex and powerful tool for creating Flash movies. It allows the author to specify the content of the movie in terms of a sequence of frames. This content is usually separated into several layers, which are displayed on top of one another. The author can create or edit one layer at a time. This layering simplifies the creation and editing processes, and allows parts of a frame to be animated while other parts remain static.

Across the top of the workspace is a list of names of menus, such as *File*, *Edit*, and *Modify*. Down the left side of the workspace are a sequence of tools for creating drawings, geometric figures, and text on the central part of the workspace, called the stage.

If the *Rectangle Tool* button is held down for a few seconds, a menu appears for drawing rectangles, ovals, and stars on the stage. Straight lines and freehand figures can be drawn with the *Pencil Tool*.

Every figure on the stage has a properties panel (displayed below the stage), on which the author can modify its characteristics, such as size, location, stroke color, thickness, and style, and fill color.

All figures should be converted to symbols, which also stores them in the library of the movie. Any number of instances of a symbol can be placed on the stage.

When a movie is completed, Flash can produce a number of different versions of it, among them Flash movies, which can be played by the Flash player, and HTML documents that include the Flash movie, which can be displayed by any browser that has the Flash player plug-in installed.

Animation is supported by creating a sequence of versions of the display stage in a sequence of frames. This is made simple by the capability of Flash to create the frames between the actual frames. For example, motion animation is created by placing the figure to be moved at the two endpoints of the motion, and then letting Flash create all of the frames between the two, with the figure in a slightly different location in each frame. As the Flash player plays the sequence of frames, the animation is realized. Shape animation does something similar with the shapes of figures.

Sound clips can be added to a movie. The length of such clips can be shortened to make the sound fit the animation of the movie.

Flash movies support user interactions through components. There are a collection of predefined components that can be dragged from a menu onto the stage. The actions of components are defined in ActionScript, which is based on JavaScript. The code is written as event handlers. The event model used is that of DOM 2, so event handlers are registered with `addEventListener`. User interactions often are used in Flash to allow the user to control various aspects of the movie.

Review Questions

8.1 What does a column of the timeline represent?

8.2 What are the two components of Flash?

8.3 What is the library of a movie?

8.4 What is the playhead?

8.5 What does a row of the timeline represent?

8.6 What are the differences between the rectangles produced by the *Rectangle Tool* and the *Rectangle Primitive Tool*?

8.7 Why are different parts of movies placed in different layers?

8.8 Describe the stroke and fill of a figure.

8.9 What is a star point size?

8.10 How is the transparency of a color selected?

8.11 What is in a file with the `.swf` extension?

8.12 Explain what the *Straighten*, *Smooth*, and *Ink* menu items for freehand drawing do.

8.13 What figures can be created with the *Polystar Tool*?

8.14 How does one specify that a text box wrap its contents?

8.15 What is the relationship betwen a symbol and a symbol instance?

8.16 What is in a file with the `.fla` extension?

8.17 What method is used to register event handlers for a Flash movie?

8.18 What is the purpose of the predefined JavaScript code in the HTML file that embeds a Flash movie?

8.19 What is an asset?

8.20 What is the basic process of animation in a movie?

8.21 What is a keyframe?

8.22 What are the two kinds of tweening in a Flash movie?

8.23 What is a blank keyframe?

8.24 What is tweening?

8.25 What aspect of a sound clip can be modified?

8.26 Which event model does Flash use?

8.27 What are the two categories of Flash components?

Exercises

8.1 Create a static Flash movie that displays your name and address and includes at least four different figures of things you like and at least six different figures that use different stroke colors, thicknesses, styles, and different fill colors.

8.2 Create a Flash movie that animates two figures: one from the upper-left corner to the lower-right corner and one from the lower-left corner to the upper-right corner of the stage.

8.3 Create a Flash movie that uses motion animation to morph a figure from a large size to a small size and back as it moves from top to bottom of the stage's right side.

8.4 Create a Flash movie that uses motion animation to show a ball bouncing continuously between the left and right sides of the top of the stage.

8.5 Create a Flash movie that plays a sound clip of some music continuously while the movie plays.

8.6 Create a Flash movie that shows some text and has a mostly transparent ball that moves from the upper-left corner of the stage to the lower-right corner of the stage and includes *Start* and *Stop* buttons that control the animation.

CHAPTER

9

Introduction to PHP

This chapter is the first of the second part of the book, the topic of which is server-side software. In the first part, all of the software discussed was executed or interpreteed on the client. Although some tasks that are done on the server could be done on the browser, most cannot.

The topic of this chapter is PHP and its use as a server-side scripting language. It begins with a brief look at the origins of PHP, followed by an overview of its primary characteristics and some of its general syntactic conventions. Next, the core language is introduced. Because PHP is similar to JavaScript, the discussion of its expressions and statements is brief. PHP's arrays, which are different from those of any other language, are then introduced, followed by a description of PHP's functions and their parameter-passing mechanisms. Because PHP uses the same regular expressions for pattern matching as JavaScript,[1] regular expressions are not described in this chapter. The form-handling techniques of PHP are discussed next, including a complete example. Finally, both cookies and session tracking in PHP are introduced.

Significant parts of PHP are not covered in this chapter. Among these are references and support for object-oriented programming. PHP access to databases is discussed in Chapter 13, "Database Access through the Web."

9.1 Origins and Uses of PHP

PHP was developed by Rasmus Lerdorf, a member of the Apache Group,[2] in 1994. Its initial purpose was to provide a tool to help Lerdorf track visitors to his personal Web site. In 1995 he developed a package called Personal Home Page Tools, which became the first publicly distributed version of PHP. Originally, PHP was an acronym for Personal Home Page. Later, its user community began using the recursive name PHP: Hypertext Preprocessor, which subsequently forced the original name into obscurity.

Within two years of its release, PHP was being used at a large number of Web sites. By then, the job of managing its development had grown beyond the abilities of a single person, and that task was transferred to a small group of devoted volunteers. PHP is now developed, distributed, and supported as an open-source product. A PHP processor is now resident on most Web servers.

As a server-side scripting language, PHP is naturally used for form handling and database access. Database access has been a prime focus of PHP development; as a result, it has driver support for 15 different database systems. PHP supports the common electronic mail protocols POP3 and IMAP. It also supports the distributed object architectures COM and CORBA.

9.2 Overview of PHP

PHP is a server-side, XHTML-embedded scripting language. As such, it is an alternative to Microsoft's Active Server Pages (ASP and ASP.NET) and Sun's Java Server Pages (JSP).

In the sense of the way its scripts are interpreted, PHP is related to client-side JavaScript. When a browser finds JavaScript code embedded in an XHTML document it is displaying, it calls the JavaScript interpreter to interpret the script. When a browser requests an XHTML document that includes PHP script, the Web server that provides the document calls the PHP processor. The server determines that a document includes PHP script by the filename extension. If it is `.php`, `.php3`, or `.phtml`, it has embedded PHP.

---

1. Actually, PHP can use two different kinds of regular expressions, POSIX and Perl style.

2. The Apache Group develops and distributes the Apache Web server, among other things.

The PHP processor has two modes of operation, copy mode and interpret mode. It takes a PHP document file as input and produces an XHTML document file. When the PHP processor finds XHTML code (which may include embedded client-side script) in the input file, it simply copies it to the output file. When it encounters PHP script in the input file, it interprets it and sends any output of the script to the output file. This implies that the output from a PHP script must be XHTML or embedded client-side script. This new file (the output file) is sent to the requesting browser. The client never sees the PHP script. If the user clicks *View Source* while the browser is displaying the document, only the XHTML (and embedded client-side script) will be shown, because that is all that ever arrives at the client.

PHP is usually purely interpreted, as is the case with JavaScript. However, recent PHP implementations perform some precompilation, at least on complex scripts, which increases the speed of interpretation.

The syntax and semantics of PHP are closely related to the syntax and semantics of JavaScript. This should make it relatively easy to learn, assuming the reader has learned that language.

PHP uses dynamic typing, as does JavaScript. Variables are not type declared, and they have no intrinsic type. The type of a variable is set every time it is assigned a value, taking on the type of that value. Similar to JavaScript, PHP is far more forgiving than most common programming languages. Dynamic typing is largely responsible for this, but the dynamic nature of its strings and arrays also contributes. PHP's arrays are a merge of the arrays of common programming languages and associative arrays, having the characteristics of both. There is a large collection of functions for creating and manipulating PHP's arrays. PHP supports both procedural and object-oriented programming.

PHP has an extensive library of functions, making it a flexible and powerful tool for server-side software development. Many of the predefined functions are used to provide interfaces to other software systems such as mail and database systems.

As is the case with JavaScript, processors for PHP are free and easily obtainable. In addition, the PHP processor is an open-source system. It is available on all common computing platforms. The Web site for official information on PHP is `http://www.php.net`.

9.3 General Syntactic Characteristics

PHP scripts are either embedded in XHTML documents or are in files that are referenced by XHTML documents. PHP code is embedded in XHTML documents by enclosing it between the `<?php` and `?>` tags.

If a PHP script is stored in a different file, it can be brought into a document with the `include` construct, which takes the filename as its parameter. For example:

```
include("table2.inc");
```

This construct causes the contents of the file `table2.inc` to be copied into the document where the `include` appears. The included file can contain XHTML markup or client-side script, as well as PHP code, but any PHP script it includes must be the content of a `<?php` tag, even if the `include` appears in the content of a `<?php` tag. The PHP interpreter changes from interpret to copy mode when an `include` is encountered.

All variable names in PHP begin with a dollar sign ($). The part of the name after the dollar sign is like the names of variables in many common programming languages: a letter or an underscore followed by any number (including zero) of letters, digits, or underscores. PHP variable names are case sensitive.

Table 9.1 lists the PHP reserved words. Although variable names in PHP are case sensitive, neither reserved words nor function names are. For example, there is no difference between `while`, `WHILE`, `While`, and `wHiLe`.

Table 9.1   The reserved words of PHP

and	else	global	require	virtual
break	elseif	if	return	xor
case	extends	include	static	while
class	false	list	switch	
continue	for	new	this	
default	foreach	not	true	
do	function	or	var	

PHP allows comments to be specified in three different ways. Single-line comments can be specified either with # or with //, as in JavaScript. Multiple-line comments are delimited with /* and */, as in many other programming languages.

PHP statements are terminated with semicolons. Braces are used to form compound statements for control structures. Unless used as the body of a function definition, a compound statement cannot be a block (it cannot define locally scoped variables).

9.4 Primitives, Operations, and Expressions

PHP has four scalar types, Boolean, integer, double, and string; two compound types, array and object; and two special types, resource and NULL. In this section, only the scalar types and NULL are discussed. Arrays are discussed in Section 9.7; objects and resource types are not covered in this book.

9.4.1   Variables

Because PHP is dynamically typed, it has no type declarations. In fact, there is no way or need to ever declare the type of a variable.[3] The type of a variable is set every time it is assigned a value. An unassigned variable, sometimes called an *unbound variable*, has the value NULL, which is the only value of the NULL type. If an unbound variable is used in an expression, NULL is coerced to a value that is dictated by the context of the use. If the context specifies a number, NULL is coerced to 0; if the context specifies a string, NULL is coerced to the empty string.

A variable can be tested to determine whether it currently has a value with the IsSet function, which takes the variable's name as its parameter and returns a Boolean value. For example, IsSet($fruit) returns TRUE if $fruit currently has a non-NULL value, FALSE otherwise. A variable that has been assigned a value retains that value until either it is assigned a new value or it is set back to the unassigned state, which is done with the unset function.

If the user is to be informed when an unbound variable is referenced, a call to the error_reporting function is included to change the error-reporting level of the PHP interpreter to 15. The following call is placed at the beginning of the script in the document file:

```
error_reporting(15);
```

The default error-reporting level is 7, which does not require the interpreter to report the use of an unbound variable.

9.4.2   Integer Type

PHP has a single integer type, named integer. This type corresponds to the long type of C and its successors, which means its size is that of the word size of the machine on which the program is run. In most cases, this is 32 bits, or a bit less (not fewer) than ten decimal digits.

9.4.3   Double Type

PHP's double type corresponds to the double type of C and its successors. Double literals can include a decimal point, an exponent, or both. The exponent has the usual form of an E or an e, followed by a possibly signed integer literal. There does not need to be any digits before or after the decimal point, so both .345 and 345. are legal double literals.

---

3. Variables are sometimes declared to have nondefault scopes or lifetimes, as discussed in Section 9.8.

9.4.4   String Type

Characters in PHP are single bytes. (UNICODE is not supported.) There is no character type. A single character data value is represented as a string of length 1.

String literals are defined with either single quote (') or double quote (") delimiters. In single-quoted string literals, escape sequences, such as \n, are not recognized as anything special, and the values of embedded variables are not substituted. (This substitution is called *interpolation*.) In double-quoted string literals, escape sequences are recognized, and embedded variables are replaced by their current values. For example, the value of

```
'The sum is: $sum'
```

is exactly as it is typed. However, assuming the current value of $sum is 10.2, the value of

```
"The sum is: $sum"
```

is

```
The sum is: 10.2
```

If a double-quoted string literal includes a variable name but you do not want it interpolated, precede the first character of the name (the dollar sign) with a backslash (\). If the name of a variable that is not set to a value is embedded in a double-quoted string literal, the name is replaced by the empty string.

Double-quoted strings can include embedded newline characters that are created by the *Enter* key. Such characters are exactly like those that result from typing \n in the string.

The length of a string is limited only by the available memory on the computer.

9.4.5   Boolean Type

The only two possible values for the Boolean type are TRUE and FALSE, both of which are case insensitive. Although Boolean is a data type in the same sense as integer, expressions of other types can be used in Boolean context. If a non-Boolean expression appears in Boolean context, the programmer obviously must know how it will be interpreted. If an integer expression is used in Boolean context, it evaluates to FALSE if it is zero; otherwise, it is TRUE. If a string expression is used in Boolean context, it evalutes to FALSE if it is either the empty string or the string "0"; otherwise, it is TRUE. This implies that the string "0.0" evaluates to TRUE.

The only double value that is interpreted as FALSE is exactly 0.0. Because of rounding errors, as well as the fact that the string "0.0" evaluates to TRUE, it is not a good idea to use expressions of type double in Boolean context. A value can be very close to zero, but because it is not exactly zero, it will evaluate to TRUE.

9.4.6 Arithmetic Operators and Expressions

PHP has the usual (for C-based programming languages) collection of arithmetic operators (+, -, *, /, %, ++, and --) with the usual meanings. In the cases of +, -, and *, if both operands are integers, the operation is integer and an integer result is produced. If either operand is a double, the operation is double and a double result is produced. Division is treated the same way, except that if integer division is done and the result is not an integral value, the result is returned as a double. Any operation on integers that results in integer overflow also produces a double. The operands of the modulus operator (%) are expected to be integers. If one or both are not, they are coerced to integers.

PHP has a large number of predefined functions that operate on numeric values. Some of the most useful of these are shown in Table 9.2. In this table, "number" means either integer or double.

Table 9.2 Some useful predefined functions

Function	Parameter Type	Returns
floor	Double	Largest integer less than or equal to the parameter
ceil	Double	Smallest integer greater than or equal to the parameter
round	Double	Nearest integer
srand	Integer	Initializes a random number generator with the parameter
rand	Two numbers	A pseudorandom number greater than the first parameter and smaller than the second
abs	Number	Absolute value of the parameter
min	One or more numbers	Smallest
max	One or more numbers	Largest

The other predefined functions for number values are for doing number base conversion and computing exponents, logarithms, and trigonometric functions.

9.4.7 String Operations

The only string operator is the catenation operator, specified with a period (.).

String variables can be treated somewhat like arrays for access to individual characters. The position of a character in a string, relative to zero, can be specified in braces immediately after the variable's name. For example, if $str has the value "apple", $str{3} is "l".

PHP includes many functions that operate on strings. Some of the most commonly used are described in Table 9.3.

Table 9.3 Some commonly used string functions

Function	Parameter Type	Returns
strlen	A string	The number of characters in the string
strcmp	Two strings	Zero if the two strings are identical, a negative number if the first string belongs before the second (in the ASCII sequence), or a positive number if the second string belongs before the first
strpos	Two strings	The character position in the first string of the first character of the second string, if the second string is in the first string; false if it is not there
substr	A string and an integer	The substring of the string parameter, starting from the position indicated by the second parameter; if a third parameter is given (an integer), it specifies the length of the returned substring
chop	A string	The parameter with all whitespace characters removed from its end
trim	A string	The parameter with all whitespace characters removed from both ends
ltrim	A string	The parameter with all whitespace characters removed from its beginning
strtolower	A string	The parameter with all uppercase letters converted to lowercase
strtoupper	A string	The parameter with all lowercase letters converted to uppercase

Note for strpos: Because false is interpreted as zero in numeric context, this can be a problem. To avoid it, compare the returned value to zero using the === operator (see Section 9.6.1) to determine whether the match was at the beginning of the first string parameter (or if there was no match).

Consider the following example of the use of a string function:

```
$str = "Apples are good";
$sub = substr($str, 7, 1);
```

The value of $sub is now 'a'.

9.4.8 Scalar Type Conversions

PHP, like most other programming languages, includes both implicit and explicit type conversions. Implicit type conversions are called *coercions*. In most cases, the context of an expression determines the type that is expected or required. The context can cause a coercion of the type of the value of the expression. Some of the coercions that take place between the integer and double types and between Boolean and other scalar types have already been discussed. There are also frequent coercions between numeric and string types. Whenever a numeric value appears in string context, the numeric value is coerced to a string. Likewise, whenever a string value appears in numeric context, the string value is coerced to a numeric value. If the string contains a period, an e, or an E, it is converted to double; otherwise, it is converted to an integer. If the string does not begin with a sign or a digit, the conversion fails and zero is used. Nonnumeric characters following the number in the string are ignored.

When a double is converted to an integer, the fractional part is dropped; rounding is not done.

Explicit type conversions can be specified in three different ways. Using the syntax of C, an expression can be cast to a different type. The cast is a type name in parentheses preceding the expression. For example, if the value of $sum is 4.777, the following produces 4:

```
(int)$sum
```

Another way to specify explicit type conversion is to use one of the functions intval, doubleval, or strval. For example, if $sum is still 4.777, the following call returns 4:

```
intval($sum)
```

The third way to specify an explicit type conversion is the settype function, which takes two parameters: a variable and a string that specifies a type name. For example, if $sum is still 4.777, the following statement converts the value of $sum to 4 and its type to integer:

```
settype($sum, "integer");
```

The type of the value of a variable can be determined in two different ways, the first of which is the gettype function. The gettype function takes a variable as its parameter and returns a string that has the name of the type of the current value of the variable. One possible return value of gettype is "unknown". The other way to determine the type of the value of a variable is to use one or more of the type-testing functions, each of which takes a variable name as a parameter and returns a Boolean value. These are is_int, is_integer, and is_long, which test for integer type; is_double, is_float, and is_real, which test for double type; is_bool, which tests for Boolean type; and is_string, which tests for string type.[4]

---

4. PHP also has the is_array function to test for arrays and the is_object function to test for objects.

9.4.9   Assignment Operators

PHP has the same set of assignment operators as its predecessor language, C, including the compound assignment operators such as `+=` and `/=`.

9.5 Output

Any output from a PHP script becomes part of the document the PHP processor is building. Therefore, all output must be in the form of XHTML, which may include embedded client-side script.

The `print` function[5] is used to create simple unformatted output. It can be called with or without parentheses around its parameter. For example, the following statement is legal:

```
print "Apples are red <br /> Kumquats aren't <br />";
```

Although `print` expects a string parameter, if some other type value is given, the PHP interpreter will coerce it to a string without complaint. For example, the following statement will produce `47`:

```
print(47);
```

Because variables that appear in double-quoted strings are interpolated, it is easy to label output. For example,

```
print "The result is: $result <br />";
```

PHP borrows the `printf` function from C. It is used when complete control over the format of displayed data is required. The general form of a call to `printf` is as follows:

```
printf(literal_string, param1, param2, ...)
```

The literal string can include labeling information about the parameters whose values are to be displayed. It also contains format codes for those values. The form of the format codes is a percent sign (`%`) followed by a field width and a type specifier. The most common type specifiers are `s` for strings, `d` for integers, and `f` for floats and doubles. The field width is either an integer literal (for integers) or two integer literals separated by a decimal point for floats and doubles. The integer literal to the right of the decimal point specifies the number of digits to be displayed to the right of the decimal point. Consider the following examples:

> `%10s`—a character string field of 10 characters
> `%6d`—an integer field of six digits
> `%5.2f`—a float or double field of eight spaces, with two digits to the right of the decimal point, the decimal point, and five digits to the left

---

5. PHP also has the `echo` function, which is similar to `print`.

The position of the format code in the first parameter to `printf` indicates the place in the output where the associated value should appear. For example, consider the following:

```
$day = "Tuesday";
$high = 79;
printf("The high on %7s was %3d", $day, $high);
```

Note that `printf` requires parentheses around its parameters.

The following simple example displays a welcome message and the current day of the week, the month, and day of the month. The date information is generated with the `date` function, whose first parameter is a string that specifies the parts of the date you want to see. In our example, l requests the day of the week, F requests the month, j requests the day of the week, and an S next to the j gets the correct suffix for the day (for example, st or nd). The details of `date` can be found at `http://www.php.net`. Figure 9.1 shows a display of the output of `today.php`.

```
<?xml version = "1.0" encoding = "utf-8"?>
<!DOCTYPE html PUBLIC "-//W3C//DTD XHTML 1.0 Strict//EN"
  "http://www.w3.org/TR/xhtml1/DTD/xhtml1-strict.dtd">


<!-- today.php - A trivial example to illustrate a php document -->
<html xmlns = "http://www.w3.org/1999/xhtml">
  <head> <title> today.php </title>
  </head>
  <body>
    <p>
      <?php
        print "<b>Welcome to my home page <br /> <br />";
        print "Today is:</b> ";
        print date("l, F jS");
        print "<br />";
      ?>
    </p>
  </body>
</html>
```

Welcome to my home page

Today is: Saturday, June 1st

Figure 9.1 Display of the output of `today.php`

9.6 Control Statements

The control statements of PHP are not remarkable—in fact, they are very similar to those of C and its descendants. The control expression used in PHP's control statements can be any type. The interpreter evaluates the control expression and, in the cases of if and loop statements, coerces the resulting value, if necessary, to Boolean.

9.6.1 Relational Operators

PHP uses the eight relational operators of JavaScript. The usual six (>, <, >=, <=, !=, and ==) have the usual meanings. It also has ===, which produces TRUE only if both operands are the same type and have the same value, and !==, the opposite of ===. If the types of the operands of the other six relational operators are not the same, one is coerced to the type of the other. If a string is compared to a number and the string can be converted to a number (it is in fact a string version of a number, for example "42"), the string will be converted and a numeric comparison will be done. If the string cannot be converted to a number, the numeric operand will be converted to a string, and a string comparison will be done. If both operands are strings that can be converted to numbers, both will be converted and a numeric comparison will be done. This is often not what is desired. To avoid this and similar problems associated with string-to-number coercions, if either or both operands are strings that could be converted to numbers, the strcmp function should be used rather than one of the comparison operators.

9.6.2 Boolean Operators

There are six Boolean operators: and, or, xor, !, &&, and ||. The and and && operators perform the same operation, as do or and ||. The difference between these is that the precedence of and and or is lower than that of && and ||. All of PHP's binary Boolean operators are evaluated as short-circuit operators.

9.6.3 Selection Statements

PHP's if statement is like that of C. The control expression can be an expression of any type, but its value is coerced to Boolean. The controlled statement segment can be either an individual statement or a compound statement. An if statement can include any number of elseif clauses. Following is a simple example of an if construct:

```
if ($day == "Saturday" || $day == "Sunday")
  $today = "weekend";
else {
  $today = "weekday";
  $work = true;
}
```

The `switch` statement has the form and semantics of that of JavaScript. The type of the control expression and the `case` expressions is either integer, double, or string. If necessary, the values of the `case` expressions are coerced to the type of the control expression for the comparisons. A `default` case can be included. As with its ancestor in C and Java, a `break` statement must follow each selectable segment if control is not to flow to the following segment. Following is a simple example of a `switch` construct:

```
switch ($bordersize) {
  case "0": print "<table>";
            break;
  case "1": print "<table border = '1'>";
            break;
  case "4": print "<table border = '4'>";
            break;
  case "8": print "<table border = '8'>";
            break;
  default: print "Error-invalid value: $bordersize <br />";
}
```

9.6.4   Loop Statements

The `while`, `for`, and `do-while` statements of PHP are exactly like those of JavaScript. PHP also has a `foreach` statement, which is discussed in Section 9.7.4. The following example computes the factorial of $n:

```
$fact = 1;
$count = 1;
while ($count < $n) {
  $count++;
  $fact *= $count;
}
```

The following example computes the sum of the positive integers up to 100:

```
$count = 1;
$sum = 0;
do {
  $sum += $count;
  $count++;
} while ($count <= 100);
```

The following example computes the factorial of $n:

```
for ($count = 1, $fact = 1; $count < $n;) {
  $count++;
  $fact *= $count;
}
```

The break statement can be used to terminate the execution of a for, foreach, while, or do-while construct. The continue statement is used in loop constructs to skip the remainder of the current iteration but continue execution at the beginning of the next.

9.6.5 An Example

The following example is meant to illustrate the form of an XHTML/PHP document, as well as some simple mathematical functions and the intermingling of XHTML and PHP in a document. The sqrt function returns the square root of its parameter; the pow function raises its first parameter to the power of its second parameter.

```
<?xml version = "1.0" encoding = "utf-8"?>
<!DOCTYPE html PUBLIC "-//W3C//DTD XHTML 1.0 Strict//EN"
   "http://www.w3.org/TR/xhtml1/DTD/xhtml1-strict.dtd">

<!-- powers.php
     An example to illustrate loops and arithmetic
     -->
<html xmlns = "http://www.w3.org/1999/xhtml">
  <head> <title> powers.php </title>
  </head>
  <body>
    <table border = "border">
      <caption> Powers table </caption>
      <tr>
        <th> Number </th>
        <th> Square Root </th>
        <th> Square </th>
        <th> Cube </th>
        <th> Quad </th>
      </tr>
      <?php
        for ($number = 1; $number <=10; $number++) {
          $root = sqrt($number);
          $square = pow($number, 2);
          $cube = pow($number, 3);
          $quad = pow($number, 4);
          print("<tr align = 'center'> <td> $number </td>");
          print("<td> $root </td> <td> $square </td>");
          print("<td> $cube </td> <td> $quad </td> </tr>");
        }
```

```
        ?>
      </table>
    </body>
  </html>
```

Figure 9.2 displays the output of `powers.php`.

Powers table				
Number	**Square Root**	**Square**	**Cube**	**Quad**
1	1	1	1	1
2	1.4142135623731	4	8	16
3	1.7320508075689	9	27	81
4	2	16	64	256
5	2.2360679774998	25	125	625
6	2.4494897427832	36	216	1296
7	2.6457513110646	49	343	2401
8	2.8284271247462	64	512	4096
9	3	81	729	6561
10	3.1622776601684	100	1000	10000

Figure 9.2   The output of `powers.php`

9.7 Arrays

Arrays in PHP are unlike those of any other common programming language. They are best described as a combination of the arrays of a typical language and associative arrays, or hashes, found in some other languages such as Ruby and Python. This makes them the ultimate in flexible, built-in data structures. Each array element consists of two parts, a key and a value. If the array has a logical structure that is similar to an array in another language, the keys just happen to be non-negative integers and are always in ascending order. If the array has a logical structure that is similar to a hash, its keys are strings, and the order of its elements is determined with a system-designed hashing function. The string keys of a PHP array are sometimes people's names; sometimes they are the names of the days of the week. They are always a collection of strings of some significance. One interesting thing about PHP arrays is that they can have some elements with integer keys and some with string keys.

9.7.1   Array Creation

There are two ways to create an array in PHP. The assignment operation creates scalar variables. The same operation works for arrays—assigning a value to a subscripted variable that previously was not an array creates the array. For example, assuming no array named $list currently exists, the following statement creates one:

```
$list[0] = 17;
```

If the script has a scalar variable named $list prior to this assignment, $list is now an array. If empty brackets are used in an assignment to an array, a numeric subscript is implicitly furnished. The furnished subscript is 1 greater than the largest used so far in the array, if the array already has elements with numeric keys. If the array currently has no elements with numeric keys, the value 0 is used. For example, in the following code, the second element's subscript will be 2:

```
$list[1] = "Today is my birthday!";
$list[] = 42;
```

This example also shows that the elements of an array need not have the same type.

The second way to create an array is with the **array** construct. We call this a construct because, although the syntax of using it is the same as that of a function call, it is not a function. The parameters to **array** specify the values to be placed in a new array and sometimes also the keys. If the array is like a traditional array, only the values need to be specified. (The PHP interpreter will furnish the numeric keys.) For example:

```
$list = array(17, 24, 45, 91);
```

This assignment creates a traditional array of four elements, with the keys 0, 1, 2, and 3. If you would rather have different keys, they can be specified in the array construct, as shown in the following:

```
$list = array(1 => 17, 2 => 24, 3 => 42, 4 => 91);
```

An array construct with empty parentheses creates an empty array. For example, in the following statement, $list becomes a variable whose value is an array with no elements:

```
$list = array();
```

The following statement creates an array that has the form of a hash:

```
$ages = array("Joe" => 42, "Mary" => 41, "Bif" => 17);
```

Some built-in functions return arrays. For example, some of the functions that access databases return arrays.

PHP arrays do not need to be purely in the form of traditional arrays or hashes; they can be mixtures of both. For example, we could have the following:

```
$stuff = array("make" => "Cessna", "model" => "C210",
               "year" => 1960, 3 => "sold");
```

9.7.2 Accessing Array Elements

Individual array elements can be accessed by subscripting, as in other programming languages. The value in the subscript, which is enclosed in brackets, is the key of the value being referenced. The same brackets are used regardless of whether the key is a number or a string. For example, the value of the element whose key is "Mary" in the $ages array can be set to 29 with the following statement:

```
$ages['Mary'] = 29;
```

Multiple elements of an array can be assigned to scalar variables in one statement, using the list construct. This is similar to the list assignments of Perl. For example:

```
$trees = array("oak" , "pine", "binary");
list($hardwood, $softwood, $data_structure) = $trees;
```

In this example, $hardwood, $softwood, and $data_structure are set to "oak", "pine", and "binary", respectively.

9.7.3 Functions for Dealing with Arrays

A whole array can be deleted with unset, as with a scalar variable. Individual elements of an array also can be removed with unset, as in the following:

```
$list = array(2, 4, 6, 8);
unset($list[2]);
```

Now $list has three remaining elements with keys 0, 1, and 3 and elements 2, 4, and 8.

The collection of keys and the collection of values of an array can be extracted with built-in functions. The array_keys function takes an array as its parameter and returns an array of the keys of the given array. The returned array uses 0, 1, and so forth as its keys. The array_values function does for values what array_keys does for keys. For example:

```
$highs = array("Mon" => 74, "Tue" => 70, "Wed" => 67,
               "Thu" => 62, "Fri" => 65);
$days = array_keys($highs);
$temps = array_values($highs);
```

Now the value of $days is ("Mon", "Tue", "Wed", "Thu", "Fri"), and the value of $temps is (74, 70, 67, 62, 65). In both cases, the keys are (0, 1, 2, 3, 4).

The existence of an element of a specific key can be determined with the array_key_exists function, which returns a Boolean value. For example, consider the following:

```
$highs = array("Mon" => 74, "Tue" => 70, "Wed" => 67,
               "Thu" => 62, "Fri" => 65);
if (array_key_exists("Tue", $highs)) {
  $tues_high = $highs["Tue"];
  print "The high on Tuesday was $tues_high <br />";
}
```

Note that PHP does not interpolate array elements embedded in double-quoted strings. That is the reason for the assignment statement in the if construct above. An array name embedded in a double-quoted string results in the word Array being inserted in the string in place of the array's name.

The is_array function is similar to the is_int function: It takes a variable as its parameter and returns TRUE if the variable is an array, FALSE otherwise. The in_array function takes two parameters—an expression and an array—and returns TRUE if the value of the expression is a value in the array; otherwise, it returns FALSE.

The number of elements in an array can be determined with the sizeof function. For example, consider the following code:

```
$list = array("Bob", "Fred", "Alan", "Bozo");
$len = sizeof($list);
```

After executing this code, $len will be 4.

It is often convenient to be able to convert between strings and arrays. These conversions can be done with the implode and explode functions. The explode function explodes a string into substrings and returns them in an array. The delimiters of the substrings are defined by the first parameter to explode, which is a string; the second parameter is the string to be converted. For example, consider the following:

```
$str = "April in Paris, Texas is nice";
$words = explode(" ", $str);
```

Now $words contains ("April", "in", "Paris,", "Texas", "is", "nice").

The implode function does the inverse of explode. Given a separator character (or string) and an array, it catenates the elements of the array together, using the given separator string between the elements, and returns the result as a string. For example:

```
$words = array("Are", "you", "lonesome", "tonight");
$str = implode(" ", $words);
```

Now $str has "Are you lonesome tonight" (which is obviously a rhetorical question).

Internally, the elements of an array are stored in a linked list of cells, where each cell includes both the key and the value of the element. The cells themselves are stored in memory through a key hashing function so that they are randomly distributed in a reserved block of storage. Accesses to elements through string keys are implemented through the hashing function. However, the elements all have links that connect them in the order in which they were created, which allows them to be accessed in that order if the keys are strings and in the order of their keys if the keys are numbers. Section 9.7.4 discusses the ways array elements can be accessed in order.

Figure 9.3 shows the internal logical structure of an array. Although arrays may not be implemented in this exact way, it shows how the two different access methods could be supported.

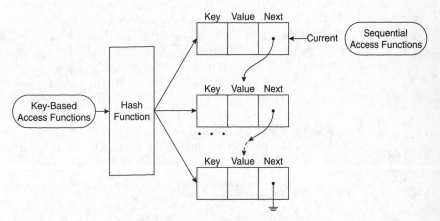

Figure 9.3   Logical internal structure of arrays

9.7.4   Sequential Access to Array Elements

PHP includes several different ways to access array elements in sequential order. Every array has an internal pointer that references one element of the array. We call this the "current" pointer. This pointer is initialized to reference the first element of the array at the time the array is created. The element being referenced by the pointer can be obtained with the current function. For example, consider the following code:

```
$cities = array("Hoboken", "Chicago", "Moab", "Atlantis");
$city = current($cities);
print("The first city is $city <br />");
```

This code produces the following:

```
The first city is Hoboken
```

The "current" pointer can be moved with the `next` function, which both moves the pointer to the next array element and returns the value of that element. If the "current" pointer is already pointing at the last element of the array, `next` returns `FALSE`. For example, if the "current" pointer is referencing the first element of the `$cities` array, the following code produces a list of all of the elements of that array:

```
$city = current($cities);
print("$city <br />");
while ($city = next($cities))
  print("$city <br />");
```

One problem with using the `next` function for loop control, as shown in the preceding example, occurs when the array includes an element with the value `FALSE`. The loop ends, but not because the "current" pointer ran off the end of the array. The `each` function, which returns a two-element array consisting of the key and the value of the "current" element, avoids this problem. It returns `FALSE` only if the "current" pointer has gone past the last element of the array. The keys of the two elements of the return value from `each` are the strings `"key"` and `"value"`. Another difference between `each` and `next` is that `each` returns the element being referenced by the "current" pointer and then moves that pointer. The `next` function first moves the "current" pointer and then returns the value being referenced by the "current" pointer. As an example of the use of `each`, consider the following code:

```
$salaries = array("Mike" => 42500, "Jerry" => 51250,
                  "Fred" => 37920);
while ($employee = each($salaries)) {
  $name = $employee["key"];
  $salary = $employee["value"];
  print("The salary of $name is $salary <br />");
}
```

The output produced by this code is as follows:

```
The salary of Mike is 42500
The salary of Jerry is 51250
The salary of Fred is 37920
```

The "current" pointer can be moved backward (that is, to the element before the "current" element) with the `prev` function. Like the `next` function, the `prev` function returns the value of the element referenced by the "current" pointer after the pointer has been moved. The "current" pointer can be set to the first element with the `reset` function, which also returns the value of the first element. It can be set to the last element of the array with the `end` function, which also returns the value of the last element.

The `key` function, when given the name of an array, returns the key of the "current" element of the array.

The `array_push` and `array_pop` functions provide a simple way to implement a stack in an array. The `array_push` function takes as its first parameter an array. After this first parameter, there can be any number of additional parameters. The values of all subsequent parameters are placed at the end of the array. The `array_push` function returns the new number of elements in the array. The `array_pop` function takes a single parameter, the name of an array. It removes the last element from the array and returns it. The value `NULL` is returned if the array is empty.

The `foreach` statement is designed to build loops that process all of the elements of an array. This statement has two forms:

```
foreach (array as scalar_variable) loop body
foreach (array as key => value) loop body
```

In the first form, one of the array's values is set to the scalar variable for each iteration of the loop body. The "current" pointer is implicitly initialized, as with `reset`, before the first iteration. For example:

```
foreach ($list as $temp)
  print("$temp <br />");
```

This code will produce the values of all of the elements of `$list`.

The second form of `foreach` provides both the key and the value of each element of the array. For example:

```
$lows = array("Mon" => 23, "Tue" => 18, "Wed" => 27);
foreach ($lows as $day => $temp)
  print("The low temperature on $day was $temp <br />");
```

9.7.5 Sorting Arrays

The `sort` function, which takes an array as a parameter, sorts the values in the array, replacing the keys with the numeric keys, 0, 1, 2, ... The array can have both string and numeric values. The string values migrate to the beginning of the array in alphabetical order. The numeric values follow in ascending order. Regardless of the types of the keys in the original array, the sorted array has 0, 1, 2, and so forth as keys. This function is obviously meant for sorting traditional arrays of either strings or numbers. Although it causes no problems, it seems to be a rare situation in which one would want to sort arrays with both strings and numbers as values.

The `asort` function is used to sort arrays that correspond to hashes. It sorts the elements of a given array by their values but keeps the original key/value associations. As with `sort`, string values all appear before the numeric values, in alphabetical order. The numeric values follow in ascending order.

The `ksort` function sorts its given array by keys, rather than values. The key/value associations are maintained by the process.

The rsort, arsort, and krsort functions behave like the sort, asort, and ksort functions, respectively, except that they sort into the reverse orders of their counterparts.

The following example illustrates sort, asort, and ksort.

```
<?xml version = "1.0" encoding = "utf-8"?>
<!DOCTYPE html PUBLIC "-//W3C//DTD XHTML 1.0 Strict//EN"
  "http://www.w3.org/TR/xhtml1/DTD/xhtml1-strict.dtd">

<!-- sorting.php - An example to illustrate several of the
     sorting functions -->
<html xmlns = "http://www.w3.org/1999/xhtml">
  <head> <title> Sorting </title>
  </head>
  <body>
    <?php
      $original = array("Fred" => 31, "Al" => 27,
                        "Gandalf" => "wizard",
                        "Betty" => 42, "Frodo" => "hobbit");
    ?>
    <h4> Original Array </h4>
    <?php
      foreach ($original as $key => $value)
        print("[$key] => $value <br />");

      $new = $original;
      sort($new);
    ?>
    <h4> Array sorted with sort </h4>
    <?php
      foreach ($new as $key => $value)
        print("[$key] = $value <br />");

      $new = $original;
      asort($new);
    ?>
    <h4> Array sorted with asort </h4>
    <?php
      foreach ($new as $key => $value)
        print("[$key] = $value <br />");

      $new = $original;
      ksort($new);
```

```
    ?>
    <h4> Array sorted with ksort </h4>
    <?php
      foreach ($new as $key => $value)
        print("[$key] = $value <br />");
    ?>
  </body>
</html>
```

Figure 9.4 shows the output of `sorting.php`.

We have now discussed just a few of the most useful built-in functions for arrays. PHP has 57 such functions, so most remain unmentioned.

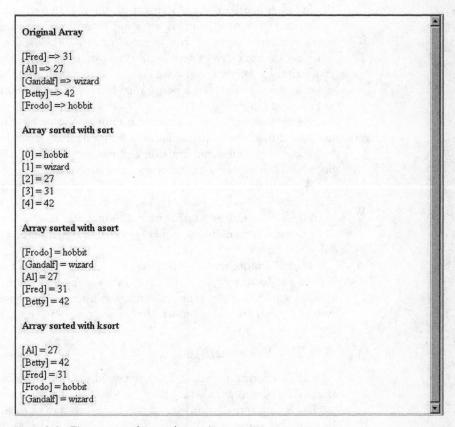

Figure 9.4   The output of `sorting.php`

9.8 Functions

PHP supports user-defined functions that are typical for C-based programming languages.

9.8.1 General Characteristics of Functions

The general form of a PHP function definition is as follows:

```
function name([parameters]) {
  ...
}
```

The square brackets around the parameters mean that they are optional. Because a function's definition does not need to appear in a document before the function is called, the placement of function definitions in a document is, strictly speaking, irrelevant. If a second definition of a function appears in a script, it is reported as an error because function overloading is not allowed and functions cannot be redefined. Function definitions can be nested, as they can in JavaScript. However, because we do not believe the benefit of nested functions is worth the additional complexity they bring to scripts that use them, they are not discussed in this book.

Remember that function names are not case sensitive. So, a document cannot have a function named sum and another named Sum. The PHP interpreter will see them as the same function and issue an error message stating that the document has two definitions for the same function.

The return statement is used in a function to specify the value to be returned to the caller. Function execution ends when a return statement is encountered or the last statement in the function has been executed. In either case, control returns to the caller. If no return statement was executed, no value is returned.

If one or more related functions are used by more than one document, it is convenient to store their definitions in a separate file and copy that file into those documents when they are requested by a client (browser). This is done using the include function, which was described in Section 9.3.

9.8.2 Parameters

As with JavaScript, we call the parameters in the call to a function *actual parameters*. We call the parameters that are listed in the function definition *formal parameters*. An actual parameter can be any expression. A formal parameter must be a variable name.

The number of actual parameters in a call to a function need not match the number of formal parameters defined in that function. If there are too few actual parameters in a call, the corresponding formal parameters will be unbound variables. If there are too many actual parameters, the excess actual parameters will be ignored. The absence of a requirement for matching numbers of parameters allows the language to support functions with a variable number of parameters.

The default parameter-passing mechanism of PHP is pass by value. This means that, in effect, the values of actual parameters are copied into the memory locations associated with the corresponding formal parameters in the called function. The values of the formal parameters are never copied back to the caller, so passing by value implements one-way communication to the function. This is the most commonly needed mechanism for parameter passing. Consider the following function definition:

```
function max_abs($first, $second) {
  $first = abs($first);
  $second = abs($second);
  if ($first >= $second)
    return $first;
  else
    return $second;
}
```

This function returns the largest absolute value of the two given numbers. Although it potentially changes both of its formal parameters, the actual parameters in the caller are unchanged (because they were passed by value).

Sometimes parameters that provide two-way communication between the caller and the function are needed—for example, so a function can return more than one value. One common way to provide two-way communication is to pass the address of the actual parameter, rather than its value, to the function. Then, when the formal parameter is changed (in the function), it also changes the corresponding actual parameter. Such parameters are said to be passed by reference.

Pass-by-reference parameters can be specified in PHP in two ways. One way is to add an ampersand (&) to the beginning of the name of the formal parameter that you want to be passed by reference. Of course, passing by reference only makes sense if the actual parameter is a variable. The other way is to add an ampersand to the actual parameter in the function call. These two techniques have identical semantics. Consider the following example:

```
function set_max(&$max, $first, $second) {
  If ($first >= $second)
    $max = $first;
  else
    $max = $second;
}
```

In this example, the first actual parameter in the caller is set to the larger of the second and third parameters.

9.8.3   The Scope of Variables

The default scope of a variable defined in a function is local. If a variable defined in a function has the same name as a variable used outside the function, there is no interference between the two. A local variable is visible only in the function in which it is used. For example, consider the following example:

```
function summer($list) {
  $sum = 0;
  foreach ($list as $value)
    $sum += $value;
  return $sum;
}
$sum = 10;
$nums = array(2, 4, 6, 8);
$ans = summer($nums);
print "The sum of the values in \$nums is: $ans <br />";
print "The value of \$sum is still: $sum <br />";
```

The output of this code is as follows:

```
The sum of the values in $nums is: 20
The value of $sum is still: 10
```

This output shows that the value of $sum in the calling code is not affected by the use of the local variable $sum in the function. The purpose of the design of local variables is simple: A function should behave the same way regardless of the context of its use. Furthermore, when naming a variable while designing a function, the author should not need to worry about conflicts with the names of variables used outside the function.

In some cases, it is convenient for the code in a function to be able to access a variable that is defined outside the function. For this situation, PHP has the global declaration. When a variable is listed in a global declaration in a function, that variable is expected to be defined outside the function. So, such a variable has the same meaning inside the function as outside. For example, consider the following code:

```
$big_sum = 0;
...
/* Function summer
   Parameter: An array of integers
   Returns: The sum of the elements of the parameter
            array
   Side effect: Add the computed sum to the global,
                $big_sum
*/
function summer ($list) {
  global $big_sum;   //** Get access to $big_sum
```

```
    $sum = 0;
    foreach ($list as $value)
      $sum += $value;
    $big_sum += $sum;
    return $sum;
  } //** end of summer
  ...
  $ans1 = summer($list1);
  $ans2 = summer($list2);
  ...
  print "The sum of all array elements is: $big_sum <br />";
```

If the `global` declaration were not included in the function, the script would have two variables named `$big_sum`, the global one and the one that is local to the function. Without the declaration, this script cannot do what it meant to do.

9.8.4   The Lifetime of Variables

In some situations, a function must be history sensitive; that is, it must retain information about previous activations. The default lifetime of local variables in a PHP function is from the time the variable is first used (that is, when storage for it is allocated) until the function's execution terminates. To support history sensitivity, a function must have static local variables. The lifetime of a static variable in a function begins when the variable is first used in the first execution of the function. Its lifetime ends when the script execution ends. In the case of PHP, this is when the browser leaves the document in which the PHP script is embedded.

In PHP a local variable in a function can be specified to be static by declaring it with the `static` reserved word. Such a declaration can include an initial value, which is only assigned the first time the declaration is reached. For example, consider the following function:

```
function do_it ($param) {
  static $count = 0;
  count++;
  print "do_it has now been called $count times <br />";
  ...
}
```

This function displays the number of times it has been called, even if it is called from several different places. The fact that its local variable `$count` is static allows this to be done.

9.9   Pattern Matching

PHP includes two different kinds of string pattern matching using regular expressions: one that is based on POSIX regular expressions and one that is based on Perl regular expressions. The POSIX regular expressions are compiled into PHP, but the Perl-Compatible Regular Expression (PCRE) library must be compiled before Perl regular expressions can be used. A detailed discussion of PHP pattern matching is beyond the scope of this chapter. Furthermore, Perl-style regular expressions are described in Sections 4.12.1 to 4.12.3. Therefore, we provide only a brief description of a single PHP function for pattern matching in this section.

The `preg_match`[6] function takes two parameters, the first of which is the Perl-style regular expression as a string. The second parameter is the string to be searched. For example:

```
if (preg_match("/^PHP/", $str))
  print "\$str begins with PHP <br />";
else
  print "\$str does not begin with PHP <br />";
```

The `preg_split` function operates on strings but returns an array and uses patterns, so it is discussed here rather than with the other string functions in Section 9.4.7. `preg_split` takes two parameters, the first of which is a Perl-style pattern as a string. The second parameter is the string to be split. For example, consider the following sample code:

```
$fruit_string = "apple : orange : banana";
$fruits = preg_split("/ : /", $fruit_string);
```

The array `$fruits` now has (`"apple"`, `"orange"`, `"banana"`).

The following example illustrates the use of `preg_split` on text to parse out the words and produce a frequency-of-occurrence table:

```
<?xml version = "1.0" encoding = "utf-8"?>
<!DOCTYPE html PUBLIC "-//W3C//DTD XHTML 1.0 Strict//EN"
  "http://www.w3.org/TR/xhtml1/DTD/xhtml1-strict.dtd">

<!-- word_table.php
     Uses a function to split a given string of text into
     its constituent words. It also determines the frequency of
     occurrence of each word. The words are separated by
     whitespace or punctuation, possibly followed by whitespace.
     The punctuation can be a period, a comma, a semicolon, a
     colon, an exclamation point, or a question mark.
     -->
<html xmlns = "http://www.w3.org/1999/xhtml">
<head> <title> word_table.php </title>
</head>
```

---

6. The first part of the name, `preg`, is an acronym for *Perl regular*, which indicates the style of regular expression used.

```php
<body>
<?php

// Function splitter.
//    Parameter: a string of text containing words and punctuation
//    Returns: an array in which the unique words of the string are
//             the keys and their frequencies are the values.
function splitter($str) {

// Create the empty word frequency array
  $freq = array();

// Split the parameter string into words
  $words = preg_split("/[ \.,;:!\?]\s*/", $str);

// Loop to count the words (either increment or initialize to 1)
  foreach ($words as $word) {
    $keys = array_keys($freq);
    if(in_array($word, $keys))
      $freq[$word]++;
    else
      $freq[$word] = 1;
  }
  return $freq;
} #** End of splitter

// Main test driver
  $str = "apples are good for you, or don't you like apples?
          or maybe you like oranges better than apples";

// Call splitter
  $tbl = splitter($str);

// Display the words and their frequencies
  print "<br /> Word Frequency <br /><br />";
  $sorted_keys = array_keys($tbl);
  sort($sorted_keys);
  foreach ($sorted_keys as $word)
    print "$word $tbl[$word] <br />";
?>
</body>
</html>
```

The output of this script is as follows:

```
Word Frequency

apples 3
are 1
better 1
don't 1
for 1
good 1
like 2
maybe 1
or 2
oranges 1
than 1
you 3
```

9.10   Form Handling

One common way for a browser user to interact with a Web server is through forms. A form is presented to the user, who is invited to fill in the text boxes and click the buttons of the form. The user submits the form to the server by clicking its *Submit* button. The contents of the form are encoded and transmitted to the server. The server must use a program to decode the transmitted form contents, perform whatever computation is necessary on the form data, and produce its output. When PHP is used to process form data, the decoding of the form data is done implicitly by PHP.

It may seem strange, but when PHP is used for form handling, the PHP script is embedded in an XHTML document, like other uses of PHP. Although it is possible to have a PHP script handle form data in the same XHTML document that defines the form, it is perhaps clearer to use two separate documents. For this latter case, the document that defines the form specifies the document that handles the form data in the `action` attribute of its `<form>` tag.

PHP can be configured so that form data values are directly available as implicit variables whose names match the names of the corresponding form elements. However, this is not allowed in many Web servers (through the configuration of PHP) because it entails a security risk. The recommended approach is to use the implicit arrays for form values, `$_POST` and `$_GET`. These arrays have keys that match the form element names and values that were input by the client. For example, if a form has a text box named `phone` and the form method is POST, the value of that element is available in the PHP script as follows:

`$_POST["phone"]`

The following is an XHTML document that presents a form for popcorn sales:

```
<?xml version = "1.0" encoding = "utf-8"?>
<!DOCTYPE html PUBLIC "-//W3C//DTD XHTML 1.0 Strict//EN"
  "http://www.w3.org/TR/xhtml1/DTD/xhtml1-strict.dtd">


<!-- popcorn3.html - This describes the popcorn sales form -->
<html xmlns = "http:///www.w3.org/1999/xhtml">
  <head>
    <title> Popcorn Sales - for PHP handling </title>
  </head>
  <body>
    <form action = "http://cs.uccs.edu/~rws/popcorn3.php"
        method = "post">
      <h2> Welcome to Millennium Gymnastics Booster Club Popcorn
          Sales </h2>
      <table>

<!-- Text widgets for the customer's name and address -->
      <tr>
        <td> Buyer's Name: </td>
        <td> <input type = "text" name = "name"
                  size = "30" /></td>
      </tr>
      <tr>
        <td> Street Address: </td>
        <td> <input type = "text" name = "street"
                  size = "30" /></td>
      </tr>
      <tr>
        <td> City, State, Zip: </td>
        <td> <input type = "text" name = "city"
                  size = "30" /></td>
      </tr>
      </table>
      <p />
      <table border = "border">

<!-- First, the column headings -->
      <tr>
        <th> Product </th>
        <th> Price </th>
        <th> Quantity </th>
      </tr>

<!-- Now, the table data entries -->
```

```
    <tr>
      <td> Unpopped Popcorn (1 lb.) </td>
      <td> $3.00 </td>
      <td align = "center">
        <input type = "text" name = "unpop"
                size = "3" /></td>
    </tr>
    <tr>
      <td> Caramel Popcorn (2 lb. canister) </td>
      <td> $3.50 </td>
      <td align = "center">
        <input type = "text" name = "caramel"
                size = "3" /> </td>
    </tr>
    <tr>
      <td> Caramel Nut Popcorn (2 lb. canister) </td>
      <td> $4.50 </td>
      <td align = "center">
        <input type = "text" name = "caramelnut"
                size = "3" /> </td>
    </tr>
    <tr>
      <td> Toffey Nut Popcorn (2 lb. canister) </td>
      <td> $5.00 </td>
      <td align = "center">
        <input type = "text" name = "toffeynut"
                size = "3" /> </td>
    </tr>
  </table>
  <p />

<!-- The radio buttons for the payment method -->
  <h3> Payment Method </h3>
  <p>
    <input type = "radio" name = "payment" value = "visa"
          checked = "checked" />
      Visa <br />
    <input type = "radio" name = "payment" value = "mc" />
      Master Card <br />
    <input type = "radio" name = "payment"
          value = "discover" />
      Discover <br />
    <input type = "radio" name = "payment" value = "check" />
      Check <br /> <br />
```

```
<!-- The submit and reset buttons -->
      <input type = "submit" value = "Submit Order" />
      <input type = "reset" value = "Clear Order Form" />
   </p>
  </form>
 </body>
</html>
```

Figure 9.5 shows the display of `popcorn3.html`.

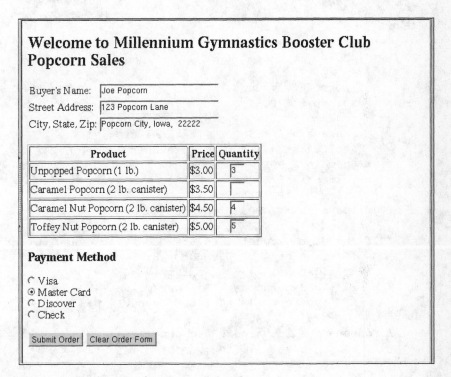

Figure 9.5   The display of `popcorn3.html`

The PHP script that handles the data from the form described in `popcorn3.html` follows. It uses the form data to compute the cost of each product, the total cost of the order, and the total number of ordered items. The product name, unit price, number ordered, and total cost for each product are presented to the client in a table. The table is defined with interwoven XHTML markup and PHP script. The table structure is described with XHTML, but the contents of some of the data cells are defined with PHP.

```
<?xml version = "1.0" encoding = "utf-8"?>
<!DOCTYPE html PUBLIC "-//W3C//DTD XHTML 1.0 Strict//EN"
  "http://www.w3.org/TR/xhtml1/DTD/xhtml1-strict.dtd">

<!-- popcorn3.php - Processes the form described in
     popcorn3.html
     -->
<html xmlns = "http://www.w3.org/1999/xhtml">
  <head>
    <title> Process the popcorn3.html form </title>
  </head>

  <body>
    <?php

// Get form data values
      $unpop = $_POST["unpop"];
      $caramel = $_POST["caramel"];
      $caramelnut = $_POST["caramelnut"];
      $toffeynut = $_POST["toffeynut"];
      $name = $_POST["name"];
      $street = $_POST["street"];
      $city = $_POST["city"];
      $payment = $_POST["payment"];

// If any of the quantities are blank, set them to zero
      if ($unpop == "") $unpop = 0;
      if ($caramel == "") $caramel = 0;
      if ($caramelnut == "") $caramelnut = 0;
      if ($toffeynut == "") $toffeynut = 0;

// Compute the item costs and total cost
      $unpop_cost = 3.0 * $unpop;
      $caramel_cost = 3.5 * $caramel;
      $caramelnut_cost = 4.5 * $caramelnut;
      $toffeynut_cost = 5.0 * $toffeynut;
      $total_price = $unpop_cost + $caramel_cost +
                     $caramelnut_cost + $toffeynut_cost;
      $total_items = $unpop + $caramel + $caramelnut + $toffeynut;

// Return the results to the browser in a table
    ?>
    <h4> Customer: </h4>
    <?php
      print ("$name <br /> $street <br /> $city <br />");
    ?>
```

```
      <p /> <p />
      <table border = "border">
        <caption> Order Information </caption>
        <tr>
          <th> Product </th>
          <th> Unit Price </th>
          <th> Quantity Ordered </th>
          <th> Item Cost </th>
        </tr>
        <tr align = "center">
          <td> Unpopped Popcorn </td>
          <td> $3.00 </td>
          <td> <?php print ("$unpop"); ?> </td>
          <td> <?php printf ("$ %4.2f", $unpop_cost); ?>
          </td>
        </tr>
        <tr align = "center">
          <td> Caramel Popcorn </td>
          <td> $3.50 </td>
          <td> <?php print ("$caramel"); ?> </td>
          <td> <?php printf ("$ %4.2f", $caramel_cost); ?>
          </td>
          </tr>
        <tr align = "center">
          <td> Caramel Nut Popcorn </td>
          <td> $4.50 </td>
          <td> <?php print ("$caramelnut"); ?> </td>
          <td> <?php printf ("$ %4.2f", $caramelnut_cost); ?>
          </td>
        </tr>
        <tr align = "center">
          <td> Toffey Nut Popcorn </td>
          <td> $5.00 </td>
          <td> <?php print ("$toffeynut"); ?> </td>
          <td> <?php printf ("$ %4.2f", $toffeynut_cost); ?>
          </td>
        </tr>
    </table>
    <p /> <p />

    <?php
      print "You ordered $total_items popcorn items <br />";
      printf ("Your total bill is: $ %5.2f <br />", $total_price);
      print "Your chosen method of payment is: $payment <br />";
    ?>
  </body>
</html>
```

Notice that the `printf` function is used to implement the numbers that represent money, so exactly two digits appear to the right of the decimal points. Figure 9.6 displays the results of `popcorn3.php`.

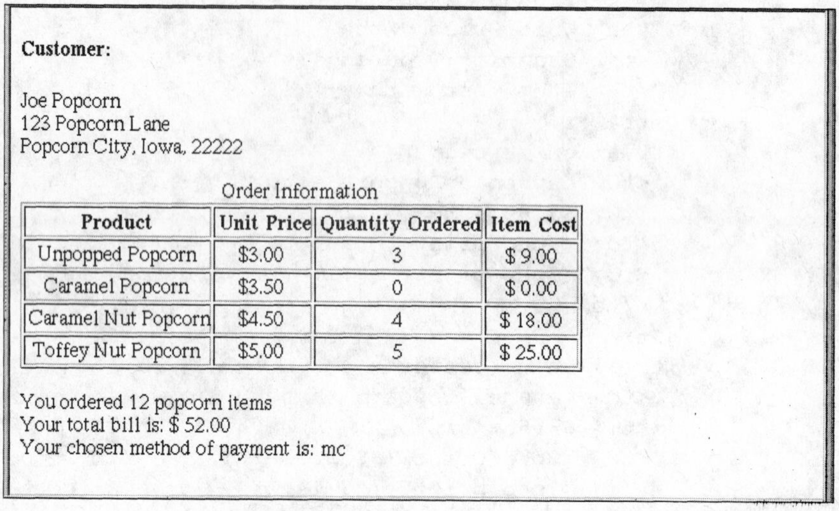

Customer:

Joe Popcorn
123 Popcorn Lane
Popcorn City, Iowa, 22222

Order Information

Product	Unit Price	Quantity Ordered	Item Cost
Unpopped Popcorn	$3.00	3	$ 9.00
Caramel Popcorn	$3.50	0	$ 0.00
Caramel Nut Popcorn	$4.50	4	$ 18.00
Toffey Nut Popcorn	$5.00	5	$ 25.00

You ordered 12 popcorn items
Your total bill is: $ 52.00
Your chosen method of payment is: mc

Figure 9.6 The output of `popcorn3.php`

9.11 Files

Because PHP is a server-side technology, it is possible to create, read, and write files on the server system using it. In fact, PHP can deal with files residing on any server system on the Internet, using both HTTP and FTP protocols. However, our discussion is restricted to dealing with files on the server itself. Furthermore, only the simple processes of opening, reading, and writing text files are covered.

9.11.1 Opening and Closing Files

The first step in some file operations is to open it, a process that prepares the file for use and associates a program variable with the file for future reference. This program variable is called the *file variable*. The `fopen` function performs these operations. It takes two parameters: the filename, including the path to it if it is in a different directory, and a use indicator, which specifies the operation or operations that will be performed on the file. Both parameters are given as strings. The `fopen` function returns the reference to the file for the file variable. Every open file has an internal pointer that is used to indicate where the next operation should take place within the file. We call this pointer the *file pointer*. Table 9.4 describes the possible values of the use indicator.

Table 9.4 File use indicators

Use Indicator	Description
`"r"`	Read only. The file pointer is initialized to the beginning of the file.
`"r+"`	Read and write an existing file. The file pointer is initialized to the beginning of the file; if a read operation precedes a write operation, the new data is written just after where the read operation left the file pointer.
`"w"`	Write only. Initializes the file pointer to the beginning of the file; creates the file if it does not exist.
`"w+"`	Write and read. Initializes the file pointer to the beginning of the file; creates the file if it does not exist. Always initializes the file pointer to the beginning of the file before the first write, destroying any existing data.
`"a"`	Write only. If the file exists, initializes the file pointer to the end of the file; if the file does not exist, creates it and initializes the file pointer to its beginning.
`"a+"`	Read and write, creating the file if necessary; new data is written to the end of the existing data.

It is possible for the `fopen` function to fail—for example, if an attempt is made to open a file for reading but no such file exists. It would also fail if the file access permissions did not allow the requested use of the file. The `fopen` function returns FALSE if it fails. The `die` function produces a message and stops the interpretation process. It is often used with input and output operations, which sometimes fail. For example, the following statement attempts to open a file named `testdata.dat` for reading only, but calls `die` if the open operation fails:

```
$file_var = fopen("testdata.dat", "r") or
            die ("Error — testdata.dat cannot be opened");
```

This form appears a bit odd, but is exactly what is needed. Because the `or` operator has lower precedence than a function call, `die` will only be called if `fopen` fails, in which case `fopen` returns FALSE.

The problem of `fopen` failing because the specified file does not exist can be avoided by determining whether the file exists with `file_exists` before calling `fopen`. The `file_exists` function takes a single parameter, the file's name. It returns TRUE if the file exists, FALSE otherwise.

A file is closed with the `fclose` function, which takes a file variable as its only parameter.

9.11.2 Reading from a File

The most common way to input a text file in PHP is to read its contents into a scalar variable as a string. Then the impressive collection of PHP string manipulation functions can be used to process the file as a string. The `fread` function reads part or all of a file and returns a string of what was read. This function takes two parameters: a file variable and the number of bytes to be read. The reading operation stops when either the end-of-file marker is read or the specified number of bytes has been read.

Large collections of data are often stored in database systems, so usually only smaller data sets are stored in files. Therefore, files are often read in their entirety with a single call to `fread`. If the whole file is to be read at once, the file's length is given as the second parameter to `fread`. The best way to get the correct file length is with the `filesize` function, so a call to `filesize` is often used as the second parameter to `fread`. The `filesize` function takes a single parameter, the name of the file (not the file variable). For example, to read the entire contents of the file `testdata.dat` as a string into the variable `$file_string`, the following statement could be used:

```
$file_string = fread($file_var,
                  filesize("testdata.dat"));
```

One alternative to `fread` is `file`, which takes a filename as its parameter and returns an array of all of the lines of the file. (A line is a string of non-newline characters, followed by a newline.) One advantage of `file` is that the file open and close operations are not necessary. For example, the following statement places the lines of `testdata.dat` into an array named `@file_lines`:

```
$file_lines = file("testdata.dat");
```

PHP has another file input function that does not require calling `fopen`, `file_get_contents`, which takes the file's name as its parameter. This function reads the entire contents of the file. For example, consider the following call:

```
$file_string = file_get_contents("testdata.dat");
```

A single line of a file can be read with `fgets`, which takes two parameters: the file variable and a limit on the length of the line to be read. Consider the following statement:

```
$line = fgets($file_var, 100);
```

This statement reads characters from the file whose file variable is `$file_var` until it finds a newline character, encounters the end-of-file marker, or has read 99 characters. Note that the maximum number of characters `fgets` reads is one fewer than the limit given as its second parameter.

A single character can be read from a file with `fgetc`, whose only parameter is the file variable. When reading a file by lines or by characters, the read operation must be controlled by the detection of the end of the file. This can be done with the `feof` function, which takes a file variable as its only parameter. It returns a Boolean value: TRUE if the last read character of the file was the end-of-file character, FALSE otherwise.

9.11.3 Writing to a File

The `fwrite`[7] function takes two parameters: a file variable and the string to be written to the file. It is possible to include a third parameter, which would be used to specify the number of bytes to be written. This parameter is rarely needed. The `fwrite` function returns the number of bytes written. The following is an example of a call to `fwrite`:

```
$bytes_written = fwrite($file_var, $out_data);
```

This statement writes the string value in `$out_data` to the file referenced with `$file_var` and places the number of bytes written in `$bytes_written`. Of course, this will work only if the file has been opened for writing.

The `file_put_contents` function is the counterpart of `file_get_contents`—it writes the value of its second parameter, a string, to the file specified in its first parameter. For example, consider the following call:

```
file_put_contents("savedata.dat", $str);
```

9.11.4 Locking Files

If it is possible for more than one script to access a file at the same time, the potential interference of those accesses can be prevented with a file lock. The lock prevents any other access to the file while the lock is set. Scripts that use such files lock them before accessing them and unlock them when the access is completed. File locking is done in PHP with the `flock` function, which should sound familiar to UNIX programmers. The `flock` function takes two parameters: the file variable of the file and an integer that specifies the particular operation. A value of 1 specifies that the file can be read by others while the lock is set, a value of 2 allows no other access, and a value of 3 unlocks the file.

9.12 Cookies

PHP includes convenient support for creating and using cookies.

9.12.1 Introduction to Cookies

A *session* is the time span during which a browser interacts with a particular server. A session begins when a browser becomes connected to a particular

---

7. `fwrite` has an alias, `fputs`.

server. It ends when the browser ceases to be connected to that server because either it becomes connected to a different server or it is terminated. The HTTP protocol is essentially stateless—it includes no means to store information about a session that is available to a subsequent session. However, there are a number of different reasons why it is useful for the server to be capable of connecting a request made during a session to the other requests made by the same client during that session, as well as previous and subsequent sessions.

One of the most common needs for session information is to implement shopping carts on Web sites. An e-commerce site can have any number of simultaneous online customers. At any time, any customer can add an item to or remove an item from his or her cart. Each user's shopping cart is identified by a session identifier, which could be implemented as a cookie. So, cookies can be used to identify each of the customers visiting the site at a given time.

Another common use of cookies is for a Web site to create profiles of visitors by remembering which parts of the site are perused—sometimes called *personalization*. Later sessions can use such profiles to target advertising to the client according to the client's past interests. Also, if the server recognizes a request as being from a client who has made an earlier request from the same site, it is possible to present a customized interface to that client. These situations require that information about clients be accumulated and stored. Storing session information is becoming increasingly important as more and more Web sites make use of shopping carts and personalization.

Cookies provide a general approach to storing information about sessions on the browser system itself. The server is given this information when the browser makes subsequent requests for resources from the server. Cookies allow the server to present a customized interface to the client. They also allow the server to connect requests from a particular client to previous requests, thereby connecting sequences of requests into a session.

A *cookie* is a small object of information that consists of a name and a textual value. A cookie is created by some software system on the server. Every HTTP communication between a browser and a server includes a header, which stores information about the message. The header part of an HTTP communication can include cookies. So, every request sent from a browser to a server, and every response from a server to a browser, can include one or more cookies.

At the time it is created, a cookie is assigned a lifetime. When the time a cookie has existed reaches its associated lifetime, the cookie is deleted from the browser's host machine. Every browser request includes all of the cookies its host machine has stored that are associated with the Web server to which the request is directed. Only the server that created a cookie can ever receive the cookie from the browser, so a particular cookie is information that is exchanged exclusively between one specific browser and one specific server. Because cookies are stored as text, the browser user can view, alter, or delete them at any time.

Because cookies allow servers to record browser activities, they are considered by some to be privacy concerns. Accordingly, browsers allow the client to change the browser setting to refuse to accept cookies from servers. This is clearly a drawback of using cookies—the clients who reject them render them useless.

Cookies can be deleted through a browser, although the deletion process is different for different browsers. The help facility of a browser can be consulted to determine the cookie deletion process on any given browser.

9.12.2 PHP Support for Cookies

A cookie is set in PHP with the `setcookie` function. This function takes one or more parameters. The first parameter, which is mandatory, is the cookie's name given as a string. The second, if present, is the new value for the cookie, also a string. If the value is absent, `setcookie` undefines the cookie. The third parameter, when present, is the expiration time in seconds for the cookie, given as an integer. The default value for the expiration time is zero, which specifies that the cookie is destroyed at the end of the current session. When specified, the expiration time is often given as the number of seconds in the UNIX epoch, which began on January 1, 1970. The `time` function returns the current time in seconds. So, the cookie expiration time is given as the value returned from `time` plus some number. For example, consider the following call to `setcookie`:

```
setcookie("voted", "true", time() + 86400);
```

This call creates a cookie named `"voted"` whose value is `"true"` and whose lifetime is one day (86,400 is the number of seconds in a day).

The `setcookie` function has three more optional parameters, the details of which can found in the PHP manual.

The most important thing to remember about creating a cookie or setting a cookie to a new value is that it must be done before any other XHTML is created by the PHP document. Recall that cookies are stored in the HTTP header of the document returned to the requesting browser. The HTTP header is sent before the body of the document is sent. The server sends the header when it receives the first of the body of the document. So, if any part of the body is created, it is too late to add a cookie to the header. If you create a cookie or change the value of a cookie after even a single character of document body has been generated, the cookie operation will not be successful. (The cookie or the cookie's new value will not be sent to the browser.)

The other cookie operation is getting the cookies and their values from subsequent browser requests. In PHP, cookie values are treated much like form values. All cookies that arrive with a request are placed in the implicit `$_COOKIES` array, which has the cookie names as keys and the cookie values as values. A PHP script can test whether a cookie came with a request by using the `IsSet` predicate function on the associated variable.

As is the case with using cookies with other technologies, remember that cookies cannot be depended upon because some users set their browsers to reject all cookies. Furthermore, most browsers have a limit on the number of cookies that will be accepted from a particular server site.

9.13 Session Tracking

In many cases, information about a session is needed only during the session. Also, the needed information about a client is nothing more than a unique identifier for the session, which is commonly used in shopping cart applications. For these cases, a different process, named *session tracking*, can be used. Rather than using one or more cookies, a single session array can be used to store information about the previous requests of a client during a session. In particular, session arrays often store a unique session ID for a session. One signficant way that session arrays differ from cookies is that they can be stored on the server, whereas cookies are stored on the client.

In PHP, a session ID is an internal value that identifies a session. Session IDs need not be known or handled in any way by PHP scripts. PHP is made aware that a script is interested in session tracking by calling the `session_start` function, which takes no parameters. The first call to `session_start` in a session causes a session ID to be created and recorded. On subsequent calls to `session_start` in the same session, the function retrieves the `$_SESSION` array, which stores any session variables and their values that were registered in previously executed scripts in this session.

Session key/value pairs are created or changed by assignments to the `$_SESSION` array. They can be destroyed with the `unset` operator. Consider the following example:

```
session_start();
if (!IsSet($_SESSION["page_number"]))
  $_SESSION["page_number"] = 1;
$page_num = $_SESSION["page_number"];
print("You have now visited $page_num page(s) <br />");
$_SESSION["page_number"]++;
```

If this is not the first document visited that calls `session_start` and sets the `page_number` session variable, this script will produce the specified line with the last set value of `$_SESSION["page_number"]`. If no document that was previously visited in this session set `page_number`, this script sets `page_number` to 1, produces the following line, and increments `page_number`:

```
You have now visited 1 page(s)
```

Summary

PHP is a server-side, XHTML-embedded scripting language. The language is similar to JavaScript. The PHP processor takes as input a file of XHTML/PHP, copies the XHTML to an output file, and interprets the PHP script in the input file. The output of any PHP script is written into the output file. PHP scripts are either directly embedded in XHTML files or are referenced in the XHTML files and subsequently copied into them.

PHP has four scalar types: integer, Boolean, double, and string. PHP variable names all begin with dollar signs. The language is dynamically typed. Arithmetic and Boolean expressions in PHP are very similar to those in other common languages. PHP includes a large number of functions for arithmetic and string operations. The current type of a variable is maintained internally and can be determined by a script through several different built-in functions. The `print` and `printf` functions are used to produce output, which becomes part of the PHP processor output file. The control statements of PHP are similar to those of other common programming languages.

PHP's arrays are a combination of the traditional arrays of C and its descendant languages and hashes. Arrays can be created by assigning values to their elements. This is often done with the `array` construct, which allows the specification of values and optionally the keys for one or more elements of an array. PHP has predefined functions for many array operations. Among these are `explode` and `implode` for converting between strings and arrays; `current`, `next`, and `prev` for fetching elements in sequential order; `each` for obtaining both the keys and values of the elements of an array in sequential order; and `array_keys` and `array_values`, which return an array of the keys and values of the array, respectively. There are also functions for stack operations on arrays. The `foreach` statement provides sequential access to the elements of an array. Finally, PHP has a collection of functions for sorting the elements of arrays in various ways.

User-defined functions in PHP are similar to those of other languages, except for parameter passing. Because PHP does not have pointers, pass-by-reference parameters must be specified in either the function call or the function definition. Variables used only in a function are local to that function. Access to variables used outside a function is specified with a `global` declaration. Static variables can be declared with a `static` declaration.

PHP's pattern matching can use either POSIX-style or Perl-style regular expressions. Form data is placed in user-accessible variables implicitly by the PHP system. This makes form handling very convenient.

Files are opened and prepared for reading, writing, or both with the `fopen` function, which returns a file variable. Every file has an internal file pointer, which maintains a position in the file where the next read or write will take place. Files can be read with `fread`, which reads as many bytes as specified in the call, up to the whole file, into a string. The lines of a file can be read into an array of strings with `file`. A single character of a file can be read with `fgetc`. The `file_get_contents` function is used to read an entire file into a variable, without needing the `fopen` function. The `fwrite` function is used to write to a file. The `file_put_contents` function writes a string to a file, without needing the `fopen` function. Interference among simultaneous file accesses can be avoided by locking a file with `flock`.

Cookies are created and set to values with the `setcookie` function, which has parameters for the cookie name, its value, and a lifetime in seconds. Cookies created or set in a previous script are available to a current script directly through the $_COOKIES array. A script can test whether a cookie exists and is set to a value with IsSet. Session tracking is relatively simple in PHP. The session_start function creates a session ID. Session variables are stored in the $_SESSION array.

Review Questions

9.1 What are the two modes of the PHP processor?

9.2 How does a Web server determine whether a requested document includes PHP code?

9.3 What are the syntax and semantics of the include construct?

9.4 What are the four scalar types of PHP?

9.5 How can a variable be tested to determine whether it is bound?

9.6 What does the chop function do?

9.7 How can you specify to the PHP processor that you want uses of unbound variables to be reported?

9.8 What is the advantage of using the unique closing reserved words such as endwhile?

9.9 How many bytes are used to store a character in PHP?

9.10 If an integer expression appears in Boolean context, how is its Boolean value determined?

9.11 Which parts of PHP are case sensitive and which are not?

9.12 What happens when an integer arithmetic operation results in a value that cannot be represented as an integer?

9.13 If a variable stores a string, how can the character at a specific position in that string be referenced?

9.14 What is a coercion?

9.15 What are the differences between single- and double-quoted literal strings?

9.16 What are the three ways the value of a variable can be explicitly converted to a specific type?

9.17 How can the type of a variable be determined?

9.18 If a string is compared with a number, what happens?

9.19 In what two ways can arrays in PHP be created?

9.20 Must all of the values of an array be of the same type?

9.21 What exactly do the `array_keys` and `array_values` functions do?

9.22 Are function names case sensitive?

9.23 What keys are used when an array is created, but no keys are specified?

9.24 Explain the actions of the `implode` and `explode` functions.

9.25 What exactly does the `in_array` function do?

9.26 What are the syntax and semantics of the two forms of the `foreach` statement?

9.27 Describe the actions of the `next`, `reset`, and `prev` functions.

9.28 Describe the result of using the `sort` function on an array that has both string and numeric values.

9.29 What is the difference betweeen the `sort` and `asort` functions?

9.30 Must all of the keys of an array be of the same type?

9.31 What happens if a script defines the same function more than once?

9.32 What are the two ways you can specify that a parameter is to be passed by reference?

9.33 What value is returned by a function if its execution does not end by executing a `return` statement?

9.34 How can a variable used outside a function be accessed by the function?

9.35 How can the value of a form element be accessed by a PHP script?

9.36 How can you define a variable in a function so that its lifetime extends beyond the time the function is in its first execution?

9.37 What is a file variable?

9.38 What does an `fopen` function return if it fails?

9.39 How can a variable be saved in a session?

9.40 Explain the parameters and actions of the `fread` function.

9.41 What is a file pointer?

9.42 What is returned by the `fwrite` function?

9.43 How can a script determine whether a particular cookie exists?

9.44 How can a cookie be created in a PHP script?

Exercises

9.1 *Parameter*: An array of numbers.

   Returns: A list of unique numbers in the parameter array.

9.2 *Parameter*: An array of strings.

   Returns: A new string added at the end of an array.

9.3 Write a PHP script to find duplicated strings in an array and list the first five duplicated strings in alphabetical order.

9.4 *Parameter*: An array of strings

   Returns: Sorted list of all the strings without duplication

9.5 Write a PHP script to find the first 10-digit phone number in the string, where the phone number must have the form of 10 digits without embedded dashes.

9.6 Write a PHP script to read contents from text file and store it in a variable.

9.7 Write a PHP script to calculate the total number of days in a given period.

9.8 Write a PHP script to show the list of files and folders in a directory.

9.9 Write an XHTML document which shows the FORM contains name, password, gender, skill, resume, and interest and that includes an anchor tag that calls a PHP document.

9.10 Write a PHP script to get the input values from the above form and print it into a new browser page.

9.11 Write the XHTML code to create a form with the following capabilities:

   a. A text widget to collect the registered user code

   b. Four checkboxes, one each for the following items and each one's cost:

   i. Motorola 3225 for $20

   ii. Nokia 8110 for $32

   iii. Siemens 322 for $25

   iv. LG 522 for $50

   c. Type of cards to pay online:

   i. Visa Card

   ii. Mastercard

   iii. Maestro Card

9.12 Write the PHP script to count the repeated word frequency in a string, which is separated by a space.

Parameter: A string.

Returns: Number of repeated words.

9.13 Modify the word frequency script and change it into XHTML table format.

9.14 Write a PHP script that computes the total cost of the items from Exercise 9.11 after adding 12 percent sales tax. The program must inform the buyer of exactly what was ordered.

9.15 Write the XHTML code to provide a form that collects user name and mobile numbers. Write a PHP script that checks the submitted mobile number to be sure that it contains 10 digits and then returns a response that indicates whether the number was correct.

9.16 Modify the PHP script for Exercise 9.9 to count the number of visitors and display that number for each visitor. *Hint*: Use a file to store the current count.

CHAPTER

10

Introduction to Ajax

This chapter provides an introduction to Ajax. As described in Chapter 1, "Fundamentals," Ajax is a process of using asynchronous requests from the browser to the server to fetch data, which is used to update a part of the browser-displayed document. The first section is an overview of the concepts and processes of Ajax. This is followed by an introduction to the basics of Ajax, including a simple but complete example of Ajax being used to help a user fill a form. Next, the issues of cross-browser implementation of Ajax are discussed. Following this, several different forms of return data are described and evaluated. In the next section of the chapter, two Ajax toolkits, Dojo and Prototype, are introduced. A complete example application using Dojo is developed in this section. The last section discusses security issues with Ajax.

10.1   Overview of Ajax

The goal of Ajax technology is to provide Web-based applications with rich user interfaces and responsiveness similar to those of desktop applications. The motivation for this goal is the great increase in the demand for Rich Internet Applications (RIAs). These applications present the user with an elaborate interface that invites and, in many cases, requires frequent interactions between the user and the server. The speed of these interactions determines the usability of the application.

10.1.1   History of Ajax

The first possibility of the Ajax approach arrived with the introduction of `iframe` element in the fourth versions of the browsers from Netscape and Microsoft. Web programmers discovered that an `iframe` element could be made to be invisible, simply by setting its width and height to zero pixels, and that it could be used to send asynchronous requests to the server. Although this worked, it was far from elegant.

Microsoft introduced two nonstandard extensions to the DOM and its Java-Script binding with the `XmlDocument` and `XMLHTML` objects, which began as ActiveX components in IE5. These were designed to support asynchronous requests to the server, thereby allowing data to be fetched from the server in the background. Such an object is now supported by most commonly used browsers, although the object now is named `XMLHttpRequest` in most browsers, including IE7.

There were some developers using Ajax technology before 2005, but there was no widespread interest in it or enthusiasm for it. Two events were the catalysts that began the rush of Web developers to Ajax in 2005 and 2006. First, many users began to experience the rapid browser/server interactions provided by Google Maps and Gmail, which were among the early Web applications to use Ajax. For example, Google Maps can quickly replace small parts of the displayed map, called tiles, using asynchronous requests to the server. This allows the user to scroll in any direction and have the map grow in that direction by means of small rectangles, without ever requiring the browser to re-render the whole screen. Most users had never used a Web application with such powerful interactive capabilities. Second, as mentioned in Chapter 1, "Fundamentals," Jesse James Garrett named this technology Ajax in early 2005. It may appear odd to some, including this author, that the acquisition of a name was an important part of the motivation for the huge growth in interest in the new approach to building Web applications, but it obviously was.

10.1.2   Ajax Technology

A typical traditional (non-Ajax) session of Web use begins with the user requesting an initial document, either by typing a URL or clicking a link on his or her browser. At that point, the browser is blocked from activity while it waits for the server to provide a new document. When the document arrives, the browser replaces the former display with a rendering of the new document. This cycle takes some time, both in network latency and in rendering time. Nothing can be done to speed this process of fetching and rendering a complete document. However, user interactions with the displayed document may require that only relatively small parts of the displayed document be modified or updated. In a non-Ajax Web application, even the smallest change in the displayed document, if it needs data from the server, requires the same process that produced the initial display. The request must go to the server, the server must construct and send back a complete document, and the whole display must be re-rendered. During this time, the browser is locked and the user can do nothing but wait. If a Web application requires many such interactions, the workflow of the user can be seriously disrupted. Clearly, this mode of operation is utterly unable to support RIAs.

As previously stated, Ajax is meant to increase the speed of user interactions with Web applications significantly. For those user requests that update only a small part of the displayed document, Ajax technology shortens the required time for both document transmission and document rendering. It does this by having the server provide only a relatively small part of the displayed document—the part that must change. This shortens transmission time because the document being transmitted is much smaller, and the rendering time because once again, only a small part of the display must be re-rendered. This is a simple idea, but one that can provide great improvements in the richness of the Web user experience, at least with applications that have frequent browser/server interactions.

Another key feature of Ajax is that requests from the browser to the server are asynchronous (the 'A' in Ajax). This means that when the browser requests a new part of its displayed document from the server, it does not need to lock while it waits for the response. Both the user and the browser can continue to do something useful during the time it takes to fetch and render the new document part.

Ajax is especially important for mobile devices. Cell phones, for example, have limited capabilities, relative to notebook and desktop computers. In particular, they have slower processors, smaller memories, smaller screens, and less communcations bandwidth. Because Ajax requires less processing and data communication, it relieves the strain on those capabilities and makes the devices more effective for Web use.

Traditional (non-Ajax) browser interactions with a server and Ajax interactions with a server are shown in Figure 10.1.

10.1.3 Implementing Ajax

Ajax is not a new programming language or even a new API. In fact, one of the most attractive characteristics of Ajax is that it does not require Web programmers to learn new programming languages or markup languages in order to build

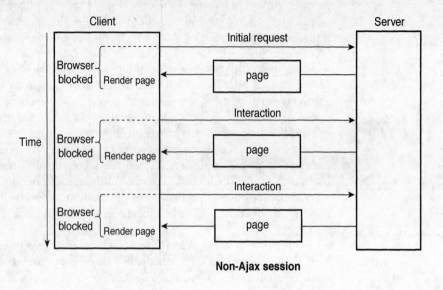

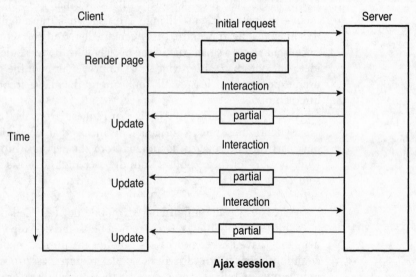

Figure 10.1 Traditional and Ajax browser/server interactions

Web sites that use Ajax. Ajax, true to its name, uses JavaScript as its primary programming language. Most Web programmers, certainly including those who have studied this book, already know JavaScript. The 'x' in Ajax represents XML. An Ajax request results in the server returning the requested data, perhaps in the form of an XML document, although other forms of data are often returned. Again, most Web programmers also already know XML. The other technologies used in Ajax are the DOM and CSS. These are also well-known to Web programmers (and readers of this book). So, Ajax is very attractive in the sense that no new technologies must be acquired or learned to use it. Furthermore, the technologies it uses are already present on the vast majority of Web browsers.

While Ajax uses JavaScript on the client side, it can work with virtually any server-side languages and technologies; for example, PHP, Java servlets, and ASP.NET.

Ajax can be implemented in a number of different ways. First, it can be implemented with just the basic tools, including JavaScript on the client (browser), the `XMLHttpRequest` object, and virtually any server-side software, using text, XHTML, or XML to transmit data.

Another way to implement Ajax is with the help of a client-side toolkit, such as Dojo or Prototype. There are also server-side tools, such as DWR and GWT. Dojo is discussed and used in an example in Section 10.4—the others are briefly introduced in that same section.

There also are frameworks for implementing applications that use Ajax, such as Adobe Flex, ASP.NET Ajax, JavaServer Faces, and Rails. JavaServer Faces is discussed in Chapter 11, "Java Web Software;" ASP.NET Ajax is discussed in Chapter 12, "Introduction to ASP.NET;" and Rails is discussed in Chapter 15, "Introduction to Rails."

For security reasons, Ajax requests using `XMLHttpRequest` can be made only to the server and site that provided the document in which the request originates. However, an application can make requests to other sites using alternative techniques, such as making requests through a proxy in the server. This is one approach used to building mashups, which are Web sites that use data from two or more sites to provide a service.

10.2   The Basics of Ajax

In this section, a Web application is developed and used to describe the basics of Ajax. Such an application includes four parts: an XHTML document to produce the initial display, a JavaScript script to produce the Ajax request of the server, a server-side program to receive the request and produce the requested data, and a JavaScript script to receive the new data and integrate it into the original document being displayed.

10.2.1   The Application

The application used in this section, which has been used previously for the same purpose,[1] is as devoid of complexity as possible but is still able to illustrate the fundamentals of the Ajax technology. The example initially displays the first part of the popcorn sales form used in Chapters 2, 9, and 15. Only the first part of the form, which gathers the name and address information from the user, is

---

1. A similar example appears in *Ajax in Action*, D. Crane, et al., Manning Publications, 2006, Greenwich, CT.

included. In a feeble attempt to make it more attractive, a small picture of popcorn has been added. The concept of this application is that it uses Ajax to help the user enter his or her address information. Specifically, a form displays the text box for the user's zip code above the text boxes for the city and state of residence. When the zip code has been entered, signaled by the DOM as the `blur` event on the zip code's text box, a JavaScript event handler function that constructs an asynchronous request to the server is called. The zip code is sent to the server in the request, which uses it to look up the city and state, which are then returned to the browser. When the JavaScript code receives the city and state, it inserts them in the city and state text boxes in the form.

10.2.2 The Form Document

The first thing needed for this application is the document to present the initial form. One requirement of this document is that the zip code text box register a JavaScript function handler for its `blur` event. The call to the handler must pass the value of the zip code text box. In the call to the handler within the text box element, this value can be referenced as `this.value`. The handler is named `getPlace`. Another requirement is that both the city and state text boxes have id attributes, so that they can be addressed conveniently by the code that must insert the values returned from the server. Finally, the document must reference the JavaScript code file in a script element in its head. The complete document, named `popcornA.html`, follows:

```
<?xml version = "1.0" encoding = "utf-8" ?>
<!DOCTYPE html PUBLIC "-//W3C//DTD XHTML 1.0 Strict//EN"
  "http://www.w3.org/TR/xhtml11/DTD/xhtml1-strict.dtd">


<!-- popcornA.html
     This describes popcorn sales form page which uses
     Ajax and the zip code to fill in the city and state
     of the customer's address
     -->
<html xmlns = "http://www.w3.org/1999/xhtml">
  <head> <title> Popcorn Sales Form (Ajax) </title>
    <style type = "text/css">
      img {position: absolute; left: 400px;  top: 50px;}
    </style>
    <script type = "text/JavaScript" src = "popcornA.js">
    </script>
  </head>
  <body>
    <h2> Welcome to Millennium Gymnastics Booster Club Popcorn
        Sales
    </h2>
```

```
      <form action = "">

<!-- A borderless table of text widgets for name and address -->
      <table>
        <tr>
          <td> Buyer's Name: </td>
          <td> <input type = "text"  name = "name"  size = "30" />
          </td>
        </tr>
        <tr>
          <td> Street Address: </td>
         <td> <input type = "text"  name = "street"  size = "30" />
          </td>
        </tr>
        <tr>
          <td> Zip code: </td>
          <td> <input type = "text"  name = "zip"  size = "10"
                    onblur = "getPlace(this.value)" />
          </td>
        </tr>
        <tr>
          <td> City </td>
          <td> <input type = "text"  name = "city"  id = "city"
                    size = "30" />
          </td>
        </tr>
        <tr>
          <td> State </td>
          <td> <input type = "text"  name = "state"  id = "state"
                    size = "30" />
          </td>
        </tr>
      </table>

      <img src = "popcorn.jpg"  alt = "picture of popcorn" />
      <p />

<!-- The submit and reset buttons -->
      <p>
        <input type = "submit"  value = "Submit Order" />
        <input type = "reset"  value = "Clear Order Form" />
      </p>
    </form>
  </body>
</html>
```

A display of the `popcornA.html` document is shown in Figure 10.2.

Welcome to Millennium Gymnastics Booster Club Popcorn Sales

Buyer's Name:

Street Address:

Zip code:

City

State

[Submit Order]   [Clear Order Form]

Figure 10.2   A display of the `popcornA.html` document

10.2.3 The Request Phase

The application requires two functions, the `blur` event handler and a function to receive the response from the server. The receiver function is called a *callback function* because the server calls the receiver function of the requestor back to return the requested data. Such a response is required for asynchronous calls. This section discussses the request phase—the `blur` handler. The receiver phase is discussed in Section 10.2.5.

The request phase of the application is entirely focused on the object used to communicate asynchronously with the server, `XMLHttpRequest`. The first step is to create an object using the `new` operator and calling the `XMLHttpRequest` constructor, as shown in the following:

```
var xhr = new XMLHttpRequest();
```

For the remainder of this chapter, we will refer to the `XMLHttpRequest` object as the XHR object. This object has six properties and six methods. However, for now only two properties and two methods will be discussed.

When the server receives a request through an XHR object, it notifies the sender several times while it is servicing the request. Like the function being called, these notifications are called *callbacks*. They are meant to inform the sender of the progress being made by the server regarding the request. There are five different values returned by the server to indicate progress, 0 .. 4. The only one of interest here is 4, which indicates that the response is complete. This indicator will be used in the receiver phase. The callback function is named `receivePlace`.

The next part of the request is to register the callback function, which implements the receive phase of the application. This function is registered to the `onreadystatechange` property of the XHR object, as follows:

```
xhr.onreadystatechange = receivePlace;
```

Note that this is not a call to receivePlace; it is an assignment of the address of the function to the onreadystatechange property. Therefore, there can be no parentheses following the name of the handler function. This handler registration causes receivePlace to be called several times while the server deals with the request, each time setting the readyState property of the XHR object to the progress value. Section 10.2.5 describes how the receivePlace handler deals with this.

The next step for the getPlace handler is to call the open method of the XHR object. The open method makes the necessary arrangements for the server request. This method takes two required parameters and three optional parameters. The first parameter, which is mandatory, is the HTTP method to be used for the request message, GET or POST. The HTTP method is passed as a literal string, so, it must be quoted. For this application, GET will be used. Recall that GET is used when there is a relatively small amount of data to be retrieved and the data is not valuable to an intruder. POST is used when there are many widgets on the form, making the form data lengthy, or when it is important that the retrieved data is secure.

The second parameter to open is the URL of the response document on the server that will either be or produce the response. In this application, the document will be the response, in the form of plain text. This URL is often just a file name without a path, because the file that produces the response is often in the same directory as the form document.

The third parameter specifies whether the request is to be asynchronous or synchronous, with true signifying ascynchronous. Because the whole idea of Ajax is to use asynchronous requests, we will always send true as the third parameter to open, even though true is the default value if the parameter is omitted.

The last two optional parameters, when used, specify a username and password. These two parameters were included to allow some authentication of requests on the server. However, because it is impossible to reliably prevent users from viewing JavaScript code, it is a poor practice to put usernames and passwords in the call to open. Therefore, these two parameters are rarely used.

Because the request handler uses the GET method and the user-entered zip code must be sent to the server, that zip code must be attached with a question mark to the URL of the response document. Recall that the catenation operator in JavaScript is the plus sign (+). Following is the call to open for our application:

```
xhr.open("GET", "getCityState.php?zip=" + zip, true);
```

Notice that a PHP document, getCityState.php, will be used to generate the response document.

The final step in the request handler is to send the request to the server. This is done with the send method of the XHR object, which takes a single parameter. The parameter could be used to send a string or a DOM object to the server to be posted, but that is rarely used. null is used as the parameter for our application, as is seen in the following call to send:

```
xhr.send(null);
```

Following is the complete request handler function:

```
// function getPlace
//    parameter: zip code
//    action: create the XMLHttpRequest object, register the
//            handler for onreadystatechange, prepare to send
//            the request (with open), and send the request,
//            along with the zip code, to the server

function getPlace(zip) {
  var xhr = new XMLHttpRequest();
  xhr.onreadystatechange = receivePlace;
  xhr.open("GET", "getCityState.php?zip=" + zip, true);
  xhr.send(null);
}
```

10.2.4 The Response Document

The response document for this application is simple—it is a small PHP script. Rather than using a database that has zip codes, cities, and states, for the sake of simplicity, only a hash with a few entries is used for testing. The actual response is produced with a PHP `print` statement. The HTTP header should have the content type set to the MIME type of the returned value, usually either `text/plain`, `text/html`, or `text/xml`. If the return document is XML, it is assigned to `responseXML`; otherwise it is assigned to `responseText`. If the content type is not set the the response, it defaults to `text/html`. If the MIME type is set to `text/xml`, but what is returned is not syntactially correct XML, the returned value is assigned to `responseText`, not `responseXML`.

The MIME type is set in PHP with the `header` function, as in the following:

```
header("Content-Type: text/plain");
```

Any output produced by the response document will be returned to the requester browser. Because the zip code text box value was sent with `GET`, it can be retrieved from the predefined PHP array `$_GET`. Following is the complete response document:

```
<?php
// getCityState.php
//    Gets the form value from the "zip" widget, looks up the
//    city and state for that zip code, and prints it for the
//    form
```

```php
$cityState = array("81611" => "Aspen, Colorado",
                   "81411" => "Bedrock, Colorado",
                   "80908" => "Black Forest, Colorado",
                   "80301" => "Boulder, Colorado",
                   "81127" => "Chimney Rock, Colorado",
                   "80901" => "Colorado Springs, Colorado",
                   "81223" => "Cotopaxi, Colorado",
                   "80201" => "Denver, Colorado",
                   "81657" => "Vail, Colorado",
                   "80435" => "Keystone, Colorado",
                   "80536" => "Virginia Dale, Colorado",
                   );
header("Content-Type: text/plain");
$zip = $_GET["zip"];
if (array_key_exists($zip, $cityState))
  print $cityState[$zip];
else
  print " , ";
?>
```

Notice that the response data is a string consisting of a city name, followed by a comma, a space, and a state name. Also, `getCityState` checks to see if it "knows" the zip code. If it does, it returns the city and state; otherwise it returns blanks, which results in the form elements for city and state remaining blank if they also are not set by the user.

10.2.5 The Receiver Phase

The receiver phase is implemented as a JavaScript function with no parameters. The function's task is to receive the server response, which in this case is plain text, split it into a city name and a state name, and set the city and state text boxes to the results.

The receiver function obviously must be able to access the XHR object, which was created in the request phase function, `getPlace`. If the XHR object is created as a global and both `getPlace` and the receiver function are placed in a file with the declaration of the XHR object, that would provide both with access. Unfortunately, that would allow another problem to occur. It is possible that more than one request could be made before the response occurs, meaning the earlier XHR object could be overwritten by the creation of another one. One solution to this problem is to register the receiver function definition directly; that is, to place the definition of the receiver function in the request function. So, instead of registering the name of a function, whose definition is elsewhere, the function is not named and its definition is assigned directly to `onreadystatechange`. The unnamed receiver function was earlier named `receivePlace` (in `getPlace`). Note that such a nameless function is sometimes called a *closure*. Such a function inherits the environment in which it is defined, which in our case gives it access to the XHR object.

The first action of the receiver function is to determine the value of the readyState property of the XHR object. Recall that a value of 4 means the response is completed. The XHR object also has a property that gets the status of the request, status. If the request was successfully completed, the status value will be 200. However, if the requested resource was not found, the status value will be 404. Also, a status value of 500 indicates there was a server error while processing the request. Therefore, the receiver function encapsulates all of its actions in the then clause of an if construct, where the if condition is xhr.readyState == 4 && status == 200. The receiver function will be called several times when the value of readyState is less than 4. For these calls, the receiver function does nothing. So, it only processes the returned value from the request when readyState is 4 and status is 200. When this happens, the receiver function gets the response text, uses the split method to separate it into city and state, and sets the text boxes for city and state to those values. The assignments to the city and state text boxes are both placed in selection constructs to prevent the overwriting of user-input city and state names for the cases where the zip code was not found on the server or the data from the server was incorrect. The complete nameless receiver function follows:

```
function () {
  if (xhr.readyState == 4 && status == 200) {
    var result = xhr.responseText;
    var place = result.split(', ');
    if (document.getElementById("city").value == "")
      document.getElementById("city").value = place[0];
    if (document.getElementById("state").value == "")
      document.getElementById("state").value = place[1];
  }
}
```

The JavaScript file, popcornA.js, includes the request function, getPlace, with its embedded receiver functions.

```
// popcornA.js
//   Ajax JavaScript code for the popcornA.html document

/************************************************************/
// function getPlace
//   parameter: zip code
//   action:    create the XMLHttpRequest object, register the
//              handler for onreadystatechange, prepare to send
```

```
//             the request (with open), and send the request,
//             along with the zip code, to the server
//    includes: the anonymous handler for onreadystatechange,
//             which is the receiver function, which gets the
//             response text, splits it into city and state,
//             and puts them in the document

function getPlace(zip) {
  var xhr = new XMLHttpRequest();

// Register the embedded receiver function as the handler
  xhr.onreadystatechange = function () {
    if (xhr.readyState == 4 && xhr.status == 200) {
      var result = xhr.responseText;
      var place = result.split(', ');
      if (document.getElementById("city").value == "")
        document.getElementById("city").value = place[0];
      if (document.getElementById("state").value == "")
        document.getElementById("state").value = place[1];
    }
  }
  xhr.open("GET", "getCityState.php?zip=" + zip);
  xhr.send(null);
}
```

Figure 10.3 shows the displayed form after the zip code has been entered.

Figure 10.3   Display of the form after the zip code has been entered

Figure 10.4 shows the displayed form after the zip code text box has lost focus and the city and state have been provided.

Figure 10.4   Display of the form after the city and state have been provided

10.2.6   Cross-Browser Support

The application demonstrated in Section 10.2.5 works correctly with FX2 and IE7 browsers. However, it does not work with earlier IE browsers. Because there are still a large number of people who use IE6 and to a lesser extent IE5, making Ajax work with those browsers must be considered.

The problem with IE5 and IE6 is that they do not support the XHR object named XMLHttpRequest. They do, however, support a similar object with a different name. So, to make Ajax applications operate correctly on both of these earlier browsers and also all contemporary browsers, these differences must be taken into account. The name of the IE5 and IE6 object is Microsoft.XMLHTTP, and it is an ActiveXObject.

Actually, XMLHTTP is the name of the original object used for asynchronous requests, invented by Microsoft. When Netscape adopted this idea, they named their object XMLHttpRequest, and other browser makers followed. Finally, in IE7, Microsoft changed to the name used by the others.

The code to create the original object (used in IE5 and IE6) is as follows:

```
xhr = new ActiveXObject("Microsoft.XMLHTTP");
```

The code can determine whether XMLHttpRequest is supported by testing window.XMLHttpRequest. If this is null (which would evaluate to false), it is safe to assume that the browser is either IE5 or IE6 and accordingly create the XMLHTTP object. The cross-browser version of the getPlace function is as follows:

```
// function getPlace
//    parameter: zip code
//    action: create the SMLHttpRequest object, register the
//            handler for onreadystatechange, prepare to send
//            the request (with open), and send the request,
```

```
//           along with the zip code, to the server

function getPlace(zip) {

// Get the object for all browsers except IE5 and IE6
  if (window.XMLHttpRequest)
    xhr = new XMLHttpRequest();

// Otherwise get the object for IE5 and IE6
  else
    xhr = new ActiveXObject("Microsoft.XMLHTTP");

// Register the embedded receiver function as the handler
  xhr.onreadystatechange = function () {
    if (xhr.readyState == 4 && xhr.status == 200) {
      var result = xhr.responseText;
      var place = result.split(', ');
      if (document.getElementById("city").value == "")
        document.getElementById("city").value = place[0];
      if (document.getElementById("state").value == "")
        document.getElementById("state").value = place[1];
    }
  }
  xhr.open("GET", "getCityState.php?zip=" + zip);
  xhr.send(null);
}
```

10.3 Return Document Forms

There are several different forms of data that can be returned from an Ajax request to the server. Among the most common of these are plain text, as used in Section 10.2, XHTML, XML, JavaScript code, and JavaScript Object Notation. Plain text is usually used for unstructured data, while the others are used for structured data. This section briefly discusses these alternatives.

10.3.1 XHTML

XHTML can and often is used as the form of structured data returned from the server. To use XHTML, an empty div element is included in the original document (the one to be updated), and the returned XHTML is placed in the div using the innerHTML property. For example, to replace a complete table element, the table element is placed in a div element, as in the following original document fragment:

```
<div id = "replaceable_list">
  <h2> 2007 US Champion/Runnerup - baseball </h2>
  <ul>
    <li> Boston Red Socks </li>
    <li> Colorado Rockies </li>
  </ul>
</div>
```

Now suppose there were a menu in the initial document that allowed the user to choose alternative sports, like football, basketball, or hockey. If the user chose football, the response XHTML document fragment would look like the following:

```
<h2> 2007 US Champion/Runnerup - football </h2>
<ul>
  <li> New York Giants </li>
  <li> New England Patriots </li>
</ul>
```

Now, if the Ajax call returns this document fragment in `responseText`, the div can be replaced by interpreting the following JavaScript code:

```
var divDom = document.getElementById("replaceable_list");
divDom.innerHTML = xhr.responseText;
```

The disadvantage of XHTML is that it is essentially a markup language for describing documents to be displayed, usually by a browser. What is often returned from the server after an Ajax request is data of some form. If that data must be processed, the XHTML document fragment must be parsed to extract the data. Also, if the XHTML is complicated, say with extensive CSS, it would be a complex task for the server to generate it.

10.3.2 XML

The name Ajax implies that XML is an integral part of the technology. Because XML is the de facto standard way of storing and transmitting structured data on the Web, this is natural. In our example, the XML document fragment would appear as follows:

```
<header> 2007 US Champion/Runnerup - football </header>
<list_item> New York Giants </list_item>
<list_item> New England Patriots </list_item>
```

When XML is used as the form of document returned from an Ajax request, the response is returned in the `responseXML` property of the XHR object. This property has the DOM address of the DOM tree of the XML document. To extract the data from the XML document, its representation must be parsed. The DOM binding provides the tools for this parsing. Some of these methods were introduced in Chapter 5, "JavaScript and XHTML Documents."

The data extracted from the XML could be used to construct a new XHTML document using DOM methods such as `createElement` and `appendChild`. If the structure of the original XHTML document need not be changed, the `innerHTML` property can be used to change the content of any element, using the data parsed from the XML document.

The process of parsing XML using the DOM methods has two disadvantages. Writing the parsing code is tedious and the resulting code is complex and error-prone. Also, support for the DOM parsing methods varies somewhat among browsers.

An alternative to this parsing the returned XML document is to use XSLT style sheets to convert it to XHTML, as illustrated in Chapter 7, "Introduction to XML." This approach is often easier and more likely to lead to reliable conversion. The converted document can then be inserted into the displayed document as in Section 10.2.

The XSLT document to convert the XML return document for our example follows:

```xsl
<xsl:stylesheet version = "1.0"
    xmlns:xsl = "http://www.w3.org/1999/XSL/Transform"
    xmlns = "http://www.w3.org/1999/xhtml" >
  <xsl:template match = "/">
    <h2> <xsl:value-of select = "header"> </h2> <br /><br />
    <ul>
      <xsl:for-each select = "list_item">
        <li> <xsl:value-of select = "list_item" />
            <br />
        </li>
      </xsl:for-each>
    </ul>
  </xsl:template>
</xsl:stylesheet>
```

10.3.3 JavaScript Object Notation

JavaScript Object Notation (JSON) is based on a subset of standard JavaScript (ECMA-262, 3rd edition). It is a textual way to represent objects, using two structures, collections of name/value pairs, and arrays of values. Our interest here in JSON is that it can be used as a simpler alternative to XML for returning data from the server in response to an Ajax request. The primary reason to use JSON instead of XML is to eliminate the complexity of parsing.

JSON is a way to represent JavaScript objects as strings. Objects are unordered sets of property/value pairs. Each object is delimited by braces. Each property/value pair consists of a property name, represented as a literal string, a colon, and a value. The property/value pairs in an object are separated by commas. The values can be literal strings, numeric literals, arrays or other objects, `true`, `false`, or `null`. Arrays are delimited by brackets. The values in an array are separated by commas, as shown in the following example:

```
{"employees" :
  [
    {"name" : "Dew, Dawn", "address" : "1222 Wet Lane"},
    {"name" : "Do, Dick", "address" : "332 Doer Road"},
    {"name" : "Deau, Donna", "address" : "222 Donne Street"}
  ]
}
```

This object consists of one property/value pair, where the property value is `employees`, whose value is an array of three objects, each with two property/value pairs.

The individual data values in such an object can be retrieved using the usual syntax for array elements and object properties. For example, the following statement puts `"332 Doer Road"` in address2:

```
var address2 = myObj.employees[1].address;
```

Because JSON objects are represented as strings, they can be returned from the server as the `responseText` property of the XHR object. The JavaScript `eval` function could be used to convert JSON strings to JavaScript objects. However, this is a dangerous practice, because `eval` interprets any JavaScript code. The returned JSON could have been modified by some malicious person to be destructive JavaScript code. Therefore, the returned JSON string must be checked to determine if it is just JSON data, and not a script. This can be done with a JSON parser. One such parser is `parse`, a method of the `JSON` object, which is available from `http://www.JSON.org/json2.js`.

The `parse` function takes a `JSON` object as its parameter. It returns a JavaScript object with the structure and data of the `JSON` object. For example, consider the following code:

```
var response = xhr.responseText;
var myObj = JSON.parse(response);
```

JSON has the following general advantages over XML: First, JSON representations are smaller, resulting in quicker transmission from the server. Second, the `parse` function is fast—much faster than the manual parsing or the use of XSLT to translate XML. Third, using `parse` is far simpler than either manual parsing or using XSLT on XML documents.

XML is clearly superior to JSON if the data being fetched with Ajax is going to be integrated, more or less intact, into the displayed document. In this situation, it is easiest to use XSLT to translate the fetched XML into XHTML. In this situation, using JSON would require the construction of the XHTML document fragment manually, using the JavaScript functions for building documents.

Of course, if the fetched data must be processed before it is integrated into some existing XHTML element, then JSON may be the better choice, because if the data is in the form of XHTML, it will need to be parsed before any processing can be done.

Be assured that the choice between JSON and XML is controversial, and that there are legions of rabid supporters of each that would not dream of using the other.

Our example return document in JSON would appear as the following:

```
{"top_two":
  [
    {"sport": "football", "team": "New York Giants"},
    {"sport": "football", "team": "New England Patriots"},
  ]
}
```

The processing of this data to place it in the XHTML document follows:

```
var myObj = JSON.parse(response);
document.write("<h2> 2007 US Champion/Runnerup" +
                myObj.top_two[0].sport + "</h2>");
document.write("<ul> <li>" + myObj.top_two[0].team +
                "</li>");
document.write("<li>" + myObj.top_two[1].team +
                "</li></ul>");
```

Note that in recent versions of the Ajax toolkit Prototype (see Section 10.4.2), it is possible to return data from the server through a special HTTP message header, X-JSON.

10.4 Ajax Toolkits

There are a large and growing number of toolkits for developing Ajax applications. Any survey of all of them would require an entire chapter of a book, and it would be obsolete long before it found the shelves of any bookstore. This section briefly introduces only two of the more commonly used toolkits, Dojo and Prototype, both of which assist in the development of client-side Ajax software.

There are also server-side Ajax development tools. Among the most commonly used of these are Google Web Toolkit (GWT) and DWR. (DWR is an acronym for Direct Web Remoting.) The GWT allows the development of Ajax software, which is normally written in JavaScript, in Java. The system includes a compiler that translates Java to JavaScript. This allows a Java developer to build Ajax applications without learning or using JavaScript directly. Another benefit is that Java code is generally thought to be less error-prone than JavaScript code.

DWR is a remote procedure call library that makes it possible and convenient for JavaScript to call Java functions, and vice versa. It also supports the exchange of data in virtually any data structure between the two languages. The server-side is supported by a Java servlet running on the server.

Neither GWT nor DWR is discussed further here.

10.4.1 Dojo

The Dojo Toolkit is a free JavaScript library of modules that support many aspects of Web applications, including Ajax requests, animation of visual effects, drag and drop of document elements, and event handling. It makes these tasks easier by providing some of the commonly needed code, in the form of functions, and by taking care of some cross-browser issues. For example, Ajax requests that work on all common browsers are greatly simplified. Another example of this simplification is the functions for manipulating the DOM. Dojo also includes a collection of widgets for creating RIAs. So, Dojo is actually a toolkit for many parts of the process of creating dynamic Web sites, which naturally includes Ajax interactions. Because our interest here is focused on Ajax, only a small part of Dojo is discussed, and that discussion will be brief.

The Dojo Toolkit can be downloaded from the following Web site: http://dojotoolkit.org. For development, Dojo can also be used directly from an AOL Web site, which eliminates the bother of the download and installation. The Web site is http://o.aolcdn.com/dojo/0.4.2/dojo.js. For software that is to be deployed, however, one should download the Dojo software and install it on the server machine. This avoids the dependence on AOL's continued support, as well as the security risk of using a third party's server and software.

The only part of Dojo described here is one of the most used Dojo functions for Ajax, bind. This function is included in the io module of the Dojo collection of modules. The name that must be used for this function in a script is dojo.io.bind. The purpose of bind is to create an XHR object and build an Ajax request.

To use any part of Dojo in a script, after downloading it and installing it, the Dojo JavaScript file, dojo.js, must be imported with an element similar to the following:

```
<script type = "text/javascript"
  src = "dojo/dojo.js">
</script>
```

This assumes that dojo.js is stored in the dojo subdirectory of the directoy where public XHTML documents are stored. To illustrate the use of dojo.io.bind, the getPlace request function from Section 10.2.6 will be rewritten using Dojo. Following is a copy of the original getPlace function:

```
// getPlace.js
//    Ajax JavaScript code for the popcornA.html document
//    This version is written to support all browsers

/********************************************************/
// function getPlace
//    parameter: zip code
```

```
//     action:    create the XMLHttpRequest object, register the
//                handler for onreadystatechange, prepare to send
//                the request (with open), and send the request,
//                along with the zip code, to the server
//     includes:  the anonymous handler for onreadystatechange,
//                which is the receiver function, which gets the
//                response text, splits it into city and state,
//                and puts them in the document

function getPlace(zip) {
  var xhr;

// Get the object for all browsers except IE5 and IE6
  if (window.XMLHttpRequest)
    xhr = new XMLHttpRequest();

// Otherwise get the object for IE5 and IE6
  else
    xhr = new ActiveXObject("Microsoft.XMLHTTP");

// Register the embedded receiver function as the handler
  xhr.onreadystatechange = function () {
    if (xhr.readyState == 4) {
      var result = xhr.responseText;
      var place = result.split(', ');
      if (document.getElementById("city") == "")
        document.getElementById("city").value = place[0];
      if (document.getElementById("state") == "")
        document.getElementById("state").value = place[1];
    }
  }
  xhr.open("GET", "getCityState.php?zip=" + zip);
  xhr.send(null);
}
```

The bind function takes a single literal object parameter. Recall that an object literal is a list of property/value pairs, separated by commas and delimited by braces. Each property name is separated from its associated value with a colon. The values can be any expression, including anonymous function definitions. The parameter to bind must have the two properties, url and load. In addition, it should have method, error, and mimetype properties. The value of the url property is the URL of the server where the request is to be sent. The value of the load property is a function that uses the data returned by the server as a result of the request. For both the load and error functions, directly defined anonymous functions are used. The value of the method property is either "GET" or "POST".

The value of the `error` property is a function that is called if there is an error in processing the request. Finally, the `mimetype` is the MIME type of the returned data.

The call to `bind` that does what the `getPlace` function does follows:

```
dojo.io.bind({
  url:  "getCityState.php?zip=" + zip,
  load: function (type, data, evt) {
            var place = data.split(', ');
            if (dojo.byId("city").value == "")
              dojo.byId("city").value = place[0];
            if (dojo.byId("state").value == "")
              dojo.byId("state").value = place[1];
          },
  error: function (type, data, evt) {
            alert("Error in request, returned data: " + data);
          },
  method: "GET",
  mimetype: "text/plain"
} );
```

10.4.2 An Example

In this section an example of using Dojo to create an Ajax application is developed. Many people now shop on the Web for virtually every kind of product. One of the many small frustrations of shopping on the Web is the following: The shopper is trying to purchase an article of clothing. After choosing a particular item, a size is selected from a list. Next, a color is chosen. If the particular size and color of the item happens not to be in stock at the time, the server returns a new document to indicate this to the user. This takes time to transmit to the browser and still more time to render. The user, when informed, must start over again. This small frustration can be avoided by having the site present only the colors of the chosen item and size that are currently in stock. Then the user can choose among the available colors, rather than possibly choosing a color that is not in stock. Using Ajax, the time required to return the available colors will be short. Furthermore, only the list of colors need be returned and rendered as a menu by the browser.

The original document for the example will be one for one specific shirt. It will include a brief description of the shirt and a menu of sizes available. It will also include a title and an empty menu for the colors. The color menu will be constructed when the Ajax request returns the available colors. The original document, named `shirt.html`, follows:

```
<?xml version = "1.0" encoding = "utf-8" ?>
<!DOCTYPE html PUBLIC "-//W3C//DTD XHTML 1.0 Strict//EN"
 "http://www.w3.org/TR/xhtml1/DTD/xhtml1-strict.dtd">
<!-- shirt.html
     Use Ajax to get the available colors of shirts
     -->
<html xmlns = "http://www.w3.org/1999/xhtml">
  <head> <title> Shirt orders </title>
    <script type = "text/javascript"
            src = "dojo/dojo.js">
    </script>
    <script type = "text/javascript"  src = "shirt.js">
    </script>
    <link rel = "stylesheet"  type = "text/css"
          href = "shirtstyles.css" />
  </head>
  <body>
    <h3> Shirt Style 425 - broadcloth, short sleeve,
         button-down collar </h3>
    <form>
      Size selection:
      <select name = "sizes"  onchange = "getColors(this.value)" >
        <option value = "14.5"> 14 &frac12; </option>
        <option value = "15"> 15 </option>
        <option value = "15.5"> 15 &frac12; </option>
        <option value = "16"> 16 </option>
        <option value = "16.5"> 16 &frac12; </option>
        <option value = "17"> 17 </option>
        <option value = "17.5"> 17 &frac12; </option>
        <option value = "18"> 18 </option>
      </select>

      <div class = "colors"
           id = "colorlist"> Colors available and in stock:
        <select id = "colorselect">
        </select>
      </div>
    </form>
  </body>
</html>
```

Notice that a script tag in this document references the `dojo.js` script and another references another JavaScript file, `shirt.js`. The `div` element at the bottom of this document will be the target of the data that will be returned by the Ajax request. This data will be placed in a select element that will be built by the Ajax callback function. The style sheet for this document follows:

```
/* shirtstyles.css - style sheet for shirt.html */
h3 {color: blue}
div.colors {position: absolute; left: 200px; top: 55px;}
```

The initial display of `shirt.html` is shown in Figure 10.5.

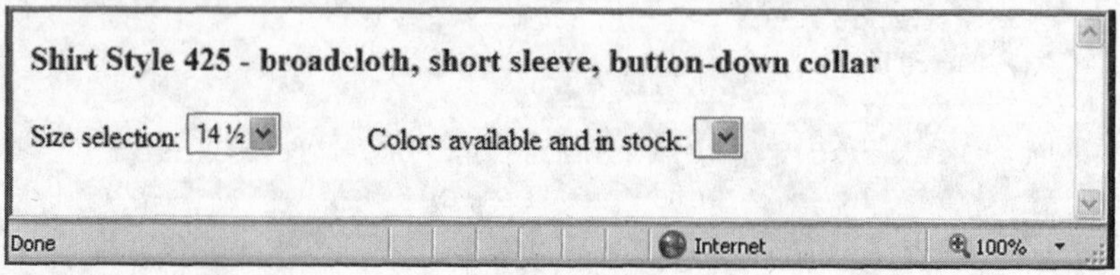

Shirt Style 425 - broadcloth, short sleeve, button-down collar

Size selection: 14 ½   Colors available and in stock:

Figure 10.5 The initial display of `shirt.html`

The JavaScript for the shirt application defines two functions, the callback function for the Ajax request, `buildMenu`, which builds the menu of colors, and a wrapper function, `getColors`, that includes the call to the actual request function, `dojo.io.bind`, which creates the request. `dojo.io.bind` comes from the `dojo.js` script.

The `buildMenu` function first gets the DOM address of the initially empty select element. Then, in case this is not the first request, the `options` property of the select element is set to 0 (to empty the select). Next, `buildMenu` splits the value returned by the request, which is a string of color names separated by commas and spaces. This places the colors in the array, `colors`. Then, it iterates through the `colors` array, building a new `Options` object for each element (color). The color is sent to the `Options` constructor and becomes the value of the option. Finally, the new `Options` object is added to the select object with the `add` method. Unfortunately, the second parameter to the `add` method is browser dependent. For the IE browsers, it must be set to −1 to indicate the option is not initially set. For other browsers, it must be set to `null`. This problem is handled with a `try-catch` clause. If `add` is called with −1 as the second parameter and the browser is not IE, an exception is raised, which executes the `catch` clause, which uses `null` as the second parameter.

The `getColors` callback function contains only the call to `dojo.io.bind`. The `url` is set to `getColors.php` with the `size` parameter attached (because the request is made with the GET method). The complete JavaScript file, shirt.js, is as follows:

```
// shirt.js
//  Ajax JavaScript code for the shirt.html document
//  Uses Dojo

// The function that builds the menu of colors
function buildMenu(type, data, evt) {
  var menuDOM = document.getElementById("colorselect");
  var nextColor, nextItem;

// Delete previous items in the color menu
  menuDOM.options.length = 0;

// Split the data into an array of colors
  var colors = data.split(', ');

// Go through the returned array of colors
  for (index = 0; index < colors.length; index++) {
    nextColor = colors[index];
    nextItem = new Option(nextColor);

// Add the new item to the menu
    try {
      menuDOM.add(nextItem, -1);
    }
    catch (e) {
      menuDOM.add(nextItem, null);
    }
  }
}

// The function that calls bind to request data
function getColors(size) {
  dojo.io.bind( {url: "getColors.php" + "?size=" + size,
                 load: buildMenu,
                 method: "GET",
                 mimetype: "text/plain"
                } );
}
```

If `shirt.html` were a real application, the response document would be produced by a program that searched the inventory and produced a list of colors for the given size that were currently in stock. To test `shirt.html`, however, a PHP script that simply returns a string of color names was used.

Figure 10.6 shows the display after a size has been selected and the request has returned a list of colors, which have been used to build a select element.

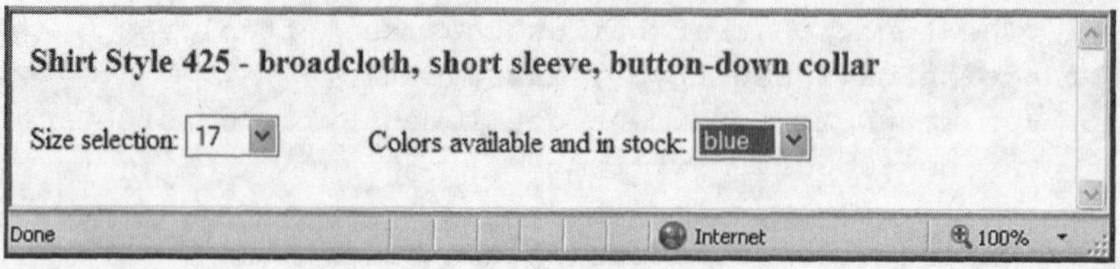

Shirt Style 425 - broadcloth, short sleeve, button-down collar

Size selection: 17   Colors available and in stock: blue

Done   Internet   100%

Figure 10.6 The display of `shirt.html` after a size has been selected

10.4.3 Prototype

Prototype is a toolkit for JavaScript. In addition to providing tools for Ajax, it extends the JavaScript language. For example, Prototype provides a more powerful way of supporting inheritance through its `Class` module. Prototype was written by Sam Stephenson, who works on the Rails team. Its original purpose was to provide the JavaScript tools needed to support the Rails framework for constructing Web software applications. In Chapter 15, "Introduction to Rails," the JavaScript tools in Prototype are used, though some of them are wrapped in Ruby methods. Prototype can be downloaded from `http://prototype.conio.net`.

The Prototype toolkit includes a large number of functions that provide shortcuts to and abbreviations of commonly needed JavaScript code. The only one of these used here is the abbreviation for `document.getElementById`, which is simply a dollar sign (`$`). For example, the following two assignment statements are equivalent in Prototype:

```
document.getElementById("name").value = "Freddie";
$("name").value = "Freddie";
```

Although a description of Prototype is a long story, our discussion here is brief, because our interest is focused on Ajax. All of the Ajax functionality of Prototype is encapsulated in the `Ajax` object. An Ajax request with Prototype is strikingly similar to one in Dojo. The request is made by creating an object of the `Ajax.Request` type, sending the relevant parameters to the constructor for the new object. Requests with `Ajax.Request` are by default asynchronous. The first parameter to the `Ajax.Request` constructor is the URL of the server to which the request is being made. The second parameter is a literal object with a list of relevant information.

The parameters, which are properties of the second parameter to `Ajax.Request`, are similar to those of the `bind` function of Dojo. The most commonly used parameters are the following: The value of the `method` parameter is either `"get"` or `"post"`, with the default being `"post"`. The value of the `parameters` property is the parameters that are to be attached to the URL of a `get` method. For example, for the zip code example, the value of the `parameters` property would be `"zip=" + zip`. The value of the `onSuccess` property is the callback function to handle the data returned by the server in response to the request in those cases where the request succeeded. The value of the `onFailure` property is the callback function for those cases where the request failed. Following is an example of the creation of an `Ajax.Request` object:

```
new Ajax.request("getCityState.php", {
  method: "get",
  parameters: "zip=" + zip,
  onSuccess: function(request) {
            var place = request.responseText.split(', ');
            $("city").value = place[0];
            $("state").value = place[1];
            }
  onFailure: function(request) {
            alert("Error - request failed");
            }
} );
```

Prototype serves as the basis for several other toolkits, two of the most popular among them being Script.aculo.us and Rico.

10.5 Security and Ajax

Section 1.8 introduced the topic of security issues associated with the Web. Ajax-enabled Web applications create new opportunities for security breaches. They also require some new approaches to Web security testing. This section introduces some of the vulnerabilities of Ajax applications and in some cases suggests ways developers can guard against them.

An Ajax application requires client-side JavaScript code, and complex applications require a good deal of it. There is a temptation on the part of developers of this code to include security controls, in part because they formerly wrote server-side code, the natural home of security controls. However, security controls in client-side software are not effective, because intruders can change the code running on the client. Therefore, security controls must be designed into server-side software, even if it also appears in the client-side software.

Non-Ajax applications often have only one or a few server-side response programs, each of which produces significant content. Ajax applications often have a much larger number of response programs, each of which is small and handles only requests for changes in one small part of the initial document. This increase in the number of server response programs increases the attack surface of the whole application., providing more opportunities for intruders.

Cross-site scripting provides another opportunity for intruders. Ajax applications often return JavaScript code to the client. Such code could be modified by an intruder to include destructive operations. To protect against this, any JavaScript code returned by the server must be scanned before it is interpreted. Another version of the problem is possible when text boxes are used to collect returned information from the server. The text box could include a script tag that includes malicious JavaScript code. Therefore, such received text should be scanned for script tags.

Summary

Ajax is a relatively new technology for building Web applications that can implement relatively quick updates to parts of documents. Asynchronous requests are made to the server, allowing users to continue to interact with the browser while the request is being handled. JavaScript code is used to create the Ajax request object. Any server software can be used to generate the response. JavaScript is again used to receive the new partial document and insert it into the currently displayed document.

Internet Explorer browsers prior to IE7 must be handled differently, because the object used to make asynchronous requests has a different name in the JavaScript supported by those browsers.

The request phase of an Ajax request for data has several tasks. It must create the object to be used for the request, register the callback function to handle the returned data, call the `open` method of the request object, and actually send the object to the server. The request object is browser dependent, so the request function must take this into account. The response document for an Ajax request can be a simple PHP script that creates the return data. It could be any program or script that returns data. The receiver phase of an Ajax communication, the callback function, is called several times by the server. When the `readyState` property of the request object is 4 and the `status` property is 200, the callback function can process the returned data. Processing ultimately uses the data, either directly or indirectly, to update part of the displayed document.

The form of the returned document, or data, varies widely. It can be XHTML, XML, pure text, or even JavaScript code to be interpreted on the browser. It could also be JSON, which is a compact data form that is part of JavaScript.

There are many toolkits and frameworks that support the production of Web sites that use Ajax. Dojo and Prototype are two of the most common of the toolkits. Both relieve the developer of cross-browser concerns and make writing Ajax requests much easier.

Ajax brings some slightly different issues to the problem of security. One of these is the temptation of developers who formerly worked on the server side to place security controls in client-side code, where they are far less effective. Another is that Ajax applications have more server-side scripts, each of which can be a security risk. Also, cross-site scripting, which is used in some Ajax applications, creates new opportunities for intruders.

Review Questions

10.1   What new software must be installed on a browser or server to run Web applications that use Ajax?

10.2   What does it mean for a request to be asynchronous?

10.3   What is the goal of the use of Ajax in a Web application?

10.4   What is a callback function in an Ajax application?

10.5   What new languages are used to program Web applications that use Ajax?

10.6   What is required for an Ajax application to run on both IE6 and the latest versions of browsers?

10.7   Under what circumstances would one use the `POST` method for an Ajax request?

10.8   What is stored in the `readyState` property of an XHR object?

10.9   What is the purpose of the `onreadystatechange` property of the XHR object?

10.10 How are parameters passed in a `GET` Ajax request?

10.11 Under what circumstances is XHTML used for the return data for an Ajax request?

10.12 What two data types provide the forms of the data in a JSON string?

10.13 What is the disadvantage of using XHTML for the return data for an Ajax request?

10.14 Explain how Ajax applications have a larger attack surface than traditional Web applications.

10.15 What are the two ways XML is used in the callback function?

10.16 For what framework was Prototype developed?

10.17   What property of the XHR object stores the JSON data from an Ajax request?

10.18   When XML is used for the return data for an Ajax request, where does the callback function find it?

10.19   What is the danger of using `eval` to process a JSON string?

10.20   For simple Ajax applications, what is the advantage of using Dojo?

10.21   What is cross-site scripting and why does it create security problems?

10.22   What are the two major advantages of JSON over XML for the response data from an Ajax request?

Exercises

10.1   Explain the two characteristics of Ajax that help it achieve its goals.

10.2   Explain why the callback function is written as an anonymous function in the request phase function.

10.3   Modify the example application of Section 10.2 to use Prototype.

10.4   Modify the example application of Section 10.2 to have it provide the addresses of repeat customers, using a hash of names and addresses.

10.5   Modify the example application of Section 10.2 to use Dojo.

10.6   Modify the example application of Section 10.2 to have it validate the zip code when it is entered to ensure that it is a valid zip code for the given city and state. The response document can be a PHP script that looks up the zip code and the city and state in a small table of examples.

10.7   Modify the example application of Section 10.6 to allow the user to select a make and model of used cars. The make must be in a menu. When a make is chosen, a menu of models must be displayed. This menu is produced by hardwired data in the original document. When a model is chosen, an Ajax request must be made to get a list of the years and colors of the chosen make and model that are available. Make up a server-resident script to produce the data from an example array or hash.

10.8   Modify the example application of Section 10.6 to use Prototype.

CHAPTER

11

Java Web Software

This chapter discusses Java server-based software, specifically servlets, JavaServer Pages, and JavaServer Faces. First, servlets are introduced, including their general structure and common uses. The servlet methods for handling GET and POST HTTP requests are then discussed. The NetBeans IDE is introduced and used to develop a complete servlet application.

Next, the chapter discusses cookies[1] and describes how they can be implemented with servlets. A complete application is developed to illustrate the use of cookies.

The last three sections of the chapter introduce technologies built on top of servlets. These include JavaServer Pages (JSP), the JSP Standard Tag Library (JSTL), JSP Expression Language (EL), JavaBeans, and JavaServer Faces (JSF). The same application is repeated four times, once with two JSP documents using EL, once with one JSP document using EL, once using a JavaBean class, and once using JSF, which also uses a JavaBean class.

---

1. Cookies are also discussed in Chapter 9.

11.1   Introduction to Servlets

This section describes the structure and uses of servlets.

11.1.1   Overview

A servlet is a compiled Java class, an object of which is executed on the server system when requested by the XHTML document being displayed by a browser. The servlet class is instantiated when the Web server begins execution. The execution of servlets is managed by a *servlet container*. The servlet container may run in the same process as the Web server, in a different process on the server host machine, or even on a different machine. The servlet request and response processes are supported with the HTTP protocol, so the servlet container must implement the HTTP specification. A servlet container might also define and enforce security restrictions on the execution of its servlets. Servlet containers are sometimes called *servlet engines*. Section 11.1.3 discusses a few of the currently popular servlet containers.

When an HTTP request is received by a Web server, the Web server examines the request. If a servlet must be called, the Web server passes the request to the servlet container. The container determines which servlet must be executed, assures it is loaded, and calls it. A servlet call passes two parameter objects: one for the request and one for the response. The servlet receives the input data associated with the request through the request object. This may include form data as well as the identity of the requesting client. As the servlet handles the request, it dynamically generates an XHTML document as its response, which is returned to the server through the response object parameter. The process of handling the request (by the servlet) is accomplished in part by calling methods on the request and response objects. When finished, the servlet container returns control to the Web server.

Servlets are often used to dynamically generate responses to browser requests. They are also used as alternatives to server extensions such as Apache modules, which users can write and add to an Apache server to extend its capabilities.

In Chapter 13 "Database Access through the Web," use of a servlet to access a database is discussed. A complete example is included.

11.1.2   Details

All servlets either implement the `Servlet` interface or extend a class that implements `Servlet`. The `Servlet` interface, which is defined in the `javax.servlet` package, declares the methods that manage servlets and their interactions with clients. The author of a servlet must provide definitions of these methods.

The `GenericServlet` class is a predefined implementation of the `Servlet` interface. The `HttpServlet` class is a predefined extension to `GenericServlet`.[2] Most user-written servlets are extensions to `HttpServlet`.

---

2. There are other extensions to `GenericServlet` (for example, to handle other protocols such as the Simple Object Access Protocol (SOAP)).

In addition to the `Servlet` interface, the `javax.servlet` package contains several other interfaces required for implementing servlets. The `ServletRequest` and `ServletResponse` interfaces encapsulate the communication from the client to the servlet and from the servlet back to the client, respectively. The `ServletRequest` interface provides servlet access to `ServletInputStream`, through which input from the client flows. The `ServletResponse` interface provides servlet access to `ServletOutputStream` and also provides a method used to send information, usually in the form of an XHTML document, back to the client.

Every subclass of `HttpServlet` must override at least one of the methods of `HttpServlet`, the most common of which are shown in Table 11.1.

Table 11.1   Commonly used methods of `HttpServlet`

Method	Purpose
doGet	To handle HTTP GET requests
doPost	To handle HTTP POST requests
doPut	To handle HTTP PUT requests
doDelete	To handle HTTP DELETE requests

The `doGet`, `doPost`, `doPut`, and `doDelete` methods are called by the server. The HTTP PUT request allows a client to send a file to be stored on the server. The HTTP DELETE request allows a client to delete a document or Web page from the server. In many cases, users are not allowed to add files to the server or delete files that are stored on the server. `doGet` and `doPost` are the focus of this section because they are the most frequently used of the `HttpServlet` methods.

The protocol of the `doGet` method is as follows:

```
protected void doGet (HttpServletRequest request,
                      HttpServletResponse response)
   throws ServletException, IOException
```

`ServletException` is a subclass of `Exception` that serves as a wrapper for every kind of general servlet problem. `IOException` can be thrown for the usual reasons. In the protocol model above, `request` and `response` are the names we have chosen to be the reference variables for the request and response objects, respectively. The `HttpServletRequest` object parameter, `request`, contains the client request; the `HttpServletResponse` object parameter, `response`, provides the means to communicate the response that the servlet sends back to the client.

The protocol of the `doPost` method is the same as that of `doGet`.

Servlet output to the requesting client is created by defining a `PrintWriter` object through the `HttpServletResponse` object, using the getWriter method. The PrintWriter object provides a collection of methods, such as println, that sends response XHTML code to the client through the response object.

Before the PrintWriter object is created, the content type of the return document must be set. This is done with the setContentType method of the HttpServletResponse object, as is shown in the following call:

```
response.setContentType("text/html");
```

Following this method call, the PrintWriter object can be created with the following declaration:

```
PrintWriter servletOut = response.getWriter();
```

Now the println method of the servletOut object can be used to generate the XHTML markup of the document to be returned to the requesting client.

We are now ready to look at a complete servlet example. This first example servlet simply responds to a call from a form that uses the GET method. The form sends no data and requires no processing. So, the only action of the servlet is to produce an XHTML document with a message to indicate that the call was received. The call to the servlet, which appears in the XHTML form tag, specifies the servlet as the value of the form tag's action attribute. The following is the XHTML document that will call the servlet. Figure 11.1 shows the display created by tstGreet.html.

```
<?xml version = "1.0" encoding = "utf-8"?>
<!DOCTYPE html PUBLIC "-//W3C//DTD XHTML 1.0 Strict//EN"
  "http://www.w3.org/TR/xhtml1/DTD/xhtml1-strict.dtd">

<!-- tstGreet.html
     Used to test the servlet, Greeting
     -->
<html xmlns = "http://www.w3.org/1999/xhtml">
  <head> <title> Test greeting </title>
  </head>
  <body>
    <form action = "Greeting"  method = "get">
      <p>
        Press the button to enact the servlet
        <input type = "submit" value = "Enact Servlet" />
      </p>
    </form>
  </body>
</html>
```

Figure 11.1   Display of `tstGreet.html`

Notice that the value of the action attribute of the form tag uses the name of the servlet class, not the name of the file that stores the servlet's code. The reference to the servlet assumes the servlet class is in the same directory as the XHTML document.

The `Greeting` servlet class extends `HttpServlet` and implements the `doGet` method, which produces the XHTML response to the browser call. Following is a listing of the `Greeting` servlet:

```
/*  Greeting.java
    A servlet to illustrate a simple GET request
    */
import javax.servlet.*;
import javax.servlet.http.*;
import java.io.*;

public class Greeting extends HttpServlet {
  public void doGet(HttpServletRequest request,
                    HttpServletResponse response)
  throws ServletException, IOException {
      PrintWriter returnHTML;
      response.setContentType("text/html");
      returnHTML = response.getWriter();
      returnHTML.println("<html><head><title>");
      returnHTML.println("A simple GET servlet");
      returnHTML.println("</title></head><body>");
      returnHTML.println(
          "<h2> This is your servlet answering - hi! </h2>");
      returnHTML.println("</body></html>");
      returnHTML.close();
  }
}
```

Figure 11.2 shows the response from the `Greeting` servlet.

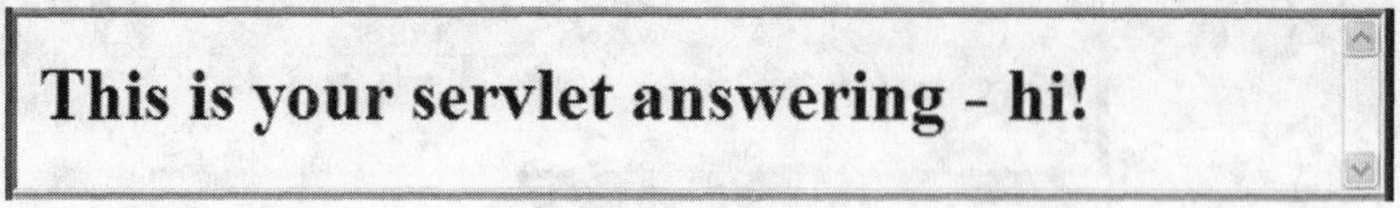

> **This is your servlet answering – hi!**

Figure 11.2 The response from the `Greeting` servlet

11.1.3 Servlet Containers

There are now a number of servlet containers available. One of the most popular is the Apache Tomcat (formerly Apache Jakarta Tomcat) servlet container, which is available free from the Apache Group at `http://tomcat.apache.org/`. Tomcat can run as a standalone servlet container or as part of another Web server.

There are also several application servers that include servlet containers. Among these are GlassFish, which is an application server for J2EE. It is distributed as part of J2EE, but it can also be obtained from `https://glassfish.dev.java.net/public/downloadsindex.html`. GlassFish, which includes a derivative of Tomcat as its servlet container, is a free open source product.

BEA and IBM developed and market commercial application servers for Java software that include servlet containers. BEA WebLogic Server is an application server for J2EE (`http://www.bea.com`). IBM's WebSphere Application Server (`http://www.ibm.com/websphere`) supports all forms of Java applications and includes a servlet container.

The servlets in this chapter were run using the application server GlassFish.

11.2 The NetBeans Integrated Development Environment

During the first part of the evolution of servlet technology, it was relatively simple to deploy a servlet for a specific server that supported servlets. The most commonly used servlet container was Tomcat. For example, in the fourth edition of this book, the servlets were deployed for Tomcat by creating a subdirectory under the main directory of the document tree and placing the compiled servlet class in that directory. The servlet was referenced with its address relative to the main document directory.

Deployment became far more complicated with the arrival and use of a collection of servlet containers. It became difficult to deploy a servlet that could be served by different servers. To alleviate this problem, a standard packaging scheme was developed with the release of the Servlet 2.2 specification in 2003. An application is now packaged as a Web Application Archive (WAR) file. WAR files can be built and disassembled with tools that build and disassemble Zip files, because they have the same structure. The file structure that resides in a WAR file is complex. Because of this complexity, people now only rarely deploy servlets by hand. We could describe how this can be done for our `Greeting` example of Section 11.1, but such a description would be lengthy and complicated. Therefore, this section describes how to use a commonly used framework for creating and deploying servlets, NetBeans, which implicitly constructs a deployment WAR file for the application being built. Of course, a complete description of NetBeans is far beyond the scope of this book. Therefore, we will only walk the reader through the creation of the `Greeting` example to illustrate the process.

NetBeans is available free from `http://www.netbeans.org`. The version illustrated in this section is 6.1.

The following narrative describes building the application that implements the `Greeting` servlet with NetBeans. After starting NetBeans, the screen shown in Figure 11.3 is displayed.

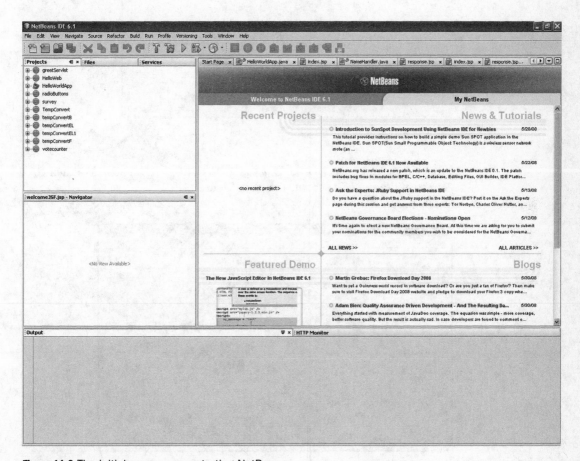

Figure 11.3 The initial screen upon starting NetBeans

The most useful part of this screen is the panel in the upper-left corner, which contains a list of the existing projects. Every project has its own directory, which is the same as the project name. Any of the existing projects can be opened by clicking its name in this list.

We select *File/New Project* from the screen shown in Figure 11.3 which brings up the screen shown in Figure 11.4.

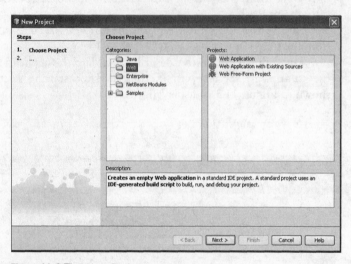

Figure 11.4 The *New Project* screen

From this screen, we select the *Web* category and *Web Application*. We then click *Next* to get to the next screen, shown in Figure 11.5.

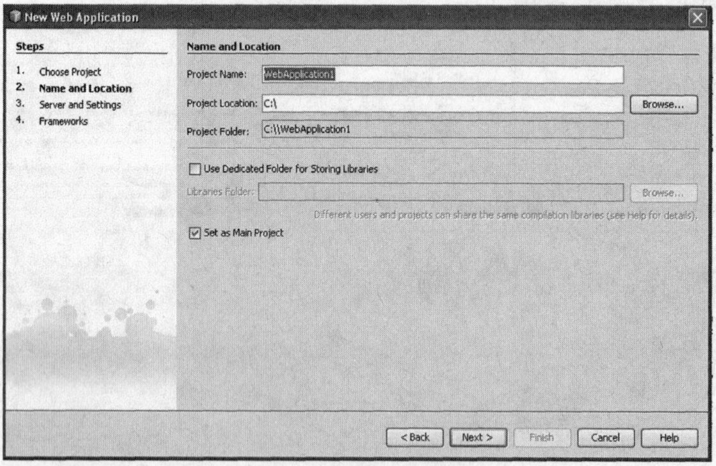

Figure 11.5 The *New Web Application* screen

In this screen, we enter the project's name, `greetServlet`,[3] and then click *Next*. This brings up the *Server and Settings* screen, on which we click *Finish*. This opens the NetBeans workspace with a skeletal version of the initial markup document of the project, which is named (by NetBeans) `index.jsp`. The document has the `.jsp` extension on its name because technically it is a JavaServer Page (JSP) document. JSP is discussed in Section 11.6. Although this is a JSP document, it will be written mostly in HTML.

A screenshot of the workspace is shown in Figure 11.6. This figure shows the workspace, which displays the initial skeletal markup document, just after creating a new project named `junk6`.

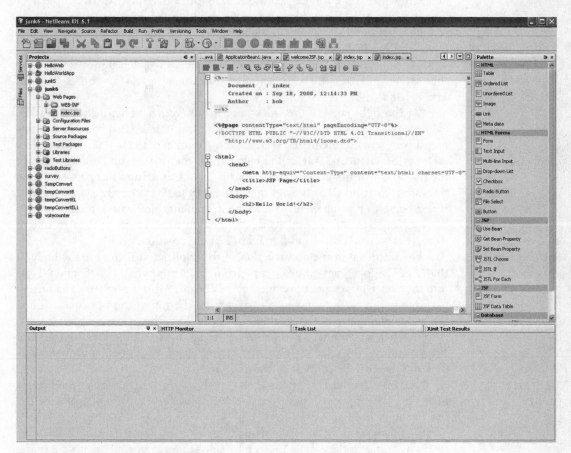

Figure 11.6 The NetBeans workspace

---

3. Note that the project name is often the same or at least closely related to the name of the servlet of the project.

There is a wealth of useful information and links to tools on the workspace screen. Across the top is a list of menus, many of which are similar to those of other systems, such as *File, Edit, Tools,* and *Help.* Immediately below these menus is a toolbar of icons, some of which we will use to construct our applications.

In the upper-left area of the screen is a window with the title *Projects,* which lists the names of projects that have been created. The junk6 item has been clicked—this displays a list of subdirectories for this project. The *Web Pages* directory has the markup files of this project; the *Source Packages* directory has a subdirectory, *<default package>,* which has the servlet class.

The center panel shows the skeletal markup document of the project, which was created by NetBeans. This document is complete, but only includes an h2 element whose content is Hello World!. Notice that the first part of the document is not HTML. At the beginning is a block of comments that are surrounded by the JSP comment delimiters, <%-- and --%>. Following the comments is a JSP directive, page, which specifies the content type and encoding of the document. The next two lines is the DOCTYPE declaration, which says this is an HTML 4.01 Transitional document whose form is that of loose.dtd.

On the right edge of the workspace is the *Palette,* which includes HTML element names, such as Table, Link, Form, and Radio Button. This is followed by a few JSP elements, such as Use Bean and JSTL If. Finally, there are two JSF elements. Any of the elements in the palette can be dragged onto the document in the center panel. This is an aid to writing markup—it allows the author to avoid some typing. It also makes it easier to get the syntax correct. If you begin to type an element into the document, NetBeans attempts to help by supplying a menu of elements that you might want, based on the first one or two letters typed. This is another aid to markup creation.

The next step in the construction of the application is to type the body of the HTML document index.jsp (from tstGreet.html in Section 11.1) into the skeletal document provided by NetBeans. After it is entered, its format is cleaned up by selecting *Source/Format* from the top of the workspace. Then the document is saved (by selecting *File/Save*). To verify that the document display is what was wanted, the project is built (by selecting *Build/Build Main Project*) and run (by selecting *Run/Run Main Project*). This opens a browser window and displays the content of index.jsp.

Next, the servlet is written. To begin this task, we right click the project name (in the upper-left panel) and select *New/Servlet,* which produces the screen shown in Figure 11.7.

On this screen, we enter the name of the servlet, Greeting, and click *Finish.* (The name of the servlet file is now Greeting.java.) This produces the workspace with a template version of the servlet in the center panel.

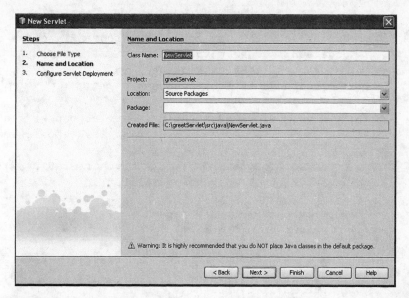

Figure 11.7 The *New Servlet* screen

This servlet is as follows:

```
/*
 *  To change this template, choose Tools | Templates
 *  and open the template in the editor.
 */


import java.io.IOException;
import java.io.PrintWriter;
import javax.servlet.ServletException;
import javax.servlet.http.HttpServlet;
import javax.servlet.http.HttpServletRequest;
import javax.servlet.http.HttpServletResponse;

/**
 *
 *  @author bob
 */
public class Greeting extends HttpServlet {
```

```java
/**
 * Processes requests for both HTTP <code>GET</code> and
 *    <code>POST</code> methods.
 * @param request servlet request
 * @param response servlet response
 */
protected void processRequest(HttpServletRequest request,
                              HttpServletResponse response)
throws ServletException, IOException {
  response.setContentType("text/html;charset=UTF-8");
  PrintWriter out = response.getWriter();
  try {
  /* TODO output your page here
        out.println("<html>");
        out.println("<head>");
        out.println("<title>Servlet junk6serv</title>");
        out.println("</head>");
        out.println("<body>");
        out.println("<h1>Servlet Greeting at " +
                   request.getContextPath () + "</h1>");
        out.println("</body>");
        out.println("</html>");
        */
  } finally {
    out.close();
  }
}


// <editor-fold defaultstate="collapsed"
//    desc="HttpServlet methods.
// Click on the + sign on the left to edit the code.">
/**
 * Handles the HTTP <code>GET</code> method.
 * @param request servlet request
 * @param response servlet response
 */
protected void doGet(HttpServletRequest request,
                   HttpServletResponse response)
throws ServletException, IOException {
  processRequest(request, response);
}


/**
 * Handles the HTTP <code>POST</code> method.
 * @param request servlet request
```

```
   * @param response servlet response
   */
  protected void doPost(HttpServletRequest request,
                        HttpServletResponse response)
  throws ServletException, IOException {
    processRequest(request, response);
  }

  /**
   * Returns a short description of the servlet.
   */
  public String getServletInfo() {
    return "Short description";
  } // </editor-fold>

}
```

This standard template NetBeans servlet includes four methods, `processRequest`, `doGet`, `doPost`, and `getServletInfo`. The `processRequest` method is called by both `doGet` and `doPost`, so it is where everything happens. Creating a servlet for an application requires the modification of `processRequest` to have it do what we want our servlet to do. Notice that `doGet` and `doPost` do nothing beyond calling `processRequest`.

Note that NetBeans puts the code of the servlet in a `try` block that includes a `finally` clause to close the output stream. This is often not necessary, and the other servlet examples in this chapter will not include the `try`/`finally`.

The standard template servlet shown is the default template, which could be modified to better the fit the needs of the developer.

To convert this program into what we want, we add the central parts of the `Greeting.java` class. When typing Java code into the workspace, the code is immediately checked for syntactic correctness. Syntactically incorrect lines are underlined in red.

We do not use `getServletInfo`, so it was deleted. We also deleted the unnecessary comments and added an initial comment line. Following is the listing of the `Greeting` servlet created with NetBeans:

```
// Greeting.java - a trivial servlet that only returns
//   a greeting
import java.io.IOException;
import java.io.PrintWriter;
import javax.servlet.ServletException;
import javax.servlet.http.HttpServlet;
import javax.servlet.http.HttpServletRequest;
import javax.servlet.http.HttpServletResponse;
```

```java
public class Greeting extends HttpServlet {
  protected void processRequest(HttpServletRequest request,
                                HttpServletResponse response)
  throws ServletException, IOException {
    response.setContentType("text/html;charset=UTF-8");
    PrintWriter out = response.getWriter();
    try {
        out.println("<html>");
        out.println("<head>");
        out.println("<title>Servlet Greeting</title>");
        out.println("</head>");
        out.println("<body>");
        out.println(
            "<h1>This is your servlet answering - hi! </h1>");
        out.println("</body>");
        out.println("</html>");
    } finally {
      out.close();
    }
  }

  protected void doGet(HttpServletRequest request,
                       HttpServletResponse response)
  throws ServletException, IOException {
    processRequest(request, response);
  }

  protected void doPost(HttpServletRequest request,
                        HttpServletResponse response)
  throws ServletException, IOException {
    processRequest(request, response);
  }
}
```

Our project is run by first building it, by selecting *Build/Build Main Project*. A trace of the building process is shown in the *Output* panel at the bottom left of the screen. Next, we run the project by selecting *Run/Run Main Project*. This results in the opening of a browser and the display of the index.jsp document, as shown in Figure 11.8.

Figure 11.8 The display of `index.jsp` of the `greetServlet` project

After clicking the *Enact Servlet* button, the `Greeting` servlet runs and produces the output shown in Figure 11.9.

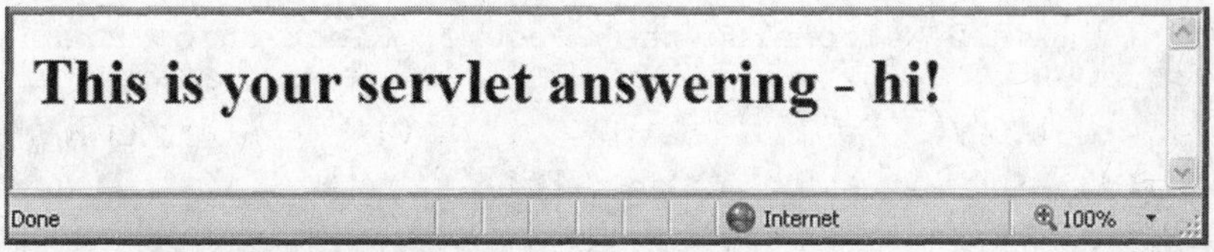

Figure 11.9 The output of the `Greeting` servlet

To support our earlier contention that the project directory structure for a servlet application is complex, we counted the directories and files generated by NetBeans for the `greetServlet` application—there were 14 directories and 19 files.

11.3 A Survey Example

The next servlet example is more complicated and interesting than the `Greeting` servlet. The initial document of this example is a form used to gather responses for a survey of potential purchasers of consumer electronics products. The example uses a servlet to collect the responses and produce the current results. The initial document for the survey follows:

```
<%--
    Document   : index (of the survey application)
    Created on : May 24, 2008, 8:37:33 PM
    Author     : bob
    Purpose    : Display a survey form for the purchase of
                 consumer electronics products
--%>
```

```
<%@page contentType="text/html" pageEncoding="UTF-8"%>
<!DOCTYPE HTML PUBLIC "-//W3C//DTD HTML 4.01 Transitional//EN"
"http://www.w3.org/TR/html4/loose.dtd">

<html>
  <head>
    <meta http-equiv="Content-Type" content="text/html;
        charset=UTF-8">
    <title>JSP Page</title>
  </head>
  <body>
    <form method="POST" action="Survey">
      <h2> Welcome to the Consumer Electronics Purchasing
          Survey </h2>
      <p />
      <h4> Your Gender: </h4>
      <p>
        <label>
          <input type="radio" name="gender" value="female"
              checked="checked" />
          Female <br />
        </label>
        <label>
          <input type="radio" name="gender" value="male" />
          Male <br /> <br /> <br />
        </label>
      </p>
      <p>
        <label>
          <input type="radio" name="vote" value="0" />
          Conventional TV <br />
        </label>
        <label>
          <input type="radio" name="vote" value="1" />
          HDTV <br />
        </label>
        <label>
          <input type="radio" name="vote" value="2" />
          MP3 player <br />
        </label>
        <label>
          <input type="radio" name="vote" value="3" />
          CD player <br />
        </label>
        <label>
```

```
            <input type="radio" name="vote" value="4" />
            Mini CD player/recorder <br />
        </label>
        <label>
            <input type="radio" name="vote" value="5" />
            DVD player <br />
        </label>
        <label>
            <input type="radio" name="vote" value="6"
                checked="checked" />
            Other <br /> <br />
        </label>
        <input type = "submit" value = "Submit Vote" />
        <input type = "reset" value = "Clear Vote Form" />
    </p>
  </form>
 </body>
</html>
```

Figure 11.10 shows the display of the initial form of the survey example.

Welcome to the Consumer Electronics Purchasing Survey

Your Gender:

- ⦿ Female
- ○ Male

- ○ Conventional TV
- ○ HDTV
- ○ MP3 player
- ○ CD player
- ○ Mini CD player/recorder
- ○ DVD player
- ⦿ Other

[Submit Vote] [Clear Vote Form]

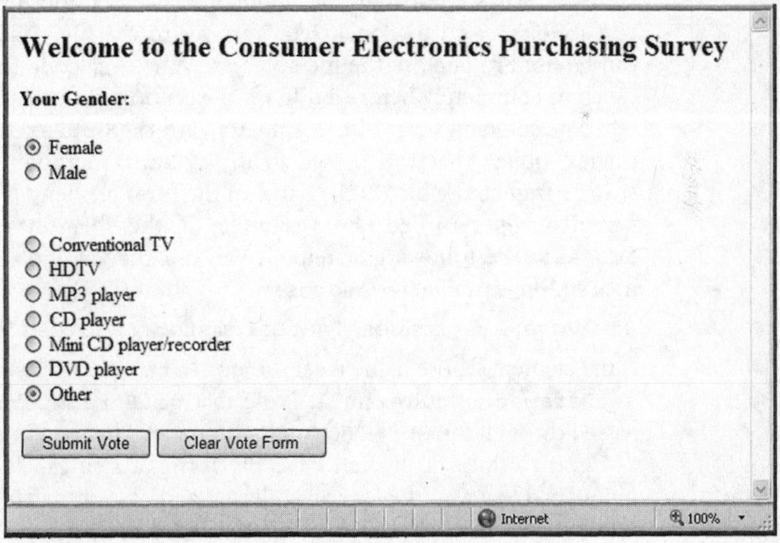

Figure 11.10   The initial form of the survey example

Because the servlet that processes the form in this page must accumulate the results of the survey, it must create and use a file to store the survey results. The first time the form is submitted, the file must be created and written. For all subsequent submissions, the file is opened, read, and rewritten. The servlet will produce the current vote totals for every client who submits a form. The survey results will be just the two sets of totals, one for each gender.

The data stored in the vote totals file is an integer array of results. The approach used is to read and write the file using the `ObjectInputStream` and `ObjectOutputStream` objects, respectively. This is a simple way to write any object to a file. When used for input, the input data object is cast to an integer array. For file output, the array object is written directly to the stream.

On all calls to the servlet except the first, the servlet must read the current vote array from the file, modify it, and write it back to the file. On the first call, there is no need to read the file first because the call creates the first vote to be written to the file. The `ObjectInputStream` object used to read the file is created by a call to the `ObjectInputStream` constructor, passing an object of class `FileInputStream`, which is itself created by passing the file's program name to the `FileInputStream` constructor. All of this is specified with the following statement:

```
ObjectInputStream indat = new ObjectInputStream(
    new FileInputStream(File_variable_name));
```

In this statement, `indat` is defined as the program variable that references the input stream.

There can be concurrent accesses to the file used here, because a servlet container can support multiple simultaneous executions of a servlet. To prevent corruption caused by concurrent accesses to the file, a `synchronized` clause can be used to enclose the file accesses. Whatever code that is in such a clause executes completely before a different execution is allowed to enter the clause.

The servlet accesses the form data with the `getParameter` method of the request object that was passed to the `doPost` method. This method takes a string parameter, which is the name of the form element. The string value of the parameter is returned. For example, if the form has an element named `address`, the following statement will put the value of the address form element in the variable `newAddress`:

```
newAddress = request.getParameter("address");
```

If the element whose name is sent to `getParameter` does not have a form value, `getParameter` returns `null`. Note that `getParameter` also works for values passed through the `GET HTTP` method, so it can be used in `doGet` methods.

Form values do not all have the form of strings—for example, some are numbers. However, they are all collected and passed as strings. So, if a form value is an integer number, it is passed as a string and must be converted to an integer value in the servlet. In Java, this is done with the `parseInt` method, which is defined in the wrapper class for integers, `Integer`. For example, to get the integer value of a parameter that is passed as the form value of an element named `price`, the following could be used:

```
price = Integer.parseInt(request.getParameter("price"));
```

We can now discuss the specifics of the servlet for processing the survey form data. The data file stores an array of 14 integers, seven votes for female voters and seven votes for male voters. The actions of the servlet are described in the following pseudocode algorithm:

> *If the votes data file exists*
> >   *read the votes array from the data file*
>
> *else*
> >   *create the votes array*
>
> *Get the gender form value*
> *Get the form value for the new vote*
> >   *and convert it to an integer*
>
> *Add the vote to the votes array*
> *Write the votes array to the votes file*
> *Produce the return XHTML document that shows the*
> >   *current results of the survey*

The servlet, `Survey`, that implements this process follows:

```
// Survey.java
//   This servlet processes the consumer electronics survey
//   form, updating the file that stores the survey data
//   and producing the current total votes in the survey.
//   The survey data file, survdat.dat, is stored on the
//   Web server.

import java.io.*;
import java.net.*;

import javax.servlet.*;
import javax.servlet.http.*;

public class Survey extends HttpServlet {

// processRequest - Processes requests for both HTTP GET
//                  and POST methods.
   protected void processRequest(HttpServletRequest request,
                                 HttpServletResponse response)
   throws ServletException, IOException {
     int votes[] = null;
     int index;
     int vote;
     File survdat = new File("survdat.dat");
     String gender;
```

```java
String products[] = {"Conventional TV", "HDTV", "MP3 player",
                     "CD player", "Mini CD player/recorder",
                     "DVD player","Other"};

// Set the content type for the response output and get a
// writer
response.setContentType("text/html;charset=UTF-8");
PrintWriter out = response.getWriter();

// Create the initial part of the response document
out.println("<html>");
out.println("<head>");
out.println("<title>Return message</title>");
out.println("</head>");
out.println("<body>");

// Synchronize a block for the votes file access
synchronized (this) {

  // If the file already exists, read in its data
  try {
    if (survdat.exists()) {
      ObjectInputStream indat =
          new ObjectInputStream(
          new FileInputStream(survdat));
      votes = (int[]) indat.readObject();
      indat.close();
    }

    // If the file does not exist (this is the
    // first vote), create the votes array
    else {
      votes = new int[14];
    }
  } catch (Exception e) {
    e.printStackTrace();
  }

  // Get the gender of the survey respondee
  gender = request.getParameter("gender");

  // Add the consumer electronics vote of the
  // response to the votes array
  vote = Integer.parseInt(request.getParameter("vote"));
  if (gender.equals("male")) {
```

```
      vote += 7;
    }
    votes[vote]++;

    //Write updated votes array to disk
    ObjectOutputStream outdat = new ObjectOutputStream(
        new FileOutputStream(survdat));
    outdat.writeObject(votes);
    outdat.flush();
    outdat.close();

  }  //** end of the synchronized block

  // Create the initial response information
  out.println("<h3> Thank you for participating in the");
  out.println(" Consumer Electronics Survey </h3>");
  out.println("<h4> Current Survey Results: </h4>");

  // Create the total votes return information for
  // female respondents
  out.println("<h5> For Female Respondents </h5>");
  for (index = 0; index < 7; index++) {
    out.print(products[index]);
    out.print(": ");
    out.println(votes[index]);
    out.println("<br />");
  }

  // Create the total votes return information for
  // male respondents
  out.println("<h5> For Male Respondents </h5>");
  for (index = 7; index < 14; index++) {
    out.print(products[index - 7]);
    out.print(": ");
    out.println(votes[index]);
    out.println("<br />");
  }

  out.close();

}

protected void doGet(HttpServletRequest request,
                     HttpServletResponse response)
throws ServletException, IOException {
```

```
            processRequest(request, response);
    }

    protected void doPost(HttpServletRequest request,
                          HttpServletResponse response)
    throws ServletException, IOException {
      processRequest(request, response);
    }
}
```

This example illustrates the use of a servlet for form handling and data storage on the server. It shows that developing servlets is not very different from writing non-Web Java applications. Figure 11.11 shows the results of running the Survey servlet after some survey responses have been received.

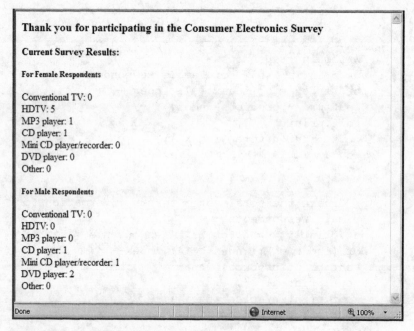

Figure 11.11 Results of the Survey servlet

11.4 Storing Information on Clients

Cookies provide a way to store information on a client machine about a previous interaction with a specific server. The javax.servlet package provides the tools for creating and using cookies.

11.4.1 Cookies[4]

A *session* is the time span during which a browser interacts with a particular server. A session begins when a browser connects to a particular server. It ends when the browser ceases to be connected to that server because either it connects to a different server or it is terminated. The HTTP protocol is essentially stateless—it includes no means of storing information about a session that would be available to a subsequent session. However, there are a number of different reasons why it is useful for the server to be capable of relating a request made during a session to the other requests made by the same client during that session, as well as previous and subsequent sessions.

One of the most common needs for session information is to implement shopping carts on Web sites. An e-commerce site can have any number of simultaneous online customers. At any time, any customer can add an item to or remove an item from his or her cart. Each user's shopping cart is identified by a session identifier, which could be implemented as a cookie. So, cookies can be used to identify each of the customers visiting the site at a given time.

Another common use of cookies is for a Web site to create profiles of visitors by remembering which parts of the site are perused—sometimes called *personalization*. Later sessions can use such profiles to target advertising to the client according to the client's past interests. Also, if the server recognizes a request as being from a client who has made an earlier request from the same site, it is possible to present a customized interface to that client. These situations require that information about clients be accumulated and stored. Storing session information is becoming increasingly important as more and more Web sites make use of shopping carts and personalization.

Cookies provide a general approach to storing information about sessions on the browser system itself. The server is given this information when the browser makes subsequent requests for resources from the server. Cookies allow the server to connect requests from a particular client to previous requests, thereby connecting sequences of requests into a session.

A *cookie* is a small object of information, usually of 1K or fewer bytes, which consists of a name and a textual value. A cookie is created by some software system on the server. Every HTTP communication between a browser and a server includes a header, which stores information about the message. The header part of an HTTP communication can include cookies. So, every request sent from a browser to a server and every response from a server to a browser can include one or more cookies.

At the time it is created, a cookie is assigned a lifetime. When the time a cookie has existed reaches its lifetime, the cookie is deleted from the browser's host machine. Every browser request includes all of the cookies its host machine has stored that are associated with the Web server to which the request is directed. Only the server that created a cookie can ever receive the cookie from the browser, so a particular cookie is information that is exchanged exclusively

---

4. The content of Section 11.4.1 also appears in Section 9.12.1.

between one specific browser and one specific server. Because cookies are stored as text, the browser user can view them at any time. The user can also alter or delete the cookies stored on the client machine.

Because cookies allow servers to record browser activities, they are considered by some to be privacy risks. Accordingly, browsers allow the client to change the browser setting to refuse to accept cookies from servers. This is clearly a drawback of using cookies—the clients who reject them render them useless.

Cookies can be deleted through a browser, although the deletion process is different for different browsers. The help facility of a browser can be consulted to determine the cookie deletion process on any given browser.

11.4.2 Servlet Support for Cookies

On the server, a Java cookie associated with a servlet is an object of class `Cookie`; on a client, a cookie is just a text data value. It is good to keep these two uses of the term *cookie* distinct.

A Java cookie object has a collection of data members and methods. Among the most commonly used data members are those for storing the lifetime, or maximum age, of the cookie and for storing the cookie's name and value as strings, along with a comment, which is a string that can be used to explain the purpose of the cookie. The most commonly used `Cookie` methods are `setComment(String)`, `setMaxAge(int)`, `setValue(String)`, `getComment()`, `getMaxAge()`, `getName()`, and `getValue()`, all of whose purposes are obvious from their names.

A cookie object is created with the constructor for the `Cookie` class. This constructor takes two parameters: the cookie name and the cookie value. For example, consider the following statement:

```
Cookie newCookie = new Cookie(gender, vote);
```

By default, a cookie exists from the time it is created until the current session ends, which is when the browser that started the session is terminated. If you want the cookie to exist past the end of the current session, you must use the `setMaxAge` method of `Cookie` to give the cookie a specific lifetime. The parameter to `setMaxAge` is the number of seconds, expressed as an integer literal. Because Java integers can have values up to a maximum of about two billion, cookies can have ages that range from one second to nearly 25,000 years. For example, the following method call gives `newCookie` a lifetime of one hour:

```
newCookie.setMaxAge(3600);
```

A cookie can be deleted in Java code by setting its maximum age to zero.

A cookie is attached to a response from a server with the `addCookie` method of the `HttpServletResponse` class. For example, the cookie `newCookie` can be added to the response object `myResponse` with the following statement:

```
myResponse.addCookie(newCookie);
```

Note that the cookie must be added to the response before any other part of the response is created, even the content type. When cookies are used, the sequence of response creation must be as follows:

1. Add any cookies to the response with `addCookie`.
2. Set the content type of the message with `setContentType`.
3. Get a response output stream with `getWriter`.
4. Place response information in the response stream with `print` or `println`.

Once again, remember that the cookie that a browser gets and stores is not a complete Java object—it has no methods; it is just some data.

The browser has little to do with cookies, at least directly. Browsers accept cookies, store them on the browser host system, and return them to the server that created them with each `GET` or `POST` request to that server that occurs before the session ends or the cookie's lifetime ends. All of this is done implicitly by the browser.

A cookie that is sent from the browser to the server must be explicitly fetched by a servlet. This is done with the `getCookies` method of `HttpServletRequest`. This method returns an array of references to `Cookie` objects. The following is an example of a cookie array declaration and a subsequent call to `getCookies`:

```
Cookie theCookies [];
...
theCookies = request.getCookies();
```

Whatever cookie processing is required can be done before the cookies are attached to the response and sent back to the browser.

11.4.3 An Example

We now consider an example of a ballot form that collects client votes in an election for the esteemed position of dogcatcher. The votes submitted through this form are recorded on the server by a servlet, which handles the form. This example uses a cookie to record, on the client, whether the voter has voted before, the objective being to prevent multiple votes from the same client. The survey form is presented with the XHTML document that follows:

```
<%--
    Document    : index (for the vote counter application)
    Created on  : May 25, 2008, 9:17:57 PM
    Author      : bob
    Presents a ballot to the user and calls
    the VoteCounter servlet for form handling
--%>
```

```
<%@page contentType="text/html" pageEncoding="UTF-8"%>
<!DOCTYPE HTML PUBLIC "-//W3C//DTD HTML 4.01 Transitional//EN"
"http://www.w3.org/TR/html4/loose.dtd">

<html>
  <head>
    <meta http-equiv="Content-Type" content="text/html;
        charset=UTF-8">
    <title> Ballot </title>
  </head>
  <body>
    <form action="VoteCounter" method="POST">

      <h3> Please choose one candidate for dogcatcher </h3>
      <p>
        <input type="radio" name="vote" value="Dogman" />
        Daren Dogman <br />
        <input type="radio" name="vote" value="Taildragger" />
        Timmy Taildragger <br />
        <input type="radio" name="vote" value="Dogpile" />
        Don Dogpile <br />
      </p><p>
        <input type = "submit"  value = "Submit ballot" />
      </p>
    </form>
  </body>
</html>
```

Figure 11.12 shows the display of the initial document for the vote counter example.

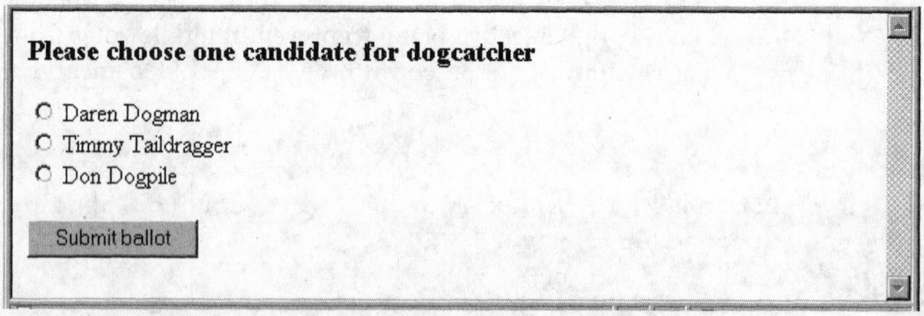

Please choose one candidate for dogcatcher

  ○ Daren Dogman
  ○ Timmy Taildragger
  ○ Don Dogpile

  [Submit ballot]

Figure 11.12　Display of the initial document

The users of the ballot form can vote for one of three persons for dog-catcher. The form presents the three choices as radio buttons and includes a *Submit ballot* button. The `action` attribute of the form specifies that it be handled by the servlet `VoteCounter`, using the `POST` method.

The vote-counting servlet has several processing responsibilities. For each ballot (request) the servlet receives, it must first determine whether a vote was actually cast. If no vote was cast, it must send an XHTML document back to the client, asking the user to choose a candidate and return the ballot form. It must also ensure that a voter does not vote twice, at least for some specified period of time. To do this, a cookie is returned to each voter. Each vote submission is checked to determine whether a cookie showing that the user has already voted came along with the ballot. If the ballot contains a vote—that is, if the form has one of its radio buttons pressed—and the voter has not voted previously, the vote must be processed. Processing a vote means reading the vote totals file, updating it, and writing it back to disk storage. Finally, the servlet must produce the current vote totals for each legitimate voter, in the form of an XHTML document. The actions of the `VoteCounter` servlet are outlined in the following pseudocode algorithm:

If the form does not have a vote
*   return a message to the client—"no vote"*
else
*   If the client did not vote before*
*   If the votes data file exists*
*   read in the current votes array*
*   else*
*   create the votes array*
*   end if*
*   update the votes array with the new vote*
*   write the votes array to disk*
*   make an "iVoted" cookie and add it to the response*
*   return a message to the client, including the new vote totals*
*   else*
*   return a message to the client—"Illegal vote"*
*   end if*
end if

Two utility methods are used: a predicate method to determine whether the client has voted and a method to create the XHTML header text. The servlet code follows:

```
//  VoteCounter.java
//    This servlet processes the ballot form, returning a
//    document asking for a new vote if no vote was made on the
```

```
//      ballot. For legitimate ballots, the vote is added to
//      the current totals, and those totals are presented to
//      the user in a return document.
//      A cookie is returned to the voter, recording the fact
//      that a vote was received. The servlet examines all votes
//      for cookies to ensure that there is no multiple voting.
//      The voting data file, votesdat.dat, is stored on the Web
//      server.

import java.io.*;
import javax.servlet.*;
import javax.servlet.http.*;

public class VoteCounter extends HttpServlet {
  Cookie cookies[] = null;
  int index;
  PrintWriter out;

  // processRequest - Processes requests for both HTTP GET
  // and POST methods.
  protected void processRequest(HttpServletRequest request,
                                  HttpServletResponse response)
  throws ServletException, IOException {
    Cookie newCookie;
    int votes[] = null;
    String vote;
    File votesdat = new File("votesdat.dat");
    String candidates[] = {"Daren Dogman", "Timmy Taildragger",
        "Don Dogpile"
    };

    // Get cookies from the request
    cookies = request.getCookies();

    // Check to see if there was a vote on the form
    vote = request.getParameter("vote");
    if (vote == null) {  //** There was no vote

      // Create the return document
      makeHeader(response);
      out.println("You submitted a ballot with no vote
                  marked<br />");
      out.println("Please mark the ballot and resubmit");
    } //** end of if (vote == null) ...
    else {  //** There was a vote
```

```java
// Check to see if this client voted before
if (!votedBefore()) {

  // No previous vote, so get the contents of the file
  // (if the file already exists)

  // Synchronize block for file input/output
  synchronized (this) {
    if (votesdat.exists()) {
      ObjectInputStream indat =
          new ObjectInputStream(
          new FileInputStream(votesdat));

      // We need the try/catch here because readObject
      // can throw ClassNotFoundException
      try {votes = (int[]) indat.readObject();
      } catch (ClassNotFoundException problem) {
        problem.printStackTrace();
      }
    } //** end of if(votesdat.exists() ...

    // If the file does not exist (this is the first
    // vote), create the votes array
    else {
      votes = new int[3];

      // Add the new vote to the votes array
    }
    if (vote.equals("Dogman")) {
      votes[0]++;
    } else if (vote.equals("Taildragger")) {
      votes[1]++;
    } else {
      votes[2]++;
    }  //** end of if (vote.equals("Dogman")) ...

    // Write updated votes array to disk
    ObjectOutputStream outdat = new ObjectOutputStream(
                              new FileOutputStream(votesdat));
    outdat.writeObject(votes);
    outdat.flush();
    outdat.close();
  }  //** end of synchronized block
```

```java
        // Attach a cookie to the response
        newCookie = new Cookie("iVoted", "true");
        newCookie.setMaxAge(5);    //** Set to 5 for testing
        response.addCookie(newCookie);

        // Write a response message
        makeHeader(response);
        out.println("Your vote has been received");
        out.println(
            "<br /><br /> Current Voting Totals: <br />");

        // Create the total votes return information
        for (index = 0; index < 3; index++) {
          out.println("<br />");
          out.print(candidates[index]);
          out.print(": ");
          out.println(votes[index]);
        }
      } //** end of if (!votedBefore() ...
      else {  // The client voted before

        // Write a response message
        makeHeader(response);
        out.println(
            "Your vote is illegal - you have already voted!");
      }  // end of else clause - client voted before
    }  // end of else (there was a vote)

    // Finish response document and close the stream
    out.println("</body> </html>");
    out.close();

  }  //** end of ProcessRequest

  //------------------------------------------------------------
  // Method votedBefore - return true if the client voted before;
  //  false otherwise
  boolean votedBefore() {
    if (cookies == null || cookies.length == 0) {
      return false;
    } else {

      // Check the cookies to see if this user voted before
      for (index = 0; index < cookies.length; index++) {
```

```
          if (cookies[index].getName().equals("iVoted")) {
            return true;
          }
        }  // end of for (index = 0; ...
      return false;
    }  //** end of if (cookies == null ...
  }  //** end of votedBefore


//------------------------------------------------------------
// Method makeHeader - get the writer and produce the
// response header
void makeHeader(HttpServletResponse response)
throws IOException {

  // Set content type for response and get a writer
  response.setContentType("text/html");
  out = response.getWriter();

  // Write the response document head and the message
  out.println("<html><head>");
  out.println(
      "<title> Return message </title></head><body>");
}  //** end of makeHeader

// Method doPost - just calls processRequest
protected void doPost(HttpServletRequest request,
    HttpServletResponse response)
throws ServletException, IOException {
  processRequest(request, response);
}
}  //** end of VoteCounter
```

The outputs of the VoteCounter servlet for the three possibilities it handles—a nonvote ballot, a second ballot from the same client, and a ballot with a legitimate vote—are shown in Figures 11.13, 11.14, and 11.15.

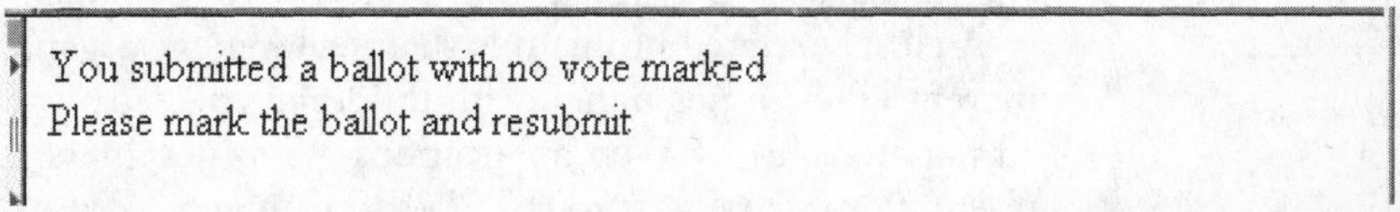

> You submitted a ballot with no vote marked
> Please mark the ballot and resubmit

Figure 11.13 The output of the VoteCounter servlet for a form with no vote

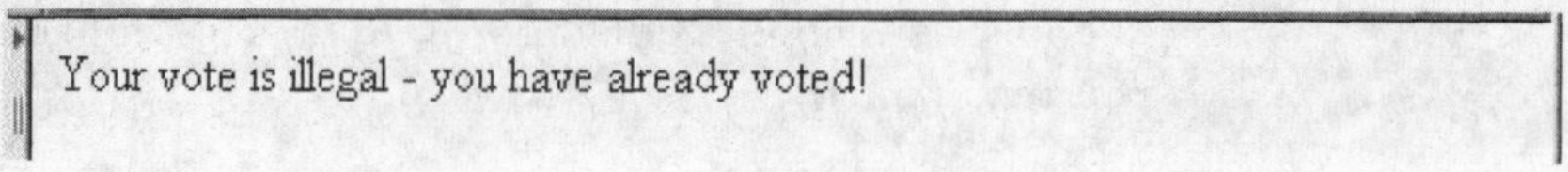

Your vote is illegal - you have already voted!

Figure 11.14 The output of `VoteCounter` for a form with a second vote from the same client

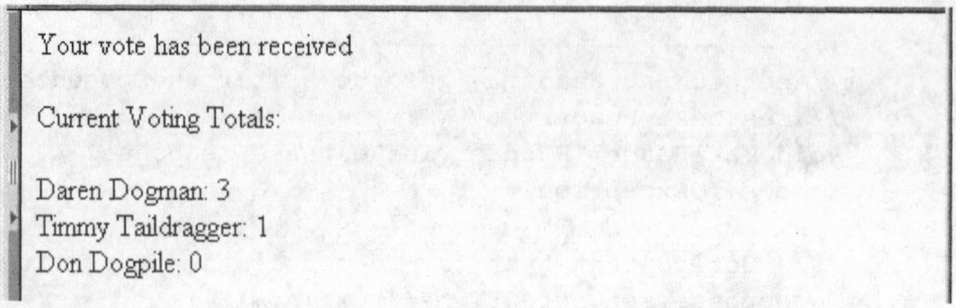

Your vote has been received

Current Voting Totals:

Daren Dogman: 3
Timmy Taildragger: 1
Don Dogpile: 0

Figure 11.15 The output of `VoteCounter` for a form with a legitimate vote

11.5 JavaServer Pages

JavaServer Pages (JSP), which are built on top of servlets, provide alternative ways of constructing dynamic Web documents. It is "ways," not "way," because JSP includes several different approaches to dynamically generate Web documents. JSP, which was designed by Sun Microsystems, is a specification rather than a product. This means that Sun does not provide code to support JSP. Other organizations are invited to implement the specification. This encourages competition among providers, which can result in better quality software.

11.5.1 Motivations for JSP

There are several perceived problems with the servlet approach, as well as other related approaches, to providing dynamic Web documents. Among these is the problem of having the XHTML response document embedded in programming code. In the case of servlets, the entire response document is created by calls to the `println` method of the `PrintWriter` class. This forces all maintenance of the user interface of the application to be done on program code.

A closely related problem is that devlopment organizations often have two different kinds of personnel, with different skill sets, work on the construction and maintenance of Web applications. Web designers focus on interface and presentation characteristics of Web documents. Programmers, on the other hand, design and maintain the code that processes form data and handles interactions with databases. Most personnel belong in one or the other of these categories rather than both. Yet having XHTML code and programming code intermixed requires people from both categories to work on the same documents. Furthermore, these mixed-code documents are difficult for people from both categories to read.

JSP can be used to develop server-based dynamic documents in which there is a clean separation between presentation (markup) and business logic. Furthermore, in some cases server-based applications that produce dynamic documents can be developed in JSP by Web designers who are not hard-core Java programmers. The same cannot be said for servlet-based applications.

The basic capabilities of servlets and JSP are the same. The basis for deciding which to use is explained in Section 11.5.2.

11.5.2 JSP Documents

There are two syntactic forms for writing JSP documents, the original way, now called *classic syntax*, and the alternative way, which uses XML syntax. The XML approach became possible in JSP 2.0, which was released in late 2003. XML syntax is useful if the JSP document will generate XML-compliant documents. However, XML syntax requires more effort and larger documents. The XML syntax of JSP documents is not further discussed in this chapter and all of our JSP document examples in this book use classic syntax.[5]

When requested by a browser, a JSP document is processed by a software system called a *JSP container*. Some JSP containers compile the document when the document is loaded on the server; others compile them only when they are requested. The compilation process translates a JSP document into a servlet and then compiles the servlet. So, JSP is actually a simplified approach to writing servlets.

In early versions of JSP, snippets of Java code were embedded in documents, similar to the way PHP code appears in documents. These snippets were called *scriptlets*. This approach retains the problem of language mixing that is inherent with servlets. Later versions of JSP, however, have capabilities that eliminate the need for scriptlets, and the use of scriptlets is now discouraged.

A JSP document, assuming scriptlets are not used, consists of three different kinds of elements: traditional XHTML or XML markup, action elements, and directives.

The XHTML or XML markup in the document is used to produce the content that is fixed. This markup is called *template text*. It is the static part of the document. Everything in a JSP document that is not a JSP element is template text. Template text is not modified by the JSP container—it arrives at the browser exactly as it appears in the JSP document. The designer choice between using a servlet and a JSP document is made on the basis of the proportion of the document that is template text. The more template text there is, the better it is

---

5. Some authors refer to JSP documents written in classic syntax as *JSP pages* and those written in XML as *JSP documents*. We will call ours JSP documents, although they are written in classical syntax.

to use JSP. If a document is mostly dynamically generated, then a servlet is the better choice.

Action elements dynamically create content. The document that results from the execution of a servlet whose source is a JSP document is a combination of the template text and the output of the action elements. An action element has the form of an XHTML element: an opening tag, possibly including attributes; content, which is sometimes called the *action body*; and a closing tag. In fact, however, action elements represent program code that generates XHTML markup.

Action elements appear in three different categories: standard, custom, and JSP Standard Tag Library (JSTL). The standard action elements are defined by the JSP specification. These include elements for dealing with JavaBeans,[6] including the response from a servlet or another JSP document, and dynamically generating an XHTML element. For example, the action element `<jsp:element>` dynamically generates an XHTML element, possibly with attributes and content defined by other nested actions. The `<jsp:include>` action element specifies a document file as the value of its `page` attribute. The document file is copied into the output document of the JSP document in which the `include` appears.

Custom action elements are those that are designed for a specific category of JSP documents within an organization. Because of its complexity, the development of custom action elements is not discussed in this chapter.

The JSP standard action elements are highly limited in scope and utility, so there are many commonly needed tasks that cannot be done with them. These limitations led to a large number of different programmers defining their own custom action elements for these tasks, which was clearly a waste of effort. This situation was remedied by the development of the JSTL, which includes action elements for many commonly needed tasks. The JSTL actually consists of five libraries. The *Core* library includes elements for simple flow control, in particular, selection and loop constructs, among others. The *XML Processing* library includes elements for transformations of XML documents, including those specified by XSLT style sheet documents. The *Internationalization and Formatting* library includes elements for formatting and parsing localized information. The *Relational Database Access* library includes elements for database access. The *Functions* library includes elements for Expression Language functions. (Expression Language is described in Section 11.5.3.)

Action elements specify actions that are described with statements in a programming language. In fact, libraries of action elements form programming languages that can be used to write dynamic actions in the form of a markup language. The difference between using the action elements and using Java is twofold: First, the syntax is completely different. Second, the special tags are simpler and easier to use than their Java equivalents. Therefore, they can be used by less experienced programmers.

---

6. A JavaBean is a special Java class that defines a reusable component. They are discussed in Section 11.6.

A directive is a message to the JSP container, providing information about the document and the sources of predefined action elements of the document. Directives can specify that content from other sources be included in a document. However, directives do not themselves produce content.

Syntactically, directives are tags that use `<%@` and `%>` delimiters. They use attributes to communicate to the container. The most commonly used directives are `page` and `taglib`. The `page` directive can include many different attributes, but only one is required, `contentType`, which is usually set to `text/html`, as in the following:

```
<%@ page contentType = "text/html" %>
```

The `taglib` directive is used to specify a library of action elements, or tags, that are used by the document. Many JSP documents use the JSTL. The URI for the JSTL is given as the value of the `uri` attribute in the `taglib` directive. Also included is the `prefix` attribute, to which is assigned the abbreviation, or prefix, that the document will use for tags from the JSTL. For example, a JSP document may contain the following directive:

```
<%@ taglib prefix = "c"
  uri = "http://java.sun.com/jsp/jstl/core" %>
```

This directive specifies the URI of the JSTL Core library and sets the prefix for its elements to `c`. Examples of the use of Core library action elements appear in the JSP examples later in this chapter.

11.5.3 Expression Language

The use of JSTL requires knowledge of its two primary technologies, the tag set of JSTL and the JSP Expression Language.

The JSP Expression Language (EL) is similar to the expressions (but only the expressions) of a scripting language such as JavaScript, at least in terms of simplicity. This similarity is most evident in the type coercion rules, which obviate most of the explicit type conversions that are required in writing expressions in strongly typed programming languages such as Java. For example, if a string is added to a number in EL, an attempt will be made by the JSP container to coerce the string to a number. This makes it convenient for dealing with form data, which is always in text form but often represents data of other types. It also makes EL easier for Web designers, who often are not Java programmers.

EL has no control statements such as selection and loop control. These are provided by action elements from the JSTL. EL is true to its name—it is just a language for simple expressions.

Syntactically, an EL expression is always introduced with a dollar sign ($) and delimited by braces, as shown in the following:

```
${ expression }
```

An EL expression consists of literals, the usual arithmetic operators, implicit variables[7] that allow access to form data, and normal variables. The literals can be numeric, either in the form of floating-point or integer values, Booleans (`true` or `false`), or strings delimited by either single or double quotes. A variable that has not been assigned a value has the value `null`. The only variables we will use are those created by the JSTL action elements.

The reserved words of EL are as follows:

```
and    div    empty   eq    false   ge      gt    instanceof
le     lt     mod     ne    not     null    or    true
```

Some of these are synonyms for symbolic operators, for example, `le` for `<=` and `lt` for `<`. This avoids any problems with having `<`, which begins tags, in a document.

An EL expression can appear in two places in a JSP document, in template text or in the values of certain attributes of certain action elements. EL often is used to set the attribute values of action elements. Because attributes take string values, the result of the evaluation of an EL expression is always coerced to a string.

EL uses data that comes from several different sources. The most interesting of these for our discussion is the form data sent in a request form, which is made available through the implicit variable, `param`. The `param` variable stores a collection of all of the form data values in much the same way JavaScript objects store their properties. To access a particular form data value, the name of the form element is used like a property name in JavaScript, catenated on the collection name with a period. For example, if there is a form element named `address`, it can be accessed with the following:

```
${param.address}
```

If the form element name includes special characters, an alternative access form is used, which is to treat the element name, specified as a literal string, as a subscript into the `param` array, as in the following:

```
${param['cust-address']}
```

EL defines a number of other implicit variables. Most of them are collections of values related to the request header, form values, cookies, and various scope variables. For example, the `pageContext` implicit variable is a reference to an object of class `javax.servlet.http.HttpServletRequest`, which has a long list of information about the request. Among these are `contentType`, `method`, which is the request method (`GET` or `POST`), `remoteAddr`, the IP of the client, and `contentLength`.

Although the values of EL expressions are usually implicitly placed in the result document, it is good to explicitly request such placement. This is accomplished by assigning the expression value to the `value` attribute of the out

---

7. Implicit variables are implicitly defined by the JSP container.

action element defined in the JSTL Core library. The recommended prefix for this library is c. To output the value of the address form element, the following could be used:

```
<c:out value = "${param.address}" />
```

The following example application, whose project is named tempConvertEL2, consists of an initial JSP document with a form that solicits a temperature in Celsius from the user. It uses another JSP document to process the form, which computes the equivalent temperature in Fahrenheit and returns a JSP document to the user to display that value. This application, like all others in this chapter, was developed using NetBeans. The initial JSP document follows:

```
<%--
   Document    : index.jsp (for the tempConvertEL2 application)
   Created on  : May 27, 2008, 9:43:43 AM
   Author      : bob
   Purpose     : To display a form to collect a Celsius
                 temperature from the user to be converted
                 to Fahrenheit
--%>

<%@page contentType="text/html" pageEncoding="UTF-8"%>
<!DOCTYPE HTML PUBLIC "-//W3C//DTD HTML 4.01 Transitional//EN"
    "http://www.w3.org/TR/html4/loose.dtd">

<html>
  <head>
    <meta http-equiv="Content-Type"
        content="text/html; charset=UTF-8">
    <title>JSP Page</title>
  </head>
  <body>
    <form action="tempConvertEL2.jsp" method="POST">
      <p>
        Celsius temperature:
        <input type="text" name="ctemp" value="" />
        <input type = "submit"
            value = "Convert to Fahrenheit" />
      </p>
    </form>
  </body>
</html>
```

The JSP document to process the form data for the `tempConvertEL2` application, `tempConvertEL2.jsp`, is as follows:

```
<%--
   Document    : tempConvertEL2.jsp
   Created on  : May 27, 2008, 9:49:07 AM
   Author      : bob
   Purpose     : To use EL to convert a given temperature
                 from Celsius to Fahrenheit
--%>

<%@page contentType="text/html" pageEncoding="UTF-8"%>
<%@taglib prefix = "c"
    uri = "http://java.sun.com/jsp/jstl/core" %>
<!DOCTYPE HTML PUBLIC "-//W3C//DTD HTML 4.01 Transitional//EN"
    "http://www.w3.org/TR/html4/loose.dtd">

<html>
  <head>
    <meta http-equiv="Content-Type"
        content="text/html; charset=UTF-8">
    <title>JSP Page</title>
  </head>
  <body>
    <p>
      Given temperature in Celsius:
      <c:out value = "${param.ctemp}" />
      <br /> <br />
      Temperature in Fahrenheit:
      <c:out value = "${(1.8 * param.ctemp) + 32}" />
    </p>
  </body>
</html>
```

This document performs the simple arithmetic computations required to convert the form data value of the component named `ctemp` to Fahrenheit with an EL expression. Both the input data value and the computed value are displayed.

11.5.4 JSTL Control Action Elements

The Core library of JSTL includes a collection of action elements for flow control in a JSP document. The most commonly used of these are `if`, `forEach`, `when`, `choose`, and `otherwise`. The form of an `if` element is as follows:

```
<c:if test = "boolean expression">
```

JSP elements and/or XHTML markup

```
</c:if>
```

An `if` element could be used to write a JSP document that served as both the requesting document and the responding document. It could determine whether the document was being processed (after being interacted with and sent to the server) by checking whether the `method` implicit variable had been set to `"POST"`. For example:

```
<c:if test = "pageContext.request.method == 'POST'}">
```

JSP elements and/or XHTML markup

```
</c:if>
```

The following is a JSP document for the temperature conversion previously done in the `tempConvertEL2` application using just one document, `index.jsp`. In this case, the document uses an `if` construct to decide which JSP code to return, the initial document that accepts the input, or the document that displays the result of the conversion.

```
<%--
    Document    : index.jsp (for the tempConvertEL1 application)
    Created on  : May 27, 2008, 2:30:02 PM
    Author      : bob
    Purpose     : Convert a given temperature in Celsius
                  to Fahrenheit. This is both the request
                  and the response document.
--%>

<%@ page contentType="text/html" pageEncoding="UTF-8"%>
<%@ taglib prefix = "c"
    uri = "http://java.sun.com/jsp/jstl/core" %>
<!DOCTYPE HTML PUBLIC "-//W3C//DTD HTML 4.01 Transitional//EN"
    "http://www.w3.org/TR/html4/loose.dtd">

<html>
  <head>
    <meta http-equiv="Content-Type"
        content="text/html; charset=UTF-8">
    <title> Temperature Converter </title>
  </head>
  <body>
    <c:if test = "${pageContext.request.method != 'POST'}">
      <form action="index.jsp"  method="POST">
        Celsius temperature:
        <input type="text" name="ctemp" value="" />
```

```
        <input type = "submit"
            value = "Convert to Fahrenheit" />
      </form>
    </c:if>
    <c:if test = "${pageContext.request.method == 'POST'}">
      Given temperature in Celsius:
        <c:out value = "${param.ctemp}" /> <br />
        The temperature in Fahrenheit:
      <c:out value = "${(1.8 * param.ctemp) + 32}" />
    </c:if>
  </body>
</html>
```

Through the browser's "view source," one can see the two versions of the body of the index.jsp document of the tempConvertEL1 project that come to the browser. The first listing below is the body of the initial document; the second is the body of the document after its form has been submitted with the input Celsius value of 100.

```
<body>
  <form action="index.jsp"  method="POST">
    Celsius temperature:
    <input type="text" name="ctemp" value="" />
    <input type="submit" value="Convert to Fahrenheit" />
  </form>
</body>

<body>
  Given temperature in Celsius:
    100 <br />
    The temperature in Fahrenheit:
  212.0
</body>
```

Checkboxes and menus have multiple values. The param implicit variable cannot be used to determine which values are set in the document that handles forms with these components. For this, there is the paramValues implicit variable, which has an array of values for each form element. The forEach JSTL action element can be used to iterate through the elements of a paramValues array.

forEach is related to the Java for-each statement—it iterates based on the elements of a collection, an iterator, an enumeration, or an array. The items attribute is assigned the data structure on which the iteration is based. The var attribute is assigned the variable name to which the structure's elements are assigned. For example, consider the following checkboxes:

```
<form method = "post">
  <label>
    <input type = "checkbox" name = "topping"
           value = "extracheese"
           checked = "checked" />      Extra cheese <br />
  </label>
  <label>
    <input type = "checkbox" name = "topping"
           value = "pepperoni" /> Pepperoni <br />
  </label>
  <label>
    <input type = "checkbox" name = "topping"
           value = "olives" /> Olives <br />
  </label>
  <label>
    <input type = "checkbox" name = "topping"
           value = "onions" /> Onions <br />
  </label>
  <label>
    <input type = "checkbox" name = "topping"
           value = "bacon" /> Bacon <br />
  </label>
  <input type = "submit"  value = "Submit" /> <br />
</form>
```

To list the checkboxes that were checked, the following could be used:

```
Pizza Toppings:
<c:forEach items = "${paramValues.topping}"
           var = "top">
  <c:out value = "${top}"> <br />
</c:forEach>
```

The forEach element can also be used to control a loop body based on a counter. For this, it uses the begin, end, and step attributes. For example, the following could be used to simply repeat the enclosed code ten times:

```
<c:forEach begin = "1" end = "10">
  ...
<c:/forEach>
```

Radio buttons must be handled differently than checkboxes. All radio buttons in a group have the same name. For this situation, JSTL has three action elements that allow the specification of a form of a switch construct. These three are choose, when, and otherwise. The choose element, which takes no attributes, encloses the whole construct. A when element specifies one of the selectable sequences of code. The when attribute, test, is set to an EL expression that describes the Boolean expression that controls entry into the body of the element. The `otherwise` element, which takes no attributes, specifies the code for the case when none of the Boolean expressions in the when elements is true. The first when element with a true `test` attribute is chosen, so if the `test` attributes of more than one of the when elements are true, only one is chosen. Consider the following example JSP document, which only displays the radio button that is currently pressed:

```
<%--
   Document    : index
   Created on : May 27, 2008, 2:51:28 PM
   Author     : bob
   Purpose    : To illustrate radio buttons in JSP.
--%>

<%@page contentType="text/html" pageEncoding="UTF-8"%>
<%@ taglib prefix = "c"
    uri = "http://java.sun.com/jsp/jstl/core" %>
<!DOCTYPE HTML PUBLIC "-//W3C//DTD HTML 4.01 Transitional//EN"
    "http://www.w3.org/TR/html4/loose.dtd">

<html>
  <head>
    <meta http-equiv="Content-Type" content="text/html;
        charset=UTF-8">
    <title> Illustrate radio buttons </title>
  </head>
  <body>
    <form method="POST">
      <p>
        <label>
          <input type="radio" name="payment" value="visa"
              checked="checked" />
          Visa <br />
        </label>
        <label>
          <input type="radio" name="payment" value="mc" />
          Master Card <br />
        </label>
        <label>
          <input type="radio" name="payment"
              value="discover" />
          Discover <br />
        </label>
```

```
        <label>
          <input type="radio" name="payment" value="check" />
          Check <br />
        </label>
        <input type = "submit" value = "Submit" />
      </p>
    </form>

    <!-- If the form has been submitted, display the payment
         method -->
    <c:if test = "${pageContext.request.method == 'POST'}">
      You have chosen the following payment method:
      <c:choose>
        <c:when test = "${param.payment == 'visa'}">
          Visa
        </c:when>
        <c:when test = "${param.payment == 'mc'}">
          Master Card
        </c:when>
        <c:when test = "${param.payment == 'discover'}">
          Discover
        </c:when>
        <c:otherwise>
          Check
        </c:otherwise>
      </c:choose>
    </c:if>
  </body>
</html>
```

11.6 JavaBeans

The JavaBeans architecture provides a set of rules for building a special category of Java classes that are designed to be reusable standalone software components. These components are called *beans*. Beans were designed to be used with visual system builders tools, such as NetBeans. To allow builder tools to easily determine the methods and data of a bean class, rigid naming conventions are required. All bean data that are to be exposed must have getter and setter methods whose names begin with `get` and `set`, respectively.[8] The remainder of the access method's names must be the data's variable name, spelled with an upper-

---

8. If the data happens to be Boolean type, `is` is used instead of `get`.

case letter. For example, if a bean has an integer variable named `celsius`, its getter and setter methods must be named `getCelsius` and `setCelsius`, respectively.

In JSP, beans often are used as containers for data used in a Web application. They are often built using JSP frameworks, such as NetBeans. Beans are written by programmers, but are often used by Web designers who do not have expertise in Java programming. When servlets and JSP are both used to build a Web application, beans are used to transmit data between the servlet and the JSP document. EL can also use the data in a bean directly.

The data stored in a bean are called *properties*. Property names are like variable names in Java, in that they are case sensitive. However, property names must always begin with lowercase letters. Properties are always private. To make them accessible to JSP documents, properties have either getter, setter, or getter and setter methods. All of these are public. The setter methods can include validation code, as well as any useful computation code. Setter methods return nothing, so their return type is `void`. Getter methods have the same return type as the property. A property that is both read and write accessible has both getter and setter methods. A read-only property has only a getter method; a write-only property has only a setter method.

Every bean class must have a parameterless constuctor. However, in Java if a class has no constructor, a parameterless constructor is implicitly provided, so the developer need not include one. The parameterless constructor allows tools to create bean instances, while knowing only the bean's class name.

To create an instance of a bean class and name it, the `<jsp:useBean>` JSP standard element is used. This element requires two attributes, id and `class`. The id attribute is assigned a name, which will be used in the document to reference the bean instance. The package name and class name of the bean class are assigned to the `class` attribute. For example, to create an instance of the bean class whose name is `Converter` and which is defined in the `org.mypackage.convert` package, the following could be used:

```
<jsp:useBean id = "mybean"
             class = "org.mypackage.convert.Converter" />
```

When a new bean instance is created with `<jsp:useBean>`, its properties only have values if they are assigned in the constructor of the bean class.

It may appear that bean instances are like Java objects. However, the two differ in purpose and use—objects are created and used by Java programs, whereas bean instances are created and used by JSP documents, without programming.

There are two other standard action elements for dealing with beans, `<jsp:setProperty>`, which sets a property value in a bean, and `<jsp:getProperty>`, which fetches a property value from a bean. The `<jsp:setProperty>` element takes three attributes, name, property, and value. The name of the bean instance (as given in the `<jsp:useBean>` id attribute) is assigned to the `name` attribute; the name of the property is assigned to the `property` attribute; the value to be given to the property is assigned to the `value` attribute. For example, to set the `sum` property of the `mybean` bean instance to the value `100`, the following could be used:

```
<jsp:setProperty name = "mybean" property = "sum"
                 value = "100" />
```

It is perhaps more common to set a property value to a value input by the user into a form component. In this case, the `value` attribute is not set in the `<jsp:setProperty>` element. If the property and the form component have the same name, no other attributes are required (beyond `name` and `property`). If the form component has a different name than the bean property, then the `param` attribute must be set to the name of the component. For example, to set the `zip` property of the `mybean` bean instance to the value of the component named `zipcode`, the following could be used:

```
<jsp:setProperty name = "mybean" property = "zip"
                 param = "zipcode" />
```

All values in JSP document are strings, as are all values input by a user to a form. If a value from a form or the value of a `value` attribute of `<jsp:setProperty>` is set to a property in a bean that has a type other than `String`, the value is implicitly converted to the type of the property.

When a `<jsp:getProperty>` element is processed by the JSP container, the fetched value is converted to a string and inserted into the document that contains the `<jsp:getProperty>` element, effectively replacing that element. The `<jsp:getProperty>` element takes two attributes, `name` and `property`, which are the same as those of the `<jsp:setProperty>` element. For example, to get the `sum` property from the `mybean` bean instance, use the following:

```
<jsp:getProperty name = "mybean" property = "sum" />
```

EL can also be used to fetch a property from a bean. In fact, this is a simpler way to do it. To get the `sum` property of the `mybean` bean instance, simply use the following:

```
${mybean.sum}
```

We now use the temperature conversion application to illustrate beans. The bean will store the Celsius and Fahrenheit versions of the input temperature. The getter method of the bean will include the code to convert the current Celsius temperature to Fahrenheit.

After creating the project and naming it `tempConvertB`, we build the initial document, `index.jsp`. This document includes a form with a text box to collect the Celsius temperature from the user. The form also has a *Submit* button to use the bean to compute the equivalent Fahrenheit temperature. The computation is part of the setter for the Fahrenheit temperature. The `index.jsp` file follows:

```
<%--
   Document    : index (for the tempConvertB application)
   Created on  : May 28, 2008, 7:51:24 PM
   Author      : bob
   Purpose     : This is the initial document for an application that
                 uses a bean in the conversion of a given Celsius
                 temperature to an equivalent Fahrenheit temperature.
--%>

<%@page contentType="text/html" pageEncoding="UTF-8"%>
<!DOCTYPE HTML PUBLIC "-//W3C//DTD HTML 4.01 Transitional//EN"
    "http://www.w3.org/TR/html4/loose.dtd">

<html>
  <head>
    <meta http-equiv="Content-Type" content="text/html;
      charset=UTF-8">
    <title> Initial document </title>
  </head>
  <body>
    <h2> Welcome to the temperature converter service </h2>
    <form name="Temperature input form" action="response.jsp"
        method="POST">
    Enter a temperature in Celsius:
    <input type="text" name="celsius" value="" size="4" />
    <p></p>
    <input type = "submit" value = "Convert to Fahrenheit" />
    </form>
  </body>
</html>
```

Next, we build the response JSP document. This document begins with a `<jsp:useBean>` element to create an instance of the bean. We name the bean mybean and give it the package name of `org.mypackage.convert` and the class name `Converter`. (We need to use these names when we create the bean class.) The next step is to include a `<jsp:setProperty>` element to move the value of the text box named celsius in the `index.jsp` document to the property named celsius of the bean. Because the text box and the property have the same name, the value attribute is not needed. Next, we insert another

`<jsp:setProperty>` element to compute and set the `fahrenheit` property in the bean. Finally, we add the `<jsp:getProperty>` element to move the value of the `fahrenheit` property to the response document. The complete response document, named `response.jsp`, follows:

```
<%--
    Document    : response (for the tempConvertB application)
    Created on  : May 28, 2008, 7:59:26 PM
    Author      : bob
    Purpose     : This is the response JSP document for the
                  tempConvertB application, which converts a given
                  Celsius temperature to the equivalent
                  temperature in Fahrenheit.
--%>

<%@page contentType="text/html" pageEncoding="UTF-8"%>
<!DOCTYPE HTML PUBLIC "-//W3C//DTD HTML 4.01 Transitional//EN"
    "http://www.w3.org/TR/html4/loose.dtd">

<html>
  <head>
    <meta http-equiv="Content-Type" content="text/html;
      charset=UTF-8">
    <title> Response document </title>
  </head>
  <body>
    <jsp:useBean id="mybean" scope="session"
        class="org.mypackage.convert.Converter" />
    <jsp:setProperty name="mybean" property="celsius" />
    Given Celsius temperature is:
    <jsp:getProperty name = "mybean" property = "celsius" />
    <jsp:setProperty name = "mybean" property = "fahrenheit"
        value = "" />
    <br />Equivalent temperature in Fahrenheit is:
    <jsp:getProperty name="mybean" property="fahrenheit" />
  </body>
</html>
```

The last step in developing the application is to write the bean class. A right click on the project (in the *Projects* list) produces a long menu. Selecting *New/Java class* switches to a new screen on which the bean class and its package can be named. We name them `Converter` and `org.mypackage.convert`, respectively, as in the response JSP document. We then type the bean into the center panel in the workspace. Following is a listing of the `Converter` bean class:

```java
// Converter - a bean for the tempConvertB application that
//             converts Celsius temperatures to Fahrenheit.
package org.mypackage.convert;

public class Converter {

  private String celsius;
  private String fahrenheit;

  public Converter() {
    celsius = null;
    fahrenheit = null;
  }

  public void setCelsius(String celsius) {
    this.celsius = celsius;
  }

  public String getCelsius() {
    return celsius;
  }

  public String getFahrenheit() {
    return fahrenheit;
  }

  public void setFahrenheit(String fahrenheit) {
    this.fahrenheit = Float.toString(
        1.8f * Integer.parseInt(celsius) + 32.0f);
  }
}
```

This completes the `tempConvertB` application. We have discussed only one very simple use of beans, but from this application the reader can gain a basic understanding of the fundamentals of beans.

11.7 JavaServer Faces

The JavaServer Faces (JSF) system adds another layer to the JSP technology. The primary contribution of JSF is an event-driven user interface programming model, for which JSP by itself has no capability. This greatly extends the ability to build interactive interfaces for Web applications. JSF is included in J2EE.

JSF includes the following specific capabilities: Client-generated events can be connected to server-side application code. User interface components can be bound to server-side data. User interfaces can be constructed with reusable and extensible components. User interface state can be saved and restored beyond the life of the server request. These allow JSF to provide an effective architecture for managing the state of components, processing component values, validating user input (through components), and handling user interface events.

As with JSP applications, JSF applications require an elaborate directory structure and two XML documents to support their deployment. And as with JSP, development frameworks relieve the developer from needing to deal with much of this. NetBeans has excellent support for JSF and is used to develop the example application in this section.

JSF documents define user interfaces with components. The values of these components are stored and manipulated with beans, which in JSF applications are often called *backing beans*.

11.7.1 The Core and HTML Tag Libraries

There are two libraries of standard JSF tags, the *Core Tags* and the *HTML Tags*. There are a total of 45 new tags in these two libraries. Nearly all JSF documents use tags from both libraries, so they include the following directives to include them and set a prefix for the tags of each. The prefixes shown are the conventional names.

```
<%@taglib prefix="f" uri="http://java.sun.com/jsf/core"%>
<%@taglib prefix="h" uri="http://java.sun.com/jsf/html"%>
```

The Core library includes 18 tags and is less complicated than the HTML library. Only one of the tags in the Core library is discussed here. The Core `view` tag is used to enclose all of the JSF tags in a document. So, most JSF documents have the `view` tag just after the body tag.

There are more than 25 tags in the HTML library, but only three of them are introduced here: `form`, `inputText`, and `outputText`. The `form` tag does nothing more than provide a container for the user interface component elements. It has many optional attributes, but none are required. The other two HTML tags discussed here are not as simple as `form`.

The `outputText` tag typically is used to display text or bean properties, using its `value` attribute. If the text is literal (though this is not the norm), it is assigned as a quoted string to the `value` attribute. If a bean property is to be displayed, it is specified with a JSF expression. JSF expressions have a form that is similar to that of JSP EL. Rather than EL's $, JSF expressions use a pound sign (#). For example, to display the `sum` property of the `MyBean` bean, the following could be used:

```
<h:outputText value = "#{MyBean.sum}" />
```

The `inputText` tag is used to specify a text box for user input, like the XHTML `input` tag with its `type` attribute set to `text`. This tag has a long list of optional attributes, although none is required. The `size` attribute of `inputText` is the same as that of the XHTML `input` tag. The `value` attribute is used to bind the value of the tag to a bean property. The property is referenced just as with `outputText`. In most applications, component values are bound to bean properties. The `onChange` attribute is used to specify JavaScript code to be executed when the component loses focus and its value has been changed since it gained focus. If the form is to be submitted when the value of the text box is changed, this JavaScript code is a call to the `submit` function. Another important attribute of `inputText`, `valueChangeListener`, is used for event handling. It is discussed in Section 11.7.2.

Following is a skeletal JSF document:

```
<%@page contentType="text/html"%>
<%@page pageEncoding="UTF-8"%>

<%@taglib prefix="f" uri="http://java.sun.com/jsf/core"%>
<%@taglib prefix="h" uri="http://java.sun.com/jsf/html"%>

<!DOCTYPE HTML PUBLIC
    "-//W3C//DTD HTML 4.01 Transitional//EN"
    "http://www.w3.org/TR/html4/loose.dtd">

<%-- (Initial documentation) --%>

<html>
  <head>
    ...
  </head>
  <body>
    <f:view>
      <h:form>
        <%-- (Form components) --%>
      </h:form>
    </f:view>
  </body>
</html>
```

11.7.2 JSF Event Handling

JSF event handling is similar to the event handling that is used for graphical user interfaces to Java applications. Events are defined by classes and event listeners are defined by classes that implement listener interfaces or by bean methods. Methods that are registered on a component as listeners are notified when an event occurs on that component.

There are three categories of events in JSF, value-change events, action events, and data-model events. Value-change events occur when the value of a component is changed. Action events occur when a button or hyperlink is activated. The topic of data-model events is complex and is not discussed here.

There are two ways an application can handle action or value-change events raised by a standard component. One option is to implement an event listener interface and register it on the component by nesting a `valueChangeListener` element or an `actionListener` element inside the component element. The alternative is to implement a method in the bean of the document that contains the component to handle the event. Such a method is referenced with a method-binding expression in an attribute of the component's tag.

Event listeners that handle the value-change events implement `javax.faces.event.ValueChangeListener`. Likewise, event listeners that handle action events implement `javax.faces.event.ActionListener`.

A class that implements `ValueChangeListener` must implement the `processValueChange` method, which takes the event object, whose class is `ValueChangeEvent`, as a parameter. This method is called by the JSF implementation when a value-change event is raised. The event object has both the old and new values of the component that raised the event. For example, the new value of the component can be accessed through `event.getNewValue()`. Following is a skeletal listener class for a value-change event:

```
public class TempChanged extends Object
    implements ValueChangeListener {
 public void processValueChange(ValueChangeEvent event)
    throws AbortProcessingException {
   ...
 }
 ...
}
```

Similar to value-change listeners, action listeners must implement `ActionListener` and the `processAction` method, which takes an `ActionEvent` parameter.

As previously mentioned, the two approaches to event handling each require their own handler registration process—if the handler is a method in a bean, it is registered with an attribute in the component element; if the handler is an implementation of the handler interface, it is registered with a nested element in the component element. Both the nested element and the attribute share the same name, `valueChangeListener` for value-change events and `actionListener` for action events. The following two skeletal `inputText` elements illustrate the forms of the two approaches for value-change events:

```
<h:inputText ...
        valueChangeListener = "#{MyBean.fixit}" />

<h:inputText ...
    <f:valueChangeListener type = "TempChanged" />
</h:inputText>
```

11.7.3 An Example Application

The example application of this section has the same purpose as the application in Section 11.6—to convert a given Celsius temperature to its equivalent Fahrenheit temperature. The difference is that in this section event handling is used to perform the conversion. Instead of the user clicking a button to cause the conversion, the conversion is performed when focus in the input text box is lost, which raises the value-change event. This application is named `tempConvertF`.

There are two ways to create JSF applications with NetBeans, one in which the developer drags XHTML, JSP, and JSF elements onto a NetBeans-generated skeletal JSF document. This approach is named the *JavaServer Faces* framework. In the other approach the developer drags JSF elements onto a JSF document. This is named the *Visual Web JavaServer Faces* framework. The visual approach (the latter) uses yet another tag library, whose conventional prefix is `webuijsf`. These documents actually use four different tag libraries, the Core and HTML JSF libraries, as well as the JSP and `webuijsf` libraries. The example here was developed using the nonvisual framework of NetBeans, in part to avoid the necessity of describing the `webuijsf` tag library.

Figure 11.16 shows the *New Web Application - Frameworks* window of NetBeans.

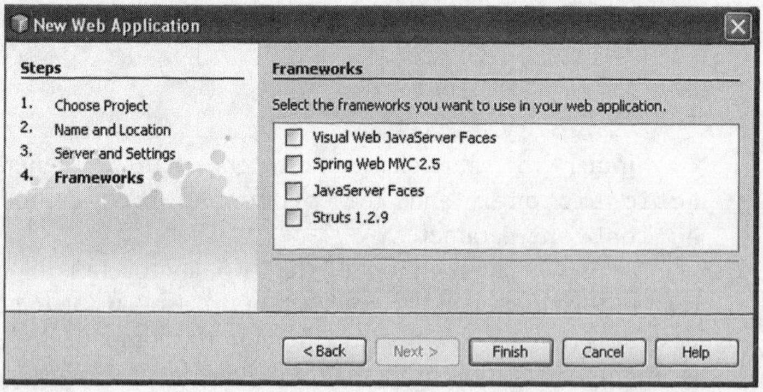

Figure 11.16 The *New Web Application—Frameworks* window of NetBeans

Following is the initial JSF document generated by NetBeans when the JavaServer Faces framework is chosen:

```
<%@page contentType="text/html"%>
<%@page pageEncoding="UTF-8"%>

<%@taglib prefix="f" uri="http://java.sun.com/jsf/core"%>
<%@taglib prefix="h" uri="http://java.sun.com/jsf/html"%>

<!DOCTYPE HTML PUBLIC "-//W3C//DTD HTML 4.01 Transitional//EN"
    "http://www.w3.org/TR/html4/loose.dtd">

<%--
   This file is an entry point for JavaServer Faces application.
--%>

<html>
  <head>
    <meta http-equiv="Content-Type" content="text/html;
      charset=UTF-8">
    <title>JSP Page</title>
  </head>
  <body>
    <f:view>
      <h1><h:outputText value="JavaServer Faces" /></h1>
    </f:view>
  </body>
</html>
```

For the example application, the user interface is added to this document, consisting of a form with an `inputText` component to collect the Celsius temperature from the user and register the event handler. The form also includes an `outputText` element to display the Fahrenheit equivalent. Following is this fleshed-out document:

```
<%@page contentType="text/html"%>
<%@page pageEncoding="UTF-8"%>

<%@taglib prefix="f" uri="http://java.sun.com/jsf/core"%>
<%@taglib prefix="h" uri="http://java.sun.com/jsf/html"%>
```

```
<!DOCTYPE HTML PUBLIC "-//W3C//DTD HTML 4.01 Transitional//EN"
                    "http://www.w3.org/TR/html4/loose.dtd">

<%--
   Document    : index (The initial document for the tempConvertF app)
   Created on  : Jun 15, 2008, 11:22:30 AM
   Author      : bob
   Purpose     : Get a temperature in Celsius from the user and
                 convert it to Fahrenheit, using an event handler
                 method in the bean as an event listener
--%>

<html>
  <head>
    <meta http-equiv="Content-Type" content="text/html;
        charset=UTF-8">
    <title> JSP Page</title>
  </head>
  <body>
    <f:view>
      <h2> Welcome to the temperature converter </h2>
      <h:form>
        Enter a temperature in Celsius:
        <h:inputText
            size = "4"
            value = "#{UserBean.celsius}"
            onchange = "submit()"
            valueChangeListener = "#{UserBean.convert}" />
        <br />
        The equivalent temperature in Fahrenheit is:
        <h:outputText value = "#{UserBean.fahrenheit}" />
      </h:form>
    </f:view>
  </body>
</html>
```

The bean for this application, named `UserBean`, is simple—it provides the storage for the Celsius and Fahrenheit temperatures, along with their getter and setter methods, and the event handler method, `convert`. The handler method has the same code as the bean used in Section 11.6. Following is the listing of the `UserBean` bean:

```java
/**
 * UserBean.java
 * @author bob
 * Purpose: To store the values of celsius and fahrenheit for the
 *          tempConvertF application. It also includes the convert
 *          method, which converts the value sent with the
 *          ValueChangeEvent event. The value is a temperature in
 *          Celsius to be converted to its equivalent in Fahrenheit.
 */
import javax.faces.event.ValueChangeEvent;
public class UserBean {

  private String celsius;
  private String fahrenheit;

  /** Creates a new instance of UserBean */
  public UserBean() {
    celsius = null;
    fahrenheit = null;
  }

  public void setCelsius(String celsius) {
    this.celsius = celsius;
  }

  public String getCelsius() {
    return celsius;
  }

  public void setFahrenheit(String fahrenheit) {
    this.fahrenheit = fahrenheit;
  }

  public String getFahrenheit() {
    return fahrenheit;
  }

  public String convert(ValueChangeEvent event) {
    celsius = (String) event.getNewValue();
    fahrenheit = Float.toString(1.8f *
        Integer.parseInt(celsius) + 32.0f);
    return fahrenheit;
  }
}
```

Figure 11.17 shows a display of the initial document of the `tempConvertF` application.

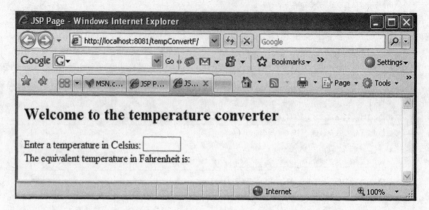

Figure 11.17 A display of the initial document of `tempConvertF`

Figure 11.18 shows the display of the `tempConvertF` application after a Celsius temperature has been entered and the focus has been shifted from the text box.

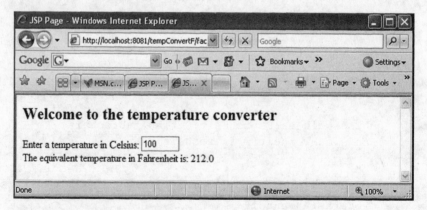

Figure 11.18 A display of `tempConvertF` after a temperature has been entered

This concludes our brief introduction to JSF.

Summary

A servlet is a Java program that resides on the Web server and is enacted when requests are received from Web clients. A program called a servlet container, which runs in the Web server, controls the execution of servlets. The most common uses of servlets are as server-side programs to dynamically generate Web documents.

Most user-written servlets are extensions to the predefined abstract class `HttpServlet`, which is a predefined descendant of `GenericServlet`, which implements the `Servlet` interface. Any class that is derived from `HttpServlet` must override at least one of its methods—most often `doGet` or `doPost`. The `doGet` and `doPost` methods take two parameters: one to get the input from the client and one to return results to the client. The `setContentType` method sets the MIME type for the return document. The `println` method of a `PrintWriter` object is used to create this document. The `getParameter` method is used to get the form values from the inquiry string of a form submission from the client. It is called through the request object parameter.

The easiest way to develop Java-based Web applications is with a framework. NetBeans is one of the most widely used Java Web frameworks.

A Web server can store information about clients on the clients themselves using cookies. A session begins with the first client request to a Web server and ends when the client's browser is stopped. Cookies are implemented on the server as objects of the `Cookie` class, which defines a collection of methods for dealing with cookie objects. Each cookie stores a single name/value pair. The server may send a cookie to the client along with the response to the client's request. Each subsequent request made by that client to that server includes the cookies (that are still alive) that have been sent by the server during any prior session. Each cookie has a lifetime, which is assigned with the `setMaxAge` method of the `Cookie` class. Cookies are destroyed when their lifetimes end. The servlet attaches a cookie to its response to a client with the `addCookie` method of the response object. Cookies are obtained from a client request with the `getCookies` method of the request object.

JSP is a collection of several approaches to support dynamic documents on the server. It is an alternative to servlets, putting some form of code in markup, rather than the servlet approach to producing markup with Java code. JSTL provides a set of action elements that form a programming language that has the form of markup. EL is a simple expression language used with JSP. The `if` JSTL element provides a selection construct; the `forEach` element provides a loop construct; and `choose`, `when`, and `otherwise` provide a multiple selection construct.

Servlets should be used when there is little static content in the return document; JSP should be used when there is little dynamic content.

JavaBeans are Java classes written using special conventions. In Web applications, JavaBean objects, called beans, are often used as containers for the data of the application. This data is exposed to JSP documents through getter and setter methods defined in the bean class. The data defined in a bean are called properties. The `<jsp:useBean>` JSP element is used to create an instance of a bean and give it a name accessible in the document. The `<jsp:setProperty>` element it used to set the value of a bean property. The `<jsp:getProperty>` element is used to fetch a property value from a bean. String values being set to properties that are not `String` type are coerced to their proper types. Non-`String` property values fetched from a bean are coerced to `String` type.

JSF adds to JSP the capabilities for building event-driven user interfaces to Web applications. There are two primary tag libraries used with JSF: the Core and HTML libraries. The form of a JSF document contains the JSF components that describe the user interface. Users create events by interacting with the components. The two most commonly used events are value-change events and action events. Events can be handled with classes that implement listener interfaces or with methods in the bean associated with the document that contains the components. JSF applications are usually developed with a framework, such as NetBeans.

Review Questions

11.1 Most user-written servlets extend what predefined class?

11.2 What is a session?

11.3 What is a servlet container?

11.4 Describe the two parameters to `doGet` and `doPost`.

11.5 What class of object is used to create XHTML output of a servlet to a client?

11.6 How does a servlet read form data values sent by a client to a servlet?

11.7 What must the first markup output of a servlet to a client be?

11.8 What are the primary benefits of using a framework for building servlet applications?

11.9 What are the purposes of the `doGet`, `doPost`, and `doPut` methods of the `HttpServlet` class?

11.10 Why would a Web server need to store information on a client about the client's previous requests?

11.11 What are the two standard tag libraries of JSF?

11.12 What is a cookie?

11.13 What exactly does the `<jsp:setProperty>` JSP element do?

11.14 What do the methods `setMaxAge`, `setValue`, and `getComment` do?

11.15 How is a cookie added to a response by a servlet?

11.16 How can a bean property be referenced in `EL`?

11.17 How does a servlet get a cookie coming from a client?

11.18 What are the two kinds of people who develop and maintain dynamic documents?

11.19 What is template text?

11.20 What are the five parts of the JSTL?

11.21 What happens during the compilation process for JSP documents?

11.22 What is the purpose of the `taglib` directive?

11.23 What is a `JavaBean`?

11.24 What is the syntactic form of an EL expression?

11.25 What are the two ways the `param` implicit variable can be used to access form values?

11.26 What is the form of a JSF expression?

11.27 Describe the syntax and semantics of the `forEach` element when it is used to iterate through a collection.

11.28 Describe the semantics of a `choose` element that includes several `when` elements.

11.29 How is the value of an `inputText` component associated with a bean property?

11.30 How are beans used by `JSP` applications?

11.31 What exactly does the `<jsp:useBean>` JSP element do?

11.32 What exactly does the `<jsp:getProperty>` JSP element do?

11.33 What is the primary contribution of JSF?

11.34 What are the two most commonly used events in JSF?

11.35 What form of constructor is required in a `bean` class?

11.36 What is the purpose and use of the `valueChangeListener` attribute?

Exercises

11.1 Provide a screen to collect the user name, e-mail id and country information. User should pickup the country from the list provided. Assign id (unique number in sequence) to every user registering.

11.2 The home page should have the option to register and login with email id. On click of login by providing the email id, check whether the email exists in the application, if so, greet the client with Name.

11.3 Revise the survey sample servlet, Survey.java, to display the results of the survey in a table, with female responses in one column and male responses in another.

11.4 Revise the survey sample servlet, Survey.java, to record the number of votes so far in the data file and then display that count every time a vote is submitted or a survey result is requested. Also, change the output table so that its data is a percentage of the total votes for the particular gender category.

11.5 Write the XHTML to create a form that collects favorite popular songs, including the name of the song, the composer, and the performing artist or group. This document must call a servlet when the form is submitted and another servlet to request a current list of survey results.

11.6 Create a Web application for shopping using Servlets and JSP. In the home page show the number of live (active) users in the application.

11.7 Modify the XHTML form for the election and the servlet VoteCounter to allow voters to vote for one additional office. The new office is named Catcatcher. Candidates for Catcatcher are Kitty Catland, Al El Gato, Kitten Katnip, Tommie Cat, and Fred Feline. The election results must be in terms of percentage of the total vote for an office. Votes are not counted if the client did not vote for both offices.

11.8 Write the XHTML to create a form with the following capabilities:
   a. A text widget to collect the user's name
   b. Four checkboxes, one each for the following items:
      i. Four 100-watt light bulbs for $2.39
      ii. Eight 100-watt light bulbs for $4.29
      iii. Four 100-watt long-life light bulbs for $3.95
      iv. Eight 100-watt long-life light bulbs for $7.49
   c. A collection of three radio buttons that are labeled as follows:
      i. Visa
      ii. Mastercard
      iii. Discover

11.9 Write a servlet that computes the total cost of the ordered light bulbs from Exercise 11.8 after adding 6.2 percent sales tax. The servlet must inform the buyer of exactly what was ordered, in a table.

11.10 Write the XHTML to provide a form that collects names and telephone numbers. The phone numbers must be in the format `ddd-ddd-dddd`. Write a servlet that checks the submitted telephone number to be sure that it conforms to the required format and then returns a response that indicates whether the number was correct.

11.11 Revise the survey example so that it displays the result as a horizontal bar, similar to a progress bar, ranging from 0–100.

11.12 Write and test a JSP document that displays the form of Exercise 11.8 and produces the same response document as Exercise 11.9.

11.13 Write an XHTML document that displays a form that collects three numbers from the client and calls a JSP document that computes the value of multiplying the three numbers together. The JSP document must use a bean.

11.14 Explain the two approaches to handling events in JSF.

11.15 Write a JSF application that accepts two numbers in text boxes and produces the sum, product, quotient, and difference between the first and the second when the second text box loses focus.

CHAPTER

12

Introduction to ASP.NET

This chapter introduces ASP.NET and discusses its use for developing Web applications on Microsoft's .NET computing platform. Before describing ASP.NET, it is necessary to introduce the .NET Framework, of which it is a part, and provide a few features of the programming language used in this chapter to discuss ASP.NET, C#. After these preliminaries, ASP.NET is introduced, including the structure of ASP.NET documents and code-behind files. Next, the server-side Web controls of ASP.NET are introduced. To describe the processing of ASP.NET pages, the whole life cycle of that processing is briefly discussed. Then page-level and control events are covered. Among the Web controls is a collection of controls used to validate form data, the validation controls. The next topic of the chapter is the use of the ASP.NET AJAX software to build Ajax-enabled applications. The last section of the chapter introduces Web services using ASP.NET. Seven complete examples are used to illustrate the concepts discussed.

The reader must keep in mind that many books have been devoted to describing ASP.NET. So, this one chapter can provide just a brief overview of this complex and powerful technology. Also, the chapter devotes about five pages only to introduce a bit of C#. If the reader is not familiar with Java, this is wholly inadequate. Such readers are advised to study Appendix A before tackling this chapter. However, because of the similarity of C# to Java, Java programmers should be able to begin to use C# for ASP.NET documents after studying this chapter.

12.1 Overview of the .NET Framework

.NET is an umbrella term for a collection of technologies that was announced by Microsoft in early 2000. In January 2002 the software to support .NET was released. It was quickly adopted by a significant part of the Web software industry. It will undoubtedly continue to be a major player in this industry in the future.

12.1.1 Background

.NET was developed in recognition that the future of a significant part of the computing business lies in Web-based software services, in which components of a software system may reside on different computers in different places on the Internet. Prior to .NET, Microsoft's technology for distributed component-based systems was named COM.

A *component* is an encapsulation of software that can stand by itself and be used by other components, without those components knowing how the functionality of the component is implemented. Components can also be created with technologies other than COM. JavaBeans is a technology developed by Sun Microsystems to support distributed component-based computing using Java. The primary difference between JavaBeans and COM components is that COM components can be written in a variety of different programming languages—they are language neutral.

The .NET Framework is exactly that—a framework for the development and deployment of .NET software. In .NET, the central concept is that a software system or service consists of a collection of components that can be written in different languages and reside on different computers in different locations. Also, because of the diversity of employed languages, the collection of tools for development and deployment must be language neutral. These ideas permeate all of the parts of the .NET Framework.

12.1.2 .NET Languages

Initially, .NET included five languages: Visual Basic .NET (VB.NET), Managed C++ .NET, JScript .NET, J# .NET, and a new language, C#. VB.NET is based on VB 6.0, a language widely used for Web programming and other software development that includes graphical user interfaces (GUIs). VB.NET differs from VB in many ways, most importantly in that it is a full-fledged object-oriented language, whereas VB is not. Managed C++ .NET is a garbage-collected version of C++. JScript .NET is based on JavaScript but also provides full support for object-oriented programming. J# .NET is Microsoft's version of Java. C# is briefly described in Section 12.2. There are now a large number of languages that run under .NET, including COBOL, Eiffel, Fortran, Perl, and Python. Work is underway to add more languages to the list.

The multilanguage aspect of .NET sets it apart from other such systems. The advantage of supporting a variety of programming languages is that there is an easy migration path from software in many different languages to .NET. Organizations that make heavy use of any of the .NET languages can easily transition to .NET. Programmers who are experienced and skilled in almost any common language can quickly become productive in a .NET environment. Although it makes reuse much more feasible, having a system composed of components written in different languages is not all good. One important disadvantage is that it complicates maintenance.

One disadvantage that .NET suffers relative to JavaBeans is that although .NET has been ported to several non-Windows platforms, such systems have seen only limited use. So, while JavaBeans is now supported on a wide variety of systems, including Windows, .NET is still used almost exclusively on Windows.

12.1.3 The Common Language Runtime

The base technology for .NET is the Common Language Runtime (CLR), which provides language-neutral services for the processing and execution of .NET software. Among the most important services of the CLR are garbage collection, type checking, debugging, and exception handling. These services are used for all of the .NET languages.

For every .NET language, the CLR has a compiler to translate source programs to a common intermediate language, which was originally named Microsoft Intermediate Language (MSIL) but now is usually called Intermediate Language (IL). After compilation, all IL programs have the same form, regardless of the original source language. Before execution, IL programs are incrementally compiled to machine code for the host machine by a Just-In-Time (JIT) compiler, which is part of the CLR. A JIT compiler translates a method to machine code only when the method is called. Once compiled, the machine code version of the method is kept for the duration of execution of the program so that subsequent calls do not require recompilation. Because some executions of some programs do not cause all of the program's methods to be called, this is an efficient approach to compilation. In .NET, it is also possible to compile a whole program into machine code before execution begins. JIT compilers are commonly used for Java program execution. One major difference between Java's approach to program execution and that of the .NET languages is that IL programs are never interpreted, as bytecode (the Java intermediate language) programs sometimes are. In fact, the .NET Framework does not include an IL interpreter, which would be similar to the Java Virtual Machine.

12.1.4 The Common Language Infrastructure

To make it possible to use the CLR for multiple languages, those languages must adhere to a set of common characteristics. These are specified by the Common Language Infrastructure (CLI), which consists of two specifications, the Common Type System (CTS) and the Common Language Specification (CLS).

The CTS defines a set of types that are supported by .NET languages. It also provides a mapping from every type in each language to its corresponding common type. For example, the CTS defines a type named `Int32`, which is a 32-bit signed integer type. The C# type `int` corresponds to `Int32`. The concept of common base types is analogous to what is done with CORBA (`http://www.corba.org`), which defines a similar set of types and gives a mapping from various languages to these common types. In CTS, types occur in two natural categories, value types and reference types. *Value types* directly refer to values in memory cells; that is, the value of a value type object is a value. *Reference types* refer to or address a memory cell that has a value. So, the value of a reference type is not a value; it is an address.

Having common types among languages is, of course, necessary if components in those languages are expected to interoperate correctly. All types of all .NET languages derive from a single type, `System.object`.

The CLS defines the language features that must be supported by all .NET languages. .NET languages can, however, include features beyond what is specified in CLS. Of course, use of such features in a program will jeopardize the possibility of interoperation of that program with programs in languages that do not support those features. Examples of CLS restrictions follow:

1. No operator overloading

2. No pointers

3. Identifiers are not case sensitive

Interestingly, the new .NET language, C#, includes all of these. However, they should not be used in C# programs that will interoperate with components written in other .NET languages that do not include them. For example, VB.NET identifiers are not case sensitive. If a C# component must interoperate with a VB.NET component, the C# component must not use two different identifiers in the interface to the VB.NET component whose only difference is case (for example, `Sum` and `sum`). To design a language that can be a .NET language, the designer must ensure that all of the CLI features are supported.

The .NET Framework includes a large collection of class libraries called the Framework Class Libraries (FCL). The initial release of FCL included more than 4,000 classes that support a wide array of application areas. For example, there are APIs for networking, reflection, Web forms, database access, and file system access. Also included are APIs for access to Windows features such as the registry, as well as other Win32 functions. These functions are called through FCL classes and are executed in the CLR.

Perhaps the most important result of having the CLI and the CLR is that components written in any of the .NET languages can use any class in the FCL. More striking, perhaps, is the result that a component in any .NET language can use classes defined in any other component written in any other .NET language. This enables a program to call the methods of a class written in any other .NET language. It also allows a program in any .NET language to subclass classes written in any other .NET language. For example, a C# program can subclass a class written in VB.NET. It can also call the methods of a class written in managed C++.

12.2 A Bit of C#

This section provides a brief introduction to a few parts of C#, primarily features that are often used in ASP.NET and that differ from their Java counterparts. It is written with the assumption that the reader is familiar with Java. C# is used for the examples in this chapter, but little of the language used will be unfamiliar to Java programmers.

12.2.1 Origins

C# is a relatively recently designed object-oriented language (released in 2002), designed to fit the needs of .NET programming. Like most other "new" programming languages, most of C# is not in fact new but borrowed from existing languages. C# can be thought of as the most recent iteration of the sequence of C-based languages. C++ was derived from C (and SIMULA 67), and Java was derived, at least partially, from C++. C# is derived from both C++ and Java, having been based on Java but including some features that are part of C++ but not Java. From Java, C# gets single inheritance, interfaces, garbage collection, the absence of global types or variables, and its level of assignment type coercion. From C++, C# gets pointers, operator overloading, a preprocessor, structs, and enumerations (although its structs and enumerations differ significantly from those of C++). From Delphi and VB, C# inherits properties. Finally, from J++ (Microsoft's version of Java), C# gets delegates. Among the new C# features are indexes, attributes, and events. Overall, C# is less complex than C++ without giving up much of the expressivity of C++, which is also the case with Java. Although C# is more complex than Java, it is also more expressive.

12.2.2 Primitive Types and Expressions

C# has two categories of data: primitives and objects. C# includes a long list of primitive types, ranging from `byte`, which is an unsigned one-byte integer, and char, which is a two-byte Unicode character, to int, float, double, and decimal, which is a 16-byte decimal type that can store up to 28 decimal digits.

Symbolic constants are defined by preceding the type name in a declaration with the const reserved word. Every symbolic constant declaration must include an initial value. For example:

```
const float pi = 3.14159265;
```

C# has the same collection of arithmetic operators as Java, so its expressions are also like those of Java. Likewise, the C# assignment statements are identical to those of Java.

12.2.3 Data Structures

The C# String type is similar to that of Java. Its StringBuilder class is the same as Java's StringBuffer class. The String class provides methods for operating on strings, including Split. The Split method separates a string value into substrings, which are placed in the returned array. The parameter to Split is an array of characters, where any of the characters that are found in the string object on which Split is called specify the places to split the string. For example, consider the following code:

```
string str = "apples,prunes carrots,grapes";
char[] delimiters = new char[] {' ', ','};
String[] substrings;
substrings = str.Split(delimiters);
```

After executing this code, the value of substrings is ["apples", "prunes", "carrots", "grapes"].

C# also supports regular expressions, like those of JavaScript, which can be used to specify the boundaries among substrings of a string in a split operation. In that case, the Split method of the regular expression class, Regex, is used.

The .NET FCL defines an extensive variety of collection classes, including Array, ArrayList (dynamic length arrays), Queue, and Stack. Although Array is a class, the syntax of array references is exactly like that of C. Because it is a class, array access is through reference variables. The following is an example of a declaration of a reference to an int array:

```
int[] myIntArray;
```

The variable myIntArray can reference any single-dimensioned array of int elements. An array object is created with the new operator, as in the following statement:

```
myIntArray = new int[100];
```

myIntArray now references an array of 100 integers on the heap.

The Array class provides a large collection of methods and properties. Among the methods are BinarySearch, Copy, and Sort. The most frequently used property is `Length`. For example, the following assignment statement sets len to 100:

```
len = myIntArray.Length;
```

12.2.4 Control Statements

The control statements of C# are nearly identical to those of Java (as well as the other C-based languages). Two differences are the `foreach` and `switch` statements. The `foreach` statement is a data-structure-controlled iterator that has different syntax than its counterpart in Java. It can be used on arrays and other collections. The syntax of `foreach` is as follows:

```
foreach (type identifier in collection) { ... }
```

For example:

```
foreach (int myInt in myIntArray) { ... }
```

The `switch` statement of C# is similar to that of Java but with one important restriction. The `switch` statements of C, C++, and Java all suffer the same problem: Although in the vast majority of cases, control should exit the construct after a selected segment has executed, the default is that control flows to the next segment after the selected segment has executed. Therefore, most segments in `switch` constructs must include a `break` statement. Leaving out the `break` is a common error in `switch` constructs. To avoid these errors, the C# `switch` requires that every selectable segment in a `switch` construct must end with an unconditional branch instruction, either a `break` or a `goto`. To force control to continue to the next segment, a `goto` is used. For example, consider the following `switch` construct:

```
switch (value) {
  case -1:
    Negatives++;
    break;
  case 0:
    Zeros++;
     goto case 1;
  case 1:
    Positives++;
  default:
    Console.WriteLine("Error in switch \n");
}
```

Note that `WriteLine` is a method of the `Console` class that is used to produce output to the screen.

C# includes a goto statement, although it cannot be used to branch into a statement block. Its statement labels are like those of C and C++.

12.2.5 Classes, Methods, and Structures

C# is a pure object-oriented programming language in the same sense as Java. There are no subprograms except methods, which can only be defined in classes (and structs) and can only be called through objects or classes. Most of the syntax and semantics of C# classes and methods are the same as those of Java. In the following paragraphs, the most important differences are discussed.

Parameters to methods can be passed by value, passed by reference, or passed by result. These three implement in mode, which is the default mode (one-way communication to the method), inout mode (two-way communication between the caller and the called method), and out mode (one-way communication from the called method to the calling method) parameter semantics, respectively. Reference variables implicitly have pass-by-reference semantics. Pass by reference is specified for value types by preceding the formal parameter with the `ref` reserved word. Pass by result is specified for value types by preceding the formal parameter with the `out` reserved word.

In some object-oriented languages, such as Java, it is relatively easy to write methods that accidentally override inherited methods.[1] This happens because the author of the new method either forgets or is unaware that a method with the same name already exists in the class ancestry. To avoid this error, C# requires methods that are allowed to be overriden to be marked `virtual`. Furthermore, any method that is meant to override an inherited method must be marked `override`. If a method is defined that has the same protocol as an inherited method but is not meant to override it, it must be marked `new`. Such a method hides the inherited version.

A struct in C++ is very similar to a class. In C#, however, a struct is quite different from the classes of the language. A C# struct is a lightweight class that does not support inheritance or subclassing. However, C# structs can implement interfaces and have constructors. Structs are value types, which means they are allocated on the runtime stack. The syntactic form of a struct declaration is identical to that of a class, except the reserved word `struct` is used in place of `class`. All C# primitive types are implemented as structs.

12.2.6 Exception Handling

Exception handling in C# is similar to that of Java. All exception classes are descendants of `Exception`, which has two subclasses, `SystemException` and `ApplicationException`. Some common system exceptions are `IndexOutOfRangeException`, and `NullReferenceException`, and

---

1. This would only happen if the author of the inherited method wants to allow it to be overridden somewhere among the class descendants. If the method should never be overridden, it is marked `final`, which prevents all descendant classes from overriding it.

`ArithmeticException`. The `try-catch-finally` structure of C# is the same as that of Java, except C# `catch` blocks do not require a parameter. Such a `catch` catches any exception.

12.2.7 Output

In contemporary object-oriented programming languages, programs have access to large, comprehensive, and complex class libraries that provide services and commonly needed types. For .NET, this is the FCL. The most commonly used part of the .NET FCL is `System`. This class defines a namespace for its constituents, also named `System`. The `System` namespace provides classes for input and output, string manipulation, event handling, threading, and collections, among others.

Output from an ASP.NET document, which becomes part of the XHTML document returned to the browser, is generated through a `Response` object. The `Response` class defines the `Write` method, whose string parameter is markup. For example, consider the following:

```
Response.Write("<h1> Today's Report </h1>");
```

If the output must be formatted, for example, to include the values of variables, the `Format` method of the `string` type (`string` is an alias for the `System.String` class) is used. For example, consider the following:

```
string msg = string.Format("The answer is: {0} <br />",
                           answer);
Response.Write(msg);
```

The notation `{0}` specifies the position in the string for the value of the variable named after the string.

The `using` statement is used to abbreviate the names of classes in a namespace. For example,

```
using System;
```

allows the program to access the classes defined in `System` without using the prefix `System` on the names of those classes.

Rather than the packages of Java, C# uses namespaces. A namespace is specified with the `namespace` reserved word, for example,

```
namespace myStuff {
    ...
}
```

12.3 Introduction to ASP.NET

ASP.NET is a large and complex topic. This section provides a brief introduction to its fundamentals.

12.3.1 The Basics

ASP.NET is a Microsoft technology for building dynamic Web documents (ASP is an acronym for Active Server Pages). Dynamic ASP.NET documents are supported by programming code executed on the Web server. Although ASP.NET documents can also include client-side scripts, we focus on the server side. ASP.NET is based on its predecessor, ASP, which allowed embedded server-side scripts written in either JScript (Microsoft's JavaScript) or VBScript, a scripting dialect of VB. Both of these languages are purely interpreted, making their execution much slower than that of code written in compiled languages. There are a few other problems with using purely interpreted code to provide server-side dynamic documents. First, documents that include both scripting code and XHTML are complex, especially if they are large. Mixing markup and programming code, which mixes presentation and business logic, creates a confusing document. Furthermore, Web markup designers and programmers must deal with the same document. Second, purely interpreting scripts before delivering documents is inefficient. Third, there is the problem of reliability of code written in scripting languages, in part because they use either dynamic typing or relaxed typing rules. Also, in many scripting languages array index ranges are not checked.

As we saw in Chapter 11, "Java Web Software," JSP offers one solution to these problems: Use Java to describe the computation associated with user interactions with Web documents. The Java language is much more reliable than the scripting languages, largely because of the strict type checking and array index range checking. Furthermore, compiled Java code is faster than interpreted scripting code. Finally, although Java can be directly embedded in XHTML documents with JSP, it is entirely separate when JavaBeans are used. ASP.NET provides an alternative to JSP. ASP.NET allows the server-side programming code to be written in any of the .NET languages.

Programming code that is part of a Web application but resides outside of the ASP.NET document (the XHTML document file) is placed in a separate file called the *code-behind* file. It is good to keep all program code separate from the ASP.NET document, for the same reasons that it is good to keep JavaScript in separate files, rather than embedded in an XHTML document.

Every ASP.NET document is compiled into a class, which resides in an assembly. An assembly is the unit in which compiled classes are stored in .NET. An assembly is also the unit of deployment for .NET. Compiling a markup document, which may or may not include embedded programming code, into a class is precisely what happens to JSP documents—they are compiled into servlets, which are classes. From a programmer's point of view, developing dynamic Web documents (and the supporting code) in ASP.NET is similar to developing non-Web applications. Both involve defining classes based on library classes, implementing interfaces from a library, and calling methods defined in library classes. An application class uses and interacts with existing classes. In ASP.NET, this is exactly the same for Web applications. Web documents are designed by designing classes.

The class to which an ASP.NET document is compiled is a descendant of `System.Web.UI.Page`, from which it inherits a collection of members. Among the most commonly used are the `Request` and `Response` objects, the `HTML-Controls` and `WebControls` classes, and the `IsPostBack` property. The `Write` method of the `Response` object is used to create output from an ASP.NET document. The two controls classes define the large collection of server-side controls that are available to ASP.NET documents. Sample documents that use the controls classes appear in Section 12.4. The `IsPostBack` property is used to determine whether the current request is a result of a user interaction with a form (as opposed to an initial request for a document). Its use is illustrated in a sample document in Section 12.4.2.

ASP.NET documents that do not use code-behind files are compiled into direct subclasses of `Page`. Code-behind files also are compiled into subclasses of `System.Web.UI.Page`. We call the class that results from compiling the ASP.NET document the *document class*. Note that a document class is pure C# source code rather than an intermediate code version.[2] Document classes that use a code-behind file are subclasses of the code-behind class. The code-behind class is an intermediate class between the document class and `System.Web.UI.Page`. So, programming code in an ASP.NET document inherits from both `Page` and the class of the code-behind file. Inheritance diagrams for ASP.NET documents with and without code-behind files are shown in Figure 12.1.

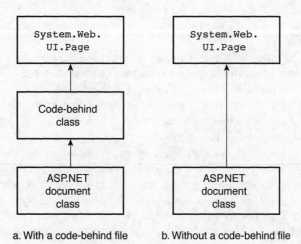

a. With a code-behind file   b. Without a code-behind file

Figure 12.1 Inheritance diagrams for ASP.NET documents with and without code-behind files

---

2. This is technically a misuse of the term "compile," although ASP.NET documents are translated from their original form to C# programs.

12.3.2   ASP.NET Documents

ASP.NET documents can include a number of different elements. First, they can contain XHTML markup, including standard XHTML comments. This markup can include static XHTML, XHTML elements made dynamic by client-side scripts, and XHTML elements made dynamic by server-side code. Second, an ASP.NET document can include one or more directives, the most common of which is `Page`, which can have any of a large number of different attributes. Directives are delimited by `<%@` and `%>`. Third, documents can have *render blocks*, which use the `<%` opening tag and `%>` closing tag and have programming code as content. This code, which cannot include subprogram definitions, is placed (by the document compiler) in a function of the class of the document when the document is translated to a class. This function's body typically consists of method calls and output statements to create the static XHTML of the document. The function is executed when the document class is executed (which produces the XHTML document that is returned to the requesting browser). Fourth, documents can include programming code as the content of script elements that include the attribute `runat` set to `"server"`. Such code is called a *declaration block* because it is not implicitly executed. Subprograms, including event handlers, are defined in declaration blocks. The code in declaration blocks is inserted directly into the class created for the document. Finally, documents can include server-side comments, which appear in elements that use the opening tag `<%--` and the closing tag `--%>`.

Directives appear in the same tag form as render blocks. For example, the general form of a directive is as follows:

```
<%@ directive-name attributes %>
```

The only directive required in every ASP.NET document that includes embedded programming code is `Page`. For these documents, the `Page` directive must minimally include a `Language` attribute, which is assigned the name of the .NET language that is used for embedded programming code in the document. This, of course, is necessary to inform the CLR which compiler is to be used to compile the document.

At this point, an example application is in order. The following simple ASP.NET document uses C# code in a render block to compute and display the number of days, hours, and minutes left in the year.[3] The `Now` method of the .NET `DateTime` class is used to get the current date and time in a `DateTime` object. The constructor for this class is then used to create the second `DateTime` object with the date January 1, 2009. The time between the two objects is computed with the `Subtract` method of the `DateTime` object for New Years Day. Then the values returned by the `Days`, `Hours`, and `Minutes` methods of that object are converted to strings to produce the output.

---

3. For simplicity, our example assumes the current year is 2008.

Following is the ASP.NET document for our simple example:

```
<!-- ex1.aspx
     A simple example of an ASP.NET document
     It displays the number of days, hours, and minutes
     left this year (2008)
     -->
<%@ Page language="c#" %>

<html xmlns = "http://www.w3.org/1999/xhtml">
  <head> <title> Ex1 </title>
  </head>
  <body>
    <h3> Days, hours, and minutes left this year </h3>
    <%
       string msg, days, hours, minutes;
       DateTime rightnow, newYears;
       TimeSpan timeSpan;

       // Set date/time of right now and new years day
       rightnow = DateTime.Now;
       newYears = new DateTime(2009, 1, 1);

       // Compute the difference in time/dates
       timeSpan = newYears.Subtract(rightnow);

       // Compute and display the differences in days, hours, and
       // minutes
       days = timeSpan.Days.ToString();
       msg = string.Format("Days: {0},  ", days);
       Response.Write(msg);
       hours = timeSpan.Hours.ToString();
       msg = string.Format("Hours: {0},  ", hours);
       Response.Write(msg);
       minutes = timeSpan.Minutes.ToString();
       msg = string.Format("Minutes: {0} <br />", minutes);
       Response.Write(msg);
    %>
  </body>
</html>
```

12.3.3 Code-Behind Files

As stated in Section 12.3.1, it is better to keep programming code separate from documents, which also separates program logic from presentation. In ASP.NET, this is done by storing programming code in code-behind files.

To illustrate the difference between declaration blocks and code-behind files, ex1.aspx is rewritten as ex2.aspx and the code-behind file ex2.aspx.cs, which are shown next. The process of ex1.aspx is written as a method and only the call to it is left in the new ASP.NET document, ex2.aspx. The code-behind file defines the class Ex2, and its method, timer.

Notice that the Page directive in this ASP.NET document includes two new attributes. The Inherits attribute specifies that this document inherits from its code-behind file's class. The name used for this attribute is the same as the base name of this file. Also included is the Src attribute, which gives the full name of the code-behind file. When the Src attribute is included, the code-behind file is implicitly compiled the first time its associated ASP.NET document is requested. If the code-behind file is changed, the next request for the associated ASP.NET file implicitly causes its recompilation.

If the Src attribute is absent, the code-behind file must be explicitly compiled and placed in the bin subdirectory of the directory in which the ASP.NET document is stored, before the associated ASP.NET document is requested. This approach has the advantage of allowing the detection and repair of syntax errors in the code-behind file before deployment.

```
<!-- ex2.aspx
     A simple example of an ASP.NET document with a code-behind
     file. It has the same functionality as ex1.aspx
     -->
<%@ Page language="C#"  Inherits = "Ex2"  Src = "ex2.aspx.cs" %>

<html xmlns = "http://www.w3.org/1999/xhtml">
  <head> <title> Ex2 </title>
  </head>
  <body>
    <h3> Days, hours, and minutes left this year </h3>
    <%
      timer();
    %>
  </body>
</html>
```

```
// ex2.aspx.cs
//    The code behind file for ex2.aspx
//    Defines a class with a method to compute and
//    display the days, hours, and minutes left
//    this year

using System;
using System.Web;
using System.Web.UI;

public class Ex2 : Page {

  string msg, days, hours, minutes;
  TimeSpan timeSpan;

  public void timer() {

    // Set date/time of New Years Day and right now
    DateTime rightnow = DateTime.Now;
    DateTime newYears = new DateTime(2009, 1, 1);

    // Compute the difference in time/dates
    timeSpan = newYears.Subtract(rightnow);

    // Compute and display the differences in days, hours, and
    // minutes
    days = timeSpan.Days.ToString();
    msg = string.Format("Days: {0},  ", days);
    Response.Write(msg);
    hours = timeSpan.Hours.ToString();
    msg = string.Format("Hours: {0},  ", hours);
    Response.Write(msg);
    minutes = timeSpan.Minutes.ToString();
    msg = string.Format("Minutes: {0} <br />", minutes);
    Response.Write(msg);
  }
}
```

The reason the using directives are included in the code-behind file but not in the ASP.NET document is that the ASP.NET code is a subclass of the class defined in the code-behind file.

The display of the output of `ex1.aspx` is shown in Figure 12.2.

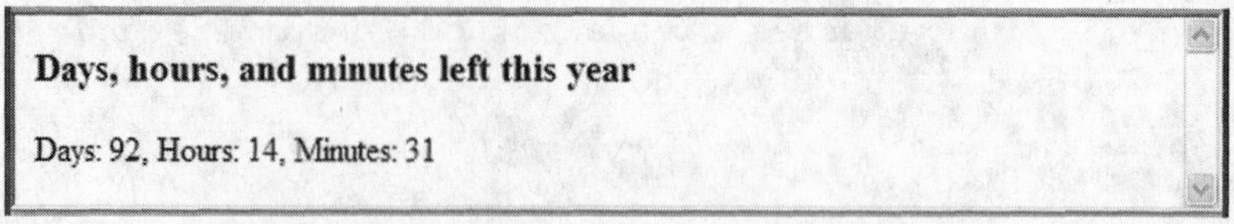

Days, hours, and minutes left this year

Days: 92, Hours: 14, Minutes: 31

Figure 12.2 A display of the output of `ex1.aspx`

12.4   ASP.NET Controls

ASP.NET controls are related to XHTML components, but they have associated program code that is executed on the server. Therefore, they are called *server controls*. There are two categories of ASP.NET server controls, HTML controls and Web controls. HTML controls are now far less used than the Web controls, so HTML controls are not covered in this book.

12.4.1   Web Controls

In addition to controls that correspond to the ordinary XHTML components, there are many more Web controls. For example, there are controls for checkbox lists, radio button lists, drop-down lists, and list boxes. In addition, there are special controls for form data validation and data binding. The most commonly used Web controls are shown in Table 12.1.

Some additional Web controls are described in the following paragraphs. All of the Web controls are in the namespace with the prefix `asp`, so the tag names are all qualified with `asp:`. For example, a text box control is specified with the following:

```
<asp:textbox id = "phone"  runat = "server" />
```

Some of the Web controls do not correspond to XHTML components and are rendered as combinations of widgets. Among these are `Xml`, `Panel`, `AdRotator`, and the list controls. The `Xml` control provides the ability to include XSL transformations on XML input as part of the output XHTML document. The `Panel` control provides a container for other controls, for those situations where you want to control the position or visibility of the contained controls as a unit. The `AdRotator` provides a way to produce different content on different requests implicitly. An `AdRotator` control is translated to an XHTML image and a link.

The `ListControl` class has four subclass controls. Two of them are familiar, `DropDownList` and `ListBox`, and both are converted to XHTML select elements. The `ListBox` control can display one or more of its items. The num-

Table 12.1 Commonly used Web controls and related XHTML elements

Web Control Type	XHTML Element
AdRotator	`<img>` and `<link>`

Button	`<input type = "button" />`
	`<input type = "submit" />`
	`<input type = "reset" />`

Calendar	None
Checkbox	`<input type = "checkbox" />`
CheckBoxList	None
DropDownList	`<select>`
Image	`<img>`
ImageButton	None
ImageMap	None
Label	None
Panel	`<div>`
RadioButton	`<input type = "radio" />`
RadioButtonList	None
Table	`<table>`
TableCell	`<th>`, `<td>`
TableRow	`<tr>`
TextBox	`<input type = "text" />`

ber of display items defaults to four but can be set to any number. A vertical scrollbar is implicitly included if the control has more items than the number it can display. More than one item in a ListBox can be selected. The DropDownList control remains hidden until the user clicks its button. The browser chooses the number of items displayed when the drop-down button is clicked. DropDownList controls do not allow multiselection mode.

The two other ListControl subclass controls are CheckBoxList and RadioButtonList. Both of these are normally translated to table XHTML elements. In both cases, the purpose is to allow programming code access to the items in the lists. This supports the possibility of adding and/or deleting list items dynamically as the result of user interaction. It also makes it possible for list items to be fetched from a database or other external source.

12.4.2 Life Cycle of a Simple ASP.NET Document

An ASP.NET document that includes a form serves both to describe the initial content of an XHTML document for browser display and to provide the event handling to process user interactions with the form in the document. So, for all ASP.NET documents that include forms, there are two kinds of requests. First, there is an initial request, which results in the requested document and its form being displayed for the client. Second, there is a request made after the form has been changed by the client. This kind of request is called a *postback* because the form values are posted back to the document on the server. C# code in a document can determine whether it is a postback request by testing the IsPostBack property of the Page class, which is true if it is a postback request.

C# code in a document can access the values of controls through the Value property of the associated object. The object associated with a control has the same name as the control's id attribute. So, if a form has a text box with the id phone, its value can be accessed as phone.Value.

To clarify the sequence of events that takes place for an ASP.NET document that includes a form, consider the following simple document example:

```
<!-- ex3.aspx
     A simple example of an ASP.NET document with controls.
     It uses textboxes to get the name and age of the client,
     which are then displayed.
     -->
<%@ Page language="c#" %>

<html>
  <head> <title> Ex3 </title>
  </head>
  <body>
    <form runat = "server">
      <p>
        Your name:
        <asp:textbox id = "name"  runat = "server" />
        <br />
        Your age:
        <asp:textbox id = "age"  runat = "server" />
        <br />
        <asp:button id = "submit" runat = "server"
                    value = "Submit"  text = "Submit" />
      <br />
      <% if (IsPostBack) { %>
        Hello <%= name.Text %> <br />
        You are <%= age.Text %> years old <br />
```

```
        <% } %>
      </p>
    </form>
  </body>
</html>
```

Notice that both the form and the controls in the form must include the `runat` attribute set to `"server"`.

ASP.NET implicitly stores the control state of a document class instance before the server returns the output of the instance to the client. This information is stored in a hidden control, which is a property of the `Page` class, named `ViewState`. `ViewState` is a reference to a `StateBag` object, which is a data structure similar to a hash. `StateBag` objects are only valid while the page is active. If the browser is pointed at a different document, the `StateBag` object is discarded. When the document is posted back to the server, the `ViewState` data is used to initialize the new instance implicitly. Of course, `ViewState` will not have form data on the first postback. After initialization using `ViewState`, the client input from the form is used for a second initialization of the instance. Therefore, any control whose value is not input by the client retains its previous value. `ViewState` provides implicit form state preservation between requests. So, it does what the HTTP protocol cannot do, save state across the round trips to the server.

Of course, saving state with `ViewState` is not free. For a large form with many controls, the resulting `ViewState` will require more time for browser/server communications, as well as storage space on the client machine.

The following is a list of the things that happen when the `ex3.aspx` document is requested, delivered to the browser, has its text boxes filled in by the user, is posted back to the server, and finally is returned to the browser. Note that many events are raised during this processing, although none is described in the following:

1. The client requests `ex3.aspx`, the original ASP.NET document.

2. A document class is created by compiling the requested document. Then the constructor of that class is invoked.

3. The control state of the instance is initialized with the `ViewState` data. (On the initial request, there is no `ViewState` data.)

4. The form data of the request is used to set the control state of the document class instance. (On the initial request, there is no form data.)

5. The current state of the instance is recorded in the `ViewState` hidden field.

6. The instance is executed and the results returned to the client.

7. The class and its instance are deleted on the server.

8. The client interacts with the form of the document.

9. The client causes a postback to the server.

10. A document class is created by compiling the requested document. Then the constructor of that class is invoked.

11. The control state of the instance is initialized with the `ViewState` data.

12. The form data of the request is used to set the control state of the document class instance.

13. The current state of the class is recorded in `ViewState`.

14. The instance is executed and the results are returned to the client; the class and its instance are deleted on the server.

`ViewState` is user-accessible, so it can be used to store state information other than form data. All controls inherit `ViewState` from the `Controls` class. Any textual data can be placed in `ViewState` with a simple assignment statement, for example:

```
ViewState["myName"] = "Freddie";
```

Accessing the values in `ViewState` is slightly complicated by the necessity of casting the value to the proper type. For example, to fetch the `myName` value above, the following could be used:

```
name = (string)ViewState["myName"];
```

To use `ViewState` for non-form data, that data must be assigned to `ViewState` before Step 13, because it is at that point that `ViewState` is finalized. In Section 12.4.3, the `PreRender` event is introduced, which is the perfect time to record non-form data in `ViewState`.

The document created by the document class that was compiled from the `ex3.aspx` document, after it has had its form filled by the client, is as follows:

```
<!-- ex3.aspx
     A simple example of an ASP.NET document with HTML controls.
     It uses textboxes to get the name and age of the client,
     which are then displayed.
     -->
<html>
  <head> <title> Ex3 </title>
  </head>
  <body>
    <form name="ctl00" method="post" action="ex3.aspx" id="ctl00">
<div>
<input type="hidden" name="__VIEWSTATE" id="__VIEWSTATE"
     value="/wEPDwUKMTQyOTM4OTczNmRkgGqzeOWp5+9PqFirn31TKZMNYGc="
 />
</div>
```

```
        <p>
          Your name:
          <input name="name" type="text" value="Mike" id="name" />
          <br />
          Your age:
          <input name="age" type="text" value="47" id="age" />
          <br />
          <input type="submit" name="submit" value="Submit"
                 id="submit" value="Submit" />
        <br />

          Hello Mike <br />
          You are 47 years old <br />

        </p>
<div>
<input type="hidden" name="__EVENTVALIDATION"
             id="__EVENTVALIDATION"
value="/wEWBAKa64qqAQL7uPQdAtCCr6oGAty7hLYEyQ+kkWxO+AfEpmRjTbk-
  loDKi/YM=" />
</div></form>
  </body>
</html>
```

This document differs from the original version of `ex3.aspx` in three areas. First, it includes the `ViewState` hidden control, which has a coded version of the form data. The code used is base64. Second, the form has an internal name and `id` (`ct100`). Third, the render block to produce the return XHTML has been replaced by its output.

The display of `ex3.aspx`, after the postback, is shown in Figure 12.3.

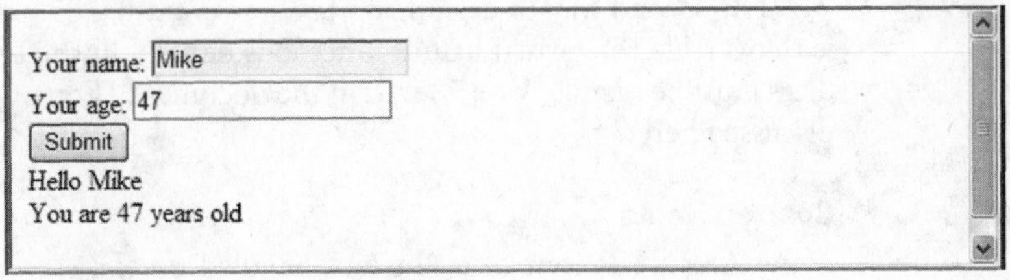

Figure 12.3 The display of `ex3.aspx`, after the postback

A postback can be initiated by a user in more than one way. Of course, a postback occurs if the user clicks the *Submit* button of a form. It also happens when any button is clicked. The user has the option of having a postback happen when a checkbox is clicked or a select item is selected. This is controlled by the `AutoPostBack` property of the control. If `AutoPostBack` is set to `"true"`, then a change in the control's value causes a postback.

12.4.3 ASP.NET Events

There are a large number of events that can be raised while an ASP.NET document is being processed and displayed. Applications, sessions, the page itself, and controls can all raise events. Application and session events are not discussed in this chapter. A discussion of page-level events and control events follows.

Page-Level Events

Page-level events are created by the `Page` class at specific times in the life cycle of an ASP.NET document. These are `Init`, which is raised immediately after a document class is instantiated; `Load`, which is raised just after the instance has its state set from form data and `ViewState`; `PreRender`, which is raised just before the instance is executed to construct the client response document; and `Unload`, which is raised just before the instance is discarded.

There are two ways to design and register handlers for the page-level events. The first is to write the handlers using predefined names that are implicitly registered when the document class is created. This implicit handler registration is called *auto event wireup*. It is controlled by the `Page` directive attribute, `AutoEventWireup`, which has the default value of `true`. If set to `false`, the implicit registration is not done, and registration must be done manually. The names of the handlers that are implicitly registered are `Page_Load`, `Page_Unload`, `Page_PreRender`, and `Page_Init`. All return `void` and take a parameter of type `System.EventArgs`. The protocols of these are as follows:

```
public void Page_Unload(System.EventArgs e) { ... }
public void Page_Load(System.EventArgs e) { ... }
public void Page_PreRender(System.EventArgs e) { ... }
public void Page_Init(System.EventArgs e) { ... }
```

The `Page_Init` handler is used in an example in Section 12.4.4.

The second way to design and register event handlers for page-level events is to override the virtual handler methods defined in the `Page` class. Such handlers must be manually registered in the document. This approach is not further discussed here.

Control Events

Many ASP.NET control events are handled on the server, although many of these are raised on the client. The XHTML events discussed in Chapter 5, "JavaScript and XHTML Documents," are both raised and handled on the client. When some ASP.NET control events occur, they cause an immediate postback to the server. In other cases, the notification is delayed until the next postback. In the case of the `Click` event, there is an immediate postback (using

HTTP POST) with the event message. When such a postback is received, the server searches for a handler for `Click` and if one is found, it executes it.

Not all events can be handled on the server, because of the time required to do it. For example, the `MouseOver` event, because of the frequency with which it may occur, cannot be handled on the server—it would simply take too much time for the postback and handling each time it was raised. So, `MouseOver` is one of the events that is still handled on the client.

Control events are either postback or non-postback, meaning they either cause an immediate postback when raised or they are saved until the next postback. For some controls, all events are postback; for example, `Button` and `Menu`. `CheckBox`, `TextBox`, and `RadioButton` are non-postback controls.

Event handlers for controls are registered the way JavaScript client-side event handlers are registered through XHTML attributes. Different controls have attributes with different names for event handler registration. `TextBox` controls use the `OnTextChanged` attribute; `Button` controls use `OnClick`; `CheckBox` and `RadioButton` controls use `OnCheckedChanged`. The handlers for controls all use the following protocol: They return `void` and take two parameters, the first of type `object` and the second of type `System.EventArgs`. This is the protocol for the `EventHandler` delegate, which provides the standard event handling approach for CLR. For example, consider the following event handler for a text box control, along with the control:

```
protected void TextboxHandler(object src,
                              System.EventArgs e) {
  ...
}
...
<input type = "text"  id = "Name"
    OnTextChanged = "TextBoxHandler"
    runat = "server" />
```

We can now revise the life cycle of an ASP.NET document request to include event creation for both page-level and control events. This time we list only a single request cycle (rather than including a postback cycle).

1. The client requests `ex3.aspx`, the original ASP.NET document.

2. A document class is created by compiling the requested document. Then the constructor of that class is invoked.

3. The `Page` event `Init` is raised.

4. The control state of the instance is initialized with the `ViewState` data. (On the initial request, there is no `ViewState` data.)

5. The form data of the request is used to set the control state of the document class instance. (On the initial request, there is no form data.)

6. The `Page` event `Load` is raised.

7. The `Page` event `PreRender` is raised.

8. The current control state of the instance is recorded in the `ViewState` hidden field.

9. The instance is executed and the results returned to the client.

10. The `Page` event `Unload` is raised.

11. The class and its instance are deleted on the server.

12.4.4 Creating Control Elements with Code

Server-side controls can be specified for an ASP.NET document in two different ways: with markup or with programing code. For example, a button can be created with the following markup:

```
<asp:button id = "helpButton"  Text = "help"
            OnClick = "OnClickHandler"
            runat = "server" />
```

The same button could be created with C# code, as shown in the following:

```
protected Button helpButton = new Button();
helpButton.Text = "help";
helpButton.id = "helpButton";
helpButton.OnClick = "OnClickHandler";
helpButton.runat = "server";
```

There are two problems with creating controls with program code: First, it requires more typing, and as as we all know, every time the keyboard is touched, there is a small but real possibility the wrong key will be pressed. Second, the placement of the control on the document display is problematic. It has to be added to something already in the document. To control the placement, a placeholder element can be defined in the markup. Then the control can be added using the id attribute of the placeholder. This gives the exact position within the document for the control. For example, the placeholder could be specified with the following:

```
<asp:placeholder id = "buttonPlace"  runat = "server" />
```

The following statement places the button at the position where the placeholder element appeared:

```
buttonPlace.Controls.Add(helpButton);
```

More than one control can be put in a placeholder. They are maintained in a property of the placeholder element, `Controls`. So, the `Controls` property is a collection of controls elements. The order in which controls are added to the placeholder's `Controls` property determines the order in which the controls will appear in the display.

Although it is easier to create elements with markup, modifying elements is a good use of program code. For example, the list items of a select element could be added with program code, after the select element had been specified in markup. This would be especially useful if the list items came from some other data source. Program code is also useful for modifying the attributes of a markup-created element.

12.4.5 Response Output for Controls

The first two sample ASP.NET documents of this chapter use the `Response.Write` method to place text in the response buffer. This is not a viable approach when there are controls in the document because the output from `Response.Write` goes to the beginning of the buffer rather than the position among the controls of the call to `Response.Write` (assuming the code is embedded in an ASP.NET document). As a more effective alternative, the text can be placed in a label control, which produces the text at the position of the label control in the response buffer. The text is assigned to the `Text` property of the label control. For example, suppose the document includes the following (at the position where the output text should be):

```
<asp:label id = "output"  runat = "server" />
```

The following places the given text at that position of the label in the response buffer:

```
<% string msg = string.Format(
              "The result is {0} <br />", result);
output.Text = msg; %>
```

In this example, the `string.Format` method is used to create a formatted string that consists of literal text and the value of the variable, `result`, which has been converted to text by `Format`. Of course, the program code could also appear in a code-behind file.

12.4.6 An Example

The following example creates a text box, a drop-down list, and a button in an ASP.NET document. It uses code in a code-behind file to fill in the list items of the drop-down list. The document also includes a label control to provide a place for the return message from the code-behind file. The code-behind file also includes a handler for the button, which confirms to the user the selected item.

The list items are added to the select element with the `Add` method of the `Items` property of the select. Each new item is created with a call to the list item constructor, `ListItem`, passing the value of the new item. For example, to add a list item with the value `"red"` to the select control with the id `mySelect`, the following could be used:

```
mySelect.Items.Add(new ListItem("red"));
```

The button handler in the example will return a message to the client, giving his or her name and the chosen select item, which in this case is a color. The client name is retrieved from the name text box of the document, using the Text property of the text box. The chosen color is retrieved from the form with the SelectedItem property of the drop-down list.

The ASP.NET document and its code-behind file follow:

```
<!-- ex4.aspx
     An example of an ASP.NET document that creates a text box,
     a drop-down list, a submit button, and a label.
     A code-behind file is used to populate the drop-down list and
     handle the button clicks. The label is used for the return
     message
     -->
<%@ Page language="c#" Inherits = "ex4" Src = "ex4.aspx.cs" %>
<html>
  <head> <title> Ex4 </title>
  </head>
  <body>
    <form runat = "server">
      Name: <asp:textbox runat = "server" id = "name" />
      <br /><br />
      Favorite Color:<asp:DropDownList runat = "server"
                                        id = "color" />
      <br /><br />
      <asp:button  runat = "server" id = "submit"
                   text = "Submit" OnClick = "OnClickHandler" />
      <br /><br />
      <asp:label id = "message" runat = "server" />
    </form>
  </body>
</html>
```

```
// ex4.aspx.cs
//    The code behind file for ex4.aspx.
//    In an OnLoad handler, it populates the drop-down
//    list created in the associated ASP.NET document.
//    It also includes a handler for the button, which
//    produces a message to the client, including the
//    client's name and the chosen item from the drop
//    down list
using System;
using System.Web;
```

```
using System.Web.UI;
using System.Web.UI.WebControls;

public class ex4 : System.Web.UI.Page {
  protected DropDownList color;
  protected TextBox name;
  protected Button submit;
  protected Label message;

  // OnLoad handler to populate the dropdownlist
  override protected void OnLoad(EventArgs e) {
    if (!IsPostBack) {
      color.Items.Add(new ListItem("blue"));
      color.Items.Add(new ListItem("red"));
      color.Items.Add(new ListItem("green"));
      color.Items.Add(new ListItem("yellow"));
    }
  }

  // Handler for the button
  protected void OnClickHandler(object src, EventArgs e) {
    string newMsg = string.Format(
        "Hi {0}, your favorite color is {1}",
        name.Text, color.SelectedItem);
    message.Text = newMsg;
  }
}
```

This example illustrates how form elements can be created dynamically with code, although in this case the content of the created element was statically defined. The example also shows a simple event handler for a text box and how dynamic output can be directed to the user without it replacing the display. Figure 12.4 shows a display of ex4.aspx after a name has been entered, a color chosen, and the *Submit* button clicked.

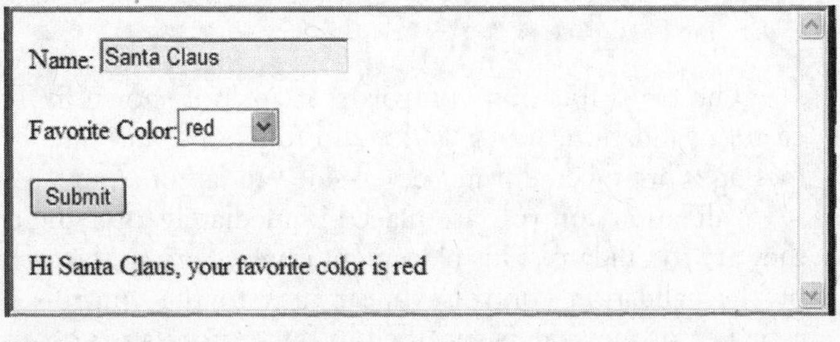

Figure 12.4 Display of ex4.aspx

12.4.7   Validation Controls

In Chapter 5, "JavaScript and HTML Documents," client-side form data validation with JavaScript was discussed. Although there are strong reasons for doing form data validation on the client, there are also reasons to do it again on the server. First among these is that client-side validation can be subverted by a devious client. Also, in some cases form data goes directly into a database, which could be corrupted by bad data. So, it is often necessary to do form data validation on both the client and the server side. In the following paragraphs, we introduce the ASP.NET Web controls designed to make server-side form data validation relatively easy.

There are six validation controls defined in the ASP.NET controls collection. The four most commonly used of these controls, along with their properties and values, are shown in Table 12.2.

Table 12.2   Validation controls and their properties

Control	Properties	Values
`RequiredFieldValidator`	None	None
`CompareValidator`	`Operator`	`Equal, NotEqual, GreaterThan, GreaterThanEqual, LessThan, LessThanEqual, DataTypeCheck`
	`Type`	`String, Currency, Date, Double, Integer`
	`ValueToCompare`	Constant
	`ControlToCompare`	Another control
`RangeValidator`	`MaximumValue`	Constant
	`MinimumValue`	Constant
	`Type`	`String, Currency, Date, Double, Integer`
`RegularExpressionValidator`	`ValidationExpression`	Regular expression

The two validation controls that are not shown in Table 12.2 are one for custom validation, which is done in functions, and one for reporting the error messages produced during server-side validation.

Validation controls are placed immediately after the controls whose values they are to validate. This placement is necessary so the error messages produced by the validation controls appear next to the controls being validated. The actual error message is specified in the `ErrorMessage` attribute of the validation control. The validation control is connected to the control it is to validate with the `ControlToValidate` property, which is set to the id of the control. The `Display` property is used to specify how the error message will be displayed. The value `"Static"` means that space is reserved on the displayed document for the message. The value `"Dynamic"` means space for the message is not reserved. The value `"None"` means no error message will be displayed, although the error is still recorded in a log. Validation controls must also include the `runat` attribute set, of course, to `"server"`.

The following example, `ex5.aspx`, illustrates some of the validation controls.

```
<!-- ex5.aspx
    An example of an ASP.NET document to illustrate server-side
    validation Web controls.
    It uses Web control text boxes to get the name, phone number,
    and age of the client. These three are validated on the
    server
    1. The name must be present
    2. The phone number must be in the form ddd-ddd-dddd
    3. The range of the age must be 10 to 110
    -->
<%@ Page language="c#" %>
<html>
  <head> <title> Ex5 </title>
  </head>
  <body>
    <form runat = "server">
      <p>
        Your name:
        <asp:textbox  id = "name" runat = "server" />
        <asp:RequiredFieldValidator
          ControlToValidate = "name"
          Display = "Static"
          runat = "server"
          ErrorMessage = "Please enter your name">
        </asp:RequiredFieldValidator>
        <br />

        Your phone number:
        <asp:textbox  id = "phone" runat = "server" />
        <asp:RegularExpressionValidator
          ControlToValidate = "phone"
          Display = "Static"
          runat = "server"
```

```
            ErrorMessage = "Phone number form must be ddd-ddd-dddd"
            ValidationExpression = "\d{3}-\d{3}-\d{4}">
        </asp:RegularExpressionValidator>
        <br />

        Your age:
        <asp:textbox  id = "age" runat = "server" />
        <asp:RangeValidator
          ControlToValidate = "age"
          Display = "Static"
          runat = "server"
          MaximumValue = "110"
          MinimumValue = "10"
          Type = "Integer"
          ErrorMessage = "Age must be in the range of 10 to 110">
        </asp:RangeValidator>
        <br />

        <input type = "submit" value = "Submit" />
      </p>
    </form>
  </body>
</html>
```

The name text box is validated to ensure that a name is given. The phone number text box is validated to ensure that it matches the given regular expression. (Regular expressions are described in Chapter 4, "The Basics of JavaScript.") The age text box is validated to ensure that the given age is at least 10 but not greater than 110.

Figure 12.5 shows the display of the **ex5.aspx** document after some of the fields have been filled incorrectly, which results in the appearance of error messages to the right of the text boxes.

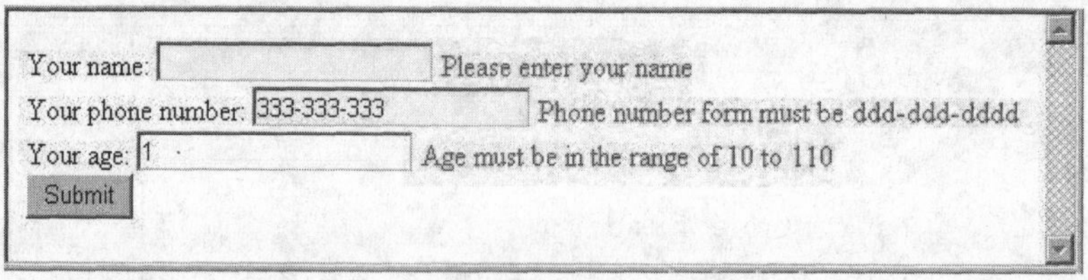

Figure 12.5 Display of **ex5.aspx** after some text boxes have been filled

In addition to the predefined validation controls, a user can define custom validation controls that are designed for some special validation. Such a custom validation is defined with a `CustomValidator` control. The actual validation can be done either with client code (for example, with a JavaScript function), server code (for example, with a C# method in the code-behind file), or both. Following is an example of a `CustomValidator` control, which in this case is to validate some characteristic of the text entered into a text box that immediately precedes the validator control:

```
<asp:CustomValidator runat = "server"
  id = "CustomValidator1"
  ControlToValidate = "name"
  ValidateEmptyText = false
  Display = "Static"
  ErrorMessage = "The text entered is not valid..."
  ClientValidationFunction = "clientValidator"
  OnServerValidate = "ServerValidator">
</asp:CustomValidator>
```

For this validator control, a JavaScript validator function, `clientValidator`, and a C# server validator function, `ServerValidator`, are both needed. The JavaScript function must appear in the markup file. The C# method must appear in the code-behind file. Both of these take two parameters. For the C# method, the first is an `object` and the second is a `ServerValidateEventArgs` type. The `Value` property of the second parameter object has the value the user typed into the text box. The same two parameters are used for the JavaScript function, although in that case the types are not needed in the function definition.

Setting the `ValidateEmptyText` attribute to `false` specifies that an empty text box is considered invalid. The default value of this attribute is `true`.

12.4.8 Master Documents

External style sheets are used to give each document on a site a consistent look and feel. In many cases, there is some content, for example a header or a footer, that should be on each document of a site. Also, there may some standard layout of information that controls the appearance of each document. With ASP.NET 2.0, these concepts can be implemented easily. A *master document* is defined, into which the content of other documents, called *content documents*, can be implicitly merged into the master document. So, if we want a particular header, perhaps consisting of one or more images and the name of the site, to appear on every one of the content documents, we define that header in a master document. Then the site consists of the master document and a collection of content documents. The browser user never sees the two different kinds of documents. When the user requests one of the content documents, that document is merged into the master document and the merged document is sent to the browser.

A simple example will demonstrate the process of building a master document and a content document. The master document will have no active controls and no code, although these could be included. The example master document simply produces a standard header, consisting of the company's name and two small images of airplanes. The ASP.NET control for images is just `<asp:image>`. The attribute for the image file is `imageurl`, rather than the XHTML attribute, `src`. All master documents need to begin with a `Master` directive. Other than that, there is little difference between conventional ASP.NET documents and master documents.

The document, named `ex6.master`,[4] follows:

```
<%@ Master %>
<!-- ex6.master
     A simple example of an ASP.NET master document
     cex61.aspx is a content document for this document
     -->
<html xmlns="http://www.w3.org/1999/xhtml" >
  <head>
    <title>Untitled Page</title>
    <style type = "text/css">
      span {font-style: italic; font-size: 30;
            font-weight: bold; color:blue;}
    </style>
  </head>
  <body>
    <form runat = "server">
      <div>
        <asp:image id = "plane1"  runat = "server"
              imageUrl = "images/plane1.wmf"
              width = "110px"   height = "45px" />
        <span>     Aidan's Used Airplanes     </span>
        <asp:image id = "plane2"  runat = "server"
              imageUrl = "images/plane2.png" />
        <br /><br /><br />
        <asp:contentplaceholder id = "TopPageContent"
              runat = "server" >
        </asp:contentplaceholder>
      </div>
    </form>
  </body>
</html>
```

Content documents must begin with a `Page` directive that includes the attribute `masterpagefile`, to which must be assigned the filename of the

---

4. All master documents must use the `.master` filename extension.

master document. The whole document, after the `Page` directive, is an `<asp:content>` element. This element must have its `runat` attribute set to `"server"`. Also, it must include the id of the `contentPlaceHolder` element in the master document. This must be assigned to the `contentplaceholderID` attribute. For example, for our example, the opening `asp:content` tag must be as follows:

```
<asp:content runat = "server"
             contentplaceholderID = "TopPageContent" >
```

The remainder of the content document is a div element that contains whatever we want to be merged into the master document. For our example, the content document, named `cex61.aspx`, follows:

```
<%@ Page masterpagefile = "ex6.master" %>

<asp:content runat = "server"
             contentplaceholderID = "TopPageContent" >
<!-- cex61.aspx
     A simple example of a content document for the
     master document, ex6.master
     -->
<div>
  <h3> Today's Special </h3>
  1975 Cessna 172, light blue & grey, 850 hours SMOH <br />
  Great condition! Price reduced! Call us! <br />
  719-444-6999
</div>
</asp:content>
```

A display of the master document, `ex6.master`, with the content document, `cex61.aspx` merged, is shown in Figure 12.6.

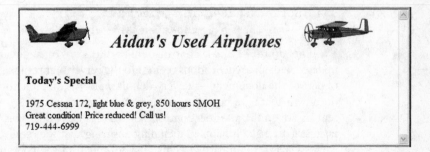

Figure 12.6 A master/content document

536   Chapter 12 · Introduction to ASP.NET

Note that the URL of a master/content document is the name of the content document.

A master document can have any number of `contentplaceholder` elements, each of which must have content documents that reference its id. There is of course much more to master documents, but those additional details are not covered here.

12.5 ASP.NET AJAX

In response to the widespread interest and positive effects of Ajax, Microsoft developed a collection of software to make its use simple in ASP.NET. Implementing Ajax in ASP.NET is especially easy when the application is constructed using one of the Microsoft frameworks for ASP.NET development, Visual Studio or Visual Web Developer 2005 Express Edition (VWDEE). The latter is a free software system. Though it sounds rather remarkable, Ajax can be implemented with these systems without the developer writing a single line of Java-Script—Ajax without using the 'j'!

Part of the ASP.NET AJAX software is the Microsoft Ajax Library, which has three parts, a type system, a components layer, and a top layer. The type system extends JavaScript by adding support for namespaces, inheritance, interfaces, and event handling, among other things. The components layer includes support for JSON, network communication, DOM interaction, and some ASP.NET application services, such as authentication. The top layer is the application model, which is event-driven. Some of these are obviously client side and some are server side. It requires an entire book to explain all of these capabilities. As should be expected, only a tiny part of these topics are discussed in this section.

The server side support for Ajax consists of server controls, a Web services bridge, and an applications services bridge. This section introduces the two most important parts of all of this, the new server controls `ScriptManager` and `UpdatePanel`. The `ScriptManager` control loads the required JavaScript libraries for ASP.NET AJAX. Every document that uses any part of ASP.NET AJAX must have a `ScriptManager` control, which has the following form:

```
<asp:ScriptManager id = "whatever"
                    runat = "server" />
```

The `UpdatePanel` control defines the area of a document that can be updated with an asynchronous request to the server that results in the re-rendering of part of the document—the very definition of Ajax interactions. The part of the document that is to be updateable through Ajax interactions is placed in the content of an `UpdatePanel` control, and the framework makes the arrangements necessary to make it happen, including ensuring that the required client-side code is cross-browser compatible. This obviates much of the code written in the Ajax applications of Chapter 10, "Introduction to Ajax."

The general form of the `UpdatePanel` control is as follows:

```
<asp:UpdatePanel runat = "server"  id = "whatever" />
  <ContentTemplate>
    (whatever is to be Ajax-updateable)
  </ContentTemplate>
</asp:UpdatePanel>
```

As is nearly always the case, a simple example is the best way to illustrate the implementation of an Ajax application with ASP.NET AJAX. Although such applications can be built by hand, it is much easier to use a framework. Recall that with JSP, the NetBeans framework constructs an elaborate directory/file structure. In the case of ASP.NET, Visual Studio (or VWDEE) helps build the aspx file and the code-behind file, as well as furnishing a complex and lengthy XML configuration file for the application. Because of this assistance, we use the Visual Studio framework to build the application. However, only the tiny part of the capabilities of this framework that are needed will be discussed (one could easily use an entire chapter to describe the capabilities of Visual Studio).

The example application to illustrate ASP.NET AJAX is a familiar one—using Ajax to provide the city and state of a form, given the zip code. Using Visual Studio, only the ASP file with the form and the C# code to provide the city and state names need be written. In Visual Studio (Visual Studio 2005 was used by the author), we begin by selecting *File/New/Web site*, which opens a *New Web Site* window, as shown in Figure 12.7.

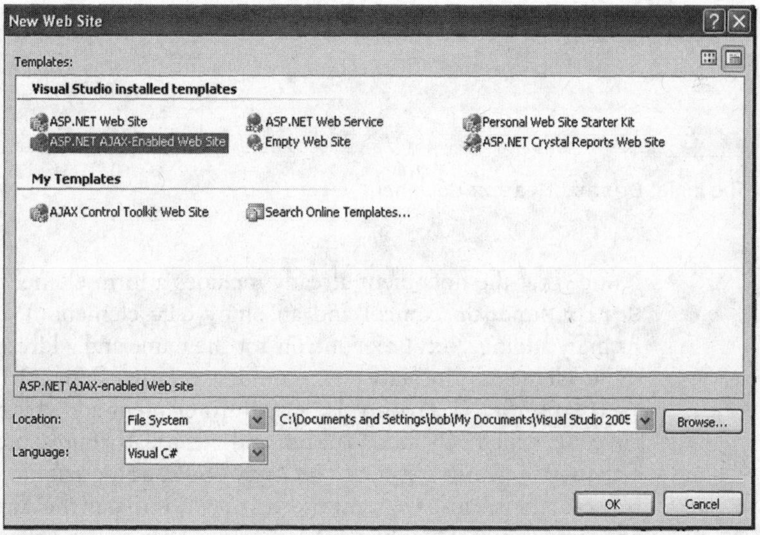

Figure 12.7 The *New Web Site* window of Visual Studio

In this window, we selected *ASP.NET Ajax-Enabled Web Site* and the C# language. This opens the workspace with a skeletal **aspx** document, as shown in Figure 12.8.

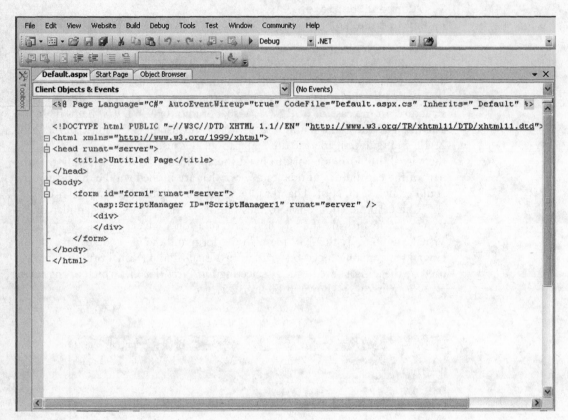

Figure 12.8 The initial `Default.aspx` document

Notice that the document already includes a form element, which contains the `ScriptManager` control and an empy `div` element. We begin building the form by adding `TextBox` controls for the name and address of the user. Because these elements are static, we could use either input XHTML elements or `TextBox` ASP.NET controls. The third element added is the `TextBox` for the zip code, which gets id, `columns`, and `runat` attributes, but also needs two special attributes. First, it needs an `AutoPostBack` attribute set to `"true"`. This is necessary because we want this text box to trigger the Ajax request for the city and state names. So, when the text box is changed and the cursor is placed outside the text box an automatic postback is done. The other required attribute is `OnTextChanged`, to which is assigned the name of the C# method in the code-behind file that is to be called when the text box is changed. We chose the name `Zip_OnTextChanged` for this method.

An `UpdatePanel` control follows the zip code text box. The only thing in the `UpdatePanel` control is a `ContentTemplate` control, in which are nested text boxes for city and state. The city and state text boxes are the ones to be filled by the data returned as a result of an Ajax request. Just to make clear that the implicit filling of the city and state text boxes is a result of only a partial re-rendering of the form, two labels are included as placeholders for time stamps provided by the code-behind file, one for the initial rendering of the form and one for each Ajax update. These labels have the following form:

```
<asp:Label id = "whatever"  runat = "server" > </asp:Label>
```

The ids of these labels are used to reference them in the C# code. The complete `aspx` document for the application follows:

```
<%@ Page Language="C#" AutoEventWireup="true"
        CodeFile="Default.aspx.cs" Inherits="_Default" %>

<!DOCTYPE html PUBLIC "-//W3C//DTD XHTML 1.1//EN"
                "http://www.w3.org/TR/xhtml11/DTD/xhtml11.dtd">

<html xmlns="http://www.w3.org/1999/xhtml">
<head runat="server">
  <title>Untitled Page</title>
</head>
<body>
  <form id="form1" runat="server">
    <asp:ScriptManager id = "ScriptManager1"  runat = "server" />
    <asp:Label id = "Label1"  runat = "server"  ></asp:Label>
    <br />
    <asp:TextBox id = "name"  columns = "30"  runat = "server" />
    Name <br />
    <asp:TextBox id = "address"  columns = "30"
                 runat = "server" />
    Address <br />
    <asp:TextBox id = "zip"  runat = "server"  columns = "30"
                 AutoPostBack = "true"
                 OnTextChanged = "Zip_OnTextChanged" />
    Zip code
    <asp:UpdatePanel id = "UpdatePanel1"  runat = "server"  >
        <ContentTemplate>
          <asp:TextBox id = "city"  columns = "30"
                       runat = "server" />
              City <br />
```

```
            <asp:TextBox  id = "state"  columns = "30"
                          runat = "server" />
        State <br />
        <asp:Label id = "Label2"  runat = "server"  >
        </asp:Label>
      </ContentTemplate>
    </asp:UpdatePanel>
  </form>
 </body>
</html>
```

Next, we build the code-behind file. We begin by selecting *File/Open/File* and then selecting `Default.aspx.cs`. This opens a skeletal C# code-behind file shown in Figure 12.9.

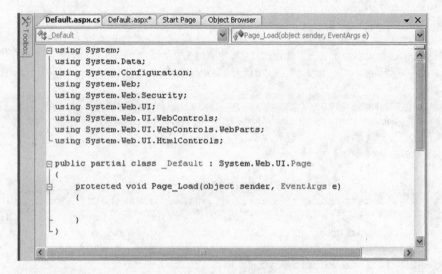

Figure 12.9 The skeletal code-behind file furnished by Visual Studio

To this partial class definition we add the handler method for the zip code text box. In this method we include a `HashTable` object that is initialized to a collection of zip codes and their corresponding city/states. The code of the method is simple—it checks to see if the hash object includes the zip code given in the form, whose name is `zip.Text`. This is done with the `Contains` method of the hash table. If the zip code is in the hash table, the city and state names are split from the value part of the correct hash table element and assigned to `city.Text` and `state.Text`, which represent the contents of the city and state text boxes.

This code is followed by the code to insert a time stamp on the document every time an Ajax request is made. The code to do this is as follows:

```
Label2.Text = "(Refreshed at " + DateTime.Now.ToString() +
              ")";
```

The `Page_Load` method is completed by adding another time stamp, this time placed at the top of the form at page load time. This time stamp must be placed in a selector that ensures that it is only executed during the initial display of the document. If the selector is not included, the time stamp will be repeated for each Ajax update, because each Ajax update raises a `Page_Load` event. The complete code-behind files is as follows:

```
using System;
using System.Data;
using System.Configuration;
using System.Web;
using System.Web.Security;
using System.Web.UI;
using System.Web.UI.WebControls;
using System.Web.UI.WebControls.WebParts;
using System.Web.UI.HtmlControls;
using System.Collections;

public partial class _Default : System.Web.UI.Page
{
  protected void Zip_OnTextChanged(object sender, EventArgs e)
  {
    Hashtable zipCityState = new Hashtable();
    char[] delimiter = new char[] { ',' };
    zipCityState.Add("81611", "Aspen,Colorado");
    zipCityState.Add("81411", "Bedrock,Colorado");
    zipCityState.Add("80908", "Black Forest,Colorado");
    zipCityState.Add("80301", "Boulder,Colorado");
    zipCityState.Add("81127", "Chimney Rock,Colorado");
    zipCityState.Add("80901", "Colorado Springs,Colorado");
    zipCityState.Add("81223", "Cotopaxi,Colorado");
    zipCityState.Add("80201", "Denver,Colorado");
    zipCityState.Add("81657", "Vail,Colorado");
    zipCityState.Add("80435", "Keystone,Colorado");
    zipCityState.Add("80536", "Virginia Dale,Colorado");

    if (zipCityState.Contains(zip.Text)) {
      city.Text =
          ((String)zipCityState[zip.Text]).Split(delimiter)[0];
```

```
         state.Text =
             ((String)zipCityState[zip.Text]).Split(delimiter)[1];
      } else {
        city.Text = "";
        state.Text = "";
      }
      Label2.Text = "(Refreshed at " + DateTime.Now.ToString() +
                   ")";
   }

   protected void Page_Load(object sender, EventArgs e)
   {
      if (!Page.IsPostBack)
          Label1.Text = "(Initially loaded at " +
                        DateTime.Now.ToString() + ")";
   }
}
```

Figure 12.10 shows the browser display of the initial screen of the zip code application.

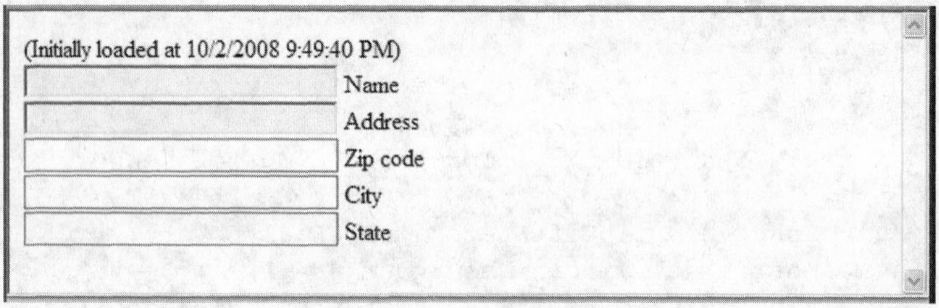

Figure 12.10 Initial screen of the zip code application

Figure 12.11 shows the browser display after entering a name, an address, and a zip code.

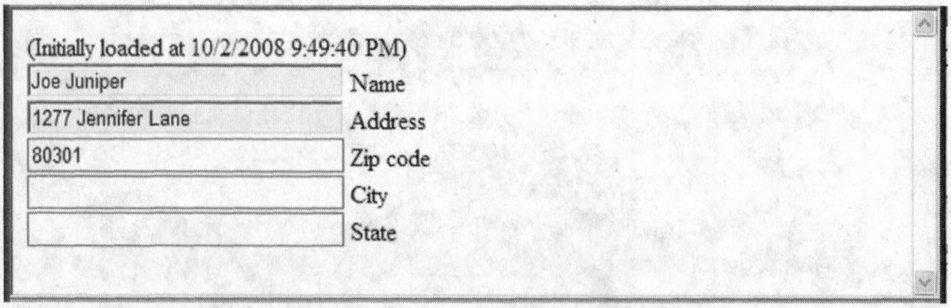

Figure 12.11 Screen after entering a name, an address, and a zip code

Figure 12.12 shows the browser display after moving the cursor out of the zip code text box.

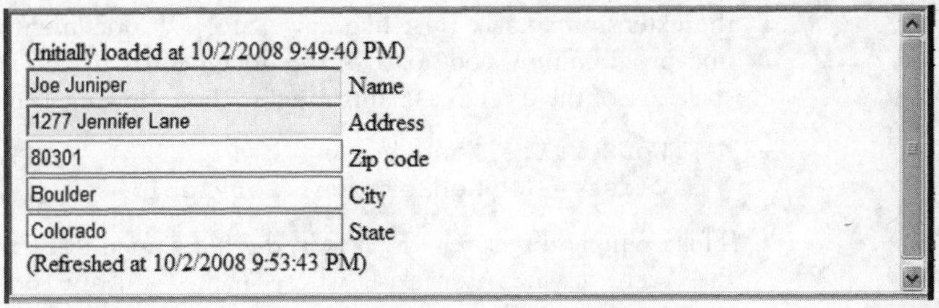

Figure 12.12 Screen after the Ajax entry of the city and state.

Figure 12.13 shows the browser display after entering a new zip code and moving the cursor out of the zip code text box. Notice that the refreshed time stamp differs from the earlier update, but the initial time stamp stays the same.

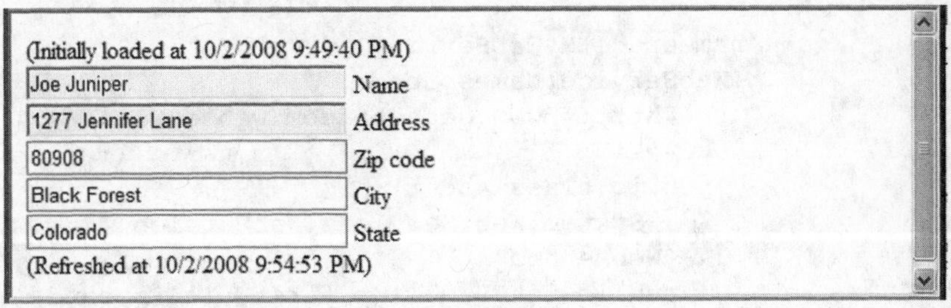

Figure 12.13 Screen after a second Ajax entry.

The example application clearly shows that an Ajax application can be built with ASP.NET AJAX without any direct use of JavaScript and without actually coding in any language the Ajax interaction with the server.

12.6 Web Services

Web services were introduced in Chapter 7, "Introduction to XML." In brief, a Web service is a collection of one or more related methods that can be called by remote systems using standard protocols on the Web.

The .NET Framework provides several kinds of support for the construction and advertisement of Web services. The most powerful .NET support tool is Visual Studio .NET, which is only briefly discussed in this book. Windows Communication Foundation (WCF) is a powerful framework for building Web Services on IIS Web servers. However, even without tools it is relatively easy to create and advertise Web services with the .NET Framework.

12.6.1   Constructing Web Services

In .NET, a Web service is simply a special kind of class, which can be written in any .NET programming language. The Web service class is stored in a file with the extension `.asmx` (just like any ASP.NET document). However, the only non-programming code part of the document is the directive at the top. The structure of the directive is illustrated in the following example:

```
<%@ WebService Language = "C#"
    Class = "MyWebService1.Service1" %>
```

This example directive, which is in the file named `Service1.asmx`, indicates the Web service is a class whose name is `Service1`, which is in the `MyWebService1` namespace, and it is written in C#.

Following is a simple Web service class, `Adder.asmx`, which defines a service method Sum3 that takes three integers as parameters and returns the sum of the three given numbers.[5]

```
<%@ WebService Language = "C#"
    Class = "MyWebService1.Adder" %>
using System.Web.Services;

namespace MyWebService1 {
[WebService(Namespace =
    "http://www.sebesta.com/webservices/")]

  public class Adder :
     System.Web.Services.WebService {
     [WebMethod]
     public int Sum3(int first, int second, int third) {
       int sum;
       sum = first + second + third;
       return sum;
     }
  }
}
```

This file imports `System.Web.Services` and inherits from the `WebService` class, which is defined in `System.Web.Services`. The `WebService` class provides various kinds of support for Web services, including the `WebMethodAttribute` class and the `Context` object, which contains information about the HTTP request that invokes the Web service.

The line that begins "`[WebService`" is used to define a namespace for Web services on this server. If it is not included, a default generic namespace is used, which could cause conflicts with other Web services. The one method of `Adder` is marked `[WebMethod]` to specify that it is to be made available as a

---

5. This is an admittedly silly Web service. However, it is useful to illustrate a Web service without much complicating clutter.

Web service. So, the `WebMethod` attribute is related to the `public` access modifier. The `WebMethod` attribute also instructs .NET to include the method in the WSDL description of the service, which is implicitly constructed (See Figure 12.14). `WebMethod` is an attribute of the `WebMethodAttribute` class.[6] A Web service class can include methods that are not Web services—they are those that are not marked with `[WebMethod]`.

```
<?xml version="1.0" encoding="utf-8" ?>
- <wsdl:definitions xmlns:soap="http://schemas.xmlsoap.org/wsdl/soap/"
    xmlns:tm="http://microsoft.com/wsdl/mime/textMatching/"
    xmlns:soapenc="http://schemas.xmlsoap.org/soap/encoding/"
    xmlns:mime="http://schemas.xmlsoap.org/wsdl/mime/"
    xmlns:tns="http://www.sebesta.com/webservices/"
    xmlns:s="http://www.w3.org/2001/XMLSchema"
    xmlns:soap12="http://schemas.xmlsoap.org/wsdl/soap12/"
    xmlns:http="http://schemas.xmlsoap.org/wsdl/http/"
    targetNamespace="http://www.sebesta.com/webservices/"
    xmlns:wsdl="http://schemas.xmlsoap.org/wsdl/">
  - <wsdl:types>
    - <s:schema elementFormDefault="qualified"
        targetNamespace="http://www.sebesta.com/webservices/">
      - <s:element name="Sum3">
        - <s:complexType>
          - <s:sequence>
              <s:element minOccurs="1" maxOccurs="1"
                name="first" type="s:int" />
              <s:element minOccurs="1" maxOccurs="1"
                name="second" type="s:int" />
              <s:element minOccurs="1" maxOccurs="1"
                name="third" type="s:int" />
            </s:sequence>
          </s:complexType>
        </s:element>
      - <s:element name="Sum3Response">
        - <s:complexType>
          - <s:sequence>
              <s:element minOccurs="1" maxOccurs="1"
                name="Sum3Result" type="s:int" />
            </s:sequence>
          </s:complexType>
        </s:element>
      </s:schema>
    </wsdl:types>
```

Figure 12.14 The first part of a service description

An `.asmx` file that defines a Web service can be viewed with an IE browser, which illustrates some of what the .NET system creates when a Web service class file is built. The display of the example Web service is shown in Figure 12.15.

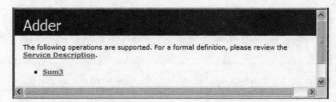

Figure 12.15 An IE browser display of the `Adder` Web service

---

6. An attribute is a way of associating declarative information with types, methods, and properties.

Figure 12.15 shows that the display includes a link (`Service Description`) to a Web Service Description Language (WSDL) description of the Web service, which has the required formats for requests and responses to the methods of the Web service. Recall that WSDL is an XML-based markup language for defining the protocols of Web services. The formats given in the service description are provided for the Simple Object Access Protocol (SOAP), HTTP GET, and HTTP POST protocols. SOAP is also an XML-based markup language. The first part of the service description for our example is shown in Figure 12.14.

Also displayed in Figure 12.15 are the names of the Web service methods. Our example has just one method, `Sum3`. Each method name is a link to a test document for the method that was written by ASP.NET. Parameters can be given to the tester, which runs the method and displays the results when the `Invoke` button is clicked. Figure 12.16 shows the tester for the `Sum3` method, including test values.

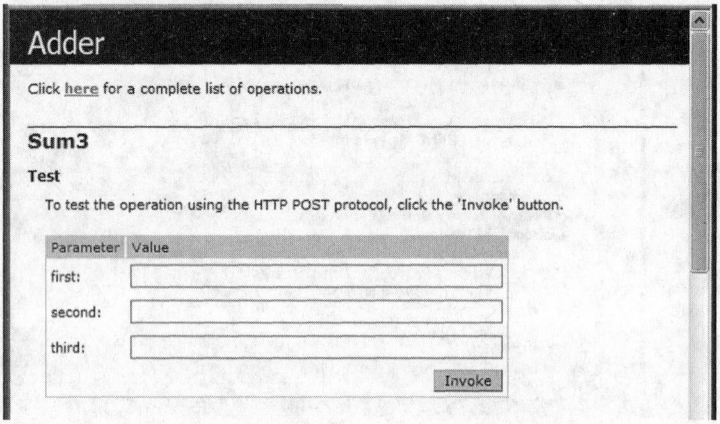

Figure 12.16 The test display for the `Sum3` service method

Entering 16, 17, and 17 as values and clicking the *Invoke* button of the `Sum3` tester produces the screen display shown in Figure 12.17.

Figure 12.17 The result of invoking the `Sum3` tester

12.6.2 Advertising Web Services

It is common that a potential client does not know the URL of a possibly useful Web service. There are two approaches used with .NET to make Web services available to clients: with a Web services discovery document and with a Web services directory written with the Universal Description, Discovery, and Integration (UDDI) language (UDDI was introduced in Section 7.11). In both cases, a directory of all Web services provided by a Web site can be made available to potential clients through a single URL on the site.

UDDI is part of Windows in the .NET Server release. It can be used to set up a UDDI server for inside an enterprise, as well as to register electronic services to make them available to the outside world. These activities are supported by the .NET UDDI SDK, which includes documentation, the `Microsoft.Uddi` assembly for the .NET Framework, and several example applications.

12.6.3 Consuming a Web Service

A Web service can be consumed by any client that can make a request over HTTP and parse the returned XML to get the result. The consumer can be a Web application, a non-Web application, or another Web service. The consumption process is simplified if a proxy is created on the client. In this case, the consumer interacts with the proxy as if it were the Web service. The proxy actually communicates with the service. The proxy, which is a class, has the same method signatures as the Web service, but hides the implementation details. The proxy can be created with Visual Studio .NET or with the Web Service Description Language Tool, whose code is in `wsdl.exe`. This file is stored in the `Bin` directory of the installation of .NET, which on our system is `C:\Program Files\Microsoft.NET\SDK\v2.0\Bin`.

Given a WSDL description of a Web service, `wsdl.exe` translates it into the proxy class. For each operation in the service, the tool creates three methods, one synchronous method and two others that can be used to call the operation asynchronously.

The `wsdl.exe` tool can be passed the URL of the Web service, rather than the actual WSDL file. The tool is also passed a switch that specifies the langauge for the proxy, the default for which is C#. For example, we can run `xsdl.exe` on the `Adder` service with the following:

```
wsdl http://localhost/svc/Adder.asmx /language:cs
```

This command produces a file named `Adder.cs` that defines the proxy service. A listing of this file is not reproduced here, due to its length and complexity.

Following is a simple C# class that consumes the `Adder` service:

```
// ConsumClass.cs - a simple class to consume the Web
//                  service, Adder.cs

public class ConsumClass {
  static void Main() {
    Adder myAdder = new Adder();
    int sum = myAdder.Sum3(15, 17, 19);
    Console.WriteLine("The sum is: {0} ", sum);
  }
}
```

This class, `ConsumClass`, can be added to the end of the file that defines the proxy class. `ConsumClass` instantiates the `Adder` class and calls its `Sum3` method, which is the Web class defined previously, and displays the returned value. To test the consumer/proxy, this combined class file can be compiled and executed.

Summary

.NET is a collection of technologies that supports the development and deployment of distributed component-based software systems written in variety of languages. The .NET Framework is a generic support structure for the .NET family of languages. The CLR is a runtime system, including JIT compilers that support the execution of .NET software. There are now 20 .NET languages, with more on the way. The CTS defines a set of types that must be supported by .NET languages. The CLS defines a minimal set of language features that must be supported by .NET languages. Software in any .NET language can interact in a variety of ways with software written in any of the other .NET languages.

C# was designed specifically for the .NET system. C# is based on Java but includes some features of other languages, notably C++, VB, and Delphi, as well as some new language features. Among its features are an improved `switch` construct, a `foreach` statement, some new controls on method inheritance, a value type struct, and properties.

ASP.NET is an approach to server-side support of dynamic documents. It is similar to JSP but is language neutral. Programming code can reside in an ASP.NET document or in a separate file called a code-behind file. In either case, the code is compiled before it is executed. Every ASP.NET document is compiled into a class before it is used, regardless of whether it contains programming code. All such classes are subclasses of the predefined class, `Page`, unless they have code-behind files, in which case the code-behind file inherits from `Page` and the class for the ASP.NET document inherits from the code-behind file.

ASP.NET documents consist of XHTML, programming code (either in script elements or render blocks), directives, server-side comments, and server-side controls. Server-side controls include the `runat` attribute set to `"server"`. The only required directive is `Page`, which must include the `Language` attribute, which specifies the language used for the programming code, either embedded or in a code-behind file. A code-behind file can be either precompiled or dynamically compiled only after it has been changed and the associated ASP.NET document has been requested. Just as JavaBeans is the best way to use Java in a dynamic document, code-behind files are the best way to use a .NET language to support dynamic documents.

ASP.NET includes a large collection of controls. These controls result in objects in the compiled `Page`-derived class, whereas the static XHTML code of a document is simply emitted by the execution of the `Page`-derived class. Different controls can raise different events, most of which can be handled by server-side code. The id attribute value of a control becomes the associated variable's name in the compiled version of the document.

The state of an ASP.NET document is implicitly maintained between requests with the `ViewState` hidden field.

There are four page-level events defined in the `Page` class: `Init`, `Load`, `Unload`, and `PreRender`. These events can be handled in server-side code. The handlers can be implicitly registered by naming them with predefined names and using the proper protocol. Alternatively, they can be subscribed to the event handler delegate, `EventHandler`.

Control event handlers are registered by referencing them on an attribute on the control.

Master documents are ASP.NET documents that are used to avoid duplication of common content on a collection of documents.

The ASP.NET AJAX provides the tools to build Ajax capabilities into an ASP.NET application. The `ScriptManager` control loads the required libraries of JavaScript code to support Ajax in ASP.NET. The `UpdatePanel` is a control that encapsulates the part of a document that can be Ajax-updateable. The actual code to specify the Ajax communication is all furnished by Visual Studio. So, an Ajax application can be written without writing a single line of JavaScript.

The .NET Framework provides significant assistance for all phases of the process of building Web services, from constructing the service itself to consuming the service.

Review Questions

12.1 What is a component?

12.2 When does a JIT compiler perform its translation of a method?

12.3 What is the primary benefit of the multilanguage aspect of .NET?

12.4 Where are C# `struct` objects allocated?

12.5   Explain how a JIT compiler works.

12.6   Describe briefly the two parts of the CLI.

12.7   Explain how the switch statement of C# is safer than that of Java.

12.8   What parameter-passing methods are available in C# that are not available in Java?

12.9   What kind of code is placed in a script element?

12.10 What characteristic is specified by attaching `virtual` to a C# method?

12.11 What is the difference between a control that includes the `runat` attribute set to `server` and one that does not?

12.12 What does it mean when a C# method includes the `new` modifier?

12.13 What are the two kinds of disadvantages of scripting languages when used for supporting dynamic documents?

12.14 What exactly is a code-behind file?

12.15 On what languages is C# based?

12.16 From what class does an ASP.NET document class that does not use a code-behind file inherit?

12.17 From what class does an ASP.NET document class that does use a code-behind file inherit?

12.18 What is the difference between a JavaBean and a .NET component?

12.19 What kind of code is placed in a render block?

12.20 Describe what is specified by the `Page` attribute `Src`.

12.21 What is the purpose of the `ScriptManager` control?

12.22 What is the syntactic difference between an XHTML widget and its corresponding ASP.NET control?

12.23 What part of a simple ASP.NET AJAX application must the developer write in JavaScript?

12.24 Why do ASP.NET server-side forms not require an `action` attribute?

12.25 What is the purpose of the `Xml` control?

12.26 What is a postback?

12.27 What is the purpose of the time stamps in the zip code ASP.NET AJAX application?

12.28 What is the purpose of the hidden control `ViewState`?

12.29 What part of the .NET system controls the execution of programs?

12.30 How can an ASP.NET checkbox control be forced to cause a postback when it is checked?

12.31 Explain how event handlers for controls are registered.

12.32 Why should form data validation be done on the server as well as the client?

12.33 What is a master document and how is one used?

12.34 Explain auto event wireup.

12.35 What is the purpose of the `UpdatePanel` control?

12.36 What are the four page-level events?

Exercises

12.1 Modify the ASP.NET document `ex1.aspx` to compute and display the number of days in your life as of today.

12.2 Modify the ASP.NET document `ex2.aspx` and its accompanying code-behind file, `ex2.aspx.cs`, to the specification of Exercise 12.1.

12.3 Modify the ASP.NET document `ex3.aspx` to use text box to get the name and use radio buttons to get the gender (male, female) and marital status of the user (single, married) and display the result along with the title Ms/Mrs/Mr, respectively.

12.4 Modify the ASP.NET document `ex4.aspx` and its accompanying code-behind file, `ex4.aspx.cs` to add the following: a multiline text box for the user's address and a drop-down list for favorite category of music (Pop, Rock, Rap, Country, Classical, Jazz), which must be populated in the code-behind file. The values of the new controls must be output when a postback is done.

12.5 Modify the ASP.NET document `ex5.aspx` to add the following: a text box for address, which the document must validate to ensure it begins with a number, which is followed by space and a text string that includes only letters; and a text box to collect a social insurance number, which must be validated to ensure it is in the form ddd-ddd-ddd, with no other characters in the text box.

12.6 Modify the ASP.NET AJAX zip code application to provide the address, zip code, city, state, and country of old customers. Use a hash whose keys are last names and first names, catenated. The information about the customer can be a single string of the address, zip code, city, state, and country all catenated together.

CHAPTER

13

Database Access through the Web

This chapter begins with brief introductions to relational databases and the Structured Query Language. Then it discusses several different architectures for database access. Next, the primary commands of the MySQL relational database system are introduced. This is followed by two sections, each of which describes a different approach to accessing databases through the Web using MySQL. First, the chapter discusses the use of server-side scripting for building systems for Web access to a database, using PHP as the sample language. Next, Java's JDBC, which provides database access from Java applications and servlets, is discussed. A complete example of both approaches is provided.

13.1 Relational Databases

A database is a collection of data organized to allow relatively easy access for retrievals, additions, modifications, and deletions. A number of different approaches to structuring data have been developed and used for databases. The most widely used are called *relational database systems*. The original design for relational databases, developed by E. F. Codd in the late 1960s, was based on Codd's mathematical theory of data. A significant number of books have been written to describe the structure and use of relational databases, so it clearly is a large and complex topic. Because just one section of one chapter of this book is devoted to it, that section can provide only a brief overview. However, it is sufficient for our discussion of database access through the Web.

A relational database is a collection of tables of data. Each table can have any number of rows and columns of data, and the data itself can have a variety of different forms. The columns of a table are named. Each row usually contains a value for each column. The rows of a table are often referred to as *entities*. The collection of values in a row represents the *attributes* of the entity. Most tables have one column for special data values that uniquely identify the rows of the table. The values in this special column are called the *primary keys* of the table. Mathematically, the entities of a table are elements of a set, so they must be unique. Both data values and primary key values in a table are sometimes called *fields*.

One way to introduce the basic ideas of a relational database is to develop a simple example. Suppose we need a database that stores information about used Corvettes for sale. We could just make a table named `Corvettes` with a column for the primary key of an entity, which could simply be a sequence of numbers. The table could have a column for the body style of the car, one for the year of manufacture, and one for the state where the car is for sale. It would also be useful to include information about the optional equipment of the cars. If six different kinds of equipment were interesting, that would require six more columns in the table.

The use of six columns of the `Corvettes` table for equipment is wasteful of memory. A better design is to use a second table—say, `Equipment`—to store the various kinds of equipment in which we are interested, such as CD players and automatic transmissions. This table could have just two columns: a primary key and the specific equipment. It would need just six rows.

To make this work, we need a way to relate cars to equipment. This need can be met with a cross-reference table, which has just two columns: one with primary keys from the `Corvettes` table and one with primary keys from the `Equipment` table. We could name this table `Corvettes_Equipment`. Each car in the `Corvettes` table could have several rows in `Equipment`, one for each specific option with which the car is equipped. This table does not need, and therefore does not have, a primary key column.

Another way to conserve memory is not to store state names in the main table. The state names could be moved to a new table—say, `States`—and have references to it in the `Corvettes` table. A primary key to the `States` table, which could be just an integer, would require far less space than a typical state name. A logical data model of the database could be as shown in Figure 13.1.

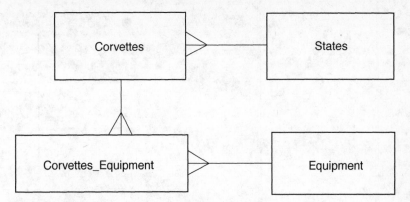

Figure 13.1 The logical data model for a database

The lines between the tables indicate the relationships between the connected tables. For example, the relationship between Corvettes and States is many to one: There may be many cars for sale in one state, but each car is in just one state. All of the relationships in our model are either one-to-many or many-to-one, depending on your point of view. Note that if we had not used the cross-reference table for this database, the relationship between Corvettes and Equipment would have been many-to-many.

The implementation of the database is illustrated with short examples of the required tables in Figures 13.2 to 13.5. This database will be used in the remainder of the chapter.

Equip_id	Equip
1	Automatic
2	4-speed
3	5-speed
4	6-speed
5	CD
6	Leather

Figure 13.2 The Equipment table

Vette_id	Body_style	Miles	Year	State
1	coupe	18.0	1997	4
2	hatchback	58.0	1996	7
3	convertible	13.5	2001	1
4	hatchback	19.0	1995	2
5	hatchback	25.0	1991	5
6	hardtop	15.0	2000	2
7	coupe	55.0	1979	10
8	convertible	17.0	1999	5
9	hardtop	17.0	2000	5
10	hatchback	50.0	1995	7

Figure 13.3 The Corvettes table

Vette_id	Equip
1	1
1	5
1	6
2	1
2	5
2	6
3	1
3	6
4	2
4	6
5	1
5	6
6	2
7	4
7	6
8	4
8	5
8	6
9	4
9	5
9	6
10	1
10	5

Figure 13.5 The `Corvettes_Equipment` cross-reference table

State_id	State
1	Alabama
2	Alaska
3	Arizona
4	Arkansas
5	California
6	Colorado
7	Connecticut
8	Delaware
9	Florida
10	Georgia

Figure 13.4 The `States` table

13.2   An Introduction to the Structured Query Language

The Structured Query Language (SQL) is a standard language for specifying accesses and modifications to relational databases. SQL was originally standardized by the American National Standards Institute (ANSI) and the International Standards Organization (ISO) in 1986. SQL was significantly expanded and modified in its early years, the result of which was standardized in 1992. This version is often called SQL-2.[1] SQL can be pronounced as either "S-Q-L" or "sequel."

SQL is supported by the databases provided by all major database vendors and is a standard that has truly become *the* standard. It is used to create, query, and modify relational databases, regardless of the particular database vendor.

The SQL reserved words are not case sensitive, which means that SELECT, select, and Select are equivalent. However, the names of tables and table columns may or may not be case sensitive, depending on the particular database. The whitespace separating reserved words and clauses is ignored, so commands can be spread across several lines if that is more readable. Single quotes (') are used to delimit character strings.

SQL is quite different from most programming languages; it is actually more like a structured form of English. It was designed to be easily understood and useful for any vendor's database. This section describes some of the basic SQL commands.

13.2.1 The SELECT SQL Command

SELECT clauses are used to specify queries of a database, which is how specific information is requested. The SELECT command has three clauses: SELECT, FROM, and WHERE. The general form is as follows:

SELECT *column names* FROM *table names*   [WHERE *condition*];

The brackets here indicate that the WHERE clause is optional.[2] The SELECT clause specifies the columns, or attributes, of a table. The FROM clause specifies the table or tables to be searched.[3] For example, the following query produces a list of all the values from the Body_style column of the Corvettes table:

SELECT Body_style FROM Corvettes;

The WHERE clause is used to specify constraints on the rows of the specified tables that are of interest. The following query produces a list of all the values from the Body_style column of the Corvettes table that have a Year column value greater than 1994:

SELECT Body_style FROM Corvettes WHERE Year > 1994;

An asterisk (*) as the SELECT clause value means to select all the columns of the specified table that meet the condition specified in the WHERE clause.

---

1. The current version of the SQL standard is SQL-3. It has not yet become widely used.

2. Actually, although the WHERE clause is often used, several other clauses can also appear in a SELECT command.

3. A SELECT command that specifies more than one table produces a join of the tables. Join operations are discussed in Section 13.2.2.

13.2.2 Joins

Suppose you want to produce a list of all Corvettes in the database that have CD players. To do this, you need information from two tables, Corvettes and Equipment. The connection between these two tables is through the cross-reference table Corvettes_Equipment. The SELECT command allows the temporary construction of a virtual table that includes information from the Corvettes and Equipment tables, using the Corvettes_Equipment table as the basis for producing the desired result. Such a virtual table is built with a *join* of the two tables. A join is specified with a SELECT command that has two tables named in the FROM clause and uses a compound WHERE clause. The WHERE clause for our example must have three conditions. First, the Vette_id column from the Corvettes table must match the Vette_id column from the Corvettes_Equipment table. This restricts the rows of the Corvettes_Equipment table to those associated with the row of interest in the Corvettes table. Second, the Equip column from the Corvettes_Equipment table must match the Equip_id column of the Equipment table. This restricts the rows of the Equipment table to those associated with the row of interest of the Corvettes_Equipment table. Finally, the value of the Equip column from the Equipment table must be CD. The complete SELECT command to extract the cars with CD players follows:

```
SELECT Corvettes.Vette_id, Corvettes.Body_style,
       Corvettes.Miles, Corvettes.Year, Corvettes.State,
       Equipment.Equip
FROM Corvettes, Equipment
WHERE Corvettes.Vette_id = Corvettes_Equipment.Vette_id
  AND Corvettes_Equipment.Equip = Equipment.Equip_id
  AND Equipment.Equip = 'CD';
```

This query produces the following result:

VETTE_ID	BODY_STYLE	MILES	YEAR	STATE	EQUIPMENT
1	coupe	18.0	1997	4	CD
2	hatchback	58.0	1996	7	CD
8	convertible	17.0	1999	5	CD
9	hardtop	17.0	2000	5	CD
10	hatchback	50.0	1995	7	CD

Notice that all references to columns in this query are prefixed with the table names. This is necessary only when the column names are not unique to one table, as is the case for the Vette_id column, which appears in both the Corvettes and the Corvettes_Equipment tables. However, even if the column names are unique, including the table names makes the query more readable.

As another example of a join, notice that the State column of the Corvettes table does not store state names. Instead, it stores row references to the States table, which stores state names. Any user who submits a query on the `Corvettes` table would likely prefer that the states' names be returned rather than the reference to the `States` table. This can be easily accommodated in SQL. For example, suppose you want to get a list of the Corvettes for sale in California. This could be obtained with the following command:

```
SELECT Vette_id, Body_style, Year, States.State
FROM Corvettes, States
WHERE Corvettes.State = States.State_id AND
      States.State = 'California';
```

This query produces the following result:

VETTE_ID	BODY_STYLE	MILES	YEAR	STATE
5	hatchback	25.0	1991	California
8	convertible	17.0	1999	California
9	hardtop	17.0	2000	California

13.2.3 The `INSERT` SQL Command

The `INSERT` command is used to add a row of data to a table. Its general form is as follows:

```
INSERT INTO table_name(column_name_1, column_name_2,...,
    column_name_n)
VALUES (value_1, value_2,..., value_n);
```

The correspondence between the column names and the values is positional: The first value goes into the column that is named first, and so forth. If `INSERT` is used on a table that has a column with the constraint `NOT NULL` and that column is not named in the `INSERT`, an error will be detected and reported. As an example of an `INSERT` command, consider the following:

```
INSERT INTO Corvettes(Vette_id, Body_style, Miles, Year,
                      State)
VALUES (37, 'convertible', 25.5, 1986, 17);
```

13.2.4 The `UPDATE` SQL Command

The `UPDATE` command is used to change one or more of the values of a row of a table. Its general form is as follows:

```
UPDATE table_name
SET column_name_1 = value_1,
    column_name_2 = value_2,
    ...
    column_name_n = value_n
WHERE column_name = value;
```

The `WHERE` clause in an `UPDATE` command specifies the primary key of the row to be updated. For example, to correct an error, you could change the year of the row with `Vette_id = 17` in the `Corvettes` table to 1996 with the following command:

```
UPDATE Corvettes
SET Year = 1996
WHERE Vette_id = 17;
```

13.2.5   The DELETE SQL Command

One or more rows of a table can be deleted with the `DELETE` command, whose general form is as follows:

```
DELETE FROM table_name
WHERE column_name = value;
```

The `WHERE` clause specifies the primary key of the row to be deleted. For example, if the car with the `Vette_id` value 27 is sold and should no longer be in the database, you could remove it from the `Corvettes` table with the following command:

```
DELETE FROM Corvettes
WHERE Vette_id = 27;
```

The `WHERE` clause of a `DELETE` command can specify more than one row of the table, in which case all rows that satisfy the `WHERE` clause are deleted.

13.2.6   The DROP SQL Command

The `DROP` command can be used to delete either whole databases or complete tables. The general form is as follows:

```
DROP (TABLE | DATABASE) [IF EXISTS] name;
```

In this line, the parentheses and brackets are metasymbols. `DROP` is used with either `TABLE` or `DATABASE`. The `IF EXISTS` clause is included if you want to avoid errors if the named table or database may not exist. For example:

```
DROP TABLE IF EXISTS States;
```

13.2.7   The CREATE TABLE SQL Command

A table in a database can be created with the `CREATE` command, whose general form is as follows:

```
CREATE TABLE table_name(
    column_name_1    data_type constraints,
    column_name_2    data_type constraints,
    ...
    column_name_n    data_type constraints);
```

A large number of different data types exist for table data, including `INTEGER`, `REAL`, `DOUBLE`, and `CHAR(`*length*`)`.[4] There are also several different constraints, which can be somewhat different among various database vendors. Constraints are restrictions on the values that can appear in a column of a table. One common constraint is `NOT NULL`, which means that every row in the table must have a value in a column that has this constraint. Another common one is `PRIMARY KEY`, which means the column that has this constraint has a unique value for each row in the table. For example, you could have the following:

```
CREATE TABLE States(
   State_id INTEGER PRIMARY KEY NOT NULL,
   State CHAR(20));
```

In some situations, table columns are referenced by position number rather than by names. The columns of a table are numbered starting with 1; that is, the first column is column 1.

We have now introduced enough SQL to make the topics in the remainder of this chapter understandable.

13.3 Architectures for Database Access

Web access to a database is provided by a client/server architecture. There are several different approaches to implementing this architecture. Client/server architectures and several of the most common of the implementation methods for Web access to databases are briefly introduced in the following sections.

13.3.1 Client/Server Architectures

The basic client/server architecture of the Web was discussed earlier in this book. In any client/server configuration, part of the work is done by the client, and part is done by the server. A client/server database access architecture is very similar. The client machines provide a way for users to input requests to a database that is resident on a computer that runs a database server. Results of requests to the server are returned to the client, which may use them in subsequent computations or simply display them for the user. A database server implements a data manipulation language that presents an interface to clients. This language can directly access and update the database. In its simplest form, a client/server database configuration has only two components, the client and the server. Such systems are called *two-tier* systems.

In some cases, two-tier systems are adequate. For example, in simple uses of the Web, the server provides HTML documents, and the client displays them. There is little computation to be divided between the two. However, some other applications require a great deal more complexity than the Web. In recent

---

4. More SQL data types and their corresponding Java data types are shown in Table 13.1 in Section 13.6.

years, large database servers have been replaced by multiple smaller servers, thus lessening the capabilities of the individual servers to deal with increasing application complexity. At the same time, client systems have grown in power and sophistication. It would seem natural for the computational load in client/server systems to gravitate toward the clients. Unfortunately, there are other problems with this solution—specifically, if any part of the application is moved to the clients, there is the problem of keeping the clients current with changes in the applications that use the database. This is clearly a serious problem if there are a large number of clients.

The most common solution to the problems of two-tier systems is to add a third component, thereby hatching a three-tier architecture. The first tier has the Web browser, which provides the user interface. The middle tier of such a system usually has the Web server and the applications that require database access. The third tier in the system has the database server and the database itself. The architecture of a three-tier Web-based database access system has the form shown in Figure 13.6.

Figure 13.6   Three-tier architecture of a Web site supported by databases

13.3.2   The Microsoft Access Architecture

Microsoft Access is a tool for implementing database applications that can access databases from virtually any common database vendor. It provides access to different database systems in two different ways: through its Jet database engine or through the Open Database Connectivity (ODBC) standard. ODBC specifies an application programming interface (API) for a set of objects and methods that serves as an interface to different databases. Each database must have a driver, which is an implementation of these objects and methods. Vendors for most common databases provide ODBC drivers. By using ODBC, an application can include SQL statements (through the ODBC API) that work with any database for which a driver has been installed. A system called the *ODBC driver manager*, which runs on the client computer, chooses the proper driver for a request on a specific database.

13.3.3   PHP and Database Access

PHP includes support for a wide variety of database systems. For each supported database system, there is an associated API. These APIs provide the interface to the specific systems. For example, the MySQL API includes functions to connect to a database and apply SQL commands against the database. Web access to a database using PHP is a natural architecture because PHP scripts are called through HTML documents from browsers. Using PHP and MySQL for database access is discussed in Section 13.5.

13.3.4 The Java JDBC Architecture

The Java JDBC architecture is a Java API for database access.[5] JDBC is very similar to ODBC, at least in terms of purpose. Both have the X/OPEN SQL Call Level Interface (SQL CLI) in their heritages.

JDBC provides a standard set of interfaces between applications that use databases and the low-level access software that actually manipulates the databases, which is supplied by the database vendor and is dependent on the particular brand of database being used. JDBC allows applications to be independent of the database system being used, as long as a JDBC driver is installed on the platform on which the application is run.

The advantages of JDBC are basically those of Java: The language is expressive and relatively safe, and programs are highly portable among platforms. The disadvantage of JDBC is that Java/JDBC programs are more complex than programs that accomplish the same things but are written in PHP.

JDBC is described in Section 13.6.

Figure 13.7 shows the most common database access architecture. Microsoft's Access architecture uses ODBC for its database API. PHP uses collections of functions as APIs for different databases. Java has JDBC as its database API.

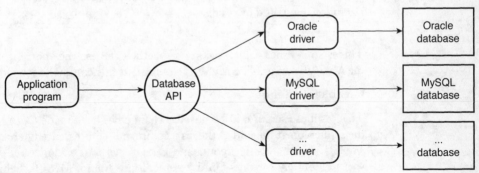

Figure 13.7 Common database access architecture

---

5. JDBC sounds like an acronym for Java Database Connectivity, but Sun Microsystems has denied this. In fact, Sun has registered JDBC as a trademark but has not done the same for Java Database Connectivity.

13.4   The MySQL Database System

MySQL is a free, efficient, widely used database system that implements SQL. It is available for all popular computing platforms. MySQL software and documentation can be downloaded from `http://www.mysql.org`. Some Linux system distributions, such as the one from Red Hat, include MySQL. This section describes a small part of MySQL. As with other software systems illustrated in this book, we do not discuss how to install or manage MySQL. These are usually system administration tasks. We cover the use of MySQL only, not its administration.

The first step when using MySQL is logging in to the MySQL system, which is done with the following command (at the command line of the operating system):

```
mysql [-h host] [-u username] [database_name] [-p]
```

The parts of this command that are in square brackets are optional. The *host* is the name of the server running MySQL; if absent, MySQL assumes it is the user's machine. If *username* is absent, it assumes that the name you used to log on to the machine is the correct username. If *database_name* is given, that database is selected as the focus of MySQL, making it the object of subsequent commands. If —p is included, it means a password is required, for which MySQL will ask.

Once you have successfully logged into MySQL, it is ready to receive commands. Although it is called "logging on," what you are actually doing is starting execution of the MySQL system.

If the database to be accessed already exists but its name was not included when logging in to MySQL, the `use` command can be used to focus on the database of interest. For example, if we want to access a database named `cars`, the following would be used:

```
use cars;
```

This is sometimes called making a specific database the "current" database for the MySQL server. The MySQL response to this command is as follows:

```
Database changed
```

This response seems odd because no change has been made to a database. Note the semicolon at the end of the `use` command—it is essential here, as it is for all MySQL commands. If a command is given without a semicolon, MySQL will wait indefinitely for one. Until a semicolon is found, MySQL behaves as if the remainder of the command is yet to be typed.

If a database is not specified when logging in to MySQL and a database command is given before `use` is used to focus on a database, the following error message will be issued:

```
ERROR 1046: No Database Selected
```

If a new database is to be created, the database itself must be created first and then the tables that will make up the database. A new database is created with the SQL CREATE DATABASE command. For example:

```
CREATE DATABASE cars;
```

This command also elicits an odd response from MySQL:

```
Query ok, 1 row affected (0.05 sec)
```

The time given varies with the speed of the host machine and its current load.

The tables of a database are created with the CREATE TABLE command, whose syntax is that of SQL. For example:

```
CREATE TABLE Equipment
   (Equip_id  INT  UNSIGNED  NOT NULL  AUTO_INCREMENT
               PRIMARY KEY,
    Equip  CHAR(10)
   );
```

The INT and UNSIGNED parts of the Equip_id column indicate the data type. The AUTO_INCREMENT is a MySQL convenience. It specifies that the values of this column need not be given when populating the table. The values 1, 2, 3, and so forth will be implicitly assigned. The value NULL is given in place of a value for a column so specified when populating the table with INSERT. A large number of different data types are possible for field values. The most common of these are CHAR(*length*), INT, and FLOAT(*total*, *fractional*), where *total* specifies the total number of characters, including both digits and the decimal point, and *fractional* gives the number of digits to the right of the decimal point.

The SHOW command can be used to display the tables of the database, as in the following:

```
SHOW TABLES;
```

If our sample database, cars, is the database of current focus, this produces the following:

```
--------------
show
--------------
+---------------------+
|                     |
| Tables_in_cars      |
|                     |
+---------------------+
| Corvettes           |
| Corvettes_Equipment |
| Equipment           |
| States              |
+---------------------+
```

The DESCRIBE command can be used to display the description of the structure of a table. For example,

```
DESCRIBE Corvettes;
```

produces the following:

```
+-----------+-----------------+-----+-----+---------+----------------+
|Field      |Type             |Null |Key  |Default  |Extra           |
+-----------+-----------------+-----+-----+---------+----------------+
|Vette_id   |int(10) unsigned |     |PRI  |NULL     |auto_increment  |
+-----------+-----------------+-----+-----+---------+----------------+
|Body_style |char(12)         |     |     |         |                |
+-----------+-----------------+-----+-----+---------+----------------+
|Miles      |float(4,1)       |     |     |0.0      |                |
+-----------+-----------------+-----+-----+---------+----------------+
|Year       |int(10) unsigned |     |     |0        |                |
+-----------+-----------------+-----+-----+---------+----------------+
|State      |int(10) unsigned |     |     |0        |                |
+-----------+-----------------+-----+-----+---------+----------------+
```

The other MySQL commands that are needed here—INSERT, SELECT, DROP, UPDATE, and DELETE—are all implementations of their corresponding SQL commands. Therefore, their descriptions do not need to be repeated in this section.

There are many tools available to aid in database administration (for example, from http://dev.mysql.com). One of these, MySQL Administrator, is a program that performs configuring, monitoring, starting and stopping a MySQL server, managing users and connections, performing backups, and several other administrative tasks.

13.5 Database Access with PHP and MySQL

PHP access to a database is often done with two HTML documents: one to collect a user request for a database access and one to host the PHP code to process the request and generate the return HTML document. The user request collector is a simple HTML document. Therefore, this section is primarily about the database connection and processing.

13.5.1 Potential Problems with Special Characters

When a query is made on a database through a browser, the result of the query must be returned to the browser as HTML. Putting database field data into an HTML document creates a potential problem. A field retrieved from the database may contain characters that are special in HTML, namely >, <, ", or &. PHP includes a function, htmlspecialchars, that replaces all occurrences of these four special characters in its parameter with their corresponding entities. For example, consider the following code:

```
$str = "Apples & grapes <raisins, too>";
$str = htmlspecialchars($str);
```

After the interpretation of this code, the value of $str has the following value:

```
"Apples &amp; grapes &lt;raisins, too&gt;"
```

This string is now ready to be made the content of an HTML tag without causing any browser confusion.

Another problem with special characters can occur with PHP scripts that get values through GET, POST, or from a cookie. Strings from these sources could include single quotes, double quotes, backslashes, and null characters, all of which could possibly cause problems if they are used in other strings in a script. To avoid these problems, the PHP system has an implicit backslashing function named magic_quotes_gpc, which can be turned on or off in the PHP.ini file. When this function is enabled, which is the default, all values received in a script from $_POST, $_GET, and $_COOKIE have backslashes implicitly inserted in front of all single quotes, double quotes, backslashes, and null characters. This avoids any problems that could be caused by those characters. For example, if the string O'Reilly is fetched from $_POST, it would be converted by magic_quotes_gpc to O\'Reilly. Unfortunately, this causes other problems. If the script compares the name to a nonslashed version, the comparison will fail. Furthermore, even displaying the name will show the backslash.

This problem is relevant here because we want to have a PHP script get SQL commands from a text box in an XHTML document. For example, suppose magic_quotes_gpc is on and the value for a query obtained from a text box on a form is as follows:

```
SELECT * FROM Corvettes WHERE Body_style = 'coupe'
```

If the name of the text box is query, its value is put in $query with the following statement:

```
$query = $_POST['query'];
```

The value of $query is converted to the following by magic_quotes_gpc:

```
SELECT * FROM Corvettes WHERE Body_style = \'coupe\'
```

Unfortunately, this string is not a legal SQL command (because of the backslashes). If it is sent to MySQL as a command, MySQL will reject it and report an error. Therefore, if complete SQL commands are to be collected from a form, magic_quotes_gpc must be disabled in PHP.ini to avoid the extra backslashes. The alternative to changing the value of magic_quotes_gpc is to remove the extra slashes in the PHP script with the predefined function `stripslashes`, as in the following:

```
$query = stripslashes($query);
```

13.5.2 Connecting to MySQL and Selecting a Database

The PHP function `mysql_connect` connects a script to a MySQL server. This function takes three parameters, all of which are optional. The first is the host that is running MySQL; the default is localhost (the machine on which the script is running). The second parameter is the username for MySQL; the default is the username in which the PHP process runs. The third parameter is the password for the database; the default is blank (works if the database does not require a password). For example, if the default parameters were acceptable, we could use the following:

```
$db = mysql_connect();
```

Of course, the connect operation could fail, in which case the value returned would be `false` (rather than a reference to the database). Therefore, the call to `mysql_connect` usually is used in conjunction with `die`.

The connection to a database is terminated with the `mysql_close` function. This function is not necessary when using MySQL through a PHP script because the connection will be closed implicitly when the script terminates.

When running MySQL from the command line, a database must be selected as the current, or focused, database. This is also necessary when using MySQL through PHP; it is accomplished with the `mysql_select_db` function, as shown in the following:

```
mysql_select_db("cars");
```

13.5.3 Requesting MySQL Operations

MySQL operations are requested through the `mysql_query` function. Typically, the operation, in the form of a string literal, is assigned to a variable. Then `mysql_query` is called with the variable as its parameter. For example:

```
$query = "SELECT * from Corvettes";
$result = mysql_query($query);
```

The return value from `mysql_query` is used to identify, internally, the data that resulted from the operation. In most cases, the first thing to do with the result is to determine the number of rows. This is obtained with the `mysql_num_rows` function, which is given the result value returned by `mysql_query`, as shown in the following:

```
$num_rows = mysql_num_rows($result);
```

The number of fields in a result row can be determined with `mysql_num_fields`, as shown in the following:

```
$num_fields = mysql_num_fields($result);
```

The rows of the result can be retrieved into several different forms. We will use `mysql_fetch_array`, which returns an array of the next row. Then the field values can be obtained by subscripting the return array with the column names. For example, if the result of a query had columns for `State_id` and `State`, we could display the results with the following code:

```
$num_rows = mysql_num_rows($result);

for ($row_num = 1; $row_num <= $num_rows; $row_num++) {
  $row = mysql_fetch_array($result);
  print "<p> Result row number" . $row_num .
      ". State_id: ";
  print htmlspecialchars($row["State_id"]);
  print " State: ";
  print htmlspecialchars($row["State"]);
  print "</p>";
}
```

The situation in which the column names are not known is considered in Section 13.5.4, which includes a complete example of accessing a database through PHP and MySQL.

13.5.4 A PHP/MySQL Example

One simple example of Web access to a database is to use an HTML form to collect a query from a user, apply the query to the database, and return a document that shows the results of the query. The form that allows users to input queries is simple. The PHP script to connect to the database and perform the query is also relatively simple—we have done all of this in Section 13.5.3. All that remains is to get the results into a form that is easy to present to the user. The example of displaying query results in Section 13.5.3 was easy because the names of the columns of the result were known and the results were not put in a table.

The rows of the result of a query are PHP arrays (recall that PHP arrays are really hashes). These result arrays have double sets of elements, one with numeric keys and one with string keys. For example, if a query gets a row with the field values (1, Alabama), the row actually stores four hash elements, two with numeric keys and two with string keys. For the `States` table of the `cars` database, the result row would actually have the following:

```
((0, 1), (State_id, 1), (1, Alabama), (State, Alabama))
```

If a row is indexed with numbers, the element values are returned. For example, if a row of the result of a query is in `$row`, then `$row[0]` is the value of the first field in the row, `$row[1]` is the value of the second field, and so forth. The rows could be indexed with strings, in which case `$row["State"]` would have the value `Alabama`. As a result of this double storage of result fields, the result rows have twice as many elements as there are fields in the result. If only the values are needed, they can be fetched from the value part of every other hash element, beginning with the second (the element with subscript 1). The following will display all of the field values in the result row in $row:

```
$values = array_values($row);
for ($index = 0; $index < $num_fields; $index++)
    print "$values[2 * $index + 1] <br />";
```

When the results are being returned as HTML content, it is always a good idea to use htmlspecialchars on the field values.

Getting the column labels from the results of a MySQL query can be confusing. From the example of the actual contents of a result array previously shown, the column labels are the keys of the odd-numbered elements of the array (State_id and State). The keys can be displayed in the same way the values were displayed previously.

```
$keys = array_keys($row);
for ($index = 0; $index < $num_fields; $index++)
  print "$keys[2 * $index + 1] <br />";
```

Following is the HTML document carsdata.html, which collects queries on the cars database from the user.

```
<!-- carsdata.html
     Uses a form to collect a query against the cars
     database.
     Calls the PHP script, access_cars.php to perform
     the given query and display the results
     -->
<html>
  <head><title> Access to the cars database </title>
  </head>
  <body>
    <p>
      Please enter your query:
      <br />
      <form action  = "access_cars.php" method = "post">
        <textarea  rows = "2"  cols = "80" name = "query" >
        </textarea>
        <br /><br />
        <input type = "reset"  value = "Reset" />
        <input type = "submit"  value = "Submit request" />
      </form>
    </p>
  </body>
</html>
```

The following HTML/PHP document, `access_cars.php`, processes a query and returns the results in a table:

```
<!-- access_cars.php
    A PHP script to access the cars database
    through MySQL
    -->
<html>
  <head>
    <title> Access the cars database with MySQL </title>
  </head>
  <body>
<?php

// Connect to MySQL
$db = mysql_connect("localhost", "rws", "");
if (!$db)
  exit("Error - Could not connect to MySQL");

// Select the cars database
$er = mysql_select_db("cars");
if (!$er)
  exit("Error - Could not select the cars database");

// Get the query and clean it up (delete leading and trailing
// whitespace and remove backslashes from magic_quotes_gpc)
$query = $_POST['query'];
trim($query);
$query = stripslashes($query);

// Display the query, after fixing html characters
$query_html = htmlspecialchars($query);
print "<p> <b> The query is: </b> " . $query_html . "</p>";

// Execute the query
$result = mysql_query($query);
if (!$result) {
  print "Error - the query could not be executed";
  $error = mysql_error();
  print "<p>" . $error . "</p>";
  exit;
}

// Display the results in a table
```

```
print "<table><caption> <h2> Query Results </h2> </caption>";
print "<tr align = 'center'>";

// Get the number of rows in the result, as well as the first row
//  and the number of fields in the rows
$num_rows = mysql_num_rows($result);
$row = mysql_fetch_array($result);
$num_fields = mysql_num_fields($result);

// Produce the column labels
$keys = array_keys($row);
for ($index = 0; $index < $num_fields; $index++)
  print "<th>" . $keys[2 * $index + 1] . "</th>";
print "</tr>";

// Output the values of the fields in the rows
for ($row_num = 0; $row_num < $num_rows; $row_num++) {
  print "<tr align = 'center'>";
  $values = array_values($row);
  for ($index = 0; $index < $num_fields; $index++) {
    $value = htmlspecialchars($values[2 * $index + 1]);
    print "<th>" . $value . "</th> ";
  }
  print "</tr>";
  $row = mysql_fetch_array($result);
}
print "</table>";
?>
  </body>
</html>
```

Figure 13.8 shows a browser display of the results of `access_cars.php` on the given query.

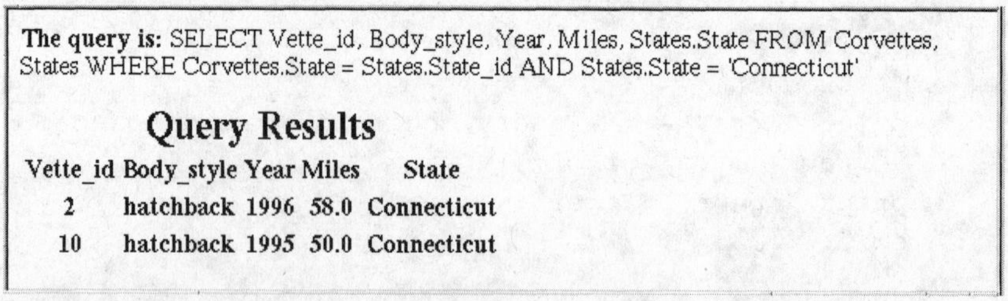

The query is: SELECT Vette_id, Body_style, Year, Miles, States.State FROM Corvettes, States WHERE Corvettes.State = States.State_id AND States.State = 'Connecticut'

Query Results

Vette_id	Body_style	Year	Miles	State
2	hatchback	1996	58.0	Connecticut
10	hatchback	1995	50.0	Connecticut

Figure 13.8 Display of the return document from `access_cars.php`

The two documents, `carsdata.html` and `access_cars.php`, which together collect a query from a user, apply it to the database, and return the results, can be combined. After inserting the XHTML markup from `carsdata.html` into `access_cars.php`, several modifications and additions must be made to the resulting document. First, the `action` attribute of the form must be changed to be self referential by changing the value to the name of the combined file. Next, there is the issue of how to get the PHP processor to produce the query collection markup the first time the document is requested and interpret the query processing code on the next request. The commonly used approach to this is to create a hidden input element that sets its value when the document is first displayed. The PHP code in the document checks the value of the hidden element to determine whether the action is to display a text area to collect a query or to apply the query to the database and display the result. The hidden element is defined with markup as shown here:

```
<input type = "hidden"  name = "stage"  value = "1" />
```

The PHP code to test the value of the hidden element has the following form:

```
$stage = $_POST["stage"];
if (!IsSet($stage)) { ... }
```

The then clause of this selector would contain the display of the form to collect the query. The else clause would contain the query processing and result display code. The combination of `carsdata.html` and `access_cars.php`, named `access_cars2.php`, follows:

```
<!-- access_cars2.php
     A PHP script to both get a query from the user and
     access the cars database through MySQL to get and
     display the result of the query.
     -->
<html>
  <head>
    <title> Access the cars database with MySQL </title>
  </head>
  <body>
<?php

// Is this the first request?
$stage = $_POST["stage"];
if (!IsSet($stage)) {
?>
  <p>
    Please enter your query:
```

```php
            <br />
            <form  method = "POST"  action = "access_cars2.php" >
              <textarea  rows = "2"  cols = "80"  name = "query">
              </textarea>
              <br /><br />
              <input type = "hidden"  name = "stage"  value = "1" />
              <input type = "submit"  value = "Submit request" />
            </form>
        </p>
<?php
} else {  // $stage was set, so process the query

    // Connect to MySQL
    $db = mysql_connect("localhost", "rws", "");
    if (!$db)
      exit("Error - Could not connect to MySQL");

    // Select the cars database
    $er = mysql_select_db("cars");
    if (!$er)
      exit("Error - Could not select the cars database");

    // Clean up the given query (delete leading and trailing
    // whitespace
    $query = $_POST['query'];
    trim($query);

    // Fix the query for browser display and display it
    $query_html = htmlspecialchars($query);
    print "<p> <b> The query is: </b> " . $query_html . "</p>";

    // Execute the query
    $result = mysql_query($query);
    if (!$result) {
      print "Error - the query could not be executed";
      $error = mysql_error();
      print "<p>" . $error . "</p>";
      exit;
    }

    // Display the results in a table
    print "<table><caption> <h2> Query Results </h2> </caption>";
    print "<tr align = 'center'>";
```

```php
    // Get the number of rows in the result, as well as the first
    // row and the number of fields in the rows
    $num_rows = mysql_num_rows($result);
    $row = mysql_fetch_array($result);
    $num_fields = mysql_num_fields($result);

    // Produce the column labels
    $keys = array_keys($row);
    for ($index = 0; $index < $num_fields; $index++)
    print "<th>" . $keys[2 * $index + 1] . "</th>";
    print "</tr>";

    // Output the values of the fields in the rows
    for ($row_num = 0; $row_num < $num_rows; $row_num++) {
      print "<tr align = 'center'>";
      $values = array_values($row);
      for ($index = 0; $index < $num_fields; $index++){
        $value = htmlspecialchars($values[2 * $index + 1]);
        print "<th>" . $value . "</th> ";
      }
      print "</tr>";
      $row = mysql_fetch_array($result);
    }  // end of the for ($row_num = 0; ...
  print "</table>";
}  // end of the else clause
?>
  </body>
</html>
```

13.6 Database Access with JDBC and MySQL

JDBC is a Java API for database access. A servlet can use JDBC to connect to a database and send SQL commands to the database as the parameter of a JDBC method. The Java interfaces that define JDBC are included in the `java.sql` package, which is part of the standard Java distribution.

13.6.1 JDBC and MySQL

This section describes the mechanisms for using JDBC to perform simple SQL operations on an existing database. The first step in developing a JDBC servlet is to establish a connection between the application and the database interface, or driver. The `DriverManager` class provides the method `getConnection`, which establishes the connection to the database. This class must select the correct driver for the database from those that have been registered.

The general form of a reference to a database for the connection operation is as follows:

```
jdbc:subprotocol_name:more_info
```

The *subprotocol_name* part is used to specify the driver for the database. For a MySQL database, the *subprotocol_name* is `mysql`. The *more_info* part is dependent on the subprotocol being used. If the database is local, it may be just the name of the database. If the database is somewhere else on the Internet, it may be the URL of the database. In the case of a database being on the same machine as the client, the *more_info* part includes `localhost` and the name of the database followed by a username and a password for the database. The username and password are attached to the database address in the same way HTML `GET` parameters are attached to a URL. For the sample MySQL database `cars`, assuming root is the user and there is no password, the reference is as follows:

```
jdbc:mysql://localhost/cars?user=root
```

A database driver may be registered in two ways, one general and the other specific. The general approach is to have the system property `jdbc.drivers` maintain a list of drivers. A servlet can add a new driver to this property by assigning the driver's class address to the property. For example, consider this statement:

```
jdbc.drivers = org.gjt.mm.mysql.Driver;
```

Here, `org.gjt.mm.mysql.Driver` is the name of the MySQL JDBC driver class that is used in the examples in this section. (The driver can be downloaded from `http://www.mysql.org`.) The only other requirement to make the driver usable is that it be loadable by the servlet, which means that it must be stored in a place where the servlet can access it. The driver manager is responsible for choosing the correct driver from those that are registered.

The less general way of registering a driver is to do it manually with the `forName` method of the `Class` class, giving the name of the driver class as a parameter:

```
Class.forName("org.gjt.mm.mysql.Driver").newInstance();
```

This approach is adequate if the servlet will be used exclusively for databases from one specific vendor.

The connection to a database from a servlet is made by creating a `Connection` object with the `getConnection` method of the `DriverManager` class. For the sample database `cars` and the MySQL database system, the `Connection` object can be created with the following statement:

```
myCon = DriverManager.getConnection(
    "jdbc:mysql://localhost/cars?user=root");
```

The `Connection` object is used to specify all database operations from the servlet.

After the appropriate database driver is registered and the connection to the database is established, a servlet can access the database using SQL commands. The first step in using SQL from a servlet is to create a `Statement` object through which one of the `Statement` methods can be used to actually issue the command. The `Statement` object is created with the `createStatement` method of the `Connection` class. If `myCon` is the `Connection` object, the following statement can be used:

```
Statement myStmt = myCon.createStatement();
```

SQL commands are created as `String` objects, as shown in the following example:

```
final String sql_com =
    "UPDATE Corvettes SET Year = 1991 WHERE Vette_id = 7";
```

From the JDBC point of view, there are two categories of SQL commands: the action commands, which include `INSERT`, `UPDATE`, `DELETE`, `CREATE TABLE`, and `DROP TABLE`; and the query command, `SELECT`. The action commands are executed through the `executeUpdate` method of the `Statement` object. For example, the previous SQL command `sql_com` can be executed with the following statement:

```
myStmt.executeUpdate(sql_com);
```

The `executeUpdate` method returns the number of rows that were affected by the command that it sent to the database.

A `SELECT` SQL command can be executed by sending it as the parameter to the `executeQuery` method of the `Statement` object. Executing a `SELECT` command differs from executing an action command in that the `SELECT` command is expected to return a part of the data found in the database. So, a call to `executeQuery` must be assigned to a program variable. The class of this variable must be `ResultSet`, which is structured to store such results and which has methods to provide access to the data of the result. Consider the following example:

```
ResultSet result;
final String sql_com =
    "SELECT * FROM Corvettes WHERE Year <= 1990"
result = myStmt.executeQuery(sql_com);
```

Objects of the `ResultSet` class are similar to objects of classes that implement the related interface `Enumeration`. In both cases, the elements of the object are accessed through an iterator method. In the case of `Enumeration`, the iterator method is named `nextElement`; in the case of `ResultSet`, it is named `next`. The `next` method is a predicate—it returns a Boolean value, depending on whether there is another element in the `ResultSet` object. Its action is to make the next element of the `ResultSet` object the current one—that is, the one that can be accessed through one of the access methods provided by `ResultSet`. Initially, there is no current element of a `ResultSet` object. Therefore, `next` must be called to make the first element current. The elements of a `ResultSet` object are typically accessed in a loop such as the following:

```
while(result.next()) {
    access and process the current element
}
```

Here, `result` is the object returned by `executeQuery`.

The actual structure of a `ResultSet` object is not visible to the application, so it is irrelevant. The information in a `ResultSet` object is extracted through a collection of access methods. Each element of a `ResultSet` object represents the information in a row of the result of the query operation. Field values in the rows can be extracted by the access methods, whose names are in the following general form:

get*Type_name*

Here, the *Type_name* part is one of the Java data types, either a primitive type such as `int` or `float` or a class such as `String`.

There are actually two of each of the named access methods: one that takes an `int` parameter, which specifies the column number, starting at 1; and one that takes a `String` parameter, which specifies the column name. For example, suppose the first row of the `ResultSet` object for the `SELECT` specified previously happened to be as follows:

```
3, "convertible", 13.5, 2001, 1
```

Assuming that the variable `style` is defined to be a `String` object, the value of the `Body_style` column `"convertible"` could be obtained with either of the following two method calls:

```
style = result.getString("Body_style");
style = result.getString(2);
```

The SQL data types do not perfectly match the Java data types. Some of the most commonly used SQL data types and their Java counterparts are shown in Table 13.1.

Table 13.1 Common SQL data types and their Java counterparts

SQL Data Type	Java Data Type
`INTEGER` or `INT`	`int`
`SMALLINT`	`short`
`FLOAT(n)`	`double`
`REAL`	`float`
`DOUBLE`	`double`
`CHARACTER(n)` or `CHAR(n)`	`String`
`VARCHAR(n)`	`String`
`BOOLEAN`	`boolean`

The get*Type_name* methods attempt to convert SQL data types to equivalent Java data types. For example, if getString is used to fetch an INTEGER value, the number will be converted to a String object.

13.6.2 Metadata

If a servlet is being developed that must work with any database—that is, the exact structure of the database is not known—the code must be able to get table names and column names from the database. Also, the types of the data in the result rows must be known. Information that describes the database itself or some part of the database is called *metadata*. There are two kinds of metadata: metadata that describes the database and metadata that describes a ResultSet object that is returned by the execution of a query.

A method of the Connection object, getMetaData, creates an object of DatabaseMetaData type, which can be used to get information about a database. For example:

```
DatabaseMetaData dbmd = myCon.getMetaData();
```

To deal with the many different database configurations, many different methods are defined in the DatabaseMetaData class. Fortunately, most of them are infrequently used, and we can illustrate the use of metadata through just one that is commonly used, getTables. Although getTables returns a variety of information, here we are interested only in table names.

The getTables method takes four parameters, only the last of which interests us. The last actual parameter to getTables specifies an array of String objects with just one element, which is set to the value "TABLE". The other three actual parameters can be null. The getTables method returns a ResultSet object that has information about the tables of the database, the third row of which has the table names. Assuming that the Connection object for a database is myCon, the code to produce a list of the names of the tables in the database is as follows:

```
String tbl[] = {"TABLE"};
DatabaseMetaData dbmd = myCon.getMetaData();
result = dbmd.getTables(null, null, null, tbl);
System.out.println("The tables in the database are: \n\n");
while (result.next()) {
  System.out.println(result.getString(3));
}
```

Adding this code to a program with access to the cars database would produce the following output:

```
The tables in this database are:
CORVETTES
CORVETTES_EQUIPMENT
EQUIPMENT
STATES
```

Fetching metadata about the result of a query on a database is more complicated than getting the table names. The metadata for a query result has a different structure than that for the general database information. For the query result, the metadata is stored in an object of the `ResultSetMetaData` class. An object of this class is returned from the `ResultSet` object when the `getMetaData` method is called, as shown in the following example:

```
ResultSetMetaData resultMd = result.getMetaData();
```

Using the `resultMd` object, the number of columns and their names, types, and sizes can be determined through the methods of `ResultSetMetaData`. The number of columns is returned by `getColumnCount`. The name of the ith column is returned by `getColumnLabel(i)`.

Using these objects and methods, the following code creates a display of the column names of the result produced by a query.

```
// Create an object for the metadata
ResultSetMetaData resultMd = result.getMetaData();

// Loop to fetch and display the column names
for (int i = 1; i <= resultMd.getColumnCount(); i++) {
  String columnName = resultMd.getColumnLabel(i);
  System.out.print(columnName + "\t");
}
System.out.println("\n");
```

The display produced by this code is as follows:

```
Vette_id     Body_style      Miles    Year     State
```

The problem of not knowing the types of the data in the result rows has a simple solution: The data can be converted to strings with `getString`, a method of the result object. This is illustrated in Section 13.6.3.

13.6.3 An Example

As an example, an HTML document that collects a database query in a text box will be used, similar to `carsdata.html`, which is used in Section 13.5.4 as the user interface to the PHP/MySQL example. The document calls a servlet to perform the query. The servlet uses its `init` method to establish the database connection and create the `Statement` object for the query method, `executeQuery`. These operations could be specified in the `doPost` method, but that would require reconnection to the database with every query. In the `init` method, they only happen once.

The `doPost` method performs the query operations and builds the return document of the results of the query. The query results are placed in an HTML table so that the output has a presentable appearance.

```java
// JDBCServlet.java
// This servlet receives an SQL query from its HTML document,
// connects to the cars database, performs the query on the
// database, and returns an HTML table of the results of the
// query

import javax.servlet.*;
import javax.servlet.http.*;
import java.io.*;
import java.util.*;
import java.sql.*;

public class JDBCServlet extends HttpServlet {
  private Connection myCon;
  private Statement myStmt;

  // The init method - instantiate the db driver, connect to the
  // db, and create a statement for an SQL command
  public void init() {

    // Instantiate the driver for MySQL
    try {
      Class.forName("org.gjt.mm.mysql.Driver").newInstance();
    }
    catch (Exception e) {
      e.printStackTrace();
    }

    // Create the connection to the cars db
    try {
      myCon = DriverManager.getConnection (
              "jdbc:mysql://localhost/cars?user=root");
    }
    catch (SQLException e) {
      e.printStackTrace();
    }

    // Create the statement for SQL queries
    try {
      myStmt = myCon.createStatement();
    }
    catch (Exception e) {
      e.printStackTrace();
    }
```

```java
  }  //** end of the init method

  // The doPost method - get the query, perform it, and produce
  // an HTML table of the results
  public void doPost(HttpServletRequest request,
                     HttpServletResponse response)
               throws ServletException, IOException {
    ResultSet result;
    String query, colName, dat;
    int numCols, index;
    ResultSetMetaData resultMd;

    // Get the SQL request command
    query = request.getParameter("Query");

    // Set the MIME type and get a writer
    response.setContentType("text/html");
    PrintWriter out = response.getWriter();

    // Create the initial html and display the request
    out.println("<html>");
    out.println("<head><title>JDBCServlet</title></head>");
    out.println("<body>");
    out.print("<p><b>The query is: </b>" + query + "</p>");

    // Perform the query
    try {
      result = myStmt.executeQuery(query);

      // Get the result's metadata and the number of result rows
      resultMd = result.getMetaData();
      numCols = resultMd.getColumnCount();

      // Produce the table header and caption
      out.println("<table border>");
      out.println("<caption> <b> Query Results </b> </caption>");
      out.println("<tr>");

      // Loop to produce the column headings
      for (index = 1; index <= numCols; index++) {
        colName = resultMd.getColumnLabel(index);
        out.print("<th>" + colName + "</th>");
      }
      out.println("</tr>");

      // Loop to produce the rows of the result
```

```
      while (result.next()) {
        out.println("<tr>");

        // Loop to produce the data of a row of the result
        for (index = 1; index <= numCols; index++) {
          dat = result.getString(index);
          out.println("<td>" + dat + "</td>");
        }  //** end of for (index = 0; ...
        out.println("</tr>");
      }  //** end of while (result.next()) ...
    out.println("</table>");
    }  //** end of try

    catch (Exception e) {
      e.printStackTrace();
    }  //** end of catch
    out.println("</body></html>");
  }  //** end of doPost method
}  //** end of class JDBCServlet
```

Figure 13.9 shows a browser display of the output of JDBCServlet on a given query.

The query is: SELECT * FROM Corvettes WHERE Year < 2001 AND Miles < 20.0

Query Results

Vette_id	Body_style	Miles	Year	State
1	coupe	18.0	1997	4
4	hatchback	19.0	1995	2
6	hardtop	15.0	2000	2
8	convertible	17.0	1999	5
9	hardtop	17.0	2000	5

Figure 13.9 Display of the results of JDBCServlet

Summary

A relational database consists of a collection of related tables of data. Most tables include a column of primary keys, which uniquely identify the rows. A cross-reference table contains no data; instead, it contains the primary keys of two data tables, providing a many-to-many relationship between the data in the two tables.

SQL is a standard language for specifying accesses and modifications to relational databases. All commonly used relational database systems support SQL. The most frequently used SQL commands are CREATE, SELECT, INSERT, UPDATE, and DELETE.

The CREATE command specifies a table name and a list of column names and their associated constraints. The SELECT command specifies one or more columns of one or more tables, along with a Boolean expression that provides a constraint on the data in the specified columns. SELECT is a complex and powerful tool. The INSERT command specifies a table name, a list of column names, and a list of values that correspond to the column names. The UPDATE command specifies a table name and a list of column name/value pairs, along with a specific primary key value. The DELETE command specifies a table name and the primary key of a specific column.

A join operation, which can be specified by a SELECT command, creates a new table by joining part of the data of one table with part of the data of another table. The objective of a join is to make information available to the user that is not stored in a single table.

A two-tier client/server architecture is common. In it, a client machine communicates directly with a server machine. The Web is an example of a two-tier client/server configuration. A third tier is used in a client/server architecture when it is better for one or both of the client or the server to communicate only indirectly with the other.

One approach to building database applications is to extend a general-purpose programming language so that it can specify SQL commands and interact with a database through them. The disadvantage of this is that such applications are not likely to be portable among the databases of different vendors. Microsoft's Access system provides a way to access the databases of most common vendors through an interface called ODBC. Because ODBC has been implemented by most vendors for their databases, this approach provides a way to develop portable applications.

MySQL is a relational database server that implements SQL. There are drivers for MySQL for most common database APIs, including PHP and JDBC.

PHP has implemented APIs for most common database systems. The MySQL API for PHP includes functions for connecting to a database (mysql_connect), executing SQL commands (mysql_query), and retrieving rows from query results (for example, mysql_fetch_array). Getting the column names for query results is a bit confusing but not difficult.

The goal of JDBC is related to that of ODBC, except that it is part of one general-purpose programming language, Java. There are drivers for JDBC for all common database systems. A servlet must create a connection to a database for which there is a JDBC driver available. Then it creates a Statement object into which can be stored an SQL command as a string. The command can be executed by passing it as a parameter to a method through the Statement object. The return value from the execution of a SELECT command is an object of ResultSet type, which stores the rows that were extracted from the database. Actual data values are obtained from the returned object through a collection of methods called through the object.

Metadata is data about the database rather than data stored in the database. It is common to need information about the result object returned from the execution of a SELECT command. This information is obtained by a method called through the result object. Specific information is obtained by methods called through the metadata object.

Review Questions

13.1 What is specified by the WHERE clause of a SELECT command?

13.2 What is the purpose of the primary keys of a table in a relational database?

13.3 What is the disadvantage of embedding SQL in a programming language?

13.4 What is the purpose of a cross-reference table?

13.5 How are string literals delimited in SQL?

13.6 What is the relationship between ODBC and JDBC?

13.7 What does the NOT NULL constraint specify in a column of a CREATE TABLE SQL command?

13.8 What does an asterisk specify when it appears as the value of a SELECT clause?

13.9 How are the column names associated with the values in an INSERT command?

13.10 What exactly is a table join, and how is one specified in SQL?

13.11 What does the PHP function mysql_fetch_array do?

13.12 What is the purpose of a third tier in a client/server configuration for Web access to a database?

13.13 Why are two-tier client/server configurations sometimes inadequate?

13.14 Explain the exact form of the value returned by mysql_fetch_array.

13.15 Explain how SQL database access can be provided by extending a programming language.

13.16 What is ODBC, and why is it useful?

13.17 What is MySQL?

13.18 How can a program iterate through the object returned by executeQuery?

13.19 What does the MySQL constraint `auto_increment` do?

13.20 What is the problem with quotes in an SQL command obtained from a form element in an HTML document?

13.21 What is the purpose of an `UPDATE` command?

13.22 What is the purpose of the PHP `mysql_select_db` function?

13.23 What is metadata?

13.24 How can a PHP program determine the number of rows in a query result?

13.25 What method of what class is used to execute a `SELECT` command?

13.26 Explain the two ways of using JDBC.

13.27 What method of what class is used to connect to a database when using JDBC?

13.28 What are the two ways column labels can be obtained from an object of metadata?

13.29 Explain the two ways to register a JDBC driver.

13.30 What method of what class is used to execute an SQL action command?

13.31 What class of object is returned from the `executeQuery` method?

13.32 What advantage does a third-tier computer provide when using JDBC?

13.33 What is the form of the methods used to extract values from the object returned by `executeQuery`?

13.34 How is the collection of metadata extracted from a database?

13.35 What purpose does a `Statement` object serve when using SQL through JDBC?

Exercises

13.1 Use MySQL to create a database of information about used houses for sale, similar to the cars database used in this chapter. Make up facilities that characterize houses.

13.2 Modify and test the program `access_cars.php` to handle `UPDATE`, `INSERT`, and `DELETE` SQL commands.

13.3 Modify and test the program `JDBCServlet.java` to handle `UPDATE`, `INSERT`, and `DELETE` SQL commands.

CHAPTER

14

Introduction to Ruby

Our primary interest in Ruby in this book is its use with the Web software development framework, Rails. However, Ruby is an interesting and useful language outside its use in Rails. This chapter takes you on a quick tour of Ruby, introducing many of the important concepts and constructs but leaving out many details of the language. In spite of its brevity, however, if you are an experienced programmer, particularly one well-versed in object-oriented programming, you can learn to write useful Ruby programs by studying this chapter. In particular, after studying this chapter and the next, you will be in a position to be an effective Rails developer. However, be warned that Ruby differs fundamentally from conventional languages, such as C++, Java, and C#, both in its syntax and because it is an interpreted scripting language. If you need more details than can be found in this chapter, there are several books dedicated solely to Ruby, as well as a Web site that includes a wide variety of information about the language (www.ruby-lang.org).

This chapter begins with the background of Ruby and a description of its scalar data types and their use in expressions and assignment statements. Next, it covers control expressions and the collection of control constructs available in Ruby. Then, it discusses Ruby's two built-in data structures, arrays and hashes. This is followed by a description of methods and how they are defined and called. Next, some of the details of classes are introduced. Finally, code blocks, iterators, and pattern matching are described. Although we attempt to introduce a significant subset of Ruby in a single chapter, do not be misled into thinking that this is a small or simple language—it is neither.

14.1 Origins and Uses of Ruby

As stated in Chapter 1 "Fundamentals," Ruby was designed in Japan by Yukihiro Matsumoto (a.k.a. Matz) and was released in 1996. It started as a replacement for the languages Matz found inadequate for his purposes, Perl and Python. Use of Ruby in Japan grew rapidly and spread to the rest of the world a few years later. The quick growth of the use of Rails, the Web application development framework that is both written in Ruby and uses Ruby, has accelerated the expansion of the language. Rails is probably the most common use of Ruby.

Learning Ruby is made easier by its implementation method, pure interpretation. Rather than needing to learn about and write a layer of boilerplate code around some simple logic, in Ruby one can write just that simple logic and request its interpretation. For example, consider the difference between a "Hello World" program in a language like C++ or Java and the Ruby "Hello World" program:

```
puts "Hello World"
```

From Perl, Ruby gets regular expressions and implicit variables. From JavaScript it gets objects that can change during execution. However, Ruby has many more differences with those languages than it has similarities. For example, as in pure object-oriented languages, every data value in Ruby is an object, whether it is a simple integer literal or a complete file system.

Ruby is available for every common computing platform. Furthermore, as is the case with PHP, the Ruby implementation is free.

14.2 Scalar Types and Their Operations

Ruby has three categories of data types—scalars, arrays, and hashes. This section discusses the important characteristics of the most commonly used types, scalars. There are two categories of scalar types, numerics and character strings.

As stated earlier, everything in Ruby is an object—numeric literals, arrays, and even classes. Although this design is much more elegant than the mixed-type design of Java and C++, it takes a bit of getting used to.

14.2.1 Numeric and String Literals

All numeric data types in Ruby are descendants of the `Numeric` class. The immediate child classes of `Numeric` are `Float` and `Integer`. The `Integer` class has two child classes, `Fixnum` and `Bignum`.

An integer literal that fits into the range of a machine word, which is often 32 bits, is a `Fixnum` object. An integer literal that is outside the `Fixnum` range is a `Bignum` object. Though it is odd among programming languages, there is no length limitation (other than your computer's memory size) on integer literals. If a `Fixnum` integer grows beyond size limitation of `Fixnum` objects, it is coerced to a `Bignum` object. Likewise, if an operation on a Bignum object results in a value that fits in a `Fixnum` object, it is coerced to a `Fixnum` type.

Underscore characters can appear embedded in integer literals. Ruby ignores such underscores. This allows large numbers to be slightly more readable. For example, instead of `124761325`, `124_761_325` can be used.

A numeric literal that has either an embedded decimal point or a following exponent is a `Float` object, which is stored as the underlying machine's double-precision floating-point type. The decimal point must be embedded; that is, it must be both preceded and followed by at least one digit. So, `.435` is not a legal literal in Ruby.

All string literals are `String` objects, which are sequences of bytes that represent characters. There are two categories of string literals, single quoted and double quoted. Single-quoted string literals cannot include characters specified with escape sequences, such as newline characters specified with \n. If an actual single-quote character is needed in a string literal that is delimited by single quotes, the embedded single quote is preceded by a backslash, as in the following example:

```
'I\'ll meet you at O\'Malleys'
```

If an escape sequence is embedded in a single-quoted string literal, each character in the sequence is taken literally as itself. For example, the sequence \n in the following string literal will be treated as two characters, a backslash and an n:

```
'Some apples are red, \n some are green'
```

If a string literal with the same characteristics as a single-quoted string is needed but you want to use a different delimiter, precede the delimiter with q, as in the following example:

```
q$Don't you think she's pretty?$
```

If the new delimiter is a parenthesis, a brace, a bracket, or a pointed bracket, the left element of the pair must be used on the left, and the right element must be used on the right. For example:

```
q<Don't you think she's pretty?>
```

Double-quoted string literals differ from single-quoted string literals in two ways: First, they can include special characters specified with escape sequences; second, the values of variable names can be interpolated into the string, which means that their values are substituted for their names. The first of these differences is discussed here; the other will be discussed in Section 14.2.2.

In many situations, special characters that are specified with escape sequences must be included in string literals. For example, if the words on a line must be spaced by tabs, a double-quoted literal with embedded escape sequences for the tab character can be used as in the following:

```
"Runs \t Hits \t Errors"
```

A double quote can be embedded in a double-quoted string literal by preceding it with a backslash.

A different delimiter can be specified for string literals with the characteristics of double-quoted strings by preceding the new delimiter with Q as follows:

```
Q@"Why not learn Ruby?", he asked.@
```

The null string (one with no characters) can be denoted with either `''` or `""`.

14.2.2 Variables and Assignment Statements

Naming conventions in Ruby help identify different categories of variables. For now, we will deal with local variables only. Other naming conventions will be explained as needed.

The form of variable names is a lowercase letter or an underscore, followed by any number of uppercase or lowercase letters, digits, or underscores. The letters in a variable name are case sensitive, meaning that `fRIZZY`, `frizzy`, `frIzZy`, and `friZZy` are all distinct names. However, by convention, programmer-defined variable names do not include uppercase letters.

As mentioned earlier, double-quoted string literals can include the values of variables. In fact, the results of executing any Ruby code can be included. This is specified by placing the code in braces and preceding the left brace with a pound sign (#). For example:

```
"Tuesday's high temperature was #{tue_high}"
```

If the value of `tue_high` is 83, this string has the following value:

```
"Tuesday's high temperature was 83"
```

Consider the following literal:

```
"The cost of our apple order is $#{price * quantity}"
```

If the value of price is `1.65` and quantity is `6`, the value of this string is

```
"The cost of our apple order is $9.90"
```

Because Ruby is a pure object-oriented programming language, its variables are all references to objects. This is in contrast to more conventional languages, such as C++ and Java, which have two categories of variables, those for primitives and those that reference objects. In Ruby, every data value is an object, so it needs references only. Because references in Ruby are typeless, there is no point in declaring them. In fact, in Ruby there is no way to declare a variable.

A scalar variable that has not been assigned a value by the program has the value `nil`.

Ruby has constants, which are distinguished from variables by their names, which always begin with uppercase letters. A constant is created when it is assigned a value, which can be any constant expression. In Ruby, a constant can be assigned a new value, although it causes a warning message to the user.

Ruby includes some predefined, or *implicit*, variables. The names of implicit scalar variables begin with a dollar sign. The rest of the name of an implicit variable is often just one more special character, such as an underscore (_), a circumflex (^), or a backslash (\). This chapter and the next include some uses of these implicit variables.

The assignment statements of Ruby are exactly like those of the programming languages derived from C. The only thing to remember is that the variables of Ruby are all typeless references. All that is ever assigned in an assignment statement is the address of an object.

14.2.3 Numeric Operators

Most of Ruby's numeric operators are similar to those in other common programming languages, so they should be familiar to most readers. There are the binary operators, + for addition, – for subtraction, * for multiplication, / for division, ** for exponentiation, and % for modulus. The modulus operator is defined as follows: x % y produces the remainder of the value of x after division by y. If an integer is divided by an integer, integer division is done. Therefore, 3 / 2 produces 1.

The precedence rules of a language specify which operator is evaluated first when two operators that have different levels of precedence appear in an expression, separated only by an operand. The associativity rules of a language specify which operator is evaluated first when two operators with the same precedence level appear in an expression, separated only by an operand. The precedence and associativity of the numeric operators are given in Table 14.1.

Table 14.1 Precedence and associativity of the numeric operators

Operator	Associativity
**	Right
+, -	Right
*, /, %	Left
binary +, -	Left

The operators listed first have the highest precedence.

Note that Ruby does not include the increment (++) and decrement (--) operators found in all of the C-based languages.

Ruby includes the `Math` module, which has methods for basic trigonometric and transcendental functions. Among these are `cos` (cosine), `sin` (sine), `log` (logarithm), `sqrt` (square root), and `tan` (tangent). The methods of the `Math` module are referenced by prefixing their names with `Math.`, as in `Math.sin(x)`. All of these take any numeric type as a parameter and return a `Float` value.

Included with the Ruby implementation is an interactive interpreter, which is very useful to the student of Ruby. It allows one to type any Ruby expression and get an immediate response from the interpreter. The interactive interpreter's name is *Interactive Ruby*, whose acronym, IRB, is the name of the program that supports it. `irb` is entered by simply typing `irb` at the command prompt in the directory that contains the Ruby interpreter. For example, if the command prompt is a percent sign (%), one can type

```
% irb
```

`irb` will respond with its own prompt, which is

```
irb(main):001:0>
```

At this prompt, any Ruby expression or statement can be typed. `irb` interprets the expression or statement and returns the value after an implication symbol (=>). For example:

```
irb(main):001:0> 17 * 3
=> 51
irb(main):002:0>
```

The lengthy default prompt can be easily changed. We prefer the simple ">>" prompt. The default prompt can be changed to this with the following command:

```
irb(main):002:0> conf.prompt_i = ">>"
```

From here on, we will use this simple prompt.

14.2.4 String Methods

The Ruby `String` class has more than 75 methods, a few of which are described in this section. Many of these methods can be used as if they were operators. In fact, we sometimes call them operators, even though underneath they are all methods.

The `String` method for catenation is specified by plus (+), which can be used as a binary operator. This method creates a new string from its operands. For example:

```
>> "Happy" + " " + "Holidays!"
=> "Happy Holidays!"
```

The << method appends a string to the right end of another string, which of course only makes sense if the left operand is a variable. Like +, the << method can be used as a binary operator. For example:

```
>> mystr = "G'day "
=> "G'day "
>> mystr << "mate"
=> "G'day mate"
```

The first assignment above creates the specified string literal and sets the variable `mystr` to reference that memory location. If `mystr` is assigned to another variable, that variable will reference the same memory location as `mystr`. For example:

```
>> mystr = "Wow!"
=> "Wow!"
>> yourstr = mystr
=> "Wow!"
>> yourstr
=> "Wow!"
```

Now, both `mystr` and `yourstr` reference the same memory location, the place that has the string `"Wow!"`. If a different string literal is assigned to `mystr`, Ruby will build a memory location with the value of the new string literal and `mystr` will reference that location. But `yourstr` will still reference the location with `"Wow!"`. For example:

```
>> mystr = "Wow!"
=> "Wow!"
>> yourstr = mystr
=> "Wow!"
>> mystr = "What?"
=> "What?"
>> yourstr
=> "Wow!"
```

If you want to change the value of the location that `mystr` references, but let `mystr` reference the same memory location, the `replace` method is used. For example:

```
>> mystr = "Wow!"
=> "Wow!"
>> yourstr = mystr
=> "Wow!"
>> mystr.replace("Golly!")
=> "Golly!"
>> mystr
=> "Golly!"
>> yourstr
=> "Golly!"
```

Now, `mystr` and `yourstr` still reference the same memory location.

The append operation can also be done with the `+=` assignment operator. So, instead of `mystr << "mate"`, `mystr += "mate"` could be used.

In the following paragraphs, other string functions will be introduced that also change a string value but leave the affected variable referencing the same memory location.

The other most commonly used methods are similar to those of other programming languages. Among these are those shown in Table 14.2, all of which create new strings:

Table 14.2   Some Commonly Used String Methods

Method	Action
capitalize	Converts the first letter to uppercase and the rest of the letters to lowercase
chop	Removes the last character
chomp	Removes a newline from the right end, if there is one
upcase	Converts all of the lowercase letters in the object to uppercase
downcase	Converts all of the uppercase letters in the object to lowercase
strip	Removes the spaces on both ends
lstrip	Removes the spaces on the left end
rstrip	Removes the spaces on the right end
reverse	Reverses the characters of the string
swapcase	Converts all uppercase letters to lowercase and all lowercase letters to uppercase

As stated previously, all of these produce new strings, rather than modify the given string in place. However, all of these methods have versions that do modify their objects in place. These are called *bang* or *mutator* methods, which are specified by following their names with an exclamation point (!). To illustrate the difference between a string method and its bang counterpart, consider the following interactions:

```
>> str = "Frank"
=> "Frank"
>> str.upcase
=> "FRANK"
>> str
=> "Frank"
>> str.upcase!
=> "FRANK"
>> str
=> "FRANK"
```

Note that after using `upcase`, the value of `str` is unchanged (it is still `"Frank"`), but after using `upcase!`, it is changed (it is `"FRANK"`).

Ruby strings can be indexed, somewhat as if they were arrays. As one would expect, the indices begin at zero. The brackets of this method specify a getter method. The catch with this getter method is that it returns the ASCII code (as a `Fixnum` object), rather than the character. To get the character, the `chr` method must be called. Consider the following example:

```
>> str = "Shelley"
=> "Shelley"
>> str[3]
=> 108
>> str[3].chr
=> "l"
```

If a negative subscript is used as an index, the position is counted from the right.

A multicharacter substring of a string can be accessed by including two numbers in the brackets, in which case the first is the position of the first character of the substring and the second is the number of characters in the substring. Unlike the single-character reference, however, in this case the value is a string, not a number. For example:

```
>> str = "Shelley"
=> "Shelley"
>> str[2,4]
=> "elle"
```

The substring getter can be used on individual characters to get one character without calling the `chr` method.

Specific characters of a string can be set with the set method, [ ]=. For example:

```
>> str = "Donald"
=> "Donald"
>> str[3,3] = "nie"
=> "nie"
>> str
=> "Donnie"
```

The usual way to compare strings for equality is to use the == method as an operator. For example:

```
>> "snowstorm" == "snowstorm"
=> true
>> "snowie" == "snowy"
=> false
```

A different sense of equality is tested with the equal? method, which determines whether its parameter references the same object as the one to which it is sent. For example:

```
>> "snowstorm".equal?("snowstorm")
=> false
```

This produces false because, although the contents of the two string literals are the same, they are different objects.

Yet another sense of equality is tested with the eql? method. It returns true if its receiver object and its parameter have the same types and the same values. For example:

```
>> 7 == 7.0
=> true
>> 7.eql?(7.0)
=> false
```

To facilitate ordering, Ruby includes the "spaceship" operator, <=>. It returns –1 if the second operand is greater than the first, 0 if they are equal, and 1 if the first operand is greater than the second. Greater in this case means it belongs later alphabetically. For example:

```
>> "apple" <=> "prune"
=> -1
>> "grape" <=> "grape"
=> 0
>> "grape" <=> "apple"
=> 1
```

The repetition operator is specified with an asterisk (*). It takes a string as its left operand and an expression that evaluates to a number as its right operand. The left operand is replicated the number of times equal to the value of the right operand. For example:

```
>> "More! " * 3
=> "More! More! More! "
```

14.3 Simple Input and Output

Among the most fundamental constructs in most programming languages are the statements or functions that provide keyboard input and screen output. The next sections introduce these as they appear in Ruby.

14.3.1 Screen Output

Output is directed to the screen with the `puts` method (or operator). We prefer to treat it as an operator. The operand for `puts` is a string literal. A newline character is implicitly appended to the string operand. If the value of a variable is to be part of a line of output, the `#{...}` notation can be used to insert it in a double-quoted string literal, as in the following:

```
>> name = "Fudgy"
=> "Fudgy"
>> puts "My name is #{name}"
My name is Fudgy
=> nil
```

Notice that the value returned by `puts` is `nil`, and that the value is returned after the string has been displayed.

The `print` method is used if you do not want the implied newline that `puts` adds to the end of your literal string.

The way to convert a floating-point value to a formatted string is with a variation of the C language function `sprintf`. This function, which also is named `sprintf`, takes a string parameter that contains a format code, followed by the name of a variable to be converted. The string version is returned by the function. The format codes most commonly used are `f` and `d`. The form of a format code is a percent sign (`%`), followed by a field width, followed by the code letter (`f` or `d`). The field width for the `f` code appears in two parts, separated by a decimal point. For example, `%f7.2` means a total field width of seven spaces, with two digits to the right of the decimal point, which is perfect for money. The `d` code field width is just a number of spaces, for example, `%5d`. So, to convert a floating-point value referenced by the variable `@total` to a string with two digits to the right of the decimal point, the following could be used:

```
@str = sprintf("%5.2f", @total)
```

14.3.2 Keyboard Input

Because Ruby is used primarily for Rails in this book, there is little need for keyboard input. However, keyboard input is certainly useful for other applications, so it is briefly introduced here.

The `gets` method gets a line of input from the keyboard. The retrieved line includes the newline character. If the newline is not needed, it can be discarded with `chomp`. For example:

```
>> name = gets
apples
=> "apples\n"
>> name = name.chomp
=> "apples"
```

This could be shortened by applying `chomp` directly to the value returned by `gets`, as in the following:

```
>> name = gets.chomp
apples
=> "apples"
```

If a number is to be input from the keyboard, the string from `gets` must be converted to an integer with the `to_i` method, as in the following:

```
>> age = gets.to_i
27
=> 27
```

If the number is a floating-point value, the conversion method is `to_f`, as in the following:

```
>> age = gets.to_f
27.5
=> 27.5
```

In this same vein, we must mention that there is a similar method, `to_s`, to which every object responds. It converts the value of the object to which it is sent to a string. However, because `puts` implicitly converts its operand to a string, `to_s` is not often explicitly called.

The following listing is of a trivial program created with a text editor and stored in a file:

```
# quadeval.rb — A simple Ruby program
# Input:  Four numbers, representing the values of
#         a, b, c, and x
# Output: The value of the expression
#         a*x**2 + b*x + c
```

```
# Get input
puts "Please input the value of a "
a = gets.to_i
puts "Please input the value of b "
b = gets.to_i
puts "Please input the value of c "
c = gets.to_i
puts "Please input the value of x "
x = gets/to_i
# Compute and display the result
result = a * x ** 2 + b * x + c
puts "The value of the expression is: #{result}"
```

A program stored in a file can be run by the command

>ruby *filename*

So, our example can be run (interpreted) with

>ruby quadeval.rb

To compile but not interpret a program, just to check the syntactic correctness of the program, the –c flag is included after the ruby command. It is also a good idea to include the –w flag, which causes ruby to produce warning messages for a variety of suspicious things it may find in that program. For example, to check the syntax of our example program, the following could be used:

>ruby -cw quadeval.rb

If the program is found to be okay, the response to this command is

Syntax OK

14.4 Control Statements

Ruby includes a complete collection of statements for controlling the execution flow through programs. This section introduces the control expressions and control statements of Ruby.

14.4.1 Control Expressions

The expressions upon which statement control flow is based are Boolean expressions. They can be either of the constants true or false, variables, relational expressions, or compound expressions. A control expression that is a simple variable is true if its value is anything except nil (it references some object). If its value is nil, it is false.

A relational expression has two operands and a relational operator. Relational operators can have any scalar-valued expression as operands. The relational operators are shown in Table 14.3.

Recall that the <=> operator is often used for comparing strings. Also, equal? is used to determine whether two variables are aliases, that is, they reference the same object.

Ruby has two sets of operators for the AND, OR, and NOT Boolean operations. The two sets have the same semantics but different precedence levels. The operators with the higher precedence are && (AND), || (OR), and ! (NOT). Those with the lower precedence are and, or, and not. The precedence of these latter operators is lower than any other operators in Ruby, so regardless of what operators appear in their operands, these operators will be evaluated last.

Table 14.3   Relational operators

Operator	Operation
==	Is equal to
!=	Is not equal to
<	Is less than
>	Is greater than
<=	Is less than or equal to
>=	Is greater than or equal to
<=>	Compare, returning −1, 0, or +1
eql?	True if the receiver object and the parameter have the same type and equal values
equal?	True if the receiver object and the parameter have the same object ID

All of the relational operators are methods, but all except eql? and equal? can be used as operators.

The precedence and associativity of all operators discussed so far in this chapter are shown in Table 14.4.

Because assignment statements have values (the value of an assignment is the value assigned to the left-side variable), they can be used as control expressions. One common use of this is for an assignment statement that reads a line of input. The gets method returns nil when it gets the end-of-file (EOF) character, so this can be conveniently used to terminate loops. For example:

```
while (next = gets) { … }
```

The keyboard EOF character is Control-D for UNIX, Control-Z for Windows, and CMD+. (period) for Macintosh systems.

Table 14.4 Operator precedence and associativity

Operator	Associativity
**	Right
!, unary + and -	Right
*, /, %	Left
+, -	Left
&	Left
+, -	Left
>, <, >=, <=	Nonassociative
==, !=, <=>	Nonassociative
&&	Left
||	Left
=, +=, -=, *=, **=, /=, %=, &=, &&=, ||=	Right
not	Right
or, and	Left

Highest-precedence operators are listed first.
The method names for unary minus and plus are -@ and +@, respectively.

14.4.2 Selection and Loop Statements

Control statements require some syntactic container for sequences of statements whose execution they are meant to control. The Ruby form of such containers is to use a simple sequence of statements terminated with else (if the sequence is a then clause) or end (if the sequence is either an else clause or it is a then clause and there is no else clause). A *control construct* is a control statement and the segment of code whose execution it controls.

Ruby's if statement is similar to that of other languages. One syntactic difference is that there are no parentheses around the control expression, as is the case with most of the languages based directly or even loosely on C. For example, consider the following example:

```
if a > 10
  b = a * 2
end
```

An if construct can include elsif (note that it is *not* spelled "elseif") clauses, which provide a way of having a more readable sequence of nested if constructs. For example:

```
if snowrate < 1
  puts "Light snow"
elsif snowrate < 2
  puts "Moderate snow"
else
  puts "Heavy snow"
end
```

Ruby has an `unless` statement, which is the same as its `if` statement except that the inverse of the value of the control expression is used. This is convenient if you want a selection construct with an else clause but no then clause. The following construct illustrates an `unless` statement:

```
unless sum > 1000
  puts "We are not finished yet!"
end
```

Ruby includes two kinds of multiple selection constructs, both named case. One Ruby case construct, which is similar to a switch, has the following form:

```
case expression
when value then
 – statement sequence
...
when value then
 – statement sequence
[else
 – statement sequence]
end
```

The value of the case expression is compared with the when clause values, one at a time from top to bottom until a match is found, at which time the following statement sequence is interpreted. The comparison is done using the === relational operator, which is defined for all built-in classes. If the when value is a range, such as (1..100), === is defined as an inclusive test, yielding true if the value of the case expression is in the given range. If the when value is a class name, === is defined to yield true if the case value is an object of the case expression class or one of its superclasses. If the when value is a regular expression, === is defined to be a simple pattern match. Note that the === operator is only used for the comparisons in case constructs.

Consider the following example:

```
case in_val
when -1 then
  neg_count += 1
when 0 then
  zero_count += 1
```

```
when 1 then
  pos_count += 1
else
  puts "Error - in_val is out of range"
end
```

Note that no break statements are needed at the ends of the selectable statement sequences in this construct—there are implied branches at the end of each when clause that exit the construct.

The second form of case constructs uses a Boolean expression to choose a value to be produced by the construct. The general form of this case is as follows:

```
case
when Boolean expression then expression
...
when Boolean expression then expression
else expression
end
```

The semantics of this construct is straightforward. The Boolean expressions are evaluated, one at a time until one evaluates to true. The value of the whole construct is the value of the expression that corresponds to the true Boolean expression. If none of the Boolean expressions is true, the else expression is evaluated and its value is the value of the construct. For example, consider the following assignment statement:[1]

```
leap = case
       when year % 400 == 0 then true
       when year % 100 == 0 then false
       else year % 4 == 0
       end
```

This case expression evaluates to true if year is a leap year.

The Ruby while and for statements are similar to those of C and its descendants. The bodies of both are sequences of statements that end with end. The general form of the while statement is as follows:

```
while control expression
    loop body statement(s)
end
```

The control expression could be followed by the do reserved word.

The until statement is similar to the while statement except that the inverse of the value of the control expression is used.

For those situations where a loop is needed in which the conditional termination is at some position in the loop other than the top, Ruby has an infinite

---

1. This example is from Thomas, et al., (2005).

loop construct and loop exit statements. The body of the infinite loop construct is like that of `while`—it is a sequence of statements that optionally begins with `do` and always ends with `end`.

There are two ways to control an infinite loop, the `break` and `next` statements. These statements can be made conditional by putting them in the then clause of an `if` construct. The `break` statement causes control to go to the first statement following the loop body. The `next` statement causes control to go to the first statement in the loop body. For example, consider the following two infinite loop constructs: ˙

```
sum = 0
loop do
  dat = gets.to_i
  if dat < 0 break
  sum += dat
  end

sum = 0
loop do
  dat = gets.to_i
  if dat < 0 next
  sum += dat
  end
```

In the first construct, the loop is terminated when a negative value is input. In the second, negative values are not added to `sum`, but the loop continues.

Ruby does not have a general `for` statement, which is ubiquitous among languages with C in their ancestry. However, Ruby includes convenient ways to construct the counting loops implemented with `for` statements in other common languages. These are built with iterator methods, which we postpone discussing until methods and arrays have been introduced. Also, there are the `for` and `for-in` constructs in Ruby, which are used for iterating through arrays and hashes (associative arrays).

14.5 Fundamentals of Arrays

Ruby includes two structured classes or types, arrays and hashes. Arrays are introduced in this section; hashes are introduced in Section 14.6.

Arrays in Ruby are more flexible than those of most of the other common languages. This is a result of two fundamental differences between Ruby arrays and those of other common languages such as C, C++, and Java. First, the length of a Ruby array is dynamic—it can grow or shrink any time during program execution. Second, a Ruby array can store different types of data. For example, an array may have some numeric elements, some string elements, and even some array elements. So, in these cases, Ruby arrays are similar to those of PHP.

Ruby arrays can be created in two different ways. First, an array can be created by sending the new message to the predefined `Array` class, including a parameter for the size of the array. The second way is simply to assign a list literal to a variable, where a list literal is a list of literals delimited by brackets. For example, in the following, the first array is created with new and the second is created by assignment:

```
>> list1 = Array.new(5)
=> [nil, nil, nil, nil, nil]
>> list2 = [2, 4, 3.14159, "Fred", [] ]
=> [2, 4, 3.14159, "Fred", []]
```

An array created with the new method can also be initialized by including a second parameter, but every element is given the same value (that of the second parameter). For example:

```
>> list1 = Array.new(5, "Ho")
=> ["Ho", "Ho", "Ho", "Ho", "Ho"]
```

Actually, this form of initialization is rarely useful, because not only is each element given the same value, but also each is given the same reference. All of them reference the same object. So, if one is changed, all are changed.

All Ruby array elements use integers as subscripts, and the lower-bound subscript of every array is zero. Array elements are referenced through subscripts delimited by brackets (`[ ]`), which is actually a getter method that is allowed to be used as a unary operator. Likewise, `[ ]=` is a setter method. A subscript can be any numeric-valued expression. If an expression with a floating-point value is used as a subscript, the fractional part is truncated. For example:

```
>> list = [2, 4, 6, 8]
=> [2, 4, 6, 8]
>> second = list[1]
=> 4
>> list[3] = 9
=> 9
>> list
=> [2, 4, 6, 9]
>> list[2.999999]
=> 6
```

The length of an array is dynamic; elements can be added or removed from an array using the methods described in Section 14.5.2. The length of an array can be retrieved with the `length` method. For example:

```
>> len = list.length
=> 4
```

14.5.1 The `for-in` Statement

The `for-in` statement is used to process the elements of an array. For example, the following code computes the sum of all of the values in `list`:

```
>> sum = 0
=> 0
>> list = [2, 4, 6, 8]
=> [2, 4, 6, 8]
>> for value in list
>>    sum += value
>> end
=> [2, 4, 6, 8]
>> sum
=> 20
```

Notice that the interpreter's response to the `for-in` construct is to display the values assumed by the scalar variable.

The scalar variable in a `for-in` takes on the values of the `list` array, one at a time. Notice that the scalar *does not* get references to array elements, it gets the values. Therefore, operations on the scalar variable have no affect on the array. Consider the following code:

```
>> list = [1, 3, 5, 7]
=> [1, 3, 5, 7]
>> for value in list
>>    value += 2
>> end
=> [1, 3, 5, 7]
>> list
=> [1, 3, 5, 7]
```

A literal array value can be used in the `for-in` construct, as in the following:

```
>> list = [2, 4, 6]
=> [2, 4, 6]
>> for index in [0, 1, 2]
>> puts "For index = #{index}, the value is #{list[index]}"
>> end
For index = 0, the element is 2
For index = 1, the element is 4
For index = 2, the element is 6
```

14.5.2 Built-In Methods for Arrays and Lists

This section introduces a few of the many built-in methods that are part of Ruby.

Frequently it is necessary to place new elements on one end or the other of an array. Ruby has four methods for this purpose: `unshift` and `shift`, which deal with the left end of arrays; and `pop` and `push`, which deal with the right end of arrays.

The `shift` method removes and returns the first element (lowest subscript) of the array object to which it is sent. For example, the following statement removes the first element of `list` and places it in `first`:

```
>> list = [3, 7, 13, 17]
=> [3, 7, 13, 17]
>> first = list.shift
=> 3
>> list
=> [7, 13, 17]
```

The subscripts of all of the other elements in the array are reduced by 1 as a result of the `shift` operation.

The `pop` method removes and returns the last element from the array object to which it is sent. In this case, there is no change in the subscripts of the array's other elements.

The `unshift` method takes a scalar or an array literal as a parameter. The scalar or array literal is appended to the beginning of the array. This results in an increase in the subscripts of all other array elements. The `push` method also takes a scalar or an array literal. The scalar or array is added to the high end of the array:

```
>> list = [2, 4, 6]
=> [2, 4, 6]
>> list.push(8, 10)
=> {2, 4, 6, 8, 10]
```

Either `pop` and `unshift` or `push` and `shift` can be used to implement a queue in an array, depending on the direction the queue should grow.

While `push` is a convenient way to add literal elements to an array, if an array is to be catenated to the end of another array, another method, `concat`, is used. For example:

```
>> list1 = [1, 3, 5, 7]
=> [1, 3, 5, 7]
>> list2 = [2, 4, 6, 8]
=> [2, 4, 6, 8]
>> list1.concat(list2)
=> [1, 3, 5, 7, 2, 4, 6, 8]
```

If two arrays need to be catenated and the result saved as a new array, the plus (+) method can be used as a binary operator, as in the following:

```
>> list1 = [0.1, 2.4, 5.6, 7.9]
=> [0.1, 2.4, 5.6, 7.9]
```

```
>> list2 = [3.4, 2.1, 7.5]
=> [3.4, 2.1, 7.5]
>> list3 = list1 + list2
=> [0.1, 2.4, 5.6, 7.9, 3.4, 2.1, 7.5]
```

Note that neither list1 nor list2 are affected by the plus method.

The reverse method does what its name implies. For example:

```
>> list = [2, 4, 8, 16]
=> [2, 4, 8, 16]
>> list.reverse
=> [16, 8, 4, 2]
>> list
=> [2, 4, 8, 16]
```

Note that reverse returns a new array and does not affect the array to which it is sent. The mutator version of reverse, reverse!, does what reverse does, but changes the object to which it is sent. For example:

```
>> list = [2, 4, 8, 16]
=> [2, 4, 8, 16]
>> list.reverse!
=> [16, 8, 4, 2]
>> list
=> [16, 8, 4, 2]
```

The include? predicate method searches an array for a specific object. For example:

```
>> list = [2, 4, 8, 16]
=> [2, 4, 8, 16]
>> list.include?(4)
=> true
>> list.include?(10)
=> false
```

The sort method sorts the elements of an array, as long as Ruby knows how to compare those elements. The most commonly sorted elements are either numbers or strings and Ruby knows how to compare numbers with numbers and strings with strings. So, sort works well on arrays of elements of either of these two types. For example:

```
>> list = [16, 8, 4, 2]
=> [16, 8, 4, 2]
>> list.sort
=> [2, 4, 8, 16]
>> list2 = ["jo", "fred", "mike", "larry"]
=> ["jo", "fred", "mike", "larry"]
>> list2.sort
=> ["fred", "jo", "larry", "mike"]
```

If the sort method is sent to an array that has mixed types, Ruby produces an error message indicating the comparison failed. For example:

```
>> list = [2, "jo", 8, "fred"]
=> [2, "jo", 8, "fred"]
>> list.sort
ArgumentError: comparison of Fixnum with String failed
        from (irb):13:in 'sort'
        from (irb):13
        from :0
```

sort returns a new array and does not change the array to which it is sent. The mutator method, sort!, sorts the array to which it is sent, in place.

In some situations, arrays represent sets. There are three methods that perform set operations on two arrays. All are used as binary infix operators. They are &, for set intersection, -, for set difference, and |, for set union. Consider the following examples:

```
>> set1 = [2, 4, 6, 8]
=> [2, 4, 6, 8]
>> set2 = [4, 6, 8, 10]
=> [4, 6, 8, 10]
>> set1 & set2
=> [4, 6, 8]
>> set1 - set2
=> [2]
>> set1 | set 2
=> [2, 4, 6, 8, 10]
```

There are a number of other interesting and useful methods that operate on arrays that use blocks. Some of them will be discussed after subprograms and blocks have been introduced.

14.5.3 An Example

The following example illustrates a simple use of an array. A list of names is read from the keyboard. Each name is converted to all uppercase letters and placed in an array. The array is then sorted and displayed.

```
# process_names.rb - A simple Ruby program to
#  illustrate the use of arrays
#  Input: A list of lines of text, where each line
#         is a person's name
# Output: The input names, after all letters are
#         converted to uppercase, in alphabetical order

index = 0
```

```
names = Array.new

# Loop to read the names and process them
while (name = gets)

# Convert the name's letters to uppercase and put it
# in the names array
  names[index] = name.chomp.upcase
  index += 1
end

# Sort the array in place and display it
names.sort!
puts "The sorted array"
for name in names
  puts name
end
```

14.6 Hashes

Associative arrays are arrays in which each data element is paired with a key, which is used to identify the data element. Because hash functions are used both to create and find specific elements in an associative array, associative arrays often are called *hashes*. There are two fundamental differences between arrays and hashes: First, arrays use numeric subscripts to address specific elements, whereas hashes use string values (the keys) to address elements. Second, the elements in arrays are ordered by subscript, but the elements in hashes are not. In a sense, elements of an array are like those in a list, whereas elements of a hash are like those in a set, where order is irrelevant. The actual arrangement of the elements of a hash in memory is determined by the hash function used to insert and access them.

Like arrays, hashes can be created in two ways, with the new method or by assigning a literal to a variable. In this case, the literal is a hash literal, in which each element is specified by a key/value pair, separated by the symbol =>. Hash literals are delimited by braces. For example:

```
>> kids_ages = {"John" => 39, "Genny" => 37, "Jake" => 23,
"Darcie" => 22}
=> {"Darcie"=>22, "John"=>39, "Genny"=>37, "Jake"=>23}
```

Notice that the order of the hash returned by Ruby is not the same as the hash literal used to create the hash. This is because the actual order of the hash in memory is unpredicatable (at least for the user program).

If the new method is sent to the Hash class without a parameter, it creates an empty hash, denoted by {}. For example:

```
>> my_hash = Hash.new
=> {}
```

An individual value element of a hash can be referenced by "subscripting" the hash name with a key. The same brackets used for array element access are used to specify the subscripting operation. For example:

```
>> kids_ages["Genny"]
=> 37
```

New values are added to a hash by assigning the value of the new element to a reference to the key of the new element, as in the following example:

```
>> kids_ages["Aidan"] = 8;

=> {"Aidan"=>8, "Darcie"=>22, "John"=>39, "Genny"=>37,
"Jake"=>23}
```

An element is removed from a hash with the delete method, which takes an element key as a parameter. For example:

```
>> kids_ages.delete("Genny")
=> 37
>> kids_ages
=> {"Aidan"=>8, "Darcie"=>22, "John"=>39, "Jake"=>23}
```

A hash can be set to empty in two ways: First, an empty hash literal can be assigned to the hash. Second, the clear method can be used on the hash. These two approaches are illustrated with the following statements:

```
>> hi_temps = {"mon" => 74, "tue" => 78}
=> {"mon"=>74, "tue"=>78}
>> hi_temps = {}
=> {}
>> salaries = {"Fred" => 47400, "Mike" => 45250}
=> {"Fred" => 47400, "Mike" => 45250}
>> salaries.clear
=> {}
```

The has_key? predicate method is used to determine whether an element with a specific key is in a hash. For example, assuming the kids_ages hash previously defined is still around:

```
>> kids_ages.has_key?("John")
=> true
>> kids_ages.has_key?("Henry")
=> false
```

The keys and values of a hash can be extracted into arrays with the methods keys and values, respectively as follows:

```
>> kids_ages.keys
=> ["Aidan", "Darcie", "John", "Jake"]
>> kids_ages.values
=> [8, 22, 39, 23]
```

14.7 Methods

Subprograms are central to the usefulness of any programming language. Ruby's subprograms are all methods because it is an object-oriented language. However, Ruby's methods can be defined outside user-defined classes, so both in appearance and in behavior, when defined outside a class, they are like functions. When a method that is defined in a class is called from outside that class, the call must begin with a reference to an object of that class. When a method is called without an object reference, the default object on which it is called is self, which is a reference to the current object. Therefore, whenever a method is defined outside a user-defined class, it is called without an object reference. This section describes the basics of Ruby's methods. Classes are introduced in Section 14.8.

14.7.1 Fundamentals

A *method definition* includes the method's header and a sequence of statements, ending with the end reserved word, which describes its actions. A *method header* is the reserved word def, the method's name, and optionally a parenthesized list of formal parameters. Method names must begin with lowercase letters. If the method has no parameters, the parentheses are omitted. In fact, the parentheses are optional in all cases, but it is common practice to include them when there are parameters and omit them when there are no parameters. The types of the parameters are not specified in the parameter list, because Ruby variables do not have types—they are all references to objects. The type of the return object is also not specified in a method definition.

A method that returns an object that is to be used immediately is called in the position of an operand in an expression (or as the whole expression). A method that does not return an object that is to be used can be called by a standalone statement.

A method can specify the value it returns in two ways, explicitly and implicitly. The return statement takes an expression as its parameter. The value of the expression is returned when the return is executed. A method can have any number of return statements, including none. If there are no return statements in a method or if execution arrives at the end of the method without encountering a return, its implicitly returned object is the value of the last expression evaluated in the method.

The `Time` object is used to obtain various aspects of time from the system clock. The `now` method of `Time` returns the current time and date as a string. This method is used in the following example methods, one with a `return` and one without a `return`:

```
def date_time1
  return Time.now
end
def date_time2
  Time.now
end
```

Consider the following calls to `date_time1` and `date_time2` and the returned values:

```
>> date_time1
=> Thu Jun 07 16:00:06 Mountain Daylight Time 2007
>> date_time2
=> Thu Jun 07 16:00:08 Mountain Daylight Time 2007
```

14.7.2 Local Variables

Local variables are either formal parameters or are variables created in a method. A variable is created in a method by assigning an object to it. The scope of a local variable is from the header of the method to the end of the method. If the name of a local variable conflicts with that of a global variable, the local variable is used. This is the advantage of local variables: When you make up their names, you do not need to be concerned that a global variable with the same name may exist in the program.

The name of a local variable must begin with either a lowercase letter or an underscore (_). Beyond the first character, local variable names can have any number of letters, digits, or underscores.

The lifetime of a variable is the period of time over which it exists and can be referenced. The lifetime of a local variable is from the time it is created until the end of the execution of the method. So, the local variables of a method cannot be used to store data between calls to the method.

14.7.3 Parameters

The parameter values that appear in a call to a method are called *actual parameters*. The parameter names used in the method, which correspond to the actual parameters, are called *formal parameters*. In effect, scalar actual parameters specify the values of objects, not their addresses. So, in Ruby, parameter transmission of scalars is strictly one-way into the method. The values of the scalar actual parameters are available to the method through its formal parameters. The formal parameters that correspond to scalar actual parameters are local variables that are initialized to reference new objects that have the values of the corresponding actual parameters. Whatever a method does to its formal parameters, it has no effect on the actual parameters in the calling program unit. The following example illustrates a method that does not change its parameters:

```
def side3(side1, side2)
  return Math.sqrt(side1 ** 2 + side2 ** 2)
end
```

Now, we consider a method that attempts to change its parameters. The intent of the following method was to interchange its parameters:

```
>> def  swap(x, y)
>>   t = x
>>   x = y
>>   y = t
>> end
=> nil
>> a = 1
>> b = 2
>> swap(a, b)
=> 1
>> a
=> 1
>> b
=> 2
```

So, you see that although `swap` changes its formal parameters, the actual parameters sent to it, `a` and `b`, are unchanged.

Actual parameters that are arrays or hashes are in effect passed by reference, so it is a two-way communication between the calling program unit and the called method. For example, if an array is passed to a method and the method changes the array, those changes are reflected in the corresponding actual parameter in the caller.

Normally, a call to a method must have the same number of actual parameters as the number of formal parameters in the method's definition. A mismatch of these two numbers results in a runtime error. However, a method can be defined to take a variable number of parameters by defining it with a parameter that is preceded by an asterisk (*). Such a parameter is called an *asterisk parameter*. For example:

```
def fun1(*params)
...
end
```

This method can take any number of parameters, including none. The passed actual parameters are placed in the array named `params` (in this example). The asterisk parameter can be preceded by other parameters, in which case only those actual parameters that do not correspond to named formal parameters are placed in the array of parameters. For example, suppose `fun2` is defined as follows:

```
def fun2(sum, list, length, *params)
...
end
```

Now, suppose `fun2` is called with the following:

```
fun2(new_sum, my_list, len, speed, time, alpha)
```

The actual parameters `speed`, `time`, and `alpha` will be passed into the array `params`. Of course, the asterisk parameter must always appear at the end of the list of formal parameters. Any normal parameters that follow an asterisk parameter will always be ignored, because the asterisk parameter receives all remaining actual parameters.

Formal parameters can have default values, which makes their corresponding actual parameters optional. For example, consider the following skeletal method definition:

```
def lister(list, len = 100)
...
end
```

If this method is called with the following, the formal parameter `len` gets the value 50:

```
lister(my_list, 50)
```

But if it is called with the following, `len` will default to `100`:

```
lister(my_list)
```

Some programming languages, for example Ada and Python, support keyword parameters. A *key word parameter* is one in which the actual parameter specifies the name of its associated formal parameter. For example:

```
lister(list => my_list, len => 50)
```

The advantage of key word parameters is that they eliminate the possibility of making mistakes in the association of actual parameters with formal parameters. This is particularly useful when there are more than a few parameters.

Ruby does not support key word parameters, but there is a way to achieve the same benefit, using hashes. A hash literal has an appearance that is similar to key word parameters. For example, if a hash literal is passed as a parameter to the `find` method, it would appear as follows:

```
find(age, {'first' => 'Davy', 'last' => 'Jones'})
```

Whenever such a hash literal is passed as an actual parameter and it follows all normal scalar parameters and precedes all array and block parameters, the braces can be omitted. So, in the example above, the braces are unnecessary.

Ruby includes a category of objects that appears in no other common programming languages, symbols. Symbols are created by preceding an unquoted string with a colon (:).[2] A symbol made from a variable name can be thought of as that variable's name. Such a symbol does not refer to the value of the variable, nor is it related to a particular instance of a variable—so symbols are context independent. All symbols are instances of the `Symbol` class. Symbols can be used to specify parameters in method calls and the keys of elements of hash literals. It has become a Ruby idiom, and even a convention in Rails, to use symbols, rather than literal strings, for the keys in hash literals when they are used as parameters. For example:

```
find(age, :first => 'Davy', :last => 'Jones')
```

Following is a method that computes the median of a given array of numbers:

```
# median - a method
#  Parameter: An array of numbers
#  Return value: The median of the parameter array
#
def median(list)

# Sort the array
  list2 = list.sort

# Get the length of the array
  len = list2.length

# Compute the median
  if(len % 2 == 1)  # length is odd
    return list2[len / 2]
  else               # length is even
    return (list2[len / 2] + list2[len / 2 - 1]) / 2
  end

end  # end of the median method
```

14.8 Classes

Classes in Ruby are like those of other object-oriented programming languages, at least in purpose. A class defines the template for a category of objects, of

---

2. Actually, many different things can be prefixed with a colon to create a symbol, for example, operators, constants, class names, and method names.

which any number can be created. An object has state, which is maintained in its collection of instance variables, and behavior, which is defined by its methods. An object can also have constants and a constructor.

14.8.1 The Basics of Classes

The methods and variables of a class are defined in the syntactic container that has the following form:

class *class_name*

...

end

Class names, like constant names, must begin with uppercase letters.

Instance variables are used to store the state of an object. They are defined in the class definition and every object of the class gets its own copy of the instance variables. The name of an instance variable must begin with an at sign (@), which distinguishes instance variables from other variables.

A class can have a single constructor, which in Ruby is a method with the name initialize, which is used to initialize instance variables to values. A constructor can take any number of parameters, which are treated as local variables, and therefore their names begin with lowercase letters or underscores. The parameters are given after the call to new.

Following is an example of a class. This class, named Stack2_class, defines a stack-like data structure implemented in an array. The difference between this structure and a stack is that both the top and second from the top elements are accessible. The second from the top element is fetched with the top2 method.

```ruby
# Stack2_class.rb - a class to implement a stack-like
#                   structure in an array
class Stack2_class

# Constructor - parameter is the size of the stack - default is 100
  def initialize(len = 100)
    @stack_ref = Array.new(len)
    @max_len = len
    @top_index = -1
  end

# push method
  def push(number)
    if @top_index == @max_len
      puts "Error in push - stack is full"
    else
```

```ruby
      @top_index += 1
      @stack_ref[@top_index] = number
    end
  end

# pop method
  def pop()
    if @top_index == -1
      puts "Error in pop - stack is empty"
    else
      @top_index -= 1
    end
  end

# top method
  def top()
    if @top_index > -1
      return @stack_ref[@top_index]
    else
      puts "Error in top - no elements"
    end
  end

# top2 method
  def top2
    if @top_index > 0
      return @stack_ref[@top_index - 1]
    else
      puts "Error in top2 - there are not 2 elements"
    end
  end

# empty method
  def empty()
    @topIndex == -1
  end

end
```

Following is simple code to illustrate the use of the `Stack2_class` class:

```ruby
# Test code for Stack2_class
  mystack = Stack2_class.new(50)
  mystack.push(42)
```

```
mystack.push(29)
puts "Top element is (should be 29): #{mystack.top}"
puts "Second from the top is (should be 42): #{mystack.top2}"
mystack.pop
mystack.pop
mystack.pop  # Produces an error message - empty stack
```

Classes in Ruby are dynamic in the sense that members can be added at any time. This is done by simply including additional class definitions that specify the new members. Methods can also be removed from a class. This is done by providing another class definition in which the method to be removed is sent to the method `remove_method` as a parameter. The dynamic classes of Ruby are another example of a language designer trading readability (and as a consequence, reliability) for flexibility. Allowing dynamic changes to classes clearly adds flexibility to the language, but harms readability. To determine the current definition of a class, one must find all of its definitions in the program and consider all of them.

14.8.2 Access Control

In a clear departure from the other common programming languages, access control in Ruby is different for access to data than it is for access to methods. All instance data has private access by default, and it cannot be changed. If external access to an instance variable is required, access methods must be defined. For example, consider the following skeletal class definition:

```
class My_class

# Constructor
  def initialize
    @one = 1
    @two = 2
  end

# A getter for @one
  def one
    @one
  end

# A setter for @one
  def one=(my_one)
    @one = my_one
  end

end  # of class My_class
```

The equal sign (=) attached to the name of the setter method means that the method is assignable. So, all setter methods have equal signs attached to their names. The body of the `one` method illustrates the Ruby design of methods returning the value of the last expression evaluated when there is no return statement. In this case, the value of `@one` is returned. When an instance variable that has a getter or setter is referenced outside the class, the at sign (`@`) part of the name is not included. For example, consider the following code that uses `My_class`:

```
mc = My_class.new
puts "The value of one is #{mc.one}"
```

Because getter and setter methods are frequently needed, Ruby provides shortcuts for both. If one wants a class to have getter methods for two instance variables, `@one` and `@two`, those getters can be specified with the single statement in the class as follows:

```
attr_reader :one, :two
```

`attr_reader` is actually a method call, using the symbols `:one` and `:two` as the actual parameters.

The function that similarly creates setters is called `attr_writer`. This function has the same parameter profile as `attr_reader`.

The functions for creating getter and setter methods are so named because they provide the protocol for object members of the class, which in Ruby are called *attributes*. So, the attributes of a class is the data interface (the public data) to objects of the class.

The three levels of access control for methods are defined as follows. Public access means the method can be called by any code. Protected access means that only objects of the defining class and its subclasses may call the method. Private access means that the method cannot be called with an explicit receiver object. Because the default receiver object is `self`, a private method can only be called in the context of the current object. So, no code can ever call the private methods of another object. Note that private access in Ruby is quite different from private access in other programming languages such as C++, Java, and C#.

Access control for methods in Ruby is dynamic, so access violations are detected only during execution. The default method access is public, but it can also be protected or private. There are two ways to specify the access control, both of which use functions with the same names as the access levels, `private`, `protected`, and `public`. One way is to call the appropriate function without parameters. This resets the default access for all following defined methods in the class until a call to a different access control method appears. For example:

```
class My_class
  def meth1
  ...
  end
```

```
...
private
  def meth7
  ...
  end
  ...
protected
  def meth11
  ...
  end
  ...
end  # of class My_class
```

The alternative is to call the access control functions with the names of the specific methods as parameters. For example, the following is semantically equivalent to the previous class definition:

```
class My_class
  def meth1
  ...
  end
  ...
  def meth7
  ...
  end
  ...
  def meth11
  ...
  end
  ...
  private :meth7, ...
  protected :meth11, ...
  end  # of class My_class
```

The default access control for constructors is private. Class variables are private to the class and its instances. That privacy cannot be changed. Also, unlike global and instance variables, class variables must be initialized before they are used.

14.8.3 Inheritance

Subclasses are defined in Ruby using the less than symbol (<).

```
class My_Subclass < Base_class
```

One distinct thing about Ruby's method access controls is that they can be changed in a subclass, simply by calling the access control functions. This means that two subclasses of a base class can be defined so that objects of one of the subclasses can access a method defined in the base class, but objects of the other subclass cannot. Also, this allows one to change the access of a publically accessible method in the base class to a privately accessible method in the subclass. Such a subclass obviously cannot be a subtype.

Ruby modules provide a naming encapsulation that is often used to define libraries of methods. Perhaps the most interesting aspect of modules, however, is that their methods can be accessed directly from classes. Access to the module in a class is specified with an `include` statement, such as the following:

```
include Math
```

The effect of including a module is that the class gains a pointer to the module and effectively inherits the functions defined in the module. In fact, when a module is included in a class, the module becomes a proxy superclass of the class. Such a module is called a *mixin*, because its functions get mixed into the methods defined in the class. Mixins provide a way to include the functionality of a module in any class that needs it. And, of course, the class still has a normal superclass from which it inherits members. So, mixins provide the benefits of multiple inheritance, without the naming collisions that could occur if modules did not require module names on their functions.

14.9 Blocks and Iterators

A *block* is a sequence of code, delimited by either braces or the `do` and `end` reserved words. Blocks can be used with specially written methods to create many useful constructs, including simple iterators for arrays and hashes. This construct consists of a method call followed by a block. In the following paragraphs, a few of the built-in iterator methods that are designed to use blocks are discussed.

The `times` iterator method provides a way to build simple counting loops. Typically, `times` is sent to a number, which repeats the attached block that number of times. Consider the following example:

```
>> 4.times {puts "Hey!"}
Hey!
Hey!
Hey!
Hey!
=> 4
```

The `times` method repeatedly executes the block. This is a different approach to subprogram control (a block is clearly a form of a subprogram).

The most commonly used iterator is `each`, which is often used to go through arrays and apply a block to each element. For this, it is convenient to allow blocks to have parameters. Blocks *can* have parameters, which appear at the beginning of the block, delimited by vertical bars (|). The following example, which uses a block parameter, illustrates the use of each:

```
>> list = [2, 4, 6, 8]
=> [2, 4, 6, 8]
>> list.each {|value| puts value}
2
4
6
8
=> [2, 4, 6, 8]
```

The each iterator works equally well on array literals, as in the following:

```
>> ["Joe", "Jo", "Joanne"].each {|name| puts name}
Joe
Jo
Joanne
=> ["Joe", "Jo", "Joanne"]
```

If each is called on a hash, two block parameters must be included, one for the key and one for the value. For example, consider the following:

```
>> high_temps = {"Mon"=>72, "Tue"=>84, "Wed"=>80}
=> {"Wed"=>80, "Mon"=>72, "Tue"=>84}
>> high_temps.each
        {|day, temp| puts "The high on #{day} was #{temp}"
The high on Wed was 80
The high on Mon was 72
The high on Tue was 84
=> {"Wed"=>80, "Mon"=>72, "Tue"=>84}
```

The upto iterator method is used like times, except that the last value of the counter is given as a parameter. For example:

```
>> 5.upto(8) {|value| puts value}
5
6
7
8
=> 5
```

The step iterator method takes a terminal value and a step size as parameters and generates the values from that of the object to which it is sent and the terminal value. For example:

```
>> 0.step(6, 2) {|value| puts value}
0
```

```
2
4
6
=> 0
```

The `collect` iterator method takes the elements from an array, one at a time, like `each`, and puts the values generated by the given block into a new array. For example:

```
>> list = [5, 10, 15, 20]
=> [5, 10, 15, 20]
>> list.collect {|value| value = value - 5}
=> [0, 5, 10, 15]
>> list
=> [5, 10, 15, 20]
>> list.collect! {|value| value = value - 5}
=> [0, 5, 10, 15]
>> list
=> [0, 5, 10, 15]
```

As can be seen from this example, the mutator version of `collect` is probably more often useful than the non-mutator version, which does not save its result.

Now we consider user-defined methods and blocks. There must be some statement in the method that "calls" the block. This statement is `yield`. The `yield` statement is similar to a method call, except that there is no receiver object and the call is a request to execute the block attached to the method call, rather than a call to a method. If the block has parameters, they are specified in parentheses on the `yield` statement. The value returned by a block is that of the last expression evaluated in the block. A method can include any number of `yield` statements, so it can cause the block to be "called" any number of times. It is this process that is used to implement the iterators illustrated earlier in this section.

When a block is used in a call to a method, part of the effect of the call is provided by the code in the method and part is provided by the block. This allows a method to have differect effects on different calls, with the different effects provided by the block atttached to the call. Consider the following example:

```
>> def get_name
>>   puts "Your name:"
>>   name = gets
>>   yield(name)
>> end
=> nil
>> get_name {|name| puts "Hello, " + name}
Your name:
Freddie
Hello, Freddie
=> nil
```

14.10 **Pattern Matching**

Regular expressions in JavaScript were discussed in Chapter 4, "The Basics of JavaScript." Because the regular expressions of both JavaScript and Ruby are based directly on those of Perl, readers who are not familiar with regular expressions are referred to Sections 4.12.1 to 4.12.3. The pattern-matching operations of Ruby are different from those of JavaScript, so they are discussed here.

14.10.1 The Basics of Pattern Matching

In Ruby, the pattern-matching operation is specified with the matching operators, =~, which is for positive matches, and !~, which is for negative matches. Patterns are placed between slashes (/). For example, in the following the right operand pattern is matched against the left operand string:

```
>> street = "Hammel"
=> "Hammel"
>> street =~ /mm/
=> 2
```

The result of evaluating a pattern-matching expression is the position in the string where the pattern matched.

The split method is frequently used in string processing. It uses its parameter, which is a pattern, to determine how to split the string object to which it is sent into substrings. For example, we could have the following:

```
>> str = "Jake used to be a small child, but now is not."
=> "Jake used to be a small child, but now is not."
>> words = str.split(/[ .,]\s*/)
=> ["Jake", "used", "to", "be", "a", "small", "child",
"but", "now", "is", "not"]
```

This statement puts the words from str into the words array, where the words in str are defined to be terminated with either a space, a period, or a comma, any of which could be followed by more whitespace characters.

The following sample program illustrates a simple use of pattern matching and hashes. The program reads lines of text in which the words are separated by whitespace and some common kinds of punctuation such as commas, periods, semicolons, and so forth. The objective of the program is to produce a frequency table of the words found in the input. A hash is an ideal way to build the word-frequency table. The keys can be the words, and the values can be the number of times they have appeared. The split method provides a convenient way to split each line of the input file into its words. For each word, the program uses has_key? on the hash to determine whether the word has occurred before. If so, its count is incremented; if not, the word is entered into the hash with a count of 1.

```ruby
#   word_table.rb
#   Input: Text from the keyboard. All words in the input are
#     separated by whitespace or punctuation, possibly followed
#     by whitespace, where the punctuation can be a comma, a
#     semicolon, a question mark, an exclamation point, a period,
#     or a colon.
# Output: A list of all unique words in the input, in alphabetical
#     order, along with their frequencies of occurrence

freq = Hash.new
line_words = Array.new

# Main loop to get and process lines of input text
while line = gets

  # Split the line into words
  line_words = line.chomp.split( /[ \.,;:!\?]\s*/)

  # Loop to count the words (either increment or initialize to 1)
  for word in line_words
    if freq.has_key?(word) then
      freq[word] = freq[word] + 1
    else
      freq[word] = 1
    end
  end
end
# Display the words and their frequencies
puts "\n Word \t\t Frequency \n\n"
for word in freq.keys.sort
  puts " #{word} \t\t #{freq[word]}"
end
```

Notice that the two normally special characters, . (period) and ? (question mark), are not backslashed in the pattern for split in this program. This is because the normally special characters for patterns (metacharacters) are not special in character classes.

14.10.2 Remembering Matches

The part of the string that matched a part of the pattern can be saved in an implicit variable for later use. The part of the pattern whose match you want to save is placed in parentheses. The substring that matched the first parenthesized part of the pattern is saved in $1, the second in $2, and so forth. As an example, consider the following:

```
>> str = "4 July 1776"
=> "4 July 1776"
>> str =~ /(\d+) (\w+) (\d+)/
=> 0
>> puts "#{$2} #{$1}, #{$3}"
=> July 4, 1776
```

In some situations, it is convenient to be able to reference the parts of the string that preceded the match, the part that matched, or the part that followed the match. These three strings are available after a match through the implicit variables $`, $&, and $', respectively.

14.10.3 Substitutions

Sometimes the substring of a string that matched a pattern must be replaced by another string. Ruby's String class has four methods designed to do exactly that. The most basic of these, the substitute method, sub, takes two parameters, a pattern and a string (or expression that evaluates to a string value). sub matches the pattern against the string object to which it is sent. If sub finds a match, the matched substring is replaced by its second parameter. Consider the following examples:

```
>> str = "The old car is great, but old"
=> "The old car is great, but old"
>> str.sub(/old/, "new")
=> "The new car is great, but old"
```

The gsub method is similar to sub, but finds all substring matches and replaces all of them with its second parameter. For example:

```
>> str = "The old car is great, but old"
=> "The old car is great, but old"
>> str.gsub(/old/, "new")
=> "The new car is great, but new"
>> str
=> "The old car is great, but old"
```

Notice from the last line that gsub does not alter the string object on which it is called. The same is true for sub. However, sub and gsub have mutator versions, named sub! and gsub!. For example:

```
>> str = "The old car is great, but old"
=> "The old car is great, but old"
>> str.gsub!(/old/, "new")
=> "The new car is great, but new"
```

```
>> str
=> "The new car is great, but new"
```

The i modifier, which tells the pattern matcher to ignore the case of letters, can also be used with the substitute method by attaching it to the right end of the pattern, as shown in the following code:

```
>> str = "Is it Rose, rose, or ROSE?"
=> "Is it Rose, rose, or ROSE?"
>> str.gsub(/rose/i, "rose")
=> "Is it rose, rose, or rose?"
```

Summary

Ruby is a pure object-oriented scripting language that is interpreted. Perhaps the primary motivation for its popularity is its use in the Rails framework for building Web applications.

Ruby has three categories of data types: scalars, arrays, and hashes. The scalar classes are Float, Fixnum, Bignum, and String. Ruby's arithmetic expressions and assignment statements are like those of other common languages. All Ruby variables are references to objects. It has no primitive types such as C++, Java, and C#. Although expressions appear in the same form as in other languages, underneath they are all executed by message passing. The String class has a large number of methods.

Ruby includes the usual collection of control statements, including two different multiple-selection statements. Arrays in Ruby are different from the more conventional languages in that they can store any objects and they have dynamic length. The Array class provides a large collection of methods, including those for implementing stacks and queues in arrays. Ruby's hashes are similar to those of Perl.

Methods can be defined in classes, but also outside classes, in which case they are much like functions. Asterisk parameters provide the means of supporting a variable number of parameters. Classes are dynamic, in the sense that methods and variables can be added or deleted at any time. Access control is provided by calling the public, private, and protected methods. Ruby includes an implicit way to provide getters and setters.

One unique feature of Ruby is its code blocks and iterators. The each and find iterators are frequently used to deal with arrays. Ruby's pattern matching operations use the same regular expressions as JavaScript.

Review Questions

14.1   What are the two integer classes of Ruby?

14.2   What is one of the most common uses of Ruby?

14.3   What is the difference between the `downcase` and `downcase!` methods?

14.4   What is the difference between the two kinds of string literals?

14.5   What is the length limit of a `Bignum` object?

14.6   What does the `String` method `replace` do?

14.7   What numeric operators in C and Java are missing in Ruby?

14.8   What are the syntactic differences between the JavaScript `if` statement and that of Ruby?

14.9   What does the `include?` method do?

14.10 In what two ways can an `Array` object be created?

14.11 What values of a variable are considered true?

14.12 Describe what the `for-in` statement does.

14.13 What is the form of a hash literal?

14.14 Describe how the concatenation operator for arrays works.

14.15 When are access control violations for methods detected?

14.16 Do method headers require parentheses?

14.17 What is an asterisk parameter?

14.18 Explain what the each method does.

14.19 What is the form of an instance variable's name?

Exercises

14.1   Write, test, and debug (if necessary) a Ruby program for the following specification:

Input: A list of numbers from the keyboard.

Output: The second smallest number in the list, along with its position in the list, with 1 being the position of the first number.

14.2 Write, test, and debug (if necessary) a Ruby program for the following specification:

Input: Three numbers, a, b, and c, each on its own line, from the keyboard.

Output: The value of the expression `10ab-((c-1)/17.44)`.

14.3 Write, test, and debug (if necessary) a Ruby program for the following specification:

Input: A list of lines of text from the keyboard.

Output: Every input line that has more than 10 characters (not counting the newline) but fewer than 20 characters (not counting the newline) that contains the string `ed`.

14.4 Write, test, and debug (if necessary) a Ruby program for the following specification:

Input: Three names, on separate lines, from the keyboard.

Output: The input names in alphabetical order, without using arrays.

14.5 Write, test, and debug (if necessary) a Ruby program for the following specification:

Input: A list of numbers from the keyboard.

Output: The median of the input numbers.

14.6 Write, test, and debug (if necessary) a Ruby program for the following specification:

Input: A list of numbers from the keyboard.

Output: Two lists of numbers, one with input numbers that are greater than zero and one with those that are less than zero (ignore the zero-valued numbers). You must first build two arrays with the required output numbers before you display any of them.

CHAPTER

15

Introduction to Rails

As stated in Chapter 14, our primary interest in Ruby in this book is its use with the Web software development framework, Rails. This chapter introduces Rails. Rails is a complex system with a large array of powerful capabilities, and this is but one chapter of a book. Therefore, only a quick introduction to a few of the most straightforward uses of Rails will be provided. The chapter begins with an overview of Rails, including its approach to bringing the MVC model of applications together with relational databases. The remainder of the chapter is a discussion of Rails through several example applications, beginning with the simplest of applications, Hello World. This application is then modified to produce simple dynamic content. Next, a small application that accesses a database is developed. Because Rails was designed to be used in an incremental approach to application development, that approach is used in this example. The first version, which is generated entirely by Rails, builds a database, but only provides database maintenance operations. The next version adds a database search operation for users. The last version includes developer-written layouts and style sheets. The last section of this chapter describes the process of implementing Ajax within the Rails system. This includes developing the initial view document, describing the helper function `observer_field` to trigger the Ajax action, and developing the controller processes to implement the application.

15.1 Overview of Rails

Rails[1] is a software development framework for Web-based applications, in particular those that access databases. A framework is a system in which much of the more-or-less standard software parts are furnished by the framework, so they do not need to be written by the applications developer. Rails was developed by David Heinemeier Hansson in the early 2000s and was released to the public in July 2004. Since then, it has rapidly gained widespread interest and usage.

Rails is a large and complex system—one book on Rails has 851 pages![2] Accordingly, this chapter only briefly introduces some of the most fundamental capabilities of the system.

Rails, like some other Web development frameworks, such as Tapestry and Struts, is based on the Model-View-Controller (MVC) architecture for applications. MVC was developed by Trygve Reenskaug, a Norwegian, in 1978–1979 while he was a visiting scientist at XeroxPARC working in the Smalltalk group. The original intent of MVC was to model graphical user interfaces, which were then being developed for Smalltalk. The MVC architecture clearly separates applications, both logically and physically, into three parts. The *model* is not only the data, but any enforced constraints on the data. For example, if a part of the data is the age of people, the model might ensure that no age value outside the usual range of possible human ages can be entered into the data storage. The *view* is the part of an application that prepares and presents results to the user. The *controller*, true to its namesake, controls the application. In addition, the controller performs any required computations. In an MVC Web application, a browser submits requests to the controller, which consults the model (which in turn consults its database). The model then reports results to the controller and indirectly to the view. The controller then instructs the view to produce a result document that is then transmitted to the client for display. The intent of MVC is to reduce the coupling among the three parts of an application, making the application easier to develop and maintain. Figure 15.1 shows the components and actions of a request and response in a typical Rails application.

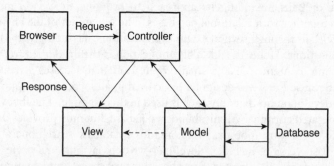

Figure 15.1 A request and response in a Rails application

---

1. The full name of Rails is Ruby on Rails, but we will refer to it simply as Rails.
2. *The Rails Way*, Obie Fernandez, Addison-Wesley, 2008.

A significant and characteristic part of Rails is its approach to connecting object-oriented software with a relational database. These two are not particularly amenable to marriage, so this is not a natural connection. For this, Rails uses an object-relational mapping (ORM) approach. Each relational database table is implicitly mapped to a class. For example, if the database has a table named `employees`, the Rails application program that uses `employees` will have a class named `Employee`. Rows of the `employees` table will have corresponding objects of the `Employee` class. The `Employee` class will have methods to get and set the various state variables, which are Ruby attributes of objects of the class. In summary, an ORM maps tables to classes, rows to objects, and columns to the fields of the objects. Furthermore, the `Employee` class will have methods for performing table-level operations, such as finding an object with a certain attribute value. The key aspect of the ORM in Rails is that it is implicit. The classes, objects, methods, and attributes that represent a database in Ruby are automatically built by Rails.

View documents are XHTML documents that can have embedded Ruby code, which is interpreted on the server when the documents are requested.

The controller part of MVC controls the interactions between the data model, the user, and the view. Some of the code to support these interactions are provided by Rails. So, much of what the developer writes for the controller is the logic of the specific application.

Rails can be and often is used in conjunction with Ajax. Rails uses a JavaScript library named Prototype to support Ajax and interactions with the JavaScript model of the document being displayed by the browser. Rails also provides other support for developing Ajax, including producing visual effects.

A Rails application is a program that provides a response when a client browser connects to a Rails-driven Web site. Because Rails uses an MVC architecture, building a Rails application consists of designing and building the three parts of an MVC system. The developer must design and build a model of the application's domain. This model must include the design of a database that represents the model. For example, if the application is an online bookstore, the model might include an inventory of books and a catalog of all books that can be ordered through the store, among other things. The developer must design and build the actions that can happen in the operation of the bookstore, such as inquiries, purchases, orders, and billing. Finally, the developer must design and build the publicly accessible views of the application domain. Of course, Rails offers a great deal of assistance in constructing an application, as will be evidenced in the example applications in this chapter.

There are two fundamental principles that guided the development of Rails. It is valuable to be aware of these when learning and using Rails. The first of these has the acronym *DRY*, which stands for Do not Repeat Yourself. In Rails, DRY means that every element of information appears just once in the system. This minimizes the memory required by the system. In addition, changes to the system are highly localized, making them both easier and less error prone. The second principle is named *convention over configuration*. Web applications with JSP require elaborate and complicated XML configuration files to specify their structure. In Rails, the structure of an application is dictated by the MVC architecture. The connections between the different parts are established and maintained by convention, rather than being specified in a configuration document. For example, the names of database tables and their associated controller classes are intimately related by convention.

Rails is a product of a software development paradigm called *Agile Development*.[3] Some of this paradigm is related to the human interactions among development team members and between the team and the customer. However, part of it is the focus on the quick development of working software, rather than the creation of elaborate documentation and then software. This is an incremental approach to development, which is facilitated by the adherence to the principles used in creating Rails.

Rails differs from the other frameworks discussed in this book, Flash, NetBeans, and Visual Studio, in that it does not use a graphical user interface (GUI). Rather, Rails is a command-line-oriented system. Commands are issued by typing them at a prompt in a DOS-like or UNIX-like command window, rather than by clicking icons on a GUI. This makes working with Rails seem old-fashioned—like using UNIX the old way.

Rails 2.0 is discussed and used in this chapter.

15.2 Document Requests

Rails is a Web application development framework. A software development framework is often constructed as a library of components that provide commonly needed services to an application in a particular application area. The specific application area for Rails is Web applications that use relational databases, which are discussed in Chapter 13, "Database Access through the Web."

Before one can use Rails, the system must be downloaded and installed on one's computer. For Windows users, the simplest way to do this is to download the complete software system named InstantRails from `http://instantrails.rubyforge.org/wiki/wiki.pl`. Instant-Rails, which was developed by Curt Hibbs, includes Ruby, Rails, MySQL, several Web servers, and everything else needed to use these technologies together. Installing InstantRails is quick and easy.

InstantRails is a self-contained system. It does not reside in the global Windows environment, so interactions with it cannot be done through a special command window.

The Leopard operating system (Mac OS X Version 10.5) for Macintosh computers was released in October 2007. This system includes Ruby and Rails, so no downloading or installation is required to use Rails on these Macs.

For UNIX systems, Rails is available from the following site:

`http://www.RubyonRails.org/down`

---

3. See `http://agilemanifesto.org`.

15.2.1 Static Documents—Hello World in Rails

This section describes how to build a Hello World application in Rails. The purpose of such an exercise is to demonstrate the directory structure of the simplest possible Rails application, showing what files must be created and where they must reside in the directory structure. InstantRails is started by clicking the red *I*, which is the icon of the InstantRails application, in the directory in which InstantRails was installed. This opens a small window, as shown in Figure 15.2.

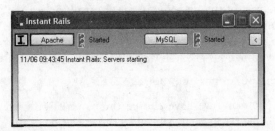

Figure 15.2   The InstantRails application window

A click on the black I in the upper-left part of this window produces a small menu. Selecting the *Rails Application* entry in this menu opens another menu. Selecting the *Open Ruby Console Window* entry in this menu opens a command line window in the `rails_aps` subdirectory of the directory in which InstantRails was installed. In our case, InstantRails was installed in the `myrails` directory. Rails commands cannot be given in a normal command window—they can be given only in a Rails command window.

If you are running Windows and the IIS server, you will need to stop it before using Rails. Also, if MySQL is running, it also must be stopped, because Rails will start its own MySQL.

Users usually create a new subdirectory of `rails_apps` for their Rails applications. We created a subdirectory named `examples` for the example applications of this chapter.

Next, we move to the `examples` directory and create a new Rails application named `greet` with the following command:

```
>rails greet
```

Rails responds by creating more than 45 files in more than 30 directories. This is part of the framework to support a Rails application. Directly under the specific application directory, in this case `greet`, 11 subdirectories are created, the most interesting of which at this point is `app`. The `app` directory has four subdirectories, `models`, `views`, and `controllers`, which correspond directly to the MVC architecture of a Rails application, and `helpers`. The `helpers` subdirectory contains Rails-provided methods that aid in constructing applications. Most of the user code to support an application will reside in either `models`, `views`, or `controllers` or subdirectories of them.

One of the directories created by the `rails` command is `script`, which has several important Ruby scripts that perform services. One of these, `generate`, is used to create part of an application controller. This script creates a file containing a class in the `controllers` directory, and also a subdirectory of the `views` directory where views documents will be stored. For our application, we pass two parameters to `generate`, the first of which is `controller`, which indicates that we want the controller class built. The second parameter is the name we chose for the controller. An important part of how Rails works is its focused use of names. Our first example of this is the name of the controller. This name will also be part of the filename of the controller class and part of the name of the controller class. In addition, it will be the name of the subdirectory of the `views` directory and a part of the URL of the application. For our example, the following command is given in the `greet` directory to create the controller:

```
>ruby script/generate controller say
```

With this command we have chosen the name `say` for the controller for our application. The response produced by the execution of this command follows:

```
exists   app/controllers/
exists   app/helpers/
create   app/views/say
exists   test/functional/
create   app/controllers/say_controller.rb
create   test/functional/say_controller_test.rb
create   app/helpers/say_helper.rb
```

The `exists` lines above indicate files and directories that are verified to already exist. The `create` lines show the newly created directories and files. There are now two files in the `controllers` directory, `application.rb` and `say_controller.rb`, which contain the `ApplicationController` and `SayController` classes, respectively. The `SayController` class is a subclass of the `ApplicationController` class. `ApplicationController`, the parent class, provides the default behavior for the controller class of the application class, which is `SayController`. `ApplicationController` was built by the initial `rails` command. The following is a listing of `say_controller.rb`:

```
class SayController < ApplicationController
end
```

Note the use of `say` in both the name of the controller file and the name of the controller class. This is another example of the use of convention in Rails.

`SayController` is an empty class, other than what it inherits from `ApplicationController`, which is in the file `application.rb`. `ApplicationController` is a subclass of `ActionController`, which defines the basic functionality of a controller. `SayController` produces, at least indirectly, the response to requests, so a method must be added to it. The method does not need to actually do anything, other than indicate a document that will describes the response.[4] The mere existence of the method specifies by its name the response document. So, the action will be nothing more than an empty method definition, whose name will be the same as that of the response document in the `say` subdirectory of `views`. With the empty method, which is called an *action method*, the controller now has the following appearance:

```
class SayController < ApplicationController
  def hello
  end
end
```

Web sites, or applications, are specified in requests from browsers with URLs. Rails applications are no different. When Rails receives the URL of a request, it maps it to a specific controller name and action method. In simple situations, the mapping is trivial—the first domain following the hostname is interpreted as a controller name and the next domain is interpreted as the name of an action method. There is no need to specify the application name, because, as we shall soon see, each application is served by its own server.

The host for our examples will be the machine on which the applications are resident. The default port for the server we will use is 3000, so the host name will be `localhost:3000`. So for the `greet` example, the request URL is as follows:

```
http://localhost:3000/say/hello
```

(Now it should be obvious why the base document is named `say`.)

Next, we need to build the view file, which will be a simple XHTML file to produce the greeting. The view document is often called a *template*. The following is the template for the `greet` application:

```
<!-- hello.html.erb - the template for the greet application
     -->
<html>
  <head>
    <title> greet </title>
  </head>
  <body>
    <h1> Hello from Rails! </h1>
  </body>
</html>
```

Note that for simplicity's sake, we have not included the DOCTYPE declaration. The extension on this file's name is `.html.erb` because the file stores an HTML document, but it may include embedded Ruby code to be interpreted

---

4. The action method could itself produce the output for this application, but then we could not also illustrate the view document.

by the Ruby interpreter, ERb (an acronym for *Embedded Ruby*), before the template is returned to the requesting browser.

The template file for our application resides in the `say` subdirectory of the `views` subdirectory of the `app` subdirectory of the `greet` directory.

The structure of the `examples` directory is shown in Figure 15.3.

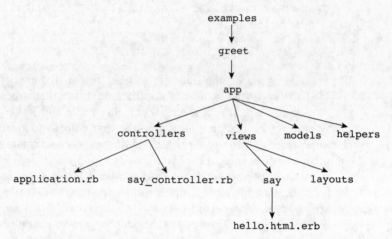

Figure 15.3   Directory structure for the `greet` application

Before the application can be tested, a Rails Web server must be started. A server is started with the `server` script from the `script` directory. Within Rails there are three different servers available. The default server is `Mongrel`, but `Apache` and `WEBrick` are also available. Because it is the default Rails server, `Mongrel` can be started with the following command at the application prompt:

```
>ruby script/server
```

Note that the server is started by a command in the directory of the particular application, in our example, `greet`. This implies that no other application can be served by this server.

Figure 15.4 shows the output of the `greet` application when it is addressed by a browser.

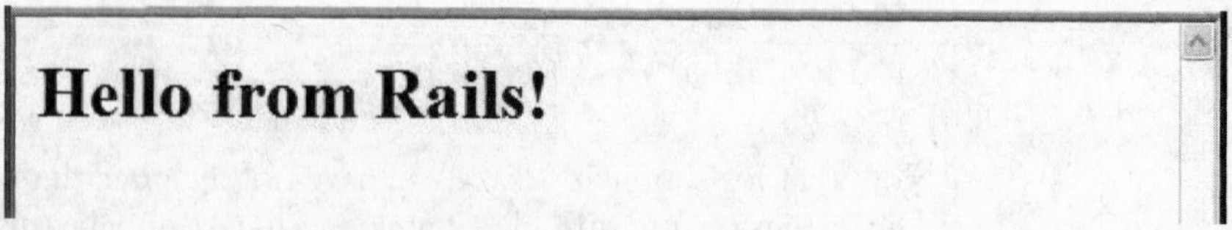

Hello from Rails!

Figure 15.4   The reponse from `greet`

The following summarizes how Rails reacts to a request for a static document: First, the name of the controller is extracted from the URL (it follows the hostname). Next, an instance of the controller class (found in the `app/controllers` subdirectory), in our example, `SayController`, is created. The name of the action is then extracted from the URL, in our example, `hello`. Next, Rails searches for a template with the same name as the action method in the subdirectory with the same name as the controller in the `app/views` directory. The template file is then given to ERb to interpret any Ruby code that is embedded in the template. In the case of `hello.html.erb`, there is no embedded Ruby code, so this step has no affect. Finally, the template file is returned to the requesting browser, which displays it. The activities of Rails in response to a simple request are shown in Figure 15.5.

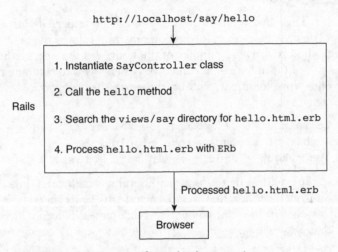

Figure 15.5   Rails actions for a simple request

15.2.2 Dynamic Documents

Rails offers three different approaches to producing dynamic documents. In this chapter, only one of these is discussed, which is to embed Ruby code in a template file. This is similar to some other approaches we have discussed, in particular PHP, ASP.NET, and JSP.

As an example of a dynamic document, we modify the `greet` application to display the current date and time on the server, including the number of seconds since midnight (just so some computation will be included). This will illustrate how Ruby code that is embedded in a template file can access instance variables that are created and assigned values in the action method of the controller.

Ruby code is embedded in a template file by placing it between the `<%` and `%>` markers. If the Ruby code produces a result and the result is to be inserted into the template document, an equal sign (=) is attached to the opening marker. For example:

```
<p> The number of seconds in a day is: <%= 60 * 60 * 24 %>
</p>
```

After interpretation of the Ruby code, this is as follows:

```
<p> The number of seconds in a day is: 86400 </p>
```

The date can be obtained by calling Ruby's `Time.now` method. This method returns the current day of the week, month, day of the month, time, time zone,[5] and year, as a string. So, we can put the date in the response template with:

```
<p> It is now <%= Time.now %> </p>
```

The value returned by `Time.now` can be parsed with the methods of the `Time` class. For example, the `hour` method returns the hour of the day, the `min` method returns the minutes of the hour, and the `sec` method returns the seconds of the minute. These methods can be used to compute the number of seconds since midnight. Putting these together results in the following template code:

```
It is now <%= t = Time.now %> <br />
Number of seconds since midnight:
<%= t.hour * 3600 + t.min * 60 + t.sec %>
```

It would be better to place the Ruby code for the time computation in the controller, because that would separate the program code from the markup. In this case, it does not amount to much code. The modified `SayController` class is as follows:

```
class SayController < ApplicationController
  def hello
    @t = Time.now
    @tsec = @t.hour * 3600 + @t.min * 60 + @t.sec
  end
end
```

The response template now needs to be able to access the instance variables in the `SayController` class. Rails makes this trivial, for all instance variables in the controller class are visible to the template. The template code for displaying the time and number of seconds since midnight is as follows:

```
It is now <%= @t %> <br />
Number of seconds since midnight: <%= @tsec %>
```

---

5. The time zone is represented as the number of hours from Coordinated Universal Time (UTC). For Mountain Daylight Time, this is –0600 for six hours after UTC.

Figure 15.6 shows the display of the modified `greet` application.

Hello World!

It is now Sun May 20 20:13:40 -0600 2007
Number of seconds since midnight: 72820

Figure 15.6   The output of the modified version of the `greet` application

15.3   Rails Applications with Databases

This section uses an example application to describe how a Rails application that uses a database is constructed. For the example database, a simple part of the `cars` database from Chapter 13, "Database Access through the Web," is used—just the main table. The operations that are implemented are simple: The user is presented with a welcome document that states the number of cars listed in the database. It also presents a form that allows the user to specify the beginning and ending model years in which he or she is interested, as well as a specific body style. The system searches the database for the entries that fit the given restrictions and displays them for the user.

For this example, we create a new application named `cars` in the `examples` directory with the following command:

```
>rails -d mysql cars
```

The d flag followed by `mysql` appears in the `rails` command to tell Rails that this application will use a MySQL database.

15.3.1   Building the Basic Application

It takes but a few commands to coerce Rails into building a complete basic working Web application that uses a database. In this section, we begin building our application by instructing Rails to do just that.

It is customary in Rails applications to use three copies of the database, one for development, one for testing, and one for production. The descriptions of three databases are constructed with the following single command:

```
>rake db:create:all
```

The Rails response to this command is as follows:

```
(in C:/myrails/rails_apps/examples/cars)
```

This creates the file `database.yml`[6] in the `config` subdirectory of the `cars` directory of our application. This file follows:

```
# MySQL.  Versions 4.1 and 5.0 are recommended.
#
development:
  adapter: mysql
  encoding: utf8
  database: cars_development
  username: root
  password:
  host: localhost
# Warning: The database defined as 'test' will be erased and
# re-generated from your development database when you run 'rake'.
# Do not set this db to the same as development or production.
test:
  adapter: mysql
  encoding: utf8
  database: cars_test
  username: root
  password:
  host: localhost
production:
  adapter: mysql
  encoding: utf8
  database: cars_production
  username: root
  password:
  host: localhost
```

This document shows that descriptions of all three databases, `cars_development`, `cars_test`, and `cars_production` were created.

Next, the following command is used to create the model, the required database migration script, the table of the database, as well as a maintenance controller and testing support files for the application.

```
>ruby script/generate scaffold Corvette
     body_style:string miles:float year:integer
```

The single table of the database, `corvettes`, was specified by the command to have three columns, `body_style`, a string, `miles`, a float, and `year`, an integer.

---

6. `yml` is an abbreviation of yaml, which was an acronym for *Yet Another Markup Language*, but subsequently became an acronym for the recursive *YAML Ain't a Markup Language*. YAML is actually a data serialization language, related to both JSON and XML.

Following is the migration class defined in the file named
`001_create_corvettes.rb`, which resides in the `cars/db/migrate`
directory:

```
class CreateCorvettes < ActiveRecord::Migration
  def self.up
    create_table :corvettes do |t|
      t.string :body_style
      t.float :miles
      t.integer :year
      t.timestamps
    end
  end
  def self.down
    drop_table :corvettes
  end
end
```

The `self.up` method is to update the table to the next version. The
`self.down` method is to back up to some previous version. To create the initial
version of the database table, the table description is included in the `self.up`
method. We could edit this method to provide some initial data for the table. To
provide the columns of the table, the `t` object methods named after the data
types are called, passing the column name in symbolic form as a parameter. For
example, `t.float :miles` is a call to the `float` method of the `t` object, passing the column name `miles`, in the form of a symbol, as a parameter. These
calls appear in the body of the `create_table` do compound construct.

Some of the operations needed by most database applications are those for
basic maintenance of the records of the tables, which are create, read, update,
and delete, which together have the catchy acronym, CRUD. These operations
are automatically generated for a table by Rails by including `scaffold` in the
command to generate the table. These operations provide the scaffolding to
make the table maintainable until more suitable operations are built, if indeed
they are needed. In most commercial applications, most if not all of the scaffolding is replaced before the application is deployed. However, it is extremely useful to have these operations provided before the developer writes any code.
They allow the developer to get a basic application that uses a database working
very quickly.

Notice that the table is named in plural form. This is required by the Rails
system, because the singular form of these names are used for the names of the
Ruby files for the models and for the classes associated with the tables.

The actual creation of the database is a result of the following command:

```
>rake db:migrate
```

This command, which causes the execution of the `self.up` method of the `CreateCorvettes` class in `001_create_corvettes.rb` produces the following response:

```
(in C:/myrails/rails_apps/examples/cars)
== 1 CreateCorvettes: migrating ===========================
-- create_table(:corvettes)
    -> 0.2030s
== 2 CreateCorvettes: migrated (0.3440s)  =================
```

The schema for the newly created database appears in the `db` subdirectoy of the application. This schema, which is Ruby code, follows:

```ruby
ActiveRecord::Schema.define(:version => 1) do
  create_table "corvettes", :force => true do |t|
    t.string   "body_style"
    t.float    "miles"
    t.integer  "year"
    t.datetime "created_at"
    t.datetime "updated_at"
  end
end
```

We modified the listing of this file, `schema.rb`, by removing the initial block of comments.

Amazing as it seems, we now have a working application with a connected database, although the database is empty. And we have yet to write a single line of code! To see what we have, we point a browser at `http://localhost:3000/corvettes` and get the display shown in Figure 15.7.

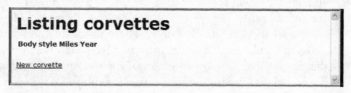

Figure 15.7 Display of the initial cars application

This document would provide a listing of the database if it contained data. It also provides a link *New corvette* that takes the user to another document for entering a `corvettes` table row, as shown in Figure 15.8.

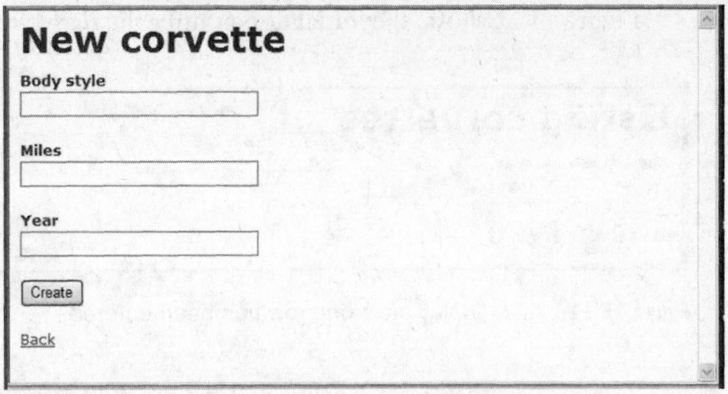

Figure 15.8 Display of the document to enter a row into the `corvettes` table

Figure 15.9 shows the document after a row of data has been entered.

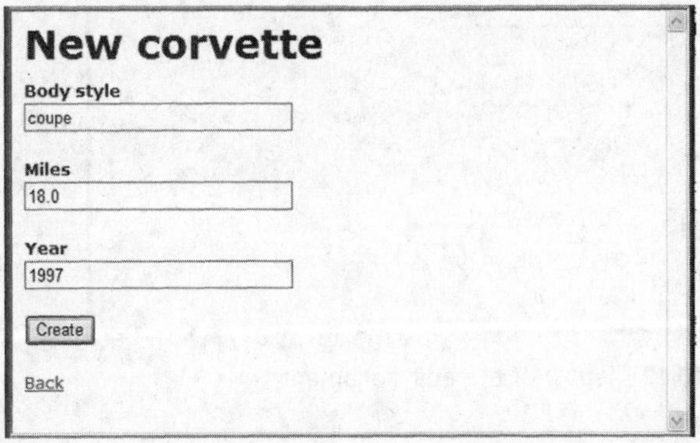

Figure 15.9 Display after a row of data has been entered

Figure 15.10 shows the result of clicking the *Create* button.

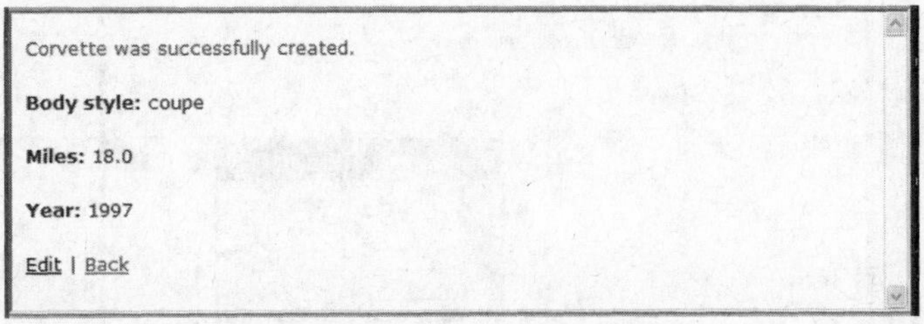

Figure 15.10 The result of clicking the *Create* button

Figure 15.11 shows the initial display after the *Back* button has been clicked.

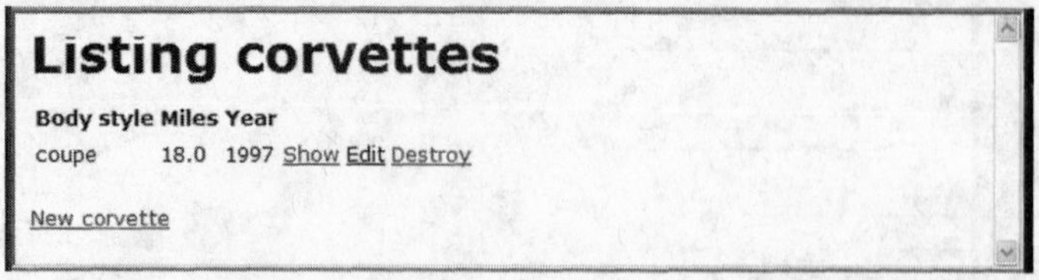

Figure 15.11 Initial display after one row has been entered

The display that results from clicking the *Edit* button on the table's only row is shown in Figure 15.12.

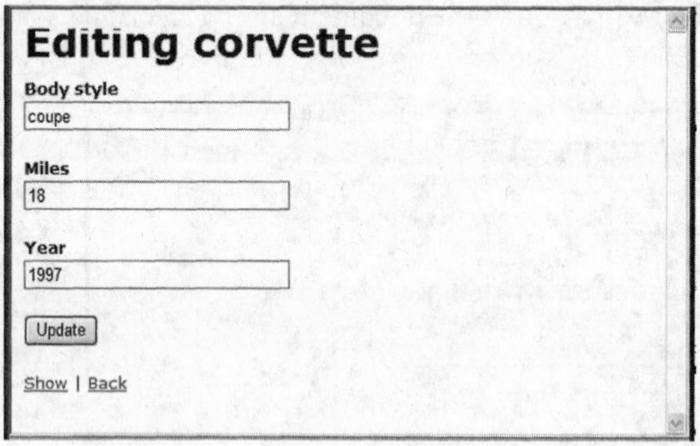

Figure 15.12 Display of the edit document

The display that results from clicking the *Destroy* button on the table's only row is shown in Figure 15.13.

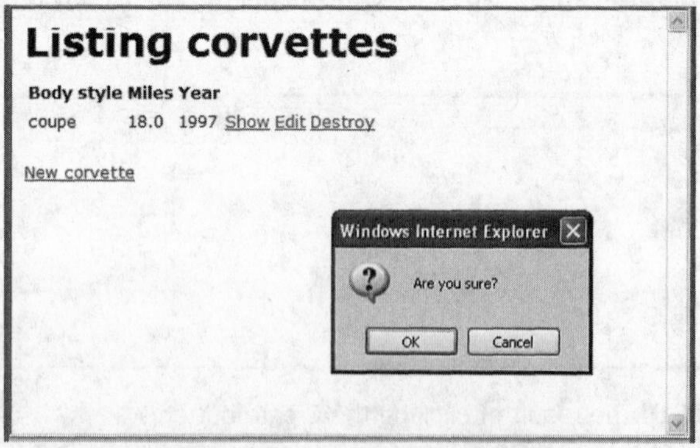

Figure 15.13 Display of the destroy document

The model file that Rails built, which is named `corvette.rb`, resides in the `models` directory, and defines the `Corvette` class is as follows:

```
class Corvette < ActiveRecord::Base
end
```

It is common to add some kind of validation to a database table. This can be done by adding a call to one of the `validates` methods. One of the most fundamental of these is the `validates_presence_of`, which takes as parameters the symbolic names of the columns of the table. When a row is added to the table with new, `validate_presence_of` ensures that all of its columns have values. An error message is issued if any are left blank. For our example, the call would be as follows:

```
validate_presence_of :body_style, :miles, :year
```

This call would be placed in the `Corvette` class of the model file.

The controller class is named `CorvetteController` by convention from the name `Corvette` given in the command that created the application. The controller file, named `corvettes_controller.rb`, is stored in the `controllers` directory and defines the `CorvettesController` class. This class defines the support methods for the database table: `index`, which creates a list of the rows of the table; `show`, which creates the data for one row of the table; `new`, which creates a new row object; `edit`, which handles the editing of a row; `create`, which handles the creation of a new row; `update`, which handles the response to a *Create* button; and `delete`, which handles deletion of a row.

There are four documents in the `views` directory. The `index.html.erb` document is as follows:

```
<h1>Listing corvettes</h1>
<table>
  <tr>
    <th>Body style</th>
    <th>Miles</th>
    <th>Year</th>
  </tr>
<% for corvette in @corvettes %>
  <tr>
    <td><%=h corvette.body_style %></td>
    <td><%=h corvette.miles %></td>
    <td><%=h corvette.year %></td>
    <td><%= link_to 'Show', corvette %></td>
    <td><%= link_to 'Edit', edit_corvette_path(corvette) %></td>
    <td><%= link_to 'Destroy', corvette, :confirm =>
          'Are you sure?', :method => :delete %></td>
```

```
    </tr>
<% end %>
</table>
<br />
<%= link_to 'New corvette', new_corvette_path %>
```

This document appears to be only a partial XHTML document—in fact, it is only the content of the body element of a complete XHTML document. So, where is the rest of the document? The answer is that Rails includes a way to supply parts of documents in a separate document. The common parts of documents are factored out and merged back in when the document is about to be displayed. The document of these common parts is called a *layout*. Layouts are an example of the application of the DRY principle—if two or more documents have a common part, do not repeat it. All of the template documents associated with the `corvettes` controller appear only as the content of the body element—the common parts, in these cases everything except the content of the body element, are in a document named `corvettes.html.erb`, which is in the `cars/app/views/layout` directory. In this case, the layout document was provided by Rails through `scaffold`. However, such documents can also be supplied by the developer. The layout document is implicitly merged into the template documents by Rails. When a template document is to be displayed, Rails first looks in the layout directory for a layout document. If it finds one, it is merged with the template document and the result is displayed.

The layout document, `corvettes.html.erb`, built by Rails for `CorvetteController` is as follows:

```
<!DOCTYPE html PUBLIC "-//W3C//DTD XHTML 1.0 Transitional//EN"
        "http://www.w3.org/TR/xhtml1/DTD/xhtml1-transitional.dtd">
<html xmlns="http://www.w3.org/1999/xhtml" xml:lang="en" lang="en">
<head>
  <meta http-equiv="content-type" content="text/html;charset=UTF-8"/>
  <title>Corvettes: <%= controller.action_name %></title>
  <%= stylesheet_link_tag 'scaffold' %>
</head>
<body>
<p style="color: green"><%= flash[:notice] %></p>
<%= yield  %>
</body>
</html>
```

The call to `yield` tells Rails where the template file belongs in the layout. The call to `stylesheet_link_tag` specifies the style sheet to be used with the layout document. In this case, the style sheet was furnished by `scaffold`.

The `new.html.erb` document is as follows:

```
<h1>New corvette</h1>
<%= error_messages_for :corvette %>
<% form_for(@corvette) do |f| %>
  <p>
    <b>Body style</b><br />
    <%= f.text_field :body_style %>
  </p>
  <p>
    <b>Miles</b><br />
    <%= f.text_field :miles %>
  </p>
  <p>
    <b>Year</b><br />
    <%= f.text_field :year %>
  </p>
  <p>
    <%= f.submit "Create" %>
  </p>
<% end %>
<%= link_to 'Back', corvettes_path %>
```

The calls to `text_field` create XHTML text boxes. The call to `submit` creates an XHTML *Submit* button. The call to `link_to` creates an XHTML link. The `show.html.erb` document is as follows:

```
<p>
  <b>Body style:</b>
  <%=h @corvette.body_style %>
</p>
<p>
  <b>Miles:</b>
  <%=h @corvette.miles %>
</p>
<p>
  <b>Year:</b>
  <%=h @corvette.year %>
</p>
<%= link_to 'Edit', edit_corvette_path(@corvette) %>
<%= link_to 'Back', corvettes_path %>
```

The embedded Ruby code, for example @corvette.body_style, fetches the input from the corresponding text box. It is possible that a user could enter any HTML markup in a text box, including a script tag that could contain malicious code. The h in the opening tag for embedded Ruby code specifies that all < and > characters are to be converted to character entities to prevent the problem.

Finally, the edit.html.erb document is as follows:

```
<h1>Editing corvette</h1>
<%= error_messages_for :corvette %>
<% form_for(@corvette) do |f| %>
  <p>
    <b>Body style</b><br />
    <%= f.text_field :body_style %>
  </p>
  <p>
    <b>Miles</b><br />
    <%= f.text_field :miles %>
  </p>
  <p>
    <b>Year</b><br />
    <%= f.text_field :year %>
  </p>
  <p>
    <%= f.submit "Update" %>
  </p>
<% end %>
<%= link_to 'Show', @corvette %> |
<%= link_to 'Back', corvettes_path %>
```

15.3.2 Completing the Application

We must now expand the example to provide its user services—to present a form to the user in which he or she can specify queries against the database, carry out such queries, and present the results to the user.

We need a new controller, which we name main, to implement the required actions for our application. The controller is created with the following command:

```
>ruby script/generate controller main
```

Next, we add an empty action method named welcome to the new controller. The template associated with the action method will provide the initial display to the user for the application. Recall that this display must include the current number of cars in the corvettes table of the database. Therefore, the welcome method must provide that number for the template. The number of rows in a table can be determined by calling the `count` method on the table's object. For example, the number of rows in the `corvettes` table is gotten with `Corvette.count`. We place the call to `Corvette.count` in the `welcome` action method and store the returned value in the instance variable `@num_cars`. The resulting controller is as follows:

```
# main_controller.rb - for the cars application
class MainController < ApplicationController

# welcome method - fetches values for the
#   initial view

  def welcome
    @num_cars = Corvette.count
  end
end
```

Every model class (therefore, every database table) supports the `find` method, which searches its table for rows that satisfy given criteria. The simplest way to use `find` is to pass it one or more primary keys. For example:

```
mycar = Corvettes.find(8)
```

If given more than one key, `find` returns an array of the requested row objects. For example:

```
list_five = (1, 2, 3, 4, 5)
first_five = Corvettes.find(list_five)
```

A `RecordNotFound` exception is thrown if any of the requested primary keys cannot be found.

In most cases, row objects of tables are needed that meet certain criteria. The `find` method can do this, too. If the first parameter to `find` is `:all`, `find` searches can be controlled by a second parameter, which is specified as the value of the `:conditions` symbol. For example, consider the following statement:

```
sixty_five = find(:all, :conditions => "year = 1965")
```

More than one condition can be specified, as shown in the following:

```
sixty_five_conv = find(:all, :conditions => "year = 1965
                       and body_style = 'convertible'")
```

This form of call to `find` is adequate only if the conditions are all literals. In many cases, the condition is at least partially made up of user input, often form data. For example, if the year condition value were in the @year instance variable, the following could be used:

```
sixty_five_conv = find(:all, :conditions =>
    "year = #{@year} and body_style = 'convertible'")
```

This approach has a critical drawback—it allows a security problem named *SQL injection attack*. So, Rails has a safe alternative, which is to use a different form of :conditions value. With this form, the value of :conditions is delimited with brackets, question marks appear in place of the user-input values, and the condition is followed by a comma and the variables that have the values. The new form of the example above is as follows:

```
sixty_five_conv = find(:all, :conditions =>
    ["year = ? and body_style = 'convertible'", @year])
```

If the first parameter to find is :first, it returns the first row object it finds that meets the specified condition.

Now we can develop the welcome template, which is stored in the welcome.html.erb file in the views directory. This document must give the initial information and then display a form that the user can fill in and submit to learn about specific cars for sale. The welcome document uses the value produced by the welcome method of the main controller, @num_cars. The welcome.html.erb file follows:

```html
<!-- welcome.html.erb - initial view for the cars application
    -->
<!-- The initial information -->
<p>
  <h1> Aidan's Used Car Lot </h1>
  <h2> Welcome to our home document </h2>
  We currently have <%= @num_cars %> used Corvettes listed <br />
  To request information on available cars, please fill out <br />
  the following form and submit it
</p>

<!-- The form to collect input from the user about their interests
    -->
<form action = "result"  method = "post" >
  From year: <input type = "text"  size = "4"  name = "year1" />
  To year: <input type = "text"  size = "4"  name = "year2" />
  Body style: <input type = "text"  size = "12"  name = "body" />
  <br />
  <input  type = "submit"  value = "Submit request" /> <br />
  <input type = "reset"  value = "Reset form" /> <br />
</form>
```

Notice that the `action` attribute of the form element in `welcome.html.erb` is set to `"result"`, which will need to be an action method in the `main` controller. Also note that the method is `post`, which is required in Rails.

Like the template document produced by `scaffold`, this template is missing its first and last parts. This will also be the case for the other template developed in this section, `result`. The other parts of these templates will be added with a layout document in Section 15.3.5.

The display of the `welcome` template is shown in Figure 15.14.[7]

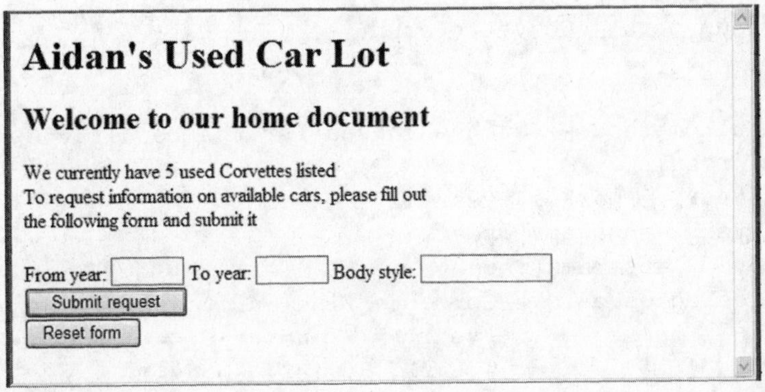

Aidan's Used Car Lot

Welcome to our home document

We currently have 5 used Corvettes listed
To request information on available cars, please fill out
the following form and submit it

From year: [   ] To year: [   ] Body style: [   ]
[Submit request]
[Reset form]

Figure 15.14   Display of `welcome.html.erb`

The next step of the application construction is to build the action method in the `MainController` class to process the form data when the form is submitted. In the initial template file, `welcome.html.erb`, this method is named `result` in the `action` attribute of the form tag. The `result` method has two tasks, the first of which is to fetch the form data. This data is used to display back to the customer and to compute the results. The form data is made available to the controller class through the Rails-defined object, `params`. `params` is a hash-like object that contains all of the form data (as well as some other things). It is hash-like because it is a hash that can be indexed with either Ruby symbols or actual keys (a hash can be indexed only with keys). The common Rails convention is to index `params` with symbols. For example, to fetch the value of the form element whose name is `phone`, we would use the following:

```
@phone = params[:phone]
```

Of course, all form data is in string form. However, some of the values are integer numeric quantities, so they must be converted to integers with the `to_i` method of `String`. The form of the statements to fetch the form data is illustrated by the following statement:

```
@num_pizzas = params[:num_pizzas].to_i
```

---

7. While you were reading, we sneaked four more rows into the `corvettes` table.

Notice that the instance variable has the same name as the form element. In this case, the value is a quantity, which is converted to an integer.

Following is the complete `MainController` class:

```
# main_controller.rb - for the cars application
class MainController < ApplicationController

# welcome method - fetches values for the initial view
  def welcome
    @num_cars = Corvette.count
  end

# result method - fetches values for the result view
  def result
    @year1 = params[:year1]
    @year2 = params[:year2]
    @body = params[:body]
    @selected_cars = Corvette.find(:all, :conditions =>
                     "year >= ? and year <= ? and body_style = ?",
                     @year1, @year2, @body])
  end
end
```

The last step of the development of the application is to design the `result` template, which is stored in the `result.html.erb` file. To provide a pleasant appearance, the information about the specified cars is placed in a table. An each iterator is used to go through all of the cars in the `@selected_cars` array provided by the `result` method in the controller.

The complete `result.html.erb` template document follows:

```
<!-- result.html.erb - the result of the user request for
                       information about cars
    -->
  <p>

<!-- Display what the user asked for -->
    Cars from <%= @year1 %> to <%= @year2 %>
    with the <%= @body %> body style
  </p>
```

```
<!-- Display the results of the request in a table -->
    <table border = "border">
      <tr>
        <th> Body Style </th>
        <th> Miles </th>
        <th> Year </th>
        <th> State </th>
      </tr>

<!-- Put the cars in @selected_cars in the table -->
      <% @selected_cars.each do |car|
        <tr>
          <td> <%= car.body_style %> </td>
          <td> <%= car.miles %> </td>
          <td> <%= car.year %> </td>
        </tr>
        <% end %> <!-- end of do loop -->
    </table>
```

Finally, the use of the `cars` application can be illustrated. Figure 15.15 shows a display of the `welcome` template, after it has been filled in by a user.

Figure 15.16 shows the `result` template, after the `welcome` form shown in Figure 15.15 has been submitted.

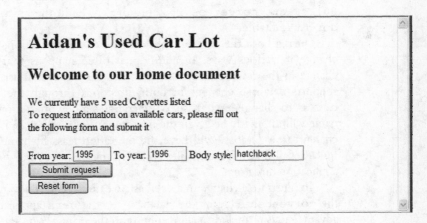

Figure 15.15   A filled–in `welcome` template for `cars`

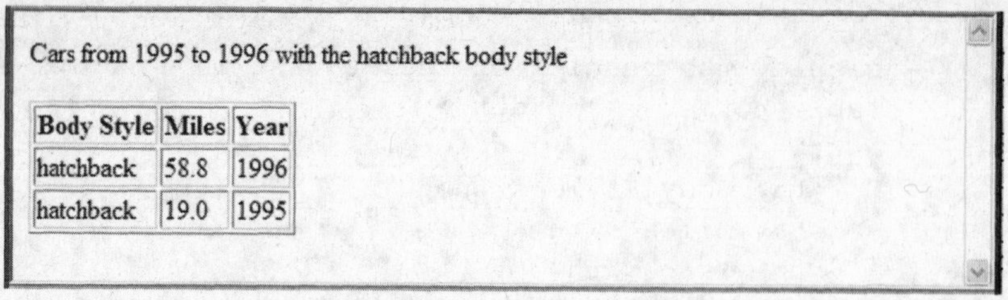

Cars from 1995 to 1996 with the hatchback body style

Body Style	Miles	Year
hatchback	58.8	1996
hatchback	19.0	1995

Figure 15.16 The `result` template for `cars`

15.3.3 Modifying a Database

The process of agile software development, for which Rails was designed, is one of creating a minimal initial version of the application quickly and presenting it to the customer. This allows the customer to see and evaluate the design and interact with the designers. In many cases, a customer thinks he or she wants some specific feature, but when presented with an implementation of that feature, the customer changes his or her mind. Incremental development, coupled with frequent interactions with the customer, characterizes agile software development.

The design of the database for an application often changes during development, due to the needs or desires of either the developer or the customer. Therefore, Rails includes effective tools for database modification. In Section 15.3.1, the initial migration file is shown and discussed. It was created by Rails in response to information provided on the command that built the initial version of the `cars` application. Recall that its filename is `001_create_corvettes.rb`, and that it built the initial version of the `corvettes` table.

During both the development and use of an application, the database may change in various ways. In addition, it often happens that a database must change in the reverse direction; that is, some changes must be undone. Rails supports database changes in both directions through the use of migration classes. To change a database, one generates a new migration class, whose file name will implicitly be given the next migration number. For example, the first changes to a database will have the migration class filename that begins with `002`. Recall that migration files reside in the `db/migrate` subdirectory of the application directory.

To illustrate a change to a database, we now create a new migration class for the `corvettes` table of the database for the `cars` application. It would be advantageous to include a state column in the `corvettes` table, to indicate the state where the car is available. We now make that change to the database, as well as the required changes to the `main` controller and its view template.

A new migration is created with a script. For our example, the command is as follows:

```
>ruby script/generate migration AddStateToCorvette
        state:string
```

The `migration` parameter tells `generate` that a migration class is to be built. The next parameter specifies the name of the migration class. The last parameter provides the name and data type of the column to be added to the table. Rails responds to this command with the following:

```
exists db/migrate
create db/migrate/002_add_state_to_corvette.rb
```

The first of these lines indicates that the `db/migrate` directory already exists; the second tells the user that the `002_add_state_to_corvette.rb` file has been created, which has the class name `AddStateToCorvette`.

The migration file created by the above command, `002_add_state_to_corvette.rb`, follows:

```
class AddStateToCorvette < ActiveRecord::Migration
  def self.up
    add_column :corvettes, :state, :string
  end
  def self.down
    remove_column :corvettes, :state
  end
end
```

Notice that the `down` method was included, which removes the column named `state`.

Now, the `rake` command, given in the application directory, can be used to update the database:

```
>rake db:migrate
```

Rails' response to this command is as follows:

```
(in C:\myrails\rails_apps\examples\cars)
== 2 AddStateToCorvette: migrating ========================
-- add_column(:corvettes, :state, :string)
   -> 0.3750s
== 2 AddStateToCorvette: migrated (0.5160s) ===============
```

The revised schema for the `corvettes` table is as follows:

```
ActiveRecord::Schema.define(:version => 2) do
  create_table "corvettes", :force => true do |t|
    t.string   "body_style"
    t.float    "miles"
    t.integer  "year"
    t.datetime "created_at"
    t.datetime "updated_at"
    t.string   "state"
  end
end
```

Now the template documents for the revised table must be modified to take the new column into account. This is a relatively simple task.

After making these changes, pointing the browser at the `corvettes` controller produces the display shown in Figure 15.17.

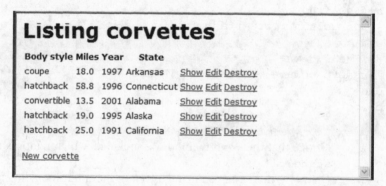

Figure 15.17 The `cars_development` database after adding the `state` column

The latest changes to the database, made by means of the latest migration class, can be removed with the following command:

```
>rake db:rollback
```

If you want to roll back the database to an earlier migration, that can be done by using `migrate` and providing a version number to which you want to return. For example, to roll back a database to its original form, the following could be used:

```
>rake db:migrate VERSION=1
```

15.3.4 Using MySQL

The scaffold-provided methods for listing database tables, creating new rows, editing rows, and deleting rows is an effective way to manage databases during the development of a Web database application. However, for creating the real data of a MySQL database, MySQL itself is a better option. This can be conveniently done in Rails.

First, MySQL must be started. This is done with the following command given at the command prompt in the `mysql/bin` directory:

```
>mysql [-h host] [-u username] [database_name] [-p]
```

All of the parameters of this command are optional (as indicated with the brackets). The host defaults to the machine being used, the username defaults to the user who is currently using the machine, and the `-p` flag, when present, indicates that a password must be used to access the database. For this application, we use the following command to start MySQL:

```
>mysql -u root
```

MySQL responds with the `mysql` prompt, at which MySQL commands can be given. At this prompt, we give the command to set the current database, which will be the focus of subsequent MySQL commands. For the `cars_development` database, the following is used:

```
mysql> use cars_development;
```

Recall that all MySQL commands must end with a semicolon. MySQL responds to the `use` command with

```
Database changed
```

Now there is a subdirectory for `cars_development` in the `mysql/data` subdirectory of the directory where Rails was installed.

To actually create the contents of the database, a file of MySQL commands are used. This file, which we named `fill_table.sql`, is placed in the `data` directory. The contents of `fill_table.sql` used here is as follows:

```
INSERT INTO corvettes values
    (1, "coupe", 18.0, 1997, "Arkansas"),
    (2, "hatchback", 58.0, 1996, "Connecticut"),
    (3, "convertible", 13.5, 2001, "Alabama"),
    (4, "hatchback", 19.0, 1995, "Alaska"),
    (5, "hatchback", 25.0, 1991, "California"),
    (6, "hardtop", 15.0, 2000, "Alaska"),
    (7, "coupe", 55.0, 1979, "Georgia"),
    (8, "convertible", 17.0, 1999, "California"),
    (9, "hardtop", 17.0, 2000, "California"),
    (10, "hatchback", 50.0, 1995, "Connecticut");
```

This file is executed with the following command:

```
mysql>mysql -u root < fill_table.sql
```

15.3.5 Layouts and Stylesheets

Recall that the templates for the `cars` application `main` controller were only partial. In this section, we develop a layout document to complete those templates.

There are two views templates for `main`, one for the `welcome` action and one for the `result` action. Both of these could use the same header information. We can build a layout to specify the header for the templates associated with both of these actions. We also include a copyright line at the bottom of both, using the layout. This new layout, which is named `main.html.erb`, is as follows:

```
<!DOCTYPE html PUBLIC "-//W3C//DTD XHTML 1.0 Transitional//EN"
    "http://www.w3.org/TR/xhtml1/DTD/xhtml1-transitional.dtd">
<html xmlns="http://www.w3.org/1999/xhtml" xml:lang="en" lang="en">
  <head> <title> Main </title>
  </head>
  <body>
    <h1> Aidan's Used Car Lot </h1>
    <h2> Welcome to our home document </h2>
    <%= yield  %>
    <hr/>
    <p> Copyright 2009, AUCL, Inc. </p>
  </body>
</html>
```

We now add an external style sheet to the layout template, just to illustrate how style sheets are used in Rails. The style sheet only sets the colors of the headings and the text box labels and the font style of the main title and the labels. The style sheet file, which is named `mainstyles.css`, is as follows:

```
/* mainstyles.css - a style sheet for the main controller */
h1 {font-style: italic; color: blue;}
h2 {color: blue;}
.labels {font-style: italic; color: red;}
```

External style sheets for template files for the `cars` application are stored in the `cars/public/stylesheets` directory.

The reference to the layout style sheet is placed in the layout for the main controller, `main.html.erb`. The reference is Ruby code that calls the `stylesheet_link_tag` method, passing the name of the style sheet, without the file name extension, as a literal string. For our example, the following is placed in the head of `mail.html.erb`:

```
<%= stylesheet_link_tag "mainstyles" %>
```

The display of the `welcome` template using `main` layout and the `mainstyles` style sheet is shown in Figure 15.18.

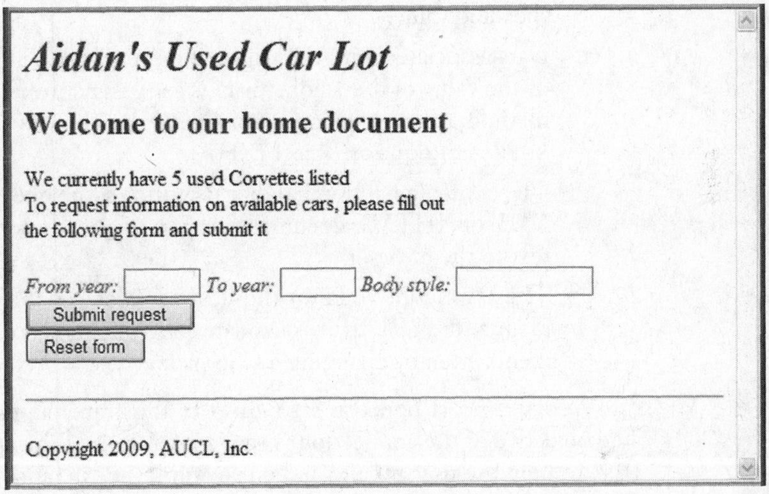

Aidan's Used Car Lot

Welcome to our home document

We currently have 5 used Corvettes listed
To request information on available cars, please fill out
the following form and submit it

From year: [   ] *To year:* [   ] *Body style:* [   ]

[Submit request]
[Reset form]

Copyright 2009, AUCL, Inc.

Figure 15.18 Display of the `welcome` template with the `mainstyles` style sheet

15.4 Rails with Ajax

In at least one sense, the idea of Rails and Ajax together does not sound very attractive. After all, Rails is all about Ruby, and Ajax uses JavaScript, and both use XHTML and possibly XML. Mixing XHTML and a programming language is an idea with some downsides, so how could mixing XHTML and *two* programming languages be good? Well, it's not as bad as it sounds, primarily because Rails includes a JavaScript library of utilities that allows most of the JavaScript to stay in the library and out of the application's listings. The library, which is named Prototype, was written by Sam Stephenson, a member of the Rails core team. It can be used in any Rails template document that includes the following directive:

```
<%= javascript_include_tag "prototype" %>
```

There are some problems with using Rails and Ajax to update a displayed document. Not all elements can be modified or replaced on all browsers using only the Rails tools. The content of an element is changed by Rails by changing the `innerHTML` property. But with Microsoft browsers, `innerHTML` is read-only for some elements, in particular most of the elements associated with tables. One element whose content can be changed successfully on all recent browsers is `div`. In fact, `div` is frequently used by Rails/Ajax applications.

Rails implements Ajax in a sequence of processes, explained briefly as follows:

1. The sequence is triggered, either by a user event, such as clicking a button or link or making changes to a form control, or a timer reaching its specified value.

2. Data associated with the triggering event, often a form element's value or the value of the whole form, is sent asynchronously to a controller method, often called an *action handler*, on the server using an `XMLHttpRequest` object (XHR).

3. The controller action handler performs some operation and returns an XML or XHTML document, or part of one, or perhaps just some plain text to the browser.

4. The JavaScript code on the browser receives the XML, XHTML, or plain text and uses it to update part of the currently displayed document, often by changing a CSS property.

We use a short popcorn sales form to illustrate the use of Rails and Ajax. The objective of the application is the same as that of the application in Section 10.2, to help the user fill a form by providing the city and state parts as soon as the zip code is entered. The entry of the zip code triggers the Ajax process of sending an XHR object to the server, along with the entered zip code. The Rails controller on the server uses the zip code to look up the city and state, which it sends back to the browser in its response. Fortunately, most of the code to support these activities is included in the Prototype library.

15.4.1 The Initial Form Document

This application is named `popcornA`. and the controller is named `popcorn`. Rails is used to generate the skeletal application, including the empty controller class, `PopcornController`. The empty method, `show_form`, is added to this controller. This initial version of the controller is as follows:

```
# popcorn_controller.rb
class PopcornController < ApplicationController
  def show_form
  end
end
```

The initial popcorn order form is presented by the template document, show_form.html.erb, which is placed in the popcorn subdirectory of the views directory of the application. This document is as follows:

```
<?xml version = "1.0" encoding = "utf-8" ?>
<!DOCTYPE html PUBLIC "-//W3C//DTD XHTML 1.0 Strict//EN"
    "http://www.w3.org/TR/xhtml1/DTD/xhtml1-strict.dtd">

<!-- show_form.html.erb
     A rails/Ajax example form;
     This describes a popcorn sales form page which uses
     Ajax and the zip code to fill in the city and state
     of the customer's address
     -->
<html xmlns = "http://www.w3.org/1999/xhtml">
  <head> <title> Popcorn Sales Form (Ajax) </title>
    <style type = "text/css">
      img {position: absolute; left: 400px;  top: 50px;}
    </style>
    <%= javascript_include_tag "prototype" %>
  </head>
  <body>
    <h2> Welcome to Millennium Gymnastics Booster Club Popcorn
       Sales
    </h2>
    <form action = "">

<!-- A borderless table of text boxes for name and address -->
      <table>
        <tr>
          <td> Buyer's Name: </td>
          <td> <input type = "text"  name = "name"
                   size = "30" />
          </td>
        </tr>
        <tr>
          <td> Street Address: </td>
          <td> <input type = "text"  name = "street"
                   size = "30" />
          </td>
        </tr>
        <tr>
          <td> Zip code: </td>
          <td> <input type = "text"  name = "zip"
                   id = "zip"  size = "10" />
```

```
              </td>
            </tr>
            <tr>
              <td> City </td>
              <td> <input type = "text"  name = "city"
                          id = "city"  size = "30" />
              </td>
            </tr>
            <tr>
              <td> State </td>
              <td> <input type = "text"  name = "state"
                          id = "state"  size = "30" />
              </td>
            </tr>
          </table>
          <p />

          <img src = "popcorn.jpg"  alt = "picture of popcorn" />

<!-- The submit and reset buttons -->
      <p>
        <input type = "submit"  value = "Submit Order" />
        <input type = "reset"  value = "Clear Order Form" />
      </p>
    </form>
  </body>
</html>
```

Notice that this document uses the `javascript_include_tag` to include the Prototype library.

15.4.2 Triggering Ajax

Rails includes several helper methods to trigger Ajax processing. Two of the most commonly used of these are `link_to_remote`, which triggers when a specific link is taken, and `observe_field`, which triggers when a specific form element is changed. The Rails helper functions for Ajax are JavaScript functions that are wrapped in Ruby methods. This explains the form of their parameters, which are often Ruby symbols.

Only the `observe_field` triggering method is described in this chapter. The `observe_field` method takes the ID of the control to be watched as its first parameter. This parameter is given as either a literal string or a symbol. For example, if `"zip"` is the ID attribute value for a control to watch, the following could be used:

```
observe_field("zip", ...)
```

The other parameters to `observe_field`, most of which are optional, appear in the form of a list of elements of a hash literal. The keys to the hash are given as symbols. The forms of the values vary among the parameters. Brief descriptions of the most commonly used parameters are as follows:

:url—Specifies as its value the URL of where the result from the server is to be posted. Given the name of the action method, and in some situations the name of the controller, as parameters, Rails builds a complete URL. The parameters are given in the form of a hash literal (a list of hash elements delimited with braces). In many cases, the value of `:url` is a hash literal with a single element consisting of the key `:action` and as the value the name of the action method of the controller that will handle the returned value from the Ajax request. For example:

```
:url => {:action => "process_form"}
```

In this example, the `process_form` action of the current controller is specified. The alternative to quoting the value of the hash element, its symbol can be used—that is, `:process_form` instead of `"process_form"`.

If the action is in a different controller, the `:controller` key can be used to specify it, as in the following:

```
:url => {:controller => :PopcornController,
         :action => :process_form}
```

:update—Specifies the `ID` of the element whose value is to be changed by the XHR response value. Note that only one element can be changed. When the `:update` parameter is specified, the controller action specified in the `:url` parameter produces the response with the `render` method. If what is to be rendered is text, the parameter to `render` is a the hash literal element with the symbol key `:text` followed by `=>` and whatever text is to be rendered. For example, the following example returns a string of text that includes two literal strings and a date/time value:

```
render :text => "<p>The time is" + DateTime.now.to_s +
                "</p>"
```

The string parameter to `render` is assigned to the `responseText` property of the XHR object.

:with—A JavaScript expression specifying the first parameter for the XHR request object. If given as a literal string, say `"zip"`, it takes the form of `"'zip'=value"`, specifying the form key to which the value should be assigned.

:frequency—The frequency in seconds at which changes to the specified control will be detected. Not setting this parameter at all or setting it to a value equal to or less than zero will use an event (`changed` for text boxes and `click` for buttons), rather than time-based observations.

:complete, :success, :failure—These are used to specify a callback function to be called when the Ajax operation is completed. The choice among the three depends on how termination occurred. If the callback function should be called regardless of how the operation finished, the :complete key is used. If the function is to be called only if the operation was completed and successful, the :success), key is used. If the function is to be called only if the operation was completed but failed, the :failure key is used. The callback function is a JavaScript function and the call takes the parameter, request, which specifies that the XHR object is to be passed to the function. Note that the :complete, :success, and :failure parameters are used as an alternative to :update. These dictate that the update is to be done by the specified JavaScript function.

The following is an example of a call to observe_field:

```
<%= observe_field("my_button",
                  :update => "name"
                  :url => {:action => process_form}) %>
```

The controller action method for our application, which is called when the XHR response appears, is named fill_city_state. The actual insertion of the city and state into the form is complicated by the fact that a controller can only produce a single value and both a city and a state are needed. One simple way around this is to have the controller action render the city and state in a string and to embed a JavaScript function in the template to process the single string of the city and state provided by the controller method. Such a function can be inserted into a document with a javascript_tag, which specifies a list of JavaScript code. The end of the code sequence is specified with the END flag, which must be specified following the javascript_tag with <<-. The function can appear in the template in the following form:

```
<%= javascript_tag <<-END
  function update_city_state(xhr) {
    result = xhr.responseText.split(', ');
    document.getElementById('city').value = result[0];
    document.getElementById('state').value = result[1];
  }
END
%>
```

The JavaScript function is embedded in this way because this document is a template document, meaning it will be processed by the Ruby interpreter, ERb. If the JavaScript had been embedded as if the document were an XHTML document, ERb would not know how to handle it.

The code block that includes the `update_city_state` function is inserted into the template file, `show_form.html.erb`, just after the text box for the zip code.

The Prototype library defines an abbreviation for `document.getElementById` method, `$`. So, `$('city')` is the same as `document.getElementById('city')`. This is simply an abbreviation, meant to reduce typing and the size of JavaScript code to be transmitted over the Internet. It was not used in `update_city_state` to avoid confusing the reader. It is mentioned here because most Rails/Ajax applications use it.

Note that in the non-Rails Ajax example in Section 10.2, updating more than one element is not a problem, because the updating is already done with JavaScript.

In the current example, instead of using `:update` to indicate which element is to be changed, the name of the JavaScript function that will update the form is given in the `:complete` parameter. Recall that `request`, which appears as the actual parameter to the JavaScript function `update_city_state`, specifies that Rails must send the XHR object to the function. The call to the function occurs when the XHR request is complete. The complete call to `observe_field` is as follows:

```
<%= observe_field("zip",
              :url => {:action => :fill_city_state},
              :complete => 'update_city_state(request);',
              :with => 'zip'
            ) %>
```

This code block is inserted in the template file, `show_form.html.erb`, between the text box for the zip code and the code block that includes the `update_city_state` function. Now the last row of the table in `show_form.html.erb` appears as follows:

```
<tr>
  <td> Zip code: </td>
  <td> <input type = "text"  name = "zip"
                   id = "zip"  size = "10" />

<%= observe_field("zip",
              :url => {:action => :fill_city_state},
              :complete => "update_city_state(request);",
              :with => "zip"
            ) %>
```

```
<%= javascript_tag <<-END
    function update_city_state(xhr) {
        document.getElementById("city".value = result[0];
        document.getElementById("state").value = result[1];
    }
END
%>
```

Notice that the value for the :complete key in the call to observe_field must be quoted, rather than appearing as a symbol. The reason is that in this case, the value is a call to a function, not the name of a function.

15.4.3 The Controller

The controller action method, fill_city_state, generates the city and the state for the form, given the zip code as a POST parameter. Recall that such a parameter is available to the controller through the params hash. If the string 'zip' is provided as the value or the :with parameter of observe_field, the controller can fetch it with params[:zip]. Then, fill_city_state can look up the city and state and provide it for the template with the render_text library function. For our example, fill_city_state includes a hash of some cities and states and zip codes, just for testing and illustration purposes. The complete controller is as follows:

```
# popcorn_controller.rb
#   The controller for the popcornA application
#   When the user enters a zip code in the popcorn
#   order form, this application puts in the city
#   and state for the user

class PopcornController < ApplicationController
  @@city_state_data = {"81611" => "Aspen, Colorado",
                      "81411" => "Bedrock, Colorado",
                      "80908" => "Black Forest, Colorado",
                      "80301" => "Boulder, Colorado",
                      "81127" => "Chimney Rock, Colorado",
                      "80901" => "Colorado Springs, Colorado",
                      "81223" => "Cotopaxi, Colorado",
                      "80201" => "Denver, Colorado",
                      "81657" => "Vail, Colorado",
                      "80435" => "Keystone, Colorado",
                      "80536" => "Virginia Dale, Colorado"
                      }
```

```
  def show_form
  end

# The fill_city_state method
# Renders the city and state

  def fill_city_state
    zip = params[:zip]

# If possible, set city_state to the city and state
    if @@city_state_data.has_key?(zip)
      city_state = @@city_state_data[zip]

# Otherwise, set it to blanks
    else
      city_state = " , "
    end

# Render it
    render :text => city_state
  end # end of the fill_city_state method
end
```

In general, as in any Rails application, the new partial document can be produced by either the controller method or in a template document, with the template document being the preferred approach most of the time. If the template document does it, the action method has the following single statement:

```
render(:layout => false)
```

The parameter is used to indicate that only a part of the displayed document is to be updated, so there is no need for any Rails layout wrappers.

If the action method is to produce the document fragment, it does it with `render`.

An alternative solution to the problem of wanting to update two elements in the form and `:update` being restricted to a single element is to replace the whole form, which would require a second template document for the updated form. Of course, that would be silly for our example, because the form is nearly the whole initial document, so replacing it would only be marginally better than requesting a whole new document without Ajax.

Summary

Rails is a Ruby software development framework for Web applications. Although it is applicable to all Web applications, it is particularly adept at Web applications that interact with relational databases. One characterizing aspect of Rails is its use of an object-relational mapping for connecting object-oriented Ruby to relational databases. Rails uses the Model-View-Controller model of software applications.

A Hello World Rails application can be built easily. A basic skeletal application is built with the `rails` command, giving the application's name as a parameter. This creates the many directories and files that support the application. A controller class can be generated by running the `script/generate` script, providing a name for the controller as a parameter. Then an empty action method is added to the controller class. The last step of developing this application is to build the view, or template file, whose name must be the same as the action method in the controller. The template file in this case is a simple XHTML document whose content is `Hello World`. After starting a Web server within Rails, this application is ready to be requested by a browser.

Dynamic documents in Rails are closely related to those constructed with PHP. Ruby code can be embedded in the template within the `<%` and `%>` brackets. When requested by a browser, the Ruby code is interpreted and its output is placed in the template, which is then returned to the requesting browser. In most cases, data and computations are placed in the controller action method, rather than in the template. All instance variables in the action method are visible in the associated template file.

Form processing in Rails is relatively simple. Form values are available to the controller class through a hash-like object. The action method extracts the form values into instance variables.

Rails applications are cleanly integrated with database servers. MySQL is part of the InstantRails package, so it is especially convenient to use. The tables of the database are accessible to the controller through classes whose names are singular forms of the table names, with the first letter in uppercase. The rows of the tables are objects of the table classes. The items in a table row are available as fields of the table objects. A Web application, including a one-table database and the basic table maintenance operations, can be built with only a couple of commands. The `find` method of the table classes provides a powerful way to extract data from the database.

Database tables are constructed with the `rake` command, which uses a migration file that provides the column names and types. A database is often the result of applying a sequence of migration files, all of which are saved. A table can also be reverted back to any existing migration file.

Layouts provide a convenient way to include boilerplate markup in all of the templates of an application. Such boilerplate markup is placed in a template file in the `layouts` subdirectory of the `views` directory.

Rails can be used to build Web applications that use Ajax. Rails includes a JavaScript library of helper functions to make this process easier. Two of the functions that can be used to trigger asynchronous requests are `link_to_remote` and `observe_field`. The `observe_field` function specifies the field to be watched, the action method of the controller to handle the request, and a timer for the watch process, among other things. The controller method whose name is given in the call to `observe_field` provides the response to the request. A JavaScript function can be embedded in the displayed document to insert the new parts in that document.

Review Questions

15.1 For what is ORM an acronym?

15.2 For what is MVC an acronym?

15.3 Explain the convention over configuration principle.

15.4 What is the intent of MVC development?

15.5 Explain the DRY principle of software development.

15.6 What must be placed in an application's controller class?

15.7 What is generated with the `generate` controller script?

15.8 In what directory are templates placed?

15.9 How are form control data gotten by an action method?

15.10 How can a template access the instance variables defined in an action method?

15.11 In what directory are style sheets stored?

15.12 In what directory are database files stored?

15.13 Why does a template file's name have the `.html` extension?

15.14 What kinds of operations are provided by the action methods generated by scaffold?

15.15 Describe the command that is used to add a column to a table of a database.

15.16 What Rails command actually builds a database?

15.17 What is described in a schema file?

15.18 What is the basis for the acronym CRUD?

15.19 What is a layout?

15.20 Explain in detail the use of `validate_presence_of`.

15.21 What kinds of support are provided by Prototype?

15.22 With what two functions can an Ajax request be triggered in Rails?

15.23 In what part of a Rails application is the code that provides the data for an Ajax change to a document?

15.24 For what purpose is the `javascript_include_tag` used in a Rails application that uses Ajax?

15.25 What is specified with the `:url` parameter to `observe_field`?

15.26 What is specified with the `:update` parameter to `observe_field`?

Exercises

15.1 Describe briefly an MVC application.

15.2 Explain how migration files help a developer manage a database.

15.3 Describe briefly the ORM used by Rails.

15.4 Build a simple Rails application to return a static document to a requesting browser, where the static document is a brief description of you.

15.5 Build a Rails application that constructs a database with a single table for well-known players from some specific team sport with which you or someone you know is familiar. The table must have columns for name, age, and team for which the person plays. The application must accept user requests for players of a specific team and age range and return a list of such people from the database.

15.6 Build a Rails application that accepts two integer values and produces the product of the two values and returns it to the client.

15.7 Build a Rails application that uses Ajax to provide a personalized greeting to a user when the user types in his or her name.

15.8 Modify the example application of Section 15.6 to add a column for position played by the person. Also modify the query form to include position played.

Introduction to Java

This appendix provides a quick introduction to Java for programmers who are familiar with C++ and object-oriented programming. It covers only a small part of Java, focusing on the features needed to understand Java programs similar to those discussed in this book. In some cases—for example, concurrency—the discussion of a topic can be found in the chapter of the book in which it is used, rather than in this appendix.

This appendix begins with a broad overview of the features and capabilities of Java. The data types and data structures of Java are then discussed, as well as the control statements. Next, it introduces the class definitions of Java, including some of the details of data and method definitions. Java interfaces, which provide a limited kind of multiple inheritance, are then discussed. This is followed by a description of Java exception handling.

A.1   Overview of Java

Java is based on C++, so it is closely related to that language. However, some parts of C++ were left out of the design of Java in an attempt to make it smaller and simpler. Other C++ features were redesigned in Java. Java also includes some constructs that are not part of C++. In comparison with C++, Java can be characterized by the following categories of differences: exclusive support for object-oriented programming, no user-defined overloading, implicit deallocation of heap objects, use of interfaces, lack of pointers, and far fewer type coercions.

C++ was designed originally as an extension to C to provide support for object-oriented programming. Because virtually nothing was left out of C, C++ supports procedure-oriented programming as well as object-oriented programming. Java does not support procedure-oriented programming. In practical terms, this means that subprograms in Java can only appear as methods defined in class definitions. The same is true for data definitions. Therefore, all data and functionality are associated with classes, and therefore with objects.

C++ allows users to define new operations that are specified by existing operator symbols. For example, if a user defines a class to support complex numbers, he or she can overload the definitions of + and − so that they can be used as binary operators for complex objects. For the sake of simplicity, Java does not allow user-defined operator overloading.

In C++, user programs can both allocate and deallocate storage from the heap. This leads to a number of different programming problems, including the possibility of dangling pointers. A dangling pointer is one that is pointing to a memory cell that has been explicitly deallocated from its previous use and possibly reallocated to a new use. Some of these problems are avoided by making heap storage deallocation a system responsibility rather than a user one. In Java, all heap storage deallocation is implicit and a technique named *garbage collection* is used to reclaim heap storage that has been implicitly deallocated.

In C++, a user program can define a class to extend two or more different classes, thereby making use of multiple inheritance. Although multiple inheritance is sometimes convenient, it has some disadvantages, among them the possibility of designing programs whose complexity makes them difficult to understand. For this reason, Java does not support multiple inheritance. In its place, Java has interfaces, which provide some of the functionality of multiple inheritance. Interfaces are discussed in Section A.4.

Pointers are notoriously risky, especially when pointer arithmetic is allowed. Java does not include pointers. Instead, Java provides references, which are also supported by C++, though in a somewhat different way. Reference variables in Java are used to reference objects, rather than memory cells, so they cannot be used as the operands of arithmetic operators. This, in conjunction with the lack of a deallocation operator for heap objects, makes references far safer than the pointers of C++.

In C++, as in many other programming languages, it is legal to assign a value of any numeric type to a variable of any other numeric type. This requires the compiler to build type conversion code, called *coercions*, into the program. Half of these conversions are narrowing conversions, in which it may not be possible to convert the value into even an approximation in the new type. For example, in C++ it is legal to assign a `float` value to an `int` variable, although this is a narrowing conversion. For example, `float` values such as `1.23E15` cannot be converted to anything close to that value as an `int` value. Java does not allow narrowing coercions in assignment statements. It is syntactically illegal to write such an assignment statement. This results in an increase in the overall safety of programs written in Java over those written in C++.

The control statements of Java are almost exactly like those in C++. One difference is that control expressions in control statements in Java must have Boolean values, whereas in C++ the control expression can be either Boolean or a numeric type. For example, in Java, the following statement is illegal:

```
if (2 * count) ...
```

Output to the screen from a Java application is through the object `System.out`, which represents the console window associated with the application. This object has two methods, `print` and `println`, which do something similar to what you would expect given their names. Both take a string parameter, but also permit variables as parameters. The values of non-`String` variables that appear in the parameter to `System.out.print` or `System.out.println` are implicitly converted to strings. The `print` method produces a string of output to the screen without attaching a newline character to the end. The `println` method does what `print` does, except that it attaches a newline character to the end. The string parameter to `print` and `println` is often specified as a catenation of several strings, using the + catenation operator. The following method calls illustrate the use of `print` and `println`:

```
System.out.println("Apples are good for you");
System.out.println("You should eat " + numApples +
                   " apples each week");
System.out.print("Grapes ");
System.out.println("are good, too");
```

If `numApples` is 7, these statements produce the following display:

```
Apples are good for you
You should eat 7 apples each week
Grapes are good, too
```

Naming conventions used in Java are as follows:

- Class and interface names begin with uppercase letters.
- Variable and method names begin with lowercase letters.
- Package names are all lowercase letters.
- Constant names are all uppercase letters, with underscores used as separators.

- Except for package and constant names, when a name consists of more than one word, the first letters of all embedded words are capitalized.
- Except for constant names, all but the first letters of embedded words are lowercase.

Java does not have an address-of operator (`&` in C++), a dereference operator (unary `*` in C++), or an operator to return the size of a type or object (`sizeof` in C++).

A.2   Data Types and Structures

In both C++ and Java, there are two kinds of data values: primitives and objects. This is a compromise design, for it provides efficiency in arithmetic operations on primitive values at the expense of complicating the object model of the language. Arithmetic operations can be done very quickly on primitive values, but are more costly when the operands are objects.

C++ has three different kinds of variables for objects: those whose value is a stack-allocated object, pointers that reference heap-allocated objects, and references that reference heap-allocated objects. In Java, there is only one way to reference an object, namely, through a reference variable. This simplicity is possible because all objects are allocated from the heap and there are no pointer variables in Java.

The Java primitive types are `int`, `float`, `double`, `char`, and `boolean`. Operations on primitive values are similar to those in other programming languages. Each of the primitive types has a corresponding *wrapper class*, which is used when it is convenient to treat a primitive value as an object.[1] The Java wrapper classes are named with the name of the associated primitive type, except that the first letter is capitalized. For example, the wrapper class for `double` is `Double`. An object of a wrapper class is created with the `new` operator and the class's constructor, as shown in the following example:

```
Integer wrapsum = new Integer(sum);
```

One of the purposes of wrapper classes is to provide methods that operate on primitive values. For example, a `float` value can be converted to a string by creating an object for it and using the `toString` method on that object. To convert the `float` value `speed` to a `String` object, the following could be used:

```
float speedObj = new Float(speed);
String speedStr = speedObj.toString();
```

As stated previously, all objects are referenced through reference variables. Reference variables are defined the same way as primitive variables. For example:

```
int sum;
String str1;
```

---

1. These classes are called wrapper classes because in effect they wrap a primitive value so it looks like an object.

In this example, sum is a primitive variable of type int, and str1 is a reference variable that can reference a String object, initially set to null.

Although an array of characters can be created and used in Java, it is more convenient to use the String and StringBuffer classes for character strings. String objects are immutable strings of characters. They can be created in two ways: either with the new operator or implicitly, as illustrated with the following declarations:

```
String greet1 = new String("Guten Morgen");
String greet2 = "Guten Morgen";
```

These two strings are equivalent. All Java String and StringBuffer objects use 2 bytes per character because they use the Unicode character codings, which are 16 bits wide.

String catenation, which is specified with the plus operator (+), can be used on String objects, as shown in the following example:

```
greet3 = greet3 + " New Year";
```

There are a number of methods that can be called through String objects to perform more or less standard string operations—for example, charAt, substring, concat, and indexOf. The equals method of String must be used to compare two strings for equality. Because strings are objects, the == operator is of no use between strings.

If a string must be manipulated, it cannot be a String object (because String objects cannot be changed). For this situation, a StringBuffer object can be used. StringBuffer objects are created with new, as shown in the following example:

```
StringBuffer greet3 = new StringBuffer("Happy");
```

The StringBuffer class has a collection of methods to manipulate its objects. Among them are append, which appends a given value to the end of the object; delete, which deletes one or more characters from the object; and insert, which inserts a value into its string object. In the cases of append and insert, if the given parameter is not a string, it is implicitly converted to a string.

In Java, arrays are objects of a class that has some special functionality. Array objects, like all other objects, are always referenced through reference variables and are always allocated on the heap. Array objects can be created with statements having the following form:

element_type array_name[ ] = new *element_type*[*length*];

For example:

```
int[] list1 = new int[100];
float[] list2 = new float[10];
```

If an array reference variable has been previously created, as with

```
int[] list3;
```

an object can be created with

```
list3 = new int[200];
```

As with other related languages, the subscript ranges of Java arrays always begin with zero. In a departure from C++, all references to array elements are checked to be sure the subscript values are within the defined subscript ranges of the array. Therefore, it is not possible to reference or assign an array element that does not exist. When a subscript that is out of range is detected, the exception `ArrayIndexOutOfBoundsException` is thrown. Java exception handling is discussed in Section A.5.

Java does not have the `struct` and `union` data structures that are part of C++. It also does not have the `unsigned` types or the `typedef` declaration.

A.3   Classes, Objects, and Methods

There are several important differences between C++ class definitions and those of Java. All Java classes have a parent class, whereas in C++ a class does not need to have a parent. The parent of a class is specified in the class definition with the `extends` reserved word. The general form of a class definition is

[*modifiers*] `class` *class_name* [`extends` *parent_class*] `{ ... }`

The square brackets here indicate that what they delimit is optional. Three different modifiers can appear at the beginning of a class definition: `public`, `abstract`, and `final`. The `public` modifier makes the class visible to classes that are not in the same package (packages are described later in this section). The `abstract` modifier specifies that the class cannot be instantiated. An abstract class is designed to be a class model that can be extended by nonabstract classes. The `final` modifier specifies that the class cannot be extended.

The root class of all Java classes is `Object`. A class definition that does not specify a parent is made a subclass of `Object`.

In C++, the visibility of variables and member functions (methods) defined in classes is specified by placing their declarations in `public`, `private`, or `protected` clauses. In Java, these same reserved words are used, but on individual declarations rather than on clauses. The meanings of these access modifiers are the same as in C++.

In addition to the access modifiers, a variable declaration can include the `final` modifier, which specifies that the variable is actually a constant, in which case it must be initialized. Java does not use C++'s `const` reserved word to specify constants.

In Java, all methods are defined in a class. Java class methods are specified by including the `static` modifier in their definitions. Any method without `static` is an instance method. Methods can also have several other modifiers. Among these are `abstract` and `final`. The `abstract` modifier specifies that the method is not defined in the class. The `final` modifier specifies that the method cannot be overridden.

Whereas C++ depends on classes as its only encapsulation construct, Java includes a second one at a level above classes, the *package*. Packages can contain more than one class definition, and the classes in a package are similar to the friend classes of C++. The entities defined in a class that are public or protected or have no access specifier are visible to all other classes in the package. This is an expansion of the definition of protected as used in C++, in which protected members are visible only in the class in which they are defined and in subclasses of that class. Entities without access modifiers are said to have *package scope*, because they are visible throughout the package. Therefore, Java has less need for explicit friend declarations and in fact does not include either the friend functions or friend classes of C++. Packages, which often contain libraries, can be defined in hierarchies. The standard class libraries of Java are defined in a hierarchy of packages.

A file whose class definitions are to be put in a named package includes a package declaration, as shown in the following example:

```
package cars;
```

The external visibility of entities in a class is controlled by the accessibility modifiers on the entities. Entities from other classes that are visible can be referenced through their complete name, which begins with the name of the package in which the class is defined and includes the name of the class in which the entity is defined. For example, if we have a package named `weatherpkg`, which includes a class named `WeatherData`, which defines a public variable named `avgTemp`, `avgTemp` can be referenced in any other class where it is visible with the following:

```
weatherpkg.WeatherData.avgTemp
```

An `import` statement provides a way to abbreviate such imported names. For example, suppose we include the following statement in our program:

```
import weatherpkg.WeatherData;
```

Now the variable `avgTemp` can be accessed directly (with just its name). The `import` statement can include an asterisk instead of a class name, in which case all classes in the package are imported. For example:

```
import weatherpkg.*;
```

A Java application program is a compiled class that includes a method named `main`. The `main` method of a Java application is where the Java interpreter begins. The following illustrates the simplest kind of Java application program:

```java
public class Trivial {
  public static void main (String[] args) {
    System.out.println("A maximally trivial Java
                        application");
  }
}
```

The modifiers on the main method are always the same. It must have public accessibility, and it cannot be extended. The void modifier indicates that main does return a value. The only parameter to main is an array of strings that contains any command-line parameters from the user. In many cases, command-line parameters are not used. When they are used, the interpreter passes them to main as strings.

In C++, methods can be defined in a somewhat indirect way: The protocol is given in the class definition, but the definition of the method appears elsewhere. In Java, however, method definitions must appear in their associated classes.

As with C++, Java constructors have the same names as the classes in which they appear. C++ uses destructor methods to deallocate heap storage for instance data members, among other things. Because Java uses implicit heap deallocation, it does not have destructors.

In some object-oriented programming languages, including C++, method calls can be bound to methods either statically (at compile time) or dynamically (during runtime). In C++, the default binding of method calls to methods is static. Only methods defined to be virtual are dynamically bound. In Java, the default is dynamic.

Objects of user-defined classes are created with new. As with array objects, a reference variable is required to access an object, but both the reference variable and the object can be created in the same statement. For example:

```
MyClass myObject1;
myObject1 = new MyClass();
MyClass myObject2 = new MyClass();
```

The two reference variables, myObject1 and myObject2, refer to new objects of class MyClass.

As is the case with C++, Java classes can have instance or class variables or both. There is a single version of a class variable per class; there is an instance variable for every instance of the class in which it is defined. Both instance and class variables that are not explicitly initialized in their declarations are implicitly initialized. Numeric variables are implicitly initialized to zero, Boolean variables are initialized to false, and reference variables are initialized to null.

Inside the methods of a class, instance variables are referenced directly. In other classes, instance variables are referenced through the reference variables that point at their associated objects. For example:

```
class MyClass extends Object {
   public int sum;

   ...

}
MyClass myObject = new MyClass();
```

In other classes that either import MyClass or are defined in the same package, the instance variable sum can be referenced as follows:

```
myObject.sum
```

Similar to class methods, class variables are specified by preceding their declarations with the static reserved word.

The following is an example of a class definition that illustrates some of the aspects of Java we have discussed. It implements a stack in an array.

```java
import java.io.*;
class Stack_class {
  private int [] stack_ref;
  private int max_len,
              top_index;
  public Stack_class() {  // A constructor
    stack_ref = new int [100];
    max_len = 99;
    top_index = -1;
  }
  public void push(int number) {
    if (top_index == max_len)
      System.out.println("Error in push--stack is full");
    else stack_ref[++top_index] = number;
  }
  public void pop() {
    if (top_index == -1)
      System.out.println("Error in pop--stack is empty");
    else --top_index;
  }
  public int top() {return (stack_ref[top_index]);}
  public boolean empty() {return (top_index == -1);}
}
```

An example class that uses Stack_class follows:

```java
public class Tst_Stack {
  public static void main(String[] args) {
    Stack_class myStack = new Stack_class();
    myStack.push(42);
    myStack.push(29);
    System.out.println("29 is: " + myStack.top());
    myStack.pop();
    System.out.println("42 is: " + myStack.top());
    myStack.pop();
    myStack.pop();  // Produces an error message
  }
}
```

We must note here that a stack is a silly example for Java because the Java library includes a class definition for stacks.

A.4 Interfaces

Java directly supports only single inheritance. However, it includes a construct similar to a virtual class, called an *interface*, that provides something closely related to multiple inheritance. An interface definition is similar to a class definition except that it can contain only named constants and method declarations (not definitions). So, an interface is no more than what its name indicates, just the specification of a class. (Recall that a C++ abstract class can have instance variables, and all but one of the methods can be completely defined.) The typical use of an interface is to define a class that inherits some of the methods and variables from its parent class and implements an interface as well.

Applets are programs that are interpreted by a Web browser after being downloaded from a Web server. Calls to applets are embedded in the HTML code that describes an HTML document. These applets all need certain capabilities, which they can inherit from the predefined class `Applet`. When an applet is used to implement animation, it is often defined to run in its own thread of control. This concurrency is supported by a predefined class named `Thread`. However, an applet class being designed to use concurrency cannot inherit from both `Applet` and `Thread`. Therefore, Java includes a predefined interface named `Runnable` that supplies the interface (but not the implementation) to some of the methods of `Thread`. The syntax of the header of such an applet is exemplified by the following:

```
public class Clock extends Applet implements Runnable
```

Although this code appears to provide multiple inheritance, in this case it requires a further complication. For an object of the `Clock` class to run concurrently, a `Thread` object must be created and connected to the `Clock` object. The messages that control the concurrent execution of the `Clock` object must be sent to the corresponding `Thread` object. This is surely an inelegant and potentially confusing necessity.

A.5 Exception Handling

Java's exception handling is based on that of C++, but is designed to be more faithful to the object-oriented language paradigm.

A.5.1 Classes of Exceptions

All Java exceptions are objects of classes that are descendants of the `Throwable` class. The Java system includes two system-defined exception classes that are subclasses of `Throwable`: `Error` and `Exception`. The `Error` class and its descendants are related to errors that are thrown by the Java interpreter, such as running out of heap memory. These exceptions are never thrown by user programs, and they should never be handled there. The two system-defined direct descendants of `Exception` are `RuntimeException` and

`IOException`. As its name indicates, `IOException` is thrown when an error has occurred in an input or output operation, all of which are defined as methods in the various classes defined in the package `java.io`.

System-defined classes that are descendants of `RuntimeException` exist. In most cases, `RuntimeException` is thrown when a user program causes an error. For example, `ArrayIndexOutOfBoundsException`, which is defined in `java.util`, is a commonly thrown exception that descends from `RuntimeException`. Another commonly thrown exception that descends from `RuntimeException` is `NullPointerException`.

User programs can define their own exception classes. The convention in Java is that user-defined exceptions are subclasses of `Exception`.

A.5.2   Exception Handlers

The exception handlers of Java have a form similar to those of C++, except that the parameter of every `catch` must be present and its class must be a descendant of the predefined class `Throwable`.

The syntax of the `try` construct in Java is exactly like that of C++.

A.5.3   Binding Exceptions to Handlers

Throwing an exception is quite simple. An instance of the exception class is given as the operand of the `throw` statement. For example, suppose we define an exception named `MyException` as follows:

```
class MyException extends Exception {
  public MyException() {}
  public MyException(String message) {
    super (message);
  }
}
```

The first constructor in this class does nothing. The second sends its parameter to the parent class (specified with `super`) constructor. This exception can be thrown with

```
throw new MyException();
```

The creation of the instance of the exception for the `throw` could be done separately from the `throw` statement, as shown in the following example:

```
MyException myExceptionObject = new MyException();
...
throw myExceptionObject;
```

Using the constructor with the parameter, our new exception could be thrown with

```
throw new MyException
    ("a message to specify the location of the error");
```

The binding of exceptions to handlers in Java is less complex than in C++. If an exception is thrown in the compound statement of a `try` construct, it is bound to the first handler (`catch` function) immediately following the `try` clause whose parameter is the same class as the thrown object or is an ancestor of it. If a matching handler is found, the `throw` is bound to it and is executed.

Exceptions can be handled and then rethrown by including a `throw` statement without an operand at the end of the handler. The newly thrown exception will not be handled in the same `try` where it was originally thrown, so looping is not a concern. This rethrowing is usually done when some local action is useful but further handling by an enclosing `try` clause or a caller is necessary. A `throw` statement in a handler could also throw some exception other than the one that transferred control to this handler; one particular exception could cause another to be thrown.

A.5.4   Exception Propagation

When a handler is found in the sequence of handlers in a `try` construct, that handler is executed and program execution continues with the statement following the `try` construct. If none is found, the handlers of enclosing `try` constructs are searched, innermost first. If no handler is found in this process, the exception is propagated to the caller of the method. If the method call was in a `try` clause, the search for a handler continues in the attached collection of handlers in the clause. Propagation continues until the original caller is found, which in the case of an application program is `main`. If no matching handler is found anywhere, the program is terminated. In many cases, exception handlers include a `return` statement to terminate the method in which the exception occurred.

To ensure that exceptions that can be thrown in a `try` clause are always handled in a method, a special handler can be written that matches all exceptions that are derived from `Exception`, simply by defining the handler with an `Exception` type parameter, as shown in the following example:

```
catch (Exception genericObject) {
...
}
```

Because a class name always matches itself or any ancestor class, any class derived from `Exception` matches `Exception`. Of course, such an exception handler should always be placed at the end of the list of handlers, because it will block the use of any handler that follows it in the `try` construct in which it appears. The search for a matching handler is sequential, and the search ends when a match is found.

The object parameter to an exception handler is not entirely useless, as it may have appeared to be so far in this discussion. During program execution, the Java runtime system stores the class name of every object in the program. The method `getClass` can be used to get an object that stores the class name, which itself can be gotten with the `getName` method. So, we can retrieve the name of the class of the actual parameter from the `throw` statement that caused the handler's execution. For the handler above, this is done with

```
genericObject.getClass().getName()
```

The message associated with the parameter object, which is created by the constructor, can be obtained with

```
genericObject.getMessage()
```

A.5.5   The `throws` Clause

The `throws` clause of Java has an appearance and placement (in a program) similar to that of the `throw` specification of C++. However, the semantics of `throws` is completely different from that of the C++ `throw` clause.

The appearance of an exception class name in the `throws` clause of a Java method specifies that that exception class or any of its descendant exception classes can be thrown by the method. For example, when a method specifies that it can throw `IOException`, it means it can throw an `IOException` object or an object of any of its descendant classes, such as `EOFException`.

Exceptions of class `Error` and `RuntimeException` and their descendants are called *unchecked exceptions*. All other exceptions are called *checked exceptions*. Unchecked exceptions are never a concern of the compiler. However, the compiler ensures that all checked exceptions a method can throw are either listed in its `throws` clause or handled in the method. The reason that exceptions of the classes `Error` and `RuntimeException` and their descendants are unchecked is that any method can throw them.

A method cannot declare more exceptions in its `throws` clause than the method it overrides, though it may declare fewer. So, if a method has no `throws` clause, neither can any method that overrides it. A method can throw any exception listed in its `throws` clause, along with any of the exceptions' descendant classes. A method that does not directly throw a particular exception but calls another method that could throw that exception must list the exception in its `throws` clause. This is the reason the `buildDist` method (in the example in Section A.5.6), which uses the `readLine` method, must specify `IOException` in the `throws` clause of its header.

A method that calls a method that lists a particular checked exception in its `throws` clause has three alternatives for dealing with that exception. First, it can catch the exception and handle it. Second, it can catch the exception and throw an exception that is listed in its own `throws` clause. Third, it can declare the exception in its own `throws` clause and not handle it, which effectively propagates the exception to an enclosing `try` clause, if there is one, or to the method's caller if there is no enclosing `try` clause.

Java has no default exception handlers, and it is not possible to disable exceptions.

A.5.6 An Example

The following example program illustrates two simple uses of exception handlers. The program computes and prints a distribution of input grades by using an array of counters. There are ten categories of grades (0–9, 10–19, . . . , 90–100). The grades themselves are used to compute indexes into an array of counters, one for each grade category. Invalid input grades are detected by trapping indexing errors in the counter array. A grade of 100 is special in the computation of the grade distribution, because the categories all have ten possible grade values, except the highest, which has eleven (90, 91, . . . , 100). (The fact that there are more possible A grades than Bs or Cs is conclusive evidence of the generosity of teachers.) The grade of 100 is also handled in the same exception handler that is used for invalid input data. Following is a Java class that implements this algorithm:

```java
import java.io.*;
// The exception definition to deal with the end of data
class NegativeInputException extends Exception {
  public NegativeInputException() {
    System.out.println("End of input data reached");
  } //** end of constructor
} //** end of NegativeInputException class
class GradeDist {
  int newGrade,
      index,
      limit_1,
      limit_2;
  int [] freq = {0, 0, 0, 0, 0, 0, 0, 0, 0, 0};
void buildDist() throws IOException {
// Input: A list of integer values that represent
//        grades, followed by a negative number
// Output: A distribution of grades, as a percentage for
//        each of the categories 0-9, 10-19, ...,
//        90-100.
  DataInputStream in = new DataInputStream(System.in);
  try {
    while (true) {
      System.out.println("Please input a grade");
      newGrade = Integer.parseInt(in.readLine());
      if (newGrade < 0)
        throw new NegativeInputException();
      index = newGrade / 10;
      try {
        freq[index]++;
      } //** end of inner try clause
```

```
            catch(ArrayIndexOutOfBoundsException) {
              if (newGrade == 100)
                freq [9]++;
              else
                System.out.println("Error - new grade: " +
                                     newGrade + " is out of range");
            } //** end of catch (ArrayIndex...
          } //** end of while (true) ...
        } //** end of outer try clause
      catch(NegativeInputException) {
        System.out.println ("\nLimits     Frequency\n");
        for (index = 0; index < 10; index++) {
          limit_1 = 10 * index;
          limit_2 = limit_1 + 9;
          if (index ==9)
            limit_2 = 100;
          System.out.println("" + limit_1 + " - " +
            limit_2 + "        " + freq [index]);
        } //** end of for (index = 0; ...
      } //** end of catch (NegativeInputException ...
    } //** end of method buildDist
```

The exception for a negative input, `NegativeInputException`, is defined in the program. Its constructor displays a message when an object of the class is created. Its handler produces the output of the method. The `ArrayIndexOutOfBoundsException` is predefined and is thrown by the interpreter. In both cases, the handler does not include an object name in its parameter. In neither case would a name serve any purpose. Note that all handlers get objects as parameters, but they are often not useful.

Summary

Although Java is based on C++, it differs from that language in a variety of ways. The primary differences are Java's exclusive support for object-oriented programming, its lack of user-defined overloaded operators, its implicit deallocation and reclamation of heap objects, its interfaces, its lack of pointers, and its lower number of type coercions in assignment statements. Most of these differences were motivated by the perceived safety risks of C++.

Like C++, Java has primitive types and objects. Character strings can be stored as either `String` or `StringBuffer` objects, where `String` objects cannot be changed but `StringBuffer` objects can. Arrays are objects with special behavior. Array indices are always checked for range in Java.

Every Java class has a single parent class. Java does not have the public and private class derivations of C++. Java class derivation is always the same. Java has an additional encapsulation mechanism (besides the class)—the package. Entities defined in classes that do not specify a visibility have package scope, which makes them visible to all other classes in the package. Only one class in a package can be public. Rather than having public, private, and protected clauses in class definitions, the individual entities in Java classes can be defined to be public, private, or protected. All methods defined for a class are defined in the class. All binding of method calls to methods in Java is dynamic, unless the method is defined to be final, in which case it cannot be overridden and dynamic binding serves no purpose.

Class variables and class methods are specified to be static. In the absence of the `static` reserved word, variables are instance variables and methods are instance methods.

An interface defines the protocol of a class, but contains no variable definitions or method definitions. Interfaces are used to provide some of the benefits of multiple inheritance without all of the complexity of multiple inheritance. A class that implements an interface provides definitions for the methods of the interface.

Exception handling in Java is similar to that of C++, except that only objects of classes that descend from the predefined class `Throwable` can be exception objects. Propagation of exceptions is simpler in Java than it is in C++. The `throws` clause of Java is related to the `throw` clause of C++, but not closely. In Java, an exception class that appears in a `throws` clause means that the method in which `throws` appears can throw exceptions of that class or any of its descendants. A method cannot declare more exceptions in its `throws` clause than the method it overrides. A method that calls a method that can throw a particular exception must either catch and handle the exception, catch the exception and throw an exception that is declared in its `throws` clause, or declare the exception in its `throws` clause.

Named Colors and Their Hexadecimal Values

The actual colors can be viewed at the following address:

http:/www.w3schools.com/html/html_colornames.asp

Name	Hex Code
aliceblue	F0FBFF
antiquewhite	FAEBD7
aqua	00FFFF
aquamarine	7FFFD4
azure	F0FFFF
beige	F5F5DC
bisque	FFE4C4
black	000000
blanchedalmond	FFEBCD
blue	0000FF
blueviolet	BA2BE2

Name	Hex Code
brown	A52A2A
burlywood	DEB887
cadetblue	5F9EA0
chartreuse	7FFF00
chocolate	D2691E
coral	FF7F50
cornflowerblue	6495ED
cornsilk	FFF8DC
crimson	DC143C
cyan	00FFFF
darkblue	000088

Name	Hex Code
darkcyan	008B8B
darkgoldenrod	B8860B
darkgray	A9A9A9
darkgrey	A9A9A9
darkgreen	006400
darkkhaki	BDB76B
darkmagenta	8B008B
darkolivegreen	556B2F
darkorange	FF8C00
darkorchid	9932CC
darkred	8B0000
darksalmon	E9967A
darkseagreen	8FBCBF
darkstateblue	483D8B
darkstategray	2F4F4F
darkstategrey	2F4F4F
darkturquoise	00CED1
darkviolet	9400D3
darkpink	FF1493
darkskyblue	00BFFF
dimgray	696969
dimgrey	696969
dodgerblue	1E90FF
firebrick	B22222
floralwhite	FFFAF0
forestgreen	228B22
fuchsia	FF00FF
gainsboro	DCDCDC
ghostwhite	F8F8FF

Name	Hex Code
gold	FFD700
goldenrod	DAA520
gray	808080
grey	808080
green	008000
greenyellow	ADFF2F
honeydew	F0FFF0
hotpink	FF6984
indianred	CD5C5C
indigo	4G0082
ivory	FFFFF0
khaki	FDE68C
lavender	E6E6FA
lavenderblush	FFF0F5
lawngreen	7CFC00
lemonchiffon	FFFACD
lightblue	ADD8E6
lightcoral	F08080
lightcyan	E0FFFF
lightgoldenrodyellow	FAFAD2
lightgray	D3D3D3
lightgrey	D3D3D3
lightgreen	90EE90
lightpink	FFB6C1
lightsalmon	FFA07A
lightseagreen	20B2AA
ligthskyblue	87CEFA
lightslategray	778899
lightslategrey	778899

Name	Hex Code
lightsteelblue	B0C4DE
lightyellow	FFFFE0
lime	00FF00
limegreen	32CD32
linen	FAF0E6
magenta	FF00FF
maroon	800000
mediumaquamarine	66CDAA
mediumblue	0000CD
mediumorchid	BA55D3
mediumpurple	9370D8
mediumseagreen	3CB371
mediumslateblue	7B68EE
mediumspringgreen	00FA9A
mediumturquoise	48D1CC
mediumvioletred	C71585
midnightblue	191970
mintcream	F5FFFA
mistyrose	FFE4E1
moccasin	FFE4B5
navajowhite	FFDEAD
navy	000080
oldlace	FDF5E6
olive	808000
olivedrab	6B8E23
orange	FFA500
orangered	FF4500
orchid	DA70D6
palegoldenrod	EEE8AA

Name	Hex Code
palegreen	98FB98
paleturquoise	AFEEEE
palevioletred	D87093
papayawhip	FFEFD5
peachpuff	FFDAB9
peru	CD853F
pink	FFC0CB
plum	DDA0DD
powderblue	B0E0E6
purple	800080
red	FF0000
rosybrown	BC8F8F
royalblue	4169E1
saddlebrown	8B4513
salmon	FA8072
sandybrown	F4A460
seagreen	2E8B57
seashell	FFF5EE
sienna	A0522D
silver	C0C0C0
skyblue	87CEEB
slateblue	6A5ACD
slategray	708090
slategrey	708090
snow	FFFAFA
springgreen	00FF7F
steelblue	4682B4
tan	D2B4BC
teal	008080

Name	Hex Code
thistle	D8BFD8
tomato	FF6347
turquoise	40E0D0
violet	EE82EE
wheat	F5DEB3

Name	Hex Code
white	FFFFFF
whitesmoke	F5F5F5
yellow	FFFF00
yellowgreen	9ACD32

Java Applets

Applets provide another way of supporting computation in Web documents. Applets can provide interactivity and dynamic content through graphical user interface (GUI) components, as well as graphics and computation. This appendix is most accessible if the reader is already familiar with the Java programming language. Appendix A provides a brief introduction to Java for those who are already conversant in C++ and object-oriented programming. However, for those without that background, the complexity of Java and object-oriented programming is a formidable obstacle to gaining an understanding of applets in an appendix as brief as this one.

This appendix begins by providing an overview of applets and their relationship to XHTML documents. Then it describes the primary activities of applets, including initialization, starting execution, and stopping execution. Following this, attention turns to the `paintComponent` method, which is used to draw text and graphics both from a Java application to a display panel and from an applet to a browser screen. Next, the appendix describes the `<object>` tag, which connects an XHTML document to an applet, and its attributes. XHTML documents can only refer to applet files because applets cannot be directly embedded in documents, unlike scripts in languages such as JavaScript. Then the appendix covers the technique for passing parameters from an XHTML document to an applet. Following this, it describes the methods of the `Graphics` class for drawing various figures and discusses how color can be used for the output of the `paintComponent` method.

Finally, interactive applets are discussed. This requires a description of how GUI components are defined in Java and how the Java event model is used to allow those components to provide interactivity.

Java 1.1 included the Abstract Windowing Toolkit (AWT), which provided basic drawing capabilities, as well as support for GUI components and an event model to allow users to interact with programs through them. Java 1.2 introduced the Swing package, which has a different set of GUI components that are similar in appearance to those of AWT but are very different internally. This appendix covers the AWT drawing facilities and the Swing GUI components. Be aware that the discussion of AWT graphics, event handling, and Swing components is brief and covers only a small portion of what exists.

All of the Java system software can be obtained from `http://java.sun.com`.

C.1   Introduction

Applets are Java programs whose execution is controlled in a way that is quite different from that of Java application programs. The purpose of an applet is related to that of client-side JavaScript: to provide processing capability and interactivity for XHTML documents.

When the browser encounters an applet in an XHTML document, it downloads the compiled version of the applet class (the `.class` file), along with any classes that the applet uses, from the server. Then an instance of the applet class is implicitly created and executed on the browser. (A more detailed description of these processes is given in Section C.2.) Because applets can include most of the Java language features, including widgets and event handling, they allow interactivity to be included in a document.

All applets must have some standard operations. The protocols for these common operations are gathered as method definitions in a predefined class named `JApplet`. All user-defined applets are written as subclasses of `JApplet`. Some of the methods inherited from `JApplet` are routinely overridden by user-defined applets.

The class header of an applet has the following form:

```
public class class_name extends JApplet { ... }
```

Although applets are good for graphics, they usually also display text and images. Rather than writing normal text to the screen, however, they must do this with a method that draws text into the browser display. All of the graphics and text display capabilities used in applets can also be used in Java application programs.

Learning to write simple applets requires the following: First, you must understand how applets are specified in XHTML documents and how documents and applets interact. Second, you must learn how the relevant graphics library classes are used to display text and graphical figures. Third, you must see how the methods of `JApplet` are used, often in overridden versions, to control applet execution within the operation of the browser.

The simplest way to test an applet is with the Sun Microsystems program `appletviewer`, which enables you to see what an applet does without using a browser and a server. This technique has the advantage of simplicity, but it lacks some of the reality of using a Web browser. Of course, it is not much more complicated to use a browser with local XHTML documents and applets.

When Java applets appeared, they provided the first way to include client-resident computational capability in an XHTML document. JavaScript and its close relatives, AppleScript and VBScript, provide much of what the first release of Java provided through its applets. The power and versatility of Java—and especially its classes to support graphical user interfaces—have grown considerably since its original release. Furthermore, Java now has a large collection of class libraries that provide far more descriptive power than the scripting languages.

Applets are the second technology discussed in this book that provides computational capabilities for XHTML documents. Both JavaScript scripts and Java applets are interpreted on the client by the browser, which is good for server efficiency. JavaScript is both simpler to learn and simpler to use than Java. On the other hand, Java is much more expressive than JavaScript, especially because of the extensive array of class libraries now available. Furthermore, Java is faster than JavaScript, so if anything beyond short and simple computations is required, Java has the advantage.

Another area in which there is an advantage for Java applets over JavaScript is graphics. JavaScript includes virtually no graphics capability. So, even the graphics available in Java 1.1 (an early version of Java) are far superior to anything available in JavaScript. On the other hand, JavaScript has an advantage over Java because it is directly embedded in XHTML documents, whereas applets must be downloaded from the server when needed.

By 2002 the initial excitement regarding applets had diminished significantly, and other technologies, particularly scripting languages, had taken over many of the former uses of applets. The decrease in popularity of applets was in part due to the inconsistency of support from the browser vendors. The Netscape 4 browsers included Java virtual machines (intermediate code interpreters) that supported only version 1.1 of Java. (Version 1.2 of Java, which included many significant changes, was released in late 1998.) So, applets either had to be written using obsolete Java, or they would not be viewable on Netscape's browsers.[1] Up-to-date Java virtual machines were available from Sun

---

1. Netscape 6 and 7 include up-to-date Java interpreters.

for these browsers, but it was a sizable download, especially for those without high-speed Internet access, so many did not bother getting it. More recently, Microsoft stopped including support for Java in their browsers, although it can be downloaded from Sun. So, for awhile, Netscape clients were required to download Java virtual machines for their browsers, and Microsoft clients now are required to download them for their browsers. Because of these problems, as well as the availability of alternative technologies, many Web sites stopped creating applets and gradually eliminated the applets they were providing.

Java has become more heavily used on the server side in the form of servlets (discussed in Chapter 11, "Java Web Software") than on the client side in the form of applets. However, for now at least, Java applets are still included in some legacy Web sites, and some applets are still being written. Therefore, it is worthwhile for Web professionals to be familiar with them.

C.2 The Primary Applet Activities

Applets must include four fundamental methods through which the browser controls their execution. All of these are inherited from `JApplet`. When an XHTML document is being interpreted and displayed by a browser and an applet is encountered, the applet class code is downloaded and instantiated. Then the browser calls the applet's `init` method, which is inherited from `JApplet` but is often overridden in the user-defined applet class. The purpose of `init`, naturally, is to allow the applet to do some initialization. For example, if the applet has user-interface components (widgets), they are normally created in `init`. Upon return from the `init` method, the browser calls the applet method `start`, which begins execution of the applet's code. The `start` method is also implicitly called when the browser user returns to a document after viewing some other document. When the browser user directs the browser to follow a link from the current page to some new page, the browser calls the applet method `stop`. When the browser is stopped by the user, it calls the applet method `destroy`, which is used to do any cleanup that might be required at the end of the applet's life.

An applet's display is actually a frame, which is a multilayered structure. We are interested in just one of those layers, the *content pane*. The content pane is where applets put their output. Note that applets do not draw anything directly in the content pane; rather, applets draw in a panel and then add the panel to the content pane. This is also true for graphics in the Java applications world. For applications, a frame is created, and the filled panel is added to that frame's content pane. For applets, the filled panel is added to the applet's content pane.

There are two distinct categories of graphics operations for applets. In one category, something is drawn using a small set of primitive drawing methods. This use of primitives, which is sometimes called *custom drawing*, is done in overridden versions of the `paintComponent` method. Custom drawing must be done outside the subclass of `JApplet`. Typically, a subclass of `Jpanel` is created and used for custom drawing. Then the applet creates an instance of the panel subclass and adds it to its content pane. The other category of graphics is the use of predefined graphics objects. Predefined graphics objects do not require the use of a `paintComponent` method. This means they can be placed directly in a panel that is created in the applet and then added to the applet's content pane. This is a simpler process.

C.3 The paintComponent Method

As previously stated, custom painting is done with the `paintComponent` method. However, when `paintComponent` is used in an applet environment, only the browser calls it; it should never be called by user code. `paintComponent` takes a single parameter: an object of class `Graphics`, which is defined in the `java.awt` package. This object, which is created by the browser, provides a collection of methods for drawing text and graphics. In a sense, the `Graphics` object provides a graphics context for `paintComponent`, similar to the device context for Windows and the graphics context in X-11. The methods of `Graphics` must be called through the browser-generated `Graphics` object. The protocol of the `paintComponent` method is as follows:

```
public void paintComponent(Graphics grafObj) { ... }
```

Initially, we discuss creating text with `paintComponent`. This is done with a method named `drawString`, which takes three parameters: a `String` literal, the *x* coordinate of the left end of the string, and the *y* coordinate of the base of the string. These coordinates are given in pixels.

Before calling `paintComponent`, the `paintComponent` method of the parent class (referred to with `super`) is called to paint the background of the display panel.

The following is an applet that displays a welcome message. It defines a subclass of `JPanel` that overrides `paintComponent`. The overriding `paintComponent` method draws the message with `drawstring`. The applet itself (the subclass of `JApplet`) creates a content pane, which is a `Container` object, with the `getContentPane` method. It also instantiates the subclass of `JPanel`, `MessagePanel`, by calling its constructor in a new clause. The `init` method, inherited from `JApplet` and overriden in the example, has just one statement, which adds the panel to its content pane by sending the `MessagePanel` object (created by the applet) to the `add` method of the `Container` object.

```
/* Wel.java
   An applet to illustrate the display of a string
   */
import java.applet.*;
import javax.swing.*;
import java.awt.*;
```

```
// The Wel applet
public class Wel extends JApplet {

// Create a content pane and the panel
  Container messageArea = getContentPane();
  MessagePanel myMessagePanel = new MessagePanel();

// The init method, which adds the panel to the applet
  public void init() {
    messageArea.add(myMessagePanel);
  }
}


// The panel class on which the message is painted
class MessagePanel extends JPanel {
  public void paintComponent(Graphics grafObj) {
    super.paintComponent(grafObj);
    grafObj.drawString("Welcome to my home page!", 50,
                       50);
  }
}
```

The call to `drawString` in `Wel` uses default values for the font parameters to display its string parameter. These parameters can be changed. The `Font` class, which is defined in `java.awt.Font`, has three variables that specify a font name, style, and size. Objects of the `Font` class can be created and used to set the instance variables in the `paintComponent` method. The font names and styles that are available depend on the implementation. We assume here that Times Roman and Courier are available in plain, boldface, and italic styles. The font styles are specified by named constants in the `Font` class, `PLAIN`, `BOLD`, and `ITALIC`. Objects of class `Font` are initialized through the three parameters in its constructor that specify the font name, style, and size. For example, consider the following instantiations:

```
Font font1 = new Font ("TimesRoman", Font.PLAIN, 36);
Font font2 = new Font ("Courier", Font.ITALIC, 24);
```

The font member of a `Graphics` object is set with the method `setFont`, which takes the `Font` object as its parameter.

The following is a revision of the `Wel` applet that uses a specific font, style, and size to display the same message as the earlier version:

```
/* Wel2.java
   An applet to illustrate the display of a string
   in a specific font, font style, and font size
   */
import java.applet.*;
import javax.swing.*;
import java.awt.*;

// The panel class on which the message will be painted
class MessagePanel extends JPanel {
  Font myFont = new Font("TimesRoman", Font.ITALIC, 24);

  public void paintComponent(Graphics grafObj) {
    super.paintComponent(grafObj);
    grafObj.setFont(myFont);
    grafObj.drawString("Welcome to my first home page!", 50,
                    50);
  }
}


// The Wel2 applet
public class Wel2 extends JApplet {

// The init method - create the content pane, instantiate
// the message panel and add it to the content pane
  public void init() {
    Container messageArea = getContentPane();
    MessagePanel myMessagePanel = new MessagePanel();
    messageArea.add(myMessagePanel);
  }
}
```

C.4 The <object> Tag

The <object> tag is used to reference an applet in an XHTML document. The <object> tag is similar to the <img> tag used to specify images. The purpose of both <object> and <img> is to create a space in the document display where something can be put. In the case of <object>, when used for an applet, that something is whatever the applet paints. The form of the <object> tag and the attributes it uses for applets is as follows:

```
<object codetype = "application/java"
        classid = "java:applet_class_file"
        width = "applet display width"
        height = "applet display height">
</object>
```

The applet file is the compiled `.class` file. The width and height specify the size in pixels of the area in which the applet will paint.

The following XHTML document defines a simple XHTML document that uses the Wel2 applet from Section C.3.

```
<?xml version = "1.0" encoding = "utf-8"?>
<!DOCTYPE html PUBLIC "-//w3c//DTD XHTML 1.1//EN"
    "http://www.w3.org/TR/xhtml11/DTD/xhtml11.dtd">

<!-- wel2.html
    A document to test the Wel2 applet
    -->
<html xmlns = "http://www.w3.org/1999/xhtml">
  <head> <title> Wel2 </title>
  </head>
  <body>
    <p>
      <object codetype = "application/java"
              classid = "java:Wel2.class"
              width = "500"
              height = "100">
      </object>
    </p>
  </body>
</html>
```

Unfortunately, there is a portability problem with the object element, even though it is part of the HTML 4.0 standard. Although Internet Explorer 6 (IE6) recognizes the `<object>` tag, it does not recognize the `classid` attribute. Instead, it uses the `code` attribute, which was associated with the deprecated `<applet>` tag. Also, if the `code` attribute is used in an object element, the `"java:"` part of the value for the `code` attribute must be dropped. The Netscape 7 (NS7) browsers do not recognize the `code` attribute. Oddly, Sun Microsystem's `appletviewer` also requires the nonstandard attribute `code`.

Figure C.1 shows a display of the output of `wel2.html`.

Welcome to my first home page!

Figure C.1 A display of `Wel2.html`

C.5 Applet Parameters

A user can pass parameters to Java applications through the command line to the `main` method. Because applets do not have a `main` method, this obviously will not work for them. Still, it is convenient to be able to parameterize applets, and in fact, parameters can be sent to an applet from the XHTML document that calls it. This is done with the `<param>` tag, which is followed by a pair of named attributes. The first attribute is `name`, to which any name you like can be assigned. The second attribute is `value`, to which is assigned the value that you want to pass to the applet. For example, you might want to pass the size of an applet display element through a parameter, as shown in the following example:

```
<param name = "size"
       value = "24">
```

The applet uses the `getParameter` method to get the passed parameter value. It takes as its single parameter the name of the parameter, as a `String` literal. For example, to get the `size` parameter specified previously, the following could be used:

```
String mySize = getParameter("size");
```

If `getParameter` is called but the XHTML document did not specify the requested parameter value, `null` is returned. This provides a mechanism for specifying default values for such parameters. For example, consider the following:

```
int mySize;
String pString = getParameter("size");
if (pString == null)
  mySize = 36;
...
Font myFont = new Font("TimesRoman", Font.ITALIC, mySize);
```

The parameter value returned from `getParameter` is a `String` object. If it is actually an integer value (rather than a string), it must be converted to an `int` value. This can be done with the `Integer.parseInt` method. So, the previous `if` statement must have an `else` clause to do this conversion, as shown in the following example:

```
if (pString == null)
    mySize = 36;
else
    mySize = Integer.parseInt(pString)
```

The code to get parameters should appear in the `init` method. The following is a complete applet that does what the applet `Wel2` in Section C.3 did, except that the size of the displayed string is a parameter that can be specified from the XHTML document:

```java
/* Wel3.java
   An applet to illustrate parameters
   */
import java.applet.*;
import javax.swing.*;
import java.awt.*;

// The panel class on which the message will be painted
class MessagePanel2 extends JPanel {
  Font myFont = new Font("TimesRoman", Font.ITALIC,
                         Wel3.mySize);

  public void paintComponent(Graphics grafObj) {
    super.paintComponent(grafObj);
    grafObj.setFont(myFont);
    grafObj.drawString("Welcome to my home page!", 50, 50);
  }
}

// The Wel3 applet
public class Wel3 extends JApplet {
  static int mySize;

  public void init() {
    Container messageArea = getContentPane();
    String pString;

// Get the fontsize parameter
    pString = getParameter("size");
```

```
// If it's null, set the size to 30; otherwise, use the
// parameter value
   if (pString == null)
      mySize = 30;
   else mySize = Integer.parseInt(pString);

// Instantiate the panel with the message and add it to
// the content pane
   MessagePanel2 myMessagePanel = new MessagePanel2();
   messageArea.add(myMessagePanel);
  }
}
```

The XHTML document that tests `We13` follows:

```
<?xml version = "1.0" encoding = "utf-8"?>
<!DOCTYPE html PUBLIC "-//w3c//DTD XHTML 1.1//EN"
    "http://www.w3.org/TR/xhtml11/DTD/xhtml11.dtd">

<!-- wel3.html
     A document to test the We13 applet
     -->
<html xmlns = "http://www.w3.org/1999/xhtml">
  <head> <title> We13 </title>
  </head>
  <body>
    <p>
      <object codetype = "application/java"
              classid = "java:We13.class"
              width = "500"
              height = "100">
        <param name = "size"
               value = "40" />
      </object>
    </p>
  </body>
</html>
```

C.6 Simple Graphics

The `Graphics` class that the `We12` and `We13` applets used to put text into a document also includes methods for drawing lines, rectangles, and ovals. Although the Swing package is now used for creating GUI components, the basic graphics capabilities of Java remain in the AWT package, which is where `Graphics` is defined. This section describes the basic drawing methods of AWT.

C.6.1   The Coordinate System

The methods that draw lines, rectangles, ovals, and arcs require the user to specify the location of those figures. Such locations are specified in terms of the `Graphics` coordinate system, which has the origin at the upper-left corner. This is exactly like the JavaScript coordinate system for positioning elements.

C.6.2   Lines

The `drawLine` method takes four parameters that specify the locations of the two ends of the line. For example, if the following `paintComponent` method were called, the call to `drawLine` would draw a line from the location (20, 10) to the location (60, 80).

```
public void paintComponent(Graphics grafObj) {
  grafObj.drawLine(20, 10, 60, 80);
}
```

C.6.3   Rectangles

The `Graphics` class provides methods for drawing rectangles and rectangles with rounded corners, where either of these can be filled or not filled. Ordinary (nonrounded corners) rectangles are drawn with either of these two methods:

```
drawRect(x1, y1, width, height)
fillRect(x1, y1, width, height)
```

In both cases, the location (`x1, y1`) specifies the upper-left corner of the rectangle, and the other two parameters specify the lengths of the rectangle's sides in pixels.

Specifying rectangles with rounded corners requires two more parameters in the method calls: one to specify the number of horizontal pixels in the rounding and one to specify the number of vertical pixels. If these two parameters are equal, the rounding is symmetric. The names of these two methods are `drawRoundRect` and `fillRoundRect`.

The following applet, `Rectangles.java`, draws the four rectangles shown in Figure C.2.

```
/* Rectangles.java
   An applet to illustrate drawing rectangles
   */
import java.applet.*;
import java.awt.*;
import javax.swing.*;

// The panel class for drawing
class MyPanel extends JPanel {

  public void paintComponent(Graphics grafObj) {
    super.paintComponent(grafObj);
    grafObj.drawRect(10, 10, 80, 60);
    grafObj.fillRect(120, 10, 60, 80);
    grafObj.drawRoundRect(10, 120, 80, 60, 20, 30);
    grafObj.fillRoundRect(120, 120, 60, 80, 40, 40);
  }
}


// The Rectangles applet
public class Rectangles extends JApplet {
  Container rectangleArea = getContentPane();
  MyPanel newPanel = new MyPanel();

// The init method for the applet - adds the panel to
// the content area of the applet
  public void init() {
    rectangleArea.add(newPanel);
  }
}
```

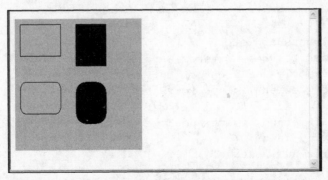

Figure C.2 A display of the output of the `Rectangles` applet

The `Graphics` class includes methods that draw so-called three-dimensional rectangles, which have shaded sides to make them appear like buttons that are either unpushed or pushed. Light shading on the left and upper sides makes a square look like an unpushed button. Dark shading on the left and upper sides makes a square look like a pushed button. The unpushed look is specified with a fifth parameter of `true`; the pushed look is specified with `false`. The name of the method for drawing these rectangles is `draw3DRect`.

C.6.4   Polygons

Polygons can be created by simply drawing a sequence of lines whose ends are connected. The points can be specified with two arrays, one consisting of the *x* coordinates and the other of the *y* coordinates. These two arrays, along with the number of points, are sent as parameters to the method `drawPolygon`. For example, an octagon could be drawn with the following applet, `Polygons`:

```java
/* Polygons.java
   An applet to illustrate drawing a polygon
   */
import java.applet.*;
import java.awt.*;
import javax.swing.*;

// The panel for drawing
class PolyPanel extends JPanel {

  public void paintComponent(Graphics grafObj) {
    int xCoordinates [] = {30, 50, 64, 64, 50, 30, 16, 16, 30};
    int yCoordinates [] = {10, 10, 24, 44, 58, 58, 44, 24, 10};
    super.paintComponent(grafObj);
    grafObj.drawPolygon(xCoordinates, yCoordinates, 9);
  }
}

// The Polygons applet
public class Polygons extends JApplet {
  Container polyArea = getContentPane();
  PolyPanel newPanel = new PolyPanel();

// The init method, which adds the panel to the applet
  public void init() {
    polyArea.add(newPanel);
  }
}
```

Figure C.3 shows a display of the octagon drawn by the `Polygons` applet.

Figure C.3 A display drawn by the `Polygons` applet

An alternative technique for specifying a polygon is to create an object of class `Polygon`, which has a constructor with the same parameters as the `drawPolygon` method. Then an alternative version of `drawPolygon`, which takes a single `Polygon` parameter, can be called, as shown in the following example:

```
Polygon myPolygon = new Polygon(
                    xCoordinates, yCoordinates, 9);
grafObj.drawPolygon(myPolygon);
```

Polygons, like rectangles, can be filled by simply calling `fillPolygon` instead of `drawPolygon`.

C.6.5   Ovals

Drawing an oval is very similar to drawing a rectangle. In fact, the parameters to the oval-drawing methods are exactly those that could be sent to `drawRect`. The four parameters to the two oval-drawing methods, `drawOval` and `fillOval`, specify the coordinates of the upper-left corner and the width and height of the oval. A circle, of course, is just a "square" oval.

C.7   Color

In Java, specific colors are represented as objects of class `Color`. The `java.awt` package includes a collection of predefined `Color` objects that represent common colors, as well as methods for creating new colors and using colors in painting applets.

The Java abstract model of color uses 24 bits, with 8 bits for each of the three primary colors, red, green, and blue. The 13 predefined colors are shown in Table C.1, along with their RGB values.

Any color possible with the 24-bit specification can be constructed by creating an object of type `Color`, as shown in the following example:

```
Color myColor = new Color(x, y, z);
```

Table C.1 Predefined Java colors and their RGB values

Color Name	RGB Value
Color.white	255, 255, 255
Color.black	0, 0, 0
Color.gray	128, 128, 128
Color.lightGray	192, 192, 192
Color.darkGray	64, 64, 64
Color.red	255, 0, 0
Color.green	0, 255, 0
Color.blue	0, 0, 255
Color.yellow	255, 255, 0
Color.magenta	255, 0, 255
Color.cyan	0, 255, 255
Color.pink	255, 175, 175
Color.orange	255, 200, 0

Here, x, y, and z are integer values in the range of 0 to 255, representing the red, green, and blue components of the color.

The color of the Graphics object can be set with the setColor method, as follows:

```
grafObj.setColor(Color.magenta);
```

The background and foreground colors for a panel can be set with methods from the Panel class, as discussed in Section C.8.

C.8 Interactive Applets

A large part of the initial interest in Java was centered on applets, and a large part of this interest came from the possibility of making XHTML documents interactive. The support for interactivity in an applet is based on the reactive GUI components (widgets) that can be put in an applet display. This section describes how GUI components can be created in an applet and how user interactions with those components can be used to trigger computations. Because you have already learned about making GUI components react to user actions with XHTML and JavaScript, this section should be relatively easy to understand.

C.8.1 Java Swing GUI Components

The Swing package, defined in `javax.swing`, includes a collection of components that are what we have called *widgets*. A label component is an object of class `JLabel`. A `JLabel` object is a static string used to label other components. For example:

```
final JLabel lab1 = new JLabel("Customer name:");
```

A button is an object of class `JButton`. The parameter to the `JButton` constructor becomes the label in the button depiction:

```
JButton myButton = new JButton("Click me");
```

A checkbox is an object of class `JCheckbox`. The constructor for checkboxes has just one parameter, the label to appear next to the checkbox:

```
JCheckbox box1 = new JCheckbox("Hamburger");
JCheckbox box2 = new JCheckbox("French Fries");
JCheckbox box3 = new JCheckbox("Milk");
```

The `JCheckbox` constructor can include a second parameter, a Boolean. If `true` is sent to the constructor, the checkbox is initially checked; otherwise, it is initially unchecked.

Radio buttons are special buttons that are placed in a button group. A button group is an object of class `ButtonGroup`, whose constructor takes no parameters. The `JRadioButton` constructor, used for creating radio buttons, takes two parameters: the label and the initial state of the radio button (`true` or `false`). After the radio buttons are created, they are put in their button group with the add method of the group object. Consider the following example:

```
ButtonGroup payment = new ButtonGroup();
JRadioButton box1 = new JRadioButton("Visa", true);
JRadioButton box2 = new JRadioButton("MasterCard", false);
JRadioButton box3 = new JRadioButton("Discover", false);
payment.add(box1);
payment.add(box2);
payment.add(box3);
```

A text box is an object of class `JTextField`. The simplest `JTextField` constructor takes a single parameter, the length of the box in characters. For example:

```
JTextField name = new JTextField(32);
```

The `JTextField` constructor can also take a literal string, which is displayed as its contents. The string parameter, when present, appears as the first parameter.

Recall that the `paintComponent` method cannot paint an applet directly. Rather, it is used to paint an object of a subclass of `JPanel`, which is then added to the content pane of the applet. Components must also be added to a panel, but in this case it is a simple `JPanel` object that can be created in the applet class because the `paintComponent` method is not needed. The following code creates the panel object we use in the upcoming discussion of components:

```
JPanel myPanel = new JPanel();
```

The background color for a panel can be set with the `setBackground` method, as follows:

```
myPanel.setBackground(Color.yellow);
```

The `setForeground` method sets the default color of everything to be drawn in the panel. For example, the following statement changes the default drawing color to blue:

```
myPanel.setForeground(Color.blue);
```

After the components have been created with constructors, they must be placed in the panel with the `add` method, as shown in the following example:

```
myPanel.add(lab1);
```

Java defines several different objects called *layout managers* that determine how components are positioned in a panel. The default layout manager for Swing components is `BorderLayout`, which places components on the borders of the panel. This is fine for some situations. However, it is often convenient to have more control over where components are placed in a panel. For this, Java offers several alternative layout managers. One of these is `GridLayout`, which divides the panel area into rows and columns of compartments, each of which can contain a component. The parameters to the `GridLayout` constructor are the number of rows and columns, and the number of pixels between the rows and columns, respectively. The layout manager for a panel is specified with the `setLayout` method, which takes a layout manager object as its parameter. For example, consider the following code, which creates a new panel named `buttonPanel` and a `GridLayout` layout manager object for the panel:

```
JPanel buttonPanel = new JPanel();
buttonPanel.setLayout(new GridLayout(2, 3, 15, 15));
```

In this example, the panel's grid layout is specified to have two rows of three components each, with 15 pixels between the components.

The following example illustrates an applet that contains some simple GUI components. It uses a `GridLayout` manager object to put the components in a single column. Notice that the components are all placed in the panel object, which is ultimately added to the applet's content pane.

```java
/* Pizza.java
   An applet to illustrate some GUI components with a pizza
   order form
   */
import java.awt.*;
import java.applet.*;
import javax.swing.*;

public class Pizza extends JApplet {
  Container contentPane = getContentPane();

  public void init() {

      // Create a panel object and set its layout manager to put
      // the components in a column
      JPanel myPanel = new JPanel();
      myPanel.setLayout(new GridLayout(20, 1, 10, 10));
      myPanel.setBackground(Color.cyan);

      // Create a label for the form heading and add it to the panel
      Label myLabel = new Label("Pizza Order Form");
      myPanel.add(myLabel);

      // Create a text field for the customer's name and
      // address and add them to the panel
      JLabel nameLabel = new JLabel("Name:");
      JTextField myName = new JTextField(30);
      JLabel addrLabel = new JLabel("Address:");
      JTextField myAddr = new JTextField(30);
      myPanel.add(nameLabel);
      myPanel.add(myName);
      myPanel.add(addrLabel);
      myPanel.add(myAddr);

      // Create radio buttons for pizza size and add them to the panel
      JLabel sizeLabel = new JLabel("Pizza Size");
      ButtonGroup sizeGroup = new ButtonGroup();
      JRadioButton s1 = new JRadioButton("small");
      JRadioButton s2 = new JRadioButton("medium");
      JRadioButton s3 = new JRadioButton("large", true);
```

```
        // Put the radio buttons in the button group
        sizeGroup.add(s1);
        sizeGroup.add(s2);
        sizeGroup.add(s3);

        // Put the radio buttons in the panel
        myPanel.add(sizeLabel);
        myPanel.add(s1);
        myPanel.add(s2);
        myPanel.add(s3);

        // Create checkboxes for toppings and add them to the panel
        JLabel topLabel = new JLabel("Toppings");
        Checkbox top1 = new Checkbox("sausage");
        Checkbox top2 = new Checkbox("pepperoni");
        Checkbox top3 = new Checkbox("extra cheese");
        Checkbox top4 = new Checkbox("hamburger");
        Checkbox top5 = new Checkbox("olives");
        Checkbox top6 = new Checkbox("mushrooms");
        myPanel.add(topLabel);
        myPanel.add(top1);
        myPanel.add(top2);
        myPanel.add(top3);
        myPanel.add(top4);
        myPanel.add(top5);
        myPanel.add(top6);

        // Now add the panel to the content pane
        contentPane.add(myPanel);

    } // End of init()
} // End of the Pizza applet
```

Figure C.4 shows a browser display of the Pizza applet.

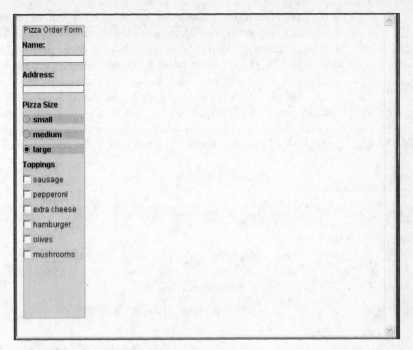

Figure C.4 Results of running the `Pizza` applet

C.8.2   The Java Event Model

GUI components are not of much value unless user interactions with them trigger computations. In JavaScript, user interactions with components create events that can be caught by event handlers, which provide the computations. In Java, a similar model is used. GUI components are event generators. In Java, event handlers are called *event listeners*. Event listeners are connected to event generators through *event listener registration*. Listener registration is done with a method of the class that implements the listener interface, as described later in this section. The panel object into which the components are placed can be the event listener for those components. Only event listeners that are registered for a specific event are notified when that event occurs.

An event generator tells a listener of an event by sending a message to the listener (in other words, by calling one of the listener's methods). The listener method that receives the message implements an event handler. To make the event-handling methods conform to a standard protocol, a Java interface is used. An interface prescribes standard method protocols but does not provide implementations of those methods. This protocol could be specified by forcing the event generator to be a subclass of a class from which it would inherit the protocol. However, the `JApplet` class already has a superclass, and in Java, a class can have just one parent class. Therefore, the protocol must come from an interface. A class cannot be instantiated unless it provides definitions for all methods in the interfaces that it implements.

A class that needs to implement a listener must implement an interface for those listeners. There are many classes of events and listener interfaces. The event classes appear in two categories: semantic events and low-level events. Table C.2 lists a few of the most commonly used classes of events.

Table C.2 Event classes

Class Name	User Actions That Create the Event Object
Semantic Event Classes	
ActionEvent	Click a button, select from a menu or list, or press [Enter] in a text field
ItemEvent	Select a checkbox or list item
TextEvent	Change the contents of a text field or text area
Low-Level Event Classes	
ComponentEvent	Resize, move, show, or hide a component
KeyEvent	Press or release a key
MouseEvent	Depress or release a mouse button, or move the cursor into or out of the component
MouseMotionEvent	Change the position of the mouse cursor over the component
FocusEvent	Get or lose focus for a component

Each semantic event listener interface prescribes one method for the handler. The low-level interfaces have several different handler methods. The handler methods for the two most commonly used semantic events are shown in Table C.3.

Table C.3 Semantic event listener interfaces and their handler methods

Interface	Handler Method
ActionListener	actionPerformed
ItemListener	itemStateChanged

As stated previously, the connection of a component to an event listener is made with a method of the class that implements the listener interface. Event listener registration establishes this connection. For example, because `ActionEvent` is the class name of event objects created by user actions on buttons, the `addActionListener` method is used to register a listener for buttons. The listener for button events created in a panel in an applet could be implemented in the panel. So, for a button named `button1` in a panel named `myPanel` that implements the `ActionEvent` event handler for buttons, we would register the listener with the following statement:

```
button1.addActionListener(this);
```

Each event handler method receives an event parameter that provides information about the event. Event classes have methods, such as `getState`, to access that information. For example, when called through a radio button, `getState` returns `true` or `false`, depending on whether the button was on or off, respectively.

All the event-related classes are in the `java.awt.event` package, so it must be imported to any applet class that uses events.

The following sample applet, `RadioB`, illustrates the use of events and event handling to display dynamic content in an applet. This applet constructs radio buttons that control the font style of the contents of a text field. It creates a `Font` object for each of four font styles. Each of these has a radio button to enable the user to select the style. The applet then creates a text string, whose font style will be controlled by the user through the radio buttons. The event handler `itemStateChanged` determines which radio button is pressed, after being informed by the `ItemEvent` object that a change has been made in the radio buttons. Then it sets the font style of the text string accordingly.

```java
/* RadioB.java
   An applet to illustrate event handling with interactive
   radio buttons that control the font style of a text field
   */
import java.awt.*;
import java.awt.event.*;
import java.applet.*;
import javax.swing.*;

public class RadioB extends JApplet implements ItemListener {

// Make most of the variables class variables, because both init
// and the event handler must see them
```

```java
    private Container contentPane = getContentPane();
    private JTextField text;
    private Font plainFont, boldFont, italicFont, boldItalicFont;
    private JRadioButton plain, bold, italic, boldItalic;
    private ButtonGroup radioButtons = new ButtonGroup();
    private JPanel myPanel = new JPanel();

    // The init method is where the document is initially built
    public void init() {

      // Set the background color of the panel
      myPanel.setBackground(Color.cyan);

      // Create the fonts
      plainFont = new Font("Serif", Font.PLAIN, 16);
      boldFont = new Font("Serif", Font.BOLD, 16);
      italicFont = new Font("Serif", Font.ITALIC, 16);
      boldItalicFont = new Font("Serif", Font.BOLD +
                                Font.ITALIC, 16);

      // Create the test text string, set its font, and
      // add it to the panel
      text = new JTextField("In what font style should I appear?",
                   30);
      myPanel.add(text);
      text.setFont(plainFont);

      // Create radio buttons for the fonts and add them to the panel
      plain = new JRadioButton("Plain", true);
      bold = new JRadioButton("Bold");
      italic = new JRadioButton("Italic");
      boldItalic = new JRadioButton("Bold Italic");
      radioButtons.add(plain);
      radioButtons.add(bold);
      radioButtons.add(italic);
      radioButtons.add(boldItalic);

      // Register the event handlers to myPanel
      plain.addItemListener(this);
      bold.addItemListener(this);
      italic.addItemListener(this);
      boldItalic.addItemListener(this);

      // Now add the buttons to the panel
      myPanel.add(plain);
```

```
    myPanel.add(bold);
    myPanel.add(italic);
    myPanel.add(boldItalic);

    // Now add the panel to the content pane for the applet
    contentPane.add(myPanel);

} // End of init()

// The event handler
public void itemStateChanged (ItemEvent e) {

    // Determine which button is on and set the font accordingly
    if (plain.isSelected())
      text.setFont(plainFont);
    else if (bold.isSelected())
      text.setFont(boldFont);
    else if (italic.isSelected())
      text.setFont(italicFont);
    else if (boldItalic.isSelected())
      text.setFont(boldItalicFont);

} // End of itemStateChanged
} // End of RadioB applet
```

The RadioB applet produces the screen shown in Figure C.5.

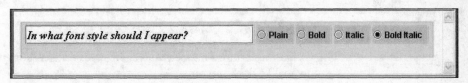

Figure C.5 The output of the RadioB applet

Summary

The impetus for Java's fast rise in popularity was the use of applets in constructing Web sites. An applet is a usually small collection of Java code defined in a class that is derived from JApplet. In objects of this class, a call is made to the paintComponent method, which can display a variety of things on the screen.

An XHTML tag, <object>, is used to inform the browser that an applet is to be downloaded from the server (or somewhere else) and run, creating something at that spot in the document. In a sense, applets are slaves to the XHTML document that calls them. The `<object>` tag also specifies the file type and the size of the area into which the applet will display and possibly some parameters to the applet.

The primary applet activities are `start`, which starts and restarts the applet; `stop`, which stops the applet's execution when the browser leaves the document that calls the applet; `destroy`, which is called when the user stops the execution of the browser; and `paintComponent`, which draws things on the screen. All of these methods are called by the browser. The `paintComponent`, `start`, and `stop` methods were described in this appendix.

Text and graphical objects are drawn by the applet with methods of the `Graphics` class. The coordinate system into which things are drawn has its origin in the upper-left corner. The `paintComponent` method takes a `Graphics` class object as a parameter. `paintComponent` calls other methods to produce the actual graphics in the applet area. The `drawString` method is used to display a character string. The `drawLine` method draws a line between two specified points. The `drawRect` and `fillRect` methods draw outlines of rectangles and filled rectangles, respectively. The `drawPolygon` and `fillPolygon` methods draw outlines of polygons and filled polygons, respectively.

Swing GUI components are implemented in Java as instantiations of their corresponding classes—for example, `JLabel` and `JButton`. The Java event model is related to that of JavaScript. Events are objects, often created by GUI components. Events are handled by methods called event listeners, which are connected to the GUI component objects. The listener object for events placed in a panel can be the panel itself. Event handlers can do virtually anything that can be done in an applet. One powerful possibility is that of dynamically changing the content of the document being displayed.

Review Questions

C.1 What three things happen when a browser finds a reference to an applet in an XHTML document?

C.2 From what class does `Applet` directly descend?

C.3 What are the two ways to test an applet?

C.4 What advantages do Java applets have over JavaScript?

C.5 What advantage does JavaScript have over applets?

C.6 What are the four fundamental methods used to control the basic operations of an applet?

C.7 How are the four fundamental methods for applet control called?

C.8 How is `paintComponent` called?

C.9   What parameter does `paintComponent` take and what is its origin?

C.10 What is the content pane of an applet?

C.11 Why is `paintComponent` used in a separate panel subclass?

C.12 Describe the parameters to `drawString`.

C.13 Describe the four required attributes of `<object>`.

C.14 Describe the attributes for `<param>`.

C.15 How are parameters from an XHTML document gotten into an applet that is referenced in that document?

C.16 Describe the parameters to `drawRect`.

C.17 How is the color of a `Graphics` object set?

C.18 How are radio buttons created in an applet?

C.19 What method places a GUI component into a panel?

C.20 Describe the parameters to a `GridLayout` constructor.

C.21 What is the event class for button clicks?

C.22 What is the event class for a checkbox selection?

C.23 What objects are sent notifications of GUI component events?

C.24 In what class is a method defined to register an event listener?

C.25 What event-handler method is used for button events?

Exercises

Write, test, and debug (if necessary) applets for the following specifications:

C.1   Modify the `Wel3` applet from Section C.5 to use parameters for the font and font style, as well as the font size. Test this applet with several different sets of parameters from the XHTML document that runs it.

C.2   Modify the `Wel3` applet to place the message inside an unfilled white circle that is centered in a filled blue square. The text must be black.

C.3   The applet for this exercise must display the Olympic logo, which consists of five overlaid circles. Below the logo must appear the text "The United States Olympic Committee." The circles must be blue, and the text must be red. The circles part of the logo must be enclosed in an unfilled green rectangle.

C.4   The applet for this exercise must display four checkboxes, labeled *Tacos*, *Chalupas*, *Burritos*, and *Nachos*. Beside each checkbox there must be a text box labeled *Quantity.* This applet does not need to deal with events or event handling.

C.5 Modify the applet of Exercise C.4 by adding event handling for the input from the user. The applet must get a number from each text box, assuming 0 if the field is not changed. It must then compute the cost of the order, assuming that tacos cost $0.79, chalupas cost $1.19, burritos cost $1.39, and nachos cost $1.29.

C.6 The applet for this exercise must display two collections of six radio buttons, labeled *Red, Green, Blue, Yellow, Magenta,* and *Cyan.* The first collection must be labeled Foreground; the second must be labeled Background. These buttons must be implemented to control the foreground and background colors of the display. So that the foreground color can be seen, include a few geometric shapes and some text.

Index